DIPLOMACY TO POLITICS

BY WAY OF THE JUNGLE

# Diplomacy to Politics

## by *Way of the Jungle*

SIR WYNN HUGH-JONES

M̧C

© Sir Wynn Hugh-Jones, 2002

First published in 2002 by
The Memoir Club
Whitworth Hall
Spennymoor
County Durham

*British Library Cataloguing-in-Publication data*
A catalogue record for this book is available from the British Library

ISBN 1 84104 063 0

While every effort has been made to assure the accuracy of the facts given throughout this book, the author welcomes word from any reader who finds errors. Otherwise it remains a true and personal memoir.

All efforts have been made to obtain permission for reproduction from copyright holders. The author regrets any omission

Designed and typeset by Carnegie Publishing, Lancaster
Printed and bound by Bookcraft, Bath

*For my Family*

# Contents

PART THREE
### Europe and Change of Career – 1970–1973

A sequel, when published, will cover:
Part Four: The English-Speaking Union and Voluntary World 1973–1977
Part Five: The Liberal Party and Liberal/SDP Alliance, 1977–1987
Part Six: Avebury in Danger and other retirement causes, 1987–2003

# List of Illustrations

# Acknowledgements

I record my gratitude to:

- Christopher Baxter, Peter Beale, Anthony Meyer, Alastair Service, Alec Stirling and Alan Lee Williams for so very kindly reading and commenting on my text and giving it such generous endorsements.

- The Public Record Office for quotable access to a number of official documents, many of them originally written by me and now released under the 30-year rule. And the Foreign and Commonwealth Office for security clearance of my diplomatic chapters under the Official Secrets Act.

- Ann Hugh-Jones for the many happy quotations from her descriptive letters home during our diplomatic and family life together.

- Joyce Pinfield and Trevor Roberts for their helpful comments on chapter 3 (Llangollen). The European Library and Mrs G. Edwards for permission to reproduce the photo of Lloyd George and Winston Churchill at Llangollen. Douglas Scott and J. Arthur Dixon for the photo of Llangollen.

- Robbie Burns and David Lloyd for their valued comments on chapter 4 (Ludlow) and permission to quote from their *Century of Change*. The *Hereford Times* for copyright permission and the heirs of George Merchant, F.G. Reeves (Mrs Myra Reeves, Gillian and Vivien) and A. Lowndes Moir for the quotations in chapter 4 from their articles and booklets.

- Leslie McLoughlin and John Evans for their good help on chapters 11 (Saudi Arabia) and 15 (Rome) respectively.

- Jean Lindsay and David & Charles Ltd for permission to quote in chapter 1 from *History of the North Wales Slate Industry*. Robert Worcester and The Foreign Policy Centre for permission to quote in chapter 21 from *How to Win the Euro Referendum*.

- The heirs, wherever they may now be, of Rose Macauley, Chester Wilmot, André Maurois, Philip Williams, Pierre Daninos, Virginia

Thomson, Richard Adloff, *Michelin Green Guides* and *Historic Ludlow Official Guide*, for the quotations I have taken from their books in chapters 1, 8, 12, 14, 15 and 4 respectively. Likewise the heirs of Mercury Staff Photographers Vincent Vaughan, Photo Keystone and Paul Wilson Photography for photographs I have reproduced in chapters 4, 13 and 14 respectively. Also Peter Richards and Conor Cruise O'Brien for the quotations from their writings I have included in chapters 6 and 17 respectively.

- *The Guardian* and *The Independent* for several quotations from their columns.

And, in particular:

- the staff of the Memoir Club for their initiative, unfailing helpfulness and high professionalism. Likewise Carnegie Book Production.
- My son Robert for his thoughtful encouragement and advice throughout.
- My wife, Oswynne, for her constant support, her hard work in typing the whole manuscript and her forbearance.

W.N. H-J.

# Preface

THESE MEMOIRS are about the life and times of my parents, including through the first World War, and about the first fifty years of my own life, including the second World War, a diplomatic career in Arabia, Europe, Africa and North America, and an inside account of Britain's entry into Europe in 1971–73. They have been written at the invitation of the publishers, The Memoir Club.

A second set will be published later, all being well, about the past thirty years, including the voluntary movement and particularly the English-Speaking Union in the 1970s; politics, the Liberal Party and the Liberal/SDP Alliance in the decade 1977–87 when today's Liberal Democrat Party was conceived; the saving of Avebury village and World Heritage Site in the late 1980s, lecturing in the United States, and a few other retirement causes since then.

I make no apology for the large number of people mentioned, in government, diplomacy, politics, education, the armed and civil services, business and industry, the media, voluntary organisations, sport, and other occupations; young people and old, male and female, rich and poor, and of many nationalities; and of course friends, colleagues and family. Indeed I am only sorry that space has prevented me mentioning more. They make the story.

I make no apology either for highlighting, throughout, my own four absorbing interests: people, politics, play and parenthood:

- People because, for all the joys and fascination of nature, the world is nothing to me without them and, as no two are the same (and, I hope, never will be cloned) I find them endlessly interesting. I happen also to like them. So I do, too, their history – another of my themes.

- Politics, aptly defined in the *Oxford Dictionary* as 'the art and science of government', because that is what makes states and communities function, and I have always found that engrossing. It is also, in a democracy like ours, that which gives us the freedom and liberty we so fortunately enjoy. In party politics I am a Liberal, with a deep belief in liberal values, and have been all my life.

- Play, by which I mean principally outdoor games, because to me they have always added that extra dimension to life that comes from the challenge, fresh air, companionship and physical fitness that sports offer.
- Parenthood because, apart from the joy a family can bring, I have often wondered what can be more important in life than bringing up the next generation – provided one is in the fortunate position to contribute, as I have been.

The past century, the twentieth by the Christian calendar, has been the most momentous in human history. I count myself fortunate not only to have lived through three-quarters of it but to find myself now still enjoying a full life in a new century and new millennium. There has been nothing calculated about my life. It has been driven mostly by circumstances and events. It has all been in public service of one sort or another, with scant monetary reward but occasional modest satisfaction, to use the wartime phrase, 'in just doing one's own bit'. There must be in any progressive society those who create wealth, and I admire them who do so industriously. To those who want to go further today by decrying public service and upholding in its place quick fixes and even quicker bucks, I would say: 'Can any material gain ever really match the satisfaction of a job well done?'

In seeking this, if I have been to interesting places, met interesting people and done a few interesting things, that is my good fortune. I recount them for whatever modest purpose these recollections and observations may serve.

PART ONE

# Family, War, Youth and War Again

# CHAPTER I

# Family

'FETCH MY CAMEL, SAID AUNT DOT' was I think the splendid opening of Rose Macaulay's *Towers of Trebizond*. Mine might more prosaically be 'Fetch my bike', for travel and perhaps venture have been the mainsprings of my life, as they have of my family for generations. From our legendary ancestor Jonathan Swift, author of *Gulliver's Travels*, to the youngsters of today, we may have lacked material gain but never, so far as I can trace, pedal-power. Nor, by and large, imagination and humour. None but Swift has achieved national fame but, from all the family papers I have inherited, it is evident that most if not all led interesting lives, as will I feel sure the younger generation today. This and the immediately following chapters are devoted to the family, and particularly to my parents. But first, when and where I joined them.

That was in 1923, in the County School House of the then Headmaster, my father, at Llangollen in North Wales. Biographies of today seem all too often to start with revelations of childhood unhappiness. Mine does not. My first years of life were as full and pleasurable as any boy could wish, at any rate to the age of 13 when my father died. World War I, with its painful separations and, much worse, the terrible slaughter, the heritage of widows, the war-disabled visible everywhere and harshly called 'cripples', and the unemployed (2 million in 1923) were in every adult mind, and remained so throughout my boyhood. But I was fortunate both in my parents, who gave my brother and me an open and liberal upbringing of thoughtfulness and devotion, and in my surroundings, the historic and beautiful Vale of Llangollen.

The school was one of a hundred and fifty such secondary schools in Wales at that time, taking children from primary to university. Selection was still the order of the day, so it was small by today's standards – two hundred or so pupils. And it was 'co-educational', meaning boys and girls mixed in every class. They came from miles around, by steam train, primitive bus, bicycle or foot and, except on Sundays and in the holidays, the place was a hive of activity, both within the red brick walls of the two late Victorian and Edwardian buildings and on the playing fields and grounds around. The Headmaster's house was in the same style, and same splendid location, high above the town (or so it seemed to a small boy). Behind it rose to nearly one thousand feet the striking hill topped by the ruined castle of Dinas Bran, built by Gruffudd ap Madog, Prince of Powys Fadog against the Norman rulers of England in the late twelfth century, on a pre-historic Dinas of Bran. It is from this historic hill that to-day's successor comprehensive school takes its name, Ysgol Dinas Bran. Behind it ranged the handsome escarpment of the Eglwyseg Rocks; while to the fore and right, across the river Dee, rose the imposing Berwyn mountains, enclosing the Vale and changing colour with every season. Alongside the school grounds lay the town recreational field, known familiarly as 'the Rec', where we kicked a football or knocked a cricket ball in season or tobogganed when the snow came. For a child it was a rural paradise.

My father Hugh was Welsh, and dedicated his life to Welsh progress. That was within the United Kingdom for Welsh nationalism was not then a live issue, and he had an international vision of society anyhow. My mother, May Normington, was Yorkshire and equally proud of her origins. If she had to be the little bit more remindful to us, that was because we lived in Wales and my elder brother Eryl and I were born in Wales, whereas Yorkshire in those days was quite remote, a day's railway journey away. I always enjoyed our visits there, particularly the dales of West Yorkshire, and still do. Like the Welsh, Yorkshire folk have their own robust culture and more's the better for it. The same of course, in differing degrees, goes for most regions of England, not to mention the Scots and the Irish. In later life, in my Liberal Party years, I was to have the opportunity of visiting and getting to know something of them all. One day each will, I hope, have its own devolved authority. It must be judged absurd by any constitutionalist that the small town of Llangollen had to wait years in the 1970s for the then Secretary of State for the Environment in London to decide whether they could have a second pedestrian crossing on little Queen Street (part of the A5 but inside their town). To-day I suppose the Llangollen District Council would have to wait on the Welsh Assembly in Cardiff. But at least, as I write, we seem belatedly to have begun to follow the rest of the Western World in practising devolution – instead of just preaching it to the European Community! It might perhaps have been different, and the twentieth-century democratic development of this country much richer, had Gladstone succeeded in establishing the sensible devolution he advocated in late Victorian times for 'Scotland, Wales and portions of England', and Home Rule for Ireland. Certainly that might have saved a century of turmoil there.

My father was born at that time, 1880. Gladstone had just begun his last full-length government before falling, after a general election, on the very issue of Home Rule, to the Tories and dissident Liberals. It was the time of the 'Scramble for Africa', and the zenith of the British Empire, before the Boer Wars in South Africa, Protectionism and, most profoundly, the Great War of 1914–18 changed all that. My father grew up in that period, and his letters which I have inherited, including from the Army in Mesopotamia and India during that War, display a keen awareness of what was going on at the time. He had an understanding of human affairs far beyond the circle of his own experience, and at one time toyed with the idea of standing as a Liberal for Parliament. He would undoubtedly have been good at it. He had all the attributes. But I do not think he would have enjoyed it. While he was firmly on Lloyd George's side, he had no time for political in-fighting and the Liberals were tearing themselves apart at that time. His preferred fields were education and voluntary organisation. His subject of study, once he had mastered English, was Human Geography and he did original research in it both in North Wales and North-West India. He liked people and always went out of his way to understand and help them on the right paths. It was his gift.

Born to a working-class family amid the slate quarries and chapels of Victorian Carnarvonshire, life must have been hard as a boy. To-day, the little town of Penygroes, where he was brought up in a cottage on the main street, still stands proudly at the foothills of Snowdonia and the mouth of the Lleyn peninsula. It is a part of the world I find takes some beating for concentrated natural beauty and good people. My father was deeply attached to it, and liked nothing better all his life than to roam the mountains there, or wherever he found their like. I have never been much of a walker myself, except with a golf club, but retain his love of the Welsh Mountains, as of Wales itself. There is to me something eternally special about the Land of my Fathers and, looking back on my own life, my two regrets are that I could not have lived there more and learnt Welsh, and that he died so young.

His father, my grandfather, was a slate-quarryman and, like so many of the workers in that industry, he, too, died young – at 50 in 1892. It was a harsh occupation, vividly described in Kate Robert's *Feet in Chains*, and more dispassionately but just as tellingly in Jean Lindsay's *History of the North Wales Slate Industry*. In its hey-day Welsh slate, though bulky and fragile to transport, was world renowned and shipped far and wide. The owners were 'nobility and gentry' (to quote the requirement of their concession applications) with names like Lord Newborough, William Oakley, Samuel Holland, W. Turner & Co., Lord Penrhyn, Lord Palmerston, Lord Pennant, and Assheton Smith. The land was Crown owned, the mining, quarry and transport rights leased by Acts of Parliament. There does not appear to have been a Welsh lessee among them. It was all determined by London in the imperial tradition of the time.

Most of the owners were divided from their workers by class, culture, language and religion. The quarrymen were mainly local, Welsh-speaking and nonconformist. Like so many others in that part of Wales then, as now, my father learnt Welsh before English. Despite three hundred and fifty years of imposed English, under the Act of Union of Wales with England, Welsh was still the language of the home and community. And their lives revolved around the Chapel. He nonetheless went on to secure an honours degree in English at the University of North Wales and to write and deliver reports, speeches, plays and poetry as fluently in English as in Welsh. At his first teaching post in Denbigh, where he was English and Senior Master before the 1914–18 War, he made it his mission to help local youngsters who could not get selected to the school, to learn English, just like those he taught in school, knowing that in the world as it was that was their only way forward. Sixty years and more on when I visited Denbigh to meet the Liberals there in 1977, an old man came over especially to tell me how much this had meant to him and others. My father's great cause was to help sustain and develop Welsh education and culture. Throughout his adult life he worked tirelessly to this end, not only in and around the substantially anglicised district of Llangollen but throughout Wales.

He was also ecumenical. Although he remained Welsh Chapel all his life, he was happy to send his sons to the English Methodist Sunday school because it was the best in Llangollen, and he chose his own burial place, alongside his first born Brian (my eldest brother, who died in infancy), in the little Church of England graveyard in the hamlet vale of Llantysilio, near Llangollen, a pearl of Welsh rural beauty that meant more to him than any sectarian divide. It is where Telford chose to draw his famous Union Canal from the river Dee, joined by the Horseshoe Falls, and the grave now also bears the names of my mother and elder brother. It is our family grave, which I too hope to join eventually.

Turning the clock back, my grandfather, the quarryman, also named Hugh, died when my father was only eleven. His wife Ann, my grandmother, was by all accounts, small, pretty and very sweet-natured. She must also have been a courageous woman, to survive widowhood at 48 with five children, two still at home – just as my mother was to do 45 years later at exactly the same age, with two children still on her hands. Neither married again. My mother certainly received proposals in widowhood. She was still 'Junoesque', according to the Ludlow School's *Century of Change 1900–2000*. I dare say grandmother Ann did too. Both declined. Both had relations of mutual devotion with their husbands and children that they found irreplaceable.

Grandmother Ann lived to 73 and saw two of her children migrate to the USA, two to London and my father, the youngest, commissioned into the War-time Army in 1914 and to Mesopotamia in 1917. He was her closest boy and she died soon after he was posted abroad. My mother lived on to 89, surviving my brother by five years. She died two weeks after the

1979 General Election, a socialist in spirit and a liberal at heart to the end. Although she had many conservative friends she could never abide the Conservative Party and, had she survived, she would undoubtedly have found Thatcherism distasteful in its extremism and probably also a betrayal of the feminist cause. Like my father she was deeply interested in people and generous of understanding, but knew her own right from wrong.

My father's two brothers and two sisters all left Carnarvonshire for pastures new, as did so many of the young there in the early part of the twentieth century. The slate industry was by then in decline, and both owner-worker and owner-tenant relations were generally woeful. Like much of British industry over the century, and even today I suspect, the owners knew how to order better than to manage. To order is to command. We British did so wherever we conquered and ruled in the world – and, by and large did so fairly effectively, America excepted, at least in comparison with most other colonial powers. To manage is in my view different. As Urwick Orr defined it in the 1950s, it is 'to get the best out of people'. That means persuasion. It is more difficult than ordering, but in civilian life much more rewarding in human response. I sometimes wonder whether the arguments that still rage in Britain today against devolution and delegation, but in favour of nationally imposed panaceas like comparability of wages (now thankfully outmoded), flexible labour markets and performance-related pay, taken with our relatively long working hours but low productivity, does not suggest that we still hanker after Empire practice in much of our management, both public and private and, with doubtless many exceptions, have yet to learn widely the wisdom of Urwick Orr – and from our own trial and experience, not just Continental and Japanese example.

Certainly it seems most of the North Wales slate industry owners at the turn of the century could have managed their companies better. Most kept wages low, profits high, health conditions grim and safety unheeded. Quarrymen were generally paid piecemeal, whether on rock face or underground. Come wind or rain (and it evidently rained quite a lot then, as now, in Snowdonia), hostel facilities and eating houses at the quarries were elementary, and the workers often made to pay for the coal heating themselves. Tuberculosis and silicosis were rampant, the latter still lacking diagnostic recognition. Accidents were rife. In the five years from 1908 to 1912 over 10% of the slate quarry workers and nearly 7% of the slate mine workers suffered injury. Deaths must have numbered some 1½% (extrapolating Jean Lindsay's figures). There was no safety legislation or workers' compensation effectively until the turn of the century.

Then came the bitter Penrhyn strike and, in 1902, the Penrhyn riots at Bangor and the High Court case in London. Lord Penrhyn's response said it all: 'Nothing is further from my intention than to invite the makers of mischief to come back into my employ.' It was perhaps little wonder that large numbers of young people decided in that period to up stumps and try the New World. Trade Union and other schemes were set up to help them. Some went to the USA, some to Australia and South Africa and some to Patagonia in the Argentine.

My father's eldest sister Marie went with her husband, Tom Llewellyn Williams, to Rome, in upper New York state and, except for the last three years of World War I when Tom served in the army in France and she came back to care for her mother, she spent the rest of her life there. We exchanged Christmas cards for many years, I as a boy and she as my New York aunt. But, sadly, we never met and they had no children. She died there on the eve of the Second World War in 1939.

My father's second brother Owen and wife-to-be Margaret also made for the New World, in 1911. Their first few years, like Marie's, must have been difficult. Like so many emigrants they found things nowhere near as rosy as they had hoped, especially in the quarries, which is where many found themselves sent, in upper New York state, Pennsylvania and Vermont. Owen and Margaret moved on west to California just as soon as they could, and eventually settled in Los Angeles. I was able to verify when visiting Los Angeles many years later that their address recorded in the old Street Directories the city kept before Telephone Directories and still keep available in the City Archives today, was exactly as I remembered it from exchanging Christmas cards as a child – 5163 Almaden Drive. Sadly it is no longer there. Nor of course are they.

Margaret came to visit us in Llangollen in 1933. Owen could not come as, in those days, 12,000 miles by rail and sea would have cost anyone lowly his job in time off let alone money. But she brought something rather special from him – two things in fact. One was an invitation to go and stay with them and see the great wide West and the huge redwood trees and everything else that California offered. Hollywood was only in its infancy. So was the automobile. And San Francisco's Golden Gate bridge had yet to be built. But there was much else. I am not sure how we could all have fitted into Owen's car, still less how we would have got there in a school holiday. But Owen had fully absorbed the get-up-and-go spirit of America (which I still find attractive) and nothing was going to stop us – except, in unfortunate succession, the Depression, or Slump as it was generally called, which we perhaps forget today brought in Britain among other miseries a voluntary cut in teachers' salaries across the board; then the shadow of War; and then my father's illness. So the Golden State was to remain a dream to me until long after Owen and Margaret had gone (they both died in their seventies during the War), indeed until 1997, when like so many other millions of visitors before me it did not disappoint.

But the very special thing Margaret brought to show us was Owen's badge of honour for saving the life of the Mayor of Los Angeles. I remember it well as a small embossed bronze plate, and my father telling me it was something to be very proud of, the American equivalent of our Freedom of the City. Innocently, as the cinema was the great novelty then, I asked my aunt if it meant my uncle could go free of charge to any Los Angeles 'Pictures' (as we then called them)? She was not impressed.

The story was that Owen, in the early days of the Slump, had given up painting and decorating to take the more secure job of janitor in the new palatial Los Angeles Mayoral offices. One day in 1932, under the administration of Mayor Porter, he walked into the Mayor's outer office to find a maniac brandishing a revolver and threatening the Mayor's Secretary and the Mayor. Like any good Welshman he did what came naturally and brought down the attacker in a flying tackle. The *Los Angeles Times* has since identified the incident for me but the press account at the time credited not Owen or any other underling, but a Police Captain, a Legionnaire, the Chief of the City detectives and two of his Lieutenants, all of whom claimed, improbably, either to have been there (the first two) or to have rushed up from the floor below (the three detectives) just in time to disarm the attacker together. So did the Mayor, reportedly emerging from his office with a gun. Some scrum, some story!

Judged by all one hears of the LA police today, things have not changed. A loyal citizen of the city remarked to me when I was there that Los Angeles probably has the only police force in the world that conducts its own foreign policy! Fortunately my wife and I had no occasion on our 1997 visit to test this (although my son Robert and a friend did, two years earlier, and found it rather unpleasant). But we did find the city administration, with the notable exception of the Archives, singularly unhelpful to our quest, in a most un-American way. Personally I have always found Americans refreshingly open, hospitable and ready to make time for a visitor. It is a main reason why I so enjoy visiting their great country. Los Angeles was different, starting with the Mayor's front man, called his 'City Constituency Advocate', whom we found indifferent to the point of rudeness. The Mayor at the time owed his election in part to a $1 million donation from the media tycoon Rupert Murdoch, who lives there. It is not my favourite American city.

Anyhow Owen had his City honour and I am witness to it. He was a man of courage and integrity, with a great love of life. He wrote us regular newsy letters, particularly at Christmas, in a delightful mix of English, American and Welsh. 'Now, Boys,' he wrote, after his first car tour of California in 1929, 'I have a little secret to tell you, Aunt Mag is a far better driver than I am. But I must not tell her! She is a fast driver too. Now can you imagine her driving the car at the rate of forty miles an hour? That's what she did from Monterey into Santa Cruz ... Gee, Boys, she did give the old bus some gas' ... 'And at 12 on Saturday the busy hour we were in the centre of the City of San Francisco, and believe me of all my experience as a driver this was my worst. We have traffic Ordinance and Regulations in Los Angeles, and the autorities is strick about them too. But Frisco they drive any old way, and being a stranger in the City made it bad for me. Anyway I am the same old pup and manage to get even with them!' That letter, like all he wrote, always began with the Welsh greeting: 'Dear Brother & Sister and the Boys', and, as always, it ended with a page or two in Welsh for my father, either about the family or about the Los Angeles Welsh community, for which he did much in his time, not least by getting the Mayor to attend their annual Eisteddfod. For all the wonders of the West I think Owen and Margaret's hearts remained in Wales. Sadly, they too left no descendants.

My father's younger sister, Siani, married another Carnarvon man, Lewis Osborne, and when he returned from the trenches at the end of World War I, they settled in the East End of London. They, too, had no children. My father's eldest brother John, known as Jack, had two sons, Jack and Edgar, old enough to enlist in the Army and Navy respectively mid-way through that War. Young Jack had his foot half blown off, but lived to walk again. Young Edgar appears to have survived too, as did the parents John and Katie, despite the frequent air raids one of their few surviving letters reveals they endured in their area of Lewisham from German Zeppelins in 1917. But what happened to them thereafter I do not know. The trail gives out a year or so after Grandmother Ann's death. John was not as close to her as Marie, Owen, Siani and my father. But they were all enterprising kinsfolk, and all true to Wales.

The maternal side of the family was as solidly Yorkshire as the paternal side was Welsh. My mother was a total stranger to Wales when she applied for and was appointed Mathematics mistress at Ruthin County Girls School in 1909. She was from all accounts then a striking young 20-year-old, straight from the heartland of Yorkshire, with rich auburn hair, a fine presence, a good (ambidextrous) tennis arm, and the distinction of being Leeds University's first female student to win a First Honours Mathematics and Physics degree. She also had a teacher's Diploma. Like my father, and so many others of their generation and social background, a professional career, particularly in teaching, was the height of ambition, and that is what she became – and, at heart, remained all her life. Knowledge and understanding were always her quest even when in old age she had to use a magnifying glass to read. Educating the young was always a duty requiring thought and preparation. Would that the high regard in which the teaching profession was then held still pertained today. The task of restoring our education standards might be a lot easier for those in it if it was. I was myself destined for that profession had not World War II intervened.

My mother's family was as dependent on the Yorkshire wool industry as my father's on Welsh slate quarrying. The wool industry was equally then in decline. Her father was a wool weaver in Halifax by the name of Charles Henry Normington. He was a humorous little man who had a hard upbringing but always managed to see the brighter side of life. His mother was called Ann. That name has popped up on both sides of the family at all ages, often without connection. She was a Swift and traced her ancestry back to the late seventeenth/early eighteenth-century dean of the Irish church, poet, political journalist and satirist, Jonathan. It may have been on the wrong side of the blanket as history relates that Swift never married his long-standing Dutch ladyfriend Esther Vanhomrigh (or Vanessa, as he coined her name). However recent research indicates he had another ladyfriend whom he may have married. Either way our family legend lives strong.

Ann, my Yorkshire great grandmother, died at the early age of 32, when Charles was still a boy. Her husband, Charles' father, was a poor but very respectable wool sorter. He was born Thomas Norminton (probably derived from the South Yorkshire town of Normanton), but introduced a 'g' into it to make it clearer to pronounce. I carry the resultant 'Normington' in my name to this day, as the trade-off between my parents for a Welsh first name. It is of course a nice if eccentric feature of Britain that we can call ourselves what we like – unless, I suppose, the change is so remote that some agency or other wants deed-poll evidence. My mother preferred, on marriage, the Welsh custom of inserting a hyphen in the name to distinguish one Jones from another. Otherwise my father might later have been called 'Jones the Head' or even 'Jones the School', like Dylan Thomas' 'Morgan the Organ'. In fact he became known in Llangollen as simply The Head. Hyphenating names is of course practised throughout Britain. It is a useful facility for those with common names or wishing to join family names. My father always preferred to be called plain Hugh Jones. So do I. But we are registered, since 1916, as Hugh-Jones.

Charles Normington married in the late 1880s a remarkable young lady called Nell (actually Ellen) Bailey, born in 1868, the eldest of eleven children only five of whom survived. Her father was David Bailey, a Yorkshire woollen mill engineer who has been variously described as 'strong, reliable and very capable', and 'difficult and tempestuous'. He was also an inventor and, in the 1890s, set off with his wife Ann to try his fortune and weaving inventions in America. Finding an interested American firm he put his principal invention and trust in their hands, and sadly never saw it again. There must have been many, on both sides of the Atlantic, who fell the same way in the early years of patent law. Perhaps there still are. Certainly there would seem to be something still lacking in that world today that permits powerful firms to force smaller companies into expensive law suits to defend their patents (as our neighbouring Wiltshire inventor of the bag-less vacuum cleaner recently had to do); and still worse to arrogate to themselves human gene patents. Anyhow, great-great-uncle

David and his wife came home from America the poorer but wiser. She was said to be a beautiful and gentle soul, slight and upright with, in later years, long white hair. She bore the American episode stoically, as she had her eleven pregnancies and six child losses in infancy. She brought up her five surviving children, four girls and one boy, to be all good chips off the Bailey block. She herself was one of twelve children, nine boys and three girls, of one William Thomas Marsden, a Quaker, whose wife's name I have failed to trace. They were all Yorkshire men and women.

All five of the surviving Bailey children stood out. They were each born among the mills and dales of West Yorkshire in the mid-Victorian era. They each lived to three-score years and more, one marrying and staying in Yorkshire, three marrying and, for different reasons, emigrating to Australia and New Zealand, and one staying single and nursing all her life. The nurse, Laura, was everyone's favourite. She went to South Africa when she was young, and served as a nurse in the final Boer War. That was before she settled in London. She came and stayed with us in Llangollen at the births of my brother and me, and brought us both into the world. She was sweetness and thoughtfulness personified.

Myra, a little older, was a strong but delightful lady who married a jeweller, Dick Edwards, in the Colne Valley and lived there all her life. Her elder daughter Lorna, like so many others of that World War I generation, never married for lack of available men. Instead, between working as an optician and later in the interesting post of Housing Officer in the new town of Crawley, she, too, became a favourite aunt and lived to be looked upon as the head of the family until her death well into her 90s. Her younger sister Muriel did marry and had three daughters, all of whom went into teaching and married teachers. One, Jenny, emigrated with her husband to University life in Canada, entered politics and became Minister of Energy in the Government of Ontario in the short-lived NDP (Labour) government there a decade ago. She is still there, with her children and grandchildren, the only present representatives of the family in North America.

The one boy of the Bailey family was great-uncle Dave. I never met him but, from all accounts, he was popular with all and not least with his nieces. He inherited his father's get-up-and-go and emigrated to New Zealand. His Bailey descendants are now in their fourth generation farming there. His youngest sister, Minnie, was only 15 when her parents went to America and had to be fostered in the family while they were away. It evidently did her no harm for in due course she married and with her husband Joe emigrated to Australia. They found a good life there in Adelaide working for the Commonwealth Government Railways.

Then there was Nell, the eldest of the five Bailey children, and my grandmother. But before coming to her, it is interesting to recall two great-great-aunts, Emma and Ada, who lived in a large house, by our family standards, at Meltham and had a croquet lawn. I never met Emma who died about the time I was born, but I well remember Ada as a gaunt and devout black-laced spinster the like of whom we rarely, if ever, see in this country any more. It was a Sunday when I was taken to see her, and no-one played croquet or anything else on the Sabbath in nonconformist West Yorkshire in those days. I still retain a vivid picture of this formidable lady rebuking my parents for not ordering me to sit silent in reverence and prayer. It was not much fun.

Nell and Charles Normington, my grandparents, were in Leeds at the outbreak of World War I. He immediately sought to join the Army but was declared too old. So he carried on working in a wool industry revived by war demand, but remained frustrated he could not see active service, although he did become a 'Volunteer' (Home Guard) when they were formed. Their three daughters, May (my mother), Nell and Laura were each by then launched in their chosen careers, two in teaching and one in nursing, and their brother Jim was away seeking his fortune in Australia. Tragedy then struck. News filtered back that Jim had contracted dengue fever in Brisbane and was in hospital. It grew worse and his best friend who had signed up for the wartime Australian Army appealed to the family to come and look after him. Mother Nell decided she must go and, in November 1916, she set sail for Australia in a troopship returning invalided New Zealand and Australian soldiers to their homes. Charles remained in Leeds to continue earning for them both and to keep the home going until she could return. She never did. Jim's condition became worse and Charles eventually decided, with the understanding and help of his daughters, that he must leave them and his beloved Yorkshire to join his wife and son in Australia. It took time for them to raise the money for the voyage and to see him and Nell through in Brisbane until he found a job. He left in April 1920 and remained there until Nell's death and his daughters clubbed together to bring him home in 1932.

I have inherited a few of Grandmother Nell's letters to her husband in the four years they were apart and to her daughters in the same period. I have more of her and Charles' letters from Brisbane in the years that followed. The family passed them around. They are extraordinary for their intimate description but stoical acceptance, and in Charles' case whimsical humour, of their blighted lives.

On arrival in Brisbane Nell rented a cottage on the outskirts of the then small market town of Ipswich and took Jim there out of hospital to care for him. Six months later she wrote, 'He is not much different but gets heavier. I have bought him a wheeled chair second hand 30 shillings so he will be able to wheel himself about the veranda ... Yesterday when I was washing him I said your mother has a lot of funny things to do for you hasn't she? He reeled off a string of curses and ended off with raising his arm with clenched fist and said, "if there is a God in heaven curse him".' Jim was a fine young man who had just volunteered for Army service when he was struck helpless, and much of the time speechless, by this painful disease. He had to be returned to hospital for long stretches. His mother, a stranger to the country, the bush and the heat, tied to the care of her son and dependant on what money Charles could send her from home 13,000 miles away, had a grim first two years. Her daughter May, my mother, wrote of her: 'Many people say she is an unusual woman, and so she is ... She always bears things so quietly ... yet has the brightest face of anyone they know ... what she always disliked was monotony and lack of social life ... which she now has to stand, unable to get out at all except Friday evenings shopping.' But Nell could still write home: 'It must be terrible by the papers, more Zeppelin raids in Yorkshire. I only hope you and all are safe', and 'It makes me very sad when I read of so many War cripples about not to mention the thousands whom no one will ever see again and who will live only in the hearts of those who have loved them.'

In time Nell found work housekeeping, wharf packing, hospital cooking (at 15 shillings per week), anything to keep going, until her husband Charles was able to join her and, in due course start a little business together in Ipswich. This was in 1920 and she wrote to her daughters: 'This will be the first time in your life I think that you have not had Dad for Xmas. Well your loss is my gain ... Dad is settling very well but oh dear sometimes I catch him looking at your photos and he will burst out with something about you ... which shows where his thoughts are.' Meantime, while Australia debated conscription to augment the already large forces of volunteers they had sent to Europe, Jim remained gravely ill and unable to join. He and his parents felt that too. It was a trapped life. Her letters ceased after a time to speak much of him, and I have no record of when he died. But in 1921 she wrote: 'Dad and I both said at Easter it is like being in a prison here. No friends to visit, no relations to go and see, just to the "pictures" that is our only refuge. The country is just bush and bush and bush hills and more bush. If I were in Brisbane I of course know people there but at present we shall have to stay here,' because of Jim and work. Two years later the drought hit Queensland, and farming, on which Ipswich depended, was devastated. 'Cattle and sheep are laid dead in thousands in the bush', she wrote. 'The "busheys" as we call them are having a very hard time and if it does not rain soon there will be no water for anyone. It is a beautiful country if there were plenty of rains. As it is one seems to be always longing for rain.'

Then in the late 1920s, of course came the Slump. Nell continued to write that they were looking forward to coming home, and to seeing for the first time their by then four grandchildren. But 'trade is bad', fares were expensive and her health was failing. She died in 1930 and the Mayor of Ipswich wrote to Charles: 'Let me say that your late wife and yourself since your residence in Ipswich have always been estimable citizens – citizens of whom any city might well feel proud.'

Grandfather Charles's great strength was his humour, never malicious, in many ways Chaplinesque; he was a perceptive observer of life. He must occasionally have been a trying man to live with in times of decision, but uplifting at all other times. His letters to his daughters from the ship on his way out to Australia held observations on everything that caught his interest, from the buildings and natives of Port Said and every other port *en route*, to the problems of a 15,000 ton ship with nearly 2000 people on board, scraping the bottom of the Suez Canal because the canal was still meant for no more than 5000 tons. Also on the heat but calmness of the Red Sea; the congenial character of his fellow 3rd-class passengers and hordes of children, and the endless series of lost and found notices posted up by the crew – to which he amused himself inventing his own additions like 'Lost 50 yards of Oriental Line, will finder return same to Mrs Fl'arty as she is washing her ten children tomorrow and wants to hang them out.'

The first job he found in Brisbane, and it took some time because there was so much post-War unemployment there, was to sell tea in the town and bush for a company of Brisbane tea merchants called Edwards & Co. They had a coat of arms inscribed 'Purity, Strength, Flavour conquer all'. He received £4 10s. per week but had to pay all his own travel expenses. When many years later I asked him about it, his response was an hilarious account of bicycling in the bush, falling off on a rough track and hearing from the tree above his first kookaburra, or laughing jackass as it is sometimes called, screeching its head off in apparent amusement. I never did discover whether he reached his next farm or sold any more tea that day.

The job did not last long, nor the next one selling pianos. Eventually he joined Nell in pioneering Ipswich's first High Street café, though there was apparently plenty of Greek competition round the back streets. They also established a little provisions shop. They lived outside the town in a lonely place on the Blue River where they could afford a house large enough to care for their son in his periods out of hospital. But grandfather Charles still found occasion to travel afield in Queensland on business when he could, and the interest to keep distantly abreast of home, Australian and international news from local newspapers and an early model radio 'that warbled'. Also to offer pungent comments on them all. After Nell's death, he wrote weekly and at length to his daughters, usually collectively 'Dear Girls'. Sometimes it would be a diary of daily encounters and conversations, sometimes his suggestions for the welfare of his daughters and particularly his grandchildren, and sometimes his views, usually ir-reverent, on political events and personalities. He much preferred Lloyd George to Baldwin even at 13,000 miles away. He enjoyed philosophising on anything and everything. Most of all he enjoyed telling stories of local people and events, always with a human interest, frequently capped with his own doggerel and, except when recounting tragedy like the local unemployment and starvation resulting from the world depression, usually with an eye for the comical.

'So you would like to know more of your ancestors,' he wrote once in answer to his daughters' suggestion that he chronicle them. 'I can tell you a lot ... The pedigree is there all right or you could not have been born ... I think my grandfather on my father's side was little of stature and as broad as he was long ... I never knew him ... My grandfather on my mother's side was tall and thin with a rather long face, noble-browed religiously inclined. I remember going to see him when a kiddie. He was a cobbler ... He had married a second time – to a red faced little thing and I don't think I liked her ... Between 60 and 70 he had a stroke and died. He stuck to his last to the last ... His first wife sported the name of Rowbotham or Rowbottom, which of the two angelic names would you prefer? I never knew the lady.' After this the daughters wisely decided to pursue their lineage enquiries elsewhere.

His wish for his grandsons was that 'they grow into great big strapping boys and be able to run, swim, jump, play cricket and football and tennis, also say grace gracefully and their prayers night and morning.' I am not sure we quite lived up to his wishes. He lived to a good age, with his youngest daughter in Leamington Spa on his return from Australia. I remember him as a kindly old man, with a twinkle in his eye, forever relighting his pipe and burning holes in his jersey, reading his weekly *John Bull* from cover to cover with the help of a magnifying glass, and always interested in people. He had a hard life but never complained.

How a man of his small stature and wife equally petite managed to produce four strapping children, all well above average height as it was then and full bodied, is perhaps just an interesting commentary on the times. Many other families of that generation did the same. The home grandmother Nell and grandfather Charles managed to create in urban working-class Yorkshire, undoubtedly put nourishment of the children first, both in food and intellect, and their own selves second. It was helpful that food, health and education facilities were so much better by then than in their youth, though still elementary compared with what we have today.

That their three daughters each found professional careers was unusual in those Edwardian and post-Edwardian times, when women had no vote and, once married, were expected to stay at home. Mrs Pankhurst and her fellow campaigners for women's rights were only just emerging. Like my mother, the second daughter Nell managed to break the mould by winning scholarships to Leeds University and emerging with a First Honours degree in English. She, too, became a teacher. She, too, was an early Socialist. She, too, remained both all her life between bringing up her family.

The third daughter, Laura, took the more conventional path, into nursing. Like, I imagine, many others of that day, she tried personal nursing first, and in later life would recall with chuckling amusement (but always maddeningly loyal discretion) her travels as companion to such notorious socialites as Mrs Cornwallis-West. After that she turned to hospital and public health nursing, rising to become the much respected District Health Visitor of that elegant midlands spa town Leamington. I remember her flat overlooking the Parade, and the Pump Room gardens with Jan Berenska's orchestra. His real name was John Smith. She knew because, like many other Leamington notables, and unnotables, she had midwifed him into the world. She was another lovely woman left without a man to marry by the slaughter of World War I. She became instead everyone's favourite until her premature death in retirement in 1963. At her memorial service she was aptly described as 'a remarkable woman who had a great influence for good ... greatly beloved ... had given her life to public service ... her help and sympathy were never sought in vain.'

The second daughter, my aunt Nell, and her husband-to-be Sam Cowan met at Leeds University just before the War but, like so many others, waited until after the conflict to get married. Much of his War was spent in the Army in France, and he was fortunate to survive unwounded. A scholarly man, he was both a gifted teacher of English and a prolific amateur artist. I still have and prize some of his paintings and drawings. Born into the Jewish faith he strongly believed in integration into the wider community, and suffered ostracism by some of his Jewish elders for the rest of his life for practising what he preached. He was also a man of great concentration. I remember endearingly how, when I was staying with them at Wandsworth Common after World War II, he went missing one evening on the London Inner Circle and eventually arrived home most apologetic. He had seen off a friend from Paddington, and then missed his underground stop three times as he went round and round the Circle totally absorbed in his book. He also had a donnish humour, enjoying recounting for instance 'the Chinese symbol for trouble is two women in one kitchen'. He felt deeply about social and racial injustice but found the militarism of the National Union of Teachers after World War II abhorrent. A teacher in his view was there to teach the youngsters their tomorrow not to politic away in an Isle of Man Conference to undermine the great Butler and Labour education reforms of the day. When he retired from Wandsworth School in 1954 after 34 years service the school paid him warm tribute as 'a schoolmaster of rare quality, of wide culture and high artistic sensitivity, and of a rich and interesting personality that enhanced any company in which he found himself ... No task was too difficult nor beneath his dignity if our welfare demanded it. Those who remember the variety of jobs he willingly undertook during the School's War-time evacuation at Woking, will not have to seek for illustrations of this characteristic, the mark of the devoted teacher and the good companion ... We miss him greatly.'

Nell could have done all sorts of things if she had wanted. She had the presence, intellect and wit. She chose to concentrate on family and teaching. I came to know her well and Sam, and their two children Cicely and Alan, after the War when, rather to my surprise, I found myself selected for the senior branch of the Foreign Service but expected to work at the Foreign Office in London on only £300 a year. I had nowhere to live but digs in outer London. They took me in as their own, and I shall always be grateful to them. No doubt I would not have been the only ex-serviceman or ex-student to have had to search for lodgings in bomb-scarred and rationed post-war London on a pittance salary. But it would have made a very much less congenial start to my new career.

The travelling instincts of the family emerged there too. First Cicely (or Laura as she preferred to be called in later life), the kindest of cousins, upped and went to help build the Brotherhood of Youth highway in Yugoslavia, and then a kibbutz in Israel, returning a year later with an Israeli husband of Austrian origin, to settle in North London, revert to teaching (including in some very tough schools not to mention classes for the disadvantaged), and between times raise a family of three girls and foster-care numerous others. She also became a Quaker, and undertook the visiting of old people and probation service. Tom died tragically in a car accident on a return visit to Israel. She, for all her gentle love of people – or perhaps because of it – remained all her life an ardent campaigner for social and racial justice. Many were the times she carried the banner at London demonstrations and meetings. British democracy and justice would not be the same without her, or the likes of her. Nor would the local Care services.

Her brother Alan broke teacher's ranks, like my own brother, and took to medicine. He did outstandingly well but, when it came to a Fellowship, encountered the brickwall of the medical establishment of the day. They did not like his then left-wing politics. So, in good family tradition, he uprooted and took his wife and four young children 'down under' where, except for medical expeditions to the Antarctic, bird-watching expeditions everywhere and an occasional visit to Britain, he has remained happily ever since. He is now a respected member of the Canberra establishment, nominally retired but, like so many doctors most everywhere, so it seems, remains for ever on call. The British medical establishment lost a good man there – not for the first or last time it seems in view of the chronic shortage of doctors in Britain today.

The Cowans also adopted a daughter, Steffi. Typically, when the call came before the War to take Jewish children from the growing holocaust in Nazi Germany, they volunteered, paraded at Liverpool Street station on a designated day in 1938 and took this little waif into their fold. She grew up with them, married and produced a happy family of her own. Poor girl, she never saw her blood parents again. In the doom-laden words of the letter my aunt and uncle eventually received from the Refugee Agency after the War 'they were removed to an unknown destination in 1943'. Amidst the horror of that fate, their one consolation must have been the knowledge that their child was safe. Genocide is a most terrible thing.

Sadly both Nell and Sam Cowan died relatively young in the mid 1950s when they were just beginning to enjoy retirement in rural St Johns, Surrey, near where they had been evacuated with their Wandsworth Schools during the War. They loved it there, though today, like so much of Surrey, it is so built up I doubt they would any longer feel it was in the country. Their travels abroad took them usually to France where they enjoyed relaxing on the beaches, painting village scenes and practising their French at such places as Wimereux and Boulogne. Those Pas-de-Calais towns are now within London commuting and shopping distance, but in pre-War days they were expeditions for the enterprising few.

My brother Eryl also travelled in his time, principally as an Army doctor first with the Royal Artillery in France and the Low Countries and then with the infantry in India in World War II. I shall come back to him in later chapters. Also to his two children, Ruth and Christopher. And especially to my own three children Julia, Robert and Katie. All five have already lived abroad for periods at one time or another, and three now have jobs that take them abroad frequently.

Travel and venture have thus been a feature of the family for at least six generations. Some have gone to stay, to America, Canada, Australia or New Zealand. Some have gone and come back, to France, Germany, the Middle East, Africa and beyond. Some have made a career of it, like me for a quarter-century and my niece Ruth who, having lectured abroad for some years for the Junior International Chamber of Commerce, now travels widely as a facilitator, helping company managers with the modern problem of mutual communication and understanding. Her daughter, Lizzie, still in her young teens, has just, as I write, paid a precocious visit to the former Soviet now independent republic of Kyrgystan in central Asia. She seems determined to carry on the family tradition, as will I dare say her engineer brother Paul, my great-nieces Helen and Olivia and my young grandson James. It must be a restless gene we all share, or the Swift/Gulliver inspiration, or something.

The other family trait is equally difficult to explain. No member in six generations has made money, or much of it anyhow. Great-great-uncle David Bailey, the inventor, had a go in the United States but failed. A great-great-grandson of his and distant cousin of mine, Ron Bailey, seems to be doing well growing avocados on a large scale in New Zealand. And my nephew Christopher, the delightful technologist of the family, seems to be on course advising national newspapers on the sophisticated modern computer equipment they need for printing. But we have no fat cats, nor even plump ones. Financial gain does not appear to have been an over-riding goal in any generation or individual member of the family. Our loss perhaps, but I hope the chapters that follow may affirm there are other things worth having in life.

# Parents in World War I, Home Front and Mesopotamia

## 1914–1917

M
Y FATHER WAS A GREAT LETTER-WRITER and enjoined everyone to do the same. From the time he first met my mother, he aged 31 at Denbigh and she aged 22 at Ruthin, they corresponded between meetings even though they were only a few miles apart. He wrote of his doings, events, thoughts, plans, and his love for her. Also of the people they knew – but never gossip, he would not abide that. Open your soul when you write, he told her. She found it difficult at first and had to be coaxed. Her training, after all, was in the Sciences, where one proceeded from the particular to the general, and wrote about practical things, not the Arts, where it seemed one could make generalisations and then seek the particular in support – she disliked that all her life – and which expected elaborative story. Also she was not a Welsh poet as he was; she was an affectionate but reserved Yorkshire woman. She learnt quickly, however, and in time became almost as fluent and diligent a correspondent as he was, both to each other when they were apart and to their wide circle of family, friends, acquaintances, and former pupils and colleagues.

She kept his letters and he kept hers. Together they make an unusual collection, particularly those exchanged when he was in the Army in Britain, Mesopotamia and India in World War I. Not all they wrote survives. None of his fell foul of the Army censor, as far as I can discern, nor did hers of course as there was no outgoing censorship. But, diligent as the Army postal services no doubt were, envelopes both of them kept show the tortuous process by which letters to and from one War front or another suffered from his frequent postings. Also there being no airmail in those days, each letter to and from the Mesopotamian and Indian fronts took weeks by sea (always, it seems, via Bombay), and there is constant reference in them to intermediate letters missing presumed sunk by the 'Hun' submarines. The surviving letters nonetheless number many hundreds and are all full, newsy and thoughtful.

The diarised extracts I have selected to publish in this and the next chapter are about the life they led and the extraordinary events of those times, rather than the romance of their relations. But the picture would be false without mention of that remarkable bond, expressed in every letter both ways and with ever fresh poetry.

Boy–girl relations in what might be called the conventional classes of those days must have been much harder to form than now – but were without doubt more durable as a result. My parents did not meet by casual introduction or accident as young things so often seem to do today. Their first encounter had to be engineered and of course escorted, over tennis. The match-maker was one of my mother's senior pupils, Dilys Edwards (later Benson-Evans) and her mother. They remained dear friends for life, as are her daughters, the elder Nerys Vaughan being like a sister to me. Dilys was later described by the great Huw Wheldon as the prettiest lady in North Wales. By then he was related through the marriage of his brother Tomos to Nerys, but I am sure he was right. Her children, grandchildren and great-grandchildren form the loveliest of Welsh families.

My parents 'went together', to use the old-fashioned phrase, for over four years before they married. Except in romantic fiction that was not unusual in those days although the War did prolong it. Marriage was for life so they took their time about it. They also had to save for it. She originally had another boy-friend in Yorkshire, called Fred Strawbridge. With due respect to his memory, I cannot but be glad that nothing came of that. My father no doubt had his share of girl-friends – he was regarded as very eligible – but probably not at school or college. Friars' School, Bangor to which he won scholarships from his primary Board School at Penygroes, was, as most secondary schools in those days, strictly segregated, boys only. The University College of North Wales, Bangor, to which in 1900 he won scholarships after a spell as student-teacher, was co-educational but the Principal, one Professor Reichel, after rusticating one student for 'philandering', imposed the following extraordinary code:

*Men students may not:*
*(a) meet women students by appointment or walk with them*
*(b) accompany women students to and from the college*
*(c) walk with women students in the grounds*
*(d) visit women students in their lodgings, or receive visits from them.*

*Reasonable association of men students and women students is permitted:*
*(a) at authorised social meetings within the college*
*(b) on the college-field during the progress of matches*

*(c) in the college itself for business connected either with the college societies or with class work.*

One wonders how all this was observed!

A feature of my parents' correspondence is that while they could each be pungent about people, events and the times, or worried about the War, family, illness and savings, or humorous about people and their ways, there was never a suggestive smut between them, nor malice about others, nor vulgarity in any form. I suppose this only seems remarkable now because, for good or bad, life is so much less restrained today. There was a much stricter code then. But their romance was undoubtedly a little special. My mother wrote much later in life that her husband had been 'the perfect lover, and never failed to write'. This has to be understood between the lines of the following Wartime extracts. So does the War background.

On 4 August 1914 Germany invaded Belgium, with the clear intention of going on to France – for the second occasion in a lifetime. Britain hesitated but, seeing the Belgians overwhelmed, stood by its *Entente Cordiale* with France and declared War on Germany. There was an upsurge of patriotic feeling and romantic patriotism it is difficult for us to comprehend today. My father volunteered right away and applied for a commission. He was accepted on 22 October 1914 and served in the RASC at different depots in Wales and England for the first two years and in Mesopotamia and India for the next two and half years, being finally discharged back to civilian life in June 1919. He and my mother married in January 1916 but, other than three months together then and an occasional visit she was able to make to him when he was stationed successively at Wrexham, Aberystwyth, Northampton, Ruthin and Hereford, they were separated all those years except by letter.

These diarised excerpts and related papers have been edited only for selection and continuity. Any imprecision of date is because in the earlier letters they were often omitted, and have had to be divined from the envelopes or contents. 'H' stands for Hughie and 'R' for Robin, the names by which they addressed each other.

## H to R Sept. 1914                                              Denbigh

*My dearest ... Great excitement in Denbigh last night – arrival of 5 German Cavalry Officers en route for the compound at Llansannan. They looked very downcast – except one. There are about 60 prisoners there altogether, amongst them is Von Tirpitz, the son of the German Admiral. He is a cheeky youth, it seems, and tried to escape from Edinburgh. So he was transported to the wilds of Hiraethog. Much good may it do him!*

**H to R Oct. 1914**                                    **Denbigh**

*(after volunteering for the Army)*

*My own ... You won't let it worry you, will you? ... I am happy to think I am only trying to do my little share. I couldn't stay on here any longer ... especially after you had given me your unselfish benediction ... I don't know how to tell poor Mam. I wrote yesterday ... I do hope she will not fret.*

**R to H Oct. 1914**                                      **Ruthin**

*Dearest ... I'm madly proud of you – you can never know how much ... This pride in you will keep me very content so don't imagine I'm fretting.*

**George R. I. 29 October 1914**              **Court of St James's**
**to Our Trusty and well beloved Hugh Jones.**

*Greeting. We, reposing especial Trust and Confidence in your Loyalty, Courage, and good Conduct, do ... Appoint you to be an Officer in our Territorial Force from the twenty-second day of October 1914. You are therefore carefully and diligently to discharge your Duty as such in the Rank of Second Lieutenant or in such higher Rank as We may from time to time hereafter be pleased to promote you to ... and you are at all times to exercise and well discipline in Arms both inferior Officers and Men serving under you and use your best endeavours to keep them in good Order and Discipline ... And We do hereby Command them to Obey you as their superior Officer and you to observe and follow such Orders and Directions as from time to time you shall receive from Us, or any your superior Officer, according to the Rules and Discipline of War ...*

**Scottish Equitable to Hugh Jones Esq.**          **Edinburgh**
**31 Oct. 1914**

> *Dear Sir ... Policy 69188 on your life*
> *Please say if you are enlisting for the period of the war or only*
> *for one of the usual terms of service.*
> *Yours faithfully*
>     *... Assistant Actuary*

[H's reply is not known! He might have been tempted to reply 'till death do us part']

**R to H 10 Dec. 1914**                                  **Ruthin**

*My dearest ... Have you ever enjoyed the exultation of sitting in an exam room supervising, with the click-cluk of protractors and the rustling of rubbers as the only sounds, and felt that every particle of knowledge – bad, good or indifferent – that the kids were putting down was of your teaching?*

**R to H 12 Dec. 1914**                                  **Ruthin**

*My dearest ... The Birch Concert was given in Ruthin last night and all the* 'quality' was there, including our Headmistress ... Apparently part of it was taken up by the singing of a recruiting song by a girl of the aristocracy (!), at the end of which a real wounded soldier made his appearance and was kissed on the stage. HM related this story with relish at breakfast, at which I murmured – disgusting!

## North Wales Times, Oct. 1914

On Wednesday, a very pleasant duty fell to the lot of the Staff and boys of Denbigh County School on the occasion of Mr Hugh Jones' departure from Denbigh to take up military duties ... The Headmaster and others spoke of his good work ... and presented him with money to the amount of £4 3s. 4d. collected by staff and boys, with which to procure a sword.

## R to H Oct. 1914                                                    Ruthin

My dearest ... I've just read the North Wales Times eulogy of you – he hasn't spared you has he? But it doesn't quite equal the Wrexham Free Press ... their report is entitled 'Purse of Gold'!

## H to R Jan. 1915                                              Aberystwyth

My dearest ... There are about 10,000 troops at present in Aberystwyth, and 5000 more coming next week. But I doubt if room can be found for them, as the town is quite full up ...

Our horses and transports have not yet arrived but I've just received my orders for tomorrow:

> 7am – Parade & drill on the Promenade
> 8–9 – Breakfast
> 9–12.30 – Route March
> –2 – Lunch
> –4.30 – Drill
> 7.30 – Dinner
> 9.30 – Men in – I have to go round & inspect
> 10 – Lights out!

Not bad, is it? Somewhat of a change from the easy life at Wrexham.

## R to H 2 and 5 Jan. 1915                                          Leeds

Dearest ... I have just been reading an article by Alex Thompson on that everlasting and ever interesting topic – the duration of the War. 1915, he is sure, will see its close. Comforting news!

Ralph P ... is now organising the publication of the Times History of the War ... He is Sam's great rival for Nell's affections. They seem to be very prepared for invasion in London. Nell says the place is in darkness and the searchlight is weirdly impressive. Almost all the men have gone, and one man we know well, a Mr N ..., is being given the cold shoulder by those young girls for not enlisting and having no reason.

*Today we went down to town to see the soldiers parade. There were the special constables and a brass band, police on horse and then the Pals Battalions who were coming to Leeds for 5 days furlough. They looked marvellously healthy and so serious – I could have wept almost when I thought that all those fine fellows were preparing for such a brutal business. There were crowds and crowds – hundreds there to watch, so keen is the enthusiasm in Leeds.*

### H to R Feb. 1915                                          Aberystwyth

[Instructions on how to get to Aberystwyth from Ruthin for a half-term weekend visit, only 70 miles as the crow flies but rather more by Mid-Wales trains.]

*My dearest ... Start from Ruthin ... Ask for cheap weekend ticket to Aberystwyth ... Change at Corwen ... Take train to Dolgelley ... You may have to change at Bala Junction ... Ask the guard ... Corwen to Dolgelley is over some very high & bleak moorland & you will find it very cold ... At Dolgelley leave the Great Western Ry for the Cambrian Ry ... The Cambrian carriages are not heated; they only have foot-warmers, which are oftener cold than warm! ... At Barmouth Junction ask guard if you have to change ... Don't go on to Barmouth ... Ask for Machynlleth ... Here I will meet you and we can come on to Aberystwyth the following day ... Bring some sandwiches and light literature. 'The way is long'.*

### H to R c. Mar. 1915                                       Aberystwyth

*Darling O'Mine ... This afternoon I have to go and be inoculated. Nearly all the men have had their doses and jolly rough doses they have been ... Then in a week's time we'll have a second dose ... It seems so absurd to make one sick for a certainty for the sake of avoiding another sickness which is not a certainty ... But it is a safeguard especially by the time we get into camp. And of course the North of France will inevitably become a very hot bed when the warm weather comes ... Anyhow the inoculations mean an extra hour or two in bed in the mornings! Cold comfort – but as the Capt. says, most comfort is cold.*

### R to H April 1915                                             Ruthin

*My dear ... Wasn't that shooting of Nurse Cavell a disgrace. It makes your blood boil – and she has such a very beautiful and noble face.*

### H to R c. April 1915                                      Aberystwyth

*My Sweetheart ... So you want me to explain to you those military terms! Here goes – A Subaltern (with accent on the sub!) is anything below a Captain i.e. a Lieut. or 2nd Lieut. In Infantry they have a battalion of 1000 men with about 10 Captains & 40 Subalterns, and 2 Majors & Adjutant – all under a Colonel. In Army Service we have Corps (not Battalion) of about 500 men, consisting of 4 companies with a Colonel, Major, Captains & Subalterns.*

*A Subaltern's life is never free here. Just as I sit down ... there comes a knock at the door ... in enters a man, there's a clank of spurs as he comes to attention (generally known as 'Shun'! or 'Hun'!), and then follows a long rigmarole which generally means my peace is interrupted & off I go on some quest or other. Bless me, a poor Subaltern's life is no joke! And there's no respite, Sunday or Weekday. But dont think I'm growling!*

### H to R 2 Sept. 1915                                                    Hereford

[H left Aberystwyth in May/June to be O/C 3rd Line Ruthin until Sept. when he was appointed O/C the newly created Admin. Centre ASC at Hereford.]

*Robin Mine ... I arrived here yesterday evening. It was with a very heavy heart I left Ruthin. How I wish you were here ... Whatever happens I am anxious we get married at Christmas ... Life seems very empty without you.*

*I had a rare send-off from the boys at Ruthin. They presented me with a silver cigarette case with my monogram engraved on it. It may have been against Kings Regulations ... but I could hardly refuse it ...*

### R to H 17 & 24 Sept. 1915                                              Ruthin

*My dearest ... There were some wounded soldiers came to tea today – poor, poor fellows.*

*Our school rooms are dreadfully crowded. In one form alone there are 32 – as you know 30 is the Board of Education limit.*

### R to H 16 Oct. 1915                                                    Ruthin

*My Dear ... The French play written by Monsieur Gouge as a review on the mistresses and another play given by the boarders made altogether 30 shillings to be sent to the Dardanelles in cigarettes. I suppose you know Sallie Davies' brother in the RAMC has been killed in the Dardanelles?*

### H to R 17 Oct. 1915                                                    Hereford

*My Sweet ... I have again offered my services overseas. As you know the first occasion was the beginning of June, and the second 4 Sept ... There are only 6 officers out of about 60 in the Welsh Divisional Train A.S.C. whose services have so far been demanded overseas.*

*Meanwhile I spend much of my time trying to heal and soothe the poor maimed fellows who are returned here to me or put in my charge. I sent one home the other day – a perfect wreck – a fine young Welshman done for the rest of his life and no more use to the Army. It wants a Heart to deal with them.*

### R to H 21 December 1915                                                 Leeds

*My Dearest ... There seems to have been a great deal of muddling over the Scarborough affair. There were trenches all along the coast and not a single man in them though they were there a fortnight ago. The sea was mined and electrical connections made with the shore but no-one set the thing going. The*

*Germans must have had perfect knowledge of the harbour. At one time they were only 600 yards from the shore ... We are fully expecting them to invade or something on Christmas Day. They are sure to go for industrial areas – but York is full of troops, and in the Aerodrome here, up Roundhay Rd, they are turning out 1 aeroplane per week.*

In the autumn of 1915 H and R decided to get married irrespective of when or whether his repeated applications to serve overseas were accepted. They initially thought of a quiet wedding in London but were advised by her Aunt Laura against this 'while the raids are on. One never knows when they are coming. The last raid was something awful.' Eventually they opted for Slaithwaite in West Yorkshire where R's family could readily foregather and dates could be changed at short notice if necessary. H applied for marriage leave for a few days in early January but had to wait until just before Christmas for approval. They were married on 6 January. 1916. They had a few days honeymoon before he had to return to duty at Hereford. She accompanied him, having obtained temporary release from Ruthin. By Easter H's posting abroad having still not come through she had to return to Ruthin. As they were together at Hereford those three months there are no letters between them for that period. But there were others:

### R. Lloyd Williams to H 10 Jan. 1916
#### 17th Battn. Royal Welch Fusiliers, France

[In Welsh] *My dear friend ... I have read of your wedding and send you my very good wishes ...* [In English] *In case Mrs Jones has not mastered the Welsh language yet I think I'd better change and write in English ... We've been out in France for over five weeks ... We've had our baptism of fire – we were heavily shelled the second day – one shell dropped about 3 yards from me – knocked me down and covered me with mud, otherwise I was alright – the man next to me was very severely wounded in the head ...*

*We had a lively time on New Year's Eve – the Germans fired two rounds each (rifle fire) when the new year came in, and our men immediately fired ten or twelve rounds each in reply ... We had a lot of fun there – the place was swarming with rats and some of the fellows were more afraid of them than of the Germans who were about 250 yards away – as a matter of fact it is rather hard to say which is the worse – a shell bursting over your head or a rat walking slowly over your face when you are just going to sleep ...*

*I hope if I survive this war, to come and see you and, after a good supper in front of a roaring good fire, to tell you about our experiences – we have seen a good many things that we daren't say anything about them in our letters.*

### R to H 7 May 1916                                    Ruthin

*My dear ... Bob E ... is over for the weekend. He has been reduced to the ranks. Injustice seems to abound in the Army. He got a new Colonel – 3 weeks old who reported on Bob and Bob's Captain that they were 'temperamentally unfit to go to the front, yet at any rate' ... The War Office replied they would be gazetted as having relinquished their commissions, so Bob resigned. This in spite of the fact his previous Colonel had recommended him for the next Captaincy. Bob moved to Kimmel Park and has been promoted Sergeant already.*

### Capt. Llwyd to H 23 May 1916     R. Welch Fusiliers, France

*My dear Friend ... [Opening in Welsh. Then, for R's sake, in English] ... When you wrote in March you were anxiously awaiting the development of events about Verdun. Now all fear seems to have been removed – and I think the struggle there has proved conclusively that it will only end in a deadlock whichever side attempts to push ... both sides have had so long to fortify they are in my opinion impregnable. Worse luck for us, because we feel it is a poor sort of warfare sitting behind sandbags, looking at one another, and being fully aware also that the people at home want a show for their money by now and that we ought to attempt a forward move.*

*It is a terrible responsibility out here, to have the lives of over 200 men and 5 officers to answer for. I feel it very much and try to do my best ... The enemy exploded a mine nearly under our front line parapet a few nights ago just where my Company was – we had quite an exciting time – but came off with few casualties considering – the crater is huge – you could put two houses in it, so you can imagine the debris – and I had my listening patrols out all around it when it went up. Young E ... went delirious with the shock – took two men to keep him from going over the top yelling 'the b——y Germans'.*

*Resting temporarily 600 yards behind the firing line ... I look at the little wooden crosses all around me, think of the 'unknown heroes' who are lying peacefully underneath them, and it seems such mockery to hear a cuckoo singing in a place like this ... Some of the men are making a wreath to put on the grave of one of our officers – shot through the neck two days ago – we all miss him very much – a teacher at Burnley, from a farmer's family near Carmarthen ... Dash these shells ... the Bosh drops them occasionally ... they make a deuce of a row – I think I'll have to get inside my dug out.*

### H to R ? May, 4 June & ? June 1916     Hereford

*Sweetheart ... Capt Scales RAMC left here for Oswestry yesterday. Just a wire on Friday evening, and he was off on Saturday. I suppose that is how my notice will come!*

*Have just finished 'Candida' – one of the silliest things I've ever read! Afraid I'm not clever enough to understand Shaw's works, and to follow the bewildering intricacies of his perverted wisdom.*

*Heard the latest? ... Will Crook's grandson asked him 'When Charlie Chaplin dies, will he go to Heaven?' – 'Yes', replied Will – 'Eh', cried the kid, 'won't God laugh!'*

## R to H 12 June 1916                                    Ruthin

*My dearest . . . I went to see Nini Williams last night. She and her daughter-in-law are most brave. Her son had returned from a raid and they could not find a Capt Brock. He said he knew exactly where the Capt was and went out to find him. Brock returned very soon, but Williams never came back. For some time they failed to find him and put up a board asking in German where he was. The reply came soon afterwards 'The officer is dead'. He was only 33.*

## H to R 19 and 24 July 1916                            Hereford

*Gentle wife . . . Just a week and you will be here. There will be plenty to keep you occupied. All are working at high pressure at the Depot . . . The poor wounded are pouring in. Over 60 landed here yesterday, 33 being stretcher cases. One poor fellow died on the way . . . I am doing RAMC as well as ASC work these days – Dr Lane does the medical, and Sgt Long and I the admin. work.*

*You will be sorry to hear Mrs Armitage's brother is reported missing. He was in the Lancs. Fusiliers and took part in the very first advance on July 1. Out of 1100 officers and men who made up the battalion, it is said that only 198 answered the roll-call. Dreadful isn't it?*

In August H & R had what turned out to be their last time together, other than a brief few days in mid-October, for nearly three years. His applications to do duty overseas were finally accepted in October but it was not to be the Western front in France but the Eastern front, against Germany's main ally, the Ottoman Empire, in the near-East. He appears to have been given only a few days notice to extricate himself from his job at Hereford, pay farewell visits to his wife in Ruthin and aged mother in Penygroes, and report to Plymouth Devonport for embarkation. But he had been well warned, that was the Army's way.

It was not however to be the Navy's way (or whichever Service was responsible for troopships – his letters do not say). On 26 October he wrote that he was 'on board Troopship', warning R 'not to be alarmed if you do not hear from me for 6 to 7 weeks – fancy spending Xmas on board a troopship!' He still did not know exactly where he was going. 'I don't think we are bound for Mesopotamia at all as there is an Indian contingent of us – and there is a separate Mesopotamia contingent at Barracks still awaiting orders to embark … The Indian contingent is very bucked to have been selected as a 'loan' to the Indian Service … as the Indian ASC has broken down under the strain of the campaigns in Europe, Mesopotamia and East Africa' … 'Anyhow we don't think we shall be out there long.'

On 2 November he was back at Rest Camp, St Budeaux, Devonport, and wrote: 'The troopship was hideous. Over 1000 men and 40 officers on board, crammed up in every corner. We officers were not so badly accommodated but the poor men, huddled like sheep in a fold. We got everything ready to start when a Staff Officer came on board for last inspection – and, Heaven be thanked, condemned the whole thing. Men and officers yelled for joy … It was an old tub, & death-trap!' But it meant not only more delay (though in the event only to 4 November) but a route around the Cape, over two months in all via Dakar, Durban, Dar-es-Salaam, Zanzibar, Bombay and then – although this was only decided at Bombay – to Basra at the head of the Persian Gulf.

Mesopotamia, the region between the great rivers Tigris and Euphrates, extending north to the Armenian Mountains, now largely Iraq, was strategically important as part of the Ottoman Empire (since 1515) and a gateway for the Turks and Germans to India. Historically it was regarded as the cradle of civilisation, extraordinarily fertile until the Turks allowed the ancient irrigation system to decline, and in former times the battle-ground of many empires – Assyrian, Babylonian, Persian, Greek, Roman and Arab. The defeat of the Turks, the destruction of their empire and the defence of 'the jewel in the British crown', India, were important British objectives in World War I, and all were achieved. H arrived there at the turn of the tide on that front.

## H to R Log 14 Nov.–3 Dec. 1916
### HM Troopship *Waitemata*, off West Africa

*My Darling … The 14 Nov was our tenth day on board. And what a chapter of incidents that 10 days contained. As soon as we got by Eddystone we ran into dirty weather and most of us had perforce to turn in. The storm was at times terrific. The ship rolled and pitched so much the propellers were often clean out of the water. Small wonder our speed averaged only about 3 to 4 knots. It was so bad the ship's pet monkey committed suicide by leaping overboard! Add to this that we were in the midst of a submarine threat … We had three alarms on Saturday night … and on Monday we were informed that a ship had been torpedoed 15 miles ahead of us. Ugh! The very name Bay Biscay makes me sick! … It took 5 days to cross it.*

*Off the Madeiras – well out to sea because of submarines – the weather improved and we began to wear our sun helmets … We put in for coal at Dakar, government centre of the French Colony of Senegal – and port for Timbuctoo! – and went ashore to visit the market … seek a cup of tea (only to be given senna!) … and see a colourful but exhausting wedding dance. Not for the world would I like to live in that God-forsaken place!*

*We crossed the Equator on 20 Nov. but it was so cold we had to change back to our Devonport clothes. It seems we are right in the S. E. Trade winds which blow from the South Atlantic. Since leaving Dakar life has been very monotonous … It is surprising what little inclination one has to do any writing. I suppose it is due to the constant rolling and pitching of the boat … I dare say it would be more tolerable if one could escape these wretched inoculations and vaccinations ... But they take good care of us on board. There are 4 doctors ... and a well equipped dispensary and hospital ... The food too is exceptionally good ... but there is a lack of opportunity for exercise – Oh for a decent long walk in the country!*

*We have formed a group that meets in the Chief Engineer's cabin every evening after dinner – an old Indian civil servant who was in the Boer war before his service in India and has rejoined the Army; a South African who took part in the capture under Botha of German South West Africa; a bank clerk from the National Bank of Egypt in Cairo; a Yorkshire Post journalist from Leeds & Lausanne ... The Chief Engineer is a New Zealander of about 50 with a very fresh and intelligent mind ... He has his own solution to the world's ills (everyone should have his own land) but is always ready with his contagious laugh to ease any tension in the group.*

*We have just passed Cape Town ... and hope to reach Durban on 4 Dec.*

### H to R Log 7–20 Dec. 1916     HM Troopship – Off East Africa

*My Darling ... We spent but a very short time at Durban, much to our chagrin – though we managed to get tea with strawberries and cream ashore. Our boat was long overdue, and another boat was waiting for us ... What a change it is from the old tub that brought us here! I didn't tell you too much in my previous letters in case it made you uneasy. She was a transformed New Zealand cargo boat, dirty, cramped and uncomfortable ... This boat is a palatial mansion ... in peacetime a pleasure boat called 'The Millionaire's Ship' ... She is luxuriously fitted and rides without rolling or pitching even in the heaviest seas. She was used in Gallipoli as the HQ of the G.O.C. General Hamilton.*

*We have had on board the first Governor of the new colony Tanganyika, formerly German East Africa. He and his two Assistant Commissioners went ashore at Dar-es-Salaam ... which was bombarded by the British fleet – some of the German vessels destroyed can be seen on the beaches ... There is still some fighting going on in the mainland.*

*We made no stay there but did at Zanzibar, which is on an island off the coast of Africa ... a very old settlement ... at one time a chief centre of the slave trade ... It has been bombarded by the British fleet more than once, and is now a British protectorate ...*

*News from home at Zanzibar told us that Lloyd George has been made Premier. This has been received with unfeigned pleasure by the officers and men on board. They all feel confident that Lloyd George will see the thing through with his usual thoroughness. They were sick of Asquith's dilatoriness.*

*The C.O. strolled up to me yesterday and addressed me in Welsh. He was born and brought up near Aberystwyth ... So with a Welsh C.O. and a Welsh Prime Minister I am cock of the walk among the other officers.*

*We have re-crossed the Equator today (15 Dec.) ... I wonder what fate awaits me at Bombay ... It is over 8 weeks since I bade you goodbye, and*

Father and Mother, just married, in 1916.

*since then we have travelled between 11,000 & 12,000 miles! ... Thank Heaven, the distance when we come home via Suez need only take 2 to 3 weeks.*

### H to R 21 Dec. 1916        Taj Mahal Palace Hotel, Bombay

*Sweetheart ... We landed here this morning, at last. We proceed to Basra on Saturday. I am naturally disappointed not making a longer stay in India, but the work is to be done in Mesopotamia, and that is where we are needed ... to help in the campaign there ... So we don't grouse. Just got your first two letters, and overjoyed to receive them.*

### R to H 31 Oct. 19 Nov. & 30 Nov. 1916        Ruthin

*My Dearest ... No letter from you, yet – except from Devonport ... so thankful you didn't sail on the condemned ship especially when I saw of the submarine action.*

*Your sister Marie has written a sweet letter and is coming home from New York to look after your mother. I am not to tell Siani or your mother, or they will worry about the trans-Atlantic journey.*

*My mother sails for Australia on Nov 11. I am going home on Saturday to say good-bye.*

*Isn't it strange that you are steaming to India, your sister to England and my mother to Australia all at the same time? I hope I shall see Marie very soon.*

*The Government have at last decided to control food supplies. We are to have no white bread, sugar for confectionary or, in particular, chocolates! As Runciman said in Parliament: 'Officers must show their affections in other ways!'*

*The Zeps got over Yorkshire and Durham. I'm hoping it won't be Leeds. Two were downed. That makes the 7th. One dropped a burning mass into the sea, and as it fell people sang 'God save the King'.*

### H to R 27 Dec. 1916        At sea, in Straits of Ormuz

*My own Darling ... We are once more on the high seas ... drawing near the head of the Persian Gulf, where we are to leave this ship and get into river steamers to take us up to Basra, for instructions.*

*Write to me as often as you can, and as long as you can. Mail to Messpot will take 4 to 5 weeks ... Your letters to me will not be censored, but mine to you will be.*

### H to R 9 Jan. 1917        Somewhere in the Messpot

*My Sweetheart ... I've done my first days work since leaving England ... It is a real relief to feel one is actually doing something, and not merely marking time ... I am stationed for duty at a river port which is also a railway head and my work has to do with both ships and trains ... The traffic is very considerable ... But one thing is awkward, we are 5 or 6 miles by road or 3 miles by river from the nearest town (Ashar) and, as it gets dark here about*

6, *there is no chance of getting there without permit, even on Saturdays or Sundays, for we work 7 days here! I wanted to go and get my photos produced at Basra, but they will have to wait. Most of the native bazaar stuff there is bare-faced Brummagem anyhow.*

*We have to do with all sorts and conditions of people here. They present a motley appearance as they work on the wharves – Hindus & Muhomedans from India, generally small and poor, but the Baboo (or Indian clerk) is quite well-educated. Then the Arab a fine type physically but you feel that, although humble to your face, he is all the time laughing up his sleeve or devising some means of cheating you. Then the Jews and other pronounced Semites, as keen on the 'dibs' as any here. Last come the Persian labourer and Kurd, the hewer of wood and drawer of water, who makes a fine beast of burden. He seems to have the strength of an Ox, and can carry prodigious weights. He wears high hats which could compare with latest English fashions.* [H appended his own sketches of them, some pointed some rounded].

*One great advantage of being stationed at a Base Depot like this is that we get wireless news everyday.*

## R to H 14 Jan. 1917                                     Leeds

*My dearly beloved ... I made a mental calculation that at least seven long weeks must drag their heavy weight before you begin to get this letter.*

*Your cablegram of 5 Jan arrived yesterday. It took 8 days.*

*It took me such a time to get used to your going to the Messpot, as you call it, and I hope you are safe. Do you remember when you were disappointed at not going to France you said 'Well, never mind, thank God I'm not going to Mesopotamia!'*

*The Government has taken power to seize any land that might be useful for potato growing etc.*

## H to R 23 Jan. 1917              Base Supply Depot Margil, by Basra
##                                   Indian Expeditionary Force 'D' Mesopotamia

*Dearest ... Our Mess is very friendly, not big, just 25 officers – 4 Majors, the rest Captains & Subalterns. Most were resident in India before the War, and are men of wide travel and experience ... They represent every shade of political opinion from the extreme caste-bound Tory to the vigorous independent-minded Social reformer ... English, Scots, Irish, Welsh ... We continually receive re-inforcements from England but they are mostly sent up the line.*

*Here we have nothing but desert and date palms – and, fortunately, the great river ... The Shatt-el-Arab is no wider than the Menai Straits ... It is a magnificent piece of port engineering carved out of the stream and desert ... but it is quite difficult to steer between the present crowd of boats & steamers.*

*My tent is spacious but the furniture is primitive – soap & petrol boxes mostly. I'm having a building set up for an office – with different layers of matting, reeds, corrugated iron, and mud – as a protection against the sun & heat.*

**General Staff Branch, 26 July 1916**                    **Simla, India**

**Notes to Officers proceeding to Mesopotamia**

*The Mesopotamia climate has great extremes of heat and cold. Dec, Jan & Feb are very cold, often cold winds but sun hot in middle of day. May to Sept is extremly hot & moist, from 100° to 125° (F). Prickly heat is very prevalent . . . a spine pad is essential, and a thick topee. Also a good pair of dark glasses with dust proof sides, as dust storms are extremely bad and glare from the water and desert extremely trying on the eyes . . . Rainfall is small, about 6 inches a year.*

*The river is the best supply of water . . . It should always be boiled or chlorinated. The other source is from wells in the desert; it is nearly always brackish and very unpleasant to taste. Some are quite good as far as organic pollution is concerned, but one occasionally finds them polluted with dead cattle.*

*Officers are advised to take the following: Clinical thermometer, Phenacitin, Aspirin, Quinine, Chlorodyne, Cascara, Citronella (for mosquitoes and flies), Keating's powder, alum and bicarbonate of soda. And the following articles of kit: Mosquito curtains, Waterproofs (for the heavy rain Dec & Jan), Camp candle lamp & candles, Berkfeld filter with candles, small emergency Cooking set, Tent & Camp bed.*

*Servants should be physically fit and able to march.*

*If private horses are taken they are at owner's risk.*

*Flies are extremely bad at some seasons . . . Most cases of enteric and paratyphoid and a good deal of desentery is caused by them.*

*It is worth leaving one's measure with a tailor in Bombay.*

**R to H 23 & 27 Jan. 1917**                              **Ruthin**

*Dearest . . . There has been an appalling munition explosion in the East end of London . . . heavy loss of life, and of munition production . . . devastation for a mile around.*

*The papers are so full of peace and yet hold out very few hopes . . . There is to be a tremendous Push in the Spring . . . The chief menace at present is the submarines. We lost 62 ships in December to our own knowledge – the Germans say 163, and may be right.*

**H to R 30 Jan. 1917**                             **Margil, near Basra**

*Dearest Wife . . . Nearly a month since we landed . . . Life so far is quite endurable . . . The natural features of the country are monotonous – the whole country is as flat as a pancake.*

*The other day I saw a most wonderful mirage. I've often read of them in deserts but never thought they were so apparently real. The whole desert side appeared to be a vast sheet of water with boats and ships on its surface. I was forcibly reminded of the tales of desert travellers we used to read.*

*We have had 3 nurses from the Basra Hospital to tea, they were so good to my colleague Dolman when he had malaria. They are rather elderly but charming.*

*People at home little think what real whole-hearted sacrifices are being made out in this desolate unfortunate country every day. One had come from New Zealand at her own expense to do war nursing – and seems quite run down by the work & conditions.*

### R to H 4 & 11 Feb. 1917                                    Ruthin

*Dearest ... You say Mesopotamia is interesting and yet it sounds to me the height of barren desolation. I do hope you are keeping well & strong.*

*The silks you sent me from Bombay are exquisite. Everyone says so. I've never seen anything lovelier than the weaving and harmonising of the colours. The scent of them is almost intoxicating too. I do so love them.*

*Germany has declared its intention to sink everything at sight, passenger ships included. No self-respecting nation can surely now keep out? But President Wilson is so ambiguous – preaching 'peace without victory' ... The California has been sunk with 2 American children among the drowned. Perhaps that will persuade Wilson, but he is a sly beggar.*

*Everyone at home is being encouraged to grow vegetables & food ... Farmers are going round seeing that everyone with space does so. The Government does not want to impose rationing because it would require such expensive organisation.*

### H to R 13 & 27 Feb. & 6 March 1917                    Margil by Basra

*Dearest Sweet Wife ... The rain has come at last. 3 days of it so far. It is a refreshing change from the heat, but the whole place is now a gigantic mud-pie of Mesopotamian clay! I can quite understand the difficulties of campaigning in wet weather here ... It is a land of mud, desert, palm trees – and howling jackals at night.*

*The pleasant news is that we have had a glorious series of successes up country – Kut, Sanna, Yat and Azizah. Our fellows are now pushing on to Bagdad. Shiploads of prisoners pass down here every day. Already 4 to 5 thousand have been captured, among them being a few Germans.*

### H to R 20 Feb. 1917                                    Margil by Basra

*Wife o'my Heart ... How I wish I was home now ... Last Friday with its bitter news ... Please do not grieve for me. My little Mother is peacefully at rest, after a long life of unselfish devotion. What a sweet gentle Mother I had. I pray I may be worthy of the love she bore me ... My O.C. offered to apply for home leave for me when I told him. He is a fine and very hard-working officer. I decided I must stick to my duty here and believe you will agree.*

### H to R 6 Mar. 1917                                    Margil by Basra

*Love o'Mine ... I've been made O.C. of my own Section of the Depot, responsible for providing food and supplies for some 15000 men and fodder for 5000 horses. The men are of 6 to 7 different nationalities, each requiring its own special kind of ration. White troops get the ordinary ration. The Indians want rice & a kind of flour called Atta, & tons of garlic & spices. The Arabs & Persians want dates etc ... Then, worst of all to feed are the Chinese. Also Egyptian, West Indian & West African. One will not eat meat; another must slaughter the animal himself; one will not eat food that has been in the shadow; and still another will not touch anything unless he has 'pinched' it! – & there are some rare thieves in this sweet Garden of Eden!*

*My O.C. at Rail & Port told me when I left, to cultivate a better opinion of my abilities, and crack myself up more. I seem to have heard that sermonette before – at home! But hope to profit by it in this job. I have a good British and Indian staff & my Kurdish, Arab & Persian coolies are quite good workers.*

*I had an amusing time with some native Arabs drawing rations this morning. 5 of them brought 10 women to carry the loads. They were quite disgusted when I remonstrated at them for standing smoking while the women worked. Even the wives repudiated – savagely – my interfering! They claimed they were stronger than the men! Labouring Arab wives are in fact the only women in Margil.*

### H to R 14 March 1917                                    Margil, near Basra

*Gentle Wife ... Great news ... we've captured Bagdad – the second most important city in the Turkish Empire, next to Constantinople. I wonder if it shows the beginning of the break-up of Turkey and its alliance with the 'Bosh'? It must certainly be a cruel fall to the pride of the Germans in their great scheme of Hamburg to Bagdad railway.*

*More & more prisoners are pouring in. 500 Turks this morning, from above Bagdad – openly declaring pleasure to be free of their own regime, especially under what few German officers there are left.*

### R to H 13 & 29 March 1917                                    Ruthin

*My dearest ... We are thrilled by the fall of Bagdad. What a prize, and what a piece of strategy it seems to have been. What next? Is our aim to join up with the Russians?*

*My exciting news is that I am actually leaving Ruthin after all. I do hope you think I am doing the right thing. Morley [West Yorkshire] have offered me a Physics & Maths post, without interview! It is near home, where Dad & Nell seem to want me, especially since Mother left for Australia. (Mother writes that she has found Jim extremely ill.) You are away. And I feel I need to go from here now. Miss R. [Headmistress] is very upset. The Governors have held an emergency meeting, and have offered an increase in salary (overdue, & for all staff!). But I've accepted Morley, and everyone is being very nice about it.*

### H to R 23 April 1917                                    Margil, near Basra

*Dearest Pal ... I feel a bit of a fraud but the Doctor told me a few days ago I had sand fly fever and insisted on my going to hospital. There are six of us – officers – down with it, all in the same ward, my C.O. included ... This fever seems to fall to nearly everybody's share some time or other. The sand-fly is a tiny winged brute, so small it can find its way through the very finest mesh ... The Hospital keeps you for a week under surveillance & then sends you to a fine Convalescent Home near here.*

*We spend our time sleeping, eating, reading – and fly-strafing! I can easily understand how the little Tailor in the fairy tale (in Arabian Nights, I believe) managed to kill 7 flies in one stroke. He must have lived in this country! So far the Major holds the record – 5 at a stroke. I've only managed 2 at a stroke.*

*I've also been trying my hand at cartoon drawing. Several now hang on the Ward walls. They seem to cheer the Sisters and some of the patients.*

*There's a plague of fleas back at the Depot. I used to shudder at the sight of the little pests but we now organise sweepstakes on flea-jumps! Every O.C. now has to have a weekly flea-chase i.e. inspection of the kits etc of all natives attached to the Depot. I promised mine a rupee for the cleanest kit. You never saw such cleaning and scrubbing in your life – even a puppy dog in one case, a Prayer-book in another, and a rat-trap in yet another, and even the Coolies!*

*You will be interested to know that the dog in one of the photos I sent you was in France with a Ghurka officer in the early days of the War until his master was killed; then in India when the regiment returned there; then with them in the Siege of Kut here in Mesopotamia, escaping to join some Tommies of the West Kents; and then, when they were invalided to India, attaching himself to one of my Sergeants here. His name is Bully, and we bow to him as supreme O.C. Margil Camp Supply Depot. He often comes with me for a walk in the evenings – provided I promise him a rat-hunt!*

### R to H Easter 1917                                        Leeds

*My dearest ... It was a great wrench saying good-bye to all at Ruthin. I had no idea I had got so attached to the place. The girls all came to see me off.*

*This Winter has been the worst anyone has known. You would be amused to see how Leeds is being patriotic. Every Sunday fields of very respectable-looking men, coats off, digging their part for dear life, to plant potatoes. And you can see from the train people doing the same on every mud patch in the Leeds slums.*

*Your last letter reached me in 5 weeks – record time! Most of them take nearly 7. One recent envelope from you was labelled 'Opened under Martial Law'. It contained only your short note and sketch of an Arab courtyard!*

*Some of your letters will help you write a book on Mesopotamia some day. Its quite like reading a book every time I get one as they are so full.*

### H to R 8 & 16 May 1917                          Margil, Messpot

*Robin Mine ... I am back at work, chirpy and cheery. My new office is finished, a neat little bungalow, – roofed with 3 or 4 layers of palm leaf matting and a thick layer of mud on top. I continue to live in a tent but have 2 very good Indian 'Boys' who know the quickest and easiest way to their Master's good will – Mulla Ahmed Din personally adorns your photo with flowers and leaves every morning! They even fan me to sleep at afternoon siesta – and woe to any mosquito or fly that hovers near – I only wish they could strafe the fleas too!*

*I am now responsible for feeding & supplying 23,000 people, but with fewer staff and nearly half of them sick in hospital. But we are meeting all demands, and the General responsible for all ASC in Mesopotamia came round yesterday, at 10 minutes notice, and found all well … Never in my life have I worked so hard.*

*I shall be very disappointed if I don't get a chance of seeing Bagdad – though all the fellows who have been there say it is dirty and uninteresting – except of course for its former great traditions.*

*Have I told you what a decent lot of fellows I have under me here? One – a cartoonist – is a Canterbury man – quite reserved but full of humour, and a good worker. Another, one of my NCOs, was manager of a big Lyons restaurant in London. Another, a clerk, is a lawyer. But in the Army one's precedents count for very little.*

*By the way, this tent of mine is becoming quite an 'open house', especially for Welsh people. Two officers on their way to India on leave, one from Liverpool and another from Bangor, dropped in yesterday. They had been told to look me up by friends up-country. It was good to see them – & to have a chat in Welsh.*

### R to H 13 May 1917                                             Leeds

*Dearest … Davenport made a statement in Parliament last week that we have enough food to last until next harvest after all – though we still have to be careful of all cereals. A great deal of land is now under cultivation – everywhere you go in the country you see ploughed fields.*

*We've been worried this last week what the Russians intend to do … We seem to be holding our own in France and expect further advances soon. Haven't the Germans got unbounded confidence? They still talk of victory and annexations!*

### R to H 19 May 1917                                             Leeds

[Took until 10 July to reach H, by then in India]

*Dearest … At Roundhay today it was perfect, the trees have suddenly blossomed, the copper beeches are getting the dazzle on their leaves … All the potato growers were gazing awe-struck at their little plots, for the shoots are just showing above the soil. We shall have enough potatoes to spare next year!*

*I told you my first days at Morley School were awful. The Physics was in a state – they haven't done any for a term. The lab was higgledy-piggledy. The senior science master was slack. So, I was told, was the whole school generally. Discipline was very difficult, especially with the boys. As you know I am used to walking into a class and getting absolute silence and obedience. This was a dreadful change … I'm glad to say I find things so different now. I'm getting into things and everybody is nice. I'm now taking chemistry as well as physics and maths. The journey from Leeds is long and the shared housekeeping at home*

*takes up time. But I've obliterated the last vestige of doubt about the move.*
*Isn't it funny you wrote as you did about Ruthin –* [saying he had long thought
she should move.]

## H to R early June 1917                                    Margil, Messpot

*Meri sabuo piari Bibi (My very dear Wife – in Hindustani) . . . You ought to*
*hear me converse with my 'Boys' & the non-English speaking Indians in the*
*Depot! When we get nowhere I resign myself to using my own tongue [Welsh]! . . .*
*I have been surprised at the 'Boys' fidelity, and they provide me no end of*
*entertainment. Ahmed Din is known to everyone as Mulla (Priest) and sees I*
*get the best of everything (His idea of 'best' anyhow). He and young Gije are*
*topping.*

*I go riding in the early morning when I can. My day starts at 5.30.*

*The heat is now overpowering in the daytime –* 107° *to* 115°F *in the shade*
*this week. A strange land this! A veritable land of extremes: too much rain in*
*the rainy season; too much heat in the hot season; too much dust when the*
*wind blows; and above all this is a land of too much Thirst. It is a tale of*
*soda-water, ginger beer and lime juice from morning till night. One can't afford*
*to drink intoxicants in this country unless one wishes to court disaster and*
*heat-stroke. A soft drink when you can get it cool is nectar of the Gods. I*
*shudder to think of the conditions when the first expedition force came here –*
*no huts, only 40lb tents; no water fit to drink; supplies only arriving fitfully;*
*and this was then a hostile country with marauding Arabs only waiting to swoop*
*on any small garrison – and worst of all, the insects (talk of the Plagues of*
*Egypt!) and the hideous desolation & monotony of it all. There is only one*
*Mesopotamia – & thank Heaven for that!*

## R to H 10 and 15 June 1917                                        Leeds

*Dearest . . . I went to the Joy's for tea last Sunday. They had a wounded*
*Tommy there. He had joined in the first month of the War and been wounded*
*twice. He is so sick of it that rather than go back to the trenches he wishes he*
*had lost a leg.*

*There is a peace conference in Leeds today – some labour members are agitating*
*& I hope they get no support. The Government has prohibited open air meetings*
*as they expected riots. It is a very small percentage of people that is so blind as*
*not to see the way of salvation for democracy.*

*We seem to be holding the Germans back and everyone trusts in Foch –*
*though 200,000 children have already been sent from Paris so they do not mean*
*to be surprised . . . If the Germans only knew the truth – England still feeding*
*well, Americans pouring over in thousands, the submarine activity not so great*
*and a sea of mines in the N. sea to counter them, Austria beginning to clamour*
*for peace. Well – we are perhaps going through the blackest cloud of all . . .*
*The Germans have drunk too deep the wine of success and are really beating*
*us now – we all know it. But it will turn. I expect we shall continue all through*

the Winter like last year. It's a slow process for the Americans to drill & equip so many. Sometimes I think 2 years is the very least before the end. Then comes a very optimistic letter from you. You may be right. You have a different point of view out there of course.

### R to H 17 June 1917                                                    Leeds

My dear ... Only 1 letter from you in 4½ weeks. They must have gone down. We had 5 from Mother in Australia yesterday. The U-boats are doing their evil business in your direction just now evidently.

Just before the war a means of telephoning by wireless was discovered. Now why wasn't the war put off for 6 months so that soldiers and their wives and sweethearts might have been able to hear each other's voices!

It must be atrociously hot when you can wear things the same day they have been washed. You see it needs a housewifely comparison of that sort to appreciate your heat.

### R to H 18 June 1917                                                    Ruthin

Dearest ... I posted my letter last night and got yours this morning. I was astounded to hear you had been in hospital for sand-fly fever. Your letter is dated 30 April and has taken 7 weeks to come. I confess I had quite a shock and do hope you are now well again.

### H to R 26 June 1917                                        Margil, Messpot

Dearest ... I'm afraid the over-work of the last three months in these conditions is telling its tale. I have re-organised the Depot in new buildings and put its work on a sound business basis with a reformed system of accounts and stock-control. But just in sight of completion, and as sick staff are returning from hospital and other vacancies filled, I find myself weak in body and have been ordered by Dr Mason to the Beit Nama (Basra) Convalescent Home. Nothing serious – just a little run-down – and one cannot afford to be 'run-down' in this country. Captain Theobald is back and insists I have a rest. He was nice enough to declare 'on my oath Jones has worked a damn sight too hard but has organised a real pukka supply Depot'. He is hoping to be transferred to Bagdad, and wants me to go with him. I should like to, but would not be much good there at present.

### H to R 27 June 1917                            No. 3 Brit. Gen. Hospital, Basra

Dearest ... Have arrived here but feel a dashed fool. It is a converted old mansion that used to belong to some Arab Sheikh, and full well did he know how to choose a site for it – delightful, overlooking the river, with hundreds of steamers & other boats passing by. I really feel alright – only a little bit tired.

### H to R Telegram 9 July 1917                                          Basra

Going India leave. Address letters Bankers Bombay. Well. Love.

**H to R Telegram 16 July 1917**                                    Bombay

*Arrived. Slight neurasthenia. No danger. Progressing splendidly.*

**R to H 16 July**                                                   Leeds

*Dearest . . . Your cable came this evening. Am anxiously waiting to know what is the matter? How long you have been ill? Whether you are suffering much? Will you recuperate in India in the hills? There has been such an outcry about Mesopotamia, it has been the chief topic here for a week. It must have been h——l let loose at the beginning. We have made some mistakes but how could we do everything at once – though some of the things that have come to light are horrible. I feel sure there has been a huge improvement there now from what you say. It is in the papers that all the officers are coming home on leave. But not you I suppose?*

**Lt Col i/c T. F. Records to R 19 July 1917**                  Shrewsbury

*Madam . . . The following report has been received today, and is communicated herewith for your information, viz:–*

*'Lieut Hugh Jones, Welsh Divisional ASC. Invalided to India from Basra 7/7/17, admitted Maharaja Gaekwar's Hospital, Bombay, 13/7/17'.*

*Any further information received will be forwarded to you immediately.*

*I am, Madam, Your obedient Servant . . .*

**R to H c. 21 July 1917**                                           Leeds

*Dearest . . . A dreadful cold-looking thing from T. F. Records Shrewsbury greeted me when I got home tonight. I gather you are at some hospital whose very name strikes terror in my heart . . . Hughie dear what am I to believe, when one day you say you are well and going on leave, then 'slightly' ill, and then this. I know you do it for my sake dearest, but now I am wanting to know quite truthfully. But what's the good of writing this when you'll get it only days & days from now? . . . It's a little hard to be separated now when I might be some use . . . but I mustn't grumble. You never do.*

*Please try and get well quickly . . . I shall be thinking of you . . . Be careful . . .*

# Parents in World War I, India and Blighty

## 1917–1919

THE ILLNESS MY FATHER CONTRACTED in Mesopotamia turned out to be more serious than he acknowledged. In addition to being run-down, common enough working day and night in those conditions, he had picked up a kidney infection and another bout of sandfly fever. He was shipped as a stretcher case from Basra to Bombay on 9 July 1917, the voyage by hospital ship taking eight days through the monsoons instead of the usual five, to add to his discomfort. He spent two weeks in a hospital for officers in the palace of the munificent Maharajah of Gaekwar outside Bombay, which he described as 'a gorgeous place, all marble and gold, situated on a hill overlooking the sea, just like Colwyn Bay, and very fine scenery, even in the monsoons – such a change from Messpot'. After a fortnight there he was transferred, with three or four other non-surgical cases, to the Officers' Convalescent Home at Nasik, the nearest hill station to Bombay – and one of the principal pilgrim shrines of India. He made good progress there and was playing nine holes of golf within a week. He also had his first encounter with the local British at a Garden Party given by the Hospital CO and found their 'condescension and affectation' unattractive – 'they would have frozen a limpet,' he wrote. He applied for and was accorded an early Medical Board, composed of a Colonel, a Welsh Major from Harley St and a Captain, who delighted him by finding nothing radically wrong but confirmed he needed convalescent leave. He was granted a place at the Crags Convalescent Home in Simla, in the foothills of the Himalayas, for three weeks and set off the 1000 miles there on 8 August.

In his last letter from Bombay he jokingly recommended to his wife a book he had found in the hospital library, *The Romance of Isabel, Lady*

*Burton*, wife of the renowned Arabian and African explorer Sir Richard Burton. They suffered long separations and Lady Burton composed her own 'Rules for my guidance as a Wife'. These included: 'Keep up the honeymoon romance, whether at home or in the wilderness' … 'Never refuse him anything he asks' … 'Cultivate your own good health, spirits and nerves, to counteract his melancholy turn' … 'Take an interest in everything that interests him, even if it be growing turnips' …'Attend much to his creature comforts'. H commented teasingly: 'I fancy she was a truly wonderful woman, don't you?!' R replied with amused scorn that Lady B 'seemed a bit of a doormat' and that she herself 'would go in for labour saving devices with a vengeance so she could be bright and cheery for him!'

## H to R 13 Aug. 1917                          The Crags, Simla

*Darling … Here I am, landed right among the wonderful Himalayas, in the summer capital of India … I have crossed the great country from Bombay, doing the journey leisurely and sight-seeing on the way. I left Nasik overnight 8 Aug … arrived Bina the following morning to learn that monsoon floods had swept away 100 villages and the main railway line, and the alternative Cawnpore and Lucknow line was unsafe, so we had to divert via Kotah on the borders of Rajputana. This meant getting back to the mainline at Muttra twelve hours late … But it took us through the most wonderful hunting grounds of India … and we actually saw a samrai (like a tiger) swoop on some small deer … The people there live in wattle and mud huts with high stockades to keep off wild beasts. You should have seen the birds – the wild peacock, kingfishers and others of gorgeous plumage.*

*At Muttra I decided to break the journey and visit Agra. I do wish you could have been with me. The Taj Mahal is the most exquisitely beautiful creation of man's mind I have ever seen. It is said that the Shah Jehan, the then mogul Emperor of India erected it in grief at the loss of his favourite wife (1629) 'to preserve the memory of their love as long as marble and ivory lasts'. And what a wondrous creation it is. I spent 2 days at Agra and bought a small Persian wool carpet and an attractively carved old brass vase for you at the bazaar.*

*From Agra the express dragged its slow way to Delhi (with its wonderful old buildings but I could not spend time there) … across lands that have known the march of conquering hordes far into the past … through Umballa, a great military station, up to Kalka in the foothills … where we were to change to the narrow gauge railway for Simla. But it had left! And, it being a Sunday afternoon, there was not another until 5.30 the following morning. So we had to make our beds in the waiting room until then. My companions – apart from the myriad mosquitos – included a Welsh RAMC Colonel and his wife, some officials – who resignedly consigned the train and its officials to some nether region of Hindu mythology, quite beyond me – and an actress and two actors, one of whom kept us entertained until the early hours – a real friend in need!*

*We also managed a visit up the mountain road to the local bazaar . . . crowded with sturdy hill-folk . . . the women some veiled, some not, one haggling with the sweetmeat vendor, others squatting and rolling out long strings of the like of vermicelli . . . a juggler entertaining the crowd with the usual basket and card tricks . . . the whole countryside seemingly in festive mood. Long trains of mules with gaudy trappings passed along the mountain road, carrying heavy packs of the good things of the Plains up to the Uplands, and even into far-away Tibet . . . their tinkling bells dying fainter as they climbed.*

*At dawn we set off on the miniature train, a six hour climb to Simla through the most wonderful hill-country, with belt upon belt of palm, mango, various species of pine, oaks and even holly . . . and here and there precarious little ledges of paddy-fields. Far in the distance we could still see the plains of the Jumna and Sutlej, sweltering in the moist heat of the monsoons; while above us height upon height, past hamlets and sanatoria perched on tree-clad ledges, through tunnels, then swaying above a sheer precipice, and all of a sudden Simla, the hill capital of a vast and ancient empire. Its very position suggests regal dignity, with the Plains below and, above, the glorious snow-capped peaks of the Himalayas dazzlingly resplendent in the Indian sunshine. It is the very heaven of a place – except when the damp, Himalayan mists come crawling up the slopes from the glens and valleys . . . and I have until the end of the month here. Then I don't know what they will do with me.*

### R to H 26 Aug. and 1 Sept. 1917                                    Penygroes

*My darling . . . Marie has welcomed me here with open arms . . . She is absolutely sterling and unselfish . . . My three letters from you from Bombay were a treasure. It made my heart ache to think of your being so ill . . . You are always trying to spare me . . . But I must know without any keeping of news back – please Hughie dearest . . . I'm so longing to know what is happening to you. If you had leave till end of August where are you now? And are you crossing back again to Mesopotamia?*

### H to R 3 and 5 Sept. 191                                               Simla

*Darling . . . The Medical Board is pleased with my recovery and extended my leave here another month on light duties. I am to work 2 or 3 hours a day at Army HQ here (which is General Army HQ for India). They have suggested I should not return to Messpot. I think this is because they found I have a perforated ear-drum. I met an old Messpot friend and his wife the other day. He was at Margil with me. He, poor fellow, had both malaria and cholera – and survived.*

### H to R 6 Sept. 1917                                                     Simla

*Dearest . . . You will want my impressions of Simla . . . Perhaps it will help you to conjure up some picture if I tell you that this summer capital of opulent India, possesses only 3 carriages and no motor-cars. There is no room for more! The* carriages are for the Viceroy, the Lt Governor of Punjab, and the C in C Indian Army. The rest of us use the Rickshaw which is quite comfy (with two coolies pulling and two pushing) or the Jhampani ... some in gorgeous livery, some in any old rag.

Simla is built on the high slopes of 3 hills and Simla proper is on a land-bridge between two heights, one crowned by the Viceregal Lodge, and the other dominated by a Hindu temple called the Jakko. I don't suppose any offence was ever meant in the juxta-position of H.E. the Viceroy's residence and the Temple of the Monkeys. But nature – or fate – ever is a grim humorist! ... The roads are nowhere wide and, running as they do along ledges carved out of the hillsides, they are scenes of constant strife between the road-mender and the land-slips ... which can become avalanches in the rainy season.

Simla life is quiet ... with a good deal of formality. Every officer on arrival must pay calls on the Viceroy, the Commander-in-Chief and the Governor. I got mine over early. Luckily they were all 'Not at home' ... Society is ultra-swanky. But we at the Crags don't mind, as we are a very happy family of about 40 officers, Colonels and down, and the Medical Officer in charge, Major Ross and his wife could not be better ... India has a tremendous charm for me – except the arid hot plains ... and has already done me lasting good.

### R to H 8 Sept. 1917          Leeds

Dearest ... Three weeks and still nothing from you except a cablegram to say you were going to Simla.

Emyr T ... was killed flying last week ... Gwilym T ... lost another brother three weeks ago and now it is his turn ... Dora T's brother is another ... I told you of Lloyd W ... Everybody seems to be getting killed. It's just dreadful and makes my heart ache.

### H to R 18 Sept. 1917          Simla

My Own ... The submarines are playing 'old Harry' with the mail-boats, so there is no knowing when or where they leave or arrive. Your letter of 26 July travelled round the Cape and Ceylon! Nonetheless welcome, I can assure you.

Tennis is a great pastime here, when the monsoons permit, and I've been doing quite well. The Indian Army officials and their families – old Regular officers, 'pukka' as they take care to inform you – are very condescending to us 'Temporaries' ( ... and are paid twice as much as we are, too!), but we hold our own ... I go down to HQ ... but am not given anything exacting ... I've not bothered to 'call' and make friends in Simla itself ... Our group at the Crags includes a flying man from East Africa, a versatile Royal Engineer, a former picture-film maker, a Somerset County cricketer, a 13th Hussar with DSO and crown to his MC, a Persian gendarme, a Major of the Administration – the wit of the party – an Irish doctor, and more. We ride and walk ... yarn ... play billiards ... put on shows for Major Ross's charities ... and at times behave like schoolboys. It is very congenial.

*Although this is Army HQ for India and the seat of Indian Government, it is very little we see or hear of War. Therein lies the charm of the place.*

### R to H 18 Sept., 2 and 14 Oct. 1917    Leeds

*My dearest . . . Fisher has spoken for the Government on educational reform . . . The Sunday Chronicle considers the teaching profession is dying for lack of salaries. Let us hope for reforms in the near future . . . I haven't had my Fisher rise yet. We expect £20 but £10 of that the school Governors will seize as they have been providing us with £10 war bonus – a mighty sum in view of the fact that everything, on average, has gone up exactly 85% since Sept 1914 – just 3 years ago.*

*My book of photos is looking ripping. The addition of the Simla ones has given it great tone.*

*I had quite a fierce debate with Marie when I was staying with her, when she informed me that the Englishman doesn't know how to fight and it is well known in America that he must be sent with a Welshman and a Scot, one to give him enthusiasm and the other sticking power! What has the poor fellow got? The source of all this has just come to light – German propaganda – it has been running through American papers.*

*I heard a magnificent lecture on Mesopotamia last week, from an educationist who had lived in Bagdad. He illustrated clearly Germany's dream of a railway system running from Berlin via Aleppo to Peking by the old silk route and by Bagdad to India (Bombay and Madras).*

### H to R 12 and 18 Oct. 1917    Simla

*My Own . . . This morning's papers brought me the cruel news of the fifth intimate friend of mine to render the supreme sacrifice – the fifth during these last few weeks – four in France but the latest in Messpot in the big fight at Ramadie. It makes me very sad.*

*We all here wish the Besant tyro and her satellites at home in Parliament would realise – as I am learning – what a vast country India is, with its millions of people, of all castes and religions, in all stages of civilisation from the modern to the primitive. It cannot be dealt with 'en masse' . . . I must say that the British Commissioners I have so far met in the Indian Civil Service have all been fine men of tact, courage and culture. They are the men who in their quiet way really govern here – not the Army, not by any means. And it is impressive to behold the allegiance they command.*

*I called on the Director General of Archaeology in India the other day, and told him of my 'stuff' (researches) and my wish to know more of the life history of the Hill-Folk in India. He was interested, offered me all help and would have taken me round the Hills here himself had he not been just off to Kashmir. He invited me to use his experience and library.*

*My leave is finally up and, on Major Ross's recommendation, the Medical Board has decided I should now go on 3 months light duty somewhere in India.*

**H to R 26 Oct. 1917**                                                Lahore

[H's service hereon, with the brief exception of his leave in Mussoorie and journey home through Bombay, was in what is today, since partition in 1947, Pakistan. Rawalpindi is now the great twin city of the capital Islamabad. Peshawar and Bannu command much of Pakistan's borders with Afghanistan. Kashmir remains divided.]

*My Own ... I left Simla last night and am on my way to Rawalpindi, in North-West Punjab ... HQ of the 2nd Indian Division and one of the biggest military stations in the country. It is known as Pindi and is considered one of the healthiest winter stations in India. I am sad to leave Simla and The Crags ... but cheerful to face duty once again.*

**R to H 21 Oct. 1917**                                                Leeds

*Dearest ... Your cable reached me ... I am glad you are not going back to Mesopotamia – till January at least ... and are going somewhere congenial ... We've been separated a whole year now ... The first weeks were indescribable misery. And yet the year has gone quickly. While the War is on we can't grumble muchly!*

*We've had reverses this weekend – a Zepp raid and none shot down, 2 destroyers gone in the N. Sea with no reason given, and the Russian fleet is surrounded. When are we going to get a complete upper hand? Russia is hopeless, but their peasantry is so ignorant and some of their more intelligent ones are so flushed with the wine of successfully overthrowing their monarchy, they can't see their drink has changed to poison – the poison of anarchy I suppose.*

*Here tea is now short and sugar rationed by ticket. Lord Rhondda says we have to eat sparingly, but its no good telling us without making us do it. I have no patience with the rulers in high places. They seem a set of sillies – except Lloyd George of course ... He is a clever man ... he will have his enemies sooner or later ... but he has become a leading figure in British political history since he came into power as Prime Minister and will live in memory whatever happens ... I make a claim on your forgiveness for my condemnation of him in the past. Perhaps he too has developed!*

**H to R 29 and 30 Oct. and c. 6 Nov. 1917**                       Rawalpindi

*Dear Wife ... I arrived here 27th, breaking my week's journey from Simla at Amritsar to see the Golden Temple of the Sikhs but it was disappointing in the rain; and Lahore, but I did not find it contained much of interest ... except the Museum where I spent some time studying Persian carpets and Indian silks ... The Curatorship was at one time held by Kipling's father ... Kipling was born there and was for years on the staff of the Lahore Gazette – and Kim's big gun stands in the Museum courtyard.*

*Can you find Rawalpindi on the map? It is well up in the North West corner of India, in the province of Punjab ... next big station to Peshawar, which is*

*right in the mountains. Here we are in the Plains, although 1800 feet up . . .
and can see the snow-covered hills of Kashmir in the distance. It is one of the
most interesting parts of India because of what our people have done here in
the way of irrigation of land and developing its resources, and because it stands
on the Grand Trunk Road from Calcutta to Peshawar and, in particular, because
of its proximity to the N-W Frontier (the Khyber Pass is only 100 miles away)
and Kashmir (the Vale is about 200 miles). I hope to visit both.*

*Pindi is a beautifully planned place – the cantonments, the European quarters,
anyhow – not big, but spacious, with wide tree-lined streets, and villas and
bungalows, with lovely gardens of poplars, orange trees etc (the oranges here
are more like tangerines). It is pleasantly hot in the day though bitter at night
at this winter season – the day-night temperature drop is as much as 30° (F)!
In Summer it becomes hot and everyone who can moves up to the hill-station
of Murree 30 miles away. My work in the Depot is so far very congenial. My
senior officers are decent, and I am still on light duty.*

### R to H 15 Nov. 1917                                                    Leeds

*Dearest . . . I hope Rawalpindi proves nice and congenial . . . You will be getting
this letter about Xmas. If so I hope you have a very happy one.*

*We went on Sat. to see 'The Better 'Ole', a play based on Bruce Bainsfather's
cartoons. It is a very clever little play. We laughed and nearly cried in turns.
No-one can appreciate it more than the Tommy himself.*

*Last week only one ship was sunk by the submarines. But the Italians have
suffered a dreadful military disaster – 200,000 taken prisoner. This week civil
war in Russia. And Lloyd George's Paris speech. Talk of a furore here! Heated
arguments in plenty. He told the truth – why we failed in 1915 & 1916. It's
what the people want – an explanation. Asquith and his followers are of course
up in arms and the whole Press is against Ll-G. Parliament's acceptance of his
creation of the War Council has alleviated things somewhat. I admire him for
telling the truth. This party political business is disgusting.*

### H to R 12, 22 and 27 Nov. 1917                                    Rawalpindi

*Robin Mine . . . I told you I could find no accommodation here on arrival – all
full. A young Scot, head of a local brewery, has now taken me in to share his
bungalow temporarily. And I have a new 'Boy', aged about 50, a 'Garwhal',
that is a hill-man akin to the Ghurkas. He knows hardly a word of English but
a dear old fellow, looks after me like a kid of 10. Like Mulla at Margil, he
knows the way to his master's affection – your photo, Sahib's own Memsahib,
is decked with flowers and pretty leaves every morning. His name is Devi Singh,
or David Coeur de Lion. All hail to the Lion-hearted, and may his shadow
never grow less – so long as he continues to serve me faithfully and truly!*

*The local men at the Depot are a very mixed lot – babus and coolies. I speak
to them in a queer mixture of English, a little Hindustani, a little Punjabi, a
little Pushtu, and a swear word or two in good old Cymraeg now and again. I*

*seem to have very little difficulty handling them and getting the work done. I am actually studying Hindustani, and am taking up painting. I am also becoming a voracious reader. Life is not very eventful here, so I have the time.*

*There is quite a good club with a fairly decent library. But I'm not in love with the type one generally meets at these purely military stations – plenty of swank and pretentiousness. And the most ridiculous thing is the petty jealousy and rivalry between different services. Mrs Colonel So-&-So regards herself as a cut above Mrs Commissioner So-&-So, and as for Mrs Inspector So-&-So of Railways, or Police – why, they are the 'giddy edge'. There seem to be four class and caste distinctions in this society: I European born and bred (we are IT) II. European born but Indian bred – known as CB (Country bred). IT cocks its nose up at CB. III. Eurasians, i.e. 'Half-castes', poor devils they are ostracised by everybody, including the Native. And IV. The Native, with whom the European has little to do here outside work, but caste is everything to them, too. The Club is all, and many are the most snobbish and affected British you could imagine. Happily there are others, in and out of the Club, as sweet and cultured as any at home.*

*You will be surprised to learn that there are 7 or 8 battalions of the old Regular Army here who have not yet seen service in this War. So we feel pretty secure, anyway! And you see the man-power of Britain is not exhausted even now.*

*However, next time anyone (like dear Marie quoted) tries to say that English troops are not doing their share in this war, please give them the lie direct from me. My experience is that in the Army actually on service, we know no distinction between English, Welsh, Scot and Irish. We may tease each other. Like that the battalion of the Gordon Highlanders who made a name for themselves in the Wazirstan campaign and are now resting here, have plenty of English, Irish and Welshmen parading in Gordon kilts! There is mixture in all regiments. We are all first and foremost British, trying to do our little best in the common cause.*

## R to H Dec. 1917                                              Leeds

*My dearest ... Since I had your last letter saying you had not heard from me for 5½ weeks I've begun wondering if you are getting anything from me. I write at least every week as ever.*

*We have just heard today that Russia is 'out of the War' whatever that may or may not mean. The mischief was done long ago when the Bolsheviks ordered the disbanding of the army before they (supposedly) realised the meaning of Germany's war aims ... Our food queues are getting dreadful. People get up at 5 in the morning to wait till the shops open for butter, margarine and tea. Something must be done soon about rationing or the people will object ... The dawn of another year: Surely 1918 will see the completion of it all.*

*I've been asked by the Head and Governers to take charge of all the Morley School maths. – as I had at Ruthin, though this is a much larger school – I wonder how I shall like teaching big boys, bigger than you some of them?*

**H to R 8, 12, 25 and 26 Dec. 1917**                          Rawalpindi

*My Own ... I do hope you are keeping confident at home. In spite of the
set-backs of Russia and Italy there can be only one issue to the War, especially
now that the USA are in with us ... The Germans aren't going to get any
grain from a peace with Russia, as the Russians haven't enough to feed themselves.
That's one great cause of the Revolution ... I'm sorry for the Roumanians,
dragged down by the Russian collapse, and only wish our people in Greece could
do something.*

*I have changed my digs and am now more central. The previous place was
2 miles out. I am sharing the bungalow of an Edinburgh man called Denholm,
who is agent for a big home firm. It is very comfortable ... Work at the Depot
goes merrily apace – and grows. I have now a staff of 40, and the OC Depot
says he is very satisfied indeed with our work.*

*Christmas morning, the sun is shining brightly, and everybody wears a helmet.
A cool breeze from the snows of Kashmir keeps the heat from becoming oppressive.
Long straggling trains of camels are slouching their way along the dusty road
from Peshawar. They bring carpets from Persia or silks from Kashmir for the
markets and bazaars of the towns of the Plains, like Delhi and Lahore. The
Unt-wala (camel driver) can be villainous-looking. To anyone interested in the
life of the 'natives' of all sorts from the low-caste coolie to the strapping independent
Pathan of the frontier, there is a bewildering kaleidoscope of people to study –
almost too much anthropology!*

*Pindi had its great Fete for the Red Cross before Christmas. The natives came
in their thousands – but very few of the Pindi Europeans, except the troops
taking part. I saw my first native dance, 40 or 50 of them from the Frontier
hills – whose ancestors fought against our soldiers in the past – dancing with
drawn swords around a huge bonfire. Their whoops and cries were blood-curdling
especially as their twisting and spinning intensified and they became more and
more acrobatic. You would have been thrilled.*

**H to R 3 and c. 10 Jan. 1918**                          Peshawar

*My Own ... This is the extreme North West corner of India, the boundary
mark of Anglo-Indian civilisation (of its kind) and Afghan and Central Asian
wild life.*

*I came here to consult a specialist in otology at the Peshawar Hospital about
my pierced ear-drum. He advised it was too much damaged to operate, but
nothing to fear as to further development. Having 4 days leave I got a lift into
Peshawar in the motorcycle side-car of a young 4th Cavalry Brigade officer,
through some of the most fertile valleys of India – oranges, apples, peaches,
junipers all the way – and past caravans of camels heading for the Khyber Pass
and Afghanistan. I tried but sadly failed to get to the Pass. Things are very
unsettled there at present and the officials dissuade people from going up ...
My visit to Peshawar was wonderfully interesting. I have been priming myself*

*on the story of the Great Mutiny of 1857 and the part played in it by the peoples of the Punjab and Frontier ... and by great men of courage and daring like Sir Henry Lawrence, John Lawrence, Herbert Edwardes and John Nicholson (to whom one fierce tribe of Frontier Mohamedans actually formed a sect of worship). The vast wonderful garden of Peshawar is actually within 5 miles of one of the most lawless districts in the world (the N-W Frontier).*

*Wouldn't you like to come out to India? Pindi was agog with excitement last week because of the arrival from home of 5 boat-loads of Officers' wives ... For a long time no women were allowed to make the voyage from home ... The Government in its merciful wisdom has at last allowed a certain number of wives and children – of Regulars.*

### R to H 9, 10, 20 and 31 Jan. 1918                    Leeds

*Dearest ... Your letters are again full of my coming out to India ... Sometimes my longing to see you makes me want to throw everything to the winds but I don't think it would be wise – at present anyhow. You don't know where you may be sent next, and the War may be going on for years yet.*

*I don't think we can begin to foretell until the Americans are got across and begin to make the Germans feel the superiority of numbers. It seems to me the Americans have been very slow ... The way Germany has received Lloyd George's speech seems to point to a death struggle. But I think the speech is most fair ... If we win and the war aims of the allies are carried out they cannot help but wipe out warfare of all kinds – for a menace from the East could be met by a union of European and American nations.*

*The Labour Conference has declared in favour of fighting on if Germany does not accept our terms. The Pacifists have no strength left because their cause is unworthy and everyone knows it.*

*You wouldn't know Britain now with its disorganisation of services, and its lame and legless men about the streets.*

*The weather is atrocious – thick inky fog ... One thing about it is there will be no air raids on London. There were 2 earlier this week – 48 people killed and 200 injured. They also seem to have done damage in Essex.*

*I wish I were 2 years older, 'cos now I can't have a vote [until age 30].*

### H to R 3 and 17 Feb. 1918                    Rawalpindi

*My own Darling ... I have had my Medical Board ... passed as quite fit for general service – nothing organically wrong now – but I'm to stay in India for another month or six weeks. After that I don't know where I shall be sent ... I feel healthy and ought to be on real service again now.*

*I have strong hopes the War is fast drawing to an end ... Everything tends to show the Germans are staking their all on a final military move, but if it does not prove an overwhelming success – which it cannot possibly do – then they cannot afford any longer to ignore their economic conditions. And then there will come the internal revolution in Hunland ... Think of the Austrians*

*with only 1% gold reserves to cover their paper issue, and think of the failure
of the submarine business, and of the unrest in Germany – the Strikes – even
if they are fizzling out – the men are evidently being terrorised to return to work
– and in Austria ... And the Yanks are pouring in ... Why, we must come
out on top, and that right soon too ... Just a few months more, just the Spring
and early Summer, and I shall be much surprised if the German collapse does
not happen.*

*There are some weird wedding festivities going on in the compound just outside
my bungalow, and you have never heard such a row ... About a dozen native
women are standing in a circle in front of the bride's house (she is aged 10!),
holding a big piece of crimson red muslin or something of the sort as a canopy,
and chanting some mysterious incantations to the accompaniment of a tom-tom
and instrument like a violin. Talk of Gregorian chants! These folk's singing is
all in chromatics and minors. Near is an impressive old beldam squatting with
philosophic calm, puffing composedly at her Hookah – or Hubble-bubble. The
natives love this pipe, and you'll often see them squatting in groups and passing
it around – every person gets so many puffs ... I've been trying to take a
snapshot of these womenfolk but they won't have it.*

*Fairy tales of Oriental life are all very well, but the romance vanishes into
thin air when you see people in their homes. The personages of the operatic
stage, and of Rabindranath Tagore, and of the Arabian Nights are of a sphere
very far removed from these poor wretches ... If you want to read something
of real life in India try F. E. Penny's novel 'Sanyasi' (who is like a faqir or
sadhu, a wandering mystic or pilgrim). It is a tale of Southern India around
Madras, but the descriptions of native life would equally well apply to many
parts.*

*It is a most remarkable country, and the longer I stay in India the more
remarkable it becomes. The people round here are strangely loyal to the Empire
– for the good reason that they are enjoying a relative prosperity that would not
be theirs if the protection, and construction, of Britain was withdrawn. Also
there is respect for the sense of fair play associated with the British. And yet,
the least ill rumour or insidious influence, and they are visibly disaffected. It is
strange to read of the tribes on the Frontier roused into open rebellion by
superstitions and talk of a German invasion of Afghanistan, even by a silly
rumour that Japanese soldiers had landed at Calcutta! They are horrified of Japs
and Chinese! They seem to regard them as man-eaters!*

*What do you think of this howler from McNamara's book: 'The Ancient
Greeks only married one wife, and this was called Monotony'!*

**R to H 23 Feb. and 2 Mar. 1918**                              **Leeds**

*Dearest ... Rationing began last week and is already going strong ... The
queues have nearly vanished and there seems to be plenty for everybody, within
reason ... My Upper School is doing the meat rationing for 20,000 people in
Morley and district. Isn't it exciting? ... Everyone in a family is to have 4*

*coupons a week (3 meatless days).*

*What do you think of the League of Nations idea? Do you think it is going to be feasible after the War? I'm afraid till we have real democracy in each country none will submit to mandates from a universal conference . . . It's the ideal thing no doubt . . . and we should give it a chance.*

*Grannie sends her love and hopes she will live to see you return – that's her message . . . Aunt Emma does nothing but condemn the Government and is furiously angry with Lloyd George because the War goes on!*

## H to R 4 and 23 March 1918                              Rawalpindi

*Dearest . . . I think I'll go in for a General Dealer's Store when I return home. What d'you think? In Messpot I had to do with all kinds of foodstuffs for man and beast . . . Here I am among pots and pans, soap, oil, cooking utensils and bedding material! I have imbibed all wisdom concerning the re-tinning of an old tea kettle and the care of woven stuffs from the mischievous encroachments of moths and such pests. Fancy a schoolmaster dealing in Coaltar and Cart-grease! But what would His Majesty's Forces do without these things? . . . Actually I've been congratulated on organising a Mobilisation Depot, with everything ready at a moment's notice . . . and have been given more sections to run. If that lecturer of yours wants some real intoning of poetry let him come to my Depot and hear the Coolies chanting as they work – always in rhythm with each extra push, pull or scrub – something like this:*

| | |
|---|---|
| *How very hot!* | *– (Burden) Yes, as hot as the Monsoon wind* |
| *How hard the work!* | *– Yes, as hard as the white ants' work* |
| *How small the pay!* | *– Yes, as small as the eye of a bunya (Money lender)* |

*Most of the people in Pindi are now getting ready for the great Summer exodus to Murree Hills. They generally leave end March or beginning of April and stay there until September or October. It is quite a sight to see the long trains of cars, tongas, camels, mules and long strings of soldiers with their bullock carts wending their way to Murree and 'coolness', to escape the coming heat of the Plains . . . leaving us poor beggars to be sizzled here! Fancy taking a house for six months then evacuating and carting everything back. I suppose that's why most bungalows you visit here are so unhomely . . . like sheds, with thick walls and hardly any windows, to protect against the heat.*

*You will have seen in the newspapers that we have a little trouble on the Frontier in Baluchistan. It is far from here and we are not bothered.*

*A colleague of mine with the delightful name of Rippin was dilating the other day on the absence of promotion in India: 'An A.S.C. officer in India has as much chance of promotion as a celluloid cat chasing an asbestos mouse in Inferno'!*

**R to H 10 and 17 April 1918**                                    **Leeds**

*My dear ... I suppose we don't intend to act on the offensive yet ... The Germans have taken Bailleul, and put in 120 divisions out of 200 ... We are probably trying to cause huge casualties to them and just holding on meanwhile. There must be some scheme in it, mustn't there? We seem at the last gasp here in England when men up to 50 have to be called up.*

*People very rarely talk about the weather. The chief topics in the shops are the ration cards, and how much brawn or bacon or sausage you can have with the little extra square, or how we are getting on on the Western Front. The Pacifists used to be discussed with venom, but they are left alone now as unworthy of a topic.*

*Dad marched 9 miles with the Volunteers on Sunday, shot there, and then marched back, getting home at 7. It was a freezing cold day. The officers had a hut to retire to at the firing range. Dad shouted 'Johnnie Walker' at them – and got a sheepish laugh. One came out, with slurred speech, and ordered them to 'fire at 3 o'clock – you understand? – 3 o'clock to the left'!*

*The tea and flour you sent me did arrive. They are a real treat.*

**H to R 29 March – 28 April 1918**                          **Rawalpindi**

*My Dearest ... On Sunday last we had a great time ... four of us set out to visit the Margalla Pass where Nicholson fought a battle in the Sikh war, and then Taxilla which has ruins going back to the time of the Persians and Alexander the Great when he invaded India long before Christ. It is a veritable Pompeii, but much older ... We found a distinguished looking Englishman in his garden who offered to show us everything ... When I remarked that he must take a wonderful interest and pride in these excavations to know so much about the antiquities of the place, he quietly replied. 'But don't you think the Director-General ought to know these things?' ... He turned out to be Sir John Marshall, one of the greatest archaeologists of today! He and his wife, who is also an authority on antiquities, then had us to tea – and croquet ... It was so enjoyable – and they have invited me back as soon as I can.*

*My mathematical wits are for ever being sharpened at the Depot ... Talk of Simultaneous Equations why I've actually caught a Babu trying to equate a deficiency in butter with a surplus in hay! ... And he succeeded, too, until I pointed out our axiom that 'things that are equal to the same thing are not of necessity equal to everything else'! He was amazed at my lack of perspicacity!*

*What dreadful days these are in France. The German offensive is striking terror to one's heart even out here. It is awful to think of the carnage, and the distress of our poor fellows in the thick of it ... The Germans are trying to force a conclusion before America has come well in, but so far have failed ... If we hold on now, there can be only one result – Germany must collapse. The economic conditions there, although so little heard of just now, will bring about an ultimate decision.*

*Turkey is absolutely knocked out and there may be defection in that country*

*at any moment ... Lloyd George's policy of unity of control is being vindi-*
*cated ... Our reserves have not been needlessly thrown waste but are still intact*
*for the final offensive ... With all their resources the Germans cannot carry*
*on at this rate much longer ... I would stake a great deal on the end of the*
*war taking place this Summer.*

*So there's to be still more taxation at home, I see from today's newspaper.*
*A very sensible budget, it appears to me. Thank goodness the Government had*
*more sense than the rag-de-luxe, the Daily Mail, for I find that worthy reptile*
*advocated taxes on tea, coffee and on working people's earnings – and let the*
*shippers and steel magnates go free, I suppose.*

*Good news – Captain Theobald, dear old fellow, is now temporary Lieut-*
*Colonel, Chief Supply Officer for the British division in Messpot ... and has*
*been mentioned in despatches ... I should be delighted to serve under him again,*
*even in Messpot.*

*Am due before the Medical Board again on Tuesday. I have no idea what*
*they will do with me.*

### H to R 8 May 1918         Bannu, North West Frontier

*My Own ... You will have had my cable but be surprised at the address ...*
*It is the very 'back of beyond', right on the Afghan frontier ... If you look at*
*a good map you will find the high mountains separating India from Afghanistan*
*have only 3 Passes – the Khyber from Peshawar, the Tochi from Bannu and*
*another from Quetta, all leading from India to Afghanistan and Central Europe.*
*That makes Bannu an important military centre. Moreover the hill tribes are*
*thrillingly uncivilised ... We have a big fort and small cantonment – and no*
*one ventures out without escort.*

*Bannu itself is a small town in a most fertile valley, but with rugged mountains*
*on three sides and desert waste on the fourth, through which runs a small*
*narrow-gauge railway. The heat is as high as Messpot (110°F and higher), and*
*moist and stifling. The garrison is about 50 officers with a similar number of*
*NCOs, and all the rest are Indian troops, and natives. There is a delightful*
*little club where we play tennis in the evening and chat and jangle after dinner*
*– notwithstanding the depredations of mosquitos, which are awful here, and the*
*flutterings of moths and fireflies. The men – there are few women other than*
*two missionaries – are a cheery and single-minded lot, with none of the snobbery*
*of Pindi. If you want to know more of Bannu and its surroundings try Pennell's*
*'The wild tribes of the Afghan Frontier'. It's a marvellous record, and reads*
*like a romance.*

*I hardly see a newspaper here ... just a glimpse of Reuters occasionally at*
*the Club ... So we know hardly anything of the progress of the War, and the*
*outside world sounds like some fairy realm far far remote.*

*The General is reputed to be one of the most efficient but considerate in the*
*Service. He's a real Welshman who can speak Welsh! Son of Lord Tredegar.*
*I haven't met him yet as he is on short leave.*

**R to H 12 and 24 May 1918**                                        **Leeds**

My dearest ... I shall be 29 at the end of this month ... I feel dreadfully old ... I do hope you are back by my next birthday.

Lloyd George has again faced the House of Commons and refuted all the base charges brought against him ... Why should he be accused of making incorrect statements? If he wished to blind the people the best way would be to say nothing ... He goes into the House dubious of his reception, makes his speech, and is acclaimed with cheers. The secret is that he has the country's welfare at heart. That's my opinion. Needless to say it seems to be no-one else's. The reason is we are in a Party-ridden country. The Liberals have Asquith as their Leader ... but he is incapable of power. The Tories put up with Ll-G because he is against Asquith – and very capable. Labour – those who are not pacifist – are working quietly for the good of the nation in different spheres, biding their time for a Labour Government ... When the War is over we can have a fool for Leader of the country without any very serious mishap. Lloyd George will go – and probably be glad of a rest ... All this underhand dealing is disgraceful.

The Americans marched through London on Sat. and received the King's salute. We are beating the Germans in the air – 1000 planes downed in 2 months!

I suppose now you feel that for me to come out to India would be hazardous as your post is again only temporary ... If you send definitely I'll come alright – at once. It's jolly to think there's a possibility.

**H to R 26 May 1918**                                        **Bannu**

Gentle Wife ... I've just returned from a most wonderful journey ... Being O.C. the Supply Depot at Bannu I have to supervise 2 other depots 26 and 39 miles right up the Tochi valley, and 5 outposts in all ... I have to visit the Miramshah and Idak depots every month, and the other outposts when I can. Miramshah is where I've just been, 6 miles from the Afghan frontier. Let me draw you a rough map of the N-W Frontier (sketch appended) ... These mountains are the home of two of the most warlike tribes on the N-W Frontier, the Wazims and the Mahsouds, and are giving our people constant trouble. They are an independent, brave, fearless lot of rascals, best thieves in the world and their greatest honour is paid not to the cultivator of what scanty soil they have nor to the owner of herds of cattle and sheep but rather to the man who has killed the greatest number of his fellow men! ... They have blood-feuds, handed down from generation to generation. I have read of such feuds but here I have contact ... The Acting Commissioner showed me the other evening an innocent looking individual who had told him, without boasting, he had shot two of his enemies on his way down to see him!

Well these are the people of the Hills through which the Tochi River runs, and up this valley Dempster and I had to go. We got a motor car and, although the road is vile, we only had two punctures ... The whole road is picketed by *troops ... lonely watch towers on the hillsides, each manned by 2 or 3 native soldiers, sharpshooters with loaded rifles. But, so far, the Wazims are untamed ... Miramshah lost two camels stolen the other day, and the sentries saw and heard nothing! The camp is on a little plain right at the top of the valley, no more than 400 square yards, hemmed in by high peaks. There are ten officers in charge. They are all cooped up day after day, poor fellows ... and glad to see any strangers!*

*The outposts I am also responsible for are on the tops or slopes of high mountains, small forts like eyries overlooking the valleys leading to Afghanistan. To get to them you have to accompany a convoy of pack mules or camels; there is no regular road, only a trackway that runs over high rocky hills and across streams (raging torrents when the snows melt) ... and from the mud walls of these forts you look down on bare valleys strewn with boulders – and you know not what wily tribesman may be lurking behind them! ... This is active service alright – very active!*

### R to H 2 June 1918      Leeds

*Dearest Man of the Hills ... You will be looking fierce and 'beardy' with a scimatar when you come home, wearing a white arrangement round you and a turban with a real diamond! ... The Frontier sounds desperate. I hope you'll be kept from harm's way.*

*The great push is on in France. Everyone is just waiting. Somehow we seem to have great faith ... No one I've met is upset or depressed we've been driven back and lost Soisson and perhaps Rheims. The Germans must be staking everything on this.*

### H to R 2 and 9 June 1918      Bannu

*My Own ... Three letters you wrote at Easter have taken two whole months to reach me in this God-forsaken 'ole ... That is one drawback here ... The other is the same routine (when not visiting the outposts) – Depot, meals, sleep, club and sleep ... It's too hot to read (over 120°F day time). Even the nights are beastly hot (up to 100°F) and muggy, even on the roof and under punkahs. Oh for the cool breezes of dear old Blighty!*

### H to R 19 June 1918      Rawalpindi

*Beloved ... Pindi once more. Bannu is one of the unhealthiest spots in India during the hot weather and anyone showing any sign of illness, they make no ado and pack him off at once ... Two other officers had bouts of sandfly fever and, of course, I must be the third and, if you please, here I am.*

*In spite of all I am not sorry to have left Bannu ... But I would not have missed the experience, not for anything, the Frontier and its romance and ruggedness and hard cruel savageries ... Everyone turned up in great style at the little railway station to see me off, all Bannu seemed to be there. I was garlanded with flowers, orange blossoms and jasmines, of all things!*

*What a decent little note from Professor Fleure. I'll try and write him a few notes on the Frontier for his Geographic Journal.*

*There is some prospect of my getting leave – I hope in Murree.*

### H to R 1–28 July 1918                                    Gharial, Murree Hills

*Beloved . . . I am up in these glorious hills again, with the sizzling, blazing Plains left far behind, enjoying a rest from Bannu and the sand-fly fever . . . We are not in Murree, which is the ultra-fashionable hill station for Rawalpindi, but at this Gharial rest camp 4 miles away – 7000 feet up on pine-covered hills, off the main Pindi-Kashmir road. Away to the north are the snows of the Hindu Kush, austere, awesome, the snow gleaming in the sun. To the east lies the deep gorge of the Jhelum River as it flows from the wondrous beauty of Kashmir to the blistering sands of Punjab and Sind . . . Such a contrast from the Plains . . . Gone are the gaspings for air and moppings of sweat. And, thank goodness, gone too are the sandflies and mosquitos, and all evil things. Do you know, I heard a cuckoo here yesterday.*

*The fellows here, 12 of us, all 'Frontiersmen' as we superciliously call ourselves, are a mad crew but fine set, including some former officals of the Indian Civil Service, all now subalterns. We walk, talk, explore, ride, take and develop photos, swot Hindustani; and I try to read up and write notes on the Frontier Geography, though books are very difficult to get . . . By the way, do not trouble to send me Punch any more, as I can get a copy almost anywhere. It is the universal paper of India . . . We are not allowed in Murree for some reason but decided yesterday to 'raid' it on hired 'tats' (small mountain ponies) and had a great day. Some of the people there possibly thought it was the long-talked-about invasion of India by wild tribes of the Asiatic steppes!*

*The monsoons are very late this year; the result is that the heat on the Plains is unusually severe. Last week alone there were 51 deaths from sunstroke among the poor troops in Pindi.*

*We are fond of dilating on the stinginess of the Indian Government especially in their treatment of temporary officers (half pay) and of frontier officers (high prices of everything). But in some things they are generous . . . this rest camp is one; working to the principle of 'prevention is better than cure' is another; and what is called War Leave to enable officers to escape the intense summer heat by relays – up to 60 days. Also they make it compulsory to have a rest cure after Frontier service . . . I had intended going on to Kashmir, with some of the fellows here, but there is no railway and a motor car is too expensive. I am not without hope of seeing what some say is the real India, the Ganges Valley and down south around Bangalore and Madras, if I can work a transfer . . . But a Pindi colleague wants me to join him for the remainder of my leave at Mussoorie in the Himalayan Hills, and I hope to do so.*

### R to H 1–10 Aug. 1918                                    Caister-on-Sea, Norfolk

*Dearest . . . 2nd epistle from this jolly place. It is August Bank Holiday so there*

*won't be much peace, and it poured last evening. I wonder where you are –
Kashmir or Pindi?*

*Foch's great counter-stroke has been eminently successful – 17000 prisoners
taken by the British and French near Amiens in 2 days ... We must wait
now ... The Americans now have 1,500,000 in France. They are making up
for lost time with a vengeance.*

*Women are not going to be allowed to enter Parliament, just as I expected.
Isn't it utterly unjust and undemocratic? We can work, fill very responsible
positions, suffer sacrifice, organise, even vote – except me (under 30) – I'm
not considered sufficiently developed for that yet – though male youngsters of
19 are! But we women cannot rule ourselves. We are to be ruled by a parcel
of fools who call themselves our superiors. But how do they get there? Money
and influence mostly.*

## H to R 14–28 Aug. 1918 Mussoorie, United Provinces

*Darling ... You'll see the scene is once more changed ... I came here through
the summer heat of Pindi and Lahore. But it is so far disappointing. Mussoorie
is considered one of the most beautiful hill-stations in India ... But I'm practically
on my own (in the Grand Central Hotel), my Pindi colleague having been
recalled at short notice to go to Messpot, and we seem more oftener than not
to be in the clouds ... There are a few nice people, but the majority are loud and
material – the 'mighty Rupee' holds sway here – and seem to think of nothing
but money, teas, dinners, scandal and backbiting. One of them, a portly and
much bejewelled dame, wife of a tobacco merchant from Calcutta, came up to
me when I was reading in the lounge the other evening to remark in a raucous
voice on my 'seclusion and aloofness', and to demand to see my book (Carpenters
'Days and Dreams' on recent major changes in scientific theory) ... Seeing the
word 'Socialists' somewhere in it she turned on me: 'You are not a Socialist
surely!' Out of cussedness I said 'I am'. She sailed out a veritable volcano of
righteous indignation! ... Then there is an old Colonel who loudly claims 30
years in India and that 'the only way to deal with the native is the Iron Hand'!
An Indian Civil Servant from Bengal and I had a good laugh at the dame ...
There seems to be little love lost between the Civil Service and the Army in India.*

*We are rather interested in the India Reforms submitted in London by Montagu
and the Viceroy ... It is awfully difficult to gain a true perspective here ...
One turns mostly in Anglo-Indian circles, which are generally characterised by
a strange conservatism and a fear of losing privileges. I have been very much
impressed by the sanity and fair play invariably shown by the Civil authorities ...
And, from my little experience, I rather think the majority of Indian people, if
they had a voice in the matter, would sooner remain under the British raj than
be transferred to the mercies of Indian 'superior personnel' as they are called ...
who seem to lack stability, authority and the respect of the peasants and lower
classes ... One thing I feel convinced of – Annie Besant's scheme for total
autonomy would soon land the country in chaos.*

**R to H 14 and 21 Sept. 1918**                                        **Leeds**

*My dearest . . . It is over my usual time to write as life has been strenuous . . .
We have removed to this house in Hamilton Avenue, Chapeltown, and it is
lovely compared with the hideous Harehills Road, Roundhay place. And I have
had school worries, but have overcome them . . . I am beginning to wonder how
we are going to set up house after the war. We should have bought things 2
years ago and stored them. It is almost impossible to get many things now. Coal
is going to be rationed, and gas. Furniture is very high in price, and second
hand furniture more than new. I am happy I got linen sometime ago or it would
be 2 and 3 times the price now – or else unprocurable!*

*We are doing wonderfully in France now aren't we? And in Macedonia and
Palestine also. But the Huns won't relinquish without a struggle, when they see
we are bent on complete conquest and forcing our war aims on them . . . Anyway
we can't stop just now can we? Thank Heaven we have some clear thinking
Americans with us and particularly that they are not hampered by any promises
in the past, as we and others probably are.*

*I read the discussions at the Labour Conference. The movement is spreading
but does not seem to be one of thought so much as of politics and the rights of
certain workers only. I may be wrong . . . There are some absurd statements
about not fighting Germany commercially after the war. They don't understand
(perhaps I don't!) how Germany organises for war and in peace, and woe betide
all other nations with Germany supreme!*

**H to R 8–29 Sept. 1918**                                        **Mussoorie**

*Dearest Heart . . . Still no Home Mail . . . I suppose the vessels have been
transferred to the Atlantic to bring every available American soldier to France.*

*My leave is gradually drawing to an end. I shan't be sorry to get back to
duty . . . Fighting has broken out with some of the tribes on the N-W Frontier,
believed to be stirred by some German agents who have come through Russia
and Persia . . . Much as I hate Bannu as a place, the duties are such that I
would jump at them without hesitation if they were offered to me again.*

*The CO of the 23rd Rifle Brigade at Bareilly, Col Turnbull, here on War
Leave like me, has struck up friendship and is delightful company . . . He is an
Edinburgh man, and on the Court of Governors of Edinburgh University, and
a great walker . . . The other evening he and I had a long and interesting chat
with the Maharajah of Patiala, the Indian prince who represented India lately
on the Imperial War Conference. He told us that what impressed him more
than anything at Home was the way in which our women were doing their
share. He swore roundly – a Sikh chief, mind you – about some women in this
country, especially the European women, thinking only of their own pleasure,
and is now recruiting a corps of them to be taken by him at his expense, to do
war work in France. Rather a wild scheme perhaps . . . but it did my heart good
to hear him speak so respectfully of our women at home.*

*The news from France is glorious . . . The Colonel declares Peace cannot*

*possibly be delayed much longer. The latest! An officer in Palestine, seeing the
sights of Jerusalem, asked a Tommy where the Mount of Olives was. The
Tommy's reply was 'I don't know, Sir . . . In fact I don't know the names of
any of the Pubs in this place'!*

## R to H 30 Sept.–14 Oct. 1918                                   Leeds

*Dearest . . . The Indian silks you sent me are simply lovely, such remarkable
workmanship, and so beautiful.*

*Wonderful news, yesterday the unconditional surrender of Bulgaria, today
63,000 prisoners in 5 days on the Western Front . . . I can't think it is going
to be very long now. I really can't sleep for excitement, to begin to think there
is an end!*

*I shall never be sorry for this separation once it is over for it has taught me
very many things, and given you such wide experience even though suffering
has formed much of it . . . I've been trying to remember your voice, not to
remember it exactly but to hear it . . . It's a dream . . . I'm frightened at what
our rulers might do now . . . The American people are fired with zeal and
enthusiasm but their country is chock full of trusts, combines and vested
interests . . . We must not just let the Germans retire to Germany . . . See what
happened in Serbia when the Bulgarians took Serbian prisoners with them on
their way home and killed them on the wayside . . . The lesson is so ingrained
– we've had throughout this War such surprises in both ways, good and bad.*

## H to R 5 Oct. 1918                                         Mussoorie

*Mine . . . The Col ASC at Brigade HQ has invited me to work there at near-by
Dehra Dunn until they move back to the Plains for the Winter at the end of
the month. Naturally I have jumped at it. I shall then rejoin 2nd Division at
Rawalpindi when they come down from Murree Hills . . . It's been rather a nice
holiday on the whole.*

*Splendid news pouring in; Palestine; much of the Turkish Army buckled up;
Macedonia; Bulgarians surrendering; Austrians staggering; and, best of all, the
Hindenberg line smashed on the Western Front . . . The collapse of Turkey is
what will exercise most influence here. India, in spite of its general loyalty to
British rule, has plenty of sedition-mongers and the chief grievance of the
Mohamedan section of the population is that we are waging war on the Turks,
the greatest Mohamedan nation in the world. Religious ties are marvellously
potent among these followers of Islam. But they have great faith in fate. When
they find we have gained the upper hand it will be 'Allah has willed it' . . . So
you can understand what a relief that news brings here . . . Today has been
proclaimed a general holiday throughout India to celebrate the surrender of
Bulgaria.*

*By Jove, there must be some flint-hearted folk still left in the old country.
Fancy that strike of railwaymen in South Wales, in spite of their leaders, and
at a time like this. It's just the same here . . . Fancy the jute merchants of*

Calcutta making 225%, and then grudging their work-people a mere pittance of a rise! There will be many an old score to pay after the war – and so thinks the Colonel too.

What do you think of this Song of the Exile, translated from an old Pathan poet?

> Gentle breeze of morn, if thou my Homeland pass,
> Should thy course be by Indus bank, by Khattak hill,
> Bear to them my heart-strains, my greetings again and again,
> Cry out to the father of waters (the Indus),
> But unto the little streamlet of Landai (Kabul) gently whisper:
> 'Soon, soon shall I gaze on my Own, my Homefolk,
> And drink of the cups of rapture'
> And Heaven knows no better than this.

> > Khusbhal Khan, the Khattak.

## H to R 15–27 Oct. 1918                                      Mussoorie

*Dearest . . . I do hope the people at home will not get impatient and force the hand of the leaders . . . Stiffen our backs a little longer and the Huns will crave for peace not on their terms but on unconditional surrender . . . That's where I am afraid of the Yanks. For the life of me I cannot bring myself to fall at the feet of Wilson, as some people do. His talk is too academic, high-falutin, to please me. It's all very well to talk large of principles and of justice and of the League of Nations; but when you come to give them practical purpose the problems are too real for vague talk. The Yank ideas will not coincide with ours or the French. For what do they know of devastation and the horror of war in their midst? The war has not yet come home to them – except in increased profits! Ugh, I love not their boasting and self-advertisement! This is a common view in India – the Picture Houses were full of it when they arrived in Britain. I hope we are not doing them an injustice.*

*I've just returned from seeing Colonel Turnbull off to Bareilly . . . He has been out in India since Xmas 1914, and his officers and men worship him . . . He has invited you and me to visit him and his wife in Edinburgh after the war.*

*The monsoon rains have failed utterly, and conditions are really very serious . . . The Government has established cheap grain shops in all populous districts, where the poor, in spite of their own blood-sucking grain dealers, can get a sufficiency of food. They are also organising throughout the country travelling dispensaries in the charge of Indian doctors, with free medicine and milk, to fight this flu epidemic. An achievement that makes one feel rather proud of the Administration, with all their faults! . . . I'm impressed too by the work of the Salvation Army . . . they do wonderful work among the poorer natives and penetrate to corners where life conditions are indescribable.*

*I have imagined myself holding converse with an old Pathan poet:*

> 'Khusbhal Khan, you boast to me of your Homeland, of your Hills that lift
> up to the heavens and shed forth a dazzling glory from their heights, of your

*glens and your "tangis" (defiles) that sink into the earth – fit lairs for the wolf-hounds of war, and of your "kaches" (upland valleys) with their ledges of green crops and the ilex and the grand deodar and the stately poplar – and the homestead perched on the height. And your men-folk, you say, are brave in the fray and know no fear, their "izzat" (honour) is dearer to them than the light of day, hefty men and free. And you hold forth about your women-folk, with their wonder-lustrous eyes and the slender bearing of the withy, so when in the mead they roam the heart of the tulip is scarred with love.*

*But I could tell you of a fair, fair country far away yond the "Kalapani" (Black Water: the Ocean) and desolate wastes, a land of Hills and Valleys smiling to the blue Heavens with a song of Spring in its heart, a carpet of lush green for the Fairies to dance on. Embosomed it is in the folds of the Sea-deity whose love sways crooning to the vasty rhythm of the deep. Its streams leap exulting down the hillsides, and its glens and meads are a-thrill with the living joy of flowers. There the songs of birds hurtle through the springy air – arrows of melody. A land of Nature's gladness – and of the deep joy of Man.*

*For it is the land where dwells my Love – She of the gentleness of the moor-ling when the autumn suns are warm, whose joy is that of the young fir branchling in the Spring – and whose Love is as Olwen's tread in the meadows – a trail of sweet flowers.*

*Oh to be with my Love watching the rippling moonbeams on the Menai, or wandering mid the wild hyacinth in the pinewoods of Moel Fama, or climbing the wondrous gorse-crags of Llanbedrog, or exulting with a wild joy on the heather-heights of Ilkley.*

*Beautiful Spirit, waft me Home soon, soon to Her who owns my Heart's Love, and fold us both in Thy beauteous joy.'*

**R to H 20 and 27 Oct. 1918**                      **Leeds**

*My dearest ... You cannot imagine what peace will mean in a thousand ways to the inhabitants of Britain. The big things at stake everyone will feel – the return of our men, the knowledge that all that bloodshed is over and we are victorious. There are also the multifarious little things – the breakdown of the tram-cars when you need them, the worry whether the coal will last or you are using the gas unnecessarily, no matches to relight the gas lamps, no vinegar when you want it, the ignominy of being told you can only have 1 pint of milk, the rush from shop to shop for little needs ... All very small annoyances of war-time life ... And yet they don't worry us much. The people are stoical.*

*The world will be a better place afterwards, for all this dreadful sacrifice and blood toll. 'Vibrant with new ideas' was said yesterday. Yes, perhaps so – I hope so for the sake of those who have given their all.*

**H to R 3 and 8 Nov. 1918**                    **Himalaya Club, Landour**

*Love ... Still in the Hills, within view of the 'eternal snows' of Badrinath and*

Kedarnath (where the Ganges rises) and Nanda Devi 25,000 feet – not much below Everest … A judge of the High Court of Calcutta and I climbed to our topmost ridge 7500 feet yesterday to see this panorama. And from my window I overlook the Dun – the Plains at the foot of these hills, with the Ganges in the distance and the little town of Dehra Dun nestling in the midst of a vast jungle – among the best hunting grounds in India. To the N-W we can see the faint track over the mountains to Simla, and the other way the pilgrim track to Tehri and the source of the Ganges … It is too wonderful for words.

I feel upset that the Labour people at home are inclined to call for conscription of wealth etc – sure roads to Bolshevism. That is not the way to raise the masses but the way to destruction … It is not for the munition workers or conscientious objectors but the poor Tommy in the trench to say what should become of the principles for which he has fought.

My monograph on the anthropo-geography of the N-W Frontier is progressing quite nicely … I suffer for want of decent books of reference … And now there's a ban on sending photos home … Also it will have to be submitted to the Censor … But I hope that peace will see these restrictions withdrawn.

My orders have arrived – I leave for Pindi tomorrow.

Last night I wooed the Muse – but this is the best she would vouchsafe me!! And it's pretty desperate!

(I)  When the war is over and gone, Robin,
        And Peace has come to its own,
     And this murderous slaughter has ceased for aye,
        – And Wilhelm quartered and drawn!
     [Rather an anti-climax! But the rhyme called for it!]
     Then what shall we do with ourselves, Robin,
        Then what shall we do, You and I?
     When the guns have ceased to spit and roar
        And the Zeppelins ceased to fly?!
           [Please, don't mind the rhythm and the syncopation that
           reminds one of Ragtimes!]

(II)  I'll tell you the first thing I'll do, Robin
         The very first thing that I'll try –
      I'll pack up my troubles with least delay,
         And away from Bombay I'll hie!
      Then a hearty adieu to the East and its hosts,
         Its heat and its 'stenches' galore,
      And hurrah for the good ship so stout and so brave
         That's to take me to Blighty once more!

(III) And when I get back to old Blighty,
         You will meet me in Town, wont you, May?
      And we'll have a right high celebration
         – With theatres and champagne – all day!!

> *[The Muse, stupid thing, rather jibbed at this – hence the*
> *lameness of the rhythm!!]*
> And if you like, I'll tell tales of Mesopotamia (?)
>   And sing you songs of Kashmir! (?)
> And we'll have a right jolly good honeymoon
>   – Just You and your hubby, my Dear!
>     *[Oh what an Anti-Climax! Can you tolerate any more? !]*
> (IV) We'll travel old Blighty all over,
>     And how we shall hug to our hearts
>   Those lovely old scenes of our Courtship
>   Whose mem'ries aye brightened my paths
>     *[Can't get decent rhyme!]*
>   – Then HOME to our own little Hearth-stone
>   Our own little Nest just for two
> And the World and its worries can go packing
>   – For all that I'll want then is – YOU.

*[Just as well the ink in my pen is giving out – or you will be consigning me to somewhere I don't wish to go! There's a New Moon!]*

'H' left Mussoorie for Rawalpindi on 10 November and learnt of the Armistice the following day at Lahore on his way through. He wrote that the Punjab capital 'went wild with celebration, with bunting flying, sirens hooting, motor horns blowing and guns from the Fort booming'. He stayed with a Lahore Inspector of Police friend and in the evening they 'lost all sense of official dignity, and went along the Mall like everyone else yelling and bawling and waving flags like mad ... Even the natives paraded the streets shouting their tumasha (celebration) hurrahs ... It was the outburst of feelings long pent up of "Thank God, it's over at last".' Later he wrote: 'In this mornings (Pindi) paper one reads of the scenes in London and the big towns at home, and it quite brought a lump to my throat.'

In Rawalpindi, the *Pindi Mail*, the largest circulation newspaper in the Northern Punjab and North West Frontier Province, fed though it was by Reuters and other news agencies, was only able to report the Armistice two days after the event. It did so of course with banner headlines, followed by agency accounts of strikes and riots in Germany, the abdication of the Kaiser, and Lloyd George's warning that Germany must expect stern reckoning.

The following day the *Mail* published the list of Heads of State to whom the King-Emperor George V had telegraphed his congratulations on the conclusion of the Armistice. We perhaps forget today who were all our allies in that Great War. Quoting Reuters the telegrams were sent to 'The King of the Belgians, President Poincaré (France), The Emperor of Japan, President Wilson (USA), the Kings of Italy, Serbia, Rumania, Montenegro,

Greece and Siam, the Sultan of Egypt and the Presidents of Portugal, China, Brazil and Cuba.' The stalwart Dominions of Canada, Australia, New Zealand and South Africa, together with India and the Colonies were not so favoured presumably because, owing allegiance to King George, their Monarch did not feel he should send telegrams to himself!

'H' found a warm welcome on his return to Pindi, but the talk was inevitably about the likely Peace terms that would be imposed on Germany and its allies; how long that would take; and particularly on demobilisation and when they would all get home. 'H' wrote to 'R' that it might not be before the Spring for him.

Meanwhile the Indian Army, in its deliberate way, organised at Rawalpindi on 27 November, a 'Thanksgiving Celebration, in honour of the Signing of the Armistice and Cessation of Hostilities Aug 4th 1914–Nov 11th 1918.' There was a parade and thanksgiving service, 'for all troops and those civilians who wished, including Massed Band renderings of an Overture Solonelle (Sullivan's 'In Memoriam'), the Allied National Anthems (listed as Italy, America, Serbia, Belgium, Japan and France), and Rule Britannia, God Bless the Prince of Wales and God Save the King'. The General Officer Commanding's Message to the troops set the scene:

> The celebration which is taking place at Rawalpindi to-day is designed to indicate in the most earnest and impressive manner not only the great victory of the British Empire and her Allies over the Central Powers but also to bear testimony to the solidarity of the Empire.
>
> The General Officer Commanding the Division wishes that the solemn import of the simple ceremony which marks the occasion may be grasped by all.
>
> The Civilian population have spontaneously come forward with a request that they may, in conjunction with the troops, do homage to the Flag of the Empire and in so doing show their loyalty to their King Emperor.
>
> It is their express wish that their presence may be taken as an appreciation of the enormous debt which India owes to the Navy and the British Army which together have borne the brunt of the great conflict now happily concluded.
>
> What India herself has done must not be overlooked. The Punjab has provided more recruits than any other Province of India and Rawalpindi heads the lists, in this respect, of all Districts of the Punjab.
>
> The Divisional Commander asks all British ranks to call to mind that Indian soldiers have fallen in France, in Mesopotamia, in Palestine and in fact in practically all theatres of the War in upholding the honour of that Flag which is for all who are assembled, whether European or Asiatics, the Symbol of Liberty.

For all his patriotisim, 'H' probably found that a bit over the top. His concern was more with the consequences and lessons of the war. He wrote: 'Even at a time like this, one's heart goes out to those poor folk who have lost dear and loved ones. What a sacrifice it has been – and all because of the fool and his satellites who ruled the destinies of Germany. I sincerely hope that he and his myrmidons will be placed on their trial before a court of Justice, just like an ordinary criminal – and that their fates will be a lesson to future generations, that it is not for dictators or magnates of any kind to tamper with the rights of peoples and nations.'

A month later 'H' wrote that there is 'still no mention of when we are to be de-mobilised although that is ever the topic of conversation. Everybody, civil and military, is anxious to get home, and great is the striving for a passage ...' As the first demobilisation announcements began to appear from other Fronts he wrote of fears in India that by the time they returned home all the good civilian posts would have been filled. He asked 'R' to look out for any teaching or administrative vacancies he might fit and to apply for him.

'R' continued to write regularly but with 'H' so much on the move and increasing pressure on the mail services as demob fever grew, many of her letters in this period never reached him. Some of his were also delayed. 'R' complained that a telegram he sent on 5 Oct about his movements took nearly seven weeks to reach her, and that it was all very exciting but frustrating not knowing when he would be home. Where should she meet him – Liverpool, London, Marseilles, or even Paris – to join the great Peace Parade planned there? Where would they then go? What sort of jobs would he be looking for? (His pre-war teaching post at Denbigh was held open to him but he had since been judged eligible for a Headship.) What of the competition for housing, few having been built during the war? Should she go on teaching at least temporarily? If so, where? – at Morley she had to give a month's notice, anyhow. Millions of other servicemen must have been going through the same ecstasy and agony, each with his or her own enormous re-adjustment to make. The Government set up schemes to help. But it was for each individual and family to find their own new lives.

In those letters that did reach 'H', 'R' could still find space to conjecture on the likely Peace terms that would be imposed on Germany and her allies; on her distrust of the Germans and the rising German Democratic Movement; on the terror of the Russion revolution and fear of Bolshevism spreading and challenging the rising Socialism in Britain; on the attractiveness of President Wilson's ideas for a League of Nations but unattractiveness of his 'voluminous praise for America only' in achieving victory; on how dreadful and 'groovy' (sic) it would be to go back to the same socially confined lives they led before the War; and on her deep concern for the 'crippled and wounded' ... 'It is so tragic,' she wrote, 'seeing them all, particularly in civilian clothes ... I hope I shall some day be able to do something to help them to get what they deserve in the way of comforts and good living. It is a duty I shall owe them for having you back safe and sound.'

In her last letter to reach him before he left India, dated 28 December, she added, 'Do you know I haven't yet heard that you know the Armistice has been signed!' and 'Your letters have been so sustaining. We will read them together some day perhaps.'

'H' finally received his orders to return home in late January 1919, under priority posting for teachers but with no assurance of immediate release. He managed to achieve his ambition of visiting Delhi *en route* but had to wait three long weeks at Bombay for a passage. He used his time there working at the University Library on his monograph on the North West Frontier peoples, and on trying to reconcile the love he had acquired for India and particularly the Himalayas and its peoples, with his dislike of the heat and the 'dread diseases of the land'. In his harder-headed moments he remembered that 'We had no sooner got over a bout of malaria than influenza and pneumonia appeared, and after that small-pox and cholera, and after that again, enteric etc.' In his nostalgic moods he remembered the joys of the hills, now under snow, the glory of the scenery, the fascinating history, buildings and antiquity, the deeply interesting agglomeration of peoples. 'Nature is so prodigal in the land – and there is such waste in this warren of humanity.' Like many British before him, and since, he had caught the magnetism of India and left Bombay wanting to return – health and circumstances permitting. He never did, but always retained a deep interest in the sub-continent, and particularly the North West Frontier.

The voyage home was anything but enjoyable. While mercifully shorter in length than the outward journey 2½ years before, it was rough in 'a converted Turkish tub' as far as the Red Sea, tedious in having to hang around Port Said for days for a change of boat, rough again in the Mediterranean, and then deeply disappointing in that, with his medical history, the Army insisted on a check-up at the Marseilles General Hospital *en route* and another at the Avenue Hospital at Liverpool on arrival there and, finally, a threatened four months 'convalescence' at the Eaton Hall Home for Officers on the Duke of Westminster's estate near Chester. He managed to get that reduced to a few weeks, then took sick leave, and was released in mid-June and formally discharged and invalided out of the Army in late July. His demobilisation from Rawalpindi had taken a full six months! The Army, to their credit, kept him under periodic medical review for two years more, recognising that his War service had probably permanently impaired his health. 'H' had nothing but praise for the Army Medical Services throughout his association with them.

On return to civilian life in June 1919 he was appointed Deputy Director of Training for the rehabilitation of ex-servicemen in North Wales based on Wrexham. Six months later, in January 1920, he became Headmaster of the County School, Llangollen. The regular letters between them of course then ceased. Eight years since engagement and four years since marriage they were at last able to set up home together.

Throughout their years of separation there is never a trace of doubt in their letters in each other's fidelity, nor a trace of rancour at their misfortune. It was hateful but their war-time duty. That was the ethos of the time.

CHAPTER 3

# Early Life, Llangollen

## 1923–1938

THE LLANGOLLEN HISTORICAL PAGEANT of 1929 achieved press and public acclaim far beyond the Vale. It declared Llangollen to be 'The World's Beauty Spot'. No one demurred then or subsequently, so far as I know. The description was, and still is, in my humble judgement, well merited.

My father wrote and produced the Pageant, and my mother chaired the 30 strong Ladies' Committee – in those days called the 'Lady Workers'. The Archdruid of Wales came to officiate and the Royal Welsh Fusiliers buglers gave the Fanfare. The whole town and district joined in as players, singers, town silver bandsmen, harpists, organisers and supporters. The Lord of the Chirk Castle, Lord Howard de Walden, attended as Patron, his wife as a bard and his five daughters as players. But the main roles went to townsfolk and to the infants of the local primary schools and children of the County School. Hundreds took part each in costumes appropriate to the episodic periods depicted. Thousands watched, including my brother and me, then aged 8 and 6. It was an historical pageant but, in the words of H. G. Wells quoted in the Programme: 'What Man has done, … and all this Story we have told, form but a Prelude to the things that Man has yet to do.' It was communal fun but also designedly educative.

My father had a way of inspiring and involving people in learning and culture. Locally, Llangollen had the Welsh imagination and the verve and talent to respond. In addition to running the School, he organised or played a leading part in countless other public events and activities there in his time – Welsh educational conferences, archaeological conferences, eisteddfodau, historical mimes, scout concerts, Welsh national theatre and more.

Llangollen was a natural venue. Two of its greatest cultural achievements of the century were in fact just before and just after my father's time. They were the outstanding Welsh National Eisteddfod of 1908, to which Lloyd George brought his then Liberal colleague Winston Churchill; and the remarkable International Musical Eisteddfod started by some of his former school and town colleagues after World War II and now a permanent event on the international cultural calendar. He would have warmly welcomed both.

His period at Llangollen, as Headmaster and townsman, straddled most of the inter-War years, 1920 to 1937. Mine was not much less, 1923 to 1938. Much has changed there since, but much remains the same. The Vale has long attracted travellers and tourists not just for its beauty but for its strategic position at the throat of the Dee valley and, over the hills, to the Clwyd valley and beyond. Also for its rich history. The 1929 Pageant singled out for historic commemoration first the coming of St Collen to the then primitive Celts and others of the area in the sixth century. (It was from him that the town takes its name.) Then it portrayed the arrival of the Cistercians and around 1200 the founding of Valle Crucis Abbey, the elegant ruins of which still stand at the foot of the Horse-shoe Pass. Third, and central to local and Welsh history, it depicted Owain Glyndwr, Lord of Glyndyfrdwy, emerging in 1401 as the unassuming but remarkable leader of Wales in its last twelve-year long war of independence against the Norman Kings of England (and the last time Wales had its own Assembly). Then, fourth, the pageant showed Llangollen as a popular meeting place around 1600 for people of the region on their way to London who wished to travel in company for protection against highwaymen and footpads. And, finally, it recalled the building of the Holyhead road (now the A5) between 1815 and 1830, another great achievement of the engineer Telford, which put Llangollen firmly on the London route to Ireland, and brought many famous people of the day to stay with the eminent if eccentric Ladies of Llangollen, Lady Eleanor Butler and Miss Sarah Ponsonby, 'the most celebrated virgins in Europe'. Their elegant Tudor house remains a sight to see in Llangollen to this day.

The Pageant might equally have included, as other Llangollen pageants produced by my father did, the prehistoric cavemen of the Eglwyseg Rocks; the coming of the Romans in the early years AD, and capitulation to them of the local Druids and Dinas Bran; the coming of the Normans and local resistance of the Prince of Powys and his castle on Dinas Bran in the early 1200s; or the building in 1346, by Bishop Trevor, of the famous Llangollen bridge over the Dee – one of the 'seven wonders of Wales' – across which I walked to primary school and town so often as a boy, which still impressively stands, in widened form, today. Other pageants he produced over those years included the siege of Chirk Castle by the Cromwellians in 1655; and the opening in 1805 of the magnificent Pontcysyllte aqueduct, which still stands proud across the lower Vale two hundred years on. Any Llangollen historical pageant now might also include

Father, Mother, Eryl and me, 1924.

the arrival of the railway in 1862, closure in 1965 but re-opening by private enterprise in the early 1970s; the visits of Pavarotti as a young man and more recently, as the world famous tenor, to the International Eisteddford; and much else. Llangollen is full of history through the ages, and no boy could be unaware of it, especially in a family like mine.

Llangollen: 'the world's beauty spot'.
Photograph by Douglas Scott, published by J. Arthur Dixon Ltd

I am apparently on record as declaring in the 4th Form that nineteenth-century history was 'good, there's plenty of "stick 'em up buddy" stuff in it.' But genuine interest in history grew with time and I would have taken it as my advanced school subject, even in preference to the sciences, had my Llangollen history teacher had her way. She made history live – and also played hockey for Wales which appealed to me. She subsequently married an Aberystwyth professor who was knighted so she became Lady Jones-Parry. But she never stopped sending me Christmas or congratulatory messages 'not to forget history'. She was convinced I would enjoy it and, like any dedicated teacher, she never gave up. It was the War, in fact, which reignited my interest, and I went back to Cambridge afterwards to do as she had advised – and have never regretted it.

Today the history and beauty of Llangollen stand as proud as ever. But it is also now a major tourist centre, and life has had to adapt. I have no doubt it is still a very attractive place to live in, especially for anyone who does not mind crowds of visitors. Certainly, with the exception of the much needed but deplorably ugly 1960s' and 1980s/90s' extensions to the old School, high on the hill, the Planners appear to have well preserved the limits and physical character of the town. It is always a pleasure to go back there.

Llangollen was a peaceful place. There was plenty going on especially on market days. Apart from the pageants, we had festivals and fairs, corn and woollen mills, fishmongers, butchers and bakers (and, thankfully, no supermarkets to gobble them up). But there were no traffic jams, and the police kept order by walking the beat, by knowing everyone and when necessary by tweaking an ear or just delivering a wigging. We had no drug problem in those days, which doubtless makes a profound difference, but with social welfare only in its infancy there was deep deprivation in such small towns just as in big, and corresponding incentive to crime. Yet the policing system seemed to work. I do not remember crime being a major local issue at any time. Nor noise. The familiar sounds were not of cars and machines and sirens, but of the splendid river Dee tumbling over its rocks, the clip-clop of the milkman's pony and heavy tread of the brewer's shire and those that pulled the old pleasure boats on Telford's canal. Also, of course, the chuffs and toots and clickety-click of the old railway trains as they plied up the valley (and are doing, again, today). Then there was the ceaseless orchestra of rural sounds we hear so much less today since the industrialisation of farming. There were birds of countless species, whose nests and eggs I am afraid we searched out in the hedgerows – but at least we knew what they were and respected their habitats (and most of their eggs). There was the dawn cockerel we hear so rarely today, and the lowing herds and bleating lambs and sheep. Lambing and calving and foaling came, as I remember, not as now with artificial insemination and the timing of man, but with the blossom of Spring.

Farming, and especially hill farming, was an uncertan occupation, open to the vagaries not only of the weather but of animal and crop diseases for which there were then few treatments. It was also, as ever, subject to changes in political policy, like Baldwin's post World War I protectionism,

Lloyd George introducing Winston Churchill and other Liberal colleagues
to the Welsh National Eisteddfod held in Llangollen in 1908.
(*Reproduced from* Llangollen in Old Picture Postcards *by Ifor Edwards, 1993,
by courtesy of the publishers, European Library*)

which in the longer term did so much more harm than good. His reason for introducing it was the crisis in agriculture as it adjusted to post-War demand and competition. This was a national issue in the 1920s and rural places like Llangollen knew it.

The countryside was of course fuller of nature than it is today. Trees and hedgerows abounded, as did butterflies and bees as well as birds. And the farm animals were all out and about, not cooped up except in the worst weather. It did not of course produce anything like the food per acre we demand today. But there was an inborn respect for nature more profound than I think we now retain, global warming notwithstanding. Environmentalism as an active body of belief was only in its infancy. I remember an elderly aristocratic lady, Mrs Aitken, who lived near Llantysilio, was considered very eccentric for going around installing litter baskets and notices of her own at picnic and other visitor sites. My father approved and, on the larger scale, himself organised a successful campaign against the plan of the Warrington Water Company to flood the beautiful Ceiriog Valley to supply more water to Lancashire. Being environmentalist however did not stop people fogging up the valley with coal burning, in the house, mill and railway. We were sadly ignorant of the causes and effects of atmospheric pollution then. We were nonetheless brought up to believe and to practise that the countryside must be protected.

I do not recall ever feeling this was in any way irksome. But I do recall occasional conflict between the beauty of the place and the beast of school examinations. Swatting for School Certificate (called GCSE I think today) on a lovely Summer evening could be a battle of concentration not always won against the alluring sound of willow, wicket and applause wafting up the valley from the town cricket field, as local heroes like Bert Iremonger bowled another visitor out or Scott Archer cut another graceful four or Ken Bruce hit another towering six. The field has now become the home and theatre of the International Eisteddfod.

Studies apart, there was somehow always something for children to do, free as we were of TV and, most importantly, free to wander unmolested – except of course when we trespassed for mischief or illicit apples. There were doubtless child abusers around then just as now. But I do not remember hearing of a single case on the highway or byways of our valley and I hope it is still so today. Perhaps we had a more in-built sense of community then. Certainly we had less violence thrust theatrically upon us by the media – boy's 'Horror' and one or two other nasty children's papers of old excepted.

School in those days provided not just lessons and homework and exams but for the boys cricket and football, and for the girls hockey, tennis and netball. Then there were athletics and the Annual Sports days. A playing field was an integral part of every secondary school. How Britain has come to sell off 10,000 in the 1980s and 1990s beggars belief. No wonder as a nation we can no longer hold our own in some traditional sports. Nor shall we perhaps until the school trend is reversed.

At Llangollen we also had school outings, plays, concerts and eisteddfods. Our teachers gave time to these activities, on top of lessons and their preparation. We were fortunate to have such a good school and dedicated staff; and I believe the exam and career successes showed it. So did the applications for any staff vacancies, I remember hearing my father say he had received many dozens for one relatively junior post, including several 1st Class Honours.

Out of school there was Anglican Church, Welsh Chapel, Methodist Sunday school, Boy Scouts and town events including carnivals on the canal with the strong men competing to climb the greasy pole for the leg of mutton on top. There was blackberry picking in the hedgerows and, on special expeditions, winberry (bilberry) picking on the Berwyn moors. There was helping stooking on the farms, or, for the mischievous, teasing the milk farmer that he was watering the milk. There was also, by the mid-1930s, 'the Pictures' for 4d. in the front rows or 6d. in the back, where at the first house Saturday night we cheered the jungle exploits of Tarzan played by Johnnie Weismuller, the original, with Maureen O'Hara as Jane. There were sweet shops galore with 'gob-stoppers' for ½d., and cake shops that would sell us late on Saturday a bag of stale cakes for 1d. before the Sunday closure. And so much else. We had opportunity to make our own pleasures more perhaps than those in the big cities – and maybe more than children have today? I do not know, but am old-fashioned enough to believe that outdoor activities, for those children who can, are just as interesting and certainly healthier, than playing computer games indoors or even surfing the internet, unless it is genuinely for knowledge. But vogues come and go.

Of course we were taught our duties too. The teaching of citizenship was not invented by yesterday's or today's Secretary of State for Education. It was taught in our school if not formally then consciously by example and guidance. I hope we responded. I think we did, though some of us were doubtless little horrors occasionally, as children always will be. Were we disciplined? Yes, of course we were. At the local primary school we were chastised with stick and cane. The stick was the one most used in my day. It was short stout hazel, wielded with vicious force on the palm of the hand. Our teacher, poor fellow, had been injured in World War I and suffered a plate in his head. We would try to soften the blow by putting a hair across the palm before he struck. I do not remember it did much, the hand still stung painfully, and for ages, although I am not sure that it was not sometimes self-prolonged by the hurt pride of being caught or the feeling it was unjust or unfair. The punishment was in any case nothing to what the really bad boys got. There were two of them at my school, and they received a caning on the bare buttocks almost every week, administered by the Headmaster in the school cloakroom. We could hear their yells of pain throughout the school. I am not sure it ever reformed them.

The County School was more progressive. There was no corporal punishment there, even in those days. The Headmaster, my father, did not believe in it. He taught respect and natural authority, reinforced when necessary by penalties of 'lines' (which involved writing out texts many times) or detention. There was also of course the extreme threat of expulsion. I do not remember him ever resorting to that although there must I suppose have been some cases in his seventeen years as Head.

The School had a very good reputation in Wales, and across the border in England too. The periodic inspections by the Central Welsh Board of Education were special events, often led by the Chief Inspector personally, and conducted in a very thorough manner. I remember younger teachers showing obvious nervousness when an Inspector sat in on their lessons. The older teachers probably felt so too, but were used to it. My father made a practice of sitting in, and sometimes joining in, the lessons of each of his staff, occasionally, as a matter of encouragement and leadership. I never heard of any teachers objecting. I suppose some might nowadays. Another difference, from what we read and hear of the system today, at least in England, is that while the Board inspections were professionally rigorous they were never acrimonious. At least that was the impression we pupils gained, reinforced in my case by hearing my father speak of them then and my mother both then and later. I have not inherited the Inspectors' reports of the '30s but I do have extracts from those of the 1920s. The interesting thing is that they were annual, with comprehensive or what were called 'Full' inspections every few years (every seventh year in that particular decade). The Inspectors were all people of high standing in the Welsh educational world, not strangers brought in from outside as seems sometimes to be the case today, at least in England. The system was smaller then of course but in Wales at any rate I believe remarkably effective. The Welsh have always had a high regard for education and learning.

The 1927 Full Inspection of the School reported very favourably but interestingly:

> The arrangements for supervision and discipline are very satisfactory, and the spirit of co-operation is specially noticeable ... The facilities provided in the Curriculum show an interesting variety, and a serious attempt is evidently made to study the special requirements of the pupils ... An admirable feature of the work in Physics is the co-ordination with the Workshop ... It is most interesting to find, year after year, a first rate tradition of advanced work in Science, for both boys and girls, fully maintained ... While the ordinary work of

instruction is well looked after, a great deal is done to foster the social and aesthetic sides of school life. In particular the School Pageants, which involve much skill and care in preparation, are a feature of which any school may well be proud. The tone and discipline were excellent and the manners of the children were most pleasing ... Under the inspiring influence of the Headmaster, well supported by the Senior Mistress and the other members of the staff, the school indubitably renders valuable service to the local community, not only in giving its pupils efficient instruction in the various branches of knowledge, but in exerting upon them a broad cultural influence which must stand them in good stead throughout their careers.

D. Vaughan Johnston, Chief Inspector, C. W. B.

I have no reason to believe that subsequent Inspection reports under my father's headship were any less favourable (or, indeed, under his successor who introduced school societies and himself became an Inspector). However the School became a Grammar School in 1945, under the 1944 Education Act, incorporating the ill-fated 11 plus entry system, and a Bilateral School in 1960 incorporating the local Secondary Modern School – an idea attributed locally to my father away ahead of his time, but in the event reportedly bungled by the Local Education Authority with bitter staff recrimination. Now the School is Comprehensive. In 1990 a stalwart little band of former County School pupils managed to track down hundreds of us and organised a great reunion. The School records had inexplicably been destroyed by the new school brooms so it was quite a task. I was privileged to be invited to propose the toast to the old school. It was a heart-warming experience to meet so many, from so far and wide, who remembered their school and teachers fifty years on, with such pride and affection.

Like everyone else who went through that school my brother and I benefited from it. He took his School Certificate with Matriculation at the age of 14 and went on to study medicine at Liverpool University at 16. He also played cricket for the school. I passed my School Certificate at 13 but, with the death of my father intervening, it was wisely decided I should consolidate in a re-run, which I did before going on at 14 to Higher Certificate at Ludlow and University at Cambridge at 17.

It was a privileged position at school to be living on the premises and the sons of the Headmaster. But my father was scrupulous; there was never any favour, and we were brought up not to expect it. In school he was Sir to us like any other boys (and girls), and on the one occasion I remember being sent by an exasperated teacher to see him with another boy, I was so visibly ashamed he had difficulty concealing a chuckle. He knew how to handle youngsters whoever they were. I remember visiting with him a Borstal Boy's Summer camp by the Union canal. They had asked him to inspect. He seemed to be able to draw good out of those young malefactors just like others.

School holidays then were much the same as they are today, two weeks or so at Christmas and Easter and seven or more in the Summer. He himself never took more than two or three weeks in August. But they were all the more enjoyable for being a precious occasion to go as a family to the seaside. I used to think this was a purely British habit born of our island tradition. From travels abroad I now appreciate it is universal for those living within reach of the sea, not least in Europe. Italian beaches in season have to be seen to be believed – or were when I lived there. The combination of sun, sea, and sand seems to much of the human race to be like the magnet is to iron filings.

Anyhow in 1935, through the enterprise of some local friends, the Lloyd-Jones family, with whom we joined, we were fortunate to find a dream place high above the Harlech coast of North Wales, that became our holiday Mecca until the War. I still visit it with pleasure occasionally now. In those days we reached it by slow steam-train to Barmouth and bus or cab thereon. We rented neighbouring cottages, with wonderful views and sunsets across Tremadoc Bay to the Lleyn Peninsula and Snowdonia, but singularly primitive plumbing and sanitation. The cottages are now one, plumbed internally and comfy – my wife and I stayed there a year or two ago – but, externally, they are still the same ivy-clad and unspoilt, and the views are still breath-taking. We were eight or nine adults and five or six children, from Llangollen, Pembroke, London and even on one occasion Sweden. We got on well together, except perhaps on rainy days, playing Monopoly when it was first invented – a disputatious game if ever there was one. We climbed the 'zig-zag' down the cliff to the shore, swam, fished and wandered the dunes and beach we had virtually to ourselves, walked the high or low road to Harlech and its magnificent Norman castle, or roamed the hills behind to the triple-echo lake and Roman steps of Cwm Buchan. They were great, if all too short, holidays.

But of course life then also had its downside. It was not always milk and honey, any more than today. There were growing problems all children to one degree or another have to face. In my case I do not remember any particular except the common affliction of shyness, though it was I think at times acute. In later life I had perforce to learn public performance. But it is not something I have ever wanted to do for a living, which is why when I eventually entered politics, it was to manage politicians, not to attempt to play their role. Nor have I ever been able to act. For good or bad my preference has always been to be oneself. I remember my father's wise words to my mother whenever she was unsure of herself: 'Just be yourself, lass.'

Then of course there was the process of living to contend with, far more laborious than today, particularly for the mother in the house, father in the garden or father at work. We had no freezers or refrigerators but, if we were lucky, a cool corner of the house called the larder, and eggs would not keep unless they were put in glutinised water in large earthenware pots. There was no washing machine or detergent but Life-buoy soap, boiler, scrubbing board, wringer and an iron heated on the fire. There was no vacuum-cleaner (until Hoover arrived), no wall-to-wall carpeting, just a hand sweeper on loose carpets, brush on boards and mop on tiles. There was no central heating but coal fires, iron grates and ovens that had to be cleaned daily and black-leaded weekly. There was electric light if you were lucky, otherwise gas but we had to light each wick with a match (so we had to go upstairs in the dark, a rather scary prospect every night to a child). Or you had paraffin lamps, as we did for six months through the Winter of 1937/38 in the hamlet of Berwyn outside Llangollen, where my mother rented a house temporarily after my father's death. Those lamps were curiously called Aladdins, and I suppose they did give magic light but the wick had a nasty habit of occasionally catching fire and belching forth acrid black smoke, requiring agility to reach and turn down before it asphyxiated us. If there are people still using them today – and I notice they are still to be seen in some hardware shops – I feel sure present models are rather more environmentally friendly.

That was the drudge my mother had to bear, in addition to the cooking, entertaining and bringing up the children without modern aids. She had a maid in the early and final years at Llangollen but during the Slump did it all herself. In the garden it was much the same for my father – no strimmers, power driven mowers or diggers, just laborious push mowers, hand clippers, spade and fork.

At work the school had a solicitor as long-serving Clerk to the Governers but the Headmaster had no secretary, typewriter, calculator or other aids. He would spend hours before term juggling in pencil on a large hand-drawn chart the timetable for each class and subject, and of course each teacher, day by day through the term. When completed, and after any necessary consultations, I suppose he had it printed in town. Many of his personal papers I have inherited, his letters, plays and pageants, human geography research, speech notes and the like are in pencil, ink being messy before modern pens, and typing was a job for the professional printer. It was all time-consuming, and I suppose extraordinary that people managed to achieve as much as they did.

There is a neat encapsulation I was given by a friend some years ago entitled 'Survivors – Those born before 1940', whose author we cannot trace – so I hope he or she will not mind my quoting the beginning and end:

We were born before television, before penicillin, polio jabs, frozen food, Xerox, plastic Frisbees and the pill. We were before radar, credit cards, split atoms, laser beams and ball-point pens. Before dishwashers, spin dryers, electric blankets, air conditioning, drip-dry clothes, before a man walked on the moon … We married first and then lived together (how quaint can you be) … We were before day care centres, group homes and disposable nappies … Pizzas, MacDonalds and instant coffee were unheard of … We must have been a hardy bunch … No wonder there is a generation gap today … but by the grace of God we have survived. Alleluia.

Health was also a primary concern just as, despite medical progress, it is today and probably always will be. We criticise our National Health Service with sometimes good cause, but it must be acknowledged that medical and public health progress has been tremendous under it. Tuberculosis was a particular scourge in my youth. We could hear the tell-tale cough in the streets, and it was easily infectious. One of our local cricketing heroes courted his fiancée for a decade and more before he was cleared of previous TB and advised he could marry. When my brother and I at an early age displayed signs of what was called cervical adenitis, this was the medical advice my nursing aunt obtained for us from some eminent authority. It speaks for itself:

> The term 'Adenitis' means inflammation of a gland. This may be due to several causes, the commonest in a child being tuberculosis. Other causes are enlarged and unhealthy tonsils … [Either way] the treatment consists of removing it [the gland] if the conditions be favourable, but if an operation is not desired, then gentle inunctions of iodex, together with cod liver oil and malt, or calcium internally, combined with good sea air, as at Margate, the gland may slowly disappear.

My parents opted for the operation, and we had a week's expedition to London to have it done. They were right. Others were not so lucky. There were of course no antibiotics in those days.

Transport was another problem. We had no car. Few did, except the wealthy, the sporty, the doctors who needed them for their rounds, and pioneering businesses like Corona, the fizzy drink people, whose open lorry called monthly at the door. Also, eventually, the butchers, bakers and grocers, with their local vans, though the bicycle delivery boy like Granville in Ronnie Barker's famous sketches, remained a feature of my home town until well after World War II.

Bicycles of course were then the fashion. My first, when I was 11, was an early Raleigh, costing £4 on mail order from Barkers of Kensington. It was a heavy black lump of a thing, with only one gear, and had to be pushed up the slightest hill. I remember it nearly finished me when, with friends on rather lighter models, we cycled over the Horse-shoe Pass to the North Wales coast resort of Rhyl and back in one foolhardy day. Now,

I gather from experts like my great-nephew Paul in Scotland and my wife's vivacious niece Josephine and her French husband Gilles in the French Dordogne, modern bicycles have as many as 27 gears. I cannot think why, but they seem to know. In my youth the crowning ambition, I recall, was to have a 3-speed Sturmy-Archer – and hope the chain would not come off. Also, we were for ever mending punctures in the inner tubes in use then. But bikes got us around faster and further than walking, and for simple convenience and exercise it can be no surprise they are back in fashion in more advanced forms today. If it were not for the controversial development of out-of-town shopping, I suppose the old sit-up-and-beg-me lady's bicycle, with its basket on the front for shopping mothers, might perhaps be too. My mother bought an early 1920s model from an elderly friend for £1 when we moved to Berwyn and Ludlow in the late 1930s and found it a great boon. Before that, I never understood how she or other women put up with the common over-the-arm shopping basket. It must have ruined many backs.

Nor can I forget the trials and tribulations of those school friends who had to spend hours a day journeying between home and school by slow trains or bus, or had to lodge the week in digs in town, or simply had to walk. For the County School catchment area stretched thirty miles and more from Chirk near the English border to Cerrigydrudion over the mountains and just short of the Conwy valley. One classmate I remember, called Thomas, walked five miles daily each way over the Bwlch (renowned as a formidable hill-climb test for early sports cars). He was never late, except once when, as he shyly had to explain to the teacher, he had spent since dawn rounding up drunken pigs. His father had apparently come home from the pub the night before with beer bottles in his pockets, and fallen into the trough. The pigs had had a ball, but not poor Thomas. How boys and girls like him found time to do their homework I do not know. They walked unescorted, too.

Telephones did exist then, but few had them. Life was somehow more ordered by convention. Unable to talk except face to face, and unable to make appointments except by letter, people resorted, as they always had, to dropping in. With my father involved in so many things, and my mother too, we had visitors all the time. The steep walk up the hill from the town never seemed to deter them. They came from far and wide, and it made an interesting little world for us boys. The only visitor unwelcome to me was our piano teacher who came each Saturday morning. Poor fellow, he was nice enough, and my brother got on well with him and derived great joy from the piano in later life. So did I come to do from music generally, but for me Saturday morning was for outdoor cricket and football not for indoor scales. My parents gave up on this eventually, and so, sadly, I never learnt an instrument. But it was my own foolish choice.

Learning to play outdoor games in those days was essentially trial and error. The pitches we played on were rough and ready, and our schools could not run to coaching. Even for school matches, whether cricket, football, hockey or tennis, pitches were not prepared as today. The school caretaker, known affectionately as Ted Bun but always addressed respectfully as Mr Williams, did not have the machinery or help that those schools which still retain playing fields and their groundsmen do today. Poor man, he also had to clean and maintain the school buildings and grounds in their entirety, helped only by his wife. They were a very dedicated couple.

So we did not grow up as stylish sportsmen, but as enthusiasts. Style, if you could call it that, came later. The sports equipment we used, except when playing for the school, was in any case primitive: rubber or old tennis balls when we could not afford or risk the hard cricket ball, single or dual wickets when the others were broken, no bails when they got lost (with plenty of resultant argument on whether they would or would not have been dislodged); tennis racquets with strings always breaking (and expensive to replace) and balls with no down left on them.

I suppose children the world over make do today just as we did then. But modern technology has changed the traditional sports more radically than perhaps we sometimes realise. Our cricket heroes like Hobbs, Hammond, Hendren, Larwood, Voce and Bradman, had much lighter bats, balls seemingly less seamed, boots as heavy as lead, pitches much more natural and correspondingly less predictable, only pads, box and gloves as protective gear, and some quite different rules from today. In football, the ball was of heavy leather laced up, and a rubber bladder within and valve to pump it up. Ours was always puncturing and when we ran out of repair patches we would fill the leather with paper instead, only to find when it got wet we could not kick it ten yards. I sometimes wonder if today's footballers, with their light plastic ball, know what our heroes Dixie Dean, Billy Wright, Stanley Matthews and the others had to put up with. Like cricket it was almost a different game. So was tennis, with its wood-framed and cat-gut rackets. Also, although the mutual hand-slapping common in cricket and tennis today appears to have originated in rural areas like Llangollen where in early times it was a peasant salute of trust, it was never a feature of sport in my youth, still less was the jumping, kissing and cuddling, like kangaroos on heat, we see in football today. We would have been dubbed silly or even cissies if we had behaved like that. Who is to say which is right? While the sportsman's code has clearly suffered in some of our sports, and money and the TV moguls have undoubtedly had corrupting influence, they have nonetheless, I suppose, helped to widen the involvement of young people, and that must be a good thing.

Our news of national events and sport came not of course from TV pictures in the home, television being still only experimental. It came from the perhaps duller but relatively more serious press and wireless of the day. As a Liberal my father took the *News Chronicle* and I gained my first insight into politics and the outside world from that slim but admirable newspaper. The wireless was a great addition to the home when it came, but a far cry from the transistors of today. Ours was a complex of coils and valves and speaker in a wooden box. It required patience to tune and to hold to BBC Daventry or Droitwich (or, for the jazz or crooning music of the time, to Radio Luxembourg). It had the irritating habit of howling or whining as the signal drifted off frequency just when the news was telling us some ominous political development in Europe or that Wolves were beating Arsenal or that Tommy Farr was winning in the ring. But it did bring a new world of news and sport and entertainment into the home, and it was every father's pride and joy who could afford it.

Saturday night Music Hall was a special treat when we all sat around the set for an hour of what today must be regarded as ponderous comedy but it made us laugh. There was Will Hay, the nutty schoolmaster, Robertson Hare, still remembered for his catchphrase 'Oh calamity, calamity', George Formby with his ukelele and mildly bawdy ballads, the Western brothers with their toffee-nosed dialogue, Jack Hulbert and Cicely Courtneidge forever bickering, and one popular crooner or another singing the romantic songs of the day (perhaps a bit treacley in retrospect but at least melodious and not ear-splitting). They were great fun. But there was also a black humour, to reflect the troubles of the time. The grimmest I remember was the ditty: 'No more money in the bank, no more naughty kids to spank, what's to do about it, let's put out the lights and go to sleep.' That was in the Slump of the early 1930s. I do not remember who wrote it but it was taken to imply despair and suicide, and shocked people widely at the time.

My memories of the Slump are few but vivid and have haunted me ever since. Those I retain are not of our own suffering, although it was hard on my father and his staff to have the school budget and meagre salaries cut, and on my mother who had to do everything without help. They are of the shocking first sight of a dole queue when the mills closed, and of men on relief road-digging, probably means-tested out of the dole because they had tiny savings, upright ex-servicemen some of them with bitterness in their bearing at what their war sacrifice had brought to them and their families. Most poignant, I remember a primary school friend, Thomas, taking me one day after school to his home down a backstreet, only to find the place fireless, almost furnitureless and foodless. His father was a carpenter but there was no longer any work. They had bread and dripping for their evening meal, and were visibly embarrassed they could not spare me any. No child could be insensitive to that. It was a bleak and, with Keynesian hindsight, appallingly ill-managed period in our national and international history. Then, in 1934, came the Gresford Colliery disaster only fifteen miles away when 265 miners and rescuers lost their lives in hideous circumstances, and a whole community was destroyed. I remember everyone for days seemed to talk only in whispers. Nationally it was recognised as a major disaster, not least to the great coal-mining industry as it then was. The Gresford Colliery owners had a lot to answer for.

So, contrary to the romantic image we sometimes hold today, did the railway industry of that time. When the Conservative Govenment of 1996 sold the railways back to private enterprise I seem to remember the Prime Minister painted a rather rosy picture of how the railways in Britain used to be under private ownership between the Wars. He was clearly too young and ill-informed to know. It is true their publicity was good. As boys we were all GWR or LMS or LNER enthusiasts, and had their toy models to play with. It is also very true that they opened up the country as never before and got us around to most corners if we needed – and had the time to change at the many junctions. But, being dependent on coal and steam, they were, as I recall, mostly dirty, noisy and liable to deposit smuts in our eyes. More importantly they were not all that safe. A newspaper cutting I have of 22 May 1929 gave the Ministry of Transport rail accident figures for that year as 460 killed and 24,210 injured, with the grim addendum: 'These figures do not include trespassers and suicides, who added another 377 deaths and 124 injured.'

The Health and Safety record of these industries must have been reason itself to take them into public ownership after the War. Today they are private again, what is left of them, and, as I write, their safety, and, in many cases, price and service record, leave a great deal to be desired. Will we ever get it right?

In contrast, another press cutting I have of the period brings light relief … It is from the *Liverpool Echo* of that time:

Eavesdropping: William Moran, 19, whose head was bandaged, was charged at Rochdale yesterday with 'Unlawfully listening by night under walls, windows and eaves of Rochdale Infirmary, to hearken after the discourse and therefrom to frame slanders and mischievous tales'. He resisted capture when caught up a spout looking through the nurses' sitting-room window and was struck on the head by an Infirmary Official. The charge was preferred under an old common law respecting 'night walkers and eavesdroppers'. Moran was bound over.

I suppose it might not be the peeping Tom but the official who hit him on the head who would be charged today?

Then the same newspaper's Personal Ads. columns carried the following:

Housekeeper, refined, good appearance, requires Post, single, to superior workingman.

We were, in fact, a deeply class-conscious and divided society.

Around us, however, the world was soon to change dramatically, and so was my own little patch. In 1936, as I approached School Certificate and the school's 1st Cricket XI, the darkening clouds of War began to gather and, at home, the cloud of my father's terminal illness.

In the great world the League of Nations had proved a broken reed in dealing with Mussolini and Abyssinia. The United States never joined, and Britain and France, both still Great Powers, failed dismally to exercise their capacity for restraint through sanctions and influence. In Germany, Hitler had secured the Reich chancellorship four years earlier and now felt his Nazi regime strong enough to march a rebuilt German army into the Rhineland, an area of great strategic importance hitherto demilitarised under the Treaty of Versailles. In Russia another ruthless dictator, Stalin, was indulging in genocide to eliminate all possible resistance to his Communist regime and rule of the Soviet Empire. In the Far East, Japan's dictatorship was invading Manchuria and China. All four of these regimes threatened peace. Each was idealogical, in different ways but all opposed to Western liberal democracy. Each was expansionist, looking to enlarge its position and influence in the World. Each was heavily re-arming, and each was already engaged in belligerence in one form and area or another. The post World War I principle of collective security was in tatters.

I remember discussion of all this in the press, on the wireless, at home and at school. But it was far from clear to us. Indeed it was all very confusing, and, it has to be said, rather remote to us youngsters. It was to affect our lives profoundly, as it was many millions of others.

Churchill's re-armament movement was only then in its infancy – and was temporarily weakened by Churchill's stubborn loyalty to King Edward VIII against parliamentary opinion through the abdication crisis. The Baldwin and Chamberlain governments wanted international appeasement, and made no secret of it. And so did most people, the politicians and the media told us. And so, I think, did most around us. Some did something about it. My mother was one of them. She actively supported for a time the Peace Pledge Union, a movement in support of peace through an effective League of Nations. It was a worthy cause scuppered by weak allied governments. My father held his council at home, though I'm sure he discussed it widely with friends and acquaintances outside and, from his occasional asides, I knew he had no illusion that without further resolve by the British, French and United States governments, war was coming again. As a liberal, a humanist and a World War I veteran he deplored the prospect deeply and was no appeaser.

In the event he did not live to see it happen. He died in April 1937, after a painful illness I would not wish to see anyone suffer. He was treated for ulcers until my mother insisted on a second opinion. That was a very difficult thing to do in those days; in a small community you did not change your doctor, dentist, solicitor or bank manager without breaking friendships and professional tradition. But it proved to be too late. He was sent to the nearest specialist hospital at Ruthin and diagnosed to have advanced cancer of the stomach. He died at home and my mother broke the news to my brother and me on the landing outside their bedroom early that morning. I can still see her. She had nursed him for months and borne to herself since Ruthin the knowledge that his illness was incurable. She now faced a future of widowhood at the early age of 47 rising 48, of finding a new home and, crucially, a new income – there was no widow's pension in the teaching profession in those days – and of protecting and launching her two sons alone. She was by common acclaim, very brave.

The School Governors and staff were admirable. They found her a mathematics post for two terms, incurring the wrath of the bureaucrats in the County Education Authority for doing so, and the Governors let us live where we were until the new Head was appointed. He, being very young and ambitious, was a little less thoughtful and gave us the boot fairly peremptorily. My mother naturally found that hurtful, but quickly created a temporary home at Berwyn and, when term started, bicycled the mile and more to school daily and taught on his staff for a term without showing her feelings. She remained totally loyal to the School.

My father's funeral was, in the words of the *Llangollen Chronicle* 'the largest seen in the town for some time, the interment being made at Llantysilio Church. Over 50 motor cars conveyed the mourners to the cemetery' from the County School House where a short service was held in Welsh beforehand. Hundreds made their own way to Llantysilio, including many who walked the mile and more from Llangollen and from the villages around. A party of 50 pupils formed the choir, led by the School staff, and many more came of their own accord or with their parents. Many mourners came from afar in Wales and from England, overflowing the little church famed for its beautiful setting and the poet Browning's seat. The service was as ecumenical as it was possible to have in those days, and bilingual. In an article by a contributor the *Chronicle* summed it up, with perhaps some poetic licence, in these words: 'A deep silence – the silence of a terrible grief, was one of the great tributes which marked the burial of Mr H. Hugh Jones on Saturday last. And nature was at its best, too, as somehow befitted the scene, for one of nature's gentlemen was being laid to rest. The little Church of course, could not accommodate all those who wished to pay their last respects, but those who remained outside in the sunshine were in that Church in spirit ... One thing was very noticeable – a bird song. Its little notes were gripping. For a while they seemed so plaintive ... And then quite suddenly the notes changed. There was triumph in its song. It seemed to sing, "There is no death". So be it.'

I missed that little bird. At the time I was seated inside the Church in the front pew with my mother and brother. But I do remember vividly the throng of good people, young and old, the solemnity of the service, the fine Welsh singing, the sunshine pouring in, the great carpet of wreaths and flowers, and the awful dawning that I had lost my father, and a much loved one at that. It took me many more years to realise the full import. Boys of thirteen do not see things as adults – at least I do not think I did. But it was at that point, I know, that I began to grow up.

The letters of condolence and messages of sympathy my mother received fill boxes. She kept them all marked: 'for the boys to read in later life to refresh their memories of their fine father.' I have re-read them again now and, filial pride aside, they do portray I think someone who in renaissance terms might have been called 'a complete man'.

Condolences came corporatively and privately from the many Welsh and British educational, cultural and heritage organisations he took part in; the local and national government authorities he cooperated with; the BBC Schools Broadcasting and Welsh National Theatre he helped to develop; and the churches, chapels, Boy Scouts, British Legion, hospital and other local bodies he helped. They came individually from most of his fellow Heads of Welsh secondary schools, hundreds of former pupils (as far back as his pre-War Denbigh days), soldiers he had commanded twenty years earlier in the War; and friends from all walks of life. The features of my father's life they most singled out were:

- His 'energy, organising ability and cheerful efficiency' …

- His 'dedication to education', 'ahead of his time in liberality', 'and to Welsh culture'; and 'his great contribution to both.'

- His 'originality and characteristic freshness of mind', 'his free and independent outlook whilst always loyal to those with whom he worked.'

- His 'readiness to help anyone in need … and any good cause.' 'A true Scout through and through.'

- His 'straightforwardness and commanding personality' … But 'kindness, understanding and genial good humour' – often 'whimsical', sometimes teasing but always 'seemed to spread a certain infectious happiness through our midst.'

- His 'gift of friendship' and capacity 'to inspire respect, love and affection – by poor and rich.'

- His 'concern for the welfare of each individual pupil, especially the poor and unfortunate.' He was 'good friend to all his pupils' and 'will be a very great loss to so many of the younger generation.' 'His pupils thought there was no one like him, and his soldiers during the War could not speak too highly of him.' He 'combined a true love of learning with a power of setting high aims before young people and being on peaceful terms with everybody.'

- 'A true gentleman.'

- 'Llangollen, Denbighshire and Wales have lost one of their finest Welshmen.' 'Would that Wales had more men like him.' 'The loss is really a national one.'
- 'His was a life of public service and self sacrifice.'

One poignant message of sympathy came from the parents of Andrew Irvine, the Himalayan explorer lost with Mallory in their ill-fated attempt on Everest in 1924. Their home was at nearby Corwen. Another was from the admirable Dr Fred Drinkwater, brought in to try to save my father at the end. He wrote: 'Never in my life have I attended so brave a man who always thought that others suffered more than he did.'

The following are extracts from an obituary in the Summer 1937 *Review* of the prestigious Association of Welsh Secondary School Headmasters and Headmistresses. They sum up my father's life and achievements as his fellows saw him:

## OBITUARY
### The late Mr H. Hugh Jones, Llangollen

But a twelvemonth ago, our energetic and genial Treasurer was busily organising and sponsoring the Summer Meeting of the Association of Welsh Headmasters and Headmistresses at his own Llangollen ... Presently disquieting reports of his health began to reach us: the end came unexpectedly after all on the 21st of April. On the 24th, on a perfect spring day, he was laid to rest in the beautiful churchyard of LlanTysilio, hard by the Dee in the Berwyn Mountains ...

His death was to me a source of personal poignancy, for we were both boys together at Friars School, Bangor ... My association with him in this County and in the Council of the Association only served to confirm my sense of his energy, his ability, his loyalty to all persons and to all causes that were true and worthy, his robust sanity and common-sense.

Mr Hugh Jones was a native of Penygroes, Caernarvonshire ... During the Great War he held a commission in the R.A.S.C. and served in Mesopotamia, being later invalided to India, where he saw service in Waziristan ... The fact that when he reached home in March, 1919 he was sent to a Nursing Home in Liverpool indicates that his warfare in torrid climates must have undermined his constitution and sowed the seeds of that insidious and deadly malady which carried him away so swiftly at the comparatively early age of fifty-six.

After demoblization he became Organiser for North Wales of the scheme for resettling ex-soldiers in suitable civilian occupations. It was while holding this post that he was appointed Head Master of Llangollen County School, over which he presided with distinction and success from January 1920 till his death.

Not long after joining the Association, he was elected to the Council. Later, he became Treasurer. He managed the finances entrusted to him with careful husbandry; his reports will be remembered for the broad humanity which he infused even to the dry details of receipts and expenses. In debate he was forceful and fearless.

His was no 'fugitive or cloistered virtue'. He touched the educational and public life of Wales at many points and it can appropriately be said of him as Dr Johnson said of Goldsmith, '*Nihil tetigit quod non ornavit*'. The high opinion held of his talent for public work is reflected in the large number of public bodies or committees of which he was a member. Besides being Treasurer and a Member of Council of the Welsh Secondary Schools Association, he was a member of the following bodies: The Joint Four Association for Wales; the Council of the Incorporated Association of Head Masters (England and Wales); the Central Welsh Board; the B.B.C. Education Committee, on which he sat as representative of the I.A.H.M. and the W.S.S. A.; the Committee for the Preservation of Ancient Monuments; the Denbighshire branch of the Committee for the Preservation of Rural Wales; the Cambrian Archaeological Society, which he induced to visit Llangollen in 1935.

But his activities were not confined to educational movements in the narrower sense. He took a lively and effective personal interest in Llangollen and its neighbourhood. He was District Commissioner of the Boy Scouts Association, Chairman of the local branch of the British Legion, and he was one of the most prominent promoters of the Welsh National Theatre at Plas Newydd, Llangollen.

Nor must we overlook the diligent and effective service he rendered to Welsh life and culture in a difficult district. He adjudicated at countless local Eisteddfodau during these seventeen years and in other ways he stoutly championed the native culture which he had imbibed from his infancy in Caernarvonshire and which he found still the same in Denbighshire, but struggling for its life on the borders of Mercia. Truly he reckoned nothing cultural to be alien from education. For him education was something infinitely greater than mere pedagogy.

He thought highly of his School; he thought highly of the Association; he thought highly of Llangollen. They also thought highly of him. One thing that particularly stands out in my memory of the Summer Meeting of W.S.S.A. at Llangollen last year is the obvious respect and affection in which the Head Master of their County School was held by his Governors and by the Urban Council. No higher tribute can be paid to his memory by the inhabitants of Llangollen or by us who were his colleagues than that silent and unconscious but eloquent tribute.

H. PARRY JONES

# CHAPTER 4

# Ludlow

## 1938–1941

OUR NEW HOME was to be across the border in the little Shropshire town of Ludlow, since described by John Betjeman as 'probably the loveliest country town in England'. It was a happy discovery, with good schools, rolling countryside and as full a history, gory and otherwise, as could be. The guide book author Edmund Vale called it 'the most complete medieval town in England'. It was to become my mother's home for the rest of her life and, of the forty homes I have had in my peripatetic round, Ludlow was the most enduring. I still retain friends there and was glad to join them in their millennium year celebration of 800 years of the Ludlow Grammar school – a record I suppose few other educational establishments in the country can match.

My mother found Ludlow, and Ludlow found her, by the process of applying for posts advertised in the Educational Supplement of *The Times* produced weekly then as now. She had to write up her curriculum vitae, admitting she had not taught for nearly twenty years except latterly the two terms at Llangollen. She had to rebuild her professional and personal references. She had to swot up her pure and applied mathematics, and her theoretical and practical physics, and catch up on twenty years development of these studies and of teaching methods. Being a headmaster's wife all those years and having two boys at school bringing back homework had saved her from remoteness. But she had to think and work her way rapidly back into the classrooms, junior, middle and senior, as also into the strait-jacket of the School and Higher Certificate examinations of the time.

She also had to rebuild her life, and most immediately her income. My brother and I were both by then old enough to go out to work. She never broached this possibility. She was determined we should have the best she could afford, and this should include university. It was a daunting challenge,

Ludlow, with its famous castle ...

not least as competition for good teaching posts was then intense. I do
not know how many she applied for but recall she reached final interview
in at least two, one at Loughborough College in the East Midlands and
the other at Ludlow High School, a girls' school founded less than thirty
years earlier but already well reputed. She was offered the senior mathematics post at that school and accepted. That is how she, and we, came
to Ludlow.

There must have been times when she craved a more familiar haven
in Yorkshire or Wales especially as, for all its attractions, Ludlow had the
reputation of being slow to accept strangers – ten years was said to be the
norm, plus a bit more for anyone coming from the other side of Offa's
Dyke, the old border enmity with Wales being still not wholly dead. Then
the lodgings we had until she found a house were not the friendliest, a
bit like a minor boot camp in fact. Furthermore the Headmistress of the
High School at that time was a product of the old school, very effective
but rather a domineering spinster steeped in the classics, scornful of
mathematics and the sciences as suitable subjects for girls (except biology,
because of the bees and the birds), and she seemed uncomfortable to have
a headmaster's widow and mother on her staff when in those days women
teachers were almost always unmarried. But my mother persevered and,
like any good teacher, won the respect and affection of her pupils year
upon year, and of her staff colleagues, the County Director of Education
and eventually of her Headmistress. They became neighbours and friends

... and 'the loveliest country town in England'. (Photo by Vincent Vaughan)

in retirement. She also soon acquired a position of her own in Ludlow, becoming, among other things, local chairman of the National Council of Women and a founder member of the much needed Ludlow Conservation Society. She became in fact a Ludlovian, and is remembered there to this day with affection.

My brother set off for university a year or two earlier than he would otherwise. There was no point in staying on to finish his Higher Certificate at Llangollen or to do so at Ludlow, when Liverpool University medical school was prepared exceptionally to take him for an intermediate year and then, all being well, for the full medical course he had set his mind on. He had an excellent school record and my mother and he did well to find and secure public and charitable scholarships to fund his fees. Such scholarships are I think still a feature of our educational world today, but more specialist than general since the advent of universal education. Before the War, when secondary schooling was still fee-paying and by selection, they were often crucial to a child's entry and progress. In my brother's case it was the generosity of the Kitchener Foundation, set up after World War I to help the children of ex-servicemen particularly in the study of medicine, which most helped him. In my case it was the Ludlow Grammar School which was generous in the disbursement of its endowments and, later, Selwyn College Cambridge and the war time State Bursary scheme for training scientists and engineers that made all the difference. Had that scheme not been introduced the very year I went to Cambridge, 1941, I would have had to rely, apart from School, County and College scholarships, on the then existent Department of Education teachers' training grant scheme – and ended up obligatorily teaching (or refunding their grant) after the War. With such a desperate shortage of teachers in many parts of Britain today I wonder why this scheme has not been revived.

My brother began at Liverpool in September 1937 and, after 1st MB, learnt his practical medicine the hard way, in the 'blitz'. I shall come back to this.

My transition to the new life was less dramatic but still quite a cultural shock. It involved two terms in digs at Llangollen to finish my school certificate before joining my mother in Ludlow, but the big leap was to gain a place at the Grammar School. It was for boys only, and I entered its 6th Form just into teenage, to be told that the High School might be within shouting distance but was for girls only and 'ne'er the twain shall meet'. To a boy accustomed to co-educational schooling this was strangely restrictive. Like so much else, it was to change with the war, and ultimately be abandoned in the merger of the two schools and creation of the present Ludlow Sixth Form College. But boys' school is what it was, and always had been, when I entered. In addition I found that from the land of rugby, where for some reason Llangollen played soccer, I had come to the land of soccer only to find they played rugby. It was a recent change for Ludlow, improbably from men's hockey, but under the inspired direction of an imported Welsh physical training and woodwork master Alfryn David (known, for some reason as 'The Beak') it was already making great progress. I was ragged at first, of course, for being Welsh but not knowing the game, and, like most newcomers before and since, was consigned for my first season to the pit of the second row. But at least it was in the 1st XV. Then there was this Ludlow reserve towards newcomers, or 'codgers' as they were called. It took a little time to break through that. But I was soon at home, and anyhow all this changed with World War II. It was as the clouds of that war gathered that we began to find the real Ludlow.

One of its charms is that although like York and Chester and Bath it seems to be magnetic to the discerning tourist, Ludlow is off the beaten track and takes time to reach. In medieval times it was perhaps the most important frontier town in England, being the centre chosen by the Normans to conquer and subjugate Wales and, at one point, also to control their campaign in Ireland. (Their campaign in Scotland of course followed a different pattern.) Then, in more recent times, Ludlow found itself on a main highway. As an old guidebook explained: 'Ludford Bridge – the older of the two town bridges over the river Teme – built between six and seven hundred years ago for the pack-horses and clumsy wagons of that period' had 'since then ... steadily shouldered the whole North-South traffic of western England.' The main road (A49) passed through the centre of Ludlow. But in the 1970s the town was finally given a bypass and, in the words of Julian Critchley, the MP and broadcaster who made the town his home: 'Ludlow is (again) a well-kept secret … a small town of 7000 people, tucked up against the Welsh hills and saved from Brummagem commuter by the Clee hills and 20 happy extra miles. Ludlow is … dilapidated, stately and very beautiful.'

That was written a quarter of a century ago. Earlier the poet A. E. Housman – whose ashes are buried there – called Ludlow, in his dismal way, the capital of his 'land of lost content'. But the slums of the lower town are thankfully now long gone; the Victorian market hall regarded by some as a midland-brick eyesore (but a useful market place and community hall in my time) has been pulled down; the 'narrows' have been made one-way; industry, unimportant since the halcyon days of medieval cloth and later glove manufacture, has returned; farming on the rich Shropshire loam has until recently boomed; so has tourism; and, although, like every prime heritage place there is doubtless a constant threat of predatory developers wishing to milk the honeypot, the Council planners and vigilant Conservation/Civic Society seem by and large to have done good work in preserving the history and loveliness of the place. Go to Ludlow just before Christmas and it is merry England at its best. Go there in late June and early July when the annual Ludlow Festival is held and it is a cultural treat. Go there any other time and, contrary to Housman, it is a town of much content.

And so it was when I found it – sleepy, yes, and shaped like the bottom of an old whisky bottle; introverted, yes, like so many proud rural towns; blasé about its extraordinary heritage, yes, like so many of Britain's historic places; but full of interest and things to do, in and around, for any youngster willing to look. There was much poverty, but very little standing around street corners – except in the cherry season, when it seemed to be the game to come into town and spit as many cherry stones on the pavements as you could manage, with sometimes perilous consequences on the foothold. Entertainment was simple but by and large healthy. There were reckoned to be over fifty pubs, rather more perhaps than needed. Situated though we were in the nonconformist belt of the borders, temperance was for the Welsh side not the English – though the Welsh came over readily enough on their prohibition Sundays. One Ludlow pub still brewed its own ale – until the publican fell in – or so the story went. It was said to be real ale too!

Ludlow has been aptly described in an old guide-book as a 'treasure-house of places of special architectural and historic interest'. It attracts visitors from all over the world to see 'an historic town unspoiled by modern development with its fine timbered buildings, narrow streets, ruined castle and beautiful church, all in a magnificent rural setting.' As a boy my short cycle ride to school took me daily over the railway tunnel, and past the old Police Station, where we knew all too well the law resided (though sadly no more – it is now a supermarket). It then took me through confined little Tower Street; through the historic 'narrows' packed with little old shops and dwellings; across the Bull Ring, where the through traffic met, often in tight confusion; past Bodenham's corner, judged by a *Sunday Telegraph* architectural panel when that newspaper first appeared, to be the finest piece of black and white Jacobean in the country (although since dated even earlier, to 1404); round the portico of the baroque eighteenth-century Butter Cross; and across the top of Broad Street, judged by the same *Sunday Telegraph* panel to contain the finest examples of Georgian in the country, and described by Christopher Hussey as: 'There is no more beautiful street, as a street, in England than this.' My ride bypassed the Church of St Laurence, whose great tower dominates the landscape for miles around, and parts of whose grandeur date from the twelfth century; but it took me through the short High Street, which is in fact, and unusually, made up of four parallel lanes each with buildings on either side. I would then ride past the old Town Hall that is no more, into Castle Square, with the elegant Georgian frontage of the High School on one side, the Castle Lodge and historic Mill Street down to the Grammar School on the other and, ahead, the great Norman castle of Ludlow. It was, and of course remains, one-way streets and pedestrianisation permitting, an extraordinary little journey through time, all in a few hundred yards. There is nowhere I have ever found, outside the renaissance and ancient cities of Italy, to compare with it in concentrated living history.

I cannot pretend I appreciated all this at the time, being then, as a school boy, rather more interested in games and in mastering my maths, physics and chemistry. But every feature remains familiar to this day and it is always a joy to go back. It is also good to hear the eternal chimes of the church clock laboriously striking the tune of the day every four hours – allegedly never to be stopped at least in day time, except during the war when Church bells were reserved for invasion warning or victory or both. In fact they must also have been suspended temporarily when the tunes were changed at the turn of the nineteenth century from the patriotic 'Rule Britannia', 'Britons Strike Home' and the like, constructed on the eve of the Napoleonic Wars, to the more sedate Psalms 104 and 113, 'See the Conquering Hero Comes', 'Home Sweet Home' and their like. The Llantysilio environmentalist Mrs Aitken recalled that event to my mother when they parted. She and her husband had chosen Ludlow, and the Angel Hotel just down from the Church, for their honeymoon in about 1901. But 'The Blue Bells of Scotland', installed that day in place of 'Highland Laddie', apparently did not like being confined to one rendering every four hours and chose, instead, to boom forth its heavy tune non-stop all night. The wayward clock and its musical director were collared the following day and, in due course, night-time playing was stopped anyhow. The Aitkens took it in good part. Ludlow would not be the same without its sonorous bells.

The castle was quite another story. To me it was the forbidding home of the cruel Norman conquerors of Wales. And, unlike all the other historic buildings of Ludlow, it was an immensely imposing but, except for the Castle House, unlived-in ruin. I never cease to admire great castles and their builders but rarely find them to be attractive objects of sight-seeing. Like the anonymous inscriber on the gate of one Edmund Vale claims to have found, I come out feeling like writing 'and Felix kept on walking'. A kindred spirit I discovered later, in Rome, was the then Foreign Secretary, later Prime Minister, Lord Home (Sir Alec Douglas-Home), who, declining to go sight-seeing with that great lover of Rome, the then Prime Minister Harold Macmillan, revealed – or rather his good wife did to mine – that on his honeymoon in the Rhineland, in the days when people holidayed abroad not just to be British but to discover other countries, he rebelled and announced 'that is the last d ... d schloss I shall visit'! Evidently one can be cultured without enjoying ruined castles.

I became more interested by force of circumstance at the beginning of the War when, joining as a schoolboy the Local Defence Volunteers, we found ourselves defending the outer castle reaches in mock battle against the regular Oxs & Bucks Light Infantry, who were temporarly stationed locally. To my discomfort I found that while it might be courageous to confront battle-hardened invaders on the outside of the Castle walls, it was foolhardy to scorn the protective purpose of those walls in the belief that the steep slope and nettles beyond would be on our side. We were roughed up, to put it mildly – though our local dentist, a former Blackheath rugby player, saved some of our honour by bringing down an attacking officer or two in fine tackles on the hard Castle square. It was all in the blackout of course.

Some months later, three of us sixth formers, members by now of the LDV's successor, the Home Guard, found ourselves commanded to guard that end of Ludlow, one night a week, from the exposed top of the Great Keep of the castle. By then we were kitted out with boots, uniform, rifle and tin hat – not the easiest outfit to carry up several flights of worn stone spiral staircase in the dark, still less down them afterwards. But at least my lonely vigils up there gave me opportunity not just to reflect ruefully on how the guards of old kept warm but to ponder how the builders and workmen with none of our modern equipment contrived to hew and mount the stones to make those great battlements and elegantly designed inner buildings. Most of all I learnt to appreciate, as dawn broke, the magnificence of the site chosen by its Norman founder, de Lacy, to command the valleys of the Teme and the Corve and beyond, with the heights of wooded Whitcliffe on one side and the distant Clee Hills on the other. Also the imposing ring of towers and baileys and gateway; and the inner moat, stone bridge, apartments, lodgings, round chapel, armoury, Council hall, well and Great Keep, combining Norman, Medieval and Tudor, and so many still standing, high, solid and impregnable. The experience was also, I have to admit, just that bit fearful, waiting alone for the Germans in that historically spooky place in the silence of the night. My colleagues and I in turn were always glad to be relieved, or to see the dawn – though that was all too often split by the blood-curdling screams of the awakening peacocks in the Lodge trees. We tried to silence their chorus occasionally with a few light missiles, but it only made them worse. As I was to learn again at Avebury many moons later, peacocks are the most beautiful birds but also the most raucous.

The stories of Ludlow Castle are of course legion. It was many years before I learnt to understand them. I suppose that if I had studied history at school or, after the war, Medieval rather than Modern History at Cambridge, I might have come to appreciate the significance of the place sooner. My history, such as it was, tended to begin with 1485 and the emergence of Britain as a self-governing nation under a Welsh King Henry VII, at last free of subjugation by Romans, Saxons and Normans, and of the civil Wars of the Roses; and, internationally, in 1492 with Columbus' discovery of the New World. According to the Rev. Lowndes Moir's admirable *Historic Ludlow Castle and those associated with it*, the Castle and Ludlow were already into the third of their four historic phases by then. The first phase had been a military castle, one of a series built by barons of the Norman conquest after 1066 Hastings, to protect land granted them by successive Norman monarchs and to subdue what peasantry remained in the forests around and, more particularly, the resistant Welsh. It was the 'Wild West' of England, speaking very different tongues from the Norman French. Various dramas marked Ludlow Castle's early growth, including a siege at one point by King Stephen, and forcible possession temporarily by his successor Henry II. But it remained in the hands of the founder family, the de Lacys, and their heirs and for primarily military purpose, for its first two hundred years. Meanwhile Ludlow began to form alongside it, a classic example of a Norman planned town which was laid out in phases during the twelfth century. The plan is still visible in Ludlow's four main streets and some of its intersecting lanes. In the thirteenth century it was fortified by an encircling wall with seven gates, one of which, the Broad Gate, still survives today together with stretches of the wall.

In what Lowndes Moir calls its second phase, the fourteenth and fifteenth centuries, still medieval but some might say its majestic period, Ludlow castle fell into the hands, through marriage, of the powerful de Mortimer family – whose name, like that of de Lacy, is still to be found without the French 'de' in the countryside around, but remembered in the annals of Llangollen and many other parts of Wales, and in Ireland, with some dread. The Mortimers developed the castle inside the walls as a great Gothic mansion, reaching its peak in the early fourteenth century under Roger Mortimer who, according to Lowndes Moir (and doubtless other authorities) 'ruled with princely splendour' his vast estates on both sides of the Welsh border and was reckoned to be 'the most powerful man in England'. He was also the gruesome murderer of King Edward II and simultaneously lover of that King's wife – a truly mighty rogue. But in 1330 he over-reached himself in entertaining the young King Edward III through the Marches (the lands bordering Wales) 'with all conceivable pomp and pageantry', arousing the envy of the King to add to his family loathing. He was seized by the King's men, when with the King's mother at Nottingham, and 'charged before the Lords with appropriating to himself royal power, stirring up dissention with Edward II and other charges'. He was condemned to the gallows, and all his properties seized by the Crown. So Ludlow Castle became a Royal Palace.

The next great drama came to Ludlow with the outbreak of the Wars of the Roses one hundred and twenty years later. Richard Duke of York, leader of the Yorkists and claimant to the throne, made Ludlow one of his military headquarters and in 1454 his army faced King Henry VI's (Lancastrian) forces across the river Teme at Ludford. The Yorkists were routed and the Lancastrians 'wrecked their vengeance on the town and castle of Ludlow'. Ludlow had been flourishing until then, a centre of political importance, and of the prosperous wool trade and cloth manu-facturing, with a wealthy Palmers' Guild and its own fine church and grammar school. Much of the town was destroyed in the sacking but, fortunately, not these institutions. Yorkist revenge was not long in coming. A year later Edward, Duke of York, son of the now dead Richard, and his Yorkist army defeated the Lancastrians under Owen Tudor at the Battle of Mortimer's Cross near Ludlow. He became King Edward IV, and, in grateful remembrance of loyal Ludlow, granted a royal charter to the town (and the status of a royal home to the Castle) in consideration of 'the laudable and gratuitous services which our beloved and faithful subjects, the burgesses of the town of Ludlow, have rendered unto us in the obtaining of our right to the crown of England, for a long time past withheld from us and our ancestors, in great peril of their lives, and also the rapines, depredations, losses of goods and other grievances, for us and our sake in divers ways brought upon them by certain of our competitors.'

That happy period lasted two and a half decades. But, with the en-thronement of the Tudors, Ludlow then found it had backed the wrong horse – as it was to do again nearly two centuries later in the Royalist and Roundhead civil war. I suppose it is as true of Ludlow today as it clearly was then that it prefers the traditional to the progressive, but rides any change well when it must. The verbal battles fought there in the 1950s and 1960s over proposals from the County to join the Boys Grammar and Girls' High schools in one may not have been as gory as those of medieval times but were certainly as hard fought.

'Edward IV like his father before him set a high value on Ludlow Castle, and realised the importance of its strategic position' (Lowndes Moir). For more than ten years his infant son, Edward Prince of Wales, and the younger brother and two half-brothers lived at the Castle. The two young Princes moved to London on the death of their father in 1483, but were intercepted by their notorious uncle, Richard, Duke of Gloucester and, as history relates, were murdered in the Tower of London. That, through Richard III's infamy and folly, proved to be the fateful end of the Yorkist royal connection with Ludlow.

The successor Tudors had other ideas for Ludlow. Welsh though they were, they readily adopted Edward IV's idea of a Council of the Marches to establish royal control of the Welsh borderland on both sides and, to the dismay of the Welsh, applied strict law and order so, in the words of a former Ludlow guide book 'the judges, lawcourts and prison in the Castle were all kept well occupied'. At first it was called the Prince's Council, and was presided over by Henry VII's son and heir, Prince Arthur, Prince of Wales. He died suddenly at Ludlow of the plague of sweating sickness soon after bringing there his Spanish bride, Catherine of Aragon. She too caught the sickness but survived to become, in due course, the first wife of Arthur's younger brother King Henry VIII, and the butt of that monarch's subsequent desire for divorce, break with the Papacy and institution of the Reformation in this country. No one can say that Ludlow has not played its part in the history of England, Britain and beyond.

Ludlow Castle continued to be the seat of government of Wales by the Council of the Marches throughout the sixteenth and most of the seventeenth centuries, under the Tudors and Stuarts, but paid in the Civil War for being the 'last Royalist garrison in Shropshire to hold out'. The Roundheads sold off all its contents and although not literally, 'one of the ruins Cromwell left behind him', it was abandoned as a garrison in 1689 and rapidly declined into a ruin thereafter. It was ultimately sold to the Clive/Powis family during the Napoleonic Wars. But the ruins still stand 'in majestic grandeur', much good restoration has been done in recent years, and I for one remain in awe of Ludlow Castle and its extraordinary history to this day.

Ludlow declined with it in the seventeenth century, but revived to become a fashionable social centre in the eighteenth century, and to add Georgian to the wealth of historic houses of all eras it has today.

The school I attended, Ludlow Grammar School, was also historic. Its origins have been traced by the distinguished Ludlow historian, David Lloyd, to two small schools around the year 1200, one favoured by the then Church Rector for scions of the wealthy to learn grammar and one favoured by the then Vicar for church choristers. It was established as a Grammar School by the Palmers' Guild in the fourteenth century. The year I entered, straight into its already overcrowded 6th Form, 1938/39, happened to be a vintage year. These things so often seem to come and go, in cycles. There were fewer than 200 boys in the school at that time but, unusually in those days, as many as 21 – over 10% – in the 6th Form. Though we were taking different subjects for our Higher Certificates we shared one classroom, each with his own well-worn little desk, like bees in a hive – except that there was no queen, only a Head-Boy named Ernie Hartland (or 'Sharky' as he was called for reasons unknown) who carried his authority with the ease of a born leader and must have been one of the best all-rounders and Captains of Rugby and Cricket the school ever produced. Tragically, after a year at Oxford, he was killed in the war flying with the RAF. So were two others, in one force or another. All 21 saw war service, most of them active service in one theatre or another. We were not of course to know this in 1938. The country was then still being lulled by Chamberlain into a false sense of 'peace for our time'.

It was a fine little school, aptly described by Robbie Burns, a former Headmaster and Principal of the successor College, and David Lloyd, the historian, in their joint Schools' and College millennium book *Century of Change 1900–2000* as: 'Both schools [the Grammar and the Girls' High] were small highly prestigious institutions where places could be paid for by parents able to afford to do so or, for a minority, obtained by those clever enough to win a scholarship ... Both schools were cohesive, tightly regulated institutions, with a clearly defined hierarchy of Head, staff, prefects and pupils. The wearing of uniform was enforced, and school life was shaped by many regulations: boys could be given detention for not wearing the school cap, and girls 'signatures' if they spoke on the staircase. Yet each school had its own distinctive culture. That of the Grammar School was robust, with manliness a much vaunted virtue, and physical sports greatly encouraged.'

I do not myself remember the regulations being particularly irksome, except the cap, and segregation. I had not had to wear a cap at Llangollen and, in my 6th Form vanity, it struck me as being *Just William* stuff. But years later when I saw middle-aged and elderly men sporting them with pride among the oarsmen of Henley, I was reminded that dressing-up is, of course, an old British custom. The regulation that boys should not be seen talking to girls in public meant that any boy so caught could find himself bawled out by a vigilant master in public – humiliating enough in itself, but doubly so in front of the girl. But, while it did make it even more difficult in those days to turn initial boy-girl attraction into a first date, it undoubtedly added spice to subsequent encounters. My first girl-friend had the happy name of Joy, and we still exchange Christmas cards. There was always the Picture House, or the 'Bread Walk' along the river or other rural places, in which to canoodle innocently on a Saturday evening when any sensible master or mistress was not on the prowl but at home or away with his or her own 'loved ones'. What a sex-obsessed race we British used to be – and maybe still are? Burns' and Lloyd's *Century of Change* records: 'One Old Girl recalls ... the rumour (unfounded) that a High School pupil had been expelled for talking to a boy in the street, though he was, in fact, her brother'!

George Merchant, long-serving French master at the Grammar School and, in retirement, author of an engaging series of 'episodes' in the life of the school and town, collectively entitled *Footsteps down Mill Street*, described the pre-War scene in rather more depressing, but realistic terms:

> Any account of life in Ludlow before the war has to be read in the light, of course, of the social conditions of those days ... The England of the twenties and thirties was not the land fit for heroes that it should have been ... The amiable caricatures of P. G. Woodhouse and his colleagues have left a charming picture for posterity which makes hilarious reading but may leave a false impression ... Although we were still the greatest country in the world in many ways ... there was a great deal of poverty ... and of general mismanagement ... We were consoled by a good deal of well meant flag-waving and it was nice to know that although, short of joining the Navy, ninety per cent of us could not afford to go and see it for ourselves, the sun never set on the British Empire ... It was an England of pride and prejudice and Ludlow was a very English community. Only shortly before the war a local landowner sacked one of his workers and deprived him of his house simply because he insisted on sending his son to the Grammar School. Grammar Schools apparently were not for the likes of his son!

On a lighter note Merchant wrote of the school cap: 'It will be no great loss if the beanie disappears, for it was a modern invention unknown in Mill Street a century ago ... never good protection against weather ... soon shrank and became shapeless. The local outfitters will not thank me for saying this ... for trade in them was always brisk.'

The school buildings I entered as a 14 year old also breathed tradition – and indeed still do. Barnaby House, incorporating then the gymnasium, where the PT Master had us hanging on bars and heaving on the scrum machine, and the little Library where a much reduced 6th Form had to be housed for part of the war, was built as a resting place for pilgrims in the thirteenth century, and was as solid as a rock. It is recorded by Merchant that when the roof was struck by a thunderbolt one day in the early 1950s, the damage was negligible – and the master supervising an examination there at the time dismissed it to the pupils as a trivial manifestation of the powers of nature. The building has more recently been modified and restored with great taste. The old School Hall, where we gathered for prayers every morning (except Catholics and Jews, who were exempted) was a town granary before the School moved in, several centuries ago, and had wonderful oak beams. Also, according to Merchant, it had tattered banners and spears captured from the Dervishes and presented by an old Ludlovian, Colonel Taffy Lewis. 'I do not know whether he captured them single handed or picked them up, either from the field after the battle or, for a consideration, from whoever was running the equivalent of the N.A.A.F.I. at that time,' wrote Merchant. In truth Lewis captured them in battle, but Merchant liked to embellish. He was President of the Old Ludlovians Association for many years, and his wit and dedication will I am sure long be remembered. Also his cricket bowling: It was a human windmill, fearfully effective and must have inspired the inventor of the old practice bowling machine. Also, in later years, his umpiring: 'I hold that if I was umpire and a batsman put his big feet between my eyes and the wicket when the bowler was bowling anything like straight, a loud and confident appeal for LBW would receive the most serious consideration, and for this I have no regrets at all.' He did not hold with the new rules ...

The School had a history of personalities. The Headmaster in my day, H. S. Breakspear, was timeless. Appointed Science Master in 1909 and Second Master only two years later, still in Edwardian times, he rose to be Headmaster in 1936, succeeding the brilliant but radical Heckstall-Smith, author of the standard textbook on electricity when I was at school and liberaliser extraordinary. Breakspear's was the long consolidating reign of Pope Paul VI after the short reformist reign of John XXIII, except that Breakspear also had to deal with all the wartime upheavals and – without disrespect to Paul VI – was in his quiet way also a reformer. It was he who established science at the school and, between his onerous Headmaster duties, helped us through our Chemistry curriculum. He was kind enough to say of me later that I had 'that rare combination of virtues, intelligence and the will to work'. I am not sure about that. The combination is not in my experience all that rare anyhow. But he was always supportive and interested in our careers and, like many others before and after me, I owe this curt but wise and kindly man a debt of gratitude.

So I do too, the young Physics master, Vincent Waterhouse, who, in a short eighteen months or more before he was called up for war service, contrived to enthuse three of us with the subject at higher level and to raise our sights to the universities we should be aiming for. I never saw him again but he stayed in touch and it was with sadness that I learnt from him in the late 1960s of the tragic accident of his son on Table Mountain, Cape Town (and of the typically uncooperative attitude of the South African authorities of that time, which only added to his and his wife Ruth's distress). Also to learn some years later that he had died at a relatively early age. He was a straightforward Lancastrian and, I understand, did much to develop the School's reputation for science when he returned after the War; also to foster the Old Ludlovians Association branch in London when he moved to a lectureship there. He was an outstanding teacher.

I wish I could say the same of the third teacher we had, F. H. ('Ben') Woolley. He was in charge of Mathematics, and was brilliant at it, a Cambridge Senior Wrangler. He was also a diligent and deeply religious little man. But for some reason we never fathomed, he did not seem to consider we needed teaching: he simply marked work we put to him, very occasionally set it, but gave us only one lesson in three years. We marked the date on some panelling somewhere, in celebration. Perhaps he thought we had our own teacher, in the High School, my mother. I of course did, when needed, but my colleagues did not. Or perhaps he believed we would learn best from the book on our own. If so, he was certainly partly right. Through the chemistry master's preoccupation with headmastering, the physics master's absence in the war and the maths master's abstinence from teaching, we certainly had to learn to study on our own, and that was valuable training for university and beyond. But I have to admit it proved a bit of a handicap when it came to working for scholarships in my final year, against others from more favoured schools. That fortunately did not stop me winning an Open Exhibition to Selwyn College, Cambridge but I think the College authorities probably took some account of student's circumstances, especially in the conditions of the war. Anyhow, it all worked out well in the end both for me and I think my colleagues.

One of them, Paul Evans, went on to Birmingham University and a distinguished scientific career first in radio and radar research at Malvern during the war and then in nuclear research at Capenhurst. We remained good friends until he sadly died of heart failure on the squash court at far too young an age, leaving his wife Joan and their baby son Hugh. The other colleague, Frank Sharp, went on to Birmingham and Southampton Universities, the Ministry of Supply and the Institution of Electronic and Radio Engineers, serving as the Editor of its journal and other publications for many years. We met again forty years on, not in school or scientific company but in Liberal Party gatherings, where he and his wife Liz have been devoted activists for many years.

Other schoolboy personalities of that time have come and gone across my path. One, R. W. Packer, was Head Boy one year, son of Ludlow's first Lady Mayor, hooker in the rugby team, fellow Home Guard, like Sharp, on the eerie Castle Tower and now, I believe, a retired Professor of Geography in Canada. He never lacked courage or, when necessary, aggression. Another was L. G. Parsons, a neighbour, rugby forward and opening bat, with whom I had some happy batting partnerships – and actually shared a girlfriend briefly at one time, I believe. He joined the RAF in the war and had a traumatic escape from a Whitley bomber, being blown out and parachuted by hand unknown when it was heading for destruction. S. E. Lewis was also a neighbour, rugby player and opening bat, who rose to become a much respected senior official of the Ludlow Council, and remains to this day an encyclopedia of all things good about Ludlow and Ludlovians. Then, in a slightly older generation was H. Peachey, subsequently a chairman of the school governors and a life-long voluntary worker for the school; and, in a slightly younger generation, Dr R. C. Humphreys, friend and neighbour for many years, who carries the OBE for his medical services in mid-Wales; J. N. Holden, one of the school's best-ever athletes, who rose to be a Brigadier in the Army Engineers, and whom I found in the Canal Zone desert when awaiting demoblisation from Egypt at the end of the war, just as he found me later in Paris when he was on secondment to the French Army at Angers and I was at the Embassy. I could go on – M. D. I. Davies, the tallest and most gregarious of his age; A. C. Jones, as good a scrum-half as the school produced who came from the level-crossing gatehouse at Onibury and went on to Cambridge; R. J. Matthews, from Tenbury, perhaps the best fast-bowler the school ever had who went on I think to play for Worcestershire.

I mention the Rugby and Cricket a lot, not because they were – and, despite the intrusion of money, still are – in my view the greatest of games, but because 1939/40 was a Ludlow Grammar School vintage year not just academically but also in these two sports. The Rugby XV must have been the best ever. It went the full season undefeated, with a total of 194 points against 9. It was a joy to play in it, even in the second row. The Cricket XI was not far behind. We even won the South Shropshire knock-out, an annual tournament of towns, villages and schools for many miles around – the forerunner I contend of the popular county and international limited overs matches of today.

The maker of the rugby team was the Welsh PT master. The maker of the cricket team was the Geography master J. J. Jones. He was a Cambridge blue, and taught me how to bat in one simple observant question in the nets: why don't you come forward? With no coaching, no one had suggested that to me before and I had been too absorbed in my own ways to notice. It transformed my enjoyment of the game. J. J. Jones also had a hand, I believe, in my aiming for Selwyn College, his college at Cambridge. He was a good example of the old team spirit of the staff at Ludlow. Because a boy was the pupil of others, that did not mean he took no interest. The staff worked together.

The History master, F. G. Reeves, was another splendid example of this. He followed my career without my knowing it, and was the first to invite me years later to address Speech Day. He made me perform from the pulpit, or from a stage alongside it anyhow, in the great Ludlow church – but came to Shrewsbury with the then Headmaster to hear me speak at some voluntary organisation meeting some months beforehand to be quite sure I had the voice. Evidently some previous Speech Day speaker had not quite had the decibels and the boys and girls, by then amalgamated in one co-educational school, and their parents had not taken kindly to that. Anyhow my effort apparently passed muster – and I learnt what a job any Minister of a large church has before a congregation of children hiding behind pillars – you simply have to direct your remarks straight at them, pillars and all, and hope they penetrate.

I came to know Fred Reeves well, in later life. He was an active Liberal
in the then die-hard Conservative Constituency of Ludlow and South
Shropshire and played a leading part with a few other stalwarts in steadily
building a Liberal challenge there. It was a remarkable achievement and
I was proud many years later, in the 1980s, to be President of the
Constituency Association for a period. Our successors have done even
better: Ludlow now, at last, has a Liberal-Democrat MP. Reeves was also
a founder member of the Ludlow Civic Society and did much to ensure
the success of that organisation, from which Ludlow has so greatly benefited.
His widow founded an annual Memorial lecture in his name, after his death,
and I was pleased to play a part in getting it going with a succession of
leading Liberal speakers. I hope it still continues. The Civic Society
remember him annually, too. He was a pioneer and worker for many local
causes.

One other personality of the period, indeed family of personalities, were
the Turpins of Julian Avenue. Mr Turpin was Inland Revenue officer for
the district, and his wife a delightful mother of three outstanding children.
The eldest, Kenneth, schooled at Ludlow and then Manchester Grammar,
rose in the Civil Service to be Assistant Private Secretary to the Deputy
Prime Minister, Clement Attlee, during the War, and then became successively Registrar of Oxford University, Provost of Oriel College and
Vice-Chancellor of the University. His sister Mary became a teacher and
then joined him at Oxford. The middle one, John, was my contemporary,
Vice-Prefect of the school, French scholar and ardent bee-keeper, who
would be called out of school whenever there was a swarm in the town,
and who, enterprisingly, subsidised his own visits to France at an early age
by acting as sales agent in South Shropshire for a bee-keeping equipment
manufacturer. I discovered many a rural ride and village of the countryside
cycling with him to deliver boxes and blowers and the other things that
made up apiculture in those days. I suppose they are still used today,
although my wife's niece's French husband Gilles Ratia in the Dordogne
now seems to be able to do it all on computer and the internet – while
his wife, Josephine, trains horses the old fashioned way with reins, brush
and pan! But of course it is well known that bees are cleverer than horses.
As the American satirist Don Marquis once wrote: 'The bees got their
governmental system settled millions of years ago ... The human race is
still groping.'

John Turpin had a way of getting to know people and places wherever
he travelled. It was he who first introduced me to the scenic and historic
wonders of Northern Italy which we toured together on leave in 1945,
just after the Germans had been driven out, he being then with the Army
in Ancona on the Adriatic and I being with the RAF in Sardinia. We
also enjoyed an amusing holiday in the summer of 1947, exploring Switzerland on £35 or thereabouts – the maximum the Attlee Government

allowed anyone for foreign holidays in those penurious post-war days. He became a doctor and is still, I know, a familiar figure in Ludlow when he visits from across the Welsh border in Newtown, and the possessor of a wide international circle of friends.

The war of course changed all these people's lives as it did most everyone else. Tucked away in rural Shropshire, Ludlow might have been expected to be a safe-haven. And so it was. But as a result, evacuees, directed and voluntary, poured in, as did schools, troops in training and military depots. Air raid training and precautions, black-out, gas masks and rationing were enforced like everywhere else, and housewives, the retired, the young, the disabled and people with any time to spare, were recruited to fill the vacancies left by those called to active service or created by the administrative demands of war-time needs and regulations. One order I know rural Shropshire enjoyed was to turn all the road signposts around, so as to confuse German paratroops when they came – and, inevitably, to confuse all 'foreign codgers' too! You had to know your way around then or you were lost – and no villager would tell you, for fear you were a 'Fifth Columnist'. We all took directions, announcements and exhortations from the Government very seriously, and with good reason. The threat to the nation was dire, as events soon revealed.

F. G. Reeves described the evacuees in his little book *Ludlow in Wartime*. He was Chief Evacuation Officer for the Ludlow district at the time, as well as Borough Councillor, school teacher, ARP warden, and in due course Home Guard and also Chairman of the Gardens and Allotments Committee formed to encourage people to grow more food and vegetables. People rallied to the call with such phrases as 'Well there is a War on, dear,' and 'We're all in it together.'

The first contingent of evacuees, according to Reeves, was 'distributed with surprising smoothness in Ludlow and the area round about. The trouble came afterwards'.

They were mothers and children from Liverpool dockside and their mode of living stunned the conservative inhabitants of Ludlow. It was found necessary to establish a de-lousing station, and despairing hostesses (that is, every household with a spare room) complained that children were not house-trained ... mattresses had to be burned and replaced ... Fish and chips were the only acceptable fare and vegetables like runner beans were treated with suspicion ... As the 'phoney-war' passed ... most drifted back home ... With the dramatic events of 1940, however ... not only were there new contingents of Government sponsored parties, but ... a flood of elderly people and of mothers and children privately seeking refuge ... The Grammar School felt the full impact ... the number of pupils nearly doubled. Then after the appalling bombings on Birmingham, St Philips School was hastily transferred to

Ludlow to share the Grammar School ... At the same time Lancing College took refuge from the South coast at Moor Park and, having no laboratory or playing field facilities, they too ... used the Grammar School's. One way and another the place seethed – although, with the shortage of fuel, not always with warmth.

Reeves' account continues:

The last evacuation remains most vividly in mind. By this time the town was bulging ... Evacuees were billeted in almost every available household ... and every derelict house had been occupied ... Then came the buzz-bomb attack on London ... and we had a message to say ... we must find room for 500 mothers and children under five ... from the East End of London ... We were given twenty-four hours ... and telephones in those days were the luxury of the few ... [On arrival] every mother seemed to be crying and certainly every child was wailing ... But within the hour the whole lot had been dispersed to their new homes ... Ludlow people, for the greater part, came out of this ordeal by evacuation very well. For an ordinary household, perhaps an elderly couple, suddenly to have to accept two or three children, sometimes homesick and often coming from a very different background, with all the difficulties of rationing to deal with, and paid a few shillings a week which could never cover the additional expenses, was a pretty heavy burden. While it had none of the horrors of living in a blitzed city, it could be a grinding daily discord ... But on the whole it worked surprisingly well. Many children became cherished members of family groups. More than one persuaded their parents to allow them to stay in Ludlow after the war was over.

He might have added another occasion when Ludlow put its all and more into helping the war distressed. This was after Dunkirk when those hundreds of thousands of troops who were thankfully saved, arrived in England and had to be dispersed for rest and recuperation. Ludlow cared for trainloads of them before they went on to their camps.

My mother being the bread-winner (there was no official category of 'working-mother' in those days), and our house being small, we were exempted from taking evacuees. But they were all around us, and in the schools. I am not sure whether teaching was officially a 'reserved occupation', meaning a teacher had to make a case for leaving his or her post to join up, probably not, but the Churchill government wisely took the long view that, whatever happened, the education of the young was vital to the future of the nation and must continue. One of the great reforms his coalition government introduced while the war was still on was the Butler Education Act. Most teachers of course did voluntary war work as well. My public spirited mother was no exception. Her one complaint was the affectation of a few of the black-out wardens, who seemed at times to enjoy humiliating any householders who carelessly left chinks of light in their curtains. Most would knock and courteously tell us to correct the omission. The few among them she felt were just 'little Hitlers' would bellow from the road, for all the neighbours to hear: 'Turn that light out!' She knew they were right, but also that command corrupts. We were all in it together so, in her book, there was no excuse for incivility. One of the better things of the war, in fact, was that it broke down social barriers and brought people together as never before. This was certainly true of Ludlow.

At school it became a very different world with the two evacuated schools imposed. The corridors became like Piccadilly Circus, the classrooms like musical chairs, the laboratories so packed for joint practicals that it became dangerous to move among crowded bunsen burners – one of the visiting schools nearly lost its chemistry master in flames on one occasion. There were plenty of problems, and the School caretaker, Tommy Allum, daily tore what little hair he had left. Prefects were given more responsibility. Pupils and staff learnt to get on with total strangers – though, inevitably, not without rivalries and occasional squabbles. The mind boggles at the organisational timetables the Grammar School Head must have had to construct and laboriously agree with all concerned, not to mention the problems of sharing supplies and finance. Like most things in war it called for ingenuity and determination far beyond peacetime. For the young it was part of a great telescoping experience that always seems to accompany war.

The evacuees also brought innovation. The urban boys from Birmingham were not to be corralled from the fairer sex as we were. They expected fraternisation and dances, and got them. So, as a result, did we – and extraordinary war-time things like black-out waltzes, which added a bit of frolic. The Birmingham school did not otherwise mix much beyond their host families, or attempt to adapt, and sadly left for home when the worst of the blitz was over with a reputation in Ludlow for avoiding rather than helping with things.

The Sussex school also maintained its isolation socially, perhaps in the tradition of public schools of that time, but emerged to enhance greatly the cricket of the area. What with them and the Molineux school evacuated to nearby Leominster, and our traditional local rivals Lucton, Hereford High and others still within petrol rationing reach, the school had one of its best cricketing seasons ever. Or I should immodestly say I did anyhow, with a couple of centuries and a record school batting average of 92.4. We also had a great rugby season, learning for the first time that at Army level an opposing fly-half does not come at you like a fleet-footed deer, side-stepping and handing off, but like a tank – the modern way, which I personally deplore. The remarkable thing is that these relatively small schools between them produced from that 1940/41 year, a post-war Captain of England rugby (Brian Vaughan), a post-war Captain of England cricket and subsequently chairman of the Cricket Board (Douglas Insole) and at least two Blues. The war drew out talent in games, like everything else. It also encouraged responsibility. I enjoyed being captain of rugby and cricket and senior prefect. It was fun.

We also learnt, among war-effort activities, to weed nursery trees for one August fortnight at a forestry camp in mid-Wales, as boring a job as anyone ever conceived, but in beautiful country delighting in the poetic address of Twiscob, Cascob, Presteigne, Rads. And in another August fortnight, to pick hops in Worcestershire for the troops' beer, equally boring but at least standing upright, and enlivened by sharing the work with migrant labour from some of the roughest parts of Birmingham. They were full of aggression if not against the busheller, who measured their output (and was in fact markedly more generous to them than to us), then between themselves. It opened my young eyes a shade to find on arrival one morning that one of the men had been chased around the huts by an axe-wielding wife that morning, and bloodied in the process – but lived.

The Local Defence Volunteers, later renamed the Home Guard, were a different matter. The Dad's Army series has written them into history in satirised form, and wonderful comedy it is too. The reality was a bit different. We had our farcical moments but we also had military training and tasks to perform which we took seriously, as I am sure did every unit up and down the land. We were in it to back up the Army against the expected German invasion. For us youngsters it was exciting. For some old soldiers of World War I, and some would-be soldiers who had never quite made it, it was too. But the gloss soon wore off when it emerged that we had no rifles or bayonets and would have to wait for them; no uniforms except one oversized camouflage denim which was soon taken from us anyhow to send to the Abyssinians; and no identification except an LDV armband – but we were proud of it, and I still retain mine. Our Commanding Officer was a bit of a put-off too. Lt. Col. Windsor-Clive was the local squire, Conservative MP and layer of foundation stones, a dutiful man but no dynamo. In the semi-feudal ways that still persisted in south Shropshire then we were expected to touch our forelocks to him anyhow. Now, by unknown process of appointment, we were expected to salute him too. Fortunately his appearances were as rare as, allegedly, his speeches in the House of Commons. The people we looked to were our Sergeant, none other than the school French master, Merchant, a trio of big ex-Army junior officers and our platoon commander Major Bennett.

Merchant, in his *Footsteps down Mill Street*, describes the trio of ex-officers as 'strapping fellows, a sight to see on parade, particularly since their soldiering in the first war had been in trenches where the object was to keep the head well down rather than well up and their posture had been neglected during the last 20 years.' But they gamely played their part.

Bennett was a local bank manager but had been an officer in the Hussars and, in Merchant's words 'retained his cavalry outlook ... and was a dashing soldier if ever there was one ... It is, of course, not very easy to bring cavalry methods to bear in guarding sewage works and the like but if anybody could bring a touch of martial glamour to such a mundane task it was Major Bennett.'

My service in the LDV and Home Guard must have been nearly fifteen months. We did regular night guard duty (2 hours on, 4 hours off) once a week, which was the tedious part, especially with school the following day. We did exercises every Sunday. The guard duty was at Ludlow racecourse until we took over the castle, and I remember the unheated and smelly back rooms we retired to between shifts as much as straining at every sound alone on the racecourse or Castle Towers. The exercises were quite different. We paraded, we route-marched against the Army, we threw Molotov cocktails (bottles of lighted paraffin bound in ladies' stockings) at targets in the old Ludlow brickworks; and, when we finally acquired a mortar we took it up the Clee Hills and fired it with enormous enthusiasm across one of the deep quarries causing, to our astonishment, a whole quarry side to collapse in a thunderous avalanche of rock and earth. We prized our mortar greatly after that – but learnt to use it with more discretion. Then, one autumn Sunday we had a great exercise out on the Windsor-Clive estate. We young bloods from school were assigned to lead the attack, and some farm lads to front the defence. In a fit of exuberance our 'Captain Mainwaring', Major Bennett ordered charge with fixed bayonets and down the hillside through the gorse we plunged, little realising the defence would fearfully fix bayonets too. There was none of the gruesome 'one, two, plunge, withdraw' we had been taught in bayonet training, just a frightened up and under if you came too close. I did not see the fellow behind a rock but he saw me and I got the point of his bayonet exactly on the collar bone. A fraction aside and I might not be writing this now. The shirt I was wearing, with the tear in the neck, remained a memento for years. It was a lesson in military folly. However we were told it showed spirit, which is what the Home Guard was all about.

One other episode remains fresh in mind, which was probably replicated across the land. One night in the summer of 1940 we were hauled from our beds in the early hours by a messenger, summoning us to man the trenches we had dug, down near the Burway playing field. There we learnt that the whole country had been put on alert by an RAF sighting of a German invasion force setting off across the Channel. We were to be ready for German paratroops, even in remote Ludlow. However, dawn came with no sign of them and no further news, and we were getting cold and bored. To liven us up Sergeant Merchant posed us the question that had evidently been preoccupying him all night: If paratroops came dressed in British uniform how would we be sure they were not Germans in disguise? None of us knew. So, turning to me who happened to be standing by him, he declared, 'You, Hugh Jones. I shall send you over the parapet to challenge them.' Merchant later said I took this in good part – probably because I had no idea how and where I would challenge. On returning home, the alert over, I inadvisedly mentioned the incident to my mother when asked what we had been doing. She was furious and, as mothers do, took up the cudgels with our Sergeant, how dare he sacrifice her son in such a way! Merchant never forgot it and a satirical version of the story appeared in his *Footsteps down Mill Street* years later – which annoyed my mother even more. I asked him long after why we had not thought of the old rural Shropshire way which was to ''eave 'alf a brick at any foreigner' anyhow. If the paratroops shot it to bits they must be German. If they just threw it back, they must obviously be just English codgers. He thought that might do in the next war. In fact the alert came to nothing. Whether the RAF mistook what they saw, or an invasion force did start out but for some reason turned back, has never to my knowledge been clarified. But it was no doubt a useful alert exercise for the whole Home Guard, and a memorable one!

Ludlow was at no time a German target. If it had been, we would have known it soon enough. F. G. Reeves records: 'the next alarm came after the devastating raids on Canterbury and Bath. Professor Joad, one of the prophets of the time, suggested in his Sunday paper column that the next obvious place was Ludlow. The reaction in Ludlow was predictable.' It apparently led to quite a confrontation between the local Emergency Committee and the Regional authorities, Army Western Command, Public Utilities, Poor Law Authority and Police when the Committee discovered the inadequacy of the others' plans for the town. Joad was a great war time personality, brilliant but politically irresponsible as academics can be sometimes. But his prediction galvanised Ludlow. In fact, as Reeves also records: 'On a moonlight night Ludlow, with its river, bridges, railway line and main road joining together, made an admirable check-point for German bombers, and the heavy raids on Liverpool and Birmingham were routed over us.' I myself remember the Heinkels and Dorniers coming over night after night. 'There goes Jerry again,' we would say, and soon after, if they were heading for Birmingham thirty miles away, we would see the bomb flashes and incendiary fires in the sky as they rained down on the poor people there. The pulsating drone of those bombers was very distinctive. I can still hear it today, if I stop to listen.

Ludlow was lucky. There was always the chance a bomber or two would drop its load *en route*, because it was in trouble or more likely wanting to ditch its load after failing to reach its target. Numerous fell in the country around but only one on Ludlow itself, and that was in the garden of the rather maverick curate the church had at the time. He lost his windows, vegetable plot and goldfish, but turned adversity to advantage by charging sixpence a time in aid of the Red Cross to see the crater.

Ludlow had its moments throughout the War. Everyone I knew followed events on the various War Fronts keenly. The great source of national information and guidance was BBC Radio. Newsreaders like Alvar Liddell and spokesmen like Lord Woolton, the Food Minister, and Dr Charles Hill, the Radio Doctor, although only minnows beside the Churchill whale, were as familiar household names as the comedians Arthur Askey and Richard Murdoch and Forces Sweetheart Vera Lynn. Everyone I remember did their bit and, as F. G. Reeves recorded in his Memories, 'there were a good many miracle workers in Ludlow during the War.' There were throughout Britain.

# CHAPTER 5

---

# Family in the Blitz

## 1940–1941

LIVERPOOL, where my brother was studying medicine, was a very different war-time scene. As Britain's premier Atlantic port it was a major German target. Some of my brother's letters home have survived. The following extracts illustrate through his eyes what that great city went through in the blitz of September 1940–May 1941, and what his life was like there. The letter heads are his student lodgings or the Royal Liverpool Hospital where he worked. Some of the dates are missing, but the sequence is clear.

### E (Eryl) to M (Mother) Winter 1940/41
#### 80 Upper Canning St, Liverpool

*I am writing this at 12.30 am. I went to bed at 11.45 after reading some King Lear, when hell let loose up above – a terrifying din, and pieces of shrapnel clanking onto the roof tops and street. One large piece I suspect landed in the back garden as it thudded onto something soft and shook the house. The raid has been on since 6pm and waves of them have been over all evening ... I don't think I've been so petrified in my life, when a bomb came I just sat up in bed, pulled the bedclothes up and waited for it to land. The interval between its start and end seemed interminable. I don't know yet where it landed but there was a terrific explosion and flash ... So much for our nearest so far. I have now decided that discretion etc., and have dressed and come downstairs, and still more Jerrys are coming over ... A few minutes ago one dropped three parachute flares which were a beautiful sight, slowly floating down in a cloudless and brilliantly star-lit sky and lighting the whole place. They ought to see something with flares like that.*

*I have been on A.R.P. duty at Smithdown Road Hospital every night Monday to Thursday ... only one raid and no casualties. However Thursday night Harold Friend and I were asked by Nurse to help with a casualty from a colliery where a fall of coal had cut his hand badly. He had to be put to sleep and Harold gave him gas, but he had just had a huge Lancashire Hot Pot – gosh, what a mess – started choking, stopped breathing, so I held his jaw and tongue forward and Dr started him off again ... came round very apologetic, and worried in case he had used bad language under the anaesthetic ... After that a young Finn came in with a pain in his tummy ... Dr told us to examine him while she changed her coat. He couldn't speak English, so we just had to prod him until he winced – and diagnosed acute appendix. We were right too as it was out before morning! ... After that about 12.30 the All Clear went and we went to bed in one of the Wards.*

*[Letter continued the following day] ... The bomb last night landed 50 yards up the road. It blew out a house and in the one next door two old friends of Miss Challoner [E's landlady], aged 72 and 84 were found with pianos and what-nots on top of them ... but are alright and after a night at the Royal Hospital have now parked themselves on us ... They have come out of it marvellously well ... So much for our longest raid 6pm to 2.30am, and for our nearest yet. I hope they don't come any nearer.*

### E to M March 1941           80 Upper Canning St, Liverpool

*This week has been very strenuous ... Exams, practicals and vivas all last week ... Mon. and Tues. again this week, then Path. and Bact. practicals and Pharmacology viva, with two Profs. questioning me on drugs and doses etc ... On Wed. night we had our second really heavy blitz. It wasn't so bad up till about 10pm but then things got going. Several hundred planes were over ... Birkenhead and Wallasey got it worst and, although I've not seen the damage, I believe it is extensive – though they didn't hit the docks or Cammell Lairds. We also got it very badly on this side of the Mersey ... We arrived at the Varsity for our vivas to find a land mine had hit the Engineer's building and badly damaged the Medical School. Both will have to come down. Also the Pathology Depts ... The Medical School was like walking through a lot of roofless and windowless arcades. I managed to get my microscope, slides and white coats out of my locker, cases scratched but otherwise all right. The Blood Bank was damaged but most of it was salvaged safely and used up straight away.*

*On the whole Liverpool centre is not badly damaged, the dock areas got it worst. The GPO got it and the upper floors are gone, so I hope you did not write any letters to me last week that might have been in there. Several warehouses and blocks of flats were demolished all over the place, including our nearest ½ mile away ... The chief trouble is that the river is mined and 3 ships got hit, one now resting on the bottom with its funnels and masts poking out of the water. No ferries are running ... In the Wirral the transport is still being sorted out with the Underground only working to Hamilton Square, all the other stations being used to house the homeless.*

**E to M March 1941**                                    **80 Upper Canning St, Liverpool**

*The last week has been very busy ... We had very big raids Tues., Wed., Sat., and several minor ones. In all we had at least 29 raids last week – with three days entirely free – and so far to 6pm this evening we have had 14 already this week. I give the numbers as I have just started counting the raids. But these are nothing to what we had two or three weeks ago when we had 7 or 8 every day. I am waiting anxiously for Sat. morning, when I can leave this hole for a few days.*

*Finishing off a few facts mentioned in your letter just received, the story about Walton Gaol is quite true. That was the Wed. raid. They also got the Nurses Home at the Southern Hospital and injured 16 nurses. Also one stick of bombs was let off at the Royal Hospital. One hit some houses causing many casualties, another the gates of the Royal sending a huge block of granite through the roof of the operating theatre. Luckily they had just finished for the day and were cleaning up, and no one was hurt. I arrived a few minutes later, after being delayed!*

*Wed. last we had our clinical exam ... it was quite nice, at the hospital and in pleasant surroundings – smoking allowed, and we gave all we knew about piles, appendices and abdominal troubles for 1½ hours.*

*Friday, after a very quiet night, we had a very good outpatients. Freddie [Mr Rawlinson – Consultant] again in very good mood – which was interrupted three times by very rowdy raids. We are so used to them now though, only a direct hit would stop things carrying on as normal.*

*Sat. four of us cycled out to Speke – near the aerodrome and Roote's factory which have been bombed nearly every time Fritz comes over, but have never been hit yet ... On the way back Fritz rather spoiled things by arriving half an hour earlier than usual – at 7.0pm ... We heard some bombs land some distance away so we dived into a shelter for a few minutes until it seemed quieter, and then resumed. But near home we heard a plane overhead and suddenly something whistling down – and did we duck! We were off the bikes and flat on the ground instantly, holding up a car behind . I looked up and saw the bomb land about mile away, with a terrific flash, fire and stupendous noise which nearly deafened us. I was never so glad to hear a bang before. The whistle makes you think the thing is going to land right on top of you, even if it may land some distance away.*

*That night's raid got T. J. Hughes' store and several buildings in central Liverpool, a tremendous goods yard fire by the docks, and one of the docks ... It was the worst raid of all so far. It must have been bad, it was even mentioned on the BBC News, which usually gives London's one bomber more publicity than the rest of the country's 1000!*

*The trams are hard hit. They have to make large detours to avoid unexploded bombs.*

**E to M 6 May 1941**                    **Royal United Hospital, Liverpool**

*I have been unable to get through to you today as all communications are cut and no telegrams accepted but I hope you are going on the old principle of no news is . . .*

*I posted a P.C. to you on Sat. but as the GPO is gutted I suppose that has gone up the shute.*

*Very briefly this is the news: Friday we had bombs at the back of the house opposite, at the corner and 50 yards up at the back of our house, and several incendiaries . . . Sat. was terrible. We started about midnight with incendiaries, one of which went clean down my chimney and into my bedroom but I got it out before any damage was done. Another fell on the roof of next door, which is unoccupied, and lodged in the gutter and the roof caught fire, but we also got that out after breaking in next door.*

*Then a land mine landed at the top of the street and removed a lot of our windows. That is all our damage. Mr Bindloss (fellow lodger) however has had a seizure with the excitement and is paralysed on his right side. Des [Farmer – later Professor of Dentistry at Liverpool University] and I had to nurse him and get him to hospital – a horrible place but the only one that will take him in. When his sister arrives he will be moved to a Nursing Home. The All Clear went at 4.30 and Des and I went in search of his Doctor but found he had been bombed out. Then, as it was too late for bed, we went to see the damage. It was really a horrible raid and the whole of Liverpool seems to have been damaged.*

*The nearest to us was damage to a margarine store, barracks and tenements at the top of Canning St which burnt fiercely all night. Smithdown Road Hospital has been evacuated as a landmine landed across the street. Mill Road Hospital had a direct hit and students, doctors and nurses – about 60 to 70 all told – are missing. The Southern Hospital (old place) got hit and is burnt out and the Northern Hospital (also old buildings) is damaged. The Royal Hospital has had more windows out by a mine which has damaged the Dental Hospital badly. University library, Social Science and Chemistry are also sufferers.*

*In town Lewis's, Blacklers, Baxendales, Horne Bros, Hope Bros, Austin Reeds, India Buildings, Dock and Harbour Board building (one of the three on Pier Head), the Art Gallery, several cinemas and shops in the centre, St George's Hall (not badly); and nearly all between the Customs House and Dale St and Castle St and Pier Head are completely gutted.*

*We have had Fire Brigades here, using the Union as a Base, from London Twickenham, Wimslow, Fleetwood, Manchester, Leeds, Bradford, Coventry, Blackpool, Littlehampton and hundreds of other places nearer in than that – there must be thousands of fire engines here.*

*Apart from lack of sleep I am quite well. Have been up to Hospital a lot. Spent last night there – 75 on Sat., and they were still operating at midnight last night. 500 at Alder Hey Hospital.*

*Gas is very low. Water OK. Electricity has come on again. Trains are running on two routes, the 1 to Garston and the 22 from two miles outside town. Exchange station is also gutted and no trains get in nearer than Seaforth.*

*Sorry to be so morbid. Hope it doesn't happen again.*

It did not, fortunately, not at any rate on quite that scale. The Blitz eased in late May '41 with the success of the Battle of Britain and Hitler's obsession with invading Russia. My brother completed his medical training at Liverpool and remained ardently loyal to that city all his life. There was never anywhere else in his judgement that had the character, tenacity, inventiveness and culture (classical and modern) to match. He was a member of both the Liverpool Philharmonic Society and the Beatles Club before the latter became known. After Army service, he chose to practise and live within reach of the city, at St Helens.

CHAPTER 6

# Cambridge in Wartime

# 1941–1943

LIKE LUDLOW, but unlike poor Liverpool, Cambridge turned out to be a relative haven during the war. So, I believe, did Oxford. They might not have been. To the leaders of Nazi Germany it must have been only a short step from bombing the great heritage centres of Bath and Canterbury to attacking the leading centres of learning, especially as both Cambridge and Oxford had some war industry adjacent. Certainly Cambridge expected this, and I believe Oxford did too. There is evidence the Nazis did think of it. An interesting account of Cambridge at war published in the University Magazine CAM many years later, recorded that Berlin radio reported at the outset of the Blitz that Cambridge had been heavily bombed, fires raging and smoke trailing far beyond the city. It was a false report, but a warning. Cambridge was hit in June 1940 and again, in one of the last air raids of the war, in 1943, with people killed in each, but fortunately neither time on any great scale. All in all, to quote the CAM article, Cambridge suffered no more than 'sporadic attention from isolated planes'. The German leadership for some reason stopped short of its destruction.

By the time I went 'up', as the University liked to call it (and of course 'down' to everywhere else at the end of term), the worst of the Blitz was over. It was nonetheless a difficult place to reach from anywhere beyond East Anglia and the Home Counties, and I found it very much prepared for the worst. We were still made to feel privileged to be there. But so we were, and so I remain. It is my Alma Mater.

My first visits were during the Blitz in December 1940 and March 1941, to take open scholarship examinations for the colleges of St John's and Selwyn. London was then virtually out of bounds to anyone transiting the country and, as the rail system of England seemed to have been built around the capital, it became a tortuous all-day journey across country from Ludlow to Cambridge. We had to change at places like Shrewsbury,

Stafford or that great but cheerless junction Crewe, and Bletchley, with compartments crowded and periodic go-slows for air raid warnings. On arrival at Cambridge, I was allotted digs for the week way out on the Chesterton Road, with a kindly landlady whose husband was a College meat-carver and son a local dance-band leader. They gave a little homeliness to my stay. I needed it. The St John's exams proved above my level. But I became interested in one chemistry question on copper valence or something like that, and, although knowing little about it, I apparently produced an original thought or two which impressed the supervising examiner. He called me in for interview before I left. I was late, walking in from outer Cambridge, but fortunately he was even later. He commended my one answer, regretted I had not done better on the other questions, but advised I try the Selwyn and St Catherine's scholarships in the Spring, and he would put in a good word for me. I later blessed him, and copper valence, about which I now know even less. My letter home recorded that the journey had cost me 32s. 6d. That was quite a lot in those days.

My next visit in March took me all round the houses again, this time via Shrewsbury, Leamington Spa, Oxford and the inevitable Bletchley (which, it used to be said, I think, was the only place where Oxford and Cambridge met other than on the fields of battle). The Selwyn exams went much better and I still have the letter from the eminent Zoologist Dr L. A. Borradaile informing me I had 'been elected to an Exhibition of £20 at Selwyn College' and that he would be my Director of Studies.

I was soon to learn however that entry through the golden gates required more than Higher School Certificate, College acceptance, Scholarships and a Director of Studies. We had to be interviewed on behalf of the University and also, improbably, to take an examination in Latin. My interview proved painless. By good fortune the Headmaster of Hereford High School was commissioned to do it and very decently suggested we met after our inter-school cricket match at Hereford. In the event we bowled his side out for 10, I being Ludlow skipper and taking 6 wickets for 2 runs, including four in four balls. I never bowled like it before or since. The interview lasted two minutes. 'I don't think we need spend much time on this, do you?' he said. Those were the days when the older Universities liked to have sportsmen as well as scholars. I am glad they still do.

The Latin, on the other hand, was little short of farce. It remained a compulsory part of the University entrance, even for scientists, which meant another examination at Cambridge. I groused at having to devote precious time that summer trying to learn a language that was not going to be of any use to me. They passed me, even though I doubt if I achieved 10%. The war demanded scientists not classicists, and by then I had also been offered a State Bursary at Cambridge on this basis. But the classical establishment had to play Lars Porsena or whatever. I hold, provocatively, that the classical tradition probably did more harm than good to British education over the previous century and more, insisting on the pre-eminence of the classics as a subject of study, to the inevitable detriment of science and modern languages. My parents, one humanities and the other science, probably shared that view. To study ancient Rome, Caesar's Wars, ancient Greece and the Greek philosophers is one thing, and valuable learning. To study the former in what had long become outside the Catholic church a dead language, and oblige school children to learn that language, was beyond my comprehension. Why not equally make Norman French compulsory? We were told that Latin was supreme as a trainer of the mind. That clearly was plain sophism, or to use the more descriptive modern word 'spin'.

Cambridge saw the light on this after the War and at last allowed students in without Latin. They also formally admitted women, having long regarded them, professors and students alike, as worthy of their own colleges and to take University courses, but not to be full members. The War released a wave of reform in so many spheres of life. But it took many more years for colleges to become mixed. In my time, it was strictly men only, and I recall one fun-loving medical colleague risking being 'sent down' (expelled) by walking a girlfriend out of his rooms at a forbidden time dressed in his clothes but forgetting her high heels might catch the Head Porter's eagle eye. He survived, and went on to become a hospital doctor and to write the brilliant *Doctor in the House* series, which we still enjoy on film today. The world of post war British comedy would have been all the poorer had the College not decided, I presume, that the war time need of doctors outweighed such indiscipline. Another fellow student was less fortunate; he was peremptorily sent down, even though he had won 'blues' (called in wartime 'half blues') in soccer and boxing for the University. He evidently went just too far. The University had its own corps of watch-dogs, and the College Porters, as I recall, were more policemen than heavers of baggage. We were kept in line.

It being wartime, any science or engineering students allowed two-year courses also risked being despatched home and into the Forces if they failed to work or to pass their exams. The Arts students perhaps had an easier time, but were only allowed one year, and no more than a so called 'War degree' at the end of it. For the science students, expected to take a 3 year Honours course in two years and an extra course in Electronics for war training purposes as well, the atmosphere was very different from all we had heard about Cambridge before the war. It was intensely serious.

This is how I found it in September 1941. But there was one more hurdle. The State Bursary scheme introduced in 1941/42 when, at the instance of some Cambridge dons, the Government awoke to the paucity of scientists and engineers coming through the universities in wartime, was given to the Board of Education to organise and a bunch of bureaucrats in Bournemouth to administer. I record that rudely because at the last moment they unaccountably directed me away from the Natural Sciences course the College and I were prepared for, and into Engineering, about which I knew nothing. Comparing notes later with others who had all been directed where they expected, I could only deduce it was either a mistake or the numbers game and my name was stuck with a pin. I was told firmly however there was no redress. There followed, instead of the elation one expected on entering the great place, an interlude as miserable as I can recall. I had first to book-learn Applied Mathematics to the Engineering entry standard, and failed – the first, and I am glad to say the only exam I ever fluffed. 'I'm afraid I haven't made a very good start up here, I've gone and pipped the exam … I'm feeling absolutely fed up,' I wrote home. To compound things it then became evident I lacked the ground work for the civil and mechanical engineering lectures and practicals that followed. It was a bemusing experience trying to understand heat engines, theory of structures, materials and the rest, and doing practicals on engines pumping up and down all around me. The sole moment of relief came when the eminent Professor Searle told us there was no engineering reason why a suspension bridge could not be built across the Channel, although the towers would have to be eight miles high! I can still see him sketching his dream. The knowledge and skill of engineers has always drawn my admiration and I learnt and practised radio and radar engineering myself. But civil and mechanical engineering remain blind spots, and the course an unhappy memory.

It lasted two weeks. I first appealed to my College Dean and Tutor, the Rev. A. C. Blyth, a dedicated but at that time rather rigid man, and received for my pains a lecture on the obligation to do what the Government said if I accepted bursary money from them. My good mother then weighed in, with letters to the Master of my College, Canon Chase, who I think tempered the Dean; to the Board of Education people in Bournemouth, which merely produced an unsigned regret and rebuttal, on behalf of 'The Secretary' (presumably 'of State for Education'); and finally to the formidable Dr Martin Wilson, Director of Education for Shropshire, who saw the point and got the Board of Education orders to all concerned – the University, College and me – changed in no time. I reverted to the Natural Sciences course forthwith. Typically perhaps, the authorisation letter from the Board of Education was in unsigned memo form, like the earlier rebuttal, whereas all previous correspondence had been normal signed letters. It was my first lesson in the ways of petty bureaucrats, an example not to be followed if I ever became one.

Selwyn was a friendly college, smaller and with less historic baggage than most. It was founded in the late nineteenth century as a primarily Anglican institution at a time when all other colleges were going multi-faith. Only a few years before I entered, students had to attend chapel regularly or be fined. Under Canon Chase, a fine Master who subsequently became Bishop of Ripon, the college adapted well to wartime while maintaining its own best traditions. Situated, like the women's college Newnham, on the Grange Road, now a centre of the University but then on the outskirts, it had its disadvantage in being farther to walk or cycle to lectures, labs and the central colleges when we were in a hurry. Also it was not on the beautiful 'Backs' of the Cam. But it did have a certain feeling of independence. Like our distinguished Bursar, Sir Hubert Sams, an ex-Indian civil servant whose place on the college High Table was always 'with but after' the Fellows, Selwyn was with but after most other Colleges. But it was none the worse for that – except that the Master could not be elected Vice-Chancellor of the University, but that changed with a successor, the Rev. Owen Chadwick, who became an outstanding Vice-Chancellor. Nor did being outside town prejudice College sporting activities. On the contrary, we had our playing field, shared I think with another college, within easy reach, and Selwyn had a great rowing tradition. I was able to play rugby, cricket and tennis in my time there and indeed captained the rugby and vice-captained the cricket, although even with a reinforcement of RAF officer cadets on six-month University courses, it could not be said the standard of play matched peacetime. For most of us, sporting activities had to be crammed in between work, as much for exercise as enjoyment.

There were steadily fewer students, too, as the war progressed and call-up age lowered. Only the women's colleges remained full. Part of Selwyn was given over to the RAF. The other four-storeyed 'Staircases' of rooms were occupied by students and a few dons. No student needed to live out. But all colleges became emptier and emptier later, I believe, the population of Cambridge only being augmented by evacuated colleges from London and by the Services – including in due course American forces, but that was long after my time. It was very different when I came back after the War. But I shall come to that later.

The College conditions were monastic. Selwyn was not a wealthy college. It had no large endowments and investments, as most of the older colleges had. The student rooms were spacious enough, two rooms each usually, but in most blocks they boasted no furniture beyond an old table, chair and iron bed, no furnishings but thread-bare half-carpets, no lamps except bare hanging ones, and no running water or lavatory except half way up the stone staircase. Being considered gentlemen, we did have college servants, or 'gyps', elderly orderlies one or two to each staircase, who woke us every weekday morning with a jug of hot water to wash and shave and a shout to raise the dead. I cannot remember what else ours did except to sell me an old wooden armchair and one or two other essentials no doubt bequeathed him by previous occupants and sold to incoming students many times over. To do him justice he probably also cleaned the rooms and staircase, and served in the Dining Hall in the evenings. I do not remember any women in the place whatsoever, except I think the Dean and Bursar had lady secretary assistants, without whom no doubt – like the great Muirfield, Troon and other men-only Golf Clubs – the administration would have collapsed, but no one was to know. In the English educational tradition of that age, it was men only – and the women's college, Newham, across the road had high walls to keep us out.

However the system worked, and worked congenially – except in one respect: 'You've no idea how cold Cambridge is,' I wrote home. The winds across the fens were one thing. Quite another were the bare rooms, with their ill-fitting windows, and no heating except a small coal fire, and this in winter only. At that stage of the war, too, the only coal available was 'smalls', which were little better than coal dust. To have a bath we had to cross the quad to the communal college tubs, down a freezing passageway, and take a cold douche to prepare for the return journey. My abiding memory of that first winter was trying to study with first the left thigh against the grate until it was hot while the other thigh grew blue, and then switching sides repeatedly until bedtime. Then, with kettle and mug and hot water-bottle, all bought second-hand, we would queue at the one gas ring half way up the staircase and fill up with hot Horlicks and water for the night. We all did this, hardy youngsters though we thought we were, including the RAF officer cadets. The following year, 1942/43, I made sure I had the one bed-sit on that staircase, tiny but with gas-fire, gas-ring and running water – and I am sure it enabled me to do twice as much work. Today Selwyn has long found the money to modernise them all, as well as to add some fine new buildings. But on the occasions when I went back in later years, fond as I was of the place, I always made a point of staying the night outside.

Food was also a problem, but that was entirely on account of the war. Rationing by then was tight and it cost too much to eat out, except, when in town at lunchtime, at the admirable British Restaurants most towns had at that stage of the war. In any case it was a rule of College to dine 'in Hall' most nights a week, a sensible and sociable rule, and I think to breakfast there too. So the College took most of our rations. For the rest I lived on dried milk and dried eggs, thankful to the good people of Canada for cutting back on their egg consumption at the behest of the Mackenzie King Government to send the dried and easily transportable product to us. It was a noble act and, in my case, appreciated almost every day of my student life. We also fed on porridge, salads, carrots (good for your eyesight in the black-out the Government told us, knowing how easy carrots were to grow!) and, occasionally, a cake from home made with the help of butter and sugar rations we saved and sent home for the purpose. Food rations were a constant preoccupation, and a major topic of conversation too. The College catering staff did well to feed us two meals a day, with the coupons we gave them and their own ingenuity. We did not feast in the peacetime College style, but we did not starve either. Nor did the country. I think history has rightly given great credit to the national supply, rationing, advisory and supervisory services of the Ministry of Food during and after the war. More is the pity perhaps that that Ministry was not retained as an integral part of Government later, instead of being subordinated to Agriculture in the so-called Ministry of Food, Agriculture and Fisheries. We might not otherwise have had to face in recent years so many animal and food health and safety problems, most arising it seems from abuses of science and technology by parts of the food and feedstuffs industries.

Cambridge adapted to wartime in a multitude of ways. Treasures like King's Chapel windows were removed to safety. Piles of sand-bags, to protect entrances against bomb-blast, lay everywhere even at Selwyn's gates. Black-out was applied rigorously – which meant our rooms at least had curtains. We always carried gas-masks. Air-raid precautions were everywhere (although only 'immediate danger' could suspend an exam!). We had to learn and practice them, volunteer for fire-watching, and join the Home Guard or Senior Training Corps (STC). That meant spending an evening a week and Sunday mornings repeating the same drill and training I had had at Ludlow, except this time, thankfully, there were no weekly night guard duties, other than for fire-watching. There was also a two-week STC camp in the vacation with all sorts of Army manoeuvres and operations, and a Certificate A to pass in firearms and things. It cost us precious studying time, but it was essential, and I was quite glad of it when I joined the RAF, even though it did lead to a mild dispute with the Officers Training Flight Sergeant when it emerged he did not like the Army style of 'shun we had been taught. The Army jumped, the RAF did not, it kept its feet on the ground!

Our work programmes were also adapted to war-time. The standard of lectures remained high, even though many of the younger science dons, and some older ones, had to go to industry, research, government or the armed forces. There seemed to be an inexhaustable supply of older, disabled and female lecturers and lab assistants in Physics heat and light, mechanics, magnetism and electricity, Chemistry organic and inorganic, Maths pure and applied, and even in the new course created for us, Electronics (or 'Radio' as many still preferred to call it). Supervisors on the other hand, that breed of dons who, with the Directors of Study and Tutors, made Cambridge so admirably devoted to giving every student personal guidance and tuition, had become scarce. The College did well to find for three of us a joint Maths supervisor of some distinction, even though the attention he could give us was limited. We also had a good joint Physics supervisor, though we had to see him on the other side of town at night after dinner, and his room, clock, and manner were like a metronome. We had a first-class Chemistry supervisor, Gerald Bulmer, a Selwyn man, to whom I owe the development of my interest in organic chemistry. He also guided me in the related subject of Biochemistry which I added to my studies in the second year. I would probably have ended up teaching or researching in that field and even genetics but for the RAF. It all seemed set in that direction at the time.

Outside work there was always plenty to do, besides sport, if we could find the time. Everyone avidly followed the events of the War. The period embraced Pearl Harbour and the entry of the Americans in late '41; the loss of Singapore to the Japanese and Tobruk to the Germans in early and mid '42; the Allied landings in French North Africa in late '42; and the turn of the tide at Stalingrad and in the North African desert in early '43. A letter I wrote home in April '43 records delight at seeing a wave of RAF bombers and fighter escort going out from the East Anglian airfields to bomb German targets in daylight at last, and Church bells being allowed again. The news was often grim but, as Allied successes began to come through it was also exciting.

Cambridge offered a wealth of scientific, political, educational and other societies to join, and open meetings, with eminent speakers like Sir William Bragg, the Nobel prize-winner, Sir Arthur Eddington the astronomer, C. H. Waddington the biologist and BBC Brains Trust member, and countless others, who gave their time freely in the great tradition of providing students with a broader and deeper education than just their chosen subject. I did not get to a fraction of those I wished, but those I attended left an abiding memory of the richness of intellectual life there, even in war-time. There were also concerts by Solomon, opera by the Sadlers Wells, and seemingly just everything to feed the mind despite the War. I wrote home in May '42, after taking my first year's exams: 'There are so many attractions here especially in Summer I can't imagine what it must be like in peacetime.' One society I did attend regularly was CUSIA, the University Society for International Affairs. That was perhaps where my interest in diplomacy was first sparked.

For all this ferment of activity and the upheaval of war, the formalities of Cambridge and College life were still observed. To be admitted to the University we had to 'matriculate', and that year of entry would appear in our records for ever more. I suppose it was once quite a ceremony. For us in war-time I wrote home disappointedly: ' We all went to the Senate house in cap and gown and signed our names in a big book, and that was all – for which we pay £5.' But gowns, short if you were an undergraduate, long if you were a graduate, remained obligatory in Hall for dinner, and for lectures. I do not think we wore them in the labs where safety came first; and war-time brought a suspension of caps (mortar boards) except on ceremonial occasions. It also led to a marked relaxation in standards of dress. Corduroys replaced flannels, and it no longer mattered if they bore multiple burn holes from the acid of the chemistry lab or pipe-smoking, as mine did. They were doubtless the forerunner of today's, or yesterday's, jeans.

Personal conduct, however, remained regulated. Only Fellows could walk on the quadrangle lawns; students walked around, and the Head Porter would be out of his gate-room in a flash, complete with bowler hat, if we trespassed. The Dean's personal permission was required to sign off dinner in Hall. Grace was always said in Latin and we took it in turns to read it. We were also expected to read the lesson in Chapel matins from time to time, and woe betide us if we had not rehearsed it. One colleague contrived to read into the lesson the instructions in the margin on one occasion. He was sternly advised by the Dean that 'that was unnecessary'. More restrictively, visitor hours were limited, so were exeats, and the gates were closed at night requiring an acrobatic act over the high garden fence to get back into college if we did not have special permission. By and large however, I do not remember any strong feeling of rebellion against the rules. I doubt that students of today would put up with them. But it was wartime, and we were brought up to be obedient. Their freedom has been hard won.

The climax of my first year was the Prelims and of my second year the degree Tripos examinations. Taking two full subjects (Physics and Chemistry) and two half subjects (Maths and Electronics) in the first year, and an additional half subject (Biochemistry) in the second, all but Maths involving practical as well as written exams, they seemed to go on for ever, especially alongside our English, History, Geography and Theology colleagues who appeared to be in and out of theirs and then enjoying themselves in no time. I later worked out the ratio was something like 14 exam periods to 4. Whether this meant the scientists were more thorough I do not know. Certainly taking History after the War, I learnt that short sharp exams in the old style could be just as testing as prolonged ones, though perhaps more arbitrary. I recall a colleague studying English complaining bitterly when he only achieved a pass degree that it was unfair to expect nightbirds to take exams before eleven in the morning. He later proved his point by rising to become Professor of English at Montreal.

I was fortunate to achieve first honours in both the Prelims and Tripos. But I cannot pretend that much if any of the scientific knowledge I acquired has stayed with me. Whatever a certain former Prime Minister may claim it does not do so unless one practises and keeps up to date, whether that be in research, industry or teaching. But the so-called 'scientific method' of observation, experiment and induction, or simply the analytical way of thinking, does, and in my experience remains for life. So, I suppose, does the basic understanding of what science is about – which to me is the discovery of nature. I have never regretted the time and effort I devoted to the sciences in my youth, even though I turned to other things after the War. That period remains as one of precious enlightenment of the physical world without which I do not think I would have since found such complementary pleasure studying the human world. 'Education is what survives when what has been learnt has been forgotten,' someone wrote. But it can also be 'the instruction of the intellect in the laws of Nature' (Huxley).

To come back to earth, I recall we celebrated the end of Prelims, a dozen of us, by going to see a film called *Helzapoppin* at the Cambridge Queen Street cinema. It was the first of the zany brand of films, long before Monty Python. We all at one point contrived to lean back in laughter at the same time with such force that our whole row collapsed. It was very Helzapoppin but, for us, just plain reaction after the long exams. For the poor people behind, and the cinema, it was perhaps rather less fun.

In the Summer vacation that followed, we were sent, after STC camp, on ten week secondments to war-time radio and radar factories to learn how the transmitters, receivers, direction and range finders, and counter devices we were going to use in the RAF, Army or Navy were made and developed. Both, as I recall, were a bit disappointing. The camps were the same old elementary drill and exercises and the radio industry, large though it was, proved unwilling to put themselves out much for us. I went to Murphy Radio in Welwyn. The workers were friendly enough and I was soon made a member of their cricket team. They taught me a thing or two about life, too. The management however chose not to give us work to do but simply left us to watch day after day the different 'shops' at work – metal-working, welding, painting, wiring and assembly, test-instruments and laboratories. 'All we do is stooge around nosing into everything and asking questions,' I wrote home. It became very boring – until one day I found a lone chemist who had been given a little hut and hose-pipe of his own and the job of making a new model Army Walkie-Talkie more waterproof, the Army having complained it leaked. His name was not Heath Robinson but it might have been. His ingenuity was to be found up and down Britain in war-time. On the other hand the disinclination of private industry to help train outsiders seemed a bit short-sighted. It was to be replicated, in my awareness, many years later in the Foreign Office, where we took in their people on secondment and gave them real jobs to do, and they took in ours but left them to make their own time and work. There was no profit in it, I suppose. I feel sure that, with all the pressures for interchanges between the civil service and industry today, things are now arranged with rather more genuine reciprocity.

In November '42, I was summoned to interview at Christ's College with a remarkable man, Dr C. P. Snow, college Master, scientist, administrator and, in his spare time, a well known novelist. I had met him before during my troubles over the Bursary scheme, which he played a part in founding, and he had proved helpful. 'Your choice of subject is entirely your own, the University is not a prison,' was his wise advice to me. This time he chaired an interview panel to decide whether, at the end of our courses, we should go into the Navy, Army, Air Force, Industry or Research. He was accompanied by a Pilot Officer Hoff, in very new RAF uniform, and some other man I think must have been from the Ministry. I met Hoff again, twenty-five years later, when he visited Canada and I was in the British High Commission there. He had by then become the organiser of the reverse brain-drain the Wilson Government had come to realise we so needed at that time – and very effective he was too, I believe, in finding British scientists in North America glad to be invited to return home. Snow and Hoff asked me my preference. I replied, 'RAF.' They replied 'Good,' and indicated the interview was at an end. I thought such an important decision in my life deserved a little more time and began asking questions about the other options. Hoff closed them promptly and Snow proffered his hand. It was one of the shortest interviews I ever had. But I wanted the RAF so I had no complaint. A few months later an RAF Commission Board of 'big-wigs' (so I wrote home) summoned me and a fellow student for interview in London and gave us each a full and friendly chat, sports predominating, followed by a medical and then a technical grilling by a Squadron Leader Signals 'even down to what composed a dry battery,' I wrote home. But I must have answered reasonably correctly for the papers went through. I was subsequently collared for another interview, this time for the new Operational Research service – the people who grilled servicemen returning from operations to advise on future mode and conduct. But the RAF took first call, and I never regretted it.

At College there was always an interval between the exams and the end of term. It gave us an opportunity to enjoy Cambridge at its summer best, punting on the river, playing College cricket and entertaining friends and family. To me it was a happy interlude of freedom, followed by an STC camp and then a hitch-hiking holiday through the Lake District and the lowlands of Scotland with a College friend, John Whinnerah, an athletics 'blue' who also went into the RAF and then teaching. I met him back at college after the War and again years later in Surrey, trying, like me, to raise money for Selwyn. I do not think either of us succeeded in raising much. But I was able to remind him of the occasion when we took a tram across Glasgow knowing we could not hitch that part of the journey, only to find from the ticket collector that a kind passenger in front had paid our fares but wished to remain anonymous. We were of course in uniform – Home Guard anyhow – and the fare was only one penny each. But to both of us it was a little act of Scottish hospitality we would not forget. Climbing Ben Nevis and tramping the Lowlands was also a good way of getting fit for the RAF. I was called up that August, 1943.

CHAPTER 7

# RAF in Wartime

## 1943–1946

Swedish friends once asked me, after enquiring about my war service and getting little response, why it was that British ex-servicemen were generally so reluctant to talk about their experiences in the War. I must have replied that it was the British way because their interesting rejoinder was: maybe, but they had also found the same among German ex-servicemen.

The truth, I suppose, is that those who survived, and we were fortunately the majority, must always feel deeply humbled by the memory of friends and colleagues and the many others who did not, as also by the sight of those who were maimed for life. Also, although packed with experience of men and places, camaraderie and conflict, war and peace, which those years telescoped for us, they were not of our choice. The great majority of us were in it for what was expressly called 'the emergency', and were glad to get back to the safety and comfort of our families and ways of life when it was over. In the RAF, and I feel sure in the other services, boasting of service exploits, or 'line-shooting' as it was called, was anyhow spurned, and anyone attempting it, especially in the Mess, would be promptly 'shot down'. Then there was the security damper: 'the enemy is listening' and 'loose talk costs lives' were the watchwords the war-time Ministry of Information drummed into us all, civilian and military everywhere, and the armed forces necessarily had their own security rules in addition. Add to this that I myself was never given, as my father would have enjoined, to 'opening my soul', and it is not perhaps surprising that my letters home, though regular and reasonably newsy, evoked periodic complaints that I 'never revealed what I was doing, nor my daily life'. Nor of course while hostilities continued, did they reveal where I was at any one time – the RAF rules on that were strict.

In fact I do not think any of the hundreds of letters I wrote to family and friends in the three years I was in the RAF ever attracted the Censor's blue pencil. As one who had from time to time to scan and if necessary censor my own troops' letters – a job I loathed, prying into their privacy as it did – I now admit that I could myself have been a bit more forthcoming in my own – and made the reading of them, and this chapter a bit more interesting! I shall recall what I can.

My RAF service was between the ages of 19 and 22, and not marked by any acts of killing that I know, nor of bravery. It covered twelve postings in England, Italy, France, Algeria and Egypt, never in any one place more than a few months and some only a matter of weeks. As a result I collected a string of service medals for being in so many theatres of war – Home, Italy, France and North Africa – which will doubtless look good on my coffin. But I gained none for gallantry, nor did I earn any. There was no occasion.

Those years remain vivid in the memory not for personal endeavour but because it was national and world tragedy and victory on the grandest scale and I lived through it. The course of that momentous period has been recorded in countless learned volumes, not least in the great man Churchill's own. Like the proverbial flea on the elephant I might occasionally have thought I knew which direction we should be taking wherever we were but, in truth, recall often not knowing whether I was on the trunk or the tail, let alone where the herd was or what we were chasing. However I did get about, if nothing else, and suppose someone must have thought it somehow contributed or I would not have been offered a permanent commission and promotion at the end. But it was marginal and minor. The rest is detail.

My RAF 'intake' was at the beginning of September 1943 at Cardington, the former airship base in Bedfordshire with its huge hangars still overshadowing the place. We were given blue battle dress, kitbag, button stick and a number – 1739095 in my case. We were registered as aircraftsmen lowest grade AC2, familiarly called 'erks', but told to report to the RAF Officers School at Cosford, near Wolverhampton – later to become famous as an athletics stadium. There we were given white bands to wear around our forage or side-caps, which marked us as Officer Cadets. For six weeks some three dozen of us were instructed in RAF administration, squarebashing, 'doubling' (the part I least liked – running at the trot with full equipment, rifle and helmet), field training (which I am on record as enjoying) and learning how to become an officer. Our instructors were a mixed but effective bunch of war-time officers stiffened by a few regular NCOs, who had developed to a fine art the manner of addressing us with the formal respect due to an officer cadet but the disdain they really felt. I still have a photo of us all together – 58 Course 'A' Squadron and Staff – a congenial enough group as I recall. We found time to organise rugby, lay on an embarrassingly amateur passing-out concert and visit Birmingham to see the Sadlers Wells Ballet with Robert Helpman and Moira Shearer (now, with her husband Ludovic Kennedy, my good neighbours in Avebury). We risked our lives to see her, the old Birmingham Bull Ring being lethal to cross at any time but most certainly in the blackout. We also survived the course, and 'passed out' to become Pilot Officers, able to wear the smart RAF officers' uniform with the thinnest of bands on the sleeve.

Half a century later, I was to be reminded that someone at that moment improbably pushed forms in front of us to sign whether or not we wished as officers to contribute to an ultimate old-age pension. As an 'erk' the State paid. As an officer it did not. With war service before me and pay of only 11 shillings a day I unhesitatingly declined. My old-age pension today is that much less for that decision. I guess most other young officers in the war did likewise. The pension scheme before Beveridge could be as mean as it was means-tested, even in war-time!

Our next posting was to the RAF holy of holies, the Staff College at Cranwell in Lincolnshire, not to become Staff but Signals Officers. It was a six month intensive course, some of it only recently instituted, to develop the corps of Signals Officers in the service. We were to learn about RAF radio and radar technically and of the communications systems on which all RAF operations depended, ground to air, air to ground, air to air and ground to ground, short, medium and long distance; also the equipment then in use and the more sophisticated direction-finders coming into service. We had to learn how to operate and service the transmitting and receiving equipment both in the air and on the ground, and of course the Morse code on which longer range telegraphy still depended. Flying was a necessary part of the training, not as pilots but as crew-members called Wireless Operators. Our first flights were for familiarity only, in an old Dragon Rapide biplane, affectionately known as the Pewkah Bomber, ever since some Canadian wag coined that name on a photo he sent home – and received a stern rebuke from some ignorant censor for revealing Air Force secrets – or so the story went. It was well named. The first page of my log book recorded in red ink a discomforting propensity to be air-sick in turbulence. Fortunately I was not alone, and soon found the cure lay in concentrating on the flying job instead of on the void below. We had great fun later in a trainer monoplane being thrown around the sky by a would-be stunt pilot, to test our nerve and to see whether we could tune a set and operate a Morse key against gravity in a loop. There were no such things as air sickness pills in those days.

Flying became the way of life thereafter; and has remained so for me ever since. The sea never held attraction beyond inshore bathing; we agreed to disagree at an early age. Flying was so much more convenient anyway. In old age I have to admit that the romance of small aircraft has now faded, as has being in the cockpit. A seat over the wing, generally the most stable part of the plane, flying high and fast for comfort, and with four good engines, is now my unexciting preference. In the war, we had no such choice. The planes before the Meteor were all slow and low flying compared with today's jets.

The job of Station Signals Officer which I was to become, involved flying up front with the pilot and other crew whenever needed or for testing equipment and facilities. But the main job was on the ground, commanding the Signals section, usually of similar strength to the Engineers, and directing both the station's air and ground communications systems and the servicing of the radio and direction-finding equipment of aircraft based there or in transit. Today much of this is done by computer. In those days it was all man-handled, riding of course on nature's electromagnetic waves but otherwise thanks to Marconi, Watson-Watt and later a few other geniuses working under the pressure of war. The Battle of Britain might not have been won, for all the brilliance and bravery of RAF Fighter Command, without the Radar detection system invented by Watson-Watt and developed by the RAF. The training ground for the thousands of Radar operators, who showed we could detect approaching enemy aircraft out of a squiggly mush on a relatively primitive oscilloscope screen, was I think Yatesbury, next door to where I now live in Wiltshire. Sadly all that remains today of that great school is a broken down hangar and a one-man hang-glider school. It should surely be memorialised.

Cranwell, for all its glory, did not become my favourite war-time place. It was rather isolated, and the Lincolnshire climate was not very friendly at that time of the year. I described it in a letter home as 'like Cambridge at its worst – cold, wet, drizzling and often foggy.' But I did add that 'the facilities of the place make up for that.' The College Mess and sports facilities were open to us and could not have been bettered. There was rugby, squash, badminton, tennis and golf and, while complaining home how hard the course worked us, I seemed nonetheless to find time to play them all (and doubtless cricket too if we had stayed the summer).

The war by this stage had at last turned in the Allied favour. September 1943 saw the Allied invasion of Italy and that country's unconditional surrender – although with the Germans well established there, we were still a long way from Rome let alone the crucial Po valley in the north. At the Tehran Conference in November, Roosevelt, Stalin and Churchill agreed that the invasion of Northern France must be the top Allied priority, the capture of Rome second (and especially its airfields from which we could bomb Southern Germany) and an amphibious landing in the South of France third. At least that is what we now know. Also that Churchill wanted to use such Allied forces in the Mediterranean as were not needed for Normandy to continue the offensive in Italy under General Alexander, but as 1944 progressed Roosevelt insisted on the South of France invasion being more important. I knew little of all this at the time but was to find myself a pawn in the great argument and change of strategy some months later.

There were some Poles at Cranwell who had escaped from their country to fight with the RAF in the specially formed Polish Air Force. One was on our course and I met the others through him. Their names held too many consonants for tongue-tied British to pronounce, so each accepted an anglicised abbreviation like Stan. They were deeply upset by the Tehran Conference and Russian proposals to annex Eastern Poland. As if to rub it in, a bunch of Polish youngsters arrived at Cranwell at that time, ostensibly to be trained for the Polish Air Force although some were officially too young; it was apparently the only way of getting them out of Russian Siberia where they had been transported in 1939/40. We were reminded that we had gone to war to save Poland from the Germans and now it was being given to their equally hated neighbours the Russians. I was to meet more of their compatriots in Italy. The Poles carried the reputation of being passionate lovers of the local girls wherever they went, but even more passionate fighters. It was bitter to see them engulfed by the Russians behind the Iron Curtain after the war, but wonderful to see them break free and lead the collapse of the Soviet bloc forty years on, and now, all being well, about to join the European Union. I do not know Poland but I do know they are a remarkable people.

The same cannot regrettably be said of a certain wartime British official who thought he could save His Majesty's Government much money and treat the Services to a special Christmas by purchasing large stocks of immature wine cheap from newly liberated French North Africa. I recall the Cranwell Mess Christmas dinner 1943 as an unmitigated disaster with the cream of the RAF college laid out in all directions. We learnt later that most messes up and down the country suffered similarly. Hitler missed a golden opportunity to invade that night. I have never heard what happened to the foolish official. His ears must have burnt from one end of the country to the other that Christmas.

Happily that was not my abiding memory of Cranwell. The isolation and climate aside, it was a very fine College to be at, a well-run course, admirable sports facilities and good company. In the distance, too, we were constantly reminded by the rumble of bomber aircraft, of one of the RAF's great contributions to the war effort. The Lincolnshire stations of Bomber Command were relentlessly active.

Before that winter was out, we were invited to state a preference for the Command we wished to join. I was tempted by both Bomber and Fighter (though not, for sea reasons, Coastal) but decided that I did not want to get stuck at stations at home, big or small, at that stage of the war, and that the most interesting work to be done as a Signals officer might be in the growing Transport Command, especially if one could get abroad. My wish was granted and, after a final scamper over the Lincolnshire countryside in a week of field exercises, I was instructed to report to Transport Command HQ at Hendon. So were three colleagues who had been with me through Cardington, Cosford and Cranwell. Five others joined us there for a group interview the outcome of which proved a happy turning point in my life.

We forgathered in a wide meeting room, with a large Mercator map on the wall, peppered with little flags. They marked Transport Command's Group and Wing headquarters and numerous Staging Posts (airfield stations) particularly in the Western World and Middle East. We were nine rookie Signals Officers. An HQ Staff Wing Commander made a stage entrance to join us and proceeded to wave a long pointer at three broad areas of the map: the UK, the North Atlantic and the Mediterranean and Middle East. 'We want three of you for each area,' he said. 'I'll take one or two questions, if you have any, and then leave you to decide among yourselves.' Someone – I think it was me – asked what the 'North Atlantic' meant. 'Anything from Belize on the equator to Nassau in the Bahamas, or Reykjavik in Iceland to Montreal in Canada,' he replied, and left the room declaring he would be back in twenty minutes to hear our decisions. It was astute man-management. In discussion, three soon diffidently staked claims to stay at home because they were married. Two others, as I recall, wanted home postings for personal reasons but accepted the married must have preference. The rest of us pondered. I remember staring at the map and suddenly seeing what appeared to be a shaft of light flash across from the UK to the Middle East and back to Italy and France. I cannot think this was a clever RAF trick to get some of us to go to the least popular of the three areas. Subliminal tricksters could doubtless do it today but not then. It must have been some form of intuition. Or so I like to think. Anyhow when the Wing Commander returned to ask our decisions, I found myself leading the field in volunteering for the Mediterranean and Middle East. Two others followed, one the stalwart son of a regular RAF Wing Commander called Bradbury, and the other a keen fellow called Gamble. I remember their names because we left Britain together three weeks later for Cairo. The six others went their various ways, one I think happy to Nassau, one unhappy to Reykjavik because he had found a girlfriend at Cranwell, one I know not where, and three to home stations. It was an extraordinary episode that determined far more for each of us than we would then know, and not least for me.

Some days later, I was in London to receive my embarkation instructions from the Hendon HQ, and decided to stay the night at the Nuffield House Officers Club in Halkin Street near Hyde Park corner. I am not sure that my intuition served me well this time, unless it was to seek adventure. No sooner had I bedded down on the top floor of the Club than wave upon wave of German bombers came over central London and the ack-ack guns in Hyde Park gave them barrage after barrage. It was bedlam. Then, the following morning a strange plane appeared overhead, low flying and slow enough for everyone to be called out to see it circle, until it suddenly dipped to explode somewhere I know not in central London. It was the first flying-bomb, the ram-jet V1, soon to be dubbed the Doodlebug. Hitler had long threatened his 'secret weapon'. This was it, and the forerunner of the more sophisticated guided ballistic V2 rocket. As my mother presciently put it: 'a horrible sign of things to come if we don't finish with wars for ever.' It was a troubling development. Thousands more were to strike Southern England in the months to come, renewing the blitz just as the Allies opened the Second Front in Normandy. They caused much fear and damage but, I have since read, could have done much worse had RAF Intelligence not already identified the launchers at Peenemunde and prepared some fighter defence against them. I can still see that sinister portent of things to come flying slowly over central London in broad daylight.

My embarkation leave was made the more memorable by the launch of Overlord – the 2nd Front – on 6 June and the manner in which I learnt of it. I had paid a brief farewell visit to my favourite UK city Edinburgh and was hitch-hiking down the A1 overnight, perched uncomfortably on the engine cowling of a goods lorry, when the driver and I noticed intense activity on all the RAF bomber stations within view in Lincolnshire and, come dawn, waves of Flying Fortresses going out from the American bases in East Anglia. It was the great event we had been waiting for but the Allied Command had maintained the time and place an extraordinarily well kept secret. By good fortune I had arranged to visit the House of Commons that morning, just out of curiosity before going abroad. Kenneth Turpin, at that time assistant Private Secretary to Clement Attlee, had kindly arranged a pass for me. Entering the House of Commons I found a buzz of excitement and was soon ushered into the gallery, with a naval officer interested in the colonial debate to follow. We were just in time to find what the buzz was about. We might have guessed, but neither of us could believe our luck. Into the crowded chamber lumbered the Prime Minister, Winston Churchill, to make his historic announcement. He first formally announced the liberation of Rome and paid tribute to the Allied forces in Italy, and then declared: 'I have also to announce to the House that during the night and the early hours of this morning the first of a series of landings in force upon the European continent has taken place ... upon the coast of France ... an immense armada ... massed airborne landings ... landings on the beaches ... vast operation ... land, air and sea forces ... There are already hopes that actual tactical surprise has been attained ...' Mr Churchill had clearly been up all night, and his speech was slurred, but he gave it his all, as ever, and it was an extraordinary occasion to witness.

My naval acquantance and I felt we could not just leave at that point. We stayed for part of the Colonial debate introduced by the then Labour Secretary of State for the Colonies Arthur Creech-Jones. It was inevitably an anti-climax, and I remember nothing of the important policies he

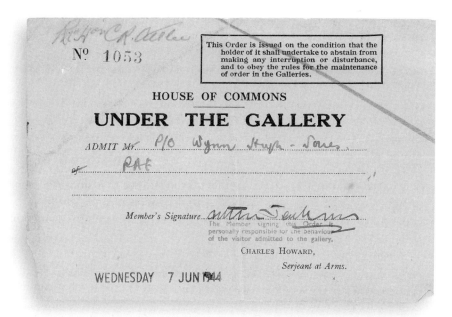

N⁰ 1053

This Order is issued on the condition that the holder of it shall undertake to abstain from making any interruption or disturbance, and to obey the rules for the maintenance of order in the Galleries.

HOUSE OF COMMONS

## UNDER THE GALLERY

ADMIT Mr. P/O Wynn Hugh-Jones

of RAF

Member's Signature

*The Member signing this Order is personally responsible for the behaviour of the visitor admitted to the gallery.*

CHARLES HOWARD,

*Serjeant at Arms.*

WEDNESDAY 7 JUN 1944

House of Commons pass issued on behalf of Clement Attlee, which enabled me fortuitously to be there when Winston Churchill announced to Parliament the opening of the Second Front.

doubtless announced. But then I too had been up all that memorable night – and still have the House of Commons pass under the Rt. Hon Clement Attlee's introduction as a reminder.

Before embarking abroad I had a last few days at home, only to find that American forces had taken over the Ludlow racecourse and that Ludlow people were finding the tendency of some GIs to drift bored around the streets, chewing gum and greeting every girl in sight, a little strange. But this was war and they were on our side so Ludlow put up with them. I also found that my brother, having finished his medical training and joined the Army Medical Service had, almost simultaneously with me, volunteered for service abroad – in his case, as it turned out, with the Royal Artillery in Normandy in early July. It was hard on our mother, all too reminiscent of when in World War I she had had to say good-bye to her husband for three years Army service abroad and her mother for ever, as it turned out, to Australia. But she took it with her usual courage, enjoining my brother by letter to be his own self, 'thorough, conscientious and careful' and 'God be with you', and to me something similar but, owing to my rapid movements once abroad and the vagaries of the service post, it apparently ended up months later 'returned to sender'. Fortunately this proved a one-off occurrence. Unlike World War I, service mail this time was not constantly lost by U-boat action, at least at this stage of World War II, and I cannot remember anyone abroad feeling they had to number their letters as my parents did in World War I to keep track of those never received.

That same momentous month, June 1944, saw my two colleagues and me on our way to Cairo via what is still today the premier RAF Transport Command base Lyneham in Wiltshire (a few miles only from where I now live), and the now derelict airfield at St Mawgan in Cornwall. It was a glorious summer's evening and the full orchestra of one of the BBC Promenade Concerts wafted across the camp from someone's radio as we waited for dark to take off. It proved a long journey, seven hours in a DC3, a wonderful war-horse but it only travelled at about 150 mph, and to avoid unfriendly enemy guns we had to take a wide circle of the Bay of Biscay to reach Gibraltar the following morning. It was not the most comfortable of flights, alternately seated on one of the metal benches either side of the cabin, with a flange stuck in one's back intended for some military purpose or other, or laid out on some 'Mae West' life jackets on the floor at the back to try to get some sleep. There were two naval captains with us; they sat bolt upright in best dress all night, like flamingos sleeping on one leg. We junior officers of the junior Service were suitably impressed. Some time later, in a letter home, I recalled that day of departure from England as 'a mad rush in the morning ... last minute attempt to insure my baggage ... feeling of elation on finding the RAF had reserved me my first-ever first-class seat on the crowded train from Paddington ... the efficiency of our handling at Lyneham and St Mawgan ... the scenic glory and splendour of the Cornish coast ... coloured every hue that only the evening sun and England can produce.'

Gibraltar in those days was a bustling fortress of strategic importance and renown. We stayed only to refuel but it looked and felt like its name 'The Rock'. Today, or the last time I visited it ten years ago anyhow, it looked and felt, sadly, like a seedy outpost of Empire and offshore smugglers' den. Perhaps some day a sensible accommodation with Spain will be found that resolves the sovereignty question while preserving self-government for the Gibraltarians

From Gibraltar we flew to Algiers, to spend a week there at a transit camp trying to get onward flight seats to Cairo. We were priority four, even lower than the crowd of Texan oilmen I eventually shared an RAF York with to Tunis, El Adem in Libya and Cairo. The Texans were going on to Saudi Arabia, where I probably met some again when I myself was posted there in the Foreign Service five years later. They had flown out from the USA to Oran and evidently had a ball there visiting local cabarets and sexual 'exhibitions' while awaiting onward flights. Their candid accounts, openly exchanged, filled our journey from one end to the other – and taught me a thing or two I had never previously imagined. Poor fellows, they were not likely to get any more of that where they were going in Arabia.

At Cairo I had to report to Transport Command HQ 216 Group, housed in a utility conversion of a palace belonging to the Belgian magnate Baron Emphraim in Heliopolis, once an ancient city of Egypt, now a residential suburb of Cairo. My two colleagues had arrived there before me, they having asserted their wish to take the first seats available from Algiers more than I had. One had promptly been sent down the Persian Gulf to a Staging Post at Shaibah, Sharjah or Bahrain, I am not sure which, all wretchedly isolated and unhealthy; and the other to Palestine. I was in luck. The Chief Signals Officer, Group Captain Watson, received me in his office, flanked by his deputy Wing Commander Long and a Squadron Leader Swaine. 'Well, do you know where you want to go?' he asked rhetorically. 'Yes, Sir,' I replied. 'Oh, where then?' he asked. 'Italy, Sir,' I heard myself reply. 'Why Italy?' he rejoined. 'Because that is where the action is, Sir,' I answered. 'Will you have him, Squadron Leader Swaine?' the Group Captain promptly asked of his colleague. 'Yes, Sir,' came the quiet reply. 'Right, then you can report to 249 Wing Headquarters in Naples,' he said to me. 'Yes Sir, thank you Sir,' I remember saying, as I saluted, turned on my heel and left, hardly believing my ears.

I dare say they had me slated for that theatre, for some reason or another, anyhow. But it was strange to see how my path was following that shaft of light on the map at Hendon. I was also to follow it to its head in France before the war in Europe was over – and then, by way of Algeria and Italy again, back to its tail, in Egypt.

Cairo struck me, like Algiers, as hot, noisy and smelly, at least at that time of the year but my week there, waiting again for an air passage, gave me a taste to revisit that city, and particularly the Pyramids. I wrote home prosaically – as I hear so many tourists say over my hedge when first visiting the great neolithic stone circle in my home village of Avebury today – 'someone must have put an incredible amount of time, energy and patience into building them.' Also enjoyable were Cairo's day and night vibrancy, and of course the absence of any blackout, but not its hygiene nor its scavenging kite-hawks. There was much more of that city and historic country to learn about when I returned eighteen months later.

Naples was a sad reflection of its former glory when I reached it on 9 July 1944. I described it home as 'a shambles – wreckage, filth and smells abound. But there is still music.' The city had long declined from the days when, before the nineteenth-century unification of Italy, it had been the capital of a Kingdom. But it was still a major Mediterranean port, and war prize for the Allies when we drove the Germans out in October 1943. The port had since been restored much damage remained. Also the great volcano Vesuvius had chosen then of all times to erupt, leaving rivers of solidified lava and sheets of black dust scarring the landscape, and destroying the coastal road south of the city. It was still a beautiful bay but anything but romantic when I reported to HQ 249 Wing, in the suburb of Portici.

My short time there was unexciting. The staff work, as a supernumerary Signals Officer, was undemanding, flies and mosquitoes plagued us day and night, so did gyppy-tummy, and a week in hospital with pleurodynia did not help. But a visit to the famous San Carlo Opera in Naples restored some spirit. And the stories of current Neopolitan enterprise kept us enthralled. One was that a public bus trapped in a crowded political meeting in one of the city's main squares, had been found, when the crowd dispersed, to be on chocks, the wheels and precious tyres having been spirited away. Another was that an epidemic of lost Allied military caps had been found by the military police to be ingenious thieving by little urchins hiding in the laundry baskets on their mother's heads. My favourite was when the leading black marketeers called a strike for more police protection for their illegal stalls in the centre of town; and won it. It was jackal land in the wake of the war, and that war was still raging north of Rome.

In early August I was suddenly told to pack my bag, help get equipment and a small convoy together and be ready by early morning to drive to the Adriatic front, north of Ancona. It was action at last. I was to be Signals Officer of a small unit, under an experienced Army liaison Lieutenant as CO, who had seen service in the abortive Norwegian campaign. A third officer was Cyphers, I had a good signals sergeant to accompany me, and there were half a dozen men. Our purpose was to establish a forward staging post (No 61 SP Det D) for RAF transport aircraft to use at a large but empty Italian airfield at Jesi. It was to be a tiny part of the great push north about to be made by the Allied Forces. The Germans were by then on their so-called Gothic defence Line, which ran across Italy from Pesaro on the Adriatic coast between Ancona and Rimini, to north of Florence in the centre and Pisa on the west coast. Despite heavy troop and equipment transfers to France, General Alexander, Commander-in-Chief of the Allied Forces in Italy, still had the American 5th Army under General Mark Clark on the west, the British 8th Army and New Zealanders in the centre and the Polish Corps on the Adriatic coast. Strongly supported by Mr Churchill, he and the Mediterranean Commander-in-Chief, General Maitland-Wilson, believed that if they could break the Gothic Line they would then command the great Po valley of Northern Italy and could not only throw the Germans out of Italy but drive on into Southern Germany and Austria, to help General Eisenhower and his 'Overlord' forces advancing through France and the Low Countries. I myself knew little of this at the time but sensed it soon enough at Jesi.

To get there took three full days, whereas today it would take less than one. For once, RAF efficiency failed. At such short notice the only vehicles we could get should all have been on the scrap heap, including the CO's jeep, my signals van, the utility truck and the inevitable bowser. They all broke down on the first leg to Rome, one after the other, and beyond our resources to repair, although my enterprising sergeant did improbably find a lady's garter on the side of the road to replace our signals van fan belt until it, too, broke. I entered the Eternal City in the early hours hitch-hiking on the back of an American Army jeep, commanded by my CO to go and seek help. The rescue was rather more competent, though my colleagues complained bitterly that Mussolini may have successfully drained the Pontine Marshes of water but not of the mosquitoes who fed on their misery half the night. The main drive Rome to Jesi went better, despite the tortuous mountain route over the Apennines via war-torn Arezzo, captured three weeks previously, and innumerable diversions off war-damaged roads. I wrote home, 'I've done quite a bit of touring recently, and seen some of the finest country and scenery outside North Wales.'

Jesi was front line and exciting. We made camp in a corner of the airfield, set up our medium and short range wireless communications (not without difficulty in that mountainous land) and awaited events. They were only hours in coming. Polish Army tanks rumbled passed all night, only to return when it was found that the Germans had conscript Poles lined up to face them. Our Poles would fight anything but, understandably, rather not their slave compatriots. The Army rapidly changed its dispositions. But then things seemed to stall. The Germans continued to shell the port of Ancona, over our heads. I had to go there from time to time for stores and found it in the words of an Army friend, 'a hole if ever there was one'. Like so many other towns across middle and southern Italy, it was badly war-torn.

The airfield and village of Jesi on the other hand, had somehow escaped serious damage. The airfield buildings had been destroyed by the retreating Germans but the runway was intact and there were no extensive minefields to contend with. An RAF Fighter Wing later joined us. We had the interesting task, as I later wrote home, 'of handling every big bug the Army has, excluding Montomery.' They seemed to come in droves, including notably Generals Alexander and Maitland-Wilson. Then came Mr Churchill himself, with General Alan Brooke CIGS. By this time the Fighter Wing CO had asserted his senior right to do the honours. So we did our little signals bit and otherwise took a back seat. But it was inspiring to see the great man again, this time so far from home – and, like us, dressed in khaki drill, for it was very hot there in August. Also to receive his familiar V-sign greeting and hear his words of encouragement. He was given a resounding cheer from all assembled. Those same troops may have largely voted against him in the following year's general election. But that was as Conservative Party leader. As war leader of the nation he reigned supreme in our respect. So I think did General (later Field Marshal Lord) Alexander, in his quiet way. I was to enjoy working briefly with him in a voluntary capacity many years later. He had the humility of true greatness.

The great push stalled not by act of the Germans but by Allied decision, insisted by the Americans against Churchill's better judgement, to withdraw seven Army divisions and a considerable part of the Allied Air Forces from Italy for the invasion of the South of France. Churchill's 'Triumph and Tragedy' dates that decision at 'early July' 1944, and his visit to the Adriatic front as 17 August. In between times Alexander and his depleted forces had nevertheless forced fourteen reinforced German divisions back to the Gothic Line from their previous line of Ancona – Arezzo – Rosignano (south of Leghorn). Churchill's tour had evidently taken him first to Maitland-Wilson's Allied Mediterranean Forces HQ at the royal palace of Caserta outside Naples, where he also held difficult discussions with Marshal Tito from Yugoslavia, and then to Corsica and off-shore St Tropez to witness the 'Anvil-Dragoon' landings on the south of France. He wrote after his meeting with Alexander at Jesi that his object now was 'to keep what we have got in Italy, which should be sufficient since the enemy has withdrawn four of his best divisions.' But he wrote also that he still hoped to break the Gothic Line, into the Po valley and ultimately advance by Trieste and the Ljubljana gap to Vienna (presumably to get there before the Russians), and that he had 'told Alexander to be ready for a dash with armoured cars.' That, we now know, is what must have been discussed at Alexander's HQ that day near Jesi.

Three weeks later I became one of those transferred from Italy to 'Anvil-Dragoon' and France. I wrote home that, the inevitable 'gyppy-tummy' aside, my spell at Jesi had been very enjoyable particularly 'being mobile, in the open, and my own boss as far as signals are concerned,' with plenty of work and full of events and action. My CO was in hospital for a while following a jeep accident, and my cypher colleague was too with malaria, so some of the time I had everything to do for the unit from operations to welfare. I also moved our Mess into a commandeered flat in the village. It was owned by a fascist lady who had fled to Rome – no doubt to join the Count Ciano coterie I was to find still in being very long after his death, when I served at our Embassy in Rome twenty years later.

The village of Jesi did not welcome us, so we had limited opportunity to fraternise. There was one occasion however when a fourth officer joined us, fluent in Italian from having been a Thomas Cook agent in Rome before the war, and he invited in three young ladies from a neighbouring flat for a drink. Bored with his monopolising the conversation I recall asking him for something to say in Italian to the nearest Signorina, but got it so disastrously wrong that all three shrieked and fled. Instead of asking her how she called herself I apparently asked her, in slang, how she performed. It brings to mind another occasion this time suffered by an Army friend later in Venice. In his best Italian he asked some local youths how he could find a gondola to cross the Grand Canal, only to find them dissolve in mirth. He had apparently mispronounced the boat

Winston Churchill arriving at our airfield at Jesi, near Ancona, Italy, with Generals Alan Brooke and Alexander, August 1944.

and inadvertently used the slang for condom. The perils of foreign languages! One other silly episode in Jesi was when I treated my fellow officers to a case of Spumante bought at a vinicole in the hills. Like the Christmas wine at Cranwell, it turned out to be freshly bottled – and proceeded to pepper us with exploding corks all evening. Some sharp Australian troops had apparently beaten me to the vinicole's good stocks. The perils of Messing Officer! But the incident did teach me something about communication. Finding some Polish soldiers in those same hills mournfully surveying the wreckage of their utility truck over the edge but fortunately none of them badly injured, we found we could converse in pidgin Italian quite easily while the local Italians who gathered around pleaded they could not understand a word we said. British, and evidently Polish, troops developed languages of their own during the war.

I reached France by air from Jesi via Naples in early September 1944, three weeks after the 7th Allied Army of French and American divisions and a mixed American and British airborne division, under US General Paton and the joint code-names of 'Anvil' and 'Dragoon', had successfully landed on the Riviera and swept up the Rhone Valley. My destination was not the sunny south but a former French Air Force training airfield at Salon in western Provence. It was in poor shape, with only a cratered grass runway, and no habitable buildings. Also, it was plagued with mosquitoes as vicious as any I have encountered anywhere, and we had to suffer them under canvas – I with no net to begin with because my kit bag had disappeared *en route*. We were sent there to establish Transport

Command's No 103 Staging Post and my job as Signals Officer was as at Jesi but on a larger scale. I was promoted to the rank of Flying Officer, a purely automatic occurrence after one year, like 2nd to 1st Lieutenant in the Army. I had a good Welsh sergeant and bunch of men who bore my youthful exuberance with respectful tolerance. When the word came that we were to move to the former French airbase at Istres because the Americans preferred Marignane, the future Marseilles airport, I took a party of them on a recce and we set about establishing a radio transmitter and receiving station there and then. The small building I chose was a partial wreck. Like all the main buildings and much of the airfield it had been mined by the Germans before they left. But it still had a roof on it, and space around for the high masted aerials we were going to need. The French Army had undertaken to clear the mines and had a platoon of sad-faced German prisoners-of-war doing the dirty work. My sergeant did not trust them. Before I had got very far inspecting the site, he called me to be careful and resourcefully found a flock of sheep, which he proceeded to shepherd over every yard with the expertise of a Welsh sheep-farmer. None blew up, so we staked the site as ours and worked that day clearing and repairing it as best we could.

Driving back along the airport road at dusk I sighted a large house in its own quad, with some signs of life within, and decided on the spur of the moment to explore it as a possible billet for the night to save returning to Salon and back the following day. On approaching it I found myself warmly welcomed by some scantily-clad ladies emerging through a beaded curtain, and sounds of merriment within. Hastily declining their invitation I returned to find my lads watching in delight. No one had ever sought to billet them in a brothel before! That place, we later learnt, remained in business through French, German, American and British occupation of Istres airfield and, for all I know may still be there. The oldest profession in the world knew no fraternisation bounds.

We were commended later by our Wing Chief Signals Officer in Naples – the same admirable Squadron Leader Swaine who had accepted me in Cairo – for our enterprise at Istres, not least in finding at neighbouring bases, and converting to our needs, abandoned German radio equipment, power generators and the like, some of it like their high telescopic aerial masts better than anything our own RAF could supply. We were to be particularly glad of those strong masts later when the Mistral winds came, blowing down the Rhone valley from the Swiss Alps as they do every winter, and across our bleak plateau with hurricane force. It was not the warmest place in the Mediterranean theatre to be that winter. I wrote home on New Year's Eve, 'Christmas morning we all had rather a shock, waking up to find a foot of snow around – South of France my eye! ... It has been freezing hard too, and now the local gales have begun again – you can guess the strength of the wind by the fact that a small wooden hut, partially sheltered, was moved bodily on its standing this morning.' (It was one of the High Frequency Direction-finding stations I had set up on the perimeter of the airfield.) Fortunately a French hutted encampment on the edge of the village remained intact so we had good if crowded accommodation, with the luxury of running water and electric light. But on the airfield it was all self-made and the cold so penetrating that I remember doing my desk-work in a greatcoat, with a Calor stove between the knees. When my brother wrote from the Army in Holland quipping me for being on the sunny Riviera, he received a rather unbrotherly reply suggesting, in the terminology of the time that he 'should get his knees browned'!

There was inevitably some feeling between forces in the Mediterranean theatre and those in Northern France and the Low Countries at the time, because the former had to serve three years abroad before getting home leave (four years if unmarried) whereas the latter, 'subject to the exigencies of the service', could apparently claim it after six months. Also, of course, the Italian theatre, in Churchill's later words, 'had made great sacrifices of whole armies for the Western Front'. But I do not remember this bothered us unduly at Istres, especially when we found we had ourselves been transferred to Home Command over our heads. We were soon busy handling more and more traffic in troops and dignitaries between the two theatres, and beyond, and I found myself with increasing communication and servicing requirements and an ever-growing section to manage. It was interesting work, fulfilling, we were told, both the war need of trooping and a peace need, paving the way for the civil airlines when the time came.

Churchill recounts that the original American proposal at the Tehran Conference for 'Anvil' was for a descent in the South of France to be just before or just after D-Day. But first we had to capture Rome. Delay in achieving that and a shortage of landing craft following transfers to 'Overlord', caused a two-month postponement to 15 August. The airborne and sea landings went very well (the former being vividly reported for the BBC by that eminent war correspondent Godfrey Talbot). The Germans were over-run, tens of thousands taken prisoner and the bulk fled up the Rhone valley, leaving few bridges intact but mile upon mile of abandoned armoured vehicles of all types. I drove up that route to Lyons, with a couple of colleagues, a few weeks later, to assist a small forward detachment of ours there. An extraordinary military scrapheap lined both sides of the road endlessly – except for tyres and other bits already salvaged by the French. We found Lyons reawakening under Franco-American occupation, after years of Vichy and German rule, but still not familiar with blue RAF uniforms. A few RAF there before us had even been mistaken for Germans! – 'most uncomfortable,' I commented home.

Operation 'Anvil-Dragoon' enabled the Americans to pour in more troops and equipment through Toulon and Marseilles once the French contingent had captured those ports (against strong German resistance), and the Allied 7th Army was able to link up with General Eisenhower's 'Overlord' forces at Sombernon in Burgundy by 11 September. It had all gone very well, because of Allied amphibious strength, pre-bombardment, air superiority, relative weakness of the German forces reduced to reinforce Normandy and local support from the French Resistance movement. It then gave Eisenhower an extra Army. As Churchill later recorded with sorrow, however, it did not achieve its original purpose because it was so late starting and, by denuding the Allied forces in Italy, it put off victory on that front until the following Spring. It was a brilliant operation but in his view (and presumably that of the British Chiefs of Staff, who had judged it 'unnecessary') it was at heavy strategic cost. The Americans believed otherwise. There was no difference while it was under way however. It seems to have been Allied co-operation at its best.

For me it was rather over before it started. There was still sniping in Marseilles when I visited that city soon after arrival, and a few pockets elsewhere. But our job was to occupy an appropriate airfield and create there a new air transport facility between Britain and the Mediterranean. By the turn of the year 1944 that task was completed, at least so far as my signals facilities were concerned. So I readily accepted an invitation to visit my new Wing HQ in Paris, and took my worldly-wise assistant, a Lancastrian called Clegg, with me. We went for three days and stayed eight, much of the time spent at the airport seeking a flight back in the difficult snow and icy conditions of the time. But 'I certainly had my fill of Paris,' I wrote home, 'and came away having got rid of an awful lot of money.' I was to get to know it much better a decade later in the Foreign Service, and it is to this day my favourite European city. On that first occasion I could only taste its vivacity, culture and entertainment, and in the most unfavourable circumstances of winter, leaking shoes, high prices and, more profoundly, the obvious sufferings of the Parisians. Only four months previously they had been under German occupation in their own capital; and they were still visibly short of food, fuel and clothing. In contrast – I wrote home – 'there seemed to be an awful lot of "voluntary" workers from Britain having a good time at government expense.' Some of our MPs had evidently noticed this too for there was an outcry about it in Parliament at the time. There always seem to be some in war, as in peace, who ride on the misfortune of others. I have no doubt, however, there were many more in and around the city quietly trying to help the French restore their capital and pride. I had the pleasure of getting to know some of them when I served there in the Embassy.

Back at Istres there occurred the first of three bad car accidents I have had in my life – and been very lucky to survive each. This one was in a jeep driving back with a colleague from a visit to Aix, along a straight stretch of road flanked by a low stone wall and deep drop on either side. In the sunshine I failed to notice that the mud farm vehicles had left on the road was wet and treacherous. The jeep skidded into the wall, lurched half over but luckily rolled back and skidded on its side until it stopped. We clambered out unscathed, to be greeted by a little old lady in black offering us a tot of eau-de-vie. Where she came from in that open countryside, and where she disappeared to once we had drunk her nectar and thanked her, I do not know. She must have been sent by the Gods. My second bad accident was in London ten years later, knocked upside down in a soft-top Austin into the Duke of Rutland's basement in Eaton Place by a speeding 'Friday afternoon' laundry van. By coincidence there was a French connection there too. My companion was a charming French lady I had just met. My third was in Rome on a hot afternoon in the early 1960s, struck by a tram whose driver had fallen asleep on a long straight stretch of road. On that occasion it was the solid frame of my old hand-built Healey that saved me. In Rome traffic you needed a tank for safety in those days. But I have been very fortunate – and long learnt that on today's roads caution is much the better part of valour.

We had many interesting visitors in transit at Istres, not least a Russian Trades Union delegation who spent a night with us *en route* to London. None of us had met Russians before and they were very formal in the Mess. We made a semi-circle around the bar in silence until one of them finally broke the ice by marching across, clicking his heels and offering me a long cigarette. Embarrassed, I remember thrusting it in my mouth and watching him as he did the same to each of my colleagues, then he turned on his heel, marched straight back to me, took the cigarette out of my mouth just as I was struggling to light it, and thrust it back in the other way. Their cigarettes had hollow cardboard stems, and lighting the wrong end smelt and tasted foul. We laughed and the Russians roared. They proved a convivial lot after that, even though we had no tongue in common. I kept the burnt cigarette end for years, as a memento of my first Russian encounter.

The rub came when home command decided my job merited higher rank and they had surplus Flight Lieutenant Signals at home. I was reminded of the old troopers' song, 'Bless 'em all … you'll get no promotion this side of the ocean …', and went off disgruntled to Algiers. I had enjoyed Istres, despite the winter weather, and had become Welfare, Entertainment and Sports as well as Signals Officer. Also I had begun to meet the local French and even attended some community dances once General de Gaulle had lifted his disapproval of such entertainment, 'while Frenchmen were fighting and dying in the front line.' I liked their animation and respected their fortitude and family spirit that had seen them through the occupation. They lacked most things but never begged.

I was now 21, having spent my coming-of-age at Istres taking the afternoon off to play football against a local side and, with colleagues, visiting the French 'pictures' and a local estaminet or two. Being still youthful but responsible for a hundred and more men, I chose to keep my age to myself. So there was no 21st party. It did not seem to matter.

Algiers was dull in comparison. We were not in the city but at the big Maison Blanche airfield some miles outside. Our unit, No 72 Staging Post, was well-established with little creative work to do but fathom the new flight control system Transport Command was developing for its own and future civil routes. I wrote home disconsolately that 'my luck seemed to have turned ... I was back overseas proper again ... faced with another two or three years before home leave ... remote from the war ... and the first time I had taken over from someone instead of starting from scratch.' But, I added optimistically, 'I know something good will come of it.' It did. Our accommodation, on an old but prosperous farm, proved to be comfort itself after Italy and France, and I was able to indulge in 'my second hot bath since coming overseas'. That was rudely interrupted by a spell in Algiers city helping out at our HQ. I described it home as, 'quite a change after living out in the wilds so long ... I have a one-room billet in the flat of an old French lady 3rd floor up in a tightly squeezed block of flats ... The street noise, cars, trams, horns and hubbub of the Arab world make a most unholy din.' But I was able to go to the opera and see some remarkably good performances in the circumstances, and back at Maison Blanche we soon had football, hockey, basketball, tenniquots, volley-ball, cricket and tennis going. They were needed not just to keep the troops fit but to buoy their spirits now that the end of the war in Europe seemed in sight and the talk was all about demobilisation. My personal comfort also benefited from the reappearance of my lost kit bag. I had last seen its contents of clothing, battledress, sportswear, writingcase and a heavy book called *The Abyss* which I inexplicably carried everywhere (without ever reading), back at Naples. I never discovered the RAF clerk who found it and brought us together again, but record my thanks to him now and forever. *The Abyss* is still on my bookshelves, but so heavy on the lap it remains unread.

Our remoteness from the war was brought home to us one day in Algiers when we heard on the Mess radio a British Government announcement: 'You are winning this war. But you can lose the peace if you associate with German civilian people. Keep away from them.' This was the non-fraternisation policy meant for those in Germany. I remarked home: 'Here we are, about a thousand miles away – some war!' V-E Day, when it came in early May, was almost as remote. We heard of great celebrations at home, but abroad, or certainly where we were, it had none of the immediacy it had in Britain and Northern Europe. The news of it was of course what we had long awaited, but it had been well trailed and first thoughts of everyone abroad were now on when they would qualify for home and release. We did celebrate V-E Day at Maison Blanche, or V-E Day plus one anyhow, with an inter-Allied athletics tournament I helped to organise. It turned out to be the hottest day of the year so far, nearly 100°F in the shade, with high humidity, preceded by a Sirocco (the summer hot wind off the Sahara) and plagued by a storm of locusts the athletes had to beat aside with their arms as they ran. It was an extraordinary sight, and not really much fun. But honour was satisfied and V-E recognised. Walking back to the Mess that evening I nearly put paid to my own future by setting my khaki jacket pocket alight with my pipe. Seeing me alone on the deserted road, beating out flames on my side, an approaching Arab just lifted his skirts with a yell and fled into the desert. I suppose he thought it was the Burning Bush, or whatever is the equivalent in the Koran. But it fair completed a strange day of V-E celebration.

Algiers city was by then out of bounds to all troops out of town. The first signs of post war revolt against French rule had erupted in city riots, a sign of things to come. Algeria was to become France's heaviest cross, even more than Vietnam, until de Gaulle gave it independence years later.

My posting back to active service came in late May. This time it was to Staging Post facilities in Sardinia for trooping to and from the Far East, where the war against Japan continued. No 63 Staging Post, or RAF Station Elmas as it was soon to be renamed, was already established. Our job was to build it up for the expected traffic both ways – not just those going out but those poor souls coming back, many liberated from Japanese prisoner-of-war camps, many released from the 'forgotten' army in Burma, and many others who had had long stretches in India and South-East Asia. They were a brave but sad sight. We were also a slip-crew staging post, where crews on these long-haul flights changed for a rest. The respected monthly magazine the *Aeroplane* described us in a July 1945 article on Trooping to India, as the first stop six hours out of England, and:

> The aerodrome at Elmas is a surprising place. Constructed in immediate pre-war days as a civil airport by the Italians, the main Headquarters building is a bright pink affair in the grandiose style so dear to Mussolini's rather pathetic neo-Roman. On one side of the aerodrome Cagliari, the picturesque but filthy capital of Sardinia, stands up on a bluff, while facing the airport is an oblong lagoon more than two miles long by about a mile wide, with a few Cants (air-sea rescue planes) of the Regio Aeronautica moored on it. To complete this theatrical decor, the lagoon is backed by a great black wall of jagged volcanic mountains. We stayed at Elmas two hours while our Dakota had an inspection and fill up of petrol ... Everything possible was done for our comfort, all ranks being treated alike ... The Station Adjutant at Elmas told me they were prepared to deal with up to 500 transients per day in the near future.

The station complement was large. It had to be for the task of controlling and servicing so many flights, and feeding, watering and when necessary accommodating so many transitting troops. My Signals section constituted about one-third, and they promoted me to Flight Lieutenant this time. We had quite a lot of Italians working for us too. Accommodation was elementary and crowded, the troops had to be housed in barrack dormitories and the officers in wards. The town was out of bounds much of the time, because venereal disease there was rampant. Entertainment on the Station was minimal. Two middle-aged dears from ENSA did their best. Thanks to them and the Italian Air Force we did have a brief visit and unaccompanied arias from the stars of the revived Rome Opera when they came to Cagliari, though the great tenor Beniamino Gigli petulantly decided he could not sing alfresco with flies buzzing around him. He was booed for his pains by our Italian airmen, and visibly irritated when we wildly cheered his colleagues who did sing for us. We did not take to the man.

The main problem we faced at Elmas was not with the Italians, or with accommodation, or with building the Staging Post facilities, or with the transients and crews and aircraft, or even with the climate, flies and mosquitoes, but with the morale of the other ranks, now the war in Europe was over and release of those in uniform had begun. Most of them now just wanted to get home and pick up the threads of civilian life again. They did not cavil at the ex-POWs, Burma boys and long-servers abroad getting priority. They did at stories that overseas service would count no more than home service for an airman's category of release, and that civilians were striking at home for more pay and thereby selfishly curtailing the transport available to bring troops back. Our Wing Padre whom I had known in Algiers, suggested on a visit that the station needed more sports and entertainment, and that I should be given the job as well as Signals Officer. The CO, a fine South African volunteer, Colonel (Wing Commander) Swanepoel, approved the idea and, with the help of a stalwart Leading Aircraftman or two, we soon had going every sport we could accommodate, even a home-made ash tennis court, though our surface somehow always defied Newton's 3rd law of Motion – every action sadly did not bounce with an equal and opposite reaction. Most of the troops joined in and, while it did not solve the problem – only fair and rapid demobilisation could do that – it certainly helped. At any rate Elmas did not join in the rash of strikes against the slowness of demobilisation that swept some Staging Posts in the Middle and Far East early the following year.

My spell at Elmas was about the longest I had anywhere in the RAF, but still only seven and a half months. It included a bout of sand-fly fever but also some enjoyable flights with the CO to Corsica, Sicily and Malta. Otherwise I suppose it was all work – though we liked to think with a purpose, not just killing time as many service units abroad then faced. I left there on posting to Group HQ in Cairo at the turn of the year 1945.

Like most others hoping to qualify for demobilisation, it was time to start thinking about one's own future. The General Election had been held at home in early July and produced the extraordinary but predictable result that the Conservatives under Churchill were out and reforming Labour was in, and with a large majority. I was personally upset not so much with the result although my party the Liberals had done poorly, as with the apparent incompetence of the service vote arrangements overseas. In those days a Cambridge (and Oxford) graduate had a university as well as a constituency vote. I received neither. My proxy vote at Ludlow was cancelled at the last minute for some mistaken reason, and my Cambridge papers only reached me months later. It was said at the time that Labour got in largely on the service vote. I cannot think how. Anyhow this big change at home was soon matched by even bigger ones abroad – the Potsdam Conference in July and then Hiroshima, Nagasaki and the Japanese surrender in August. The war was now truly over. My own demob number was announced as 54, which looked like at least two more years before release, and as leave became subordinate to demobilisation it did not look like I would get home in that period either. So there seemed nothing else but to soldier on.

One day at Elmas however an Air Ministry Order fell across my desk inviting applications for the Foreign Service and Home Civil Service under special 'Reconstruction' regulations which took account of war-interrupted education and would favour ex-servicemen. I knew nothing of the Foreign Service and my science and small town background hardly seemed to fit. But the authors, the Civil Service Commission, sounded reformist and open to the unorthodox, and RAF service had already fired me with a desire to travel and deal with people abroad. By coincidence, there then appeared at Elmas on a flying visit an enthusastic RAF Education Officer who, as I wrote home somewhat unbelievingly, 'thought my youth and qualifications stood an excellent chance.' I pondered it for three months, meanwhile exploring with Cambridge whether I could return there to take a Part ll Tripos degree, which I was still determined to do, possibly changing to History or Economics. The reply was encouraging. The question was could I do both? I decided to apply and see what happened. There was plenty of time, and the Foreign Service was anyhow still remote.

The mainland of Italy meanwhile again beckoned, this time on leave. My old friend John Turpin, then an Army Education Captain in Ancona, suggested we met in Rome and, in a utility car he would arrange, we would explore central and northern Italy, war-torn but now liberated of the Germans. We did just that in August 1945, and that tour would make a book in itself. Suffice it that from Rome we travelled up the west coast to Grossetto, Leghorn, Pisa, La Spezia and over the hairpin pass to war-damaged Genoa, then to elegant Turin and beautiful Lake Maggiore, up to the Swiss border and back to Lake Como; then to imposing Milan (with *La Traviata* at the Scala Opera's temporary home in the Castello Sforcesca), Lake Garda, Verona, Padua, glorious Venice, Bologna, Assisi (staying the night, improbably, in the Nun's Convent) and finally Siena, where we were royally entertained by some of Turpin's Italian friends and joined in the festivities of the famous (or notorious, depending on your equestrian sympathies) Palio. We parted there as he had to return to Ancona while I had to get to Rome – once again entering its gates by hitch-hike – and fly to Naples, where V-J night was being celebrated, and back to Sardinia. I was to enjoy visiting some of these great places again, on holiday after the war and from the Embassy in Rome some years later. Italy is an incomparable country and its people most gifted. Of Sardinia, however, I wrote on leaving – prophetically as it turned out – 'I shall never re-visit this island but I shall not regret my stay here ... not least the view across the Elmas lake in the early morning, the weather in Spring and Autumn (though not the Summer heat), the self-dependency that the isolated nature of the place forced upon us and, personally, the independence I had there, virtually my own boss.'

My last posting in the RAF was the converse. It was to be staff not line, terminative not creative, and the flesh-pots of Cairo not the war-torn encampments of the Western Mediterranean. I was able to send my kit bag and camp kit home and, in due course, indulge in regular hours and free Sundays for, as I wrote home, 'the first time since I was a kid'. It seemed to me strange when, with the onset of Cairo's hot, humid summer in April, and the disagreeable camseen winds off the desert, our official hours were reduced to 38 per week (with early start, and afternoons off), 'as if it was peace-time, while troops are being held back from demobilisation.' But I had to admit 'I would not be human if I did not enjoy it.'

HQ 216 Group was where I had started in the Middle East and Mediterranean, and I had come full circle. It was still housed in a baroque palace in the residential Cairo suburb of Heliopolis, and turned out to be a congenial place, under the command of an Air Commodore, formerly the dynamic Anglo-American Whitney Straight, then one I think called Cousens. My chief was still Group Captain Michael Watson. He had his wife out, and they mixed in high Cairo circles. His deputy was still Wing Commander Long, a shrewd and friendly old-timer, who would drag me out for tennis at the Heliopolis Club every free afternoon through the heat of the Summer, diligently weighing himself before and after and declaring he had lost 4 lbs, before putting it back on again with iced shandy. I did the same of course, until one day we discovered the changing-room attendant fixing the weighing machine to register our 4lbs losses irrespective. We carried on tipping him just the same, for his pleasing ingenuity. The W/Cmdr tragically died on the courts later, I heard. He was an airman of the old school who would never give up. The other Signals colleagues were a regular Squadron Leader Alsop and three war-time

Flight Lieutenants like me. We messed together in a nearby flat, looked after by a family of some Mediterranean minority or another, like so many in that area at that time. A teacher of French from Alexandria I came to know seemed to epitomise that cosmopolitanism. He was of Algerian origin so his family language was French. Talking to his sisters who were at the English School in Alexandria he spoke English. Talking to his mother he chose Italian because she knew it and he considered it the softest language. Arguing politics with his father, was always he said in their most vehement common tongue, Arabic. He was fluent in all four.

Politics came alive in Egypt and particularly Cairo at that time. The Wafd party had begun campaigning for a revision of the Treaty with Britain and, now the war was over, for the withdrawal of Britain's right to station troops on the Suez Canal. Riots broke out in Cairo in February and the British Forces Command put the city temporarily out of bounds to all troops. That did not bother us unduly. Except for the lively Cairo markets and night life, we had all we wanted in Heliopolis – restaurants, shops (though prices were inflated by the war), dances, cinemas and the sports club, all the things I had barely seen for seemingly an age. Except for the climate and the hygiene, it was luxury, and I enjoyed as intense a period of playing and organising games – cricket, tennis, swimming, hockey, soccer and even athletics – as I had ever had or was likely to again.

The work was undemanding. I was supposed to be the HQ Signals technical expert, to whom our several Wings and thirty or forty Staging Posts, from the Persian Gulf to Austria and from upper Egypt to Greece, appealed for advice on technical signals matters, and through whom Air Ministry modifications to equipment were conveyed. Fortunately for me, it also involved visits to many of these units for inspection and, in a few cases, to cost cheaply what we were planning to leave to the locals when we pulled out. Usually with Alsop and others, I was able to visit Luxor (and of course Thebes and Karnak), Rhodes, Beirut, Nicosia in Cyprus, Lydda and Haifa in Palestine, and, in the Western Mediterranean, Rome (for my fifth time), Naples (and, this time, Pompeii), Catania and Taormina in Sicily and Malta. It could sometimes be tedious flying those distances back and forth in the slow and bumpy little planes then at our disposal, and writing reports afterwards. But it was all grist to my mill, and Alsop and the others were thoroughly good company. Such ventures however had to come to an end. From May onwards they did so rapidly.

In June HQ 216 Group was suddenly found surplus to post-war require-ments and absorbed in the mighty Middle East HQ in Cairo. I was left to wind down the Signals side, dispose of the records and wrap things up. 'Amazing as it may seem', I wrote home, 'having started two years ago as the most junior of Signals Officers in the great RAF Transport Command empire of the Mediterranean and Middle East, I have ended in the capacity

Awaiting demobilisation, Cairo, 1946.

of acting Chief Signals Officer, though it is now but a shadow.' Threatened with an arduous Wing HQ job in the field when I had finished, but by now hoping for earlier than expected release to return home, I was fortunate the job lasted until July. I had declined the Group Captain's kind invitation to be put up for a permanent commission with promotion, in favour of University again and possibly the Foreign Service. Timing was the problem. It would have been difficult to start out in the field again at that point even with added rank. That dilemma was fortunately resolved for me by the timely introduction by the Government of a Class B Release scheme, under which servicemen whose studies had been interrupted by the war, and who had done three years in the Services, and who wished to return to University, could apply to do so for that Autumn term instead of waiting for the normal Class A Release. I found I qualified. It would involve some financial loss, as much as £100, because HM Treasury, with its usual stinginess, had made it a condition that those taking advantage of the scheme should forfeit half their paid release leave and all their overseas paid leave supplement, for the privilege. But I applied and, thanks to the Dean of Selwyn, was able to write home joyously at the end of July: 'It has come! Class B release. And I have accepted it. So now I am on my way home and out of the Service.' I had also, thanks to my College, been accepted for re-entry to Cambridge to take a Part ll Tripos of my choosing, with the prospect of a state bursary to help financially – and no nonsense about taking preliminary Engineering or Latin this time!

It remained of course to decide: what then? This posed a dilemma, not just what career I should be seeking after Cambridge, but whether, if anything came of my application for the Foreign Service, they would want me to break my return to Cambridge, which would not only be thwarting but, more seriously, invalidate my Class B release and postpone my return home by months. I agonised long on this. Faced with an invitation to take the Foreign and Civil Service preliminary written exam in Cairo in July, I found the Civil Service Commission had a representative there (as, no doubt in the other centres they had chosen which I later learnt were Naples, Baghdad, Delhi and Singapore), and he advised I had nothing to lose by going ahead and seeing what happened.

So, after three years in uniform, I found myself on 2 and 3 July 1946 sitting with a couple of Army Captains and half a dozen civilians from our Middle East Embassies, Schools, Supply Centres and the like in a bare room in Cairo furnished only with tables and chairs, the temperature rising to 90°F and sand blowing everywhere, trying to be an exam student again, but this time without studied preparation. I still have the questions. Some were:

*English:*  Would you agree that without reform of the individual there can be no reform of society? (Time allowed 2 hours)

Write a 300 word summary of the given 1100 word extract from Ross's 'Foundations of Ethics'. (¾ hour)

Answer seven questions on the given passage adapted from Hobson's 'Free thought in the Social Sciences'. (¾ hour)

*Arithmetic:*  Questions on tax, relative speed, population growth and shapes. (1½ hours)

*Intelligence:*  (1 hour) (My own description afterwards) '58 short questions in 20 minutes, followed by another heaven knows how many in 10 minutes, and more in 10 minutes and finally still more in 20 minutes: ... including all sorts of amazing questions and problems, from comparisons of proverbs and sayings to counting the number of blocks in given 3-dimensional piles and how many faces of each were completely covered ... By the time the fellow next to me finished that question, he told me later, his face was nearly on the paper and he was seeing blocks floating about all over the place.'

*General:*  Answer three questions in 1½ hours from the given choice of twelve like 'Examine the view that there is no danger of large-scale unemployment in Great Britain during the next 10 years' and 'Consider the possible consequences for the British Empire of the growth of Arab nationalism in the Middle East'.

That exam turned out to be just the first of five different tests and interviews candidates had to face before selection to the Civil or Foreign Services, and we were told there would be only 200 places in the Foreign Service. I wrote home that while I had decided on the type of career I wanted to follow, 'one that will involve action, responsibility and travel', I was relaxed about the Foreign Service, it would be some months before the results of the written exams emerged anyhow. For the rest, it was easier to say what I did not now much want to do, namely teaching, science, commerce or the RAF, than where specifically I was heading after Cambridge. Time would tell.

I left Cairo for the Canal Zone and home in mid-August, sad to be leaving the RAF and the many friends and colleagues I had come to know, and with the highest regard for that Service. It was now to be behind me. But in the continued contacts I have had with serving and retired members of the RAF over the years since, I have never had cause to waver in my admiration of its professional standards, and camaraderie. It was a privilege to be a member for those years.

CHAPTER 8

# Family in the Army

## 1944–1947

MY BROTHER ERYL joined the Royal Army Medical Service (RAMC)
in April 1944 from medical school and hospital doctoring at Liverpool,
in time for the 2nd Front invasion of France. After a brief six weeks
Officers and School of Hygiene training at Aldershot and the RAMC
College in London, he was attached to a medium artillery regiment, the
107th RA South Notts Hussars, who had already seen service in the
Western Desert, Tunisia, and Sicily. He embarked with them for France
as their Medical Officer in mid-July, a month after the first landings, and
remained with them, in General Dempsey's 2nd British Army, through
Normandy, up the Channel coast, through Belgium and Holland, and
ultimately into Germany.

In June 1945, the war in Europe over, he was transferred home and in
July to India where he served for a year and a half as Medical Officer of
the Green Howards. Most of that time was spent in and around Calcutta.
The war with Japan ended as he arrived, but the partition and independence
of India loomed and the Army's main task became one of trying to keep
the peace amidst the riots and internecine fighting that broke out between
the different Calcutta communities. It was a task that involved treating
the victims of violence in the streets as well as the injuries and ills of his
own unit soldiers in an uncongenial climate. He came home on demobilisation in February 1947.

Some of his letters home from North-West Europe and India survive.
The following are edited extracts. The addresses in Europe have been
divined from the contents and research of the course of the war, it being
forbidden at the time of course to disclose unit locations.

### E (Eryl) to M (Mother) 28 July 1944
#### 107 Med. Regt. RA, BLA (Normandy beaches)

*We are allowed to write a fortnight behind the news so I can now give you an idea of our trip across ... We came over in a convoy of merchant ships with the sea like glass, following the coast within sight of Beachy Head and then Isle of Wight before turning south across the Channel and anchoring off the beachhead for the night ... It was an incredible sight, thousands of ships all over the place: cargo boats, tank landing craft, hospital ships, and the Navy sprinkled liberally around ... That night we had a few planes over and the sight of all the guns opening up and red tracers in a sky already lit up by searchlights and flares was almost beautiful ... Next day we unloaded all day and as it was not finished by night we missed the tide, spent the night on a landing craft and charged the shore next morning, landing in about two feet of water ... After that the regiment spent a day finding itself, having sailed in two separate boats each unloading onto about a dozen landing craft beaching at widely separated points ... Next day we had the superb good luck [sic] to go slap up to what is being described as the greatest battle of the war so far ... you will have read about it in your papers ... The weather and fanatical Hitler Youth slowed the whole business down to a standstill however.* [This must have been the assault on Caen. Montgomery announced a breakthrough but did not in fact attempt all that Eisenhower and the Air Forces wanted, though Churchill supported Montgomery's achievement of securing at less cost the vital bridgehead through Caen.]

*Our regiment has been fighting very successfully since we came in. We've had bouquets from the front line Infantry and Tank regiments ... When all the guns around us are firing it is quite stupendous ... Our chief worry however is not Jerry bombs or shells but a particularly virulent type of French mosquito, which has scored a decisive victory from the Col. down to the lowest gunner! ... The countryside has been terribly battered around, but the Pioneers and Engineers are doing a magnificent job clearing roads, renovating water supplies, erecting bridges, repairing railways etc. The organisation is truly remarkable.*

### E to M 20 Aug. 1944     107 Med. Regt. RA, BLA (Normandy)

*Jerry made the little village we were in when I last wrote so hot that we had to withdraw. We were in a bulge and were plastered from three sides, and bombed nightly ... In spite of all we had very few casualties – odd chaps who stopped little bits before they could duck ... We moved back into a town, and for a few days into a house where I was able to transfer my R.A.P. (Regimental Aid Post) from my 15 cwt truck – and also sleep in a four-poster! ... I also had to look after a lot of chaps from other regiments around, and French civilians.*

*We are now moving forward frequently, in increasing distances each time ... Pause for a break: six ME 109s came nosing over just then, but two have been shot down, great excitement ... Our own (RAF) fighters are overhead most of the time, keeping them away ... We have just spent a night in a beautiful chateau, in which a German General has been living. They evidently left in a hurry, and the place was in a filthy state – it took us hours to clear up – I've never seen so many flies on the food they left.*

*Yesterday we had the worst day since coming across. Orders were to move at 8am ... After being delayed all morning we got about 5 miles on the road when a message came that the positions we were to occupy were filled with Jerry tanks which had broken out. Also that our Colonel was missing last seen in a tank that had been hit ... He was killed sadly.*

*Today the ferocity of the shooting has to be seen to be believed ... We're dead hot on Tiger tanks as our 5.5 guns are the only ones that have any effect on them, and our Armoured Division, whom we support, send for us to shift them when their own tanks are held up ... Jerry is leaving bunches of tanks all over the place in a desperate attempt to keep the neck of the pocket from closing. Between firing on them, our guns are potting at the thousands of vehicles in long dusty streams as they pass along the few remaining roads open to them in this district ... There are hundreds of very shattered Jerry prisoners coming in past us, but many more still holding out viciously. They are incredibly tough fighters considering the pasting they are getting.*

[This must have been the battle of the Falaise Pocket, east of the river Orne, between Argentan and Falaise, involving the 1st Canadian, 2nd British and 1st and 3rd US Armies against the German 7th Army composed of some 100,000 remnants of fifteen and more divisions. Chester Wilmot records in his *Struggle for Europe* that Hitler suspected the German Commander Von Kluge, of seeking to capitulate to the Allies, and replaced him by Model from the Russian front just at this moment. It did not save the Germans. Many escaped, but they lost some 10,000 dead, 50,000 taken prisoner, 'gruesome heaps' of horse-drawn transport and a 'holocaust of blazing vehicles and exploding ammunition' ... 'sacrificed on the altar of blind obedience to the Fuhrer's command.']

## E to M 6 Sept. 1944        107 Med. Regt. RA, BLA (Normandy)

*The battle is now moving too fast for us to keep up and as we haven't been needed we are having a rest ... I'm very thankful for my lean-to tent, opening out on both sides of my truck, daytime for my RAP, night-time I have one side and my orderlies and driver sleep in the other. Better than the slit trenches I had in July which in the rains had at least 3 inches of water in them!*

*I've just been on a liberty trip ... to a city with a famous old cathedral ... and the least damage of any I have yet seen. We were the first British troops there and have had a superb welcome ... besieged by excited French people ... all the men taken off to homes and sightseeing and generally given the time of their lives ... Three other officers and I were taken in charge by a half-English lady who gave us a full sightseeing tour and celebration party ... Food has been very short and high priced ... no wonder they look pale and thin, the babies and young kiddies terribly so as milk has been almost non-existent ... In spite of all they have been through they are cheerful, and it seems very few collaborated with the Germans. I hope when we occupy Germany we don't meet a great passive resistance, like the Germans evidently encountered here from the French and must have found exasperating.*

[The city must have been Rouen]

### E to M 26 Sept. 1944      107 Med. Regt. RA, BLA (Seine-Maritime)

*We are now in an area that has received considerable attention from our bombers and big guns and is like a blasted heath with large craters all around . . . and it is blowing a constant gale so the craters are like lakes and the tracks muddy rivulets . . . I was lucky the other day to get into a Jerry naval barracks and pick up a useful pair of wellingtons and a very good stock of quality medical equipment and drugs.*

*The press and radio amuse and annoy us at times. They are so horribly enthusiastic. The mere fact that one man may have got into a town and come out rather hurriedly, means to the Mirror and Express that we have captured it! . . . The utter nonsense the 'headline rags' print! We get our papers usually about 3 days late . . . and are sometimes led to believe we really are wonderful, brave and heroic! . . . The munition workers at home are not popular here either, with their demands for higher pay and, this morning, we had three 'prematures' – faulty shells that exploded in the barrel. Fortunately only one casualty but I had to give him chloroform and put a Thomas splint on.*

*Our life remains one of intense activity followed by equally intense boredom waiting for the next attack to start. It is not as the papers portray, one of terrific continuous work. There is a definite routine with each attack . . . first the bombers, then our AA guns, to soften up defences, then the infantry and we fire at anything that may hold them up. Then, all being well, we wait for the next attack.*

### E to M 6 Oct. 1944                107 Med. Regt. RA, BLA (Belgium)

*I can now mention what jobs we were doing while you imagined us in the thrust to Arnheim. We were working up the Channel coast of France, helping to clear the flying bomb and cross-Channel gun areas and capture the ports. One fine day we could see the white cliffs of England. The Jerry big gun sites are stupendous. One was turned on us in one battle – like an express train hissing through the air, but luckily did little damage . . . We've been through many of the places that were famous in the last war.*

*The Belgians are being very good to us . . . We are staying in farms and the owners cannot do too much for us . . . When we arrived here we were just over a kilometre from the canal that formed the front line but in spite of the terrific battle raging before us and the huge quantity of stuff Jerry lobbed at us none hit our guns . . . One night we beat off four counterattacks which were threatening our infantry up front . . . Incidentally two of our troop commanders have been awarded the M.C. for their work in the Falaise battle . . . Everyone is now getting ready for a winter campaign ... The Padre and I have bought sheepskins from a local farmer to cure and then fix inside our leather jerkins. Our Mess Bombardier was a furrier before the war and is doing the cutting and fitting for us.*

## E to M 25 Nov. 1944    107 Med. Regt. RA, BLA (Holland)

*We have now been in this country two weeks, so I am allowed to tell you where we were last ... We were helping to clear the Scheldt estuary so as to be able to use the port of Antwerp. We started off clearing a German pocket bounded by a canal and were actually firing from Belgium into Holland. Then we moved into the captured area which was flooded in parts, hopelessly wrecked and a horrible part of the world ... When that was finished we fired across the river and supported the attacks across the causeway, and the sea landings on the Islands ... At one place, standing on a dyke, we could watch the battle over on the other side, landing craft going across and our own shelling, with all the Jerry guns potting back at us. We were very thankful to leave that bleak countryside, and we had a long journey across Belgium and Holland to where we are now.*

[The battle to clear the Germans from both sides of the great Scheldt estuary took over 60 days and minesweeping it up to Antwerp another three weeks. It was a complex operation, led by the Canadians with British army, marine, naval and air force support and involving among other things fighting over land deliberately flooded by the Allied bombing of the Walcheren dykes. The Germans resisted strongly, access to Antwerp port (already in Allied hands) being crucial to each side. Churchill records in 'Triumph and Tragedy' that, after the Arnhem thrust, clearing the Scheldt and opening Antwerp was the first priority. The canal E mentions was doubtless the Leopold Canal.]

## E to M 8 Dec 1944    107 Med. Regt. RA, BLA
## (Holland near the German frontier)

*For the Regiment this is a pleasant change, supporting British troops again and our chaps meeting old friends from Middle East and other campaigns. Personally I would prefer to be back supporting the Canadians, their medical units were so helpful, well stocked and none of the red tape we now have ... We've collected bouquets from the Divisions we have supported, and now from General Ritchie – and an extra rum ration from our Brigadier on the strength of that ... It was the Brig's 50th birthday the other day. With due ceremony he ordered his regiments to fire on their first target in Germany. We were first to be ready and to fire!*

*We have managed to get ourselves billetted in houses etc. The real battle here is not so much one of gaining land from the Germans as of gaining accommodation before other regiments – a battle of real estate! We have in fact been fortunate for the past month ... Here we are in a big Dutch house, with its windows intact, and open grates protruding into the room so we are kept warm at nights. The people, three families in all including seven children, are very friendly ... each evening we all foregather to sing lustily (and drink our tea and smoke our cigarettes!) ... I am trying to learn Dutch from them but cannot manage the throaty pronounciation ... I'm told that our next positions will not be so fortunate, we shall have to get under canvas again, a horrible thought! All the houses in Germany it seems have been razed to the gound either by us or by the Germans themselves.*

*I've just had a batch of very despondent news: one of my Liverpool friends killed, another missing, Holden wounded and paralysed, Bunty's John back with a leg off, two chaps from our survey party here have today lost a foot and a leg on mines, and I've just had to send a man to hospital with malaria, which has been one of my main bugbears in this unit ... Jerry is now shelling our gun positions.*

**E to M 8 Dec. 1944**                    **107 Med. Regt. RA, BLA**
                              **(Holland, on the German frontier)**

*The battle here now is amazing, not like the newspapers portray (except the Mirror has it right) ... Everything is frighteningly peaceful when you get up to the front line, except now and again you hear the guns behind open up, or a crackle of a machine gun or the crack and whine of a bullet passing near ... The further back you go the more noisy it becomes, there you get the bombing and shelling, and the big guns, and the endless procession of supply columns grinding their slow way up, and the tanks wheeling around as they move up into position or come back out of the line for a rest. Except when there is a battle on, the front is the quietest place on earth. You even measure how far forward you are by the degree of quietness – its a sinister, frightening silence which brings a cold sweat on you as you wonder 'God, was that the right turning I took way back?', and then the odd shell or a bullet whining over makes your mind up for you, you wheel the truck round in record time and get to hell out of it, with an uncomfortable feeling of having made a bog-up of your map reading. I may add for your comfort I don't make a point of this all the time!*

*I hope you have a good Christmas. Don't worry about me. Its not so rigorous here, though I wish to God it would end, I'm fed up with the boring routine and cold, wet and mud. It was interesting and thrilling at first, now it is neither.*

**E to M 4 January 1945**                  **107 Med. Regt. RA, BLA**
                              **(Holland on the German frontier)**

*I'm now up to my eyes ... Have taken on Mess Secretary. Its a frightful business, paying for NAAFI supplies in French francs, billing in Belgian francs, being paid half in that currency and half in Dutch guilders, and having to balance the books in sterling! On top of that I'm being inundated with bumph – inoculation and vaccination returns, V.D. returns, malaria returns, sick returns etc. etc. – the penalty of being an Army doctor! ... Add to this that under the demobilisation scheme the Government has just announced my number is 57, so I fancy my chances for Burma are quite promising. My chaps have already altered the meaning of B.L.A. to 'Burma Looms Ahead'.*

*We had a rather good time at Christmas. When the Yanks got pushed back we were terrified we would have to retire also, not that we might have a sticky time but that we would have to leave this house! ... Christmas Day was the men's day and we served them with early morning tea and Xmas dinner, and arranged a party for them in a pub across the road with a band (hired for 200 cigarettes) ... The weather was cold and frosty but clear and sunny. Since then it has snowed and thawed, and we have mud and slush ... Boxing Day was our big day ... The Army did us proud then too. The food and drink were first-class – even the men said so! And entertainments had been organised all round – including a Pantomime, Aladdin, and an 'Arty Party' – I never realised we had so much talent in the Regiment ... On Sat. we had a visit from the General ... and that evening we had our Brigadier to dinner (in our house). It was terrific, with the table laid by one of the Dutch family and their silver lent to us for the occasion. Afterwards it became a bit noisy and I had to vamp at the piano while the Brig. sang 'Rolling home' in a loud and untuneful voice. Anyhow he enjoyed himself and everything went well.*

*On Jan 1st at one second past midnight all the guns in this Army plastered Jerry, but he retaliated next morning by sending his planes over, and they had a terrific reception, some flying high and diving and twisting and turning to dodge the AA fire, whilst others flew just at tree top height, screaming past us – two gave me an awful shock as they strafed down the road barely 30 yards away – and flying just over the houses, whilst everyone in the neighbourhood fired at them with everything they'd got. We saw five brought down, but got ten in our vicinity and 150 odd all told. Jerry hasn't shown up since then! ... It was rather disconcerting this morning when the kids of the house bombarded our men with snowballs when they were lined up on parade – but the chaps got their own back when they had been dismissed!*

## E to M 31 January 1945          107 Med. Reg. RA, BLA (Germany)

*We have had several moves up [into Germany], each one into a more bleak part of the countryside. It is all flat 'upland' with small villages dotted about and all smashed to blazes ... There are no civilians about, so we find an odd room in a house which looks as if it might keep the snow and wind out and not leak too badly, and we move in and patch it up. In this village hardly a house has not had a shell through it. When we moved in we had to move out some dead bodies to make it sanitary again. How they stank ... I am now having to inoculate the whole Regiment – a job I detest as much as do the men themselves.*

*I was visiting Regimental HQ the other day – it is in a 3-ton truck with 4 wireless sets, 3 telephones, map boards etc – and as they were short handed they put me 'on duty'. We had to fire at some Jerry tanks. The 'Red Tab'* came round later to congratulate our CO on our speedy and accurate shooting. The CO replied that they had been training the Doctor to take his first shoot, or they could have been still faster!

Important news: I have drawn home leave in the ballot and will be home some time in March.

**E to M 8 Feb. 1945**                      **107 Med. Reg. RA, BLA (Germany)**

The country here is pretty frightful again – low-lying, flooded and wet, and very muddy ... We've had to ferry our stuff up by half-tracks ... We have a farmhouse to ourselves, with windows intact, so we are very comfortable.

You will know from the wireless that things went wrong all over the place a month ago. Monty came along soon after to dish out some MCs to some of our officers and said that if Jerry had got through nothing could have stopped him reaching Antwerp. We were very apprehensive at the time. Everyone was running around digging trenches and emplacements etc, and dozens of local attacks were broken up by our guns. Thankfully our main attack got in before Jerry's. It was a terrific battle.

We were otherwise very happy at that Dutch town. It was delightful country and the town clean, tidy and colourful. The people gave us a terrific reception. One day we had a football match against their team. Thousands turned out to watch and cheer and the band started off with the Anthems. The Burgomaster gave a speech, and all the men were presented with silver spoons. And all this happened within 2 miles of the front line!

**E to M 7 March 1945**                      **107 Med. Reg. RA, BLA (Germany)**

There's very little news ... We are to have our first rest since we came over – except for the unofficial one after Falaise when the battle went on too fast for us. Then I have leave, beginning 29 March. I should be home by the 31st all being well.

Men coming back from leave are very perturbed about the attitude at home. They say everyone has lost interest and thinks the war is as good as finished. I don't know whether this is true. Maybe we here do not read our Mirror, Mail and Express enough to know what we are doing! The amount of clap trap and half truths printed in those rags is just no one's business.

St David's Day was made the subject of a large celebration here – by myself, in the face of considerable opposition from our Scottish Adjutant, Irish Padre and English CO. They eventually ordered the leeks decorating the Mess to be put to better use, to wit eaten. They were German leeks anyway!

**E to M 6 May 1945**                      **107 Med. Reg. RA, BLA**
                      **(Between Bocholt and Münster, Germany)**

I so enjoyed being home ...

Our war has now ended, at least the fighting part of it. Now the worst part begins – the Army of Occupation. We have just finished our first week of it *and I do not like it. All spit and polish, and non-fraternisation, and cold aloofness on the part of the Jerries … Fortunately we are conveniently near the Dutch frontier, and have set up a Rest Centre in a town over there.*

*You need not worry about me any more. We live in a small peaceful town, in the school, and have a comfortable mess and all amenities. The countryside is flat but pretty, and very well farmed. These Germans can work! The more I see of these people the more incredible it seems that we ever won this war.*

**E to M June 1945**          **107 Med. Reg. RA, BLA**
**(Coesfeld, near Münster, Germany)**

*I have a nice little house for my RAP but have to make it 10 bed for my minor patients, and I've only one orderly. The chief worry at present however is that the Regiment is taking over the supervision of eight camps of Russian ex-prisoners and displaced persons (the so-called foreign workers – the forced labour). There are 4200 of them. I have also been helping out at a nearby hospital, and doing quite a lot of minor surgery. Up to now American hospital units have been looking after the Russians. I have to take over from them … and have only 3 orderlies to help and none of us speak a word of Russian …*

*Anyway I have now found a Serbian officer who knows something about 1st Aid, a Russian military nurse – a grand lass – an Italian medical orderly and two Russian volunteers, and a Russian doctor. I have set myself up as Consultant … I have my own sick parade and then go from one Russian camp to another, the outer two being about 30 miles apart!*

*Our Mess is in the large country house of a steel magnate from Gelsenkirchen in the Ruhr. It is beautifully furnished with priceless china and ornaments, a library of old books and special editions, a music room and Steinway, lovely old prints and paintings, and beautiful gardens … The old boy (the owner) of course hates us but the others put up with us. They are terrified of the Russians, who loot, plunder, rape and assault seemingly for something to do. Our patrols have to be sent out to protect our enemies from our allies!*

*The most difficult thing here of course is the rule of non-fraternisation with the German civilians. The idea is sound, but it is a terrible temptation to the men to see pretty girls and beautiful little children obviously just asking to be friendly. Fair play the men are observing the orders very well.*

E's letters from Germany ceased at this point. On 18 June he received orders to return to the UK for leave, medical and transfer to 'an Eastern Theatre'. On 28 July he embarked from Southampton for India on the troopship *Durban Castle*. Having been promoted Captain in April, he was made Medical Officer of the ship. They reached Bombay three weeks later. There he learnt he had to proceed to Calcutta to join the 2nd Battalion The Green Howards at Barrackpore.

Like his father before him, he travelled slowly across India by train, ten days in all, and was immediately taken with the immensity of the country, the changing scenery, the seething towns and the great variety of people he encountered or saw. He also had his first introduction to Indian politics. Pandit Nehru joined the train at Delhi and stayed on it until Allahabad. At each stop he was hailed by crowds of enthusiastic young supporters, shouting, chanting and carrying banners – 'even when he was having breakfast,' E noted, and commented, 'He must be a great patriot to put up with it all the time.' Crossing the Ganges at eventide E wrote that the sunset was like a gigantic fire reminding him of the blitzes 'but more vivid as it sank deeper behind the hills and the colours got darker and richer. I have not seen such colouring even at Harlech's best.' He reached Calcutta on 1 Sept.

There are no letters from him extant between then and the following June. It is clear however that, like his father before him in Mesopotamia, he threw himself into his work on arrival (in this case looking after the troops medically of course) with scant regard for his own health in that insalubrious climate, and paid a price for his conscientiousness. He did the same in the Calcutta riots in the late summer and autumn, but recovered his enjoyment of the better sides of Army life and India before finishing his time there in early 1947.

### E to M 27 June 1946
#### 2nd Bn. Green Howards, Barrackpore, 12 APO

*This past month has been a fight for the health of the troops. At the end of May I had over 90 men in hospital and over 80 treated in barracks – 170 men ill in a Battalion of 600! I did a report to the CO (who is a Regular) and told him he was grossly overworking the men in the climatic circumstances of this place and that morale was the lowest I had met in any unit. The CO is a good man. He lacks imagination but saw the point and altered his training programmes the next day . . . A good thing too, for the Major-General had just woken up to the situation and we had the answers for him when he asked. Another 100 men are to be sent to us, to release a company at a time for relief training in the hills.*

*I am writing this in hospital where I am being treated for prickly heat that has gone septic – penicillin jabs every 3 hours – for 16 doses – which are almost as painful as the pimples and boils. It is like sleeping on a bed of needles . . . My ADMS sent me here and I am then to be posted for two weeks or so to Lebong, near Darjeeling (in the mountains bordering Nepal) . . . Tomorrow I shall be on the North Bengal express and then mountain railway to Darjeeling. I do not anticipate having much work to do there. It will be a rest cure in the cool mountain air and I am much looking forward to it.*

### E to M 27–31 August 1946
#### 2nd Bn. Green Howards, Calcutta, 12 APO

*I hope you received the cable and the two short notes I sent you last week . . .*

We are still in the middle of Calcutta. There are now only one or two incidents daily and yesterday we did not have to open fire at all ... I have never seen anything like this party before. It was sheer unmitigated civil war between Hindus and Moslems with both sides to blame equally. The leaders have been inciting the mobs to this for a long time, and when it started they were impotent to do anything about it ... 4 British battalions were called in straight away, and had to be reinforced by 5 others later. There are now a total of 45,000 troops in Calcutta.

We were given the worst area and even before I at the end of the column had got off the bridge into Calcutta, our forward troops were firing over the seething fighting mobs. The whole thing was sheer mass murder, for a change completely communal and not anti-British ... It was distasteful to see the Quit India followers smarming up to us for protection of their shops, houses and selves. Needless to say they got exactly the same treatment from us as the poor bazaar shopkeepers and the street cleaners.

I see in today's paper they have so far accounted for 3000 stiffs, which means the police estimate of over 6000 killed must be fairly accurate. Add to that between 20 to 30,000 injured and you can imagine what it has been like. Bodies and refuse all over the place, shops and houses looted and burnt – the fire brigades went out to 1600 fires and many more remained unanswered. You can imagine the smell from putrifying bodies and a week's accumulation of garbage. I went round with six stench masks over my nose ... One night we were ordered out on body disposal at 2am. The CO called for volunteers and he, the Adjutant, the Coy. Commander, the Padre, I and about 20 lads went out collecting putrefying corpses, – to save the face of the incompetent poops of this blasted Bengal Government – may they all rot in hell for their actions over the last two weeks.

31st Aug. We are still here, browned off. We expect trouble again on the 2nd when the Assembly meets, on the 12th when they meet again and on the 18th when there is a Hindu holiday – We just wait and wait and wait for something to happen, knowing full well it won't whilst we are here but would start again if we went.

The CO and 2 i/c had dinner with the Governor last night. We are at present living in his band's quarters. He and his wife are apparently a sincere and genuine couple but at a loss amongst the artificiality of this place (that's his statement not mine). He remarked that the first Bengal Governor, Warren Hastings, had to fight his way in, and it looks as if he, the last Governor, may have to fight his way out.

If we quit India now I am sure there will be civil war between Hindus and Moslems, the riots here are only a beginning and the numbers killed in 3 days bear witness to the vicious ferocity of communal feeling. The political leaders and the press have whipped up a frenzy which was bound to lead to this, and now they are incapable of stopping it ... They call for British troops to leave, but criticise us for not coming into Calcutta sooner ... It's as stormy as Palestine, *where the Army is sitting between Jews and Arabs and getting slanged by both sides whatever it does.*

## E to M 4 Nov 1946
### 2nd Bn. The Green Howards, Calcutta, 12 APO

*The last ten days have been bad ... As you probably heard on the BBC or saw in the papers, Calcutta has flared up, so has Dacca in East Bengal, Bombay, Patna, Lahore, Lucknow and dozens of other places throughout India ... We here have degenerated into a sort of Fire Brigade – alarm, pack up and move into town, settle the trouble, sit on the spot until everything is quiet again and move back, only to come back a day or two later to some other area. One Coy. turned out 16 times in one night, and had to return again the next two nights ... This sort of thing has now been going on since mid-August ... alternately patrolling and picketting in Calcutta and catching up back at Barrackpore ... And we are now losing fifty men a month on demobilisation ... Can you wonder that many of the lads are so tired and demoralised as to be almost beyond caring?*

*I am sorry for anyone having to join up now. The whole spirit of the Army has changed. It used to be everyone working hard towards one purpose. Now everyone is wondering how soon they can get out of it. The best and most experienced men have left and most of the others, hard worked and short staffed, are only waiting for the day they can get out.*

*The weather fortunately is now pleasant. It is the end of the monsoons and everything at Barrackpore is a lovely green. The days are still hot but at night one can sleep again without the everlasting fan ... I suppose when one thinks of the nasty cold wet miserable English November I should be glad to be having a few more months here.*

## E to M 2 January 1947                2nd Green Howards, Barrackpore

*My demob has come through and I leave here on 12 Jan for Deolali and Bombay. All being well I should be home by mid-February.*

*We came out of Calcutta just before Christmas ... The big Muslim festival of Muharram in the first and second week of December gave us quite a lot of trouble, and there were two or three ugly situations. I'm quite certain that if we had not been there it would have started all over again. It seems fairly peaceful now, and we hope we will not have to go back.*

*My last few weeks at Barrackpore have in fact been enjoyable. Apart from the better weather, my work has gone well, my orderlies are now fully trained, and I seem to have the confidence of both the officers and the men. Now that I'm leaving, the bouquets are almost embarrassing. Even from my old CO – and as he has remarkably little good to say of any of his officers, I take that as a great compliment. I have just realised too that I have liked being in the Army and am going to miss the life and the friendliness and comradeship. On the whole I have enjoyed being an Army doctor. It has not taught me much medicine, but it has taught me a lot about the world and to know men and how to deal with them. I even thought of staying on for a while, but decided it is about time I saw something of you and home again, and as I'm not going to stay in the Army the sooner I get a hospital job and make my mind up what I'm then going to do, the better. Also I could not stand another couple of months like last May and June here – they were most miserable!*

*I have also been tempted with the thought that if I were offered a decent job out here I might accept it ... I get on well with the Indians and have made many friends among them ... The Indian other rank is a grand fellow, simple and always happy ... I like the people and the country. But after Calcutta I hate the administrators and, after last May/June, the hot weather – which is a pity.*

E left Bombay, by the troop transport *Queen of Bermuda*, in mid-January, after a 1200 mile train journey again across India, and had a good voyage home via the Suez Canal. He had nothing but praise for the arrangements made by the Indian Army to get people home when their demobilisation numbers came up. He was released on 3 February 1947 and officially three months later, with the honorary rank of Captain. After leave he returned to doctoring in his beloved Liverpool.

CHAPTER 9

# Cambridge, Post-War

## 1946–1947

CAMBRIDGE AND SELWYN looked just the same when I returned to register in August 1946. After all it was not the first war they had survived. But that was in vacation time. Term proved very different. It soon became evident that, from a state of unusual quiescence in the latter stages of the War, the University was not only active again with fellows and staff returning and students coming up, but erupting with thousands of ex-servicemen taking advantage of the imaginative release and bursary scheme offered by the Government to those wishing to resume their education.

I was one of them and, in a letter home, described the scene as 'Many of my former colleagues are back ... Many of them married! The place is packed and the lectures are one seething mass of humanity. Many seem old and many have war injuries. It is an amazing sight ... History faculty lectures are overflowing, with students crowded on steps, floors and benches ... The women strike me as being exactly as before ... But the men include the bald, the bearded, the bewhiskered, the maimed and even the blind ...' It was an extraordinary mixture of the mature and the young, the former eyeing the latter as having a big advantage, fresh from school, little realising (nor did I until later) that the youngsters viewed with equal awe the hoary ex-servicemen returning with their cups supposedly full of worldly wisdom. For beneath the great picture of students of many ages pouring in from everywhere, of happy reunions and of Cambridge bouncing back with a vengeance, the atmosphere was soon one of intense competition. It was as plumb serious as '41/'43, and even more so. There was obvious concern that jobs had to be found at the end, families of those married to be supported, and the disabilities of those handicapped to be overcome. Voices of worry at the depth of this competitive trend were soon to be heard. In November 1946 an Oxford don, Muir, caused a stir by a talk on the wireless about it. He acknowledged the studiousness of post-war university students but warned that university education should not degenerate into a quest for degrees as just commercial assets. There was more to university education than set-piece examinations. The 'lighter side' of university life should be revived. By that he made plain he was not referring to the story-book activities of pre-war university life at Oxford and Cambridge, but to the extra-curricula intellectual and sporting activities that so enriched student life there. His plea won our immediate support in principle, but none in practice. The time and circumstances were too compelling.

I returned to take a Part II Tripos not in Chemistry, as was my intent after taking Part I Natural Sciences in 1943, but in History. It was a big change, which I had tried to rationalise in a letter home from Cairo as a desire for three things: added qualifications, educational and cultural value, and acquisition of more knowledge of history especially as that would be of use to me in the Foreign Service if I joined. In fact it was more than that. War service had made me realise I was fundamentally more interested in animate objects, people, than in inanimate objects, things. Some might say the distinction was false, or at least oversimplified, and they would be right. The bio and medical sciences are all to do with living organisms and social studies have since acquired the status of a science. But I returned with little desire to spend the rest of my life in laboratories or classrooms, as I had previously planned, and a strong desire to learn and travel among peoples. A study of history seemed the obvious starting point, especially as the subject had long interested me. I had taken the first exam for the Foreign Service but my letters home confirm that Cambridge and History were my priorities, and the rest could wait.

My return to Selwyn that August was straight from the RAF demobilisation camp, somewhere in the Midlands, with a generous travel voucher to Ludlow via Cambridge. The RAF demobilisation people were very good. We were all anxious to get home, and streaming with colds, after a tedious five day troopship voyage from Alexandria to Marseilles, a miserably cold train journey across France in war-worn and partly windowless trains, a crowded ferry crossing of the Channel and a further cold train journey from Dover. They met us, they fed us, they kitted us out with a free sports jacket and trousers, they formally discharged us, and they met my request for a roundabout journey home with exemplary courtesy and despatch. Anything the RAF did they did well in my experience and I am sure this is still so.

Selwyn College, by contrast, turned out to be in the calm before the storm. The Master, Dean and leading Fellows were their usual dignified selves, although the Master was about to move up the Church hierarchy and, in Selwyn's tradition, to be replaced by another eminemt churchman, Canon Telfer. The Bursar's office however was a different scene. They were in a whirl. Term started in a month and the expected invasion of ex-servicemen, augmenting those already there, was about to come. Accommodation in College was already fully booked, I was told, and I would have to find my own. The fact that I had applied for readmission weeks ahead from Cairo and been accepted, and that I was a graduate and Scholar (though I think I had forgotten that myself), counted for nothing. So, still in uniform, I shamelessly pulled rank, grabbed the addresses of two or three likely lodgings on the College list, over the protests of the Bursar's secretary, and ran. It was every man for himself, and I was lucky to find a welcoming little family in Grantchester Street, within short cycling distance of the College and lectures. Some students had to lodge two and three miles out. Cambridge, like I suppose most educational institutions that find themselves suddenly growing too fast, whether university, polytechnic, college or school, struggled to maintain its cohesion, and also its soul. At least that is how it struck me as my year progressed. The University became temporarily a glorified student sausage machine.

The Selwyn dons were personally most welcoming and helpful, the Dean, the Rev. Blyth, going out of his way at relative short notice to arrange my re-entry and Class B release from the RAF to do so. The old theological Fellow, Professor Marsh, proffered his hand and beaming smile whenever we met. The Master and Fellows contrived to maintain some Collegiate unity. They were a bit taken aback by my wish to change subjects so dramatically, but rallied in support. I was referred to the Senior History Fellow, Dr G. Perrett, whom I remembered as being somewhat elderly even when I was last up. Indeed there was a charming story of his equally elderly wife driving her little box Austin gently along the straight Ely to Cambridge road, on the wrong side, when she bumped into a lorry whose driver had by that time stopped, astonished at the prospect before him. No one was hurt, but Mrs P. endeared herself to the Magistrates and all when it emerged that her response to the driver's challenge 'What the h—— do you think you are doing?' had been: 'Oh dear, Oh dear, I have just been to lunch with the Bishop of Ely.' The College was very fond of her, and her husband. When we met he remarked that in all his many years he had not heard of anyone taking the Part II History Tripos in one year without previous study of the subject. But he saw no reason why I should not try, and do reasonably well if I worked at it. So I gave it a try.

It was half term before I came fully to appreciate the task. Choosing the subjects on which to concentrate was relatively easy. With the helpful advice of my designated supervisor, Dr T. G. W. Spear OBE, an ex-Indian Civil Servant, I opted for Modern European History, English Constitutional History and a new course called The Expansion of Europe. Reading and learning the facts in such short time would be one thing. Learning historical analysis would be another. But, in addition, under the influence of the previous Regius Professor G. M. Trevelyan and others, the Tripos was now demanding a high literary standard – and I had had no training in that, or essay-writing since mid-school. It was a fair challenge with, once started, no going back. It left me no time for anything else that year, no Societies, no socialising, no games except I think a couple of rugby matches and one cricket net. It was unremitting study, and preparations for the Tripos exam. But then so it was for most of that year's students. The fun had to wait for May week.

There were also numerous practical problems. Books were in short supply, both in the shops and in libraries. Fortunately for me the resourceful history mistress at my mother's school in Ludlow found me books even the University Library said were not available, or not for more than a mere two weeks at a time anyhow. Clothing was still on coupons and after buying the essentials there were too few left for a suit. So I had to appear at the College's annual Commemoration Service and Dinner the following April in my RAF battledress converted by a spiv firm of tailors I had found outside the RAF demobilisation camp, into a so-called suit with every ounce of surplus cloth gone, including most pockets and all lapels, and dyed with something very like ink. It must have reduced me to the likeness of a skin diver. It seems there are always a few sharp boys around in and after a war who make money from salvage. Another little problem was the level of prices. It seemed to have risen substantially while we were away, not least for my pipe tobacco. Fuel was also very short, not helped by the Cambridge cold and the national electricity cuts of that winter. And food was still very much on ration. Most of us found this the most trying restriction at first. Whatever hardships ex-servicemen had endured in the war care was always taken to feed us – an army marches on its stomach, Napoleon or someone shrewdly said. I think we complained at first that the College was taking half our rations and only giving us a poor dinner every night. But I later had to acknowledge in writing home that the obligatory dining 'in hall', which still held force, was 'at least filling'. Also my little landlady, Mrs Withers, did wonders for me with my remaining coupons. And the admirable British Restaurants still existed when we were in town. So we soon re-learnt to put up with the shortages suffered all along by the civilian population. It was not to be all White Cliffs of Dover after all but hardship Britain, which had won the war but was now paying for it.

At Cambridge, money too was scarce. The War Gratuity ex-servicemen were paid – in my case about £60 – helped. But service pay had not allowed of much saving. And the benighted Department of Education contrived to take half the year before paying our ex-servicemen's university bursaries. That fell particularly hard on the married students. However, all I knew survived. There was an air of determination not to let little things bring defeat where bigger things had failed to do so. I wrote to my brother, still in the Army in India: 'You will find Britain awfully dreary when you get back – the gloomy faces and skies strike one first. But I never realised before what a pleasure our green fields and trees can bring to eyes grown unaccustomed to them ... Even in the rain ... And it poured from the moment I reached the Release Centre to the time the cold I had collected left me a month later. I scorned those who told me I would need an acclimatisation period ... But it is all right now ... We are all ruddy Englanders again, and I even find the Cambridge east winds invigorating after the lazy heat and depressing stench of Cairo.' My literary aunt, Nell, epitomised it another way; in a card to my mother on her birthday she wrote: 'I am sending a little box of chocs – greater love hath no man that he lay down his sweet coupons —.' That was Britain in 1946/47.

There were of course happy features. It was good to be home and to see family again. It was liberating to be free of uniform and service routines. It was great to be doing something new, and of one's own choice. It was flattering to be ceremonially sworn in as a College Scholar – even if I only had the converted RAF battledress to wear. It was fun to meet old college friends and in some cases like the athlete John Whinnerah his charming wife, even if I did comment home that 'they seemed so young. Or perhaps it is just I cannot get used to people of my age being married. No fetters on me anyhow – at least until I feel more in the settling-down age.' It was touching to receive a little card and cheque from the Ludlow Welcome Home Fund. What thoughtful and kindly people they were who organised and contributed to that. I suppose it was done countrywide. I hope so. Above all there was the relief of knowing the war was over, victorious against hideous tyranny, and personally that we were back, alive and in one piece – the fortunate some of us anyhow. There was a lot to be thankful for, and Cambridge opened its doors as never before.

There were those who wondered where all these students were going to end. Our college Fellows at Selwyn worried about this. Our Dean in particular kept tactfully counselling us. There was full employment in those days, so all doubtless would find jobs. But the Fellows' concern was that we found careers – a vital distinction. The students I knew seemed all to have set their sights either on the Administrative (i.e. Senior) branch of the Civil Service or Foreign Service, or on teaching. The circles we frequented did not seem to be long on other professions, still less on industry and business. The ethos of both in those days, outside a few enlightened companies, did not demand graduates beyond scientists and engineers, and in some cases scorned them. In any case, with the Attlee Government intent on nationalising the major utilities, the best prospects for employment looked like being in the public services, and especially the Civil Service which was going to administer it all. The competition, however, was intense. My letters home were littered with mention of people I had met or heard about who had already tried the Civil and Foreign Service 'Reconstruction entry' and failed.

My own chance came with an invitation to the Civil Service Commission in London, soon after my return to Cambridge, to follow up the written examination I had taken in Cairo. It emerged I had done well in that exam in the arithmetic and the intelligence questions and, gratifyingly, in the essay, but comparatively poorly in the English. My interviewer, whom I described in writing home afterwards as 'an elderly, very thoughtful and kindly gentleman', drew me into conversation about everything from the revival of liberalism in Italy to rugby and then, courteously, asked why I had not done better in the English paper. 'Well, Sir, if I might excuse myself,' said I, embarking on an explanation of the torrid conditions in which the exam had been held and, more importantly, my lack of training in English. 'Oh,' he interrupted gently, 'There's no need to excuse yourself, this interview does not affect the written exam at all. You got more than the required 300 marks altogether and you therefore qualified.' He just wanted to know about the English, and concluded, 'It just shows how unreliable written examinations are.' After further conversation he then mused, 'Yes, you will do well to carry on.' Apparently I was a borderline case and this was the Commission's way of judging and counselling. I found it very thoughtful and sensible at the time, and such subsequent dealings I had with the Civil Service Commission left me in high regard of it throughout my public service career.

My interviewer also, gratifyingly, saw virtue in my plan to finish a year of history at Cambridge, and to postpone until then the remaining parts of the Civil and Foreign Service entry exams – the language oral, the 'Country House' and the final interview. In the officialese of the time I would 'seek deferred entry'. The Civil Service Commission subsequently confirmed their agreement to this. It was a relief. I could now concentrate at Cambridge solely on my studies.

The Tripos year was actually only eight months, with two vacations at Christmas and Easter included. That helped to concentrate the mind. The subjects proved absorbing; the lectures crowded but of high quality; the notes I made laborious (I still have them); and the supervision, after initial resistance to my inevitably targetted approach, was constructive and thoroughly helpful. The whole was an interesting if demanding experiment. But it worked. I did not achieve a first honours. My Tutor and Supervisor kindly commented that that would have been asking too much. But the examiners gave me a 2(1), and all concerned seemed to think that was quite a good result in the time available. Whether it contributed one jot to the principle of mixed disciplines at Cambridge I do not know, though I hold that principle to be desirable, if only to counter the modern narrowing of studies and the trend to what I would term the 'gold-fish bowl society'. For me personally, however, it was a satisfying achievement, with more benefit to my future life and outlook than I could remotely have foreseen at the time. It was a turning point.

Of course we all come out of examinations moaning about something. I was no exception. It seemed to me to be carrying them to the ultimate to test an academic year's study of large subjects in four three-hour papers, concentrated into a few days. I wrote home that I was going to write to the authorities to suggest they spread things over more papers and time in future, like the Natural Sciences people. But I never did. By then I was enjoying a May Ball and a college cricket tour in Kent. Study was behind me, a holiday in Switzerland ahead and then the remaining Foreign Service entry examinations, or whatever. It was fun to be free at last of exams and war service and more exams, and yet still only 23. That summer went like a flash, until the Civil Service Commission caught up with me at Geneva University, supposedly learning French but without exams. I vowed never to take any more in my life (except the remaining Foreign Office entry), and kept that vow. I had had enough.

Cambridge nonetheless remains my intellectual home, as no doubt to the millions of others who over the centuries have studied there. I have re-visited it and Selwyn College whenever I could, and always with pleasure. There is a magnetism about the place that the then Dean of Selwyn, the Rev. Blyth, drily summed up when I went for dinner on High Table ten years later. I was about to assume charge of my own diplomatic mission for the first time, in Guinea, West Africa, and as we sat around the Senior Common Room, passing the port, I made bold to invite him and the other Fellows present to come and stay with me if they were ever in those uncongenial parts. 'We do not have to,' rejoined the Dean, 'you see, everyone comes to us!' And so I suppose we do. That is Cambridge.

# PART TWO

# Diplomatic Service

# CHAPTER 10

# The Foreign Office, London,

# 1947–1949

THE FOREIGN OFFICE I joined in October 1947 was in transition from the rather elitist pre-war to the more widely embracing post-war Service. There were still leading Ambassadors who on retirement entitled their memoirs 'The Ruling Few' or 'The Inner Circle'. But there were also reformers in the senior ranks who had won their case in the Anthony Eden White Paper of 1943, and they had a powerful ally in the Labour Secretary of State for Foreign Affairs, Ernest Bevin. The 'reconstruction period', including broadened recruitment, was well under way when I entered the great portals. The aura was still sedate, but inside I discovered a ferment of activity. Post-war world problems were being grappled in every corner.

I had the best part of two years there before being sent abroad, and three more spells later in differing capacities between foreign postings. All in all my diplomatic career spanned twenty-six years and followed the unusual cycle of Foreign Office – 'Wilderness' – 'Fleshpots' three times round, ending with special assignments in the Foreign Office, Lord President's Office and the Cabinet Office on Britain's entry into the European Community. It finished eleven years short of normal retirement at my choice, for family reasons, and I then took up home-based voluntary and political service. If one counts each appointment in the Foreign Service as a separate job, which they are in terms of most that matters – the country you are in, the subjects and people you are dealing with, the life you are leading – my tally reached 13. I was fortunate that they were all interesting, and few more than my initial spell in what everyone liked to call the FO.

For those who may not know it, the FO and its successor the FCO (Foreign and Commonwealth Office) have long been housed in that splendidly solid and Italianate building on Whitehall opposite No. 10

Downing Street, overlooking the lovely St James' Park and within walking distance of Parliament and the Palace. It was designed by George Gilbert Scott in the 1860s, and in my time the FO occupied just half of his great quadrangle. Before the war it was only one quarter. Today it is the whole, the FO having successfully resisted attempts to barrack them elsewhere in modern glass and concrete, and merged with the Commonwealth and Colonial Offices into one FCO – and one Diplomatic Service. Since 1991 the FCO has also brought into the quadrangle its previously out-housed departments and restored the whole building. The restoration is beautifully illustrated and described, together with a history of the building, in Anthony Seldon's *The Foreign Office*. The Grand Staircase, Locarno Rooms and Durbar Court are sights to see and, happily, are now occasionally opened to the public.

In the post-war years, and indeed throughout my time in the Service, the FO was, to the outside world, a prestigious but rather mysterious and secretive place. It was open only to its occupants and official visitors. If friends had the temerity to call on us there we saw them in the front door lobby, under the eye of the main door guards (or 'messengers' as they were called). We would not dream of receiving them in our offices. Nor would we ever talk about our work outside, other than to colleagues. If asked by curious friends or family what we actually did, we would change the subject. This was not just for security in the formal sense, which was tightened after the Burgess and Maclean defection in the early 1950s. It was because in dealings with foreign governments it was felt it could be prejudicial if they learned our government's position through other than the official diplomatic channels. Of course this still applies today. But with the advent of modern communication systems and of more freedom of official information the days have no doubt passed when a frustrated press could jibe: 'If you are not more forthcoming you will go to your grave tagged Secret.'

Inside, the bewildering thing to a new entrant was not so much the secrecy or the methods of diplomacy or even the substance of the work. We soon learnt, if we did not already know it, that diplomacy and its concomitant, negotiation, were like the law, engineering, medicine, teaching, banking, business or good management, were not something acquired at birth or effortlessly, they were professional skills mastered only by hard work and experience. Office and service procedures, however, had to be learnt at the outset, and most of us on entry, I think, found those of the FO perplexing. They had been largely inherited from before the war.

Paper dominated everything. Diplomacy demands records both because, like most other facets of government, it relies on the 'collective memory', but also because it involves communication with other governments and interests abroad through its own Missions, and detail matters. Within the FO, paper communication between the many regional departments (Western Europe, Eastern Europe, Eastern and Levant, American and so forth) and the functional departments (Economic, European Cooperation, Treaty and Nationality, Consular etc) and the administrative departments (Personnel, Establishment and Organisation, Security etc) and, of course, up the line to Under-Secretaries, Deputy Under-Secretaries and Ministers, went by locked boxes and pouches carried by uniformed messengers, augmented for urgent papers by a system of high pressure air tubes much like those that used to be found in department stores. Today it is by computer and every F.O. desk seems to be graced with one. In our day we were not even supplied with typewriters although we could later get dictaphones on application. Instead we relied on pooled shorthand typists. We also occasionally walked around to see each other. But I suppose that still happens for, thankfully, computers have not yet replaced legs.

Communication with posts abroad was by telegram, encyphered or open according to the content, or by savingram (mailed telegrams), letter or formal despatch carried in sealed diplomatic bags by King's (later Queen's) Messengers. Every substantive report, on receipt in the Foreign Office, was given a file of its own, on which minutes were written with pen and ink. Messy new things like the early biros were banned. We signed our minutes in full if we were addressing them across to other FO departments or up the line to our superiors. We initialled them off if we did not think they required further action. It was all pigeon-carrier stuff compared with the 'single on-line global network' the FCO is apparently developing today – enabling it, to quote a Chief Clerk's Newsletter 'to roll out a combination of Firecrest alongside FTN to give internet browsing access to our nascent Intranet and rapid Restricted and public e-mail,' and, it is hoped, a 'single, Intranet-based way of storing and retrieving information.' That sounds impressive and will no doubt transform the already rapid way in which the Foreign Office traditionally tries to keep ahead of events, just as the development of the telegraph, telex and cypher machine did before and during the war. One just hopes that the high standard of English proudly maintained by the FO throughout its history will not suffer in the process!

The modernising changes under way when I joined were in both the work and the staffing. There were three driving forces. The first was a major enlargement of demand on British diplomacy because of the development of international organisations and, paradoxically, because of Britain's weakened position in the world. I shall come back to that. The second was the advent to the Foreign Secretaryship of Ernest Bevin. The third, and perhaps most important, was the reform initiated by the Foreign Office itself in 1943, which foresaw not just the necessity to replenish and expand ranks starved of career recruitment during the war but the need to unify in one Foreign Service the separate Diplomatic, Commercial Diplomatic and Consular Services; also to widen the diplomatists' range of experience and knowledge to include not just political but economic, financial and social affairs; and, most radical of all, to broaden the base of recruitment.

Since the foundation of the Foreign Office by Charles James Fox in 1782 membership had been largely confined to the best public schools and people with private income. In 1937 all but five of Britain's ambassadors and one third of the junior diplomatic secretaries were reportedly Old Etonians. By contrast, in the post-war 'reconstruction' entry nearly 40% of the first fifty chosen came, to quote *The Times*, 'from schools whose position in the social scale is delicately indicated by the description "grant-aided".' That is how many of us came in. The senior jobs obviously remained in the hands of diplomats of the old school, both at home and abroad, and many of them found rapid promotion in the suddenly expanded service, as did some members of the former Consular and Commercial Diplomatic Services. They also benefitted, like the newcomers, from improved terms of service introduced at the same time – although on a scale starting at £300 per annum for a 3rd Secretary and £100 per annum for a shorthand-typist, those terms were still meagre. By and large I think we 'reconstruction' entrants found the older diplomats accepted the democratisation of their service with grace and encouragement, as did former members of the Commercial Diplomatic and Consular Services, glad at last to be part of one Foreign Service. In the old tradition they took us as they found us, and we, mostly ex-servicemen with war service behind us, took them in the same spirit. It provided an infusion of new blood at a time when it was most needed, while perhaps retaining the best of the old services, the high standards and public-spiritedness anyhow.

Ernest Bevin was later criticised for overlooking the provision of the White Paper to retire early those diplomats judged too elderly or hidebound to adapt. In the words of the *News Chronicle* 'those who know him well think he finds it hard to throw out a man who, according to his lights, has served his country faithfully and has won his promotion patiently, even if he does think the Beveridge Plan is just a new method of bottling port.' The White Paper exhortation 'to plan ahead to avoid congestion at the top' was thus frustrated from the start, as we were to discover later. On the other hand when the then Head of Protocol produced a booklet on Foreign Service conduct, for us raw recruits and wives, in the condescending Edwardian style of 'how to be a gentleman (or lady) and how to mix in society', Bevin not only banned it on sight but had all copies destroyed. He would not tolerate elitism, nor of course anything that brought press mockery on the Office. It did in fact contain some useful tips, but in a style that made it more a book of mirth than advice. We relinqushed our copies with reluctance.

I never actually met Bevin. There were too many layers of officials above me for that. But his presence was everywhere, ably assisted by his Minister of State Hector McNeil, who died even more prematurely, and his Parliamentary Under-Secretary, Christopher Mayhew, whose political and golfing friendship I came to enjoy in later life. Bevin's rise to fame from very humble origins is well known. Somewhat unprepossessing in appearance and manner, especially after the suave elegance of Eden, Halifax and most of his other predecessors; unversed in foreign affairs except through his Trade Union contacts and as Minister of Labour in Churchill's war-time coalition; and at times surprisingly inarticulate, he nonetheless took to the job like a duck to water and few would deny, I think, that he ranks as the greatest Foreign Secretary Britain has had since the war. That is while his health held anyway. His nose for foreign affairs was extraordinary, and his contribution to European-Atlantic security and European economic recovery immense. He was also a practised administrator, and the success of the FO reforms owed much to the energy and understanding he put into them. If he failed to produce a lasting settlement in Palestine it was not for want of trying, and to this day no one has yet done so in that unhappy land. The Foreign Service took him to heart as no other, and mounted a bust of him opposite the Grand Staircase in fond memory. By contrast his successor, Herbert Morrison, although a great figure in both Churchill's war-time coalition and Attlee's successor governments, found himself lost in the job and able to contribute little but indecision. Bevin had something special, and in my first years he reigned over the FO benign and supreme.

We have to remember of course that, although it is little more than fifty years ago, Britain then still bore the responsibilities of a world power. The Empire survived. But in 1947 India and Pakistan achieved independence and, soon after, the British Commonwealth of Nations, formed in 1931 with the white Dominions, was replaced by today's open association of Commonwealth nations. Imperial Conferences became a thing of the past. The India Office and Service ceased to exist and, soon after, the Dominions Office and Service were enlarged to become a Commonwealth Relations Office and Service. The 'reconstruction' entry applied to them too – and figured on my application form as my second preference. Meanwhile the Colonial Office, which administered our Colonies worldwide and, like the India, Dominions and Commonwealth Relations Office, was housed in the same George Gilbert Scott quadrangle as the FO, was promised a spanking new building of its own opposite Westminster Abbey and moved out to Church Street in anticipation. But it was not to be. Successive governments found it less and less timely to be planning an expensive new symbol of empire, and the site remained an eyesore car park for years until the present Conference Centre was built there. The merger into an all-embracing Foreign and Commonwealth Office and Service came in the 1960s.

Back in the immediate post-war years all this was in the future. Hopes of national recovery and a pivotal position in the world remained high. The FO already had too much on its plate to covet more. In addition to its traditional task of handling the country's bilateral relations (with now an increasing number of countries), there were world-wide defence interests still to tend, especially in the face of the new Soviet and Chinese threats and the movements for independence in the colonies. There were also world-wide commercial and financial interests to rebuild from a base impoverished by the War, and we had to adapt to a world now dominated by the USA and the Soviet Union. Part of the answer was to be found in more and more multilateral cooperation with like-minded countries, for common peace-keeping, defence, economic, financial, trade, labour, health, food and agriculture and even cultural purposes. The international organi- sations created post-war seemed to be endless – the United Nations and its regional and specialised agencies; the Brussels Treaty Organisation and then NATO; the Organisation for European Economic Cooperation; the Council of Europe and its Human Rights Court; the European Coal and Steel and Atomic Energy Communities; the International Monetary Fund and International Bank for Reconstruction and Development, both ema- nating from the Bretton Woods Conference of 1944; and countless lesser bodies down to individual subjects like whaling, locusts and the Colorado beetle. International cooperation on a permanent peace-time basis came of age in one great rush. It was a natural and necessary sequence to war-time collaboration between the Allies. The diplomacy involved was not without precedent in peace-time. I suppose it could be said to have been pioneered in the Congress of Vienna, the Versailles Peace Conference and the League of Nations, but never remotely on this scale and intimacy. It created a whole new dimension to the work of the Foreign Office.

So, in a different way, did the Government's perceived need, in the parlous economic circumstances of the country, to maintain tight control of our overseas trade and balance of payments. To achieve this the Foreign Office, Treasury and Board of Trade, jointly with other interested Depart- ments, had to plan, negotiate and maintain up-to-date a great network of trade and payments agreements not only with our main trading partners but with any countries from whom we wished to import or to whom we wanted to export. This added yet another dimension to the work of the FO, as also of course to our Embassies, Legations and Consulates abroad. Then, as if that was not enough, there was the new task of administering the occupation of Germany, jointly with our American and French Allies and the troublesome Soviets, and with our armed services in the British Zone. The largest front-line section of the FO when I joined was devoted to Germany; the second largest to the Middle East and specifically the Palestine crisis; and the third to the newly created economic side, dealing with both bilateral and multilateral economic affairs, including the great Marshall Aid plan for Europe. It was into that economic mill that I was to find myself pitched on arrival. It was a whole new world.

The 'reconstruction' entry proved very popular to aspirants in the services and universities. The FO found no difficulty in recruiting to all its four branches (senior, clerical, secretarial and messengers). From being 'woefully understaffed' so Parliament was informed in 1943 and 'even shorter of trained staff' at the end of the war, it was soon up to its planned 6000. Some 4000 of these would be abroad, in 25 Embassies, 26 Legations, 5 Offices of Political Representatives to ex-enemy countries, several Delegations to the new International Organisations, and countless Consulates. That was still small by comparison with the Home Civil Service, significantly less than 1% in fact. How it stands today, I do not know. Against a great increase in the number of countries demanding diplomatic presence there have been continual economies and now I believe a growing custom of sharing representation both across posts and with some of our European and Commonwealth friends. There has also been a sea change in the advancement of women. Although they occupied more than half the jobs at home and abroad in 1947, all but a handful were secretarial and administrative. The reconstruction regulations debarred them from the senior branch. But Bevin soon changed that, and several admirable young ladies, and one or two older ones too, appeared on the scene in quick time thereafter – although for a long time only on the discriminatory condition that they must resign on marriage.

From being male, Etonian, private income dominated and specialising in political diplomacy, the FO thus changed its composition and functions, its staff and work, with remarkable agility in those few years after the war. We newcomers found ourselves in the company not just of established diplomats, consuls and long-serving staff but a few former members of the Indian and Sudan Civil Services, of the Home Civil Service and international business, as well as of course fellow ex-servicemen. Some of the latter had distinguished war records including a submarine commander with the DSO and DSC, two or three organisers of resistance behind the German lines in Italy and Yugoslavia, several former prisoners-of-war from German and Japanese camps, and one former RAF pilot who among other exploits had clipped part of the great name-plate off the hangar of my former station at Maison Blanche Algiers with the wing of his Wellington but survived. There were also a few from the Dominions, the entry being open to them too.

In retrospect, it was an extraordinary achievement to bring together and induct all these people in such quick time bearing in mind that the reconstruction process could not begin until the war in Europe was over. Moreover the induction needed was not just of the newcomers to the ways and work of the Service. It was of everyone to the requirement of the White Paper that 'Economics and finance have become inextricably interwoven with politics; and an understanding of social problems and labour movements is indispensible in forming a properly balanced judgement of world events.' All officers were now enjoined to help promote the export trade. Not all achieved this metamorphosis over-night, and the planned training envisaged by the White Paper took many years to develop. Under the pressure of events and growing workload there was only one way of induction, and that was the old one of throwing people in at the deep end and, with minimal but intelligent guidance, giving them their head to swim. It is a method I think still has merit.

It was into this world that I embarked at the preliminary examination in Cairo and interview in London in 1946, little knowing where it would lead nor, in truth, what it would involve. I had never met anyone from the Foreign Office, nor for that matter anyone from the other great Departments of State other than the Air Ministry and, in childhood, those in the Board of Education and Welsh Office my father had to the house. London was unfamiliar except for brief visits. Most of all, the international affairs I would be dealing with were an unknown world. I had read newspapers and there was an informative little newsheet from the British Society for International Understanding I subscribed to regularly. Also of course my RAF service abroad and history course at Cambridge had given me a background. But, contrary to my own normal habit, I barely prepared for any of the entry tests. In retrospect I think it was probably the simple challenge, plus perhaps the unexpected encouragement I found at each hurdle, that drove me on.

The language oral was a case in point. I took it in September 1947, at the Civil Service Commission offices in the Burlington area of central London. My telegram home afterwards read. 'Unbelievable I passed the oral.' It was a one-to-one chat with a friendly grey-haired Frenchman who did all the talking, in French of course, to see if I had 'the ability to learn foreign languages.' I was very lucky. My knowledge of French was still no more than '*la plume de ma tante*', if that. I heard my interviewer at one point mention Ludlow in a tone of affection, and then ask a question I fortunately understood: what were the local trees whose fruit everyone ate in the streets? '*Cerisiers*,' I replied, remembering the cherry-stones every-where in season, and groping for probably the only fruit tree I could remember in French at that time. It saved me, and I have been ever grateful to the cherry, and to the kindly interviewer. I am not a good linguist, nor ever have been, but at least justified his faith in me by learning French on the job later in France, Guinea and the Congo.

Within days of the oral we were summoned to the famous Country House 'test of personal qualities' at Stoke d'Abernon in Surrey. There must have been thirty of us, most aiming for the Home Civil Service, one or two for the Northern Ireland Civil Service or the Clerkships in the House of Commons or the London County Council, and the remainder for the Foreign and Commonwealth Services. We were told the two days there would not determine our entry but reports would be made on each of us to the Final Interview Board. To quote *The Times* it was: 'to provide tests based on the War Office methods of selecting officers developed during the war. Character, skill and behaviour are studied from every angle, to be tested further at final interview. Under this system it is claimed that the man with nothing more to him than the academic qualifications for the "good paper-writer" is eliminated. As Mr Bevin has put it, he wants "more in the way of personality".'

The Country House was a stately home, converted in utility fashion for war-time use, with pre-fab outhouses and rather unkept grounds but a certain faded grandeur. The Director greeted us once we were assembled. He was a retired Colonel who might have pioneered the system. He had that natural authority that comes of experience and intelligent command, and the gift of putting people at ease. We were divided into three groups, with a chairman, observer and psychiatrist attached to each. We were to be put through a forty-eight hour programme of individual and group tests, to 'string us apart'. But we were to get to know a bit about them too. The Colonel, whose name I regrettably cannot now trace, impressed us all and I count myself fortunate that he chose to chair my group. The observer we had was a quiet academic who clearly knew what he was doing but did not mix in the bar after dinner or reveal anything of himself at any other time. Some of the other chairmen and observers were more forthcoming but as they were not assigned to my group I remember little of them. The psychiatrists were a breed apart, one retiring, one a tall gaunt lady who psychoanalysed during the day and talked economics in the bar at night, and the third, the one assigned to my group, a pale faced rather self-conscious intellectual whom I did not take to but who turned out to be a man of parts. I shall come back to him.

The Colonel thoughtfully assured us at the outset that what the Civil and Foreign Services were looking for was round pegs for round holes, so any candidate rejected by the Final Interview Board should not take it to mean he or she was a failure but just not quite what they were lookng for. In particular, they were not seeking Assistant Principals or 3rd Secretaries but potential Permanent Under-Secretaries, Ambassadors and Consuls-General. He also assured us that, contrary to anything we may have heard before coming, off-duty would be off-duty, and there would be no microphones under our beds! It was nice to know.

The tests ran, one after the other, from morn till night. They included written problem solving and what the cynics called 'noughts-and-crosses exams', one-to-one interviews with the psychiatrist, group discussions on some moral or topical issue, mutual assessment, and 3-minute speeches on our own subject to the assembled throng. Our examiners were not averse to the odd trick. Our observer, sitting in the back when I was delivering my little speech, deliberately dropped pens and things with a clatter to see if it threw me. But, comparing notes with fellow interviewees in the train to London afterwards I think we nearly all found it, as I wrote home afterwards, 'terribly searching, but fair'. There was one dissenter I remember who enthusiastically declared it to have been 'very stimulating'. I do not know what became of him!

Before we left, the Colonel reminded us that the tests were still experimental and they would welcome any comments or criticisms we cared to make. I was one who volunteered, but was disconcerted to find myself directed to the same psychiatrist whose test I thought questionable. At interview he had asked me to tell him my life story in a matter of minutes and 'not in chronological order but in the style of Lytton Strachey'. Never having read anything of Strachey, and not being introspective, I found it very difficult to respond, and questioned afterwards whether it was a fair test. He defended his corner by contending that I must have met and quizzed at Cambridge many who had already been through this mill, so I knew what was coming. I had to disabuse him; there had been other things to do at Cambridge than analyse one's past and prepare for his test. We agreed to disagree. It was my first encounter with psychiatry and I thought how unworldly he was. I was wrong. The following weekend, walking in the grounds of Hampton Court with some friends, a rustling behind the bushes caught my attention and there, rolling in the long grass (unmown because of petrol rationing) was the same pale face but this time with the handsome red-haired housekeeper of the Country House; and a few weeks later *The Times* announced their engagement. There was evidently more wordliness in psychiatry than I credited, even in those early days of that now distinguished science.

The fifth and final entry test to the Foreign Service was an Interview Board at the Civil Service Commission on 1 October. Between times I had thought it only prudent to go and see the University Appointments Board at Cambridge to explore other careers, and came away with plenty of literature but nothing that immediately appealed. So into the interview I went to be grilled for an hour by a dozen or more distinguished men and women gathered together by the Civil Service Commission from, I suppose, the Civil Service, Foreign Service and Academia. They were seated sternly but observantly at tables in a horse-shoe across a large bare room, entered by a huge oak door through which, at the bidding of a messenger I gained my first sight of them – and they of me. Their job, according to the regulations, was 'to award each candidate a mark for his intelligence, personal qualities and record', the places available going to those with the highest marks, or Civil Service Commission decision if there was a tie. It was strictly competitive and, although borderline candidates could have a second attempt (provided they paid their £1 entry and were still no older than 31), the Interview Board came to be termed 'Final'. Out in front of them was a lonely little table and chair for the candidate and a flask of water in case he ran dry. In the words of my father, the atmosphere on entry 'would have frozen a limpet'. The Chairman, I remember, kindly sought to put me at ease, but it took the best part of the hour to produce a thaw. I wrote home afterwards: 'The interview went off quite well though I've absolutely no idea what impression I created (or failed to create). One or two of my remarks were a bit fatuous; also, as about one third of the one hour's grilling centred on my theory of education I was a little flummoxed by the Chairman's final remark that the *Times Educational Supplement* had an article in its August edition on the British Educational System "which is based very much on your theory". Was he implying my theory was a cribbed one? Heaven knows ... Most of the interviewers questioned me in turn, on subjects ranging from Education to Anglo-Russian relations, the character of the Italian people and their post-war economic and political problems, the future of the Italian colonies, the difficulties of the Ministry of Supply in peace-time (I waffled on that) and the problems involved in Britain in subsidising food.'

On two successive questions I remember replying frankly that I did not know, I had not had the opportunity to study the subjects. That was accepted, but I knew that whatever the next question, ignorance could not be pleaded yet again. It came in challenging tone from a distinguished grey-haired man I had already picked out as the scourge among them if anyone was. 'What would you do with the Italian North African colonies?' he asked. 'Put them under United Nations Trusteeship,' I replied, remembering having read this suggestion somewhere. 'Bah,' he said loudly, or so it sounded to me, and I remember thinking I had blown it. It was in fact a popular solution at the time although not among those who doubted the United Nation's competence. Happily the next question was on the character of the Italian people and, having exhausted the little first hand knowledge I had of them, I found myself recounting how the Neopolitan black marketeers had struck for police protection of their stalls, and secured it. Somehow this broke the ice. The remainder of the interview went swimmingly and I hereby record my thanks to those Neopolitan rogues for providing me with a timely anecdote. The 'Bah' man nonetheless got in his most telling question: would I be prepared to serve in small and distant posts? He had clearly marked me down for the wilderness rather than the flesh-pots if I got in. The idea in fact quite appealed to me, with the promise in small posts of more down-to-earth work and responsibility, and I said so. He did not bah at that but mm'd approvingly. The interview then ended with the chairman's remarks about my education theory – which I am sure in retrospect he meant to be complimentary, though I cannot now recall what the theory was!

The news that I had qualified came to me at Ludlow a fortnight later in a letter from the Foreign Office Personnel Department inviting me to come and see them 'as soon as possible to discuss your future work and training'. My mother held afterwards that when she woke me with an official-looking envelope and read out the contents at my request, all I did was grunt and go back to sleep. This may be apocryphal but there is no doubt I felt by now it was somehow predetermined. On 24 October 1947, I presented myself to the uniformed doorman at 8 Carlton House Terrace, the home then of the Foreign Service administration wing, and was invited to wait standing by a window in the narrow entrance corridor until summoned. Suddenly a familiar figure burst through the front door, paused, turned on his heel and declared 'Well done Hugh-Jones,' and swept on. It was 'Bah', who turned out to be the legendary Sir David Scott, Chief Clerk (Chief of Administration) and great reformer, who knew everyone in the Service and never forgot a face or name. Considering that he had only seen me at Board interview, in a sequence of many others, and dealt with countless people daily worldwide, and that I was standing silhouetted against the window when he passed, I could not but feel that if this was the British Foreign Service then it was the place for me. It was a happy introduction.

The next step was less so. They sent me on a French course at a crammer's school in Kensington for a few weeks with two others who had the grounding I lacked, and my results were poor. The new head of Personnel Department, being of the old school, decided I had been lazy and recorded a black mark start to my two years probation. Discovering this I pointed out that as a student of science and history not languages and as an ex-servicemen, it was a little unreasonable to be expected in only six weeks to discourse freely in French and know how to translate obscure things like 'Scotch mist'. The thought of anyone entering the Service without languages was obviously still novel to him. But he quickly took the point and removed the black mark. I got to know him many years later, as Sir Roddie Barclay, one of the 'Flying Knights' who sought to negotiate British entry into the European Community. He was a very able diplomat.

It emerged later that I had also qualified for the Home Civil Service, but my first preference, the Foreign Service, took precedence, which was a good thing. It was travel and people abroad and international affairs that drew me. Home affairs were to come later.

My first day of work in the Foreign Office proper was after Christmas and had me up early at the Wandsworth Common home of my aunt and uncle where I was staying, don my newly tailored suit (costing an arm and a leg in money and coupons), white shirt with starched and boned collar, black and white morning tie and polished shoes. It was then a quarter of a mile walk past the grimly forbidding Wandsworth gaol, to catch the No. 77 or 88 bus to Whitehall. This became my routine for two years, except that in due course I found the wherewithal to join those in the FO who wore short morning dress and carried a rolled umbrella. The bowler hat or 'Anthony Eden' homburg or military trilby most of my colleagues sported did not appeal. I have never worn a hat since leaving the RAF, except briefly when appointed head of post for the first time in Guinea, but that did not last long as the hat, being dark and of clerical shape, was exactly what the locals liked to wear, sometimes two and even three at a time, and it was soon 'borrowed'. In the post-war FO we were expected to dress soberly and smartly, and of course behave with decorum. From the moment we entered the great doors and climbed the grand staircase, we were, after all, representing our country, no matter how lowly the job.

Mine was indeed on the bottom rung of the so-called 'desk' jobs. I was assigned to the relatively new Economic Relations Department which, under its dynamic head Roger Stevens, later Ambassador to Tehran, dealt with almost everything economic from bilateral trade and payments agreements world-wide to multilateral organisations like the General Agreement on Tariffs and Trade, IMF, International Bank, Food and Agriculture Organisation and, until the advent of Marshall Aid, when a new European Economic Recovery Department was created, our Department had that big subject too. It also had the sensitive subject of Atomic Energy. As the new boy I was assigned to deal with the United Nations regional economic organisations in Europe, the Far East and Latin America. They had been founded the previous year with high hopes among the idealists of assisting the post-war economic recovery and development across Europe including the Soviet bloc, across Asia and the Far East, and across Latin America. But they had rapidly become more political pressure groups than effective economic organisations. Britain's interest in them was marginal. Why my Department dealt with them when there was, around the corner, an efficient UN Economic and Social Department, alongside a UN Political Department, I am not sure. But it gave me the opportunity to learn a bit about countries all over the globe and of Britain's interests in each region; also experience of briefing delegates to international meetings.

The job also taught me a bit about how the FO worked. The Economic Commission for Asia and the Far East was still at a formative stage, and the full membership not yet agreed. I assumed that with the territories and interests Britain still had in that great region we would want full UK membership, and briefed our representitive to fight for it. 'I don't like this,' wrote Foreign Secretary Bevin across the telegram of instructions I had drafted when it was shown to him. 'Why not?' I asked the Head of my Department. 'We don't know,' he replied, 'but the Secretary of State has an extraordinary intuition and you may be sure he has good reason.' So I reluctantly redrafted the telegram to settle for whatever membership the regional members wanted. Bevin was right of course. On the morrow of British withdrawal from India and with all that was going on in the region – the Mao communists advancing down China, war destruction and turmoil in the British, Dutch, French and Portuguese colonies, the defeat of Japan and large American presence on the Pacific rim – there were far more important British interests to defend than membership of a regional 'talking shop'. That seems obvious now. It was not to my seniors any more than to me then, but Bevin foresaw that post-war Britain could not much longer pose as a great power there.

The job also brought me personal baptism in the world of international conferences, an experience to be multiplied many times in the years ahead. The occasion was the annual meeting in Geneva of the UN Economic and Social Council, a body of elected membership which was not going to change the world but in those early United Nations days held out hopes for many deprived nations. I was made secretary of the UK delegation jointly with another newcomer, Keith Matthews who had been a District Commissioner in the Indian Civil Service before joining the Foreign Service. We were under the guidance of a remarkable lady, Barbara Salt, who older members of the Service will remember was a war-time temporary who became established when the Service eventually admitted women to the senior branch. She went on to be appointed Britain's first woman Ambassador (to Israel I think), but tragically fell ill and was unable to take up the post. She was nonetheless made a Dame and lives in the history of the Service as the first 'Her Excellency'. She took us in hand at Geneva, taught us the ropes, and thrust us in turn into the UK delegate's seat to learn to speak (to the briefs we had ourselves written!). This was to a conference of thirty and more, including a Soviet Ambassador, his sad Bulgarian acolyte, and representatives of China (still the pre-communist Kuomintang), Canada, France and other countries of Europe, the Middle East, South-East Asia and Latin America. It was a happy induction although, on the first occasion I was made to speak, my intervention was apparently so ambiguous my colleagues asked me politely afterwards which side I was on! It was conference lesson number one: think before you speak. Lesson number two was on my return to Northolt airport, a little one-ringer Customs Officer out to get someone, picked on me. He did so I think, because I had proudly plastered my bags with 'On His Britannic Majesty's Service' labels. He ordered me to the back of the queue and then searched my luggage with a fine tooth comb even to the beading on my tennis racquet cover. 'What's the matter,' I finally asked in exasperation, 'don't you trust a civil servant?' That tore it. Drawing himself up to his full five feet he declared angrily, 'I am a civil servant'! And so of course he was, and I never forgot it. It does not matter so much nowadays as customs have more sophisticated ways of picking out the smuggler. But throughout my travels I have always since followed the old adage: choose an experienced two-ringed customs officer if you can, avoid the zealous one-ringer at all cost.

On return to London I found a long questionnaire awaiting me from the Ministry of Labour asking, allegedly for the Scientific Register, what I was now doing, was I in research or industry and if so which of a long list? I wrote home that I was sorely tempted to tick the gas industry, as perhaps the nearest to my new profession after the experience of that conference.

Two other interesting little experiences I recall in that job were my first conclusion of an international agreement and my first receipt of a diplomatic démarche. The agreement was between a small clutch of countries led by Britain (on behalf of certain colonies), to fight together against the red locust, a virulent strain of that long-standing scourge of Africa and the Middle East. The promoter of the agreement was an extraordinary British scientist of Russian origin, Dr Uvarov, who made the locust his life's enemy and built up an international network of services to counter it. He operated from a corner of the Natural History Museum in Kensington. I was to see first hand when later stationed in Arabia, the effectiveness of his shoestring organisation against the desert locust. My job on the red locust was to see that the instrument of agreement was properly prepared by our experts in Treaty and Nationality Department, and to arrange the signing ceremony in the Minister of State's office with the Ambassadors of the other countries concerned. The Minister's Private Secretary, Fred Warner, later Ambassador to Tokyo, knew the drill and re-wrote the short speech I had prepared for the Minister, Hector McNeil, to give at the ceremony. He skilfully lifted the tone and content of my first effort at speech-writing, but came to discuss it to ensure I learnt and was not upset. That was the way of the Foreign Service then, and I dare say it still is. Diplomacy starts at home.

The first diplomatic representation, or démarche, I received was from the Counsellor of the Embassy of Chile in London, asking on behalf of his government for British government support in the International Whaling Commission to allow Chile a higher annual quota of whale fishing. He rather overplayed his hand by pleading that without more whale meat Chileans would starve and turn communist. By unhappy coincidence I had that lunchtime, with a couple of colleagues, sampled whale meat for the first time at a cheap restaurant off Leicester Square, and we had found it nauseating. Innocently I felt impelled to tell the Chilean Counsellor this, only to find his Ambassador complaining to the Head of my Department the following day that I had rather rudely rejected their démarche. I maintained he had it coming to him for overstating his case, but was gently instructed it might be better next time to respond simply that 'we would consider the Chilean representations' – which is exactly what we were going to have to do with the other interested departments anyhow. So ended another lesson.

Things were changing on the economic side of the FO when I joined. It remained headed by the tall commanding figure of Roger Makins, as Deputy Under-Secretary (Economic), later to become successively Ambassador to Washington, Permanent Under-Secretary of the Treasury, and Head of the UK Atomic Energy Authority. Beside him, as Under-Secretary, worked Eric Berthoud, an import from Shell via war-time work in one of the home departments. He later became I think Ambassador to Poland

and his son followed him into the Service also to become an Ambassador. I remember playing in his village cricket derby one bank holiday at his invitation somewhere in Essex. The Marshall Plan was by then launched and a European Recovery Department, later renamed Mutual Aid Department, was created to deal full time with it. Roger Stevens moved over to head that department, ably supported by people like John Henniker-Major, Colin Crowe and Gordon Burrett, each of whom I would enjoy coming to know in later years and who went on to eminence in the British Council, the Foreign Service and the Civil Service respectively. The new Head of my Department, Oscar Morland, was a quiet man, member of the former Consular or Commercial Diplomatic Service and as thoughtful and competent a chief as I could have wished. He later became Ambassador to Tokyo, and one or more of his sons also did well in the Service. His assistant Head, also very much representative of the reformed Foreign Service was, first, a distinguished member of the Indian Political Service, Humphrey Trevelyan, who went on to be Ambassador to Iraq and then Governor-General of Aden, and then Roger Jackling who had come into the Service from a law office in New York and went on to be Ambassador to West Germany. Others I remember from those days include John Barnes with whom I worked closely again in later years and who went on to become Ambassador to Israel and then The Netherlands, Kenneth Pridham and Ivor Vincent who attained Ambassadorships to Poland and Nicaragua; Frank Brenchley who, after Poland, was appointed Ambassador to Egypt but whose wife tragically fell ill and he was unable to take up the post; and my first mentor, John Rob, a young First Secretary of the old Diplomatic Service, who watched over my initiation with exemplary patience and courtesy, but who also tragically died young, of I believe multiple sclerosis. The Foreign Service was hard on health.

There was also among us for a while one of the first women diplomats, Jenny Turner, but that bright interlude lasted only months before she married a fellow from the Treasury and was obliged to resign. But of course there were other women about too. The Under-Secretaries had personal assistants, and each Department had two or three shared secretaries, ruled by a 'Departmental Lady', who was often a figure of awe. Ours was a Mrs Barcroft, a refined and kindly lady but not one to cross. The Foreign Office tempered its formality by pioneering the modern use of christian names up and down the hierarchy and the secretaries were part of the family. I still keep in touch with one, Betty Moore. But the Departmental Lady was, with the Secretary of State and Ministers, above the familiarity of first name calling, rather like a Matron.

All on the economic side in those days were housed in the old Locarno rooms on the first floor, except for a third department called General which dealt with international maritime and air transport and, for lack of space inside, had to be outhoused. Reporting on the restoration of the Locarno Suite forty and more years later, the *Independent* commented:

> The Locarno suite of three rooms – the Cabinet Room and larger and smaller Conference rooms – was specially designed by George Gilbert Scott to evoke a feeling of grandeur, 'a kind of national palace, or drawing room for the nation'. It was renamed after the Treaty of Locarno was signed there in 1925 ... With the outbreak of the second World War the chandeliers were shrouded and the suite taken over by the cyphering branch of the Communications Department. Shortage of space in the post-war years led the rooms to be divided up into cubicles under a false ceiling ... The splendour remained shrouded behind anonymous plasterboard.

That is where we and our successors worked, with the archivists occupying the half floors above, all of us unaware of the grandeur behind the plaster – until it was restored in 1991.

After Geneva I was told to hand over my desk to a newcomer, Peter Marshall (who went on eventually to become Deputy Secretary General of the Commonwealth), and to take on the work of overseas trade and payments. It may be difficult for anyone accustomed to today's world of free trade in goods and vast free trade in money, to visualise the tight restrictions of the immediate post-war world, when protection of industry recovering after the war and of desperately drained currency reserves, was the order of the day. Trade and payments were a constant preoccupation of Ministers in Committee and Cabinet, and the full time concern of the Overseas Negotiating Committee, chaired by the Foreign Office and including senior officials of the Treasury, Board of Trade, Ministries of Supply, Food and Agriculture, other interested departments and the Bank of England.

The control was in extraordinary detail. Many were the hours the ONC and its sub-groups spent working out how much beef we could authorise our Embassy negotiators in Buenos Aires to agree with the Argentinian authorities and our importers to take from the Argentine in the next quarter, or the number of oranges we could afford from Brazil, not to mention commodities like oil and minerals. Ominously rising deficits in the balance of payments and declining sterling reserves were a constant reminder of the task. Tight control was an essential part of the austere economic policy pursued by Sir Stafford Cripps, Chancellor of the Exchequer, and the Government of the time. It did work. With the help of devaluation and Marshall Aid the economy steadily improved. But there were times when I for one wondered whether there was not a shade too much official fear of giving up war-time controls and allowing trade to develop again without all-embracing licence. Habit grows hard. I put a paper up to this effect after a time, specifically on the Argentine trade agreement, so important to us as a beef-eating nation then, and found agreement among my immediate superiors (that is FO'ese for 'bosses') but little in Whitehall. Part of the problem lay I believe in the powerful, some might say almost obsessive, attachment of the Treasury and City of London to protecting sterling as a primary currency of world trade. But we did at that time still hold the reserves of many countries of the so-called Sterling Area and that imposed obligations. The whole system took many years to open up, beginning after Cripps and then with the abandonment of domestic rationing. (I still have in my inherited papers a food ration book of my mother's of 1950/51.) In my time, the trade and payments control system occupied the energy and talent of a whole army of officials senior and junior and much time of Ministers too. But there was a common spirit of fighting for recovery, and very much what is today I think called 'joined-up government'.

That does not mean there were no occasional inter-departmental squabbles. Of course there were, and, in the nature of all dynamic organisations, there always will be. But we had a camaraderie and a will to sort them out, and usually did so amicably. The chairmanship of the Overseas Negotiating Committee fell to the Foreign Office because, even down to oranges, we were dealing with foreign countries, and I dare say Ernest Bevin insisted anyhow. To put it in perspective however, this trade and payments army constituted but a fraction of the government services of the day. By 1947 the 'reconstruction' had already brought the total number of Civil Servants reportedly up to 700,000, which was more than twice the pre-war strength, although they were expected to fall back to 650,000 when rationing ended. The run-down of war-time services administering the armed forces, the armaments industry, information and the like, was outweighed by the huge new administrative demands of social security following Beveridge, education following the 1944 Butler Act, the new National Health Service and the nationalised industries. They were all largely centralised in London in those days. Then there were Parliament, the London County Council and its Boroughs to administer. The capital was awash with officials. Inevitably there were occasional envies and jealousies, and the Foreign Office being, in the public image, a rather glamorous place, drew its fair share. I recall one rather silly occasion – how could a new recruit forget it? On the regular bus from Wandsworth one day I heard an official of the Ministry of Supply and another from some corner of the Board of Trade, both identifiable because they always talked in a loud voice, discussing what they thought of the FO. It was illuminating. On arrival at Westminster the elder concluded triumphantly, 'The trouble with the Foreign Office is that they are just a bunch of pseudo-intellectuals who read the *New Statesman!*' I often wondered, but never found any who did.

The old tradition of the Foreign Office was apparently to deplore anyone who 'works too hard' or 'shows too much zeal'. Whatever it may have been pre-war, there were few I encountered in those post-war years, and later, who did not put in many hours beyond the official eight hour, five and a half day week. We lunched in a rationed canteen or, when we could afford it, a West End club, commonly The Travellers, and went home late most evenings. The same applied widely in the Civil Service, at least in those Departments we dealt with. Some of the Press was inclined to be snide, as now, but there was a measure of public appreciation, which I feel sure today's Civil Service equally merits but rarely gets. The good old *News Chronicle* was particularly understanding. In January 1947 the columnist A. J. Cummings wrote: 'These 4000 administrators at the top are the nation's Brains Trust, and in general they are shamefully overworked.' Three years later, in 1950, the Political Editor Paul Bareau wrote:

> Pity the men who run our lives ... You will see him as he catches his train home in the evening, probably nearer eight than seven pm, pallid of countenance, red rims round the eyes, carrying an ancient bulging black dispatch case with the royal insignia in faded gold – the trade mark of the higher civil servant ... The business of administration has become increasingly complex ... and, in addition, the civil servants now have to tend the huge increase in international organisations with which the world is beset ... There is a strict injunction in the book of rules of the Civil Service that no secret papers my be taken away from the office. If it were observed the administration of this country would collapse tomorrow! ... The higher civil servant is not the tyrant, the kill-joy depicted by so many cartoonists. He is an underpaid, over-worked fellow, driven by a machine which often makes intolerable demands on him; driven also by a loyalty and devotion which few outside the machine will ever suspect.

That was indeed how I found most of them. In these pages I may from time to time indulge in criticism of the petty officialdom and even chicanery I encountered at times in one Department or another. But I can record that in all my dealings with other countries over the years I never found a Civil Service quite to match ours in integrity, competence and hard work, although the Canadian and French came close. How it is today, especially after the depredations of the Thatcher, Major and now the Blair years, I no longer know but have little doubt that our Civil and Foreign Services remain national assets admired abroad if not always adequately at home.

One subject of foreign affairs that fascinated me in those early days, and still does though I have never had the opportunity to go there, is China. At the Geneva UN Conference I met – and did not like – the Kuomintang Chinese. They had some large public works project they wanted supported by the UN, that seemed very fishy to young bloods like me and my Canadian colleague, John Halstead, whom I was to meet again in a senior position in Ottawa many years later. We were eventually persuaded by wiser heads to make our point but then recognise that the Chinese delegation had cleverly secured the majority of votes and we would lose support on matters of more importance to us if we persisted in trying to block them. It was a lesson in committee diplomacy. On return to London I found a different and much bigger China problem on my desk. The Mao communists were sweeping the country from the North and threatening Shanghai where we had huge investments – some £300 million as I recall. Should we try to defend them, and if so how? Our China experts, the 'Old China hands' as they were called in Whitehall, reckoned there was nothing we could do. Representing the economic side of the Office and, I suppose, righteous youth, I argued for action in the form of sanctions and negotiation. The 'do nothing' viewpoint prevailed, though not without prolonged discussion, including of course with the companies concerned. 'The Chinese always take the long view and so should we,' was the philosophy of the old hands. How much we actually lost I never discovered. But the shipping, trading, banking and I think oil companies concerned survived, the leading ones anyhow, and have doubtless since recouped many-fold through Hong Kong and the opening up of China since Mao. It was an illuminating if frustrating exercise in foreign policy.

If life in those days revolved very much around work, there was also a lighter side. The Foreign Office had a Sports Club at Swakeleys House, Ickenham in North London, and it had a rugby team just that season started by two stalwarts, Geoff Hardy and 'Hooky' Walker from GCHQ, then at Eastcote and under the aegis of the FO. I joined and we had a splendid two seasons culminating in the annual Middlesex Seven-a-sides. I had by then graduated, or retreated whichever way you look at it, from second-row forward through fly-half and centre to full-back, my favourite position, and they made me Vice-Captain. I never did discover what my team-mates did at work until 50 years on, in 1996, they found and invited me to attend the half-centenary celebrations of the FO Sports Association RFC and its successor the Cheltenham Civil Service Rugby Club. It flourishes and I understand now has four teams. We also played cricket and tennis at Swakeleys. Whether the FO still has a sports club there or elsewhere I do not know, but hope so.

Life with my aunt and uncle and cousins at Wandsworth Common was also fun. They had come back to London from evacuation with his school in the Spring of 1946, to find their house in Ellerton Road, after five years absence and requisitioned occupation by others, in what she could only describe as: 'an appalling state … ceiling lathes and plaster exposed … floors crumbling … windows broken and blocked up with black cardboard … the Ideal boiler knocked squiffy and the paint a horrid chocolate brown ...' They had restored it bit by bit by the time I came to stay with them, and had refound their feet and friends in London. 'There is a strange rightness in being back,' Nell wrote. 'I feel we shall never want to move again as this is our home and the thought of moving is nightmarish.' London was also beginning to come back to life. 'The damage done and the big open spaces laid bare have to be seen to be believed,' wrote my grandfather Charles Normington on a visit there in the Summer of 1946. 'There are still hundreds of shops without windows,' he added. There was also the restrictive rationing of food and fuel to contend with. But within those limitations there was always something going on in the Cowan household, whether it be discussion of politics, education or the news; or visits to exhibitions, concerts, heritage sites or the East End markets, as far as restricted public transport permitted; or *The Times* and *Observer* crosswords. They suffered neither fools nor the idle gladly but were ever thoughtful of others, and always of good humour. They were a delight to live with.

My first car added a bit more freedom although the petrol ration covered but 30 miles a week, and the car only lasted a few months. It was a pre-war Austin 10 saloon, of indeterminate mileage and ownership, bought, on local recommendation to my Leamington aunt, from an ex-Sergeant of Police in Warwick. He turned out to be just a front-man for one of the many spiv dealers who popped up after the war to salvage anything with wheels, repair the engines, paint over the rust and sell them to mugs like me on a market starved of cars. I rashly took it on a three week holiday on the Continent and, despite finding myself with a dead battery on the then unfriendly Yugoslavia border, dead windscreen wipers in a snowstorm on the Pack pass in Austria, and a hole in the side you could put your fist through when an accidental scrape revealed little but rust under the paint, I contrived to cover 3000 miles, only to find the insurance condemning it on return. The chassis was rusted right through. With the help of a local friend in Leamington I was able to shame the dealer and ex-Sergeant into reimbursing me much of the cost. But it was another lesson learnt, elementary today but still novel in those days: beware of second-hand car salesmen you don't know. That holiday I also experimented with a moustache, only to find it viewed on return with such horror by a lady colleague that I felt obliged to remove it forthwith. To be likened to an errand-boy was a snobbish but effective way of dismissing such vanity in those days. Beards were rare in the Foreign Service; I do not remember anyone sporting one. Moustaches were not uncommon but had to be mature. We were very conformist, I suppose. But my aunt observed to my mother that her son 'seems very happy, and well except for his usual Rugger limp which he seems to regard as good for him. I do not know how!'

Altogether those two years gave me an absorbing introduction to London,

Government, the world of diplomacy, and international affairs. Once that probation period was over I was granted a Commission, signed personally, for some strange historic reason, by both HM the King and the Prime Minister of the time, and reading as follows:

(Signed) GEORGE R

GEORGE the SIXTH by the Grace of God, of Great Britain, Ireland and the British Dominions beyond the Seas, King, Defender of the Faith, etc, etc.

To All and Singular to whom these presents shall come, Greeting ... KNOW YE ... that We have constituted and appointed ... Our Trusty and Well beloved Wynn Normington Hugh-Jones Esquire to be an Officer of the Ninth Grade of our Foreign Service at any of our Diplomatic or Consular Establishments abroad or in the Department of Our Principal Secretary of State for Foreign Affairs or elsewhere as aforesaid. Giving and Granting to him in that Character, all Power and Authority to do and execute all necessary Writings, Memorials and Instruments, as also to assist our Ambassador ... or Our said Principal Secretary of State for Foreign Affairs ... And we therefore request all those whom it may concern to receive and acknowledge our said Trusty and Well beloved Wynn Normington Hugh-Jones ... and freely to communicate with him upon the things that may appertain to the Affairs of our Embassy ... or to those of Our Foreign Service at large.

GIVEN at Our Court of St James's the Twenty-first day of November in the Year of Our Lord One Thousand Nine Hundred and Forty-nine and in the Thirteenth Year of Our Reign. (with effect from the Twentieth day of November, 1947)

By His MAJESTY'S COMMAND

(Signed) C.R. ATTLEE

CHAPTER 11

# Saudi Arabia

## 1949–1952

W ELL, I'm not sure I really mind where they send me,' I concluded. We had just spent an entertaining evening, my aunt, uncle and I, going through the atlas to decide where I would most like to go on my first diplomatic posting. I had been told in the office that morning that Personnel were after me to go abroad and wanted to see me tomorrow. I could state my preferences ... but there was no guarantee.

'Every Embassy seems to have good and bad about it,' I conjectured, after showing off the little knowledge I had acquired about each and all in my two years in the Foreign Office. If the country was interesting the job was not, or the social life, or the climate, or the altitude, or the sports facilities, or the reputation of the Ambassador or his wife. I would probably not get much choice anyway. Post preferences were merely a sop to democracy, said the cynics.

So I retired to bed prepared for anything – until an afterthought struck. 'Jedda,' I called down to my aunt and uncle, 'that is the one place I do not want.' 'Why not, where is it'? they asked. Out came the atlas again. We found it in tiny print, half way down the Red Sea, the diplomatic capital of Saudi Arabia. A real little hell-hole from all accounts.

The next evening – 15 July 1949 – I returned home to be greeted expectantly: 'Well, somewhere really nice?' 'Not really,' I replied – 'Jedda!' They did not believe me. But so it was, and so it was to be.

The 1st Secretary in Personnel deputed to break the news to me did so skilfully. He had been there himself, and spun me a good story of congenial company and fine sunsets. He later rose to be Ambassador to Egypt, I think. Not that he left me any choice, still less occasion to express any preference. The FO Selection Committee wanted me to go to Jedda, and I had no health or family reason to argue. We had in any case all signed to go anywhere in the world – and I took that to be a solemn pledge.

My dear mother was very distressed at the news and wanted to know the full why and wherefore. I sought to reassure her, writing:

> The interview was not rushed and most of the questions you raised did in fact go through my head. I probably could have got a better post if I were better at bluffing (to put it crudely), but that sort of thing never appealed to me ... I am in any case a fatalist at heart and Jedda has perhaps been hanging over my head since one of the fellows on the French course got out of a posting there (he had a wife and baby but ended up in a not much better place) ... I keep an open mind about my future and am no careerist ... For an artist or a doctor or a lawyer the quest to find their purpose in life may be relatively simple. For me it isn't, because I did not find my natural bent easily. I think I have found it in the work of the Foreign Service. I am not perfectly sure, but I find much of the work interesting and some of it fascinating, and it seems to provide the natural medium for what I know are my chief interests, politics and people (for want of a better expression). Time and experience will prove or disprove this ... I know well the discomfiture of heat, flies and sand will lessen my zest for life and capacity to live and learn. To that extent it will involve a certain waste of time which I cannot contemplate with equanimity at this stage of life ... I did think of resignation. Probably in three, six or twelve months time I shall wish that I had done so. But if my second post is more attractive climatically (as it should be) I think my acceptance of this appointment will appear justified ... It will only be for 1½–2 years.

If truth be known, I soon got over the shock and began to find the challenge of Jedda quite exciting. Still young and single, I was ready to taste adventure again, after three deskbound years in Cambridge and London. Given only three weeks to prepare there was no time to mope anyhow. It took longer to get ready in those days because most things went by sea and there were provisions to order, domestic equipment to acquire, a car to purchase and so forth. There was also tropical clothing to obtain, a course of inoculations to endure, farewell visits to Lords and Wimbledon to fit in, and of course to family and friends, all by public transport. There were established suppliers like Saccone & Speed for drink and Mr Smith of Hawes Bros in Faringdon Road for clothing – he was the recognised expert on tropical outfitting even though he had never been east of Dover. I remember him showing me a tropical suit he had made for a Colonial Governor by the splendid name of Sir Hilary Blood. I declined one with reluctance. There would be no occasion for a suit in Jedda. There was, however, a white tropical diplomatic uniform to be made, with braided cuffs and collar, and spiked-top topee. Every moment was filled, and my aunt recorded that I only caught the airport bus at the old Airways House terminal at Victoria by seconds.

It made it interesting that the Middle East was high in priority in British foreign affairs at the time. I had tasted North Africa, Egypt and Palestine during the War but not reached Arabia. I was not an Arabist, and had no wish to become one, but my job was to be Commercial Secretary, so there might be scope for some initiative. Also, being a modest cog in a small wheel might be more interesting at this stage than a small cog in a big Embassy. Anyhow Personnel had assured me it would not be for long. They would, of course! In fact it was to be three years and more; much longer than was usual in such a place, and, as it turned out, the longest of my diplomatic career.

Saudi Arabia was then at an early but interesting stage of development. It had only emerged from centuries of desert tribal conflict in the space of a lifetime, and the population of five to six million was still mainly nomadic. Today, 50 years on, it is of course one of the world's wealthest nations per capita, the foremost producer of oil and a powerful state in Middle East affairs and beyond. It is also an important market. While democratic progress and human rights remain deplorably lacking by our standards, economic progress has been phenomenal.

The creator of this state, King Abdul-Aziz Ibn Saud, still ruled supreme. I was to meet him many times during my stay and although he was by then getting old and infirm, he never failed to impress by his regal bearing, his natural authority, his courtesy, his mastery of detail and his wisdom. I was to find he was one of those rare people whose presence you could feel when entering his audience chamber before you even knew he was there. He was a big man in every sense of the word, and all Arabians revered him. An historian of Arab affairs told me recently that I am now one of only a few people alive outside Arabia who knew him. That must date me, and I was of course no more than aide to successive Ambassadors and distinguished visitors at those encounters. But we were always included, and I count myself fortunate to have been there.

Ibn Saud was perhaps unique in contemporary history, in being a warrior chief who united his country, created his own Kingdom, and won worldwide respect for it in his own lifetime. Churchill and Roosevelt recognised this and his friendship by inviting him to special meetings in Egypt towards the end of the war. Born in 1876, he was the eldest surviving son of a dynasty that had ruled central Arabia on and off since the eighteenth century and proselytized the strict Wahhabi Moslem faith. At the age of 25 he set out to reconquer Riyadh and his grandfather's domains from rival rulers, and then, step-by-step, to capture Eastern Arabia from the Turks, Northern Arabia from the Rashidis and Western Arabia, including Mecca, the birthplace of the Prophet Mohammad and Medina, the Prophet's burial place, from the Hashimites. He formally established his kingdom and secured recognition by Britain and other countries in 1932. By then he had won over all the tribes and, by prolific procreation (he

King Ibn Saud and Winston Churchill in Cairo, February 1945.

eventually had over sixty children – by of course innumerable wives), and importantly, by bringing them up as a band of brothers (and sisters), he was already well on the way to creating the dynasty that continues to rule Saudi Arabia today. (The present King Fahd is the fourth of Ibn Saud's sons to rule in succession.) This was evident when I was there. Like the courtiers of European monarchs of old, all the family lived in the capital to be near the King. Social intercourse with westerners was limited by the King's refusal to have non-Moslems living in Riyadh and by prohibition of both alcohol and anything resembling political gatherings. Several of his sons and even grandsons however had already begun to travel and occasionally appeared among us in Jedda.

This was but seventeen years into the life of the Kingdom. Ibn Saud had not wasted time. He granted an oil concession in Eastern Arabia to CASOC, the forerunners of the Arabian American Oil Company (ARAMCO) only a year after creating his state. Oil started flowing five years later. World War II checked development but by the time I found myself reporting on the Saudi economy, oil production was already soaring and revenue pouring into the Saudi coffers. Under this bonanza the crude financial administration of the State was soon crumbling and the Royal family becoming profligate. This was the downside. Despite his age, war wounds, arthritis and blindness in one eye, the King remained sole executive, except for financial affairs which he delegated to his trusted but also aged friend Abdulla Suleiman. The national budget was rudimentary, there were few statistics, and the finance, customs and tax administrations were elementary. Those responsible carried most everything in their heads. Their capacity to do so never ceased to amaze me. Many Jedda merchants were the same. A few, usually to be found seated cross-legged on a raised rug in their small open shop, ran huge currency exchanges, I discovered, involving Indian rupees, silver and gold coins, via the Lebanon, Persian Gulf and India, on small margins but large profits, without any accounting or reading literacy. Their memory for figures and for mental arithmetic was astonishing. But the administration of the State could obviously not continue like that. Pressure for reform grew strongly while I was there, from internal and external advisers, but major change had to await the demise of both the King and his Finance Minister, and also the ultimate abdication of the King's immediate successor Saud.

Ibn Saud in his prime was a formidable ruler, described by that distinguished orientalist, Sir Ronald Storrs, as a 'benevolent despot, cast in heroic mould, the wisest-living Arab, founder of his own Kingdom, and a war-proved friend of Great Britain.' He was also very shrewd. He selected his ministers, regional governors, advisers and senior officials with care and rarely found cause to change any of them over the years. He chose his friends in the world similarly, and, once established, remained loyal. So it was in his relations with Britain. He cherished the British support he had received and never forgot it, nor let any of his entourage do so.

Britain was of course the dominant power in the Middle East before the 1939/45 War and had recognised Ibn Saud since 1927, after anguished debate following the withdrawal of the Turks from Arabia and collapse of the Ottoman Empire in the 1914/18 War. Even during the 1939/45 War Britain had found shipping, food and minted silver riyals to keep Saudi Arabia going. After the War, we no longer had the wherewithal. Saudi Arabia had in any case found its own feet, with the development of oil and revival of the Haj pilgrimage, and the Americans had moved in, following ARAMCO. As in most other parts of the world, we found we were not so much representing the victor of World War 2 as a declining power with worldwide responsibilities far outstripping resources. We had to adjust. We learnt locally, as nationally, to punch above our weight in defence of British interests when we could and realistically to seek the cooperation of others when we could not.

In post-War Saudi Arabia we had to look after not just British interests but those of every other Commonwealth country that wanted any trade or consular assistance there including many Commonwealth Asian and African nations with Moslem communities who sent pilgrims to the annual Mecca Haj. In addition, and importantly, we represented the many states bordering Saudi Arabia which were still under British protection – Kuwait, Qatar, Bahrain, the Trucial Sheikdoms, Oman, Hadramaut and Aden on the Arabian peninsula, and Sudan and Eritrea across the Red Sea. We also had a Military Mission training the Saudi Army at Taif in the hills behind Jedda; a Desert Locust Mission fighting the locusts of Arabia and based near Jedda; two long-established trading and shipping companies; a few visiting construction companies; and subsidiaries of the former British Overseas Airways serving each side of the country from Aden and Bahrain respectively. Commercially there was growing British interest in the country as the oil and Haj revenue developed. Politically, there was always the critical situation in Palestine and, bilaterally, the running sore of ill-defined and oil-rich boundaries with our protectorates, to consult and argue about. There was still plenty of substance in common British and Saudi interests to keep the relationship special – as indeed it seems to have remained, off and on, almost to today.

So this is where I found myself in the early morning of 21 August 1949, having flown by a lumbering old BOAC York from London to Tripoli and Cairo the previous night, and by a slow and bumpy Aden Airways DC3 overnight from Cairo to Jedda. The Foreign Office had secured Treasury permission for me to travel by air rather than the still normally prescribed sea, for the simple reason that there was no passenger sea service to Jedda, even from Liverpool, the then popular port of Britain which still published sheets of daily sailings. It seemed anyhow that the days of regarding air flights as exotic were passing, even among the skinflints of HM Treasury.

My diary for that day reads. 'Arrived Jedda. Stinking hot. Very steamy day.' And so it remained. I was to find that the climate, while free of the extremes of hot and cold inland in the desert, and a bit better in winter than in summer, never relented, particularly in its high humidity – and attraction to insects. With irritating winds and only very rare rain, it was not made for human habitation – not, at any rate, without the good housing, air conditioning, running water and other facilities and comforts that now abound there. It was also monotonous, with no let-up at night. We sweated, suffered prickly heat, 'gyppy tummy', flies, mosquitoes and the rest, without much relief. The saving grace, I suppose, as in most such places, was that we all suffered together – and determinedly made the best of it. The people one really felt for were the 100,000 pilgrims who came from all Moslem corners of the globe in overcrowded ships and planes, or on foot, for the annual Haj. Our suffering was as nothing to theirs. Jedda's reason for being was in fact as port to the Moslem Holy Land and because Mecca and Medina were prohibited to non-Moslems.

My first sight of the place as we came in to land was enough to make any but a pilgrim's heart sink. It was just a small sun-drenched clump of dirty white buildings, between the sea and the desert, more like a fishing village than a diplomatic capital. The airport was but a strip, half a mile out of town, with an elementary control tower and one radio operator. A year later I discovered him listening to Cairo pop singing on the principle that if an aircraft was going to crash that was the will of Allah so why should he worry? An Aden Airways passenger plane had gone missing in the Sudan desert, across the Red Sea. My discovery that no-one had been listening was just in time to prompt a belated rescue operation. The passengers and crew were in rather a bad way when found but at least they survived. Jedda air traffic control was subsequently internationalised.

The town, as I first entered, looked as if it had been shaken by an earthquake long ago and never straightened up. Hundreds of crazily leaning houses, mostly four storeys high, with latticed balconies stuck out at all angles, crowded together around narrow alleyways and a teaming *suq* (market). Built of relatively soft coral rock it was only the mosaic of rough-hewn wooden beams in each structure that held it together. The town wall which for centuries had assured its defence, had just been pulled down, and a few modern offices and houses had begun to appear. The only paved road was that to Mecca. There was no piped water, although it was under construction from the hills. Coolies delivered our water daily to pots on the top floor, and it trickled down to us through primitive plumbing. When we had a shower it involved standing in a laundry tub under a rusty rose. The coolies were all bow-legged, poor fellows, from pulling a bowser round town and carrying the cans of water up four flights of such houses daily. It was inadvisable to inspect the pots for fear of finding the many nasties usually drowned in them. I did it once, but never again. There was a municipal electricity supply of sorts; but the Embassy had its own small generators and a resident engineer to service them.

Movement was by foot or, for goods, by myriad coolie-carts, except for the few who could afford cars. Mine was a little open-topped Morris Minor, as tough and splendid a car as Morris ever produced. But I had to borrow most of the £300 cost, and wait three months for delivery. Incongruously a few huge American cars had begun to appear, owned by Saudi Royals or leading merchants or the growing American oil and construction community. Horses were no substitute; they could not stand the coastal climate. It was a town of growing contrasts, with everything but the basic sorghum and fish imported, with living costs correspondingly high, and nowhere to go but the sea and desert.

What a dump it seemed to be at first sight. But still worse was to come that first day, when I was shown my designated flat. My predecessor had described it to me in detail when offering its contents for sale. This was the tradition in those days. Maybe it still is. Only the bare furniture was provided by those officially responsible for our housing, the late Ministry of Works. All staff below Head of Mission had to provide their own domestic ware wherever they went. My predecessor had said it was a spacious flat rented in an old building which 'faced the wrong way'. Bring plenty of Harpic, he said. It turned out to be on the lowest habitable floor of an old building, closed in by others, airless, rather foul smelling, with ceilings of brown stained planks and walls of dark green oil-paint, as depressing as anyone could have chosen. I vowed to get out of it before it drove me to drink.

The other Embassy buildings, the Ambassador's Residence and the Office (called the 'Embassy' and the 'Chancery' respectively) and most of the other staff flats were at least open to the sea since the destruction of the old wall. In due course I was able to move into one of them, sharing it with the equally newly arrived Embassy accountant. It was at least habitable though still primitive. The Chief Inspector of the Foreign Service visited us in early 1950 and reported that in all his experience he had never seen a post worse housed or more neglected. As a member of the old Consular Service and an experienced Inspector, he knew what he was talking about. Sir Alexander Hutchen was his name. A quiet Scot and fine man.

Although it was not really my job, but with the support of my colleagues, I began before he arrived to explore the possibility of securing at a reasonable rent, some new buildings under construction in a good location opposite the Embassy. The fact that they were being built for the Minister of Finance personally and that he expected rent in gold sovereigns (still, with the silver riyal and silver Maria Theresa dollar, the currency of Saudi Arabia then) would raise some objections at home. But the Chief Inspector lent his full support and I was given freedom to redesign and negotiate them to our needs, and in due course the staff and Chancery were rather better housed as a result. I tried but failed to persuade the Ambassador that a third new building in the same compound should be made the new Embassy residence. But the Ministry of Works scuppered that. They had promised to build a new one for him – they loved architecting and building their own, anywhere they could afford in the world. It took them in this case, I believe, the best part of twenty years.

Their record on air conditioning was little better. The room units we eventually persuaded them to supply in 1951 turned out to be huge contraptions that must have been built in a moonlighting ordnance factory. They were certainly made more for warfare than comfort, with crude fan belts that came off regularly at night and woke the living with a clattering against the casing like a pneumatic drill. I am told that when they were eventually replaced by the American room units everyone else used, they had to be unceremoniously dumped at sea. No one wanted them even for scrap. Many times later in my career I would come to wish we could have got rid of the Ministry of Works' dead hand on government overseas property everywhere at the same time. I was pleased to have the opportunity, twenty years on, to play an initiating part in achieving this. Whether the successor Agency proved better I do not know. I hope so.

On the brighter side, my colleagues in Jedda turned out to be a stalwart lot. So did most of the small European, American and Diplomatic community. Few local Arabs mixed socially with the foreign community in those days, and their wives were confined to the harem. But those who did were as welcoming as everyone else. There was a rugged solidarity, and moaning about the place was tactfully discouraged. We worked hard – 6½ days a week, early morning to early afternoon and frequent evenings. Being a Moslem country the Sabbath was Friday. But our weekly diplomatic bag arrived by air from Cairo that day, so opening and reading mail took up the Sabbath morning. Socially, we lived in each other's flats. There was not much to talk about. But it was congenial and that made it tolerable.

My first Ambassador, Alan Trott CMG, was a scholarly man of dry humour who had served his whole diplomatic career in the Middle East and spoke Persian and Arabic fluently. His first love was Persia where he had been Oriental Secretary at the Embassy until the Shah, in some momentary pique with the British Government, declared him persona non grata (P.N.G.), which meant he had to leave the country for good. He had been accused of spying in some allegedly sensitive area outside Tehran, but a more improbable spy it would be difficult to imagine. His hobby was bird-watching in the hills and deserts around and the taxidermy of birds he shot with an 0.22. Anyone commissioned to fetch a drink from his refrigerator would as like as not find it part full of stuffed pigeons. His wife was the daughter of a missionary. They made a kindly if administratively slightly absent-minded couple. As the most junior Secretary I was often called upon to help at their diplomatic parties, all too frequently at short notice to fill the 14th place at table because they had ended up with the unlucky 13. But when at our annual King's Birthday party they gave for the Diplomatic Corps before their main party for the British Community, they asked me to organise the drinks from their wine store (where, for obvious reasons, no servant was allowed to tread) and then found, too late, we were toasting King George VI in pomagne not champagne, I was rebuked only with a chuckle. The French Minister's face had been a sight to see.

The Trotts retired a year or more later, sadly disllusioned with Arabia and with the Service after all they had put into it. A very different couple, Clinton Pelham and his wife Jeannie took their place. He was neither an Arabist nor experienced in Middle East affairs. He had been our man in Madagascar during the War and most recently Commercial Counsellor in Madrid. Full of bonhomie but shrewd, he had clearly been appointed to sharpen up our dealings with the Saudis. I am not sure whether he succeeded. He arrived to find our long-serving Vice-Consul, Cyril Ousman, had just been murdered by a crazed young Prince of the Royal household, and had the difficult task of seeking Saudi justice at the same time as presenting his credentials and making his mark. Our boundary dispute with the Saudis over the oil-rich area of Buraimi between Oman and Saudi Arabia was also bedeviling. I had a year with him, and he and his wife descended on me in Paris on their eventual way home, but I am not sure I ever got to know him. He ended his career as Ambassador to Prague, behind the iron curtain. It must have been almost pleasurable after Jedda.

Ambassador Trott and Jedda Embassy staff in tropical diplomatic uniform for King Ibn Saud's New Year reception, Jedda, 1951. On the left is Cyril Ousman; on the right Don McCarthy and me.

Personally I have always found life happier if one looks for the good in people, and, cynic though I may have become in old age, I still hold to that. The Counsellor and number two in the Embassy in my first year there proved the exception. He was doing his penance in return for promotion, and did little to endear himself within or without the Embassy. He later achieved an Ambassadorship in South America, and I understand ended his life literally under a bus. None of us would have wished him that. Life can be very cruel.

His successor Derek Riches on the other hand was one of the finest men I ever met in the Service. It was a pleasure to work under him especially when he was Chargé d'Affaires in the period between Ambassadors and when the Ambassador was on leave. An ex-consular service Arabist, he was humble but wise about the Middle East and about life in general. It was typical of the man that he took time out of his home leave to write me a letter of appreciation when I left, and I still retain it. He later became successively Ambassador to Libya, to the Congo and finally to the Lebanon when that now sad country was beautiful and thriving, and he was knighted. We stayed in occasional touch for many years.

The life and soul of the Embassy, however, were my two colleagues in Chancery, Michael Errock, 2nd Secretary and Consul, and Don McCarthy, 3rd Secretary, both post-war entrants into the Service, and both trained Arabists. They sat me between them in a three-sided square of worm-eaten desks, on a mite-eaten carpet, in a large room open to the Counsellor's and Archivists' rooms on either side, the staircase ahead and a window and balcony behind. Nothing conformed to any geometric pattern. The building was four-storey coral rock and wood. The Consular office was on the ground-floor, with dual entrances, so rioting – usually Somali – pilgrims could sweep through without damage! The small accounts and typing offices were on the mezzanine; the central Chancery on the 2nd; flats on the 3rd; and water pots and laundry on the top. Everything, including safes, had to be carried up the steep spiral staircase, with steps as uneven as the floors. It was a decrepit place that was to be my office for the two years until the new building was ready. The Ambassador sensibly worked in the Residence. We took it in turns to walk papers back and forth to him by the coast road. Security was as much faith as fact.

A good feature of Jedda in those days was that there was no crime. Consignments of silver and gold coinage arrived by ship under guard but, to the astonishment of the crews, were met by coolies, taken without guard to the banks (one Dutch, one French and later one British), emptied on the floors and counted openly. There was no such thing as burglary, at least not until just before I arrived when one poor fellow was caught thieving from a car. The usual penalty was to chop off a hand or arm or, in the worst cases, public execution. I say 'usual' but the new Governor of the Hejaz, Prince Faisal, second son of the King and also Minister of Foreign Affairs, had stopped this gruesome practice in this part of Arabia a year or two previously. In this petty case, however, Riyadh, presumably wanting an example, overrode the Governor and decreed execution. Justice was swift and the poor thief was beheaded by the sword in public – and in a botched and gory mess from all accounts.

I heard much of this on arrival and was to learn more, all too intimately, a week or two later. Not having left myself time in London to have a hair cut, I asked my colleagues where to go, and received the ready response that a Turkish barber would come and do me at my desk if I wished. And so he promptly did, a great bearded hulk of a man, shrouded in Arab dress, who wasted no time. He was soon thrusting his mirror before me to approve his handiwork. It was then I saw his fierce countenance, razor and scissors still in hand bearing down on me. It was not a pretty sight – until I noticed Errock and McCarthy in stitches. I had apparently had my hair cut by none other than the stand-in executioner! He had been roped into that job when neither the official executioner nor his deputy could be found. My haircut was passable. But I made sure to find another barber next time.

Errock had a brillant intellect, a wicked sense of humour but a masterly concentration when he chose. I saw him swat up and perform a marriage of two South Africans who for some obscure reason wanted to be spliced in Jedda. He did it to perfection, never having even assisted at one before

– and the rules and procedure are, I learnt, far more complex than they seem. He went on to be Consul-General in Jerusalem, but sadly died young.

McCarthy was a solid Irishman, recruited like me from an ex-service background and expected to spend much of his career in outposts. In fact he rose to be a successful Head of Arabian Department in the Foreign Office, achieving the near-impossible of getting on well with that most mercurial of Foreign Secretaries, the Rt. Hon George Brown, and ending his career as Ambassador to the United Arab Emirates in the Persian Gulf. His passions were music and keeping fit, both great assets in the wilderness. It was not he but some other colleague I think who wisely counselled: eat yoghourt every day and keep your bowels open and you will be all right in the tropics. But it was he who on home leave discovered the first long-playing gramophone on the market and proceeded to despatch to me the turntable, amplifier and speakers with instructions to build and make them worthy of the new classical records he was bringing out. In fact he did most of the work himself on return, and great was the excitement when he announced the launch. We all assembled. We all waited. We all gasped. Improbably, the turntable would only go round the wrong way. We summoned Aramco's electrical engineer to advise. After a stiff drink he could only endorse an irreverent suggestion of mine, drawn from RAF experience, that we should drop it from a great height, and hope that that might reverse the polarity, or something. McCarthy wisely would have none of that and chose instead to write to the makers EMI. The reply was disbelieving and rude, implying that he had perhaps been too long in the desert. Undaunted, McCarthy persevered, and eventually won a replacement that went round the right way. Stranger tales of the Arabian nights hath no man told!

Errock was also enterprising. Deep in the Embassy archives lay a Treaty which still gave us the right to manumit any slaves in the Hejaz from British or British Protected states we could find. We knew there were still many in the country, particularly from Nigeria, the Sudan and Southern Arabia (the Hadramaut). Discovering who and where they were and their circumstances was a different matter. Most would be in domestic service and the doors were closed. We had to wait for an approach. Early in 1950 our local staff in the Consular Section reported that a Hadrami woman in slavery in Jedda wished to be freed. Errock and McCarthy went to great lengths to help her, only to discover that her master was none other than the highly regarded Arab Secretary of the American Embassy! The American Chargé d'Affaires at the time took it well when approached by our Chargé d'Affaires and acted swiftly. It would not have looked good in the UN or in Washington if he hadn't. My colleagues had succeeded in manumitting a slave, a rare achievement in that day and age. They were resourceful fellows, popular in the community, and Don McCarthy remained a good friend until his death.

In due course Errock was replaced by another 2nd Secretary and McCarthy by a bright young 3rd Secretary. Both, like their prececessors, had learnt Arabic at the Centre of Arabic studies the Foreign Office ran in Shimlan, Lebanon in those days. The former brought a wife and two young children, our new housing being available by then. I cannot think who advised this; Jedda with its prickly heat, flies, mosquitoes, frequent malaria and occasional smallpox epidemics, dust, dirt, lack of sanitation and of places to go was hardly the place for unclimatised little children. They eventually had to leave, and the experiment abandoned. Young John Thomson, the new 3rd Secretary, on the other hand throve. Grandson of the Nobel prize-winning mathematician J. J. Thomson and son of the Nobel prize-winning physicist Sir George Thomson, he had broken the family tradition of the sciences and Cambridge to take to the arts and diplomacy. Able and ambitious he eventually became High Commissioner to India and UK Permanent Representative to the United Nations in New York. His father set a parental first by visiting us in Jedda. I can still see his frown of displeasure at what he found his son enduring. It was better by then than it had been two years before, but still a long way from the gentle Cam.

Space does not allow me to pay tribute individually to the series of accountants, administration officers, archivists and typists, who came and went in my time there. They were all without exception hard-working, and all, except one whom I recall as a bit of a shop-steward, willing and uncomplaining. And so were the few wives. Life was not much fun for any of them.

Every Embassy also had in those days, and no doubt still does, some locally engaged staff – people recruited locally on local terms. Outstanding among ours were Cyril Ousman, the Vice-Consul, and his wife Dorothy who slogged away at the typewriter for us. They had lived in Jedda since about 1929 and 1934 respectively, and had come to know everyone up to and including the King. An ex-Army engineer he had originally come to run Jedda's first water desalination plant. He was appointed British Pro-Consul in 1934 and Vice-Consul a few years later. Among his accomplishments was, I believe, the delivery by desert track from Jedda to Riyadh of the Rolls Royce built as a gift to King Ibn Saud from the British Government of the time. It had special running boards on either side for the King's guards. Sadly however Rolls Royce had refused to believe the King liked to ride next to his driver and was a big man. They made the front seating to their design, not his. So, when I eventually saw it in Riyadh, it was in the proud possession not of the King but of his much smaller brother Abdullah. But at least it was still running. Ousman remained very fit for his long years in Jedda yet I never saw him take exercise. He liked his tipple, as did we all. His secret was to drink large quantities of water. I learned to do the same – as now have American sportsmen – 'keep the body cool, keep up your liquid intake,' I hear them say. Ousman had ceased to travel when I knew him. Young royals liked to call on him and Dorothy occasionally when they were in Jedda, and it was through them I met several. He made an effective Vice-Consul, with his experience, dry humour and equable temperament, well able in particular to cope with the thousands of pilgrims who besieged the Consular office for help in one form or another during the annual Haj.

One other locally engaged member of staff stands out in my memory, one Hassan Malik, a Persian by origin but head of our small band of Arab locals. He came to me one day when I was acting Head of Chancery, with tears in his one eye, and a tragic story of losing all his savings in a fire in his flat, high in the back streets of Jedda. They were stuffed in his mattress. I believed him and organised a whip round the Embassy staff to help him out. The last I heard of him, forty years on, was that his grandson had got to Eton and done splendidly there ending as a prefect. I like to think our few pounds helped. As things turned out, the commercial work of the Embassy took little of my time, once it was organised. Business visitors were few and business enquiries not much more in those early days. So I took on as well the economic and financial reporting to the Foreign Office, Board of Trade, Treasury and Bank of England, the writing of *Board of Trade Journal* articles, and the encouragement of British companies interested in the many construction projects the Saudis were beginning to develop now they had some wealth. I do not remember being trained to this work in any way, except for my two year desk initiation at home. We were not in those days sent on courses to learn business, economics, finance, trade promotion or whatever, as may happen now. My instructions telling me I had been 'selected' for the Jedda appointment, asked me to see various Foreign Office Departments about administrative matters and the Eastern Department about Saudi Arabia but, beyond a business contact or two that a newly created one-man FO Training Section struggled to provide, that was it. It was again a case of being pitched in at the deep end and told to swim. In fact I only remember receiving in Jedda one telegram of instructions I could not understand, nor could the Ambassador or my colleagues. It was to do with £ sterling payment aspects of the famous Saudi take-over of 51% of ARAMCO in 1951. Having had to deal in London with the Board of Trade and Treasury gobbledegook of the time, I rashly thought I could telegraph back on behalf of the Ambassador for plainer English. We got rather more of it than I expected!. For the rest of the time, it was a matter of learning on the job. As I wrote home, 'Heavens how time flies, aged 26 and I'm still only beginning to learn my job!'

It was not always easy in the Saudi Arabia of that time to discuss things with officials, or to make representations, or for that matter to find out what was going on. For any important business the Ambassador had to go to Riyadh to see the King (except during the Haj month when the King came to Jedda or Taif). He would fly to Riyadh by Dakota or Bristol Freighter of the newly formed TWA-run Saudi Airlines and would take one or two of us with him. Every visit took at least two days. But that was quick compared with the pre-Airlines times when it required a 600 mile expedition by desert track, and at least a week. A previous British Ambassador had once commented that Saudi Arabia must be the only country in the world where it was more difficult to communicate with the Government to which he was accredited than to his own. It was a bit better than this when we were there. The Head of the Foreign Office in Jedda, Taher Redhwan, and his few staff, tried to be helpful. But they were governed by Riyadh where not only the King but the Minister and Deputy Minister of Foreign Affairs resided.

When it came to economic and financial relations, however, the problem was not remoteness by distance but by secretiveness. The Finance Minister and small Ministry of Finance were in Jedda but did not always encourage foreign access, did not publish anything but an outline annual budget, and kept things to themselves anyhow. I was fortunately able to build up co-operative relations with the newly appointed Deputy Minister of Finance, Najib Salha, a very able man of Lebanese origin; with the Head of ARAMCO's government relations office, Gary Owen; with the Banks and leading merchants; and of course the British trading and construction companies operating there. Also, later, with the American Point 4 aid adviser Arthur Young, who paved the way for a Saudi Arabian Currency Board our own Bank of England had previously recommended, and ultimately for a Saudi Arabian currency once the King's opposition to paper money died with him. (The King's objection was to usury, on religious grounds.) An American historian, Dr F. J. Stanwood, who researched the period for a book on Abdullah Suleiman in 1985, told me then that my reports, just published by the Public Records Office under the 30 year rule, were 'unique ... the only consistent regular set of economic reporting on Saudi Arabia' for that period. I am glad someone found them useful. Whether the Departments at home and, through them, British business did at the time I do not know, but I seem to remember an occasional favourable response. The Foreign Office was always good at that.

My first encounter with the great man King Ibn Saud was formal. He came to the Hejaz for the Haj, in October 1949, and received the Diplomatic Corps at his palace in the desert outside Jedda. The Corps was quite small in those days: British and American Embassies; French, Dutch, Italian (and, later, Pakistan) Legations; and I think, an Egyption Consulate-General. All diplomatic staff were invited. I wrote home: 'We queued up to shake hands with the fine old man and sat around the great reception room for half an hour while the Doyen held conversation with the King. Arab coffee came round.' This was poured with great skill and panache by a berobed servant, from an ornate metal pot held at shoulder height in his right hand into tiny handless cups in his left. You had to waggle your cup when he came around again if you did not want more, and watch your dregs being disdainfully pitched across the carpeted floor. My letter home continued: 'This was followed by a rather synthetic lemonade, while the imposing bodyguard with their guns of all types and ages and their gold-sheathed swords, squatted in half-circle around the end of the room farthest from the King. We filed past to shake hands again on leaving. Ibn Saud is an imposing-looking old monarch, partly chair bound but of large stature and authoritative appearance, His diseased eye and steel-rimmed glasses give him a slightly wicked look. He is a crafty old bird.'

I am not sure that that exactly did him justice! My respect for him grew with every subsequent meeting, beginning with the extraordinary naval visit to Jedda in January 1950, of the then Commander-in-Chief Mediterranean Admiral Sir Arthur Power in his flag ship destroyer, accompanied by Lieutenant Mountbatten, HRH Duke of Edinburgh, commanding his own frigate. The programme we had laid on with the Saudis unfortunately had to be curtailed because a smallpox epidemic broke out in Jedda as they sailed down the Red Sea. We were all heavily vaccinated and doubtless so were they, but the British Public Health adviser to the Saudi Govenment counselled caution, so the two charming ladies they had brought with them, Lady Power and Lady Pamela Mountbatten, and both crews stayed on board out in the harbour. There were still no wharfs at Jedda for vessels bigger than lighters.

I wrote home: 'Fortunately the Duke of Edinburgh and the C-in-C turned up trumps at their two interviews with King Ibn Saud – my estimation of the Duke has gone up immensely. We had a magnificent Royal dinner at the Palace, were presented to the King again and met the Duke and C-in-C at the Ambassador's residence. The ladies of Jedda were a bit mad when the Duke and C-in-C left before they arrived for the late evening party but a spot of hard work on our part turned the party into quite a successful affair, and everything ended reasonably happily.' The Duke and C-in-C were only doing what the doctor ordered.

I might have added, and am partly indebted for this to the C-in-C's Admiralty report now in the Public Records office, that the King received in solitary state except for a kneeling Sudanese interpreter and at the other end the usual horde of squatting guards, though, in his traditionally open way, all doors soon filled with seemingly anyone and everyone who wished to be present. The King was of course in full Arab dress with gold agal headcord. He discoursed on Middle East defence, the Jews (whom he intensely disliked) and Communism (which he likened to 'things that creep along under the ground and must be killed without hesitation'); and, humourously, about his common interest with the Prophet in prayer, beautiful women and perfume. He had quite a twinkle in his good eye when amused and laughed easily. He was the perfect host. Some thirty of his sons were present at the dinner, but no ladies. They were entertained separately by the King's four wives. The King respected British naval tradition by giving pride of place at the audiences to the C-in-C above Lt. Mountbatten, but when it came to the dinner he signalled the future Queen's consort to sit in royal line next to him and the Royal Navy was put in its place. Presents delivered by trusted couriers the following day, in his generous Arab tradition, included pearls, swords, daggers, wrist-watches, perfume, Arabian garments and a flock of sheep, together worth a small fortune, principally for Princess Elizabeth, but also the Duke, C-in-C and his wife. The C-in-C and the Duke together returned some silver spoons and our resourceful Vice-Consul headed the sheep off the gang-plank just in time to give them to charity. It was a memorable visit, which I understand Prince Philip still recalls.

Between times, in late 1949 and early 1950 tragedy struck the Embassy three times, a foretaste of things to come. Our Arab Secretary, a backbone of the Embassy since 1931, died of cancer in Cairo after we had rushed him to hospital there. Our long-serving and popular Accountant Willie Horne retired and was promptly killed in an air crash at home. His replacement, John Lee, a Northumbrian, fellow member of the Foreign Office Cricket Club in London and my flat-mate when I found new accommodation in Jedda, suddenly collapsed after tennis with frightening paralysis. The British Public Health doctor immediately diagnosed polio-myelitis. We propped him up with sandbags and nursed him as best we could until a military aircraft and nurses summoned from the Canal Zone in Egypt arrived to take him to the British Military Hospital there. Happily, he confounded the medics not only by surviving, when they reckoned his time was up, but by steadily recovering in England to rejoin the FO, marry and have a happy family life. He was as brave and determined a man as I have known.

In addition to limited tennis, we did have a few, very basic, sports facilities to help keep us fit. There was fishing for those who wished (a sport I never mastered); swimming for those who did not mind sea mites clinging to the skin; and golf for those who, like me, had a club or two and a few old balls to bash about the desert where someone long ago had marked and oiled three 'greens'. There was gazelle shooting in Desert Locust Mission jeeps in the sand, scrub and gravel wastes ten and twenty miles inland – a sport I eventually gave up in deference to those beautiful animals, but not before one had led us a merry dance into soft sand, where I learnt the hard way what being stranded in the blistering desert was like, with mirages and no water for a day until we were found. It took a couple of weeks and more to recover. Then, importantly, there was cricket, of a sort. We challenged every ship we could find, from India or home, usually on a Friday Sabbath afternoon, in all I suppose four or five times a year. Clothed correctly in white we played on old coconut matting pegged down in the desert for the match, on a flattish strip of the old Medina road, which was not surfaced but simply baked sump-oil on sand and gravel. Vehicles using the road usually steered around us. Camel trains did not; the drivers took the view it was their track and straight down our pitch they drove leaving us to rescue the wickets, clean the mat, and wonder how the MCC would have reacted to that. But it was good fun.

So indeed was Jedda social life, though it could get monotonous. My first introduction to it was a seemingly endless series of farewell parties given to a popular member of our Embassy on his posting home. Unfortunately for him the weekly flight to Cairo did not arrive to take him away, nor the following week, so the farewell party round was mounted again and again until we were at last able to pour him onto a plane and take to Lent (my high church and Catholic colleagues anyhow – though I did once catch them sniffing the cork, in turn!). The foreign community was only about 150 strong, and, leaving aside the Bechtel construction camp and the gold-mining Saudi Arabian Syndicate, who mostly kept to their own times and routines, less than a hundred mixed socially. But that was enough to provide parties sometimes night after night, at least in the Winter. Wives, and those due for leave escaped home in the Summer if they could. In the old tradition we always dressed for parties. Shorts and shirt in the daytime gave way to black tie and cummerbund in the evening – for drinks as well as dinner. Once my car arrived I learnt to tie the black tie while driving, but do not think I ever quite mastered the cummerbund that way. Everyone drove in the middle of the road anyway.

The life we led could no doubt be mirrored in many a tropical outpost elsewhere in the world. But ours did have unique features. One was that we all worked on different times (and calendars). Many of us, for Saudi reasons, set our watches at 6.00 p.m. every evening as the sun set over the Red Sea (occasionally with a distinctive green flash). But the Saudis themselves set theirs six hours different (and had their own calendar). ARAMCO were one hour different, to be closer to the oil camp time in Eastern Arabia, and Bechtel two hours different, to start construction earlier in the morning. Appointments could, and did, become endlessly confused. It might be concluded that Saudi Arabia was the only country in the world where it was possible to defeat time; duck behind a sand-dune at sunset and you could just deduct another half-hour. I suppose that this interesting peculiarity has long been ironed out.

In March 1950, the Ambassador decided to visit Riyadh and Eastern Arabia and take with him a retinue of his wife, the Counsellor, an archivist and me. So I met the King again, this time in his Riyadh town palace. His custom of hospitality was to receive his visitors immediately they arrived in Riyadh for a courtesy welcome, and then receive them again for business the following day. There was no question of whisking in and out, even if we had wanted. The proceedings were always dignified and

we were lent Arab dress to don over western clothes. This time the King
was indisposed and so was his first son (and subsequent king) Saud, so we
were received by his second son Faisal (also subsequently king). But we
called on the King twice the following day, once for business and once
to say farewell, and this time I was enormously impressed. He was in his
own capital and larger than life. I wrote home: 'He is probably the greatest
man of Arabia since the Prophet and he exudes history. He looks every
inch the part, a great figure … who fills the great reception room with
his presence. He was in fine fettle and kept us for a full hour … talking
of past episodes in his life between the business we came to discuss'
(probably the Palestine and the Buraimi crises at that time). Mrs Trott
meanwhile did her duty by calling on the King's wives, only to find the
King courteously joining them in due course to receive her too. She came
away wrapped in a large gift of black lace-net with sequin borders, from
which, I wrote home, 'it took us half an hour to unravel her.'

My job on these occasions – apart from carrying the gin – was to record
the Ambassador's official discussions with the King, and any follow-up
discussions with the Minister of Foreign Affairs, Prince Faisal, if he was
there, or the Deputy Minister of Foreign Affairs, Sheikh Yusuf Yassin who
was always there. In the diplomacy of those days, wherever we were in
the world, it was considered discourteous to take notes at such meetings.
We might leave an Aide Memoire of what the Foreign Office wanted us
to say. But the discussion itself had to be committed to memory and
recorded immediately afterwards. This discipline was to prove for me, over
the years, a wonderful memory trainer, and I have been thankful to find
it remaining into old age. The practice of writing copious notes at encounters and, still worse nowadays, of taping them, is one of America's
less endearing exports, I find.

That visit was also memorable for my first sight of what were to become
the world's most prolific oilfields – though in fact they were little more
than taps and pipes and refinery, the oil being so rich – and for two other
remarkable personalities we met who, like King Ibn Saud, we may not
find the like today. The first, the Emir bin Jilawi, was Governor of Hasa,
the Eastern (and oil) province of Saudi Arabia. He received us at Hofuf
and lunched us, squatting on the floor, in Arab style. I recorded home: 'a
frightening man. His eyes and beard are black and his ruthlessness renowned.' His father had been at Ibn Saud's side in their warrior days, and
our host was the only man to whom Ibn Saud still delegated the judicial
power of life and death, which he used fairly frequently. I recorded at the
time that it was 'one hell of a good meal' despite the squatting, which
never has been my forte 'the only trouble was that we found his brother
had laid on dinner in the same style for us when we arrived at the Gulf
Coast, an hour's flight away.' At Bahrain, the Ambassador, Mrs Trott and
I (the other two had returned to Jedda) were received by, as I wrote 'an

almighty body called Sir Rupert Hay with a wife and jolly daughter.' He was British Political Resident Persian Gulf (as the Gulf was then called), ex Indian Political Service and, without doubt, the uncrowned King of the Gulf. When he visited Kuwait or Qatar or the Trucial Sheikhdoms, all then British protectorates, all now prosperous and independent nations, it was said the Sheikhs quaked. He was viceregal, full of pomp, unbending but effective in keeping the peace of the Gulf at that time. He was the last of an historic line of British rulers there.

We were in Riyadh again, the Ambasador and I, to see the King within three months. This time I wrote: 'it was awful. The task was not too pleasant (the Buraimi boundary dispute) and the place was like a blast-furnace. Everyone was fasting during the month of Ramadhan and the air trip back was as rough as any I've ever had.' Fortunately the plane came via Taif 4000 feet up in the Hejaz mountains, and I was able to stop off and spend a few days with our Military Mission there. Brigadier Baird was another fine outpost character, ex-Arab Legion, fluent in Arabic and a dynamic head of that training Mission. One of his officers, Major St John Armitage, also ex-Arab Legion and an Arabist, later joined the Foreign Service, to become in due course Consul-General Dubai, and in retirement is now a distinguishd authority on Arabia. I later, back in Britain, had the pleasure of being his best man, and we still keep in touch.

By September 1950, a year of going hard at it in those trying conditions finally caught up with me. Prickly heat was the curse of the humid tropics before air-conditioning, with everyone having his or her own ineffectual palliative and no-one having a cure – except to get into air-conditioning or high above the humidity in a plane or up a mountain. Mine went septic, so I had to get out. We had a small local leave entitlement and I persuaded an American friend and Middle East scholar Bill Peyton to show me the Levant. He was at that time in the not very onerous position of official representative to the Saudi Arabian Government of John Paul Getty who had secured the oil concession to one half of the neutral zone between Saudi Arabia and Kuwait. Peyton was the 'quiet American' and knew the Middle East as few others did. He was a splendid companion; we saw great sights and met interesting people in Beirut, Damascus, Amman and Jerusalem, and returned to Jedda healthy and refreshed. He later settled in England, married and worked for the *Economist* and Shell. Sadly, he died relatively young.

1951 saw major developments in the Middle East, in Saudi Arabia and locally in Jedda that all affected us. Egypt's unilateral abrogation of the 1936 Treaty in November was an assertion of independence and slap in the face to Britain that, I suppose, led eventually to Colonel Nasser's nationalisation of the Suez Canal and the Anglo/French/Israeli war with Egypt in 1956. That, in turn, led to a prolonged breach in our relations with Saudi Arabia. We were to learn that for all Saudi friendship with

Britain, Arab solidarity came first. But that was away ahead. In 1951 we felt only the first rumblings, but we felt them none-the-less. I found myself in Cairo, on my way back from home leave, the day the Treaty abrogation was announced, and saw at first hand some of the anti-British riots in support. They were no doubt officially inspired and probably largely 'rent-a-mob', but there was equally no doubt that the retention of British forces in the Canal zone was being challenged. In those days of course it was believed that not only peace in the Middle East but control of the Suez Canal were vital to British interests. The Egyptian challenge was another subject for our periodic meetings with Ibn Saud.

The bombshell in Saudi affairs was the announcement of agreement with Aramco that the Saudi Government was taking a majority holding in the company. We had had no warning of this, nor had London nor, I later learned, had the US Government in Washington. Nor had any other oil producers of the world, among whom of course it immediately set the fashion. The Saudis and Aramco kept their negotiations tight and secret. It was still possible to do that in those days, for there were no chattering classes in Riyadh and no free press anywhere in the country. Our interest was not only in the repercussions on BP, Shell and other British oil producers, and of course on the oil market, but also on sterling because it was still a major currency of trade and reserves in the area and the Saudis prescribed that part of ARAMCO payments must be made in sterling. It gave me quite a lot of work extracting from the Saudis and ARAMCO all London wanted to know, but it was an interesting time.

Locally in Jedda, Ambassadors and staff came and went but I seemed chained, doing some of the political as well as the economic and commercial work and ending up as Head of Chancery. The new accommodation developed and seemed popular and successful. I had enjoyed designing the interior layouts, in negotiation with the builder and his Italian foreman – and finding that mathematics can make up a lot for ignorance of building! The builder, interestingly enough, was one Mohammed bin Laden, a shrewd little Yemeni who made his life's work and fortune building palaces, houses and roads for the Government, the King and Royal family, the Minister of Finance, and anyone else with money. He begat, among fifty and more children the notorious terrorist of today Osama bin Laden. I doubt if the old man would have approved one bit of his offspring's cause and use of inherited wealth. He was, in my short acquaintance with him, an Ibn Saud man and a builder, no more and no less, and in those days spent his money frugally.

My next project was less successful, but for a rather extraordinary reason. It was to create Jedda's first Sports Club, with a simple 9 hole golf course in the desert, a tennis court or two and perhaps even a hard matting cricket pitch; and an elementary clubhouse. Never could such an idea have received such a spontaneous welcome. The local Aramco head Gary

Owen, a leading Saudi businessman and later government Minister Mohammed Ali Reza and I formed a working group and in no time had ready an outline plan and a draft constitution (adapted from my London sports club, The Hurlingham). Still more, we had offers of money embarrassingly in excess of what was needed, from everyone we canvassed including local Saudi merchants who knew none of these games. Team sports were forbidden until popular Saudi demand for football was finally conceded by the King that same year. The problem for our club was to get official permission. It had to go to the King. Gary Owen was going to see him anyhow, so he put it to him from us all. But the King said 'No'. He considered it would only encourage people to drink and talk politics, and he would not have either. So what must have been the most generously endowed sports club ever conceived was still-born – and it was left to a charitable American Ambassador in later years, I understand, to create the golf part privately.

Between times I was allowed home leave and, having shipped my little Morris Minor by cargo boat to Barletta in Southern Italy, spent the Summer of 1951 happily touring Europe and then the UK visiting friends and family, attending the newly created Llangollen International Eisteddford and Liverpool's (and Sir Thomas Beecham's) splendid contributions to that year's great Festival of Britain. On return by air in early October – with the Foreign Office still rule-bound to prove to the Treasury there was no sea passage available – we were held up *en route* by sandstorms over Egypt and I had to telegraph my colleagues in Jedda to say, 'Delayed Rome by bad weather.' They never really believed me. I suppose it did sound improbable from Jedda.

I came back to intimate tragedy the like of which I had not encountered since the War and was not to see again until the Congolese Katanga fifteen years later. It was as if the British community in Jedda, for all its resilience, was suddenly cursed. In the space of six months we lost in fatal gun, car and swimming accidents, illness and a murder, nearly 10% of the community. It began with the death of the British pathology adviser to the Saudi Government Dr John Manifold, killed in a shooting accident on medical expedition in the Asir, and climaxed in the murder of our Vice-Consul, Cyril Ousman, defending his wife and himself from a maniacal young son of the King, Mishari, on 16 November. At the community's New Year's Eve gatherings, the fear of who next was palpable, and the prayers that it should end were fervent. It did end there, fortunately. But it fell to our Chargé d'Affaires to conduct the funerals and arrange the enquiries where appropriate, and to us to help.

I undertook the report on Ousman's murder. There were some accusations levelled posthumously at him, and his wife, to excuse the Prince, and again in an absurd article in the *Observer*, trying to match the *Sunday Times* scoop on the Arnot case, thirty years later. They were false and malicious. I made that plain at the time and in the published letter I wrote to the Editor of the *Observer* in October 1980 which secured the Editor's full and published recantation of the offending article. The Ousmans were pillars of the British community in Saudi Arabia, with a wide circle of Saudi friends, including many in the Royal family, and were people of kindness, integrity and high personal standards.

The morbid facts of the murder were that on the afternoon of Friday 16 November 1951 Mishari called on the Ousmans when they were having their siesta and, unaccountably, first threatened them, and then rushed out to his car for a gun and came back and shot Cyril twice through the open window of their spare room. Their flat was on the ground floor of the new building we had just occupied, immediately below mine. It was still only partly furnished, and had scaffolding and unmade-up ground around. Cyril had clearly dashed into the spare room to save Dorothy, and had sought what protection he could there by locking the door and pushing the only furniture, a flimsy wardrobe, against the outer window, I found him dead on the floor, shot in the groin and neck, while a friend, St John Armitage, who was with me, found Dorothy in a state of shock in their bedroom.

We had just come back from cricket and passed a large open American car tearing out of our compound with screeching tyres. It contained two men, both of more African than Arab complexion, identified by servants who greeted us with the news there had just been a shooting, and by Dorothy, as Prince Mishari and his driver. No one but he could say what got into him; he was known as the odd sheep of the Royal family, and unstable, but we were never to my knowledge given any interrogation report by the Saudis. The Minister of Foreign Affairs simply expressed the Government's deep regret and assured our Ambassador that Mishari had been found and would be incarcerated in a Riyadh dungeon. A pension was paid to Mrs Ousman in blood money. The King was not told as it was feared his health might fail with the shock. Cyril Ousman was buried in the little Christian cemetery in Jedda and Dorothy retired to a widowed life in Durban, South Africa until her death in 1987. She was helped financially in her old age by a compensation award some of my old Jedda colleagues (McCarthy, Armitage and a former head of the Locust Mission, John Hewitt), extracted for her from the *Observer* after the Editor's recantation. She wrote to us all, deeply touched to find how old friends had surfaced unsolicited, to defend the good name of the Ousmans after so many years. It was the least we could do for her after all she had suffered.

Mishari is believed to have been released from prison a year or two after the murder, possibly in a general amnesty, and to have led a full life. He even appeared once in an official Saudi mission to London. He died in June 2000. A Saudi press bulletin then reported he had been given 'funeral prayer by the present King, attended by many dignitaries, at the holy

Mosque in Mecca'. That does not in my book say much for Saudi justice. I like to think that King Ibn Saud, had his family had the courage to tell him at the time, might not have imposed the death penalty on his murderer son but would at least have banished him.

I met the old King again several times more in 1951 and 1952. There was always some Foreign Office reason for one Ambassador or another to go and see him. One occasion was to accompany a visiting official from the Foreign Office, my former Deputy Under-Secretary Sir Roger Makins. Except that he had some difficulty in keeping his Arab head-dress on, a problem not uncommon to the uninitiated and bald, Makins clearly enjoyed his visit, made his mark and, through his report, put Arabia and the Persian Gulf rather more on the Foreign Office map than they had been.

In my last year, 1952, King Ibn Saud became less and less well. He died the following year, 1953. By then I had left Jedda for pastures new, but only after becoming for a full year, following Ousman's death, the longest serving member of the Embassy. My eventual departure was timely in another respect. Prohibition on drink was declared absolute in Saudi Arabia in October 1952. I was able to bequeath my poor successor John Heath and his wife Patricia only one bottle of champagne and the dregs of three bottles of Bols liqueurs. They survived well – we still keep in touch – but I felt for them.

One's first post is I suppose always special and although my letters home referred to it often in unflattering terms, I look back on it now as an experience I would not have missed. The Saudis were always kind to me, even though I never mastered their tongue (there were simply no teaching facilities then in Jedda), and the Ministry of Foreign Affairs gave me an unusually nice send-off dinner when I left. I could not pretend, however, that the climate and conditions were kindly. The American Ambassador, Ray Hare, a most delightful and able diplomat who subsequently became US Ambassador to Egypt, gave a farewell dinner for me, and I forgot it. His 1st Secretary came in search and found me writing in my flat. I dressed in haste and arrived shamefaced. He passed it off forgivingly as 'Jedda Memory'. I had been there too long.

CHAPTER 12

# Paris

## 1952–1956

'WHICH was your best post in the service?', I have often been asked. My reply has always been: 'If you mean the most interesting it would be Guinea' – a chapter yet to come. 'If you mean the most enjoyable it would be Paris.' If asked the reasons I would be less sure. Finding Paris again was certainly a joy. It was the fleshpots after the wilderness, but it was also the most spirited and cultured city I knew. Finding excellent sporting facilities, and good company there were other attractive reasons. So was finding a place in a big Embassy for the first time. And so was finding the French, the most off-putting of people on first acquaintance but the most stimulating when you get to know them. I may find other reasons, as I recall those days in this chapter, but that is already quite a list.

When the FO told me I was to be released from Jedda, there was no beating about the bush, just: 'We hope you will feel that your patience has finally been rewarded.' And so I did. I was to be 2nd Secretary, on promotion, in the Commercial Section of the Embassy, no great shakes in a staff of hundreds, just a small cog in one of the biggest of our wheels abroad. And I would now really have to learn French. But never having enjoyed the bright lights for any length of time through the War, penurious post-war London and desert Arabia, the prospect was exciting. They gave me six weeks notice this time, extended further to await my successor. But with the Ambassador and several others on leave from Jedda at the time, there was no opportunity for me to go to Beirut or somewhere to acclimatise *en route*. So at the end of November I flew direct, with short stops just to change aircraft at Beirut and London.

The result was near disaster. After two weeks I wrote home: 'I am still dazed and not quite registering things.' After two months I wrote: 'The change has been even more difficult than I expected.' It was in fact three months and the Paris Spring before I woke up, like Rip van Winkle, to find where I was and the glories around me. Friends and acquaintances from Arabia kept looking me up on their way through to remind me of what I had left, and the immensity of the change grew with every day. It was bewildering, and not helped by the sharp change in climate – from the upper 80s in temperature and humidity and the curse of prickly heat in Jedda to winter and a particularly cold snap in Paris. We do not turn a hair at this today because, apart from conditioned aircraft we have air-conditioning at one end, central heating at the other, and adaptable modern clothing. At that time Paris was still recovering from the War and occupation and was short of everything including fuel and heat. My first letters home complained of the shivering cold, the frugal hotel accommodation until I found a flat, and the difficulty of finding warm clothing and household needs in a city still low on consumer goods and high on prices. I was eventually offered the rented family flat of my predecessor but wrote home: 'It is impeccably located in the 16th arron-dissement and full of elegant Louis this and that furniture, but big and gloomy, and the owner wants to sell it anyhow. So I am back to flat-hunting and, even with the help of the Embassy, it is quite a game – there are so few available.' There was also a car to get. As British diplomats we were expected to buy British and this time I chose a soft-top Austin A40 that seemed suitably dashing for my purse and Paris. It was one up on the Morris Minor I had reluctantly left in Arabia but nowhere near as robust, as I discovered in a rather dramatic accident in it in London three years later. So my hard earned savings of £100 accumulated in Arabia soon went and, as in all subsequent foreign posts, I started in debt. All that and, as I wrote home, 'having to learn this wretched language in short time on the job', made for a rather discontented start.

It was not in fact all cheerless. Everyone in the Embassy proved wel-coming, at least from the Minister (Commercial) down, and across in the Chancery and the Consulate-General. I did not meet the Ambassador, HE (His Excellency) Sir Oliver Harvey or his deputy, HMM (Her Majesty's Minister) William Hayter, for many weeks. Nor did I ever get to know them. They were both rather unbending old school. In due course they were replaced by Sir Gladwyn Jebb and Patrick Reilly, as fine an Ambassador and Minister as I could have wished. But that was some time ahead.

My job carried a degree of independence which was encouraging. I was charged with reporting on the French economy, industry and commerce, and liaison with the Quai d'Orsay (the French Foreign Office) on a few matters like war reparations no-one else wanted. The Minister (Commer-cial), his deputy the 1st Secretary, a 3rd Secretary and two locally-engaged officers, devoted their time principally to export promotion and especially to our trade and payments agreements with France, which loomed quite large in our foreign trade. I was also charged with liaising on economic

matters with our delegations to NATO (then based in Paris) and the
OECE (successor to the Marshall Aid organisation), which brought me
into contact with colleagues there and their multilateral concerns. Then,
most demanding at first but ultimately rewarding, I had to study and extract
anything of interest in the French economic press and publications. It
meant my learning journalistic and technical French as well as colloquial,
all in one. I took to reading aloud at night in my hotel room and then
my flat, to atune my ear as well as to help understand the articles I found
in the economic and business sections of *Le Monde* and other French daily
newspapers or the heavy weekly magazines *L'Usine Industrielle* and *Le
Commerce Exterieur*. What my hotel and flat neighbours thought of these
nightly readings I never knew. They probably dismissed them as just another
eccentric habit of *Les Anglais*. I never found the French much given to
curiosity about strangers' doings as we Anglo-Saxons are, some of us
anyhow. Their upbringing was to take more interest in each other and
things of the mind. That did not stop them being very practical people
nonetheless. At the national level their post-war reconstruction demonstrated that. At the domestic level the apartments I viewed all seemed to
be built around the kitchen and the bedroom, with the drawing room
often furnished for reception rather than comfort. But that was their way.

My Embassy colleagues were a talented and hard-working lot. The
Ambassador, and consequently the Embassy, suffered from the brooding
shadow of the former Ambassador, Alfred Duff Cooper, a distinguished
conservative politician who had resigned over Munich and later been
appointed by Churchill as Minister Resident in Algiers following the Allied
invasion of North Africa, and then to Paris. He and his famously glamorous
wife, Lady Diana, could not bring themselves to leave the scene of their
triumph as Britain's first Ambassador to France after the liberation. They
lived out at Chantilly but near enough to inspire Nancy Mitford's amusing
book *Don't tell Alfred* and her '*entresol*' principle: beware the host and
hostess – or anyone for that matter – who decline to leave the field free
to their successors. Sir Oliver Harvey and his charming Welsh wife did
not have untrammelled happiness as Ambassador and Ambassadress in
Paris as a result.

My immediate chief, Ernest Mecklereid, the Minister (Commercial),
was a dapper product of the old Consular Service, reserved and much
travelled. He had an apt little story of the demands of the Service which
I have since found quite useful in constraining assistants wishing to absent
themselves more often than seemed reasonable. Serving as HM Consul in
southern Siam (as it was then called), he found it congenial and just
occasionally necessary to slip over the border into northern Malaya to
weekend with his British colonial and army friends there. But it was
irksome that he had to seek permission from his Ambassador in Bangkok
every time he had to leave his consular district to do so. Emboldened to

ask for blanket permission he received the curt ambassadorial reply, 'Certainly, so long as you are always on the end of the telephone when I want you!' That of course was before the invention of the mobile phone. His wife was French and charming but tragically invalided by a fall through the floor of an unsafe old house they had been viewing to buy for eventual retirement. His deputy, the 1st Secretary, Bernard Cook when I arrived and John Lloyd later, were both also ex-consular service, family men and congenial to work with. Lloyd was a great one for a yarn and a laugh but he and his devoted wife Nell also bore a tragedy in having an invalid child needing constant care. Like the Mecklereids, they never complained. The 3rd Secretary when I arrived was an intense young man of the post-war generation who did not stay long in the Service but moved into candidate politics and then more happily I believe into the church. The FO's recruitment process of finding round pegs for round holes was evidently not infallible. His successor Kenneth Uffen, on the other hand, soon found his feet and in the process also a lovely wife, Nancy, then personal assistant to HM Minister. The diplomatic service was quite a marriage bureau. Uffen went on to be Ambassador to Colombia where I believe he suffered siege by local terrorists but happily survived, and then Ambassador to the OECD in Paris. But that of course was years later.

The Embassy was fortunate to find after the liberation many British, Anglo-French and French residents willing to work for us on meagre locally-engaged terms. Some had fought in the French Resistance. Others had suffered the Germans in other ways. One of these working in the Commercial Section on export promotion, poor Ted Oddy, died at his desk of heart failure while I was there. 'Finding him seemed for a moment like Jedda again,' I wrote home. The revived British Chamber of Commerce was another help. There were several in the British community with stories of hardship and bravery, not least the CBI representative in Paris, Yeo Thomas, the 'White Rabbit' of the Resistance. But few carried it on their sleeves. The preoccupation of daily life in the circumstances of post-war France was too pressing to be forever re-living the nightmare of the past.

We were especially fortunate in the Commercial Section to have, in addition to two lively secretaries from home, whom I remember as Barbara and Minty, two local ladies, Jocelyne and Patsy, both Anglo-French, bilingual, and vivacious. They took me in hand from the start, guided me through those first confused months and helped me into the work, the language and the life of Paris. They even made up a party at my request, to show me a Montmartre nightclub with a cabaret of statuesque nude ladies. Sadly my testosterone level had sunk so low over the years of enforced celibacy in the War, Cambridge, London and Jedda, that Les Naturistes left me cold. I remember one of the ladies was quite pretty too. Arguably the female form has to be seen in movement (or tantalisingly veiled) to achieve full beauty. But I doubt even that would have stirred my turbid blood at that time. It was winter anyhow and, as another of Nancy Mitford's books once portrayed, love does not come easily in a cold climate. Jocelyne eventually taught me to overcome that too, in the natural French way, and we had a lot of fun before she was taken into the Diplomatic Service and posted afar. She eventually married and settled in France I believe, as also did Patsy earlier – indeed we were all *garçons* and *demoiselles d'honneur* together at her wedding, I recall.

Finding a flat and, as it turned out, a rather delightful one, also made a difference. I fell on it, with the help of the Embassy, at the end of February. It was on the top floor of one of those fine stone buildings that make up one side of the Rue de Rivoli, overlooking the formal gardens of the Tuileries on the other side. It was only minutes from the Place de la Concorde, and short walking distance from the Embassy in the Faubourg St Honoré. The owner was a French businessman who had made his fortune in refrigeration in Morocco and lived with his family in one of the apartments below. Being still in a daze I took a taxi from the Embassy

The view from my Paris flat in the rue de Rivoli, overlooking the Tuileries and Place de la Concorde. Bastille Day, 1953.

to see it one lunch-time, and the cunning cabby took me half way around Paris to get there. I fell for it on sight, even though the furnishings were sparse, and I was able to negotiate an acceptable rent there and then. Still unaware of where I was, I took another taxi back to the Embassy, and this time was taken around the other half of Paris to get there. When, weeks later, I finally realised what I had stumbled upon, I wrote home: 'It is in the very centre of Paris, with a wonderful view taking in most of the monuments of inner Paris … spacious and convenient enough for official entertainment … and perfect for guests … I've already had acquaintances from across the globe spying my spare bed-room and will have to choose whom I invite or be inundated … I've also secured the services of a little cook/maid, Giselle, whose account-keeping leaves something to be desired but knows what to do … All I need now is a wife but though this place is swarming with adorable creatures (there's a film of that name that would probably shock you) I have yet to find one that fits.'

Paris in the Spring for a diplomatic bachelor, soon in social demand because there were so few of us, was in fact hardly the place to be seeking matrimony. It was just that I had reached 30 and that always seems to be a shock to the youthful system. Also all my friends and colleagues seemed to be married and I was accumulating rather too many positions of bestman and godfather for comfort. But there were soon many other things to think about. It was hard work in the Embassy but time to play hard too. The first thing was to find a sports club, and again it was just there for the asking. The Standard Athletic Club in the forest of Meudon was British but internationally composed and, improbably, provided cricket as well as tennis in the Summer, and hockey in the Winter. It had a sensible wooden clubhouse and as enterprising, congenial and multinational a membership as anyone could wish. It later achieved fame in Willie Rushton's comedy sketch on cricket in Paris and as one of the pioneers of cricket in France. (There are today, apparently, 26 French cricket clubs, with between them over 1000 members.) I shall come back to that remarkable Club, which was destroyed by the Germans during the war and had just been rebuilt.

My first year in Paris was eight years after the War and thirteen since the outbreak. To many in France, as in Britain, that war period was a life-time. The gallant Free French and Resistance apart, they had not as a nation had to suffer the supreme hardship of holding out alone for victory. But in addition to the humiliation of defeat and Vichy they had suffered the devastation of war across their land not once but twice and the pain of occupation, bombing and insurrection in between. France lost in the War over 600,000 in battle, resistance (including 30,000 shot by German firing squads), civilian casualties, deportation to German concentration camps and missing, plus several hundred thousand victims of starvation diet and other indirect effects of the war and occupation. The task facing France in 1945, apart from recovering its pride, was described

The Standard Athletic Club's first men's hockey team, Paris, 1953/54
(minus me taking the photograph!).

by André Maurois in his *History of France*, written at the time, in these terms:

> The ravages of war had turned the country upside down ... There were fewer French people than in 1939 (and many refugees) ... Millions of dwellings were destroyed or damaged ... Almost all bridges, railway stations and dams had to be rebuilt ... Many factories had been stripped of their machinery ... Everything was lacking – clothing, agricultural machinery, fertilisers, fodder ... Payments to the Germans as occupation costs (three hundred billion francs) and war expenditures had brought on considerable inflation ... American Lend-Lease helped but only until hostilities ceased ... Poor in man-power [numerically], poor in energy and raw materials (France has always lacked both) ... the problem [of economic recovery] was above all a problem of industrial equipment ... France never lacked ingenious scientists, skilful diplomatists or clever artisans ... what was needed was a far-sighted Government, having the courage and intelligence to make a continious effort of organisation.

He might have added: also generous Marshall Aid from the United States and the genius of French administrators to run the country almost irrespective of the politicians.

'In all the ages of her history', Maurois quoted an American historian as saying, 'the French have given proof of an inexhaustible vigour, of a capacity quickly to raise themselves out of disaster, of a courage and persistence which the worst misfortunes have been unable to beat down. How many times in the course of the centuries have we not seen France, torn with internal stife or prostrate at the feet of her enemies, immediately astonish the world by her wonderful powers of recuperation?' Maurois added:

> The Frenchman is no less stubborn than the Englishman, but he cannot be so in the same fashion ... The Englishman does not admit that he can be beaten ... The Frenchman knows that his country from time to time runs the chance of being overwhelmed by a superior force ... Because France happens to lie at the western extremity of the European continent she has throughout her history been threatened and invaded ... and from this has sprung her desire for a strong authority ... But never has the conquest been of long duration ... each time the enemy has been driven forth. Once invaded France pulls herself together; resistance is a classic phenomenon in her history ... Her awakenings are as miraculous as her crises are troublesome.

The country I found in 1953 was already demonstrating both post-war economic miracles and political troubles. For centuries our historic enemy but, since the turn of the century and the Entente Cordiale, our close ally in two world wars, and now partners in the Dunkirk, Brussels, North Atlantic and United Nations Treaties, we had every reason to want to see France strong again, most especially in the face of the post-war Soviet threat. Economically by 1953 there was still destruction to repair, heavy industry to modernise (several of the larger industries had been nationalised, along with the mines, banks and insurance companies); the public debt to be brought down and the franc reserves rebuilt. But order had already been restored in the rural areas, the transport system repaired, bridges rebuilt, and the flagship railways were making great strides – and running to time. Food and fuel still lacked. But, under successive national economic plans, and a strong measure of traditional *dirigisme* from the centre, the capacity of the French to bounce back was already evident.

Anglo-French relations at the popular level were another matter. War or no war they remained as before and as they still are today – more love-hate than love-in. We did not have the *Sun* screaming obscenities across the Channel in those days. It was more gentlemanly. But the first book I was given to read – by friends outside not inside the Embassy I hasten to add – enjoyed the provocative title: *Mesentente Cordiale*. It was a witty account of the daily differences between our two peoples as seen by an Anglo-French couple, she being French he English but each looking at their national idiosyncrasies through the eyes of the other. Regrettably no copy now seems extant. But the next, *Les Carnets du Major Thompson*, became a classic and best-seller in English and French. Written by a Frenchman, Pierre Daninos, with cartoons from *Punch*, it satirised the French and English through the eyes of a caricature English major. It began with the claim of a French brain surgeon, friend of the Major, that on opening the brain of an Englishman he had found a royal breast plate, an umbrella, a cup of tea, a Dominion, a policeman, the rules of the Royal and Ancient, a Coldstream Guard, a bottle of whisky, a Westminster Hospital nurse, a cricket ball, a fog, and a piece of earth over which the sun never set. To this, according to the Major, a nurse who claimed to have attended the operation and was now living in South Africa, rejoined that the surgeon himself later suffered brain surgery and they found 19 ex-Presidents du Conseil (Prime Ministers), three dancers of the Folies-Bergère, a box of over-ripe Camembert, a Maginot Line finally completed, and a Légion d'honneur. There was much more in the same vein of mockery of each other's national habits and particularly of the French. I remember the concern in the Embassy that the French would take it badly – forgetting perhaps that it was written by a Frenchman. In fact there was no such reaction. Anglo-French humour had finally come of age, not quite like Anglo-Irish humour but starting that way anyhow. Also it revealed that we were not the only people in the Channel who could laugh at ourselves, after all. (The Dutch and the Belgians could too.)

If there was so much that bound Britain and France together in the post-war world, there were nonetheless also important issues between us. Political stability was one. Colonial policy another. European integration a third. My job in the Embassy did not involve me directly in any of these to begin with but, as time went on, I became sucked into all three, and found them absorbing.

In his *Politics in post-war France*, written at the time, the Oxford historian Philip Williams began: 'The British have never had much respect for the political capacity of their nearest neighbour ... There is little under-standing of the deep differences between the British and French outlook on politics, or the fundamental reasons for these differences ... The political structure of France is the result of her historical and geographical background. No country can rid itself of its past.' The clerical issue permeated politics in France long after it did in Britain. Historically the French, unlike the British, came to expect 'not merely [periodic] changes of government, but changes of the whole political regime.' But the administrative structure remained solid, 'without fundamental alteration since the reforms of Napoleon. It is a tightly centralised system ... closely controlled from Paris ... far greater than in Britain.' (That of course was then. Today, with the growth of centralisation in Britain and a measure of devolution in France, one could argue comparison of the systems has been partly reversed.) 'Geographically,' Williams continued 'the experience of an invasion in every generation has engendered in France an uncertainty about the future ... The [resultant] instability which so appals Anglo-Saxon observers – who greatly exaggerate its real importance – is accepted by democratic Frenchmen as the price which a country with their history and traditions must pay for freedom. [To the French] Governments can never be trusted and must always be checked; their aims and methods are alike questionable. "The State is not a referee but a player – and probably a dirty player".'

That last caustic interpretation of the French outlook was actually a quotation from the most eminent British authority on France at the time, Professor D. W. Brogan. It probably still reflects the average Frenchman's attitude to government today. Happily however that political instability is now a thing of the past. Since General de Gaulle's return to power in 1958 (for nine years) and creation of the 5th Republic, France has enjoyed relatively stable government. The post-war 4th Republic we had to deal with was a nightmare in comparison. In the seven years 1946–53, following the collapse of de Gaulle's provisional and first elected administrations, France had twenty short-lived governments. The key figures – Bidault, Blum, Ramadier, Schuman, Queuille, Pleven, Faure, Pinay, Mayer, Laniel – barely changed. They just played musical chairs and, fortunately for France's allies, the Foreign Ministry stayed in the hands of only two men, Bidault and then Schuman. But no government survived for more than nine months, and two only lasted a matter of days.

It was the infighting of the political parties that no one seemed able to stem. There were six main parties by 1953. The first post-war elections had put the Communists in the lead, followed by the left-wing MRP, the Socialists and the Radicals. The Convervatives were far outnumbered. By 1947 the Communists had been manoeuvred out of coalition government into opposition, and the pattern of politics shifted also as the gaullist RPF emerged and the Radicals and the Conservatives, the parties of the pre-war 3rd Republic, revived to take control. The French voters went to the polls twelve times in the four years 1945–49, counting referenda and local as well as general elections, and a new cycle began in 1951. The local elections were all fought on a national basis. So, throughout my time in France, the political atmosphere was one of almost permanent electioneering. It was also one of perpetual government changes, and an everlasting stream of Prime Ministerial candidates being summoned to the Élysée Palace (in the same street as our Embassy) to be charged by President Auriol or his successor President Coty to try to form the next. On one occasion, I recall, he got through so many so fast that a search party had to be sent out for a remote contender who, embarrassingly (even for France), was found with his mistress. The press, perhaps hypocritically, made sure he was not invited again for some time.

Looking back, it seems astonishing that the French achieved anything remarkable in those years. But they did, by dint of their able underpinning administration, entrepreneurs and technicians, and the brilliance of two or three political leaders. One was Mendes-France, who got them out of Indochina after their disastrous colonial war there. Another was Robert Schuman who fathered Franco-German reconciliation and, with the great planner Jean Monnet, and Adenauer of Germany, de Gasperi of Italy, Spaak of Belgium, Stikker and Luns of Holland and Beck of Luxembourg, laid the foundations of the future European Community.

Those years in Paris brought home to me personally both the need for some permanent European structure to prevent further German wars, and the determination of the Schumans and Monnets and their Benelux, German and Italian counterparts to achieve it. Also, that our British interests lay with them, not outside. The concept popular in London at that time, that Britain's future lay proud and independent at the intersection of three circles – the Atlantic, Commonwealth and Europe – seemed to me wishful thinking. Of course we were part of all three and should remain so, but to try to make a living of it in the post-war world would be the act of an ageing juggler. We were a European nation, whether we liked it or not, and it seemed to me perfectly possible to join in the vision and creation of a peaceful and prosperous Europe without excluding close association with the United States (who supported European integration) or the Commonwealth (who could benefit from it). Nor could I see any threat there to national character or culture. That was clearly not the European aim and the French would not stand for it anyhow. As for the pooling of sovereignty, had we not already blazed that trail ourselves in the creation of the Brussels and North Atlantic Treaty organisations for mutual defence, and found it beneficial? As Adlai Stevenson brutally observed: Britain had lost an empire but failed to find a new role in the world. This was surely it.

What first led me in this direction was following the affairs of the new European Coal and Steel Community, created by the six in 1951 to coordinate the recovery of those great industries in peace instead of military confrontation. We in Britain had refused an invitation to join this first experiment in post-war European integration, principally because it was supranational, providing for the will of the majority to prevail, whereas we found consensus co-operation more to our independent liking. Whitehall regarded its creator Jean Monnet as 'the evil genius of Europe'. Studying how it worked in practice I discovered that it was not only proving successful but, far from imposing votes on the unwilling, it actually worked by consensus (reinforced of course by the knowledge that the statutes allowed of majority voting on certain matters if necessary). This was hardly the ogre it was made out to be in London. In time our own people at home came to appreciate this and first sought official British relations through a UK Council of Association and later full membership. But it took a depressingly long time.

The European Defence Community was the next project to reach Treaty form among the Six but, like yet another idea, a European Political Community, that was also floating around European circles in the early 1950s, it proved to be too far ahead of its time. Promoted by a French Prime Minister Pleven from Alsace, it provided for the integration of revived German forces in common European services, but that meant the French would have to set an example by relinquishing much authority over their own. The Assemblée Nationale was deeply divided on it. Government after Government waited for an opportunity to put it to them for ratification. The will-they-won't-they calculations of how the Deputés would vote became a full-time occupation for all interested press and diplomatic observers. Our Embassy expert was Sir Anthony Meyer, a very able 1st Secretary in Chancery who later in life entered politics and, when Mrs Thatcher turned anti-European, he had the courage to stand against her and force a party leadership election. He remained a leading member of the European Movement in Britain for many years. I watched with interest how he got to know the French Parliament and assessed the ebb and flow of opinion – and remembered it when I came to do the same in our own Parliament over our entry into the European Communities twenty years later. But on that occasion Parliament voted in favour. On this occasion, when Prime Minister Mendes-France, himself unenthusiastic about the European Defence Community, finally put it to the French Assemblée on a free vote, the project was lost.

There was much weeping on the Continent when the EDC fell. The cause of European integration had suffered a severe set-back. There was unashamed rejoicing in London. Our Government, Foreign Office and Armed Forces had never liked it, and we had not only refused an invitation to join but made it plain we considered it a crack-pot scheme. But it left a defence vacuum in Europe, and something had to be put rapidly in its place. German and Italian expectations of being admitted to the community of Western defence had been raised and now thwarted, and the Soviet menace from the east hovered ever more menacingly over Europe. Eden promptly seized the initiative and toured Europe with a Foreign Office scheme to admit Germany and Italy into NATO and the Brussels Treaty organisation, the latter to become known as the Western European Union and to have control of the levels and content of German rearmament. It was a brilliant plan and in the aftermath of the collapse of the EDC it found ready acceptance Europe-wide, and in the USA. I found myself dealing with some of its creations when I was posted back to the Foreign Office two years later.

They were stirring times to be in Europe in those years 1953–56. Undaunted by the EDC defeat, the European leaders soon came up with yet another project, this time providing for a European Economic Community based on the concept of a Common Market but dedicated to 'ever closer union among the peoples of Europe'. Again Britain was invited to join in working it out. Again we not only declined, but had the temerity to advise it would not work and the Six should drop it. Convinced this was mistaken I set about compiling a case for London to think about, as seen from Paris. The first shot would have to be a letter at official level to start the process of persuasion. I drafted it for the Ambassador, Sir Gladwyn Jebb, to send to the highest responsible FO official, Sir John Coulson. It argued, with evidence, that the EEC project was widely regarded as not just visionary but level-headed and that there was growing political momentum behind it. We would do well to keep the door open instead of closing it on ourselves. The Ambassador received it well, agreed it and sent it. The impact in the FO was an embarrassed 'yes we take note'. But Eden and Whitehall would have none of it. An observer was sent to the Messina Conference of the Six where the EEC Treaty was to be agreed, and the official chosen was not a diplomat but a die-hard sceptic from the Board of Trade called Bretherton who not only reported back that it would fail but apparently wrote to the convenors of the conference before returning home: 'I leave Messina happy because even if you continue meeting, you will not agree; even if you agree, nothing will result; and even if something results, it will be a disaster.' So Britain stayed out, and neither Sir Gladwyn Jebb nor any of us lesser fry could persuade London otherwise – until the European Common Market proved itself such a success that the Macmillan government eventually saw the light – though it was many years before we joined.

Sir Gladwyn was a big man in every way, with a commanding presence, towering intellect, combative spirit and a grasp of world affairs that had few equals. He enjoyed grandeur and at his crowded Memorial Service at St Margaret's Westminister on his death many years later (he lived well into his nineties) he was described by the historian and politician Lord (Roy) Jenkins as 'the nearest thing to Lord Curzon we shall see in our lifetime'. But I found him also, when his ever-active mind was not on higher things, a man of humble kindness and thoughtfulness; and once a friend, always a friend. I count myself fortunate to have had him as Ambassador in Paris. It mattered not to him that I was a junior on the commercial side, when my draft on Europe was put to him by my chief. He grilled me on the subject for the best part of an hour, with only one welcome breather when he took a telephone call from London. He had only recently come from being the hero of the United Nations, the first acting Secretary-General and then, after a spell in the FO, the first UK Permanent Representative to the UN. The Security Council had just been opened to American television and there Americans saw for the first time someone publicly standing up to the Soviets. They liked it and he became famous for it. In Paris I think he was probably just looking for a cause beyond Anglo-French relations and the hosting of Ministers, Royalty and the rest at the historic Embassy. He had doubtless already focussed on the European divide as the big issue. My draft and interview were timely. He thereafter pursued the subject with growing vigour and, not long after retirement in 1960 when he was raised to the peerage, he joined both the Liberal Party and the European Movement and became a powerful voice in the land for each. I had the pleasure of working with him again, in both, when I myself retired from the Service some years later.

The Embassy Minister, subsequently knighted to become Sir Patrick Reilly, was also one of the Service's best, and went on to be Ambassador to Moscow and later to Paris. As his obituarist wrote on his death much later, his 'feel for French traditions and susceptibilities was outstanding ... He was held in high regard by General de Gaulle ... He was a man of high and generous quality.' I had the pleasure of working again with him, too, in later years, and he could not have been more helpful.

Other colleagues I have not mentioned but would not want to forget, because we had good times together in those days in Paris, included Anthony Rumbold, then Head of Chancery who was later my Under-Secretary in the FO and ultimately Ambassador to Austria; John Beith who succeeded him and went on to be Ambassador to Belgium; Michael Wilford, a New Zealander and, like me, a man of science originally – or, in his case, engineering – who became Ambassador to Japan; and Antony Duff, a submarine commander and DSO in the war who rose to be High Commissioner to Kenya and tried twice to retire but was called back first to guide Christopher Soames in negotiating the final settlement in Rhodesia, and later, at 65, to take over MI5 as Director General to shake it up. There was also a splendid Consul-General I remember at Paris who retired and then unashamedly reappeared selling lavatories for some maker or other. 'One had to supplement one's pension somehow,' he proclaimed. There were also good colleagues and friends in the Delegations to NATO and the OECE, in the Diplomatic Corps, in the Quai d'Orsay, and in French industry, business and agriculture. I was privileged to join a regular luncheon gathering of the leaders of the French agriculture, food and wine associations and had some jolly times with them.

There were also visits and liaison to maintain with our Consuls-General and Consuls in the main provincial cities of France. Their economic reporting was my charge to co-ordinate. They were all a pleasure to work with – except perhaps one. We had at Lyons a remarkable Consul-General called Robert Parr, known locally as Sir Parr. He had spent much of the war as HM Consul Brazzaville on the Congo river and, not having much to do beyond aiding the Allied air supply route from Takoradi to East

Africa, he learnt to affect an Edwardian style of dress and manner. Appointed to Lyons after the liberation, he was an instant success as the eccentric English gentleman, and represented us splendidly. But economic reporting was to him demeaning, and in my time he never contrubuted a single one. Challenged on this when he eventually passed through Paris on retirement he proclaimed that his Secretary had had a breakdown (which was true, poor girl) and he had discovered his reports stuffed under the carpet! He received a knighthood for his pains. The Service was tolerant of eccentrics in those days. I hope, fibbers apart, they still are.

Life in Paris became fuller and fuller as time went on. Writing home in July 1953, seven months after arrival, I was able to say: 'I've grown very fond of this place and happy in it now. You'll see that when you come.' I had invited my mother and her younger sister Laura to be among my first guests. Unusually in the family, she had only been abroad once before, on a continental bus tour. Her place had so often been to hold the fort at home – for her parents, her husband and her sons – and Paris was an adventure. I was able to meet them at Boulogne, house them in my flat, show them Paris (the little I knew by then, anyhow), suggest where to go when Embassy demands called me away, and introduce them to the delights of Paris bistros, boulevard cafés and the Bateau-mouche on the Seine. They lapped it up, as I suppose any Normington would, and went home reassured that diplomacy was not a bad profession for me after all. They were followed by a succession of old friends that summer. All seemed to enjoy themselves. Certainly I did, being able to have them to stay in such a place.

The autumn brought a health problem that, somewhat unnecessarily as it turned out, cast a small cloud over my stay in Paris. The Embassy doctor, contracted locally after the liberation, had a better bedside manner than he had knowledge of medicine. He diagnosed and treated what turned out to be simple appendicitis, first as amoebic dysentery, presuming that was only to be expected of someone coming from Arabia, and then, when the Tropical Diseases Hospital in London found no such thing, he insisted that, as I was now living in France, it must be liver. His young locum when he was away, was no better, contributing only a new treatment called antibiotics but dispensing them with total disregard of dosage. The doctor was finally sacked by the Embassy, others having found him equally useless. My appendix grumbled on until I finally had it out, in London on return. That was my only experience of the French health service. It was in a poor way, like most other services at that time. It is now, from all accounts, second to none.

There was also a small problem of a different character and that was the number of acquaintances from home and the Middle East wanting to 'look me up'. I did not mind most, and indeed enjoyed seeing them again. But I had to be selective and that was not always easy. One from the oilfield area of Eastern Arabia disturbed me greatly over lunch by rolling his eyes in an extraordinary way. I brought the lunch to a hasty conclusion, presuming he had become a victim of the old liquor-stills we had heard some enterprising Americans had brought out from former prohibition cellars at home to use illicitly in Saudi Arabia after the imposition of the Government ban on alcohol. Stories had reached me that some of these stills had produced some strange results. Hastily walking my visitor away up the rue de Rivoli, he suddenly stopped, pulled something out of his eye and complained, 'These new contact lens really don't fit very well'! I had done him a grave injustice. On the other hand, encountering one night in a Paris night club the majestic figures of two leading Saudis I had known well in Jedda and receiving – rather to the surprise of my companions – a great bear-hug from each, I was reminded that there had been some very durable friendships made there.

There would be in Paris too, I soon found. We all came to learn that, usually, the first year at any post was one of settling in, getting to know the people and country, and mastering the job. The second year was the most productive and enjoyable. In the third one should be able to coast a bit but rarely did so for one reason or another. Then came another posting, to start the cycle all over again. Paris was no exception. But there were always new factors. The change in Ambassadors made a big difference to my working life. Being drawn into the mainstream of the Embassy work added greatly to the interest. So did involvement occasionally in the Ambassador's heavy programme of entertainment even if it did sometimes mean little more than being a glorified footman to the Duke and Duchess of Windsor when they came to dinner. I had met the Duke years before, as a boy Cub when he visited Llangollen as Prince of Wales. In Paris he was a sad reflection of his former self. The Royals and Government Ministers the Ambassador often had from London were much more fun to meet, as of course were his many French guests. I was called in whenever a bachelor was needed at table.

I also found myself drawn into the Ambassador's annual Queen's Birthday party and recall that, finding a staff argument going on about the need to cut it down to size, I rashly argued the contrary, only to find it resulted in the greatest traffic jam the Paris Police (and the poor officials of the President's Palais up the street) had ever encountered in the Faubourg St Honoré! The following year someone had the presence of mind to open the garden entrance as well, so the Paris Queen's Birthday party remained a great affair – as I think it should be, and hope it still is.

Another factor, in my final year, was the arrival of a new Minister (Commercial), Bobby Isaacson from Washington, when Meiklereid left to assume his own Embassy. He too was a delight to work for and I was only sorry it was for such a short time before my own time for posting arrived. Between all the to'ings and fro'ings of Embassy life however there was always more of Paris to explore. The best way of discovering everything, from the Louvre to the Sèvres, the opera to the Montmartre night clubs, and so much else, was to take visitors. They dragged me out willingly. I think we found between us a fair trove of the treasures of Paris (It would take a lifetime to find them all.) That was curbed for a while in my final year when my cook/maid left. She had her mother with her in a room on top and it did not work out. It was August when she left. As most Parisian families were then on holiday and took their maids with them, I was persuaded to advertise and say 'Diplomatic bachelor seeks housekeeper ...' The response was instant. They came in their droves from all over Paris, every conceivable 'housekeeper', from a single Polish mother complete with child to an elderly 'white Russian' who admitted she could neither cook nor clean but 'would lawve to teeach yo Rawshan'! Paris was very cosmopolitan. That was one of its charms. I eventually found a living-out housekeeper and she saw me through to my departure.

In season the Paris social round was hectic. If someone had bothered to invite me I felt I should always make time to attend, – even if it meant criss-crossing Paris two and three times of an evening and, all too often, weaving through jams of impatient French drivers, all klaxoning each other like fury. That was a challenge in itself, especially around the Arc de Triomphe where all roads met. I recall being reduced to playing bumps there one evening with French drivers front, back and side, to get out of a five- and six-lane bottle-neck. Those like me who had cheap cars already scratched had the advantage! I also recall appearing at a party one evening in some block of flats somewhere west of the Arc and, after several minutes of chit-chat with my French host and hostess and some of their guests, realised I had never seen any of them in my life before. Withdrawing in confusion, I eventually found the party I wanted, on another floor. My unknown host and hostess were charming throughout, as only the French can be, and invited me back if I failed to find my destination.

The weekends were another thing, or Saturday afternoon and Sunday anyhow, for we still worked a 5½-day week in the Embassy. There was time to go down the Loire valley to see the great chateaux brought to life by the new invention of 'son et lumiére'. Or to Versailles or Fontainebleau or Chartres. Or, on longer weekends and occasional holidays, skiing in the French Alps or in Switzerland or Austria, which I had never done before, or visiting the sunny French 'Midi' or the vineyards of Burgundy or Bordeaux or even the Italian Alps. I was fortunate to find a charming lady colleague to share some of these delights initially, and some very good friends, Peter and Annie Urlik who were always full of enterprise, fun, knowledge and kindness, to share many more. He died tragically of cancer a few years later, and she had to bring up their three young daughters alone, while earning a living hospital midwifing. She did a fine job of it, too, and we still keep in touch. I have an extraordinary picture postcard of her on our shelves leading a crowd of happy students down the Champs Elysées from the Arc de Triomphe on the official liberation day in 1944. She found it on sale on the fiftieth anniversary of D-Day – which the French commemorated far more extensively, and with far more expressions of gratitude to their Allies than the British media reported in this country.

The Standard Athletic Club was another source of happy companionship as well as sport. It was going through one of those cycles when a wealth of talent and enterprise fortunately appeared on the scene all at once. The captain of cricket was a Welshman, Charles Wildblood, an industrialist and a natural leader. The secretary, improbably, was an American in Paris, Mike Vail; the star player an Indian diplomat Prem Sharma; the wicket-keeper a Dutch journalist, Eric Peerboom; another star player a Canadian diplomat and Cambridge blue, Basil Robinson (whom I was to meet again in Ottawa years later); our two leg-spinners both English economists in the OECE, David Thompson and John Stone; a Sikh Indian diplomat, H. S. Jassel; a couple of Army Captains from the NATO Military HQ then at Fontainebleau; a Scottish insurance assessor, Ian Campbell; an English artist from the 'Latin Quarter', Len Hunting; and our one splendid French-man, Henri Natanson. We were as international a cricket side as there could ever have been. We were also not a bad side, especially at home on our own matting wicket in the forest of Meudon. We played as far afield as Brussels and Geneva, against the British community teams there and Rotterdam against the famous Dutch Flamingos. On these occasions families and friends came too.

Skiing with my good friends Peter and Annie Urlik at Arosa, 1955.

Annie Urlik (centre, in white) leading the student celebrations through
the Arc de Triomphe on the liberation of Paris, August 1944.
(Photo Keystone, Collection Debarquement 1994)

The club had been founded in the 1890s, and after the first World War
there were half a dozen other teams in a Northern France Cricket League,
founded by the War Graves Commission – which of course had staff
wherever there were war cemeteries. The French found it very confusing.
The *Guardian* newspaper claimed to have found one in 1954 who wrote:
'There are three batons driven into the ground, supporting two pieces of
moulded wood. When the ball attains them – each protected by a guardian
who holds a wooden racquet and whose legs are in white armour – and
the moulded pieces of wood fall, the guardian sees himself eliminated.'
The Scorer was 'a referee who holds on his knees a sort of logarithmic
table.' According to the same source, when the game was once demonstrated
at Meudon to a group of French Army officers in the hope they might
take it up, their very Gallic response was, 'We might do something with
it if you can allow all 22 men to play at the same time'!

The Meudon grounds were a charming sight at a weekend, alive with
players of cricket and tennis and families, surrounded by bushes and trees,
through which perplexed French families picnicing in the woods could be
heard to say; '*Qu'est-ce que c'est que ça, Papa?*' '*Ça, mon enfant, ça c'est
le baseball anglais*'! In my first winter, copy Paris region and beyond, and
surprised ourselves by rising rapidly over two seasons up the 3rd and 2nd
divisions into the 1st. Our Indian and Pakistani colleagues had a lot to
do with that. We even ambitiously entered an international tournament

at Reims but sadly came to grief against the sober Dutch, our team having been rashly introduced the night before to a particularly potent local wine called Blanc de Blanc, then the base of Champagne but little known because it did not travel. (It does nowdays, but in much inferior quality.) My team-mates made me centre-forward and run off my feet that day, for leading them astray. We had a lot of fun together.

The highlights of the sporting year, however, were the cricketing visits of the Notts Casuals, Yorkshire Colts and the Cricketing Society of Great Britain. There was always a County player or two and County coach with each. Arriving in time to play us twice, on the Saturday and Sunday, they usually knocked spots off us in the first match. We then ensured they had a great time Saturday night in the bright lights of Paris, and we knocked spots off them in return on the Sunday. They were memorable weekends and the visitors always went away happy. The Standard Athletic was a splendid club, and I hope it and all the friends I made there wherever they may now be, still flourish.

One other reason why Paris proved so enjoyable was the natural delight in finding female company after so many years of enforced celibacy. A charming young lady, daughter of some good American friends, took me aback recently, as she left us to revisit her own pleasures of Paris, by asking whether I had had many girl-friends there. Only an American would have the temerity to ask such a question. But if truth be told, I suppose I did, and I remember them all with affection. I would like to pay tribute to them by name but must respect the old convention that that might embarrass those long married with families. So that they know I have not forgotten them if they chance to read these pages, I shall record just their first name initials: J, B, S, R, P, S, P, S, V, J, E, J, M, S. They were of several nationalities, and all lovely. I hope they have had fulfilling lives and still thrive.

At the beginning of 1956 I was transferred to the FO in London, to work on what were called the Western Organisations, the complex of international bodies created after the war for European political and defence co-operation. It was what I had asked for, a job at home on the political side and preferably dealing with Europe. It meant too that I could come back to France occasionally on conferences, and keep up with friends there. I left Paris in a whirl of farewell parties. It had been a memorable three years.

# CHAPTER 13

# Foreign Office, London

# 1956–1959

L ONDON SEEMED a social desert after Paris. No one would deny its
greatness as a city or its myriad attractions or its magnetism as a place
of work. In time I enjoyed living and working there again. But unlike
Paris and other flat-dwelling cities, London social life beyond theatre-land,
the debutante set and of course inner-city estates moved out with the
commuters at night and weekends to their houses and gardens in the
suburbs. London clubs were all men only, and morgues at night. This at
any rate was how I found it in 1956 and, with the loss of Embassy life
too, it was quite a come-down from Paris. I re-joined the Hurlingham
Club in Fulham, then reviving from the war, shorn of its previous polo
by local Council land acquisition, but modest in price and good for tennis,
cricket, par–3 golf, croquet (which I never played but observed was a
rather more combative game than it was made out to be) and parties.
That helped. So did my acquisition of a studio flat in Ashley Court, near
Westminster Cathedral at £3 a week unfurnished. It was a bit claustrophobic
after the Rue de Rivoli but cosy once furnished, and just walking distance
across Victoria Street and St James' Park to the FO. Compensation lay
too in the work, which proved eventful, as did life itself soon enough;
and, of course, in being near family and old friends again after six and
more years abroad.

It began in fact not in the FO but in St George's Hospital, Westminster
where I was taken by friends to lose my long-rumbling appendix in the
nick of time. It then continued in Morocco where I went for a fortnight's
convalesence. This was the one country of North Africa I had not seen
during the war and, happily, 1956 was one of those rainy winters when,
if it was not exactly green from the Mediterranean to the Atlas mountains
it was very nearly so. French army officers I met at Agadir made haste to
remind me that when, at the turn of the previous century, the British

government had sent Sir Eyre Crowe, head of the Foreign Office, to scout out Morocco with a view to challenging France and Spain (and Germany) for this strategically placed land, the rains had totally failed and the country looked like desert from one end to the other. So Crowe had advised his political masters in London not to bother – but to challenge the French at Fashoda for the Egyptian Sudan instead. Anglo-French legends do live on! Those soldiers at Agadir also apparently contrived suspicions of me, which turned out to my advantage because they invited me to party after enjoyable party in order – so I soon learnt locally – to keep an eye on me. It was straight out of Evelyn Waugh. They did not find it plausible that a lone British diplomat versed in French affairs would choose to convalesce in Morocco at the very time when – actually unbeknown to me – the French government was about to set Morocco free on the road to independence. It was the first and only time in my life that I was taken for a spy and, since their surveillance involved giving me a good time, I rather enjoyed it.

There were very few other visitors at Agadir at the time. Large hotels were rising at most Moroccan resorts, as French money found its way back from Indochina, but growing political turbulence discouraged the growth of tourism. I was lucky at Rabat, the capital, to run into the lady who ran the Moroccan tourist office in London, accompanied by two British travel agents all doing an official tour. They took me with them to visit fascinating Marrakesh and the resort of Agadir. There we stayed at the new Saida hotel, empty but for one other group, somewhat improbably the managing family of the famous – or notorious whichever way you looked at it – Windmill theatre in London. That theatre's proud boast was that it never closed during the war. It evidently must have done at this time! Tragically, that delightful and historic part of southern Morocco was totally destroyed by earthquake a few years later. I fear some of those I came to know in my convalesence must have died with it.

Returning to Rabat, I found myself enveloped in the Sultan's triumphant return from Paris with kingship and independence in his grasp. The country went wild for three days in non-stop partying, parading and dancing in the streets. I went to the old Islamic city of Fez to see them celebrate there and observed for the first time the exhilaration of independence. I was to experience more of that in Guinea three years later.

Tangiers, my final port of call on that holiday, was in those days an exciting place to visit, not only for its Roman remains, its strategic location on the Strait of Gibraltar and its past history of being held successively by so many powers, but for its unique international zone status and multinational administration since 1923. Shackled governmentally by the need for condominium agreement on everything, and the squabbling that led to each of the four or more administering powers having their own stamps on sale and police on show, it had become a haven of smuggling and international crime, in the best Barbary pirate tradition of the coast. It lost that status only months later when, by international agreement, it was ceded to Morocco on that country's independence. I suppose I must have been one of the last foreign visitors to Tangiers as it was, and still retain as a souvenir a beautiful yellow and gold brocade wedding gown I was able to pick up for a song. It was exquisite Moroccan workmanship.

Settling to life in London and work in the FO and Whitehall took a little time after all that. The adjustment was not helped by a further health problem arising out of the appendicitis. Short-term I had to learn as everyone else does and as my nursing aunt had warned me, that it was one thing to be pitched out of a hospital desperate for beds, only days after an old-style operation, but it was quite another to resume full activity immediately. 'When the abdominal nerves are cut it takes a year to heal fully,' declared my aunt, and she was right. Today, key-hole surgery avoids that, and is a great blessing. In addition, the ill-diagnosis and treatment administered to me in Paris was found to have left its mark, in the form of a spastic colon, which has remained with me ever since but, happily, I have learnt to live with it as other sufferers know one can. So I was instructed to ease up, which was not welcome. It lasted only a short boring time however – and that fortunately is the only health story I have to tell of myself in this book. I was then 33.

The FO had by now promoted me to 1st Secretary and placed me in one of the most interesting of departments, the Western Organisations. My office was again on the coveted first floor but this time overlooking Downing Street and, in fact, directly opposite No. 10. It was a large high-ceilinged room I shared with two others, and through its great window we could see all the Prime Ministerial comings and goings. One of the most memorable I recall was looking down on the first visit to the West of the Soviet leaders President Bulganin and Party 1st Secretary Khrushchev, induced by Prime Minister Eden to come out of their stronghold to visit Britain (and subsequently the USA). They cut strange figures, two stocky little men draped in ill fitting khaki raincoats down to their ankles, but rulers of a huge area of the globe and would-be rulers of much more. Khrushchev was already embarked on his programme of reform, and of destalinisation in the destruction of the image of his predecessor Joseph Stalin. Taken to visit Oxford and specifically I think Magdalen College, the irreverent students of that establishment greeted him with a full-throated rendering of 'Poor old Joe'! Khrushchev is alleged to have joined in heartily, no one having the nerve to tell him the words, or to shut up the students! The visit was nonetheless historic, no Soviet leader, I think, having previously been seen east of Potsdam since the Bolshevik Revolution. A lesser historic occasion we watched later in that year was the sad figure of Clarissa Eden arranging the removal from No. 10 when her husband was obliged to resign the Prime Ministership, a broken man.

That FO room is still there, I know, though now furnished with modern desks, chairs, computers and fitted carpet. The old fireplace has gone. We had to stoke it up daily in the winter to supplement the old-fashioned central heating. So, perhaps, has the daily departmental tea we took it in turns to arrange with cake and biscuits and which was attended religiously and congenially by everyone from the Assistant Under-Secretary down. In modern jargon I suppose it might have been called team-building or bonding; to us it was just a natural way of meeting and chatting about things daily. The only downside was the inevitable sprinkling of cake crumbs which fed the mice nestling beneath our floorboards. After some months I rashly tracked down a Ministry of Agriculture rodent officer in Beaconsfield and called him in to rid us of the pest. He came one afternoon, looking for all the world like a human mouse, and proceeded to lay little trays of poisonous powder under the boards. 'Where will the mice go to die?' we asked. 'Right there,' he declared, baring his teeth in a Tom and Jerry grin of triumph. And so they did, until the FO administration eventually found someone to remove the malodorous carcasses. I suppose every large organisation has its rodent officer or equivalent, probably now called a Pest Resources Executive or some such Business School title.

My first job in that Department was to look after British membership of the Council of Europe, a Europe-wide body which included neutrals and was created after the war on the initiative of France, Britain and Benelux, with an inter-governmental Executive and an inter-Parliamentary Assembly 'to achieve greater unity … and facilitate the economic and social progress' of its members. Germany was invited to join, as its 14th member, in 1951. Although excluded from matters of defence, which were to be the preserve of NATO, it was originally conceived as the great white hope of European reconciliation. By the time I came to deal with it the initial enthusiasm had faded. The Ministerial Council had been superseded by the councils of the Six, the Western European Union (WEU), the North Atlantic Treaty Organisation (NATO) and the Organisation for European Economic Co-operation (OECE). The Council of Europe Assembly however was still attractive to some Continental and British parliamentarians, and set the pattern for similar Assemblies in the Western European Union, the European Community and, less formally, the Atlantic Alliance. It is still active today, having enlarged its membership to include Eastern Europe and beyond, and given birth to a few important offspring, notably the European Convention on Human Rights. We in Britain at long last incorporated that Convention into the law of the UK in 2001. In fact British representatives played an important part in originally drafting it, also in creating the parallel European Court of Human Rights (often confused with the Court of the European Community, which is quite different). It is the first modern Bill of Rights we have had in this country, and much needed to counter the growth of 'elective dictatorship' (as Lord

Hailsham called it). In my view we should be thankful for it, and to the Council of Europe.

That aside, it was not a very exciting body. Our Parliamentary delegation to the Assembly expected me to be there as adviser but they tended to know it all themselves, as MPs sometimes do, so for me, as I wrote home, it was rather: 'Off to Paris tomorrow, there to catch a train for a tedious six hours to Strasbourg. All for the sake of hanging around an Assembly that can very well get on without me. However the boss wants me to go with him, so I shall make the most of what Strasbourg has to offer.' It was, in fact, an anti-climactic period for all there, with the fading of the initial idealism. That rogue politican but brilliant orator, Bob Boothby, once described his visits there as 'Strutting the streets of Strasbourg in a state of black despair'. However, my visits took me also to Paris, Bonn and Brussels. So, in Maurice Chevalier's immortal words 'I remember it well'.

So I do, too, but less kindly, the unusual weekend of Friday 13 July 1956. Superstition has it that that combination of day and date is unlucky. To me, and the charming French lady I was taking out to lunch for the first time, that day was 'nearer thy God' than either of us would have wished. I have mentioned in a previous chapter the three car accidents of my youth. This was the second and, as the newspaper picture reproduced elsewhere in these pages illustrates, it was rather dramatic. Match-making friends on both sides of the Channel had urged me and Regine, comptesse daughter of the distinguished French diplomatic family de la Barre de Nanteuil, to meet. She was then working at the Western European Union headquarters in Belgravia. We eventually got together over a pub lunch in Rochester Row, Victoria. Driving her back to her office in my car it was drizzling and Friday afternoon and we were struck by a large laundry van, obviously in a hurry as people tend to be just before the weekend, at the intersection of Eaton Place and Belgrave Place. The impact projected us helpless across the road and, as *The Times* and other newspapers reported the following morning: 'into the (rotten) railings of the Duke of Rutland's house in Belgrave Place, somersaulting and landing upside down at the bottom of the 20 ft well.' 'Lucky diplomat and his lady passenger,' declared the press, 'to have escaped such an accident, in a soft-topped car, on Friday 13th, with only scratches and stitches.' That was nicely British of them. We would have felt luckier if we had not been hit at all! But we were indeed fortunate. To the accompaniment of theatrical 'oo-oohs' from the flock of local ladies who quickly gathered from nowhere to see the blood, the firemen arrived in what seemed no time (probably because, falling on our heads we were a bit concussed) and extracted us from the wreck alive and well. I remember we were taken into the adjacent cellar of the Rutland house, sat on the stairs and a doctor appeared from nowhere. 'I know you,' I recall saying. 'You are my doctor.' 'Yes, yes,' he replied soothingly. But in fact he was, by coincidence. I had registered with his practice and

Upside down in the Duke of Rutland's basement on the corner of Belgrave
Place and Eaton Place. 'Friday 13 [July 1956] was lucky for this diplomat
and his lady passenger,' the press said. 'They escaped with minor injuries.'
(Photo: Paul Wilson Photography)

shaken his hand only a few months previously. Remembering people has
always been a pleasure to me though I prefer not to be concussed, this
being the second time in my life, the first being in rugby at Cambridge.

We were treated at St George's Hospital casualty and discharged by a
raw young house surgeon, who practised a few stitches on us but was

otherwise reassuring in his indifference. He was in fact correct. We both miraculously emerged without damage. The car did not. It was a complete write off. Many months later however I was surprised to receive from HM Customs and Excise a demand to pay some £30 duty on 'the sale of my car within one year of bringing it into the country from France'. Enquiries revealed that the London Victoria garage commissioned by the firemen or police to remove the car from the Duke's basement, and then by my insurers to condemn it to the scrap heap, had not in fact done so but sold it on for 'restoration'. Also that, after passing through three sets of hands, it had eventually been sold on the market for some £300, doubtless as 'good as new'. I paid the duty but only on condition the Customs and Police traced and warned the new owner about it. I took the manager of the Victoria garage (which was part of a national chain), to task, but he denied all knowledge. It was a dirty business.

The day after the accident I was due at Cambridge by mid-day to be best man to my old friend from Arabia, St John Armitage, and his lovely bride Jennifer, daughter of an eminent Cambridge professor. We were to meet at the University Arms hotel where the bridegroom and his family were staying the night. To steady his nerves over breakfast his family gave him the *Daily Mail* and there, to his dismay, he read on the front page of my accident. He woke me at my flat in London with an urgent call to learn if he still had a best man. I was fast asleep, having foolishly gone with friends to the Hurlingham Ball the night before still partly concussed. I assured him I would be there, forgetting I now had no car, but managed to do so by train and in full morning dress. In the rush his studs went missing and by the time we had borrowed the Hotel Manager's there was nothing to do but jump into the beribboned Rolls at the hotel entrance and drive rapidly to the church while Jennifer and her father took a roundabout route to let us arrive first. Half way there I remember looking around the Rolls and asking St John: 'Are you sure this is our car?' 'No it isn't,' he replied reflectively. 'Never mind,' we chorused, and drove on. We never did discover how the other wedding fared, but heard nothing further so all must have been well. Back at the hotel I found the events beginning to catch up on me and could only manage a few chosen words for the bestman's speech. The Professor tactfully observed afterwards that although it might be the shortest speech he had ever heard it was full of meaning! He was a kindly man. His daughter and son-in-law will no doubt read this account of their wedding with a happy chuckle. They remain among my oldest friends.

Ever challenging fate, as the young do, I replaced the lost Austin by an open top Healey Abbott four-seater sports, second-hand of course. It was one of a small number hand-built by Healey in the early 1950s before he went in with Austin to design the smaller and popular Austin Healey. The Healey-Abbott is now a classic, to be seen only in museums and perhaps occasional rallies. I had mine for nearly ten years, in London, Rome and London again until family needs and the introduction of metered parking and traffic wardens in central London prevailed and I had to sell it to another buff who came all the way from Derby for it. Why do we treat cars as symbols of human virility when most are in fact just lethal monsters and, in North American terms, polluting 'gas-guzzlers'? They do not in my view need to be any of these things if governments would only internationally take a grip on the power-worship of the motor car industry. I exclude from that Mr Healey, he was a master designer!

On the world stage events were now moving to change Britain's position profoundly partly because of that very craving for motor vehicles. Oil had already been a major world preocupation for a generation and more. In the 1950s it was booming, proven by the War to be vital to defence as well as development. But, outside the Americas, the supply was concentrated east of Suez. A waterway linking the Mediterranean with the Red Sea had been the dream of many men since the time of the Pharaohs and had finally been achieved in 1869 by the efforts of the French diplomat de Lesseps and support of the then Viceroy of Egypt Mohammed Said. Initially Britain opposed the scheme, dubbing it 'inexpedient and impracticable', but Disraeli came to see financial benefit in buying a large British shareholding in the concession holder, the Suez Canal Company, and potential advantages to Empire and trade in this shortened route to India and the Orient. Once opened, the Suez Canal became the gateway between East and West, and had to be steadily enlarged to take increasing traffic. By 1950 the largest commodity passing through was oil from Persia, Iraq and Kuwait, and this despite the opening of a trans-Arabian pipeline from eastern Saudi Arabia to the Mediterranean.

The Canal belonged to Egypt but the agreements guaranteed that the operating concession belonged to the Suez Canal Company until 1968, and that the Canal 'shall always be free and open, in time of war as in time of peace, to every vessel of commerce or of war, without distinction of flag ... and shall never be subjected to the exercise of the right of blockade.' In 1956 the then ruler of Egypt, Col. Nasser, flouted these guarantees, nationalised the Canal and challenged the share-holding powers, and notably France and Britain, to recognise his authority. International negotiations dragged on for months until the patience of the Eden government in Britain and Mollet government in France snapped. On 26 October they mounted, with a willing Israel, a military invasion of Egypt to recover the Canal. The sad story of that ill-conceived expedition has been endlessly recounted and analysed. As a recent article by Hywel Williams in the *Guardian* reminded us:

> Eden was proud of a reputation for morality and honour. But oil and
> trade supplied his motive for military action ... Many applauded his

(statement) that appeasing dictators never worked ... What undid Eden was collusion. The private agreement was that Israel should issue Egypt with an ultimatum to withdraw ... in terms that invited a rebuff. Britain and France would then have a cloak of morality to come in and 'separate the combatants' ... He lied to the House of Commons about this collusion ... And he crazily presumed on the support of the United States, which in November demanded (and secured) the withdrawal of the Anglo-French force. It was the end of Britain as a great power.

The Foreign Office at large was not party to it. The negotiations with France and Israel, and the planning and decision-making were kept by Eden to a secretive little Ministerial and official group at what we used to term (and perhaps still do) 'the highest level'! The nearest I came to involvement was when the Anglo-American row was at its height I was invited as dogsbody to a dinner given by the Lt. Governor of the London region in his elegant Mayfair house for the American Ambassador to meet senior officials of the FO privately to try to smooth things over. It was my first experience of that select London circuit, more commonly used by inner circle politicians. The curious feature was that it required a well-housed wealthy patron to host, and this remains so today. The days of rival political town houses are long past. That particular dinner was obviously inconclusive but I saw its use.

The Foreign Office at lower level was in ferment over the Suez venture, and the corridors buzzed with condemnation. It even overspilled into the Travellers Club downstairs luncheon room, where members of the Office who could afford the Club subscription but not the upstairs dining room liked to gather (I could afford neither at that time). Unfortunately the day the news broke, there was an MP among them none had noticed, one Nigel Nicholson, son of Harold Nicholdson the author and former diplomat, but a shadow of his famous parents. He returned to the Commons that afternoon and foolishly declared to the chamber that the FO was in revolt. That took some living down! It was an unhappy time for all, and not least of course for the country. Eden resigned. Butler, his natural successor, failed to win over the Tory king-makers, and never recovered. Only Macmillan came out of it well, neatly shedding his initial association with the venture and going on, against the odds, to win a further Tory term of office on the disingenuous but popular slogan 'You've never had it so good'. Those events, and the European Community dispute, were the major issues of those years 1956–59, and they had a profound effect on our foreign policy and the future work of the Foreign Service.

1957 saw the 'special relationship' with the United States in shreds, the Suez Canal in Egyptian hands (but run competently once the war wrecks had been cleared), our standing in the Middle East in tatters (and, in some cases like Saudi Arabia, in diplomatic suspense) and, to crown it all, a major difference with our one European ally in it all, France, and the rest of the Six over the embryo European Community. It was a time to review commitments and begin laboriously to rebuild trust in Britain abroad. But in Europe the government chose to flay around seeking both a new defence policy and ways of out-flanking the EEC as it came into being with the signature of the Rome Treaties in March 1957. I was given a little part in these ventures by being assigned to desk responsibility for the Western European Union and the political aspects of European integration. It proved an interesting but frustrating year.

The Foreign Office had changed since I was last there. The predominance of the German departments had gone with the end of German occupation, and of the Middle East departments with the decline in our responsibilities there. South East Asia and the Far East were now East of an Egyptian-controlled Suez and, with Australia, New Zealand, India, Pakistan and now Malaya independent in the Commonwealth, our relations in those regions were more the responsibility of the Commonwealth Relations Office than the FO. Interest in Latin America was secondary and in Africa yet to emerge. The focus of foreign policy was over-ridingly on the East–West cold war and Europe, and particularly on the Western Organisations where policy was concerted with our allies. The principal departments concerned were Western Orgs, as we called it, a new unit called the Permanent Under-Secretary's department, the European Economic department and the Northern (Europe) department. Relations with the United States were not handled in the North American department but across the board. So most new initiatives to try to restore Britain's position after Suez came our way, and we had a direct line to the Secretary of State Selwyn Lloyd and the Minister of State David Ormsby-Gore through our Under-Secretary, the Viscount (Sammy) Hood.

Selwyn Lloyd was a survivor. He was in on Suez with Eden but recognised as a diligent, hard-working Foreign Secretary and was retained by Macmillan until he fell with others in the 'night of the long knives' later. I saw quite a lot of him in those three years. He had an image problem after Suez and lacked humour, so he engaged a public relations adviser – the first Minister to do so I think – but the fellow had the sins of his trade and tried disastrously to spin Lloyd's sense of humour instead of his obvious strong points. Lloyd nonetheless steadily won respect abroad and at home and was good to work with. He was much later elected Speaker of the House of Commons. Ormsby-Gore was also a pleasure to have as Minister, and later made a very good Ambassador to Washington, as a political appointee by Macmillan at the time of President Kennedy. There were also two junior Ministers, one a peer who did very little and the other a billy-bunterish figure who came to grief over some alleged liaison in the bushes of St James' Park.

The Viscount Hood was a distinguished figure in Western diplomatic circles and London society in those days. Tall, elegant, wealthy and single, he was brilliant at his job but preferred only the inner circle of posts and so never reached beyond Minister in Washington and Deputy Under-Secretary at home. He was good to work with, especially as he commanded the respect of Ministers and officials alike. Pat Hancock, the head of Western Orgs when I was there, was cast in the same courtly mould and, except for spells as Ambassador to Israel and Under Secretary at home, really found Dorset and fishing more to his ultimate taste. They were both of the pre-war school, as was Sir Anthony Rumbold, who replaced Hood as Under-Secretary and had been a colleague in Paris. All the others in my first spell in Western Orgs (I was to return as Assistant Head a few years later) were, like me, post-war entrants. Some were older than others. Anyone like me, still in his early 30s, was barely out of short pants in the eyes of the FO in those days, war service notwithstanding! Several nonetheless went on ultimately to be Ambassadors of one grade or another, John Bushell, the Assistant Head and a good golfing friend, became Ambassador to Viet Nam and then Pakistan; Clive Rose, UK Permanent Representative to NATO; John Lambert Ambassador to Tunisia; John Drinkall, a Cambridge golf blue, Ambassador to Afghanistan and then High Commissioner to Jamaica; Charles Booth, a colleague again in Rome later, Ambassador to Burma and then High Commissioner to Malta; John Cambridge, Ambassador to Kuwait and then Morocco; Ken Scott, Ambassador to Yugoslavia and then deputy Private Secretary to the Queen, and Juliet Collings, one of the first dozen women Ambassadors in the Service (to Luxembourg) and later Mistress of Girton College, Cambridge. None of the others made the grade as far as I know, two changing career to academia and writing, two falling from grace, and three or four disappearing out of the reference books. Altogether they were a talented crew, or to be precise, succession of crews because they came and went. The department seemed to be involved in all major issues of the day, from the East-West conflict and the future of Germany, to the Atlantic, defence policy and, not least, the future of Europe.

Faced simultaneously with the humiliation and fall-out of Suez and the growing realisation that the Eden government had also been wrong on European integration of the Six, the Macmillan government determined on three major initiatives in Europe and Defence. All involved Western Organisations. The first was a fundamental review of defence policy conducted by the then Minister of Defence, Duncan Sandys. Whitehall gossip had it that the White Paper he eventually produced with the support of his colleagues, went through twenty-five and more drafts. But the conclusion was profound. It was to abolish conscription by 1962 and make the armed forces wholly professional. This was not new to Britain, conscription having been introduced only in World Wars and . But it was new to much of the Western (and Eastern) world. The United States followed only when the Viet Nam war was over, a decade and a half later.

An immediate consequence of the review, dictated also by the need to economise after Suez, was a decision by the government to reduce the level of British forces stationed under Alliance defence strategy in Germany. Nothing could have more upset the Six. To achieve agreement on Eden's plan in 1954 to bind Germany and Italy into western defence by welcoming them into NATO and allowing them forces of their own again under agreed controls, Britain had had to reassure the French and Benelux by guaranteeing to maintain British forces in Germany at set levels. Now, less than three years later, we wanted to reduce this Brussels Treaty commitment, maintaining that our restructured professional forces would be more effective anyhow. The argument was conducted in the Western European Union, composed of Britain and the Six at Foreign Secretary level with Selwyn Lloyd in the chair, and the Americans, Canadians and Supreme Allied Commander Europe invited as observers.

This was my field and I shall not forget those meetings, especially that in February 1957 when Selwyn Lloyd used a form of diplomacy I had never seen before. Having put forward the British proposals and explained them, he sat there, in the chair, like a sphinx, hour after hour, while his European colleagues argued the reverse, sought compromises and gradually grew silent in frustration and weariness. A communiqué was finally agreed in the early hours of the morning, recording that the examination of the British proposals would be concluded at a further meeting. But Lloyd had won acquiescence, deeply aggrieved though the Six were. When the Macmillan government sought still further reductions in our forces in Germany later that year, they were this time sunk in a NATO review and renegotiation of Germany's contribution to local costs.

The Macmillan government's second initiative in Europe, in which I also became involved although only marginally, was to create a European Free Trade Area (EFTA) around the periphery of the European Economic Community (or 'Common Market' as it was popularly called). The EFTA was to encompass, besides Britain, 'the Scandinavians, Swiss, Austrians and perhaps also the Irish, Portuguese and others' (Spain was still then under Franco) …'so as to avoid the economic division of Europe inherent in the Six-Power Common Market and probably inherent in any simple association of the United Kingdom with that grouping.' (That is a quotation from an FO despatch to European posts of October 1957.) The EFTA was not welcomed by the Six for the obvious reason that it was born of British distrust of them and their community schemes for Europe. But the Scandinavians and others responded well; negotiations with the Six were sensibly conducted in the wider OECE; and EFTA eventually came into being in reasonable harmony with the Community of the Six. It still exists today although, as most of its members peeled off eventually to join the European Economic Community after all, it now encompasses only Iceland, Norway, Switzerland and Liechtenstein and all of them except Switzerland have now formed a European Economic Area with the EEC. My involvement was internally in the FO arguing, when the opportunity arose, for the alternative of UK association with the Six; and externally in the WEU and Council of Europe Assemblies, accompanying the responsible Minister Reginald Maudling when he went to promote the scheme among European Parliamentarians. He was pleasant company and a very skilled advocate, in his laid-back way, and I suppose it might be claimed for EFTA that at least it saved us from isolation during the decade of de Gaulle's veto on our joining the EEC ...

The third Macmillan government initiative in Europe involved me, up to the hilt. It was Ormsby-Gore's idea, which Selwyn Lloyd latched onto, that we should offer a sweetener to the Six, to make EFTA and the reduction of forces in Germany more palatable. It started with a vague, almost throw-away, remark by Selwyn Lloyd in his address to the annual Ministerial meeting of the North Atlantic Council in Paris in December 1956. I was there and had to report it to the FO, but was frankly surprised to be asked on return home to flesh it out into a substantial proposal of three elements. One was that we and the Six should get together more often at Ministerial level, in the WEU, for political consultations on anything that would be helpful to our mutual relations. That was sensible enough, provided it did not waste people's time by duplicating consultations in NATO, the OECE, the Council of Europe, and EFTA/EEC meetings. The second element, also added in time, was closer cooperation in the research, development and production of non-nuclear armaments, which was already a function of WEU. That too was sensible enough, although everyone knew from experience the difficulty of getting multilateral agreement in Europe on common requirement and specification of weapons. The art was still at a very early stage in WEU, NATO and bilaterally. It was to be nearly a decade before we in Britain achieved a major break-through in the joint Anglo-French development of the Jaguar strike aircraft. I was to find myself involved in that too, on return to Western Orgs in the mid-1960s.

The third element of the third Macmillan government initiative – this is beginning to sound cartesian! – was a proposal to simplify the network of European and Atlantic organisations that had grown up since the war and particularly their associated Parliamentary Assemblies, of which there were now four – Council of Europe, WEU, European Economic Community and, less formally, NATO. This was the Ormsby-Gore plan, dubbed The Grand Design. Unfortunately, while it sounded sensible enough in pragmatic London and was at least a constructive initiative, it failed to thrill the Six because in Paris, Bonn, Brussels, The Hague and Luxembourg it looked mighty like a British attempt to cramp the development of the EEC or at any rate its Parliamentary Assembly. I was given the job of working it out for discussion in the WEU and promotion through our Embassies in Europe and North America.

I spent a weekend on it. The first part was easy enough to write: that was the statement of the problem – the confusing plethora of Western organisations now taking up so much of the time of Ministers, Officials and Parliamentarians in Europe. So was the third part: the Grand Design with one Parliamentary Assembly operating in functional committees of differing membership like the United Nations but – inevitably – no power to control the executives of any of the different organisations including the European Commission. That was not my idea and I knew it would not work. But, as W. S. Gilbert wrote of civil servants: 'The privilege and pleasure that we treasure beyond measure is to run on little errands for Ministers of State!' It was the middle part that stumped me: how to marry the prescribed solution in part three to the problem in part one. I spent all Sunday trying to square that circle and it was not until late at night that the solution dawned. It came in a flash: forget my scientific upbringing of logical argument from the evidence, just bring the statements of the problem and the solution together, with no middle linkage at all, and see what your colleagues think of it.

So I did that. There was no alternative. To my surprise my colleagues thought it 'very good'! They too knew their duty. So it went to the WEU and all around Europe, and I and my WEU opposite numbers in the Embassies of the Six in London spent hours, days and weeks arguing diplomatically about it, until one day Hood told me it had served its purpose, I had done my job, the Six were persuaded we were sincere even if, in their view, misguided, and we could drop it. So began and ended the fleetingly famous Grand Design for European Organisations.

In October 1957 Ministers eventually authorised the FO, goaded by Sir Gladwyn Jebb in Paris and, I like to think, a few others of us, to acknowledge, in the despatch I have already mentioned, to all our posts in Europe and Washington, Ottawa, Moscow and the UN, that 'Her Majesty's Government are fully conscious of the important political implications of the Rome Treaties, the ratification of which is now virtually complete ... They recognise that when this union begins to take shape the UK will have to come to terms with it. Those terms would seem most likely to involve a much closer association of the UK with Europe than exists today ... HMG are prepared for that to the extent that it can be achieved without damage to UK relations with the Commonwealth and the United States.'

That, to me, marked great progress. The despatch went on to say that 'In present circumstances the UK could not contemplate sinking its identity completely in Europe even if otherwise this seemed desirable and feasible.' That was in fact an odd thing to say as there never was, nor is there today except among extreme 'federalists', any question of any member state of the European Community losing its national identity in some uniform whole. Not even Russia achieved that in the Soviet Union, not permanently anyhow, and that was under totalitarian communism. In any case the French, Germans, Italians and others simply would not have it, as anyone who has lived among them must know. However British relations with the European Community have all along been bedevilled by semantics. The words 'integration', 'federation', 'supranational', 'identity' and 'sovereignty' still mean different things to different people. What mattered more in that FO despatch, however, was that for the first time it declared: 'On the other hand HMG consider it to be in the UK's long-term economic and political interest that she should do so partially (sink her identity in Europe). That is the logic of the UK's geographical proximity to continental Europe, and of the relative decline in her position and that of other European countries in the modern world. The problem is not so much one of intent as of timing and method.'

That was a great advance towards British government realism on Europe, compared with the post-Messina and pre-Suez outlook a year and more previously. Little more than three years on from then the Macmillan government came around to applying for British membership of the European Community. It was a tragedy we had taken so long, and even greater tragedy that de Gaulle was by then back in power in France and chose to block British membership for a further decade. I shall come back to that in a later chapter.

If those particular years in the FO 1956–59 were frustrating, because of Suez and the slow acceptance of Europe, they were nonetheless gratifying to anyone working in Whitehall to see recovery after Suez and progress on Europe. They were also personally enjoyable because we had a happy team in the Office and, once I had found water-holes in the London social desert, there was a fulfilling life outside too. There was cricket, playing for a team called the Nomads who had no ground of their own so we travelled around London and the Home Counties to play clubs on their grounds, or occasionally had matches at Hurlingham which had its own delightful little ground with a huge chestnut (I think) at mid-wicket. I had a good season, reaching an even higher batting average than I had at school until I was run out in the last match of the season, which reduced it to 83. That was still a Nomad's record although hardly something to boast about. The truth was that club cricket in the London area had reached a low of heavy-booted caution at that time, whereas the cricket I had been playing on coconut matting abroad taught quick footed batting – I actually wore tennis shoes, much to the scorn of the MCC opponents we occasionally encountered. So I had the advantage and it was rather fun.

Fielding long hours in the outfield one day, however, I found myself wondering if golf might not be more my game for the second half of life. Casting around I found friends of like-mind and we soon formed a golfing group, including John Bushell from the Office and Heather Stileman, an active Hurlingham member. We joined the Hindhead Golf Club on the borders of Surrey and Hampshire, a longish drive from London in those days, but worth it for the scenic beauty and welcome we found there. It is now I think Peter Alliss' club and the subscription must be two to three hundred times what we paid – which, as a Country Member, was £8 per annum as I recall. I managed to win the Captain's prize there the following year but before handing it to me the Captain without ceremony announced he had cut my handicap from 24 to 18. That is how it was done in those days, by human authority not calculating computer. I have never won a Captain's prize since! Heather Stileman achieved particular fame in my book by scoring a hole-in-one at Sunningdale but standing her ground against the mob of stockbrokers who appeared in the bar demanding the traditional free drink from her. 'That is not a rule of the Ladies' Golf Federation,' she stoutly declared, and left them speechless as well as drinkless. We had a lot of fun together.

I was also able to do quite a lot of travelling, and not just about Europe but – something a diplomat rarely had the opportunity to do – around Britain. There was an enterprising little publishing company in Bristol in those days, who compiled and published a diarised catalogue of local events throughout Britain every year. It seems not to exist any more, which is a pity, because it opened up towns and villages, ports and resorts, dales and vales, fêtes and festivals, games and sports throughout the country for every weekend in the year, which added incentive to travel. We perhaps forget that this was not possible during and after the War because of petrol rationing, which was only ended in 1957.

I was also able in 1958 to re-visit Scotland, and to pay my first and memorable visit to Ireland. To do so by car was an expedition in those days, the Western seaboard of Ireland being still a land of crofts and poverty. At Galway we attended the races to see, in fabled fashion, a snow-white Fairy Queen streak ahead of the field only to fade up the final straight and come in last – to the distress of the farm lads punting their last punts and probably their year's savings on the fantasy. That same evening we found a small hotel restaurant in town for dinner only to be told by the pretty little Irish waitress with distant blue eyes I can still see today, that she was very sorry but they did not serve it. 'So what are those people over there having?' I asked. It was obviously the staple dish of boiled beef and boiled potatoes. 'They're having high tea,' came the reply. 'Could we then please have high tea?' I asked. 'I'm very sorry, but we don't serve high tea after 8 o'clock,' she said. It was by now long gone 8 and other restaurants might be the same. In despair I asked: 'I don't mind what you call it, but could we please have what they are having?' She thought for a long time, gazing with those lovely eyes through the window. 'We-ell, you can have law-wnch if you like,' she replied helpfully. 'And what is law-wnch?' I asked. 'Boiled beef and boiled potatoes,' she replied.

So we had lunch, and she served it just like high tea but at dinner time. I always think that was so very Irish: charming, a little inconsequential but delightfully willing. They are an extraordinarily talented people I find, with a tragic history that now, we hope, is at last steadily being put behind them. They are also now prospering, within the European Community, which is wonderful to behold. Good luck to them, South and North.

My companion on that holiday consented to become my wife later in the year. So I have Ireland to thank for that too. But that is for the next chapter.

# CHAPTER 14

## Guinea

## 1959–1960

'I F PARIS WAS THE MOST ENJOYABLE, Guinea was the most interesting of my posts.' That was my choice, and remains so. One reason was surmised by my mother in wishing me Godspeed as I set off for the unknown in January 1959: 'It will be interesting for you, who likes responsibility, to be tackling this new job and with no precedents.' I was to have my own Embassy, however small and, unusually, to start it from scratch. But there were other reasons too. There was the engaging enthusiasm of a nation finding its own independence. It was difficult not to share their exhilaration. Then there was the struggle for their hearts and minds that had to be mounted against the cold-war efforts of the Soviet Union and its communist allies to make Guinea the first Cuba of Africa. It was a close run fight, the forerunner of Angola, Somalia, Ethiopia and so many other cold war battles for Africa that followed, and indeed of Cuba itself. It was also the first scene of Sino-Soviet competition in Africa.

'How, where and why' were the questions I was asked by family and friends alike when my appointment was announced as HM Chargé d'Affaires, Conakry. Few had heard of the place. I had to do some rapid homework myself, although I already knew something of it from the FO telegrams that had been flying about for weeks past between London, Paris and Washington. Talk of the French pulling out in pique and leaving a vacuum and of our opening a post there to help fill it, intrigued me and I was not surprised when, on enquring of Personnel Department what they had in mind for me after three years in London they 'threw a fly over me about it' (to use an old FO expression). I agreed to think about it. There were personal and family concerns I had to weigh. The FO needed to do some thinking too. Their initial concept, emanating from an African Department anxious to get representation into Guinea but under pressure from the European side of the Office not to offend the French, was to send a (male) diplomatic officer and (female) secretary to live in the bush and report! I had to point out the absurdity of that and we agreed that whoever went would need to establish an Embassy proper in the capital Conakry and be in charge as Chargé d'Affaires. It would be for a tour of eighteen months and subject only to the appointment in due course of a non-resident Ambassador to visit occasionally for the sake of form. I agreed to go on that basis. The FO later told the press that I had volunteered. That was not correct. But as so often in my career, it seemed pre-determined. That answered the 'how'.

The 'where' required study of the map. It was a West African coastal state shaped like a pan-handle, and coloured on the map as part of the French empire. It lay between, to the east, the British colony of Sierra Leone, then quietly moving towards independence under its outstanding Governor Sir Maurice Dorman, and the independent slave-founded state of Liberia; and, to the west and north, the backward Portuguese colony of Guinea-Bissau and the large French colonies of Senegal and Soudan (later Mali – which includes the city of Timbuctoo). It was not to be confused with New Guinea, the large south-west Pacific island divided between Indonesia and Papua, nor even with the Gulf of Guinea, the 'armpit' of Africa where the continent bends inwards off Nigeria and the Cameroons; still less with guinea pigs, which are domesticated rodents from South America, or human guinea pigs who are of course people used in experimentation. It was known to early European travellers as Les Rivières du Sud, because of its many streams emptying into the sea from the mountainous interior of the Fouta Djalon. It became a French colony in 1883 and took the name of Guinea soon afterwards. The guinea fowl was indigenous, but so it was elsewhere in Africa. So that answered the 'where'.

Finding anyone who had been there was more difficult. Indeed I never did until I reached the capital Conakry. The French Overseas Administration and those French companies active there knew it of course, but those sources of knowledge were closed to me by French objections to my appointment. There were a few British who had been there. By coincidence I met one recently forty years on, who told me he was working for ICI in West Africa at that time and paid regular sales visits from his base in Nigeria to each of the ten French, four British and two Portuguese colonies which then made up the region with Liberia and newly independent Ghana (formerly British Gold Coast). But the usually well-informed FO did not know of them, nor that – as a friend later discovered for me – there was a standard work on French West Africa in English by Virginia Thompson and Richard Adloff. As their study recorded: 'Few (but the French) ventured into the vast and important tropical areas under French administration.' To us in London it was unknown territory.

In area Guinea was the same size as the United Kingdom but in population only one twentieth of ours. It encompassed mountains in the north, plains on a central plateau, forest in the pan-handle and richly arable but swampy and tsetse-fly ridden lands along the coast. It had bauxite mines, minerals, diamonds and timber. It also had, in the coastal area and sea, an abundance of natural food, fruit and fish, augmented by the cattle of the central plains. In my Annual Review of Guinea for 1959 (a chore the FO imposed on Heads of Mission everywhere in the world every year to make us think above the daily round, and to print for the information of Ministers), I felt able to comment: 'The basic economic fact of this country revealed in the temporary hiatus in trade immediately after Independence in 1958, is that it is impossible to starve in Guinea except through idleness.' I might in fairness have added, 'or grave misfortune.' But, except in the mountains and deep in the jungle, the country could have supported a far larger population than its 2½ million, if the dominant tribe, the Peulhs (or Fulani) of the centre and north had favoured the cultivation of agriculture and industry instead of preferring 'their independent existence as herders and [Islamic] religious contemplatives' (Thompson and Adloff); or if the French had been able to put more into the country in their eighty years of colonisation. The more negroid tribes of the coastal plain, mostly Mandingos and only superficially Islamised, and the peoples of the forest in the north-west were, with individual exceptions, largely subordinate. The Peulhs never fully accepted French domination, and it was perhaps historically predictable that, under their leadership, Guinea would be the first French colony in West and Equatorial Africa to strike for independence. Thompson and Adloff commented a year and more before that happened that 'Guinea, with its great reservoirs of unemployed in the towns and its promising future as the most industrialised territory of the Federation remains the most dangerous powder-keg in French West Africa.' That proved prophetic.

There was also an immediate reason for that prediction. It centred around a trade union organiser by the name of Sekou Touré, 'an able and forceful grandson of the (Peulh) conqueror Samory, far less imbued with French culture than the other (emerging) leaders of French West Africa ... had frequent conflicts during his early youth with the (French) authorities, received little formal education and (officially) had been to France only since election as a deputy to the (French) Assembly in 1959' (Thompson and Adloff). He had risen rapidly in the Guinea ranks of the Rassemblement Democratique Africain (RDA) party, now burgeoning across French West Africa and, in local elections, had already defeated the more conservative and French-controlled Rassemblement du Peuple Francais (RPF), and taken a radical turn that differentiated him from the other RDA leaders like Felix Houphouet-Boigny in the Ivory Coast and Leopold Senghor in Senegal. It was French policy in those days to regard the French empire as part of greater France, with the intellectual elite of each colony educated to become Frenchmen called evolués and each colony enabled to elect representatives to the French Assembly in Paris. Sekou Touré had no time for the *evolué* concept. He, and several of his Guinean trade union and RDA colleagues, had been singled out years earlier by scouts of the powerful French communist trade union the CGT, and trained secretly in unionism, political campaigning and marxism.

The question when they rose to power, was whether they were convinced communists bent on spreading the gospel in West Africa, or radical socialists with close connections with the communist world but first and foremost African nationalists with an Islamic background. Either way, as I later wrote in my 1959 Annual Review. 'A year and more of living among the Guineans has convinced me that they would have sought their independence at an early date and gone left in their form of state with or without General de Gaulle's impulse. They had been preparing for it since 1946, and those in the French administration who told us in Paris in 1953 and 1954 that nothing ever happened in this part of Africa, that it was all politically dead were, it now seems, woefully wrong.'

The occasion for declaring independence came suddenly in the summer of 1958. General de Gaulle had resumed power in France, called from retirement – as he always expected to be – to resolve the political instability of the 4th Republic and the civil war in Algeria. He achieved both in time, establishing in the process the present 5th Republic. He also conceived a new form of French Union (or Community as he called it) allowing self-government to many of its constituent parts and the choice of being in or out. He toured French West and Equatorial Africa to obtain agreement from the colonies he thought fit and secured it from all except one, Guinea. Sekou Touré, by then the elected local leader, received de Gaulle, listened to him, saw him off at Conakry airport and there dramatically declared the Guinean reply to be '*Non*'. De Gaulle was mortified and unforgiving. He immediately ordered the withdrawal from Guinea of all French administrators, judiciary, army and aid, and suspended trade and franc zone support. Many French teachers, lawyers, doctors and small businessmen also left. Some of the officials even took their light bulbs with them. The French, unlike the British, had long encouraged people from the home country to go out and settle in their West African colonies. So even hairdressers and taxi drivers in Conakry were mainly French. Although many French businesses hung on and there were also many Lebanese, Syrians and Greeks who remained, as did the Canadian and South African mining companies and the Patterson Zochoni trading house, the French sanctions and exodus left Guinea stranded in independence.

It was inevitable that the Guineans would immediately appeal to their Soviet and other communist friends. This was the vacuum that so disturbed the Foreign Office, bearing in mind the extent of British interests along the West African Coast. Representations were made to the French to think again but de Gaulle would not hear of it – until the FO announced that in that case we would open representation there ourselves, whereupon the French, ever suspicious of *Perfide Albion*, came rapidly off de Gaulle's high horse although only to save face and trade. That was the 'why'. It was into this hot-house that I was invited to go, in November of that year.

My first concern was family but they took it well. My second, perhaps understandably, was how I would cope without a wife. I assumed that, as at Jedda, there would be some sociable ladies about but it would not do to get involved. I consulted my doctor – Raymond Rowntree, a wise man who had sorted me out medically after Paris and was reckoned to be one of the best diagnosticians in London. Rejecting any idea of prescribing me the sort of bromides we were given during the war, he bluntly advised: 'get married'! So did the head of my department in the FO, Pat Hancock who sensing my dilemma remarked to me one day in his elegantly detached way: 'You know, Hugh, marriage is not a bad thing. It is really a partnership.' I took their advice and asked my very good friend Ann Purkiss, with whom I had been 'going for some time' – to use that nice old-fashioned phrase – if she would marry me and come to Guinea. She consented, and always joked that I would not have married her but for Guinea. The only truth in that was that we would have done it in more leisurely fashion! As it was we were wed by Christmas and had no honeymoon. She had been married before so knew a little about it although the experience had been brief and in her youth. For my part, having entered the stakes late owing to the war and Jedda, and still enjoying my independence, I undoubtedly needed wise advice and a kick in the pants. Guinea provided it, and I was fortunate to find Ann willing. She had been told by a Spanish fortune-teller that she would marry a diplomat one day and she had the intelligence, wit, travel experience and looks to enjoy it. She was also an author and, at the time, foreign editor of the London publishers Heinemann. We had a lot of fun together over fifteen years, sometimes tempestuous but always interesting, and raised three children who remain our bond, pride and joy.

So Guinea did me that great service. It also helped shake the FO out of its silly concept of a bush post when I announced I was taking a wife. My secretary-to-be Kay Lusmore welcomed the news when I met her and she and Ann became good friends. Neither in fact was able to come until nearly two months after my departure, Ann because of appendicitis, Kay because of chickenpox, and both because the FO, with the Treasury for ever on their backs, preferred they came by the cheapest means, which was still the Union Castle boat from Liverpool to Freetown. By then I had found a rented house for a Residence, flats for the staff and a small but adequate office in town, all – unlike Jedda – with very necessary air-conditioning. I was also launched into the ferment of Guinea politics. But it made all the difference to have Ann with me.

The third concern back in November had been how to organise an

Embassy from scratch. No one in the FO knew. No one around had done it. Arranging travel and credentials was one thing and we had an honorary Vice-Consul in Conakry, Spyros Tsiantar, the deputy manager of Patterson Zochonis, who could help locally. But there was accommodation to find and adapt, office furniture and equipment to acquire, safes and official stationery to ship out, cypher books to supply under escort, vehicles of British make to purchase, uniforms for locally engaged staff to arrange and a thousand and one other things, not forgetting of course the Union Jack and pole for the office and pennant for my car. There was also the official accounting to establish (the FO was hot on that), rent and other local allowances to be assessed and agreed with London, and consular facilities to be organised – we were in fact inundated from the start with requests for consular help from citizens of Sierra Leone and other British colonies along the coast who found themselves in Guinea, as also from visiting journalists, salesmen and mafia attracted like bees to this newly independent country in the news.

Fortunately I found a man in the FO who had foreseen the need. He was a retired Brigadier, Charles Steel by name, head of our ultra efficient Conference Department, and in his drawer he had the makings of a plan. We worked on it together and he appointed one of his staff, David Edwards, to help and in due course, at my urging, to go ahead with vehicles and supplies by sea to Freetown and rough laterite road to Conakry. That was a great help.

Yet another concern of course was staff. Bureaucracy does not work like business in such ventures. You do not draw up a plan and budget, get it agreed and then it is up to you. You have to make your case for everything and argue it through point by point. It was clear to me from the outset that if I was to establish relations with the leading Guineans and play any useful part in the rapidly evolving scene, I could not afford to get bogged down on book-keeping, minor administration and daily consular services. Reluctantly Personnel eventually agreed I must have a Vice-Consul and they appointed one, Bill Wright, to go out with Edwards ahead of me. It was not quite his scene but he helped where it mattered. The Secretary they gave me, Kay Lusmore, proved a gem: personable, equable, efficient and ever thoughtful, she remained a pillar throughout. She later married a senior British Treasury official and we stayed in touch for years. Then there was another Secretary, also called Kay. She was a tough little lady who had served around the globe and was as helpful as could be in the difficult early days when we needed all hands to the pump.

So that, together with a few locals we recruited, was the sum total of my Embassy staff, and it remained that small throughout my time. There was no point in having more, even to cover illness and leave. In that unhealthy climate and those tense circumstances, it was wise to keep staff to the very minimum. We were lucky I suppose to cope right through without serious mishap, although I did have to send the Vice-Consul home ahead of his leave when he lost his cool and was in danger of being declared persona non grata (PNG). In the Service at large, to be so declared was sometimes an accolade, like being thrown out of Moscow in tit-for-tat diplomatic expulsions. In other cases, like this, it threatened gratuitously to harm relations. His successor, Geoff Windle, I had known in Jedda and was a man I could leave in charge when I travelled or finally left. It was not always easy to keep one's marbles in those conditions. All but the one did so admirably and formed a good little team.

There was one more hurdle to surmount before I actually reached Guinea, and it was French. Their policy was to let Guinea stew in its own juice until General de Gaulle felt prepared to lift the trade and payments sanctions and allow Guinea back into the franc zone. They did not believe the Soviet bloc could supplant them nor, of course, that it was necessary for Britain or any other Western country to move in. Despite fair FO warning they were shocked when my appointment was announced. I was summoned to lunch by the French Ambassador in London, Monsieur Jean Chauvel, and found myself subjected to a head-shrinking as only the French could conceive. I knew the Ambassador and most of his senior staff from working together in European circles, and particularly Francis Huré, the 1st Secretary (political) who was my opposite number in the West European Union. But the atmosphere was frigid. I was the only guest and the Ambassador signalled me to sit at the bottom of the table, flanked on either side in ascending order of seniority by his 1st Secretaries, Counsellors and Ministers, with himself at the head. He made little effort to converse, nor did any of his staff except Huré, other than to take note that I was going to Guinea and that French interests there were naturally paramount. The lunch was brief, almost a snack by French standards, and coffee was taken at table. Over that, the Ambassador cleared his throat and announced that Huré would be coming to Guinea. He then rose and left, followed by his staff except poor Huré who took me off to another room to explain.

It appeared that the Ambassador had that morning been asked by the head of the Quai d'Orsay, M. Joxe, to designate a member of his middle-ranking staff who knew me, to go and open a French Embassy in Guinea before I or any other Western diplomat reached there first. Huré was the obvious choice and, having a wife but no children and a good health record, he had no option but to accept. He was understandably appalled at the prospect and pleaded with me: 'Could you possibly postpone your departure to give me time to pack, brief myself in Paris, and get to Conakry first?' I was sympathetic, knowing how rushed I had been myself over several weeks and that briefing took time (I had been required by our rather over-zealous Personnel to visit some twenty Departments, from political to security). But I was already booked, inoculations taken, flat let, Ann's hospitalisation arranged, my advance party on its way and the

Guineans told when to expect me. He was dismayed. I knew the FO would not object to my letting him arrive first if possible. They would be only too glad that the French were seemingly coming to their senses. But I knew, too, they would not want me to postpone my arrival. They had recently received a visit from a young Guinean envoy, Diallo Telli, who had impressed them, from the Secretary of State Selwyn Lloyd down, with his intelligence, humility and the urgency of filling the vacuum without delay. I suggested a compromise to Huré: he should fly out direct to present his credentials while I kicked my heels at Dakar for a day or two *en route*, and he would then return to Paris for his briefing and organisation, and come back to Guinea when he could. He reluctantly agreed, and did just that. So the French were able to mark with the Guineans that they were, after all, the first Western nation to recognise Guinean independence with the accreditation of a Chargé d'Affaires of Embassy (and promise of early negotiations on assets, trade and payments). And we were able to keep our undertaking to be there without delay. In fact we were the first working Embassy there from any country and the Guineans always viewed me as the first diplomat to arrive and stay. We were ahead even of the first Soviet bloc Ambassador – from Czechoslovakia. That added a little extra pioneering responsibility to my job.

I suppose that after that extraordinary lunch at the French Embassy in London, the Ambassador felt able to report to Paris that he had had me in, made it clear to me that French interests in Guinea should be respected, extracted from me agreement that the French representative should go in first and briefed Huré to keep an eye on me. It was all rather silly, but at least obliged the French to resume some measure of responsibility. Franco-Guinean agreements on assets, trade and payments were concluded in January. But Huré only stayed a few months and no one replaced him until an Ambassador, Pierre Siraud, was eventually appointed. It was a difficult assignment, caught between President de Gaulle's bitter antipathy and President Sekou Touré's glorification of his famous 'Non' (which in fact inspired other French African states soon to negotiate independence). 'Better poverty in independence than slavery in dependence,' was the popular Guinean song. Those of us who hoped for reconciliation between France and Guinea were disappointed.

I arrived in Guinea on 24 January reasonably prepared for the unexpected. I had my Letters ready in French, a short address to deliver to the President in case he invited me straight in to see him (not the usual diplomatic custom but the Guineans might make their own); and some remarks to make publicly in case of need – my pleasure to be there, greetings of my government, congratulations on independence, and our determination to develop friendly relations 'founded on Britain's deep interest in West Africa, and in the defence of peace and democracy'. What I did not expect at the airport was a military band playing God Save the Queen, a guard of honour to inspect, a line of Guinean officials to meet me and, a little disconcertingly, a Radio Guinea microphone thrust in my face as I touched Guinean earth at the foot of the aircraft steps. The only thing missing, I later discovered, was the person of the Secretary of State for Foreign Affairs, Cissé Fodé, who caught up with me later with all apologies, he had overslept. I got to know him well in the months ahead and enjoyed working with him; he had a shrewd head but disarming humility and, like many of his colleagues, particularly the few from the coastal region of Guinea, a great sense of humour.

Seeing the reception party through the aircraft window as we taxied to a stop, I remember looking around to see who was the African dignitary on board. Then it dawned it was me, and I was thankful to have my little speech ready, a trilby had to doff (my first – and last) and my RAF training in inspections behind me. Also for my advance party who were there ready to escort me to the President, who was awaiting me.

He received me in the former Governor's Residence, generally called the Palace because it also housed reception rooms and offices. He looked the part, young (in his mid-30s), agile and handsome but reserved and dressed for the occasion in flowing Peulh robes and his trademark leopard-skin side-cap. He met me at the top of the stairs, led me into his lounge and, with barely a word, left the floor to me to present my credentials and letter of goodwill I had brought from the Foreign Secretary, Selwyn Lloyd, and to deliver my address that I intended to work for the betterment of relations between our two countries and hoped to have the pleasure and honour of meeting him frequently. To all that he replied, '*D'accord*,' and that was it. I was to find that he was a man of few words, except of course when speech-making, and a good listener. Also that '*d'accord*' from him did not mean 'I agree' but 'I understand'. Many newcomers fell foul of that.

I was to learn soon that he harboured high hopes of my mission, at minimum as an example to the French and others. Also that in those parts, as indeed in much of Africa, you had to be seen to be working in the common cause, and seen frequently, or it was assumed you had turned against. It was Diallo Telli who advised me of that, when I had been there a fortnight, taken up largely with establishing the Embassy administratively, and the President was evidently wondering why I had not been to see him again. I promptly found a reason, gave him a presumptuous little homily on the dangers of accepting any and every Soviet bloc overture and aid without circumspection and told him I proposed to work for more Western representation and aid to come to Guinea. He replied with his usual enigmatic '*d'accord*', and I made a practice thereafter of always seeing him every two to three weeks, somewhere or other and if only for a few chosen words. It proved helpful to do so, and he never refused me or found excuses. It was the same with his leading Ministerial and Bureau Politique colleagues. It paid to see them regularly, if less frequently, as well. At the pace of

# RÉCEPTION DU CHARGÉ D'AFFAIRES ANGLAIS

**Le Président Sékou Touré présentant M. N Famara
Keita sous-secrétaire d'Etat à la Défense Nationale, à M.
Hugh Jones, chargé d'affaires anglais, au cours de la soirée
donnée en l'honneur de M. Jones.**

With President Sekou Touré (centre) at his reception for me soon after my
arrival in Guinea, 1959.

events it was essential to be in close touch to have any hope of exerting
influence.

Within three weeks of my arrival the President sent word he wished to
give a public reception for me at the Residence with all his colleagues,
wives and press present. I was naturally pleased to accept but intrigued to
know the purpose. Marxists did not give parties for fun. It would have
been discussed in the Bureau Politique or Cabinet amidst vastly more
important subjects like rebuilding the state, socialising the economy,
securing aid and promoting the Guinean cause in Africa. I assumed it was
to encourage others, perhaps cock a snook at the French, and to show his
people that newspaper and bush-telegraph stories of Soviet bloc visitors
and aid pouring in were balanced by growing Western attention. Whatever
the reason, it was a good party and when I sought permission to ask his
wife for a dance and received the customary 'd'accord', and from her, I
had the impression that he regarded that as a test of attitude, and he

approved. My assistants, Edwards and Wright then took to the floor with Ministers' wives, as I did too, and the party went with a swing.

The first few weeks were a testing time. Aside from creating a working Embassy in quick time we had to establish good working relations with the Guinean authorities at all levels and make them feel we were supportive while at the same time getting to know the remaining French and other business communities. I found myself well received and, whenever I posed questions to the Guinean authorities about protocol or security or consular facilities, their engaging reply was more often than not: 'We are new to this. You tell us!' That made things easier.

Ann joined me in mid-March. I went to Freetown to meet her and Kay and, as on the brief liaison visit I had already paid there, we were given British colonial honours. She was very impressed. We flew to Conakry and went straight to the rented house I had secured for us, half way between the airport and town. It was small but adequate, enough for guests and entertainment and it had a large tropical garden overlooking the sea. It was a relief to be there after two months in Conakry's one hotel, the Hotel de France, surrounded by Soviet bloc delegates, visiting journalists and buccaneers sniffing out the post-French prospects. But I had vowed to await Ann's arrival before moving in. It was after all to be our first home together. She took to it instantly and, with perhaps a little author's licence, wrote home later:

> I am overflowing with things to tell you. First and foremost our house and garden ... the most beautiful white villa in the world set at the edge of the sea in a garden of wonder, not the soft-catkins-snowdrops type but a vivid rioting bower of scarlet, yellow and brilliant green ... the drive flanked by purple and red bougainvillea ... the wide entrance steps crowded with huge scarlet hibiscus ... coconut palms waving against the sea (sometimes with black and grey monkeys leaping about hysterically knocking the coconuts down!), and enormous flowering cactus as tall as me ... and avocado pears growing in the garden and loofahs in the trees – what a magical world! ... and a lovely little sea beach curving right into the garden with a big frangipani tree covered in richly scented yellow blossoms growing on it, and a view of a little island just offshore, with brown-sailed fishing smacks drifting across the water ... That day Hugh had had the painters and gardener painting the garden chairs and swing hammock and little wrought-iron tables white and red, and the cook and house-boy he had engaged were there smiling waiting for us. The house has bright yellow and red and green cushions and contemporary wooden furniture, and black and white squared tiled floors and curtains of a smart gay black and yellow contemporary design floating in the breeze in the archways – all combined to make a picture of paradise.

Later we were of course to discover that there were tropical nasties to temper the delights of the garden – vipers, green mambas (the deadliest) and whistling snakes, and an almost prehistoric looking curiosity, monitor lizards who fed off mammals, snakes and small lizards. Also the beach was not of sand but mud and flotsam from the coastal mangrove swamps. And the cook contrived to misunderstand duck for dog when he shopped for our first dinner party (the words are similar in creole English)! He also managed to blow up the Butagas stove. So his smile had to be replaced. Then there were the inevitable insects – although nature sometimes had its own remedies. Ann wrote:

> The place is full of tiny dramas ... The very first night we sat down to dinner together we turned round to see through the arch, isolated in

Handle with care! With a pair of coiled boa constrictors at the Institut Pasteur, Kindia, Guinea.

the middle of the main floor, a little green toad. He looked absurd sitting there in the expanse of black and white tiles and didn't seem to want to go even when Hugh with the help of Maurice (the house-boy) and a broom handle tried to edge him towards the door. He stopped at the top of the steps and looked reproachful, then did a somersault down two of them. The loss of dignity however didn't deter him, within an hour he was back, and the next night he was there with his wife and daughter (Winnie and Agnes, christened by Hugh). Apparently they eat the mosquitoes and flying-ants ... Last night there was a plague of those ants. We had been for cocktails with a French architect who has built a beautiful 'African' house like a kraal, and came back to find these pests in clouds around every lamp. We went round doping them with the flit-bomb thing but in the morning the floors were carpeted with thousands of them. Cookie says it presages the rains. Before they are upon us, however, we're going upcountry for a short tour, by car, to the Fouta Djallon, the mountainous region to the north.

We did go upcountry, to Labé, the capital of that region, and enjoyed the sunshine and cleaner air, away from the perpetually overcast and sticky coastal climate. The journey was hair-raising, riding the narrow and corrugated laterite roads in a light British Ford not built for such conditions. In the end we piled rocks in the back of the car to give it more stability. My driver was on Ramadhan which made it purgatory for him, with all the heat and dust, so I took the wheel. Asked what were the birds we could hear in the bush crying mournfully, he did not know (they were in fact hoopoes) but replied, equally mournfully, in French: 'They are not eatable.' The visit was nonetheless successful in enabling me to meet some of the newly appointed regional administrators and, more especially, the political party officials of the RDA now renamed the Parti Democratique de Guinée (PDG) who, as at national level in Conakry, had become, communist fashion, the real rulers of the country. Sekou Touré was of course leader of the Party and chairman of the national Bureau Politique as well as President of the state.

It was diplomatic custom in those days – and perhaps still is – for newly arrived heads of diplomatic mission to call on those already in post for a courtesy chat – with strictly no business discussed. As more and more missions opened in Conakry, particularly from the Soviet bloc, it became an additional task for me to receive them and then to return their calls. It was also the custom, or I conceived it to be, that a head of mission's wife should call on the wives of the President and Secretary of State for Foreign Affairs. Ann did both and wrote home:

I went to pay my courtesy call on Mme. Sekou Touré at the palace at 5 p.m. on Monday. She is very elegant and also beautiful. She served pineapple juice and we chatted for an hour (in French), and her tiny daughter, Andrée, 2 years old, with gold rings in her ears, came in a little white frock and shook my hand, curtsied, said Bonjour, and skipped out again. Then on Friday (Good Friday for us) I went to call on the two wives of the Secretary of State for Foreign Affairs, the Mesdames Cissé Fodé. They, like Mme. Sekou Touré, are Muslims and on Ramadhan, so they could not eat or drink. But they received me cordially with champagne, little cakes cooked by themselves, a dish of mango fruit, and they also put on African music records for me (music from the African Ballet of Keita Fodeba, who is now Guinea Minister of the Interior – Hugh and I saw this ballet at the Edinburgh Festival in 1957). They were charming and delightful, one young, like a beautiful black swan, the other older and the mother of the two children – whom they both referred to as 'our children'. We laughed a good deal but when I asked them confidentially what they did with themselves they confessed they were bored much of the time. We hope to have them to dinner one of these days.

Some time later when I had come to know Cissé Fodé well, I plucked up courage to ask him one evening how he coped with two wives when I found it as much as I could do to cope with one! He laughed, that infectious West African belly laugh and rejoined: '*Il faut être sportif, mon ami!*' By that he actually meant 'fair', and explained that his wives took it in turns, day in day out, to enjoy official functions or fulful duty chores. But his words were choice. He was in fact one of the few leading Guineans still practising polygamy. One of the first acts of the Guinea government had been to ban it but allow grace to those already so married for the sake of the wives and children. In addition Sekou Touré declared 1959 to be the year of the organisation of youth and the emancipation of women. The former bounded forward. The latter, the emancipation of women, proved much harder going against the habits of centuries and there were still no women in any position of national responsibility when I left – although they had certainly learnt to march in impressive order on parade days.

Another endless source of interest – and work – throughout my time in Guinea was the stream of visitors attracted by this maverick state, increasingly in the news for its spurning of General de Gaulle and France, for its acceptance of Soviet bloc overtures and aid on an increasingly worrying scale, and for the dash it was cutting in Africa to foster the anti-colonial movement. 'Africa for the Africans' was Sekou Touré's call. It evoked a great response. I reported after a year there: 'With the help of the Soviet Bloc Guinea has survived the break with France with such success that it can look back not only on survival but also some economic progress, considerable internal political progress towards their chosen monolithic party state and the achievement of a position of leadership in the new emergent Africa. Conakry has ceased to be a backwater, the capital of a tiny unimportant colony of 2½ million largely illiterate inhabitants. It has become in fifteen months of independence a rival centre to Cairo and Accra for the attentions of African nationalists and Eastern and Western Powers.'

President Nkrumah of Ghana was the leading African visitor. At his suggestion Guinea and Ghana formed a nominal Union and the two leaders a blood bond. They were of course sowing their seeds of anti-colonialism and 'positive neutrality' in black Africa at a fertile time. 1958 was the year of Prime Minister Macmillan's famous 'Wind of Change' speech, marking British government support of independence for African states. The difference was that while Macmillan envisaged them all being democratic, friendly and playing cricket in British tradition, Sekou Touré and Nkrumah preferred authoritarian one-party states, in the African tribal tradition, professed neutrality in the cold war, and distinctly pink not blue politics.

Other state visitors who poured into Conakry included President Soekarno of Indonesia, whose majority Muslim faith the Guineans respected but whose Presidential arrogance in publicly conveying the greetings of 200 million Indonesians to 2½ million Guineans caused gratuitous offence to his sensitive hosts. King Hussein of Jordan impressed much more, as he did everywhere. So, in his own cigar-smoking way, did President Tubman of Liberia. President Boukassa of the Central African Republic, an evil little man bedecked with medals, did not. Nor greatly did the first Chinese mission, who also displayed arrogance – and whose acrobatic show they brought with them nearly ended in disaster when their multiple-ring act came adrift and wayward rings only missed President Sekou Touré's ear by inches. And many many more. My diplomatic colleagues and I spent an unconscionable time at Conakry airport and the Residence summoned to parade and party for all these foreign visitors. But so did Sekou Touré and his colleagues. It was all grist to the Guinean mill. I suppose I met more Presidents, Kings and Prime Ministers there in eighteen months than I did in the rest of my diplomatic career.

There were also constant comings and goings of foreign personalities we fortunately did not have to salute – but we knew about them: African politicians come to organise the All African Peoples' Conference (forerunner of the OAU), and the African Bloc in the United Nations, in both of which Guinea played a leading part; African Trades Unionists come, at Guinean invitation, to challenge the longer-established and more staid UGTAN; countless officials from the Soviet bloc; and, inevitably but always discreetly, marxist mentors from the French CGT.

British press interest soon developed too. First to come was Hella Pick of *Africa Today* and later the *Guardian*. Then Colin Legum of the *Observer*, perhaps our foremost Africa correspondent of his day. In time, as FO and

Commonwealth Office representation in independent Africa developed and it became for a time the continent to serve in, he even produced a full page spread 'Our Men in Africa' – describing me rather curiously as 'a serious shrewd young Welshman who has made his reputation ... much liked by the touchy Guineans'. That aside, I welcomed their visits as contributions both to knowledge of the Guinea problem at home and to Guinean awareness of our interest. In particular there was Patrick Cross of Reuters, commissioned to create a Reuters chain through emerging Africa. He started in Guinea – and flatteringly always claimed it was my tactical advice not to hang around attending on the Guinea response but to make them anxious by buzzing off to other interested countries and then come back, that did the trick – both in Guinea and elsewhere in Africa. I cannot think it did. But it worked in Guinea, and helpfully brought the Guineans for the first time into daily contact with a world news service. Cross was a remarkable man, whose friendship, and his wife's, we were to enjoy again in Rome, where he was based. The local Agence France Presse correspondent was also a frequent visitor to our house. He was always well informed and liked to exchange news and views. Much of our information on Guinean affairs came from the official Guinea newsheet. They liked to publicise developments, speeches, aid agreements and visits inward and outward, to encourage Party activists at home and foreign interest abroad. Otherwise the information I gathered was from comparing notes with such other observers as I could trust and, most importantly of course, from personal daily contact with the leading Guineans.

I had to report to the FO as events occurred but periodically sent them surveys. In early 1960 I commented:

In a small semi-totalitarian and rumour-ridden country of this nature, signs of change, real or imaginary, in the health and relative authority of the President and other leaders are inevitably the subject of exaggerated attention and 1959 brought its full crop of stories that Sekou Touré was failing in health or was falling into the hands of some of his more extreme colleagues. In fact he remained in good health with only occasional lapses of tiredness from overwork, and the end of the year found him entrenched as undisputed leader ... and no serious divisions in the Bureau Politique ... There were occasional signs that the 'Young Turks', the President's half-brother Ismael Touré, Minister of Communications and Keita Fodeba, Minister of Defence, together with those in the Bureau holding no Ministerial portfolios, were asserting themselves ... notably when, against the President's better judgement, it was decided to open the flood-gates temporarily to the Soviet Bloc in July-August; and when a Fodeba-led mission to Eastern Europe in February accepted a Czech offer of far more arms, including tanks, than they were authorised ... and when a Diallo Saifoulaye and Ismael Touré mission to Moscow went beyond their brief in August by initialling a 140 million rouble Soviet loan agreement without prior reference home ... The fault however has lain not so much in deliberate branching out as in lack of experience in dealings abroad, briefing and communications. There is still a frightful gap in the Guinean administration between decision and execution, and it is here that the Soviet Bloc has found itself able to force the Guinean hand.

The FO in its formal way decided in June 1959 to fulful the protocol of appointing our Ambassador in Liberia to be also non-resident Ambassador in Guinea. I had to explain this to President Sekou Touré who far from welcoming it found it disturbing. 'Why not you?' he asked. I had to explain that by FO standards I was too young. 'Unbelievable,' he responded, adding that we were the same age. I assured him I would remain in charge, except when the Ambassador visited from Monrovia; and that I was sure he would find Guy Clarke sympathetic. He replied, 'D'accord,' without conviction. As I had also recently had to introduce to him Adam Watson, our man in Dakar, and explain that the FO had given Adam a co-ordinating role among our missions in West Africa, he just put it down to British eccentricity – and he and his colleagues continued to call me *Monsieur L'Ambassadeur* or *Excellence*, as they had chosen to do from the start.

Watson and his wife, full of adventure, drove the length of Senegal and around Gambia and Portuguese Guinea, by Land Rover, only to find themselves arrested on entering northern Guinea by the country's newly created security force. It was monetary reform day and despite the clearance authority I had obtained for them, they were taken for smugglers and spent an uncomfortable night in gaol before I could get them released. They both took it in good part. Guy Clarke's visit on the other hand went without hitch. He concluded there was nothing he could add to what I was already doing and proposed just to pay a duty visit occasionally but not to interfere. He was a delightful guest. His visit coincided with my first Queen's Birthday party in June and the Summer rains were due but the FO declined permission to postpone it to the dry season. Ann wrote home this description:

Invitations to 300 people were issued so you can imagine the flap. For days beforehand we had Little Men here painting the flag-pole, turning the old tennis-court into a car park, putting up a huge awning in case of rain. At 5.30 p.m., one hour before the Guinean dignitaries and everyone else arrived the skies opened and the first big deluge of the season was upon us! Within 10 minutes it threatened to send everything awash ... We had ten boys helping, several of them borrowed from friends and all in their best uniforms. In the middle of the schimozzle the caterer's van arrived ... and the fun was then to get the canapés out of their ice-boxes onto trays without drowning … Hugh had a wonderful system of chauffeurs and umbrellas operating on the front steps to protect the guests as they arrived and to take their cars off to the car park for them. I wish you could have seen the scene.

The party was I think the first diplomatic national day celebrated in independent Guinea and, despite everything, it was adjudged a success. There is nothing like cramming people together with drinks in their hands while the storm rages, to make a party go! The FO or Palace, whoever made these decisions, relented the following year. I was allowed to hold it in dry April.

By late 1959, despite all our efforts, the position of Guinea in the cold war was perilous. I felt obliged to report:

The Soviet Bloc have now virtually secured their bridgehead in West Africa. By stepping into the breach so rapidly and forcefully when the French abandoned Guinea in October, 1958, they secured an immense amount of good-will on which they have steadily built ever since. Their campaign has been co-ordinated and has drawn in all members of the Bloc, notably Czechoslovakia, the USSR, East Germany, Bulgaria, Hungary, Poland and now, alongside, China and North Viet Nam, and Outer Mongolia to come. We have seen every method of peaceful penetration employed: barter and preferential trade agreements; exchanges of cultural missions, teachers, students and scholarships (there are now several hundred selected young Guineans studying in Soviet Bloc countries); constant exchanges of good-will missions at all levels and in all spheres; gifts of arms and agricultural equipment and foodstuffs; cultivation of the Guinea trades unions, the youth movement, the women's movement, hard pressed officialdom, and the middle echelons of the Party in general, on whose impressionableness the Bloc countries had by the end of the year begun to make a deep and evident impact. Press, radio, pamphlet, cinema and other propaganda media have all been used, and we are now promised a visit by Mr Khrushchev … Guinea is well on the road to becoming if not a neo-communist satellite, at any rate a very favoured friend, and it will need a determined effort on the part of the West and more especially on the part of more reliable African states to keep her in 1960 from going over the brink. The strongest bulwarks she has of her own are President Sekou Touré, who despite his Marxist leanings sees clearly that Guinea's place is in Africa, and the Mohammedan faith of the majority of her population. Paradoxically though it may seem, the West may in this struggle find a convenient ally in the Egyptians whose manner of standing up to the Communists at the recent Afro-Asian Solidarity Conference in Conakry did not pass unnoticed by several of the Guinean leaders … We and the Americans (whose performance now they are here has so far been disappointingly tangled in disagreement over an aid agreement) are now faced with the prospect of either exerting an even greater effort or of abandoning Guinea to the Soviet Bloc and taking the consequences in neighbouring and still friendly African states.

I could have added to the methods the Bloc used: substantial loan agreements, technical experts in strategic positions, exclusive arms and bank note agreements and political support through communist front organisations in Africa. Their programme, jointly mounted, was formidable.

Guinea was also the first country in tropical Africa to receive a Chinese Embassy, and they immediately offered their own economic and technical aid. This was the year of Khrushchev's disastrous meeting with Mao Tse-tung in Beijing and the beginning of the Sino-Soviet split. The first Chinese diplomat to arrive in Guinea called on me but spoke no language I knew, nor did his so-called interpreter. We had a seemingly hilarious meeting in my office trying to discourse on air-conditioners and time-zone differences – at least that is what I thought we were talking about – but my China-wise staff member Kay C advised me afterwards that his giggling would not have signified amusement but embarrassment! His Ambassador, when he arived, scorned such diplomatic courtesies so there was no repeat problem. He kept to his stiff self even from his bloc colleagues. I do not think he enjoyed being there and, like some of his Soviet bloc colleagues, used it as a base to explore openings in other West African states as much as to proselytize the Guineans.

The Soviet Ambassador, Daniel Solod, was a senior diplomat well known for his activities in Egypt, the Yemen and Libya, where he had secured the notorious Soviet-Libyan arms agreement that sent shock waves through the Mediterranean and NATO at the time. I came to know him quite well and when I called to say good-bye on my eventual posting away from Guinea, he openly discoursed to me on his study of the states of Senegal and Mali to the north and the important sections of their populations he was convinced were ripe for conversion to communism. He even illustrated this to me on a map, and was obviously just about to send his findings and recommendations to Moscow. I challenged his premises not in any hope of dissuading him but to draw him out, and he obliged. He had, as Marx counselled, looked for and found conflicting economic and social conditions, applied dialectical materialism and drawn the necessary conclusions. He did not say, but implied, that his recommendation to Moscow would be to mount a campaign in each country, using Guinea as a base. They did in fact do so, I believe, but found stony ground. The Soviets made many such mistakes in Africa, and the Chinese even more so. They seemed to assume that the model of communism their own totalitarian systems and aggressive foreign endeavours portrayed was as attractive to the poor and colonised African as it was to the converted. Many Guineans did fall for it, as did many other Africans at the time. But the majority happily did not, including in the end Guinea.

The strategy we pursued was in essence the same as we had adopted in our former colony Ghana and now in dependent Nigeria, Sierra Leone and Gambia, and that was to ride with the wind of change. Unlike the French, Belgians, Spanish and Portuguese, who at that time seemed intent on hanging on to their dependent territories, our colonial servants in West Africa were under instructions to prepare for independence and work themselves out of their jobs. Membership of the Commonwealth meant free association not dependence. Nor, unlike France over Guinea and, to come, the United States over Cuba, did we uphold sanctions as a way of trying to prevent such territories from going communist. The policy I recommended for Guinea, which was followed, was to muster as strong a Western presence, constructive influence and aid programme as we could, to enable those who genuinely wanted 'positive neutrality' to hold the line against those who wanted, from conviction or drift, to fall into the Soviet web. The great argument was whether the Guinean leader Sekou Touré, with enough of his colleagues, was in the first or the second of those camps. The French maintained he was in the second, beyond the pale. I early formed the opinion that he was not, but warned that 'he would not hesitate to break his lines with the West if the West in general was at any time to adopt the French attitude towards Guinea.' It was touch and go for the eighteen months I was there and, although sadly the country subsequently went sour in a different way – it steadily turned in on itself – history bears witness that our strategy worked and the Western effort succeeded.

That effort was more political than economic. Western material aid never attained more than a fraction of that of the Bloc. The first aim I recommended was to get the Americans, as leaders of the West, involved, together with any European nations willing and able to help. The United States responded and in mid 1958 appointed as resident Ambassador John Morrow, Principal of the University of South Carolina, with no previous diplomatic experience but a fine presence, intelligence and interest. His charming wife Rowena came with him and it was a joy to have them. We became close colleagues. He soon made his mark with the leading Guineans but encountered two problems. The first I have already mentioned: his masters in Washington at first wanted to give Guinea aid on terms the Guineans found too demanding by comparison with the Bloc. The second was personal and came later. Like so many black leaders in America at that time, I think he harboured an image of emerging Africa as pure and oppressed as their enslaved forebears. As the Guineans shed their engaging exuberance in independence and entered the serious business of establishing the Party-run state they wanted, and their new-found but controversial place in the world, so they started jockeying among themselves, and Sekou

Touré began on the path of internal repression. None of us liked it but John Morrow perhaps more than most felt deceived. He did not expect Africans to indulge in torturing their own kith and kin, particularly with the aid of Czech experts. One place it was done was in an army compound within earshot of his house in Conakry – so, on occasions he could sit of an evening helplessly listening to screams of pain. This was in 1960 just before I left, and disillusioning to me too. Morrow nonetheless did a fine job and played a vital role. So to a lesser extent did a representative of West Germany whose government saw red in the activities of East Germany there and sent him to help.

Moderate West African statesmen also played their part, indeed a very important part, not necessarily always in ways we favoured, like Nkrumah's loan to Guinea when we were subsidising Ghana, or his anti-colonial outbursts against Britain. But in his own way he helped restrain Guinea, as did Tubman of Liberia, Senghor of Senegal and Houphouet-Boigny of Ivory Coast. They carried weight with Sekou Touré especially when, as Guinea reached the brink, some started openly drawing away, so confining Guinean leadership in Africa more and more to the extremists. Sekou Touré took that message and it probably marked the turning point in his meteoric rise to fame in Africa.

There was little Britain could do for Guinea by way of aid. Our limited resources were stretched across the new Commonwealth. I managed to squeeze out of London a teacher of English who was very well received as the Guineans had by then lost most of their teachers from France and had decreed English should be taught alongside French in all schools. Also they attached great importance to education; they built hundreds of new schools by voluntary labour in their first year of independence, and they were full day and night. However a gramophone English course I presented from the British Council to the Minister of Education, Barry Diawadou, a distinguished Guinean who had formerly been Sekou Touré's rival for the leadership, ended in the laughter bin. It began in dowager tones like Edith Evans: 'Come into the garden, George. We will have tea among the roses.' The Minister fortunately saw the funny side. The British Council and I had failed to take the precaution of checking it before presentation. A sense of humour in the people we were dealing with, and a sense of the ridiculous as many Guineans had, was – and doubtless remains – a great help to diplomacy!

More constructively, we also made our mark with the first Western trade and payments agreement with Guinea. I had brought with me from the Board of Trade a rough model, thinking it might come in useful some time. Falling upon some pre-independence Guinean trade statistics and comparing them with our own the Board of Trade had given me, I had a shot at constructing an agreement and found the Board of Trade willing and the Guineans delighted. The Minister of Economic Affairs, M. Beavogui, and I then negotiated it, secured approval on both sides, signed it (with what treaty people call 'full powers', that is written authority), and announced it. There was much applause from London and in Guinea. I do not know how much trade resulted, but it provided a useful incentive to appropriate British business and the Guineans to get together, and I think inspired other Western countries to follow suit.

Two big events in the continuing conflict of 1959, however, lay in the invitations Sekou Touré secured from Britain, the United States, West Germany, the Soviet Union, Czechoslovakia and Morocco to visit those countries, and the visit to Guinea of the Secretary-General of the United Nations, Dag Hammarskjöld. This was little more than a year before he was killed in an air crash in the Congo, and the crisis in that country was already about to dominate the African scene. Guinea nonetheless demanded his attention. The Western end of President Sekou Touré's 'world tour' on the other hand, began in London. This was because we had been the first diplomatic mission in Guinea. It provided not a little drama. I went ahead to prepare and, as Mme Sekou Touré and two or three Ministerial wives were going to accompany their husbands, Ann came with me. The Guinean Ambassador to Western Europe, Nabi Youla, based in Paris, laid the ground work with the FO. It was to be a five-day visit with a call on the Queen, meetings with the Prime Minister and Foreign Secretary, a lecture to the Royal Institute for International Affairs at Chatham House, banquets and luncheons, and visits to Scotland Yard, Kew tropical gardens and the Sadlers Wells ballet. I had strongly urged this visit on the FO who had done a good job in getting it agreed.

That reckoned without the French. At the last moment Paris made strong representations to London that to lionise Sekou Touré would be to offend France and that he was now beyond redemption anyhow. Selwyn Lloyd, with Macmillan's agreement, immediately downgraded the visit, and I was shocked to discover on arrival home that it was to be just bare courtesy after all. I considered the French were wrong and a sham reception would do real harm. Archie Ross, the Under-Secretary (and subsequently Ambassador to Sweden) and Christopher Ewart-Biggs, the acting head of African Department (later, tragically assassinated by the IRA in Dublin) supported me, so did Brigadier Geoffrey McNab, head of government hospitality (and previously with me in Paris as military attaché). Also, importantly, we won over John Profumo, then Minister of State in the FO (but later the central figure of the Keeler scandal). He and his wife, the actress Valerie Hobson, agreed to host and hostess in place of Selwyn Lloyd. That was step one.

The second and key feature was to get the Prime Minister on side. It took a threat from Sekou Touré to quit after the first day and representations from me and his private secretary Philip de Zulueta to win him round. It had by then become a hairy visit, not helped by the frozen limpet demeanour of the upper crust of our government at that time. At the airport, Macmillan and Lloyd did their duty by lining up to meet the Guinean President and party on the tarmac, but as their official guests descended the aircraft steps and walked the thirty yards towards them, none moved, neither they nor their accompanying officials. They just stood like robots. Someone had to break the ice, so I walked forward from the back to greet the Guineans and introduce them. As I did so, I saw the look of relief on Sekou Touré's face. He must have thought he was in Paris! Macmillan's voice could then be heard asking Selwyn Lloyd in surprise, 'Who's that?', and the reply came back up the line, 'Our Chargé d'Affaires.' After the introductions I took the relieved Guineans off to the luxury of Claridges, where they were to stay as HM Government's guests, all twelve or so of them.

The main event of the visit was to be a meeting at No. 10 with Macmillan and selected colleagues. It started reasonably well, with Sekou Touré explaining Guinea's accession to independence and 'positive neutrality' for Africa and Macmillan responding with 'wind of change' remarks. With interpretation, that took an hour, and the Guineans were ready for discussion. Instead Macmillan looked at his watch, rose and closed the meeting. That evening there was a dinner at No. 10. I went to fetch Sekou Touré. On the way he made it plain that he had spared the time to come to London to hold constructive discussions about Guinea, Africa and the world and if the afternoon's meeting was all the Prime Minister envisaged then he would leave tomorrow. I relayed this to Macmillan during the course of the evening with a strong plea that he made more time in the days ahead. He returned a reluctant 'yes'. Sekou Touré was assuaged, a further meeting was held before the end of the visit, which both sides pronounced a success. So was the lecture Sekou Touré gave to a large audience at Chatham House in a logical presentation of the case for free and neutral Africa. He did so without notes. If his argument was not wholly to the audience's liking he nonetheless impressed them as a thinker and nationalist. He also enjoyed his call on the Queen, and visit to the Sadlers Wells ballet. On the other hand I know he found the indifference of Scotland Yard when he visited their operations room a little off-putting (so did I!), as also the authorities at Kew. And he found some of our customs strange.

At the Prime Minister's dinner at No. 10, it was the turn of Mme Sekou Touré to face the frozen limpets. While her husband was taken off by Macmillan for photographs and I was marshalling his accompanying Ministers, she and her accompanying ladies and my wife were directed into the drawing room, there to find – as Ann recounted to me afterwards – a semi-circle of Ministers, shadow Ministers, officials, Chiefs of Staff et al. standing even more robotic than the line-up at the airport. No one moved to greet and introduce the ladies. Ann, from behind them, thought they were going to turn and flee, and went forward to take them round.

Fortunately the Mountbattens were among the guests and that remarkable lady Countess Edwina broke ranks to skip across the room and take them in hand – which she did throughout the evening. The dinner otherwise passed off well, although the Guineans ate little having prudently lined up a rice dish feast to their own taste at Claridges on return.

The formality at Buckingham Palace also perplexed Sekou Touré. I took him there and left him and his Ambassador, Nabi Youla, to go in while I waited for them in the car. Surprised he called out, 'Aren't you coming with me?' Before I could explain that the Queen received one-to-one the Marshal of the Diplomatic Corps, who had met us, took it upon himself to reply in stentorian tones, 'No, he cannot – he cannot come in!' – which seemed to both of us gratuitously rude – but then we do sometimes pick them in this country, don't we?! Driving around London, however, Sekou Touré also observed another side to our protocol. We had a motor-cycle escort, but it was an innovation, just introduced for visiting heads of state, following the demand of Marshal Tito of Yugoslavia when he had visited London earlier that year. The police were still not allowed to clear the way, as was the custom in most other countries. The escort merely tried to lead the official cars through traffic jams. This mystified the Guineans. 'What about the Queen?' Sekou Touré asked. I explained it was the same for her. He laughed incredulously. 'This is democracy gone mad!' he commented.

On return to Conakry, after also visiting Washington, Moscow, Prague and Bonn, the President went out of his way to tell me that he and his colleagues (who formed a careful cross-section of his government including the 'young turk' Fodeba) had found their visit to London 'positive'. It had evidently been worth our effort.

That 'world tour' was the crest of Guinea's triumph and the turning point of their extraordinary story. The President and his party returned to a delirious welcome. As Ann wrote home: 'He was greeted by about 30,000 cheering people. We were invited to be among the leading official cars winding slowly back the twelve kilometres from the airport into town where there was a short reception at the palace. After waving and smiling for over an hour along the cheering route, my face was aching! Very difficult to keep the same smile like that, even though one definitely feels like smiling. I really wondered how the Queen does it all the time! I just had to massage my face for a little while afterwards! At the reception the President made a point of coming up and talking to Hugh.' But Sekou Touré was soon to find that a month away at that stage had brought out the problems of their headlong rush into everything at home. Some of the Bloc aid was proving ill-chosen (mountains of cement gone hard on the docks) or cast-off (machinery lacking parts) or not what was expected (even, on the bush telegraph, stories of snow ploughs arriving!). Certainly the Guineans were finding it difficult to spend the Soviet, Czech and

Ghanian loans effectively. But that was largely administrative. The exhilaration of independence was waning. Endless conferences, meetings and rallies and the political education of the cadres had come to take precedence over the hard grind of management and training of administrators – a familiar story in the communist world.

The Bloc diplomatic and trade representation by now outnumbered all others and was of some quality; the experts they had brought in were assigned to key areas like Security, the Army, the Service des Mines, the aviation and transport authorities, the youth movement, education and the state-owned radio. They had also begun to use Guinea as a base for communist-front organisations in West Africa – three conferences already. Typically, they were also working with the Guineans on a three-year economic plan, inevitably orientated to their own penetration. When that plan finally emerged in the Spring of 1960 we diplomats had to spend a whole week at a conference up country at Kankan with the government and Bureau Politique, listening all day to it being read out, and then more days to political speeches about it. The gilt was by now coming off the gingerbread and, as happened subsequently to Cuba, initial neighbourly support or respect in the region had begun to be mixed with fear. But unlike what was to happen to Cuba, which had the sustained wrath and sanctions of the United States to provoke cussed internal unity, the anger and sanctions of France had receded from Guinea leaving no menacing enemy from without for the Guineans to blame for their problems. Factions, real and imaginary, began to emerge, together with the seemingly inevitable concomitant of the totalitarian state, alleged plots and repression. President Sekou Touré became in time a tyrant. His state did not become the Cuba of Africa. That was very narrowly avoided. Instead it turned in on itself for twenty years until, after his death in 1981 and a few subsequent years of military government, it re-emerged the multiparty state of today.

I left at the turning point and count myself fortunate to have been there in the exciting time of Guinea's emergence and the successful struggle to save her joining the Soviet bloc. I enjoyed the pioneering, the creation of the Embassy and being in the thick of things. My wife wrote home that I was 'in my element', there, whatever that might mean! Also enjoyable was the constant flow of interesting visitors. Even the Vice-Chairman of the British Civil Service Commission, Jack Goldsmith, came to look. So did enterprising friends like Eric Bruton, Editor of the *Gemological Journal* and his wife Ann, a great pal of my wife's, not to mention the FO Chief Inspector – although I believe the average taxpayer at home would have gazed in disbelief at the intimate examination of our lives and personal expenditure we had to undergo for his benefit, even in the midst of political crises and already long hours! Perhaps today's diplomatic service still endures the same process. I hope not. It was absurdly intrusive.

However, the accolade for the most unusual visit must go to the British

Commander-in-Chief South Atlantic in HMS *Puma* in February 1960, the first white uniformed and colonial-looking crew the Guineans had seen since independence. Admiral Dymock Watson looked every bit the part – as the Guineans told me afterwards – but found it distressing to have hastily devised Guinean protocol superimposed on ours which they had already accepted. As a result the Admiral was accorded more gun salutes than the Queen, which rather shook him! When we called on President Sekou Touré who had never seen me dressed in starched whites, pith helmet and sword before, and was taken with mirth, as I am afraid so was I, the Admiral was shocked! At the end of the visit he condescendingly said he would report to the Admiralty it had gone well in the circumstances but perhaps I would get the Guineans to respect British naval protocol next time! I refrained from reminding him that, contrary to my assurance to the Guineans that the British Navy always docked on time, he had arrived four hours early because the crew had foolishly played rugby at their previous port of call, Bathurst, and one of the team was found to need medical treatment so they had steamed all night – and required some Guineans and me on board when we should have been elsewhere. That did however mean that I was with them when an excited Lieutenant poked his head into the Captain's cabin to announce that the Queen had given birth to a second son, Prince Andrew, whereupon that strange cry went up 'splice the mainbrace'. The Captain was a splendid fellow but will remain nameless because he got so sloshed at our dinner party for the Admiral that evening – he had been at the helm all the previous night, poor fellow – that on leaving he saluted my wife, with 'So ve-e-ry nice of you to come' – and collapsed in my car. I have always held the Senior Service in the highest regard – gentlemen to the last!

I left Guinea in August 1960, sad to conclude such an unusual episode in my life and to leave the Guineans who had made it for me, also my remaining staff who had been admirably supportive, and our pretty villa, which I had embellished with a do-it-yourself swimming pool, built by my gardener and night watchman under my amateurish direction (but sadly destroyed by the Lebanese owner and our Ministry of Works afterwards, as unauthorised!). It made up for the one thing that was really missing in Conakry, which was sport. I had to go to Freetown to play squash and golf – and unbend as far as one could in that town of Graham Green's depressing *Heart of the Matter*. But the FO finally accepted my recommendation that to keep up with the Soviets we must appoint a resident Ambassador, for even though the Guineans always addressed and treated me as one that could not be handed on. Nor, by the rigid FO rules, could they appoint me 'acting unpaid' like the armed services would have done. It was all rather silly. But I was ready to go. I had done my job and, with the climate, tension and work-load, probably reached my useful limit. Ann had too, and wisely left for home a month earlier. She had enjoyed it too.

In my final days I made a point of paying farewell calls on all the leading Guineans. They had planned to come and see me off at the airport. But I preferred it my way, and they were appreciative. I might have known that, in the tradition in which they had been trained, many of them would co-ordinate what they wanted to say to me. When I realised what was happening I made notes afterwards. I shall quote a few, the first group because they were common to many and nice to have; the second group, those with named attribution, because to me they summed it all up:

> We regret your departure ... We have learnt of it with surprise ... We thought you would remain permanently the representative of your country ... You came here at a difficult moment and appreciated straight away our aims and aspirations ... You came to understand us ... We shall miss you ... and your honesty and friendly smile.

> We have no complaint against you, neither personally nor in relations with your country [that was from the Director-General of Security] ... We attach importance to good relations with your country ... We count you among the most 'seducteur' of diplomats, you and M. Knap [Czech Ambassador]. [That was from Diallo Saifoulaye, the very reserved and influential President of the National Assembly and Political Secretary of the Party] ... I have told your Minister of Foreign Affairs in London they are making a big mistake in transferring you. We are 'un pays nerveux'. You have understood us fully ... always calm ... we much regret your departure. [That was Diallo Telli, then Guinea Ambassador to Washington, subsequently Secretary-General of the Organisation of African Unity, based in Addis Ababa, but eventually and tragically destroyed by Sekou Touré] ... And, typically brief: D'accord, bon voyage et merci [President Sekou Touré].

It was nice, too, to have tributes from colleagues, particularly my former Under-Secretary, Lord Hood, then in Washington but about to become Deputy Under-Secretary at home: 'Congratulations on being given an independent mission at what must be the record age in youth and, what is more praiseworthy, on making such an outstanding success of it ... I was delighted when even the old Foreign Office brought itself to pay tribute in an official despatch to your achievements in making friends with Sekou Touré. That is something you can always remember with pride ... My warm congratulations too on being appointed to Rome ... I picture you applying yourself with renewed ardour to plans for unifying the [EEC] Six and the [EFTA] Seven.'

# CHAPTER 15

# Rome

## 1960–1964

R OME IS AN INCOMPARABLE CITY to visit, but not to work in – there are too many distractions!' That was my early conclusion on settling there, and I do not think I had cause to change it over the three years that followed. Even more than London, the secret of appreciating its greatness was to get out into the countryside and beyond regularly or it could overwhelm. My job, as Embassy Head of Chancery, was interesting but did not altogether help in that direction, as it entailed always being at my desk. Our Consuls in Venice and Florence, as in Rome, were similarly fixed by their responsibilities, and understandably complained of the misplaced envy they sometimes attracted for being stationed amidst such glories when in fact their lives were largely taken up with dealing indoors with the demands of British tourists out there enjoying it all. I was spared that. I was also fortunate in starting with a fondness for Italy and the Italians, and in having at least a passing acquaintance with Rome, from my service in Italy during the war. Much of course had changed since then, generally for the better as peace healed wounds. Through it all, however, remained the amazing richness of the Italian heritage, the ebullience (and happy noisiness) of its people, the beauty of its scenery and the relative warmth of its climate. Also enticing was the sophistication of Rome after Guinea, tempered though it was by the well known blaséness of the modern Romans whose city has seen it all.

I was gently reminded of all this in Guinea before leaving. Amidst telegrams about the cold war and wind of change was one from our Ambassador in Rome, Sir Ashley Clarke, welcoming me to his staff and my announced intention to fly home via Rome, and adding, 'I hope you will feel able to attend a Garden party I am giving on that date?' How courtly, what a different world. It would be almost as big a change as from Arabia to Paris, once again it was from the wilderness, and this time jungle, to the fleshpots.

As Head of Chancery, that is head of both the political section and of administration, my job this time would be 'a key one in a large Embassy', Sir Ashley wrote. But it was also to be pivotal while he and others did the travelling. That was made clear to me when, on arrival, I blithely started planning visits to the regions of Italy and our eight or so Consulates and was reminded that I had 'to make a case'. Anticipating constraints – there were bound to be some as number three in a grade one mission after running my own little grade four affair – I wrote home before leaving Guinea: 'I view Rome with mixed feelings. It is a wonderful place and will be a welcome change from the very trying conditions here. The job will also be different. I much prefer running my own show. However it is a job much sought after in the Service and I am sure we shall enjoy it.' And so we did, although as much for the unexpected as the expected.

1960 was but seventeen years since the Allied invasion of Italy had brought about the deposition of 'Il Duce' Mussolini and the break-up of the German-Italian Axis; and fifteen years since the death of Mussolini, at the hands of the Italian partisans in Northern Italy, and of Hitler in Berlin and the end of the war in Europe. Memories remained fresh. Italy had lost a very great deal by her foolish alliance with Germany and cheap stabbing of France in the back when France was down. Hundreds of thousands of Italian troops had been killed or taken prisoner in North Africa, the Horn of Africa, on the Russian front and against the Allied forces in Italy itself. Some 100,000 partisans and civilian supporters had lost their lives in the final Italian resistance movement against the Germans. Italy had lost its colonial empire of Tripolitania, Cyrenica, Ethiopia, Eritrea and Italian Somaliland in Africa and Albania in the Balkans. The country had suffered devastation from Sicily in the south to Lombardy and Venezia in the north, as the Allied forces advanced and German forces retreated. Although the Italians had made some amends for joining with the Germans, by switching sides after the fall of Rome and mounting partisan resistance forces behind the German lines, the hard fact remained that they had chosen the path of fascism and alliance with German nazism against the Western democracies and lost humiliatingly.

Unlike the Germans it was not in the Italian character to dwell on this publicly afterwards, still less of course to converse about what had gone wrong. I had noticed this in 1944/45. It was still evident in 1960. Whether people one met had collaborated with Mussolini's black-shirts and the Germans, or courageously opposed them or, like the great majority, simply acquiesced (Mussolini was quite popular until he started copying Hitler in 1936), the wish was clearly that it all be forgotten and that, as a 1961 textbook put it: 'The resistance movement was the moral purging that gave Italy once more the right to her place in the civilised world.' No one liked humiliation, the Italians more than most. 'Bella figura' (or 'face' as we call it) mattered to them. So, on the nice side, did their innate desire to please, but that meant they tended to avoid controversy even in friendly discussion of history. The war was a closed book and, except for a few on the far political right, so was the fascist period.

In the full panoply of Italian history fascism was of course but an episode, even if a recent and nasty one. An old edition of Michelin Italy I possess succinctly described Italy's part in the ancient civilisations thus: 'Since 2000 BC and throughout antiquity Italy, the meeting-place of races, has seen the Etruscan, Greek and Latin civilisations flourish on her soil. Two thousand years later, Western civilisation is still impregnated with them.' The Renaissance, the Revival of Learning after 'the Dark Ages' of medieval Europe, was another extraordinary Italian achievement, starting in the fifteenth and sixteenth centuries with a flowering of literature, art, architecture, invention, humanism and learning that spread throughout Europe and still graces our lives today. A delight of Italy we discovered in our time in Rome whenever we could get into the countryside around, was to find that every village, every church had its own works of art and often its own masterpieces. As Michelin again put it: 'Italian art ... has given the world such a profusion of marvels that a journey to Italy becomes a "pilgrimage to the sources" which every man who cares for culture ought to make.' We did not have to make the pilgrimage, we were happily posted there. And we did not really have to go searching. If knowledgeable friends did not take us they always readily pointed the way, or if they did not, our many visitors found it for us. To list our expeditions and findings over three years, within Rome and easy reach of Rome, would fill a guide-book. I shall not attempt it, beyond a few favourites later.

Modern Italian history was also full of interest. Unification was only achieved in 1870 and, to quote Michelin again: 'The leading feature of Italian social life is its intense provincialism, a survival of the times when Italy was divided into States whose capitals competed with one another. The élite do not gravitate to the capital, as they do in other countries. Rome remains a residential city inhabited by officials, while Milan claims the role of an economic capital and Florence that of a cultural centre. Turin, Venice, Naples and Palermo, formerly capitals of independent states, keep their own character.' Given these centrifugal forces we might have expected to find the country plagued with political division, and so it was – and still is – not least between the prosperous European north and the poverty-stricken Mediterranean south. But, that apart, we soon learnt that that very provincialism had perversely given the republican democratic constitution adopted after the war a framework of local administration which, like France under its post-war 4th Republic, sustained the whole while the politicians could play musical chairs at the centre. I personally found the manoeuvrings of the Christian Democrats and their sometimes-allies-sometimes-not Social Democrats, Radicals, Republicans, Liberals and eventually in the famous 'opening to the left' the Socialists, so byzantine as to be best left to our Embassy expert to follow and interpret for us.

Since the Communists had narrowly failed to take power in 1948 (and much alarmed the rest of Western Europe and particularly the United States in the process), they remained by 1960 influential but now safely out of power (except in places like Bologna). In any case there was perhaps much truth in the saying that, leaving aside the Moscow-trained and dedicated activists: 'Scratch an Italian communist and you will find a catholic underneath. Scratch a French catholic and you'll find a communist underneath.' We forget perhaps what a very powerful force communism was internally in continental Western Europe post-war, nurtured by the Soviet Union before, during and after the war. The resistance movement in Italy was largely communist.

My first Ambassador in Rome, Sir Ashley Clarke, was a distinguished member of the Service of pre-war vintage, a highly cultured man who loved Italy and was greatly respected by the Italians. He suffered the desertion of his wife half way through his stint but never faltered – and, to everyone's pleasure, married in retirement his former secretary Frances Molyneux, whom we all admired. They continued to work for Anglo-Italian causes, not least Venice in Peril, to the end of his days. His successor, Sir Jack Ward, was also a pre-war entry but a very different character, bluff and hearty with an admirable ex-WRAC wife Daphne. He made a slightly improbable Ambassador in that refined post but evidently performed it to FO satisfaction. We had a year together and got on well, as did Ann with his wife. More was my surprise, I recall, when the very day he was giving a farewell dinner party for us, he invited me over to the residence at lunch time and proceeded to tell me, without introduction, that the Service was the last stronghold of dictatorship and that I should avoid unorthodoxy or it might prejudice a good career. Considering everything I thought this a bit rich and told him so. That night he made amends with a glowing tribute to me in front of a distinguished gathering and I never heard another word, until years later the FO Permanent Under-Secretary told me Ward had reported on me with unqualified praise! I think he had meant well but somehow skipped his lines, which was not very diplomatic. Or he may have been thrown by my refusal to share his lunch time gin. I never liked the stuff, preferring wine and whisky, and after sundown. Whatever the reason his gaffe did in fact foretell in ways neither he nor I could have then envisaged, a later turn in my career – which is why I here recount the incident.

The FO view of my future at that time was apparently rosy. On a visit to London a few months previously I had called on the new head of Personnel, David Muirhead, to review staff matters at Rome, only to be told in a confidential manner that the Administration had decided to promote one of my age-group (from 1st Secretary to Counsellor) as evidence of their concern at the log-jam, and they were thinking of choosing a colleague Michael Palliser who had been deputy head of Mission at Dakar when I was head at Conakry, and was older than me. 'Would you mind?' Muirhead asked, to my surprise. 'No,' I replied, wondering why he had asked me, 'I think highly of him.' It was only later I was informed that I had been the next in line – and perhaps missed a trick by not replying 'Why only one, why not two or more?!' – which is what a year later they were obliged to concede.

The FO Administration had become rather hidebound at that time. I had not myself joined in the demands for reform, being too preoccupied with Guinea and Rome. With the departure to higher things of people like John Henniker-Major, an outstanding head of Personnel in the David Scott tradition, they seemed to have come to think more of empire building in an overdue merger with the Commonwealth and Colonial Services, than of foreseeing ever tighter economies and the corresponding need to thin out the pre-war survivors at the top or stifle post-war talent under-neath. For myself, I had no complaint. They had so far given me a succession of interesting and absorbing jobs, and I trusted that would continue. I was apparently now looked upon as a 'high flier', whatever that novel term meant, which was nice to know. I was learning the price of success. Michael Palliser went on to become Permanent Under-Secretary. My future took a more unorthodox course. But that is for later chapters.

The Minister at the Rome Embassy, Denis Laskey, was also a high-flier, but of an older age-group. He had been Private Secretary to the Secretary of State in London, always a key post. He and his wife Perronelle became good friends and we remained in touch for years. He went on to be Ambassador to Romania and then to Austria. Others on the Embassy staff I particularly remember – there were 150 including the locally engaged and I came to know them all and their wives and children – included a remarkable locally-engaged officer called Guy Hannaford, who knew every-one in Italian politics, and his home-based successor Mondi Howard who became similarly expert in penetrating that labyrinth. Kym Isolani was another outstanding local recruit as Information Officer. He sadly fell foul of FO citizenship rules because although his mother was British his father was Italian, and he had to kick his heels in Britain for four years or more before the FO could engage him fully in the Service. Another colleague I remember was Charles Booth, who had been with me in the FO Western Organisations Department. He was my assistant in the Rome Chancery, and a highly efficient one, too. John Patterson was both a member of Chancery and Private Secretary to the Ambassador. He served with me again in the FO Western Orgs Dept later but sadly had to leave the Service for family reasons although he did well in the Treasury instead. Then there was a bright young man who came as my assistant when Booth left. His name was Douglas Hurd. We only had a few months together but met again when he and I both eventually left the Service for different reasons, and he became personal assistant to Edward Heath as Leader of the Opposition and then as Prime Minister. His distinguished political career thereafter is well known – Northern Ireland Secretary, Home Secretary, Foreign Secretary and very nearly Prime Minister. The post-war British Diplomatic Service was full of hidden worth. Indeed by the mid 60s, it came under public criticism for hogging talent beyond its needs.

In the early 1960s the Embassy was housed, as it had been since the War, in the Villa Wolkonsky outside the city to the south-east. It was splendid as an Ambassadorial residence and had extensive grounds. But the offices – the Chancery – were in out-houses and prefabricated shacks, and had been so for fifteen years waiting for the Ministry of Works to rebuild. The old offices had been at the Porta Pia, within the Aurelian walls in north-east Rome, but had been blown up in 1947 by Jewish terrorists in protest at events in Palestine. Choosing their time well, they had brazenly closed the Via Nomentana to traffic without anyone suspecting their motives, and entered the Embassy grounds to lay their explosives under the buildings without challenge. No one was hurt but it caused a political storm at the time. I remember it in the newspapers at home. In due course the Ministry of Works appointed Sir Basil Spence, architect of Coventry Cathedral and a recognised leader in his field in Britain, to design a new Chancery on the old site. He turned out to be a self-opinionated prima donna 'whose progress into the upper reaches of the architectural establishment', according to the writer and critic D. J. Taylor writing in the *Independent* magazine some years later 'seems to have been marked by, on the one hand great brilliance and, on the other hand an ingrained inability to admit that other people's suggestions might be of the smallest value.' Invited on television in the early seventies to answer criticisims from dwellers in the concrete tenement blocks his firm had designed in the early sixties he – to quote the same article – 'declined, on the grounds that he could discuss architecture only with professionally trained architects'!

He appeared at the Embassy one day in 1962, accompanied by his apprentice son and a sizeable model of his proposed new British Embassy in Rome. He proceeded to explain to us, in theatrical manner, how, being on stilts with moonlight reflecting on a lake of water beneath, it would match the great Aurelian walls of Roman antiquity alongside, and fulfil his dream project after Coventry Cathedral. Ashley Clarke went white with cold rage. I can still see him. Laskey and I did too, in our own ways. It was outrageous. Spence had apparently visited Rome many times to plan it, armed only with Treasury figures of square footage (based on the expected number of staff and their ranks!) and had not come near us to consult the intended users. Still worse, in Ashley Clarke's architectural view the design would be out of keeping with Rome and, in my administrative view,

Ann with Harold Macmillan, Rome, 1960.

it was obviously functionally impractical. Spence dismissed our criticisms. He had been appointed by none other than Prime Minister Macmillan, and he knew his architecture and his Rome! – though he then revealed his ignorance of the Rome climate by telling us how his extraordinary window shields of travetine slab would protect us from the hot winter sun as well as that of the summer. He also seemed to be under the illusion that he was building an Embassy, not just the Chancery – and that the Queen would come especially to open it. As for functionalism, that was simply of no concern. He then repaired to his hotel in high dudgeon while Ashley Clarke retired to draw his own design.

We had a further meeting the following day. Spence appeared complaining he had had ulcers all night as a result of our previous encounter. Ashley Clarke presented his design, but Spence declined to bend, and went home determined in his own right. By the time he next visited Ashley Clarke had retired and I was somehow left with the baby. I decided to give a dinner party for him to meet representative Italians of the Belle Arte, Municipality and Rome society. Ann wrote home afterwards: 'It was a difficult dinner. We had to work hard to protect Sir Basil Spence from the opposition of the Italians to his proposed ultra-modern design.' There was in fact a practical reason for putting it on stilts, to save it being dwarfed by the Aurelian walls. But the rest, in our view, and that of many

With Ambassador Sir Ashley Clarke and Rome Embassy colleagues in full
diplomatic uniform after paying a May Day call on the President of the
Italian Republic, 1963.

discerning Italians, would be more a monument to Spence in Rome than
a Chancery or Embassy to be proud of. However I believe he won through
after our time, though with modifications, and that is where the Embassy
offices are now housed. I hope they are rather more fitting and functional
than his first design. God Bless the Prince of Wales. I share his view of
much of modern British architecture.

The administrative structure of an Embassy in those days was no different
in essence from that of any comparable sized organisation in the business
of communication. Probably that still remains so today. The principles of
management and organisation are after all universal. At Rome, as at Paris,
we had a Commercial Section to promote our trade and payments with
Italy and to report on the Italian economy. We had an Information Section
to handle information and press relations; Service Attachés to liaise with
the Italian military and promote the export of British arms; a Rome
Consulate and others in the field to handle our consular responsibilities
for British and dependent peoples in Italy; a separate but closely allied
office of the British Council to handle our cultural relations (headed in
my time by an outstanding Council officer, Harry Harvey-Wood, formerly
I think the founding director of the Edinburgh Festival); and a separate
but commonly administered Legation to the Holy See, headed at the time
by Sir Peter Scarlett, a former head of the FO China Department. (It was

not he I think but one of his predecessors who liked to say that that job would have been enjoyable if he had not had to spend half his life on his knees!)

The core work of the Embassy was handled by the political section, confusingly called the Chancery like the whole office complex. This included reporting on internal political events and developments, handling official visits, of the Queen, Prime Minister, Ministers, MPs and officials; and consultation and negotiations with the Italian Government on international matters of common concern, especially on Europe, NATO and the UN, but also on subjects like support for the newly independent Somaliland (formerly part Italian part British). We also had in the Embassy Labour and Civil Aviation Attachés, a Visa Section and a section for intelligence liaising with the Italians. Underpinning the whole was an administration and accounting department, headed by a diplomatic officer but supervised by the Head of Chancery. It was he – in this case me – who bore the responsibility for advising the Ambassador whether he could sign the monthly accounts to the FO. It was a responsibility not to be taken lightly, especially since a fraud had been discovered in the accounts of I think the Cairo Embassy and the Ambassador and Head of Chancery there had been severely reprimanded. A Service that, by any business standards, lived on a shoe-string, could not anyhow afford to do otherwise.

The Head of Chancery also bore a measure of responsibility for co-ordination of the work of the Embassy, and for welfare which for one reason or another was much in need of attention when I arrived. Apart from active work on both I always made a point of keeping an open door – as I have in all my managerial posts. I would not wish to be in any of the corporate organisations one hears of today who require consultant 'facilitators' to come in and show senior managers how to talk to each other. Perhaps the computer, for all its benefits, may be partly to blame. But perhaps E-mail and the Internet will at least get people to write to each other again.

Overall direction of the Embassy lay of course with the Ambassador. We addressed him as 'Sir' and, on paper, as H. E. (His Excellency) or Y. E. (Your Excellency). In his absence it fell to his deputy, the Minister, who was known as HMM but, as in the FO, could be addressed by christian name. The theory of treating the Ambassador in such an exalted way was that everything should be done to build him up in the eyes of the people to whom he was accredited. I sometimes think we carried that too far. One result was that it was not always easy for some Ambassadors to come down to earth on retirement. On the other hand I still myself cringe at the habit of some modern youth in addressing the elderly by their first names without a by-your-leave. Anyhow, to come back to the Rome Embassy organisation, every day started, as at Paris, with a meeting of the senior staff with the Ambassador, to review events and the telegrams the

FO had sent us or other Embassies had copied to us. Long gone were the days when an Ambassador had discretion to do almost anything he judged to be in his country's interest except declare war. Diplomatic life had become very different by the 1960s, with telegraphic reports and instructions flying around in such volume that at a key departmental desk in London we could be faced daily with hundreds circulated for our information only, in addition to those for our action. The mind boggles at the thought of coping today with 'single on-line global network' and 'Firecrest' and 'nascent Intranet' communication systems. But at least I suppose they are more on screen than paper, and so the telegrams or their equivalent take up less space in one's in-tray (if such primitively useful things are still employed in the FO).

British interests and influence in Italy in the 1960s were important. They probably remain so, the present unpredictable Berlusconi period notwithstanding. We had had one experience in our lifetime of the 'Mother of Europe and child of the Mediterranean' (as the textbook I have already quoted described Italy) turning against us and we did not want another. She was now a member of NATO and WEU in her own right, and we wanted her to remain so. She was also, on her own initiative (and particularly that of her great post-war statesman, de Gasperi) a founder member of the European Economic Community. Britain was not of course, but at least we had come round to recognise that the fundamenal purpose of that great venture was to heal the wounds of successive European wars and bind Germany and Italy into Western Europe in peaceful union. Moreover, for all their political instability, romantic fervour, love of intrigue, infamous accounting system and craze for fast cars, the Italians had – and still have – an infectious vitality, a lovable congeniality, a deep respect for family, a nimble athleticism, a brilliant inventiveness and a creative artistry second-to-none. They were also, in Michelin's words 'born builders, so much so that post-war reconstruction was carried out with phenomenal speed.' By 1960, with the added stimulus of the European Common Market, the economy was set on boom for much of the decade – and called the Italian 'economic miracle' – even if it was also a time of inceasing social tension and division between the north and south. Italy was becoming an important trading partner to us and, in due course, became a member of the world 'Group of 7'.

We carried some influence there because, despite Britain's post-war decline, particularly in the Mediterranean since the Suez débâcle, and our failure to join the European Community, and the predominance of the United States (especially with its large Italian emigré community), it was, they remembered, Britain and the Commonwealth who had stood success- fully against the Germans and them in the early years of the war; it was British leadership that had driven them out of their empire in North Africa and the Horn of Africa, and turned the tide of the war by inflicting defeat on the Axis there; it was under British command that the Allied forces had driven the Germans out of Italy after the Italian surrender; and, more positively, it was on British initiative that Italy had been rehabilitated into the North Atlantic Alliance and Western European Union in 1954. Further back, one could find many other links – not least, to a British Celt, that while Italy's Roman ancestors had failed to conquer us completely they had knocked our neighbouring tribes into a nation called England – and the rest is history! But I never found an Italian prepared to take responsibility for that! They did remain modestly proud, however, of the renaissance they had given us and the world later. We had much in common, and still do.

The recognition the Italians much wanted was a state visit by HM The Queen and Prince Philip. This was set for May 1961. When I joined the Embassy the previous October the arrangements were already advanced. In their usual efficient way Buckingham Palace officials had been out months beforehand to agree an outline programme with the Italians and us, and to brief us in their tactful way on the form to follow and details to remember. The visit was to last several days, initially in Rome with meetings, dinners and receptions at the President's palace (the Quirinale), the Embassy and the Municipality of Rome, followed, as I recall, by visits to Milan, Florence and Venice and a final day in Rome again. To make the most of a Royal visit, everything had to be organised down to the last detail, not just the events and timing but the people she should meet and mingle with, the important media coverage to be sought, the arrangements for her transport, security, accommodation, meals and an occasional rest, and for the availability of safe hands to ensure no paparazzi caught a cheap scoop of the Queen losing her foothold in a gondola or of some over-curtseying guest toppling backwards before her. Buckingham Palace rightly expected perfection. With all her commitments at home and abroad it would be years before she could come again. Every minute of her time with us was valuable to Anglo-Italian relations.

I happen to believe, in today's debate on the future of the Monachy, that it is a very good thing for Britain. I also have great admiration for Queen Elizabeth, and all those members of the Royal family who day in day out uncomplainingly do their duty at home and abroad and encourage public service up and down the country – and who, unlike most of us, have no freedom to do other things, or to say what they think, or to marry whom they wish, or even to retire without a political furore about the succession. Like our system of parliamentary democracy, the monarchy has its faults (and needs, within reason, to be kept up to date), but no one to my knowledge has thought of anything genuinely better for Britain, or for the Commonwealth. I sometimes think it is a pity that those who carp cannot be given the opportunity to try it for a day or at least make the effort to observe the Royal Family at work. They might then come to realise that royal jobs are hardly cushy. At any rate that has been my conclusion, after a lifetime's observation from afar and occasionally from near, and no more so than after watching the Queen and Prince Philip perform their arduous duty so admirably on that visit to Italy. As a nation and Commonwealth we are, in my view, extraordinarily fortunate to have the House of Windsor willing and able to perform their demanding roles so well.

With that homily I now have to admit a minor vested interest. At the end of the Queen's visit to Rome, although I had played no particular part beyond attending functions, fending off a few of the less worthy members of Rome society who complained they 'had still not received their invitations', and otherwise just keeping the work of the Embassy going while others were involved, I was wheeled in to see Her Majesty and Prince Philip privately and, to my surprise, presented with an elegant little medal which she kindly explained to me was an MVO (Member of the Royal Victorian Order). Prince Philip in his best naval manner, then thrust a pair of leather-framed photographs of the Queen and himself, duly signed, into my other hand, and out I went, still bemused. It transpired that Ashley Clarke, Denis Laskey and the FO had decided I merited some honour for my work in Guinea and as I was too young to qualify for the traditional CMG, they recommended this to the Queen instead and, the Victorian Order being personal to the Queen, she was kind enough to confer it on me. I had to enquire of my colleagues to learn why.

Honours recommendations were played very close to the chest in those days, and to some extent still are. I came to know more about the system when it fell to me to advise and in some cases make my own recommendations at various diplomatic posts, for worthy British subjects abroad, and to do the same in the voluntary and political organisations I worked for later at home. I believe in the system as an encouragement to public service beyond the call of duty. I do not believe in it as a populist gesture to over-paid film stars and footballers. But that sounds a little churlish, so I shall not pursue it.

'Rome is an incomparable place to visit,' I was minded to say at the outset of this chapter. Our visitors came in droves, official and personal. Family and friends from home were a joy to have, as were friends and colleagues from France, Arabia, Guinea, the United States and beyond. So were interesting officials from Whitehall, attending conferences or accompanying Ministers (who usually lodged with the Ambassador). It was the sons of friends of friends who became a bit much, eating us out of house and home on their hitch-hiking way to Greece, or somewhere, and then returning for more! We had found a wonderful penthouse at the top of the Palazzo Theodili, in the centre of Rome, after three months of searching when we first arrived, and, as Ann wrote home at the end of our three years there, 'it seems to have become quite famous.'

The flat enjoyed spectacular views of Rome from any of the rooms, terraces and turret we had at four different if charmingly crazy levels. We also became known, I think, for the entertainment we were able to give with the help of a hearty Abruzzi cook called Italia and maid Maria both of whom became part of the family. The palazzo was in Via Ara Coeli just off the Piazza Venezia and from our place on top we could look up to Mussolini's 'Wedding Cake' and, more interestingly, to the Roman Campidoglio, hiding the Forum, Coliseum and Palatine hill beyond; or across the city to its other six hills and the Pantheon, St Peter's and the countless spires and piazzas between; or behind to the Palazzo Doria and Via del Corso; or down below to the headquarters of the Jesuits, Christian Democrats and Communists; or beyond to the Campo di Marzo and its maze of little streets, like the Via Coronari where you could see antiques being made and other fascinating Roman activities.

The only drawback was four flights of travetine steps to climb, but they were easy enough for all except heart cases and, on one occasion, the wife of the Thai Ambassador, a golfing friend who made her nobly gyrate the whole way up in her tight oriental gown rather than miss the party. We even held formal dinners with one table in the small dining room and another on the higher little terrace beyond connected by way of an open window and stair-box to form a virtual extension. It may not have been orthodox but the Italians loved it. As for our staying guests, we enjoyed

The Campidoglio – one of the splendid panoramic views from our flat in Rome.

planning each day's expedition with them, standing on the turret and deciding which line of glories they should explore that day. It was like an old-fashioned panoramascope and, when my brother suggested this and was challenged by his 8 and 6 year old children to make one he spent every spare hour for weeks back home drawing a complete panorama in twelve parts from his photographs. His son Christopher has them still and I have framed copies. They are remarkable. He had never drawn before – and would have been the first to say modestly that Rome does that to people.

My mother was also a visitor, with her sister Laura, and, although she was by then lame with arthritis and Laura was sickening with what turned out to be a terminal illness, they ploughed their way through all the antiquity and renaissance they could reach on foot or Ann could drive them to, like early explorers. So, with different degrees of determination did most of our guests, personal and official. We liked to take them of an evening, when we could, to open-air opera at the Castel Sant' Angelo or Caracalla's Baths or indoors to the Opera House; or to the Son et Lumière at the Forum or any illuminated piazza or, of course, the Trevi Fountain; also to one or other of our favourite little restaurants to dine in the open (and to be addressed by the owners in ever ascending Italian flattery as Signore, Dottore, Avvocato, Commendatore, even Eccellenza!). At week-ends we would picnic with them in the Alban Hills overlooking Diana's mirror (Lake Nemi) or amidst the sights of Tivoli, Ostia Antica, Bracciano, Palestrina and so many other places of interest within an hour of Rome; or, further afield, to Spoleto or even Naples. Over the three years I suppose the occupancy rate of our two spare rooms must have rivalled that of any hotel. But it was always interesting to hear their experiences at the end of the day if we had not been able to accompany them. Rome was not a place to work in, as I have said, but we could still share the fun of our visitors.

Their experiences were not of course invariably uplifting. Like any city Rome had its fair share of rogues. But they were somehow different from others. The amorous ones were probably the worst. My secretary, Jennifer Maddock, a pretty fairhaired girl – the type Roman Casanovas seemed particularly to favour – found herself one lunch-time stranded in her little Fiat on the Fori Imperiali. By the time she got it started again she had nearly twenty young Italian men in unwanted attendance. I found her in tears poor thing. My aunt, exploring the Chiesa di Gesu, found herself escorted by an unwanted guide who pestered her for payment and then made a pass at her behind the altar! She repulsed him firmly. The founder of the Jesuits, Ignatius of Loyola, must have turned in his grave beneath that very place. But we had to marvel at their cheek, and I suppose it was better than today's muggings. An old spinster friend of my mother's wrote to her before she came: 'I hope you have a lovely holiday in Rome. It will be warm and so interesting. However I have no love of the people. I cannot forget how they treat their animals, though perhaps they use motor cars now instead of donkeys, mules and horses. I hope so.' We all have our ways, and preconceptions!

Official visits were another matter. They took up a great deal of our time. If the Queen's visit was foremost, three others also stand out. First, in order of time, came the British Minister of Aviation, Peter Thorneycroft accompanied by Bill Stephens, director of our ill-fated programme of the time to build an independent British ballistic missile and space launcher. In 1961 the Macmillan government decided to abandon this ambition on grounds of cost and to buy ready-made American missiles instead. But we had Blue Streak, which had cost a lot to develop. European-minded all of a sudden, the government decided to offer it to Europe as the first stage of a European Launcher Development Organisation (ELDO). Thorneycroft, with his own matrimonial Italian connections, knew the Italians might be intrigued. We prepared the ground – it was one of my first tasks on arrival at the Embassy. Thorneycroft and Stephens came out, and succeeded. The French, Germans, Belgians and Dutch then also joined. So was born the organisation that later grew into today's European Space Agency. We played our little part.

Then came the historic visit of Archbishop of Canterbury Fisher to the reforming Pope John XXIII. It was the first time Primate and Pontiff had met since the Reformation four hundred and more years before. The visit went well and I think much encouraged the ecumenical movement at home. There was great media interest and, at the Archbiship's request, we laid on a press conference for him in the Embassy ballroom, our Legation to the Vatican being too small for it. The room was full and there was one question on everyone's lips: 'After 400 years who spoke first and what did he say?' The Archbishop was bound to silence by the Vatican rule he had accepted that no one ever publicly disclosed conversations with the Pope. For an hour he parried every attempt to draw him out, talking instead about the significance of the occasion. At last, as he made move to close the conference, one of the British journalists made a last plea: 'Come on, Your Grace, who spoke first and what did he say?' With a twinkle in his eye, Fisher responded, 'Well, it might have been me.' Great excitment ensued. Notebooks at the ready, they all called, 'And what did you say?' 'Well,' replied the Archbishop, 'I might have said: Doctor Livingstone, I presume!' The room erupted in mirth, spoilt only by the Archbishop's humourless press secretary who jumped up to wag a finger and call, 'Off the record ... Off the record!' I feel sure someone in that room must sometime have ignored that injunction. If not, let me be the first. I was there.

The most intriguing visit, however, was undoubtedly that of Prime Minister Macmillan and Lord Privy Seal Heath in February 1963. Macmillan loved Rome and, like so many others before him, drew inspiration from its timeless grandeur. He came several times while I was there. On this particular occasion, however, he needed it. The world seemed suddenly to have collapsed about Britain and him. President Kennedy had refused him Skybolt, the weapons system upon which the independence of the British nuclear deterrent was planned for years to come. The Americans had decided to ditch it themselves and turn to submarine based (and of course land based) systems. This was after the Cuban missile crisis the previous year. Kennedy was in no sense anti-British (except perhaps where Ireland was concerned) and he was to suffer tragic assassination later that year. But when Macmillan came to Rome the future of Britain as a nuclear power was suddenly in doubt and there was crisis in Anglo-American relations. By unhappy coincidence, there was also crisis in each of the other two great circles of our international standing, the Commonwealth and Europe. The Commonwealth Leaders Conference of 1961 had, under pressure from the newcomer, President Nkrumah of Ghana, and Macmillan's own 'wind of change' initiative, driven South Africa into withdrawal from the Commonwealth, the first serious breach in that free and fast growing association of former British territories. Worse still, after all the trauma of Britain's conversion to seeking membership of the European Economic Community and months of negotiation, President de Gaulle had imposed his veto. We seemed suddenly to be isolated in the world and Macmillan, the very proponent of the concept of world interdependence, saw his whole house of cards collapsing. He came to Rome officially to consult with the friendly Italians but privately to seek solace and perhaps inspiration.

He did find both, as we were witness, but seemed to us dramatically to go half gaga in the process. On the Saturday he was due to meet the Italian Prime Minister Fanfani, we gathered in the small Rosetti room of the Embassy – Heath, Ward, Laskey, Lord Hood from the FO, Heath's private secretary and me – for a briefing meeting with him beforehand. For a time he did not appear so we went ahead with Heath. Eventually he shuffled in, sat himself down on the same antique sofa as Heath, and said not a word. So we continued our meeting. Suddenly, he came to life and called out rhetorically, 'Rome wasn't built in a day!' We went silent, and waited. Nothing happened. So, led by Heath, we resumed our discussion. Suddenly again he interrupted with the call, 'Rome wasn't built in a day!' And then a third time, after which he lapsed into silence until it was time to go. We knew he was under great strain but this was worrying. Heath and the Ambassador took him off to see Fanfani, but the meeting was conducted entirely on our side by Heath. They then flew back to London, after visiting a few more of his favourite Rome sights, and we waited for news of his illness or something. We need not have done so. On the Monday he made a great speech in Liverpool. He told the people of Britain all that had gone wrong. But he held out the hope that, with patient endeavour, everything would be put right again. His punchline of course was: 'Rome wasn't built in a day!' He was the consummate politician and it was absorbing, if not perturbing, to see him operating in such adversity. It was also interesting to observe the relationship between the two men and realise for the first time that Heath was his Dauphin. Macmillan did not succeed in pulling through, but resigned in ill-health six months later. His weekend with us was a political cameo.

I was moved to give Heath and Hood on that visit some written suggestions on our future relations with Europe and the USA and Commonwealth in the light of these setbacks. I recommended that at all costs we should not withdraw hurt but, on the contrary, take positive initiatives to restore and strengthen our alliances with the USA, with NATO, with the Six through the WEU, with outer Europe in EFTA, and with the Commonwealth. The purpose was five-fold: to find new accord with the Americans; to reaffirm the solidarity of the Alliance, weakened against the Soviet bloc by Anglo-American discord and by de Gaulle's undermining policies; to reaffirm our determination to be a cornerstone of Europe and continue to conduct our affairs with the goal of joining the European Community; to revive economic co-operation in the Commonwealth, and play an active role both in the Kennedy round of world tariff negotiations and in the new impetus for international commodity agreements, so widening our markets at the same time; and of course, to restore our international standing in the process. I listed specific initiatives we could take to these ends, and was pleased to see most of them and the general thrust emerging as Government policy by April. The only exception was that for internal political reasons Ministers did not want publicly at that point to say that eventual membership of the European Community was still our goal. They preferred to bide their time before making that announcement. Public opinion at home had taken quite a knock and had to be nursed back to this concept. It was good for us to find, however, that official minds at home were set in that direction and that positive initiatives were to be taken in Europe, the Atlantic Alliance, Commonwealth and World trade. It would have been so easy for the Government to have retreated into negative policies of 'Little England' and stultifying isolation. There were many at home who advocated this, particularly in the Labour Party and Trade Union Movement. It was to the credit of Macmillan and his colleagues that they did not succumb.

On the personal level there was nothing special to achieve in Rome, beyond doing the job competently. It was not pioneering like Guinea. But there were a few little accomplishments I remember with pleasure, notably the resolution of the Embassy's long-standing health and welfare problems, the creation of a Rome Sports Association and the arrival of our first child Julia. The first of these, the Embassy health problem, was chronic, my predecessor warned me. We had a proportion of staff who were recovering from unhealthy post service, and the Rome surgeons were notoriously quick with the knife. Our head of Registry went into hospital with an upset stomach and came out with his appendix in a bottle – and a staggering bill. I found the solution with the help of Dr Medvei, the Treasury Medical Adviser (who curiously enough was the only consultant to whom the Diplomatic Service had official access). We worked out it would actually be cheaper as well as medically better to send problem cases home, where Medvei would ensure they were looked after under the National Health, or privately if they had health insurance, which we encouraged to be certain of getting beds. The system worked well and, I believe, was adopted by other similarly placed posts. The welfare problem was not chronic but unhappy. We solved it by the usual means of creating a representative committee and enthusing everyone to organise communal activities, including of course the wives and children. That helped local as well as home-based staff. Life in Rome was not all milk and honey, especially for those on low pay and allowances, as most were.

The Rome Sports Association was a Commonwealth community venture which later became Italian – and probably still exists in different form

Julia, aged 1, Rome, 1964.

today. It was based on cricket and, I like to think, represented a real invasion of the Roman heritage. Between the ancient and the modern, the people of Rome must have seen every other Western game imaginable – but not the 'noblest of them all'. There was plenty of tennis, swimming, football and even golf. Cricket was the poor relation, confined to occasional games on a rough little field in the woods of the English College for priests in the hills.

The golf at the old Acqua Santa course south of Rome or the new Olgiata course north of the city or at a little summer course in the hills at Fuiggi, was good fun but the core membership at Aqua Santa and Fuiggi at that time was from the circle of the former fascist Minister Count Ciano and was inclined to make its own rules. It required a concerted effort by the rest of us to break through their competition arrangements to win anything – as I was fortunate enough to do once, with some rude remarks about my handicap but a silver Abruzzi cup to show for it. It also required vigilance. There was a charming story of two American priests playing in a Sunday competition (between Masses). Taking a penalty drop at a water hazard they were told by their little caddies there was no need to do so, it had not been done by other players earlier. Challenged by the elder priest to reveal who had so ignored the rule, the first caddy parried, with a cherubic grin, 'Oh no, Father, I'll tell you the sin but not the sinner'! But I have to say it was only a tiny minority who misbehaved. The rest were a delight to play with. Moreover those few were not the only players to be condemned as sinners. So, I recall, were the British Embassy Head of Chancery and Military Attaché, and from the pulpit, by none other than our hard-pressed Anglican Canon, for playing on Sunday morning instead of attending his services! He informed us later that the Pope had once told him he was watching this little Protestant enclave through his back window. I think the Canon was a little obsessed.

Cricket of course was a different matter. The hierarchy of the English College – Monsignor Tickle who went on to be Catholic Chaplain to the Armed Forces, and Monsignor Clarke who went on to be Catholic Bishop of Norwich – were more relaxed about Sunday games. Ever desirous of promoting the game I conceived the notion one weekend picnicking with Ann and some visitors in the private grounds of the Villa Pamphili on Rome's eighth hill, that the summit field there, beautifully surrounded by trees, would make a delightful cricket ground. It might also be a contribution to the Eternal City, not to mention our own pleasure, if we could make it so. The owners were the Principessa Orietta Pugson Doria Pamphili and her English naval husband Frank. They agreed the moment I put it to them even though they were not personally fans of the game. We convened an open meeting in the Palazzo Doria and found keen support in the British and Australian communities and a willing squad to lay a matting-on-concrete pitch and to clear the outfield. We made Frank Doria President, they made me Chairman and we appointed my good friend John Evans, a Briton working in the Australian Embassy immigration office, as Secretary. We called it, ambitiously, the Rome Sports Association, and, thanks to the hard work of Evans and others it flourished for many years, regularly entertaining sides from Britain and, twice, the Australian Test Match sides on their way home from the Ashes in England. The Rome Municipality eventually took over the Villa Pamphili, in payment of death duties I think, and with it the sports ground we had created. By 1980 there was an Associazione Italiana Cricket and by 1987, I read then in the *Independent*, there were as many as 500 cricketers in Italy, with a growing league of clubs who were sending teams to England to play some of ours. Viva the Associazone Italiana Cricket! I hope it continues to flourish.

The achievement which gave us the greatest pleasure, however, was the adoption of our first child Julia. We named her that to remember the Roman connection. Adoption was quite a normal practice in those days when, on the one hand, medicine did not know how to overcome simple impediments to family procreation and, on the other, single women did not have the protection of the pill and were ostracised for bearing a child out of wedlock. So there was natural demand and supply. It is all very different today, and I sometimes think our Social Services have swung far too far in preferring temporary guardianship for children in need instead of, where the blood mother willingly agrees, permanent adoption into a totally devoted family. We adopted twice, and produced a son in between, as sometimes happens. The process of adoption was not easy. We had to persuade the charitable society most recommended to us in London to accept us at our relatively advanced age (by their lights) and being resident abroad, and it took a year in each case. In addition Ann had to spend three months in the UK and I one month with our baby, each time, in a form of probation until the Society was satisfied and could advise the Court to certify adoption. But re-reading our letters of the time I know we were delighted with the care and competence and sensitivity which that experienced Adoption Society gave to their calling, and particularly to us. Our two daughters are living proof of that. They were born to us as far as we are concerned and I know they feel that too. They boss us about of course, as daughters do! They bring and have brought us great happiness. Some Rome friends followed the same path with the same wonderful result while we were there, and with the help of the same Society. I hope it still exists, both for the good it did and for the example it set in this ever-needed service to the community.

We left Rome on transfer to London in January 1963. Before Christmas and the farewell parties were upon us, Julia had her first birthday. Afterwards she wrote a four-page letter about it to her grandmother, through Ann's ever-inventive pen. It seems apt to conclude this chapter with a few quotations:

4 Via Ara Coeli, Rome
21 November 1963

Darling Grannie,

I just thort I would write and tell you what a wunderful birthday I had. It went on for sevril days as first of all a very x–iting Parcel arrived two days before and as it rattled my mother could not resist encurridging me to open it so I did. It was a green cart on yellow wooden weels full of gorgeous bricks from my Granny and Granpa and on top was a perficktly Dear little Squeeking Animal wot I adored straightaway from my Cousin Carol, so I threw all my other ole toys out of the way and squeeked and trundled to my hearts-content and ate the lovely paper the parcel was rapped in and blew my nose on my sock just out of the shear joy of being nearly One …

Well then the nex day was Saturday and they told me when I woke up that although I would not be One until tomorrow, I was giving my Birthday Party today so they got Maria to take me for a trific long walk in the morning to tire me out and then they bludgened me into having a trific long sleep – but not before I had had a wale of a time at lunch-time opening seven envelopes the postman had brought me with the help of my Daddy whose omlet got cold wile he read out all the messidges and stood up all the cards on my tray and showed me my very first cheque – a lovely one from my Granny in Ludlow. A cheque is a thing that looks like any ole bit of paper you might like to chew up any day of the week but wich is akshully a magic paper wich you can take to a shop and get whatever toy you want for, wich I thort was a heavenly idea really …

They carried me upstairs and I was so astonished when they got me into the salon that I just broak off all conversation and stared – the hole room had been changed about and looked like a speshul nursry in Harrods or London Airport or something. My Daddy had said the little Horrors must not get a chance to reck the decent chairs so he had moved half of them out and hidden them and his secretary Barbara who I had invited had arrived and the 2 of them were sitting in the middle of a hole lot of toys and play-pen and my walking-machine and everything, despritly trying to get the balloons blowed up … My birthday cards were standing all round the walls, and the yellow rosebuds my Daddy had bought me that morning in the middle of the table …

I was just thinking how nice it was when there was a terrible noise and a ror on the stairs and in came that huge boy Tom in a bright red knitted suit. He is very tall and 18-months old, a big tuff boy … Fortunately there was a diversion as someone else arrived, Nicholas in brown velvet drawers and gold curls who made a grab at the bowl of Smarties and began cramming them into his mowth the norty boy …

Then Amy Louise arrived which gave me confidence as she is a month yunger than me and still nothing but a Baby, in a knitted white lace dress with ribbons, and a present of a pair of white slacks for me which I threw over into the playpen without a thort much to my mother's embarrisment and ate the paper wich was delishus. Daddy got out the bubble-blowing apparatus and blew soap bubbles all over the place in the general pandimoniun and stepped on a balloon and Nicholas fell off the African stool and had to be taken out on the terrace for a Diversion by his Father (there were 21 peeple including mothers and fathers) and Tom roared under a chair to try and get a soap bubble and bumbped his head so my mother said it was time for Tea ... When I blowed out the candle everyone started singing Happy Birthday To You wich astonished me, singing in the middle of Tea like that ...

They all said it had been a trific party as they backed dwon the stairs and my Daddy said he was more exhorsted than having 150 people for cocktails. I was so excited I felled asleep sitting up in my cot.

The next morning was Sunday and I was akshelly really One this time (and had Jus Begun, as that idiot Cristofer Robbin would say) and I certainly felt One by this time ... I hardly saw my parents except for an hour or so becos they had to go to a reception at the Embassy at 5.30 to help with the Brittish delegation of the European Movement and talk a lot of politicks and eat nuts and things, a thing wich my father says I shall have to be helping with too before long so I mite as well get used to things like that hapening on my birthday ...

Well then ... that evening wot should turn up but a yuge paper parcel wich the porter's wife brort up saying someone had left it there for Signorina Julia Hugh-Jones. It turned out to be a great red horse with a saddle and peddles from Oddone Colonna wot had bronkytis and I neerly faynted when it reered its grate head out of the paper and started galloping at me as it was considerably taller than me and had Snorting Nostruls and Bailful Eye. I screemed and rushed off and my parents have tackfully hidden it somewhere until I'm bigger than it is and can snort back at it. (Though of course we did not admit this to Oddone when I went to his party on Monday, we just thanked for it and said it was magnificent, wich is wot is called Diplomasy.)

Well anyway now I am One and I am shore nobody else in my age-group has got such a lot of wonderful Relations and Frends that all together have made it such a trific birthday and made me feel that it's about the best age anyone could possibly be and I send hundreds and thowsands of love and

XXXXXX from Julia

CHAPTER 16

# Foreign Office, London

## 1964–1966

WE ARRIVED HOME from Rome in mid-January 1964. Ann and Julia came by air. I followed by road, up the west coast of Italy familiar from my memorable leave from the RAF near the end of the war. The route was then across France to Paris where I stopped to visit my old friends Peter and Annie Urlik and old colleague Anthony Rumbold, then Minister in our Embassy; and to call on our Delegation to NATO to bring myself up to date on their affairs for my new job. I enjoyed the long drive, knowing it would probably be the last in my old Healey-Abbott, by now affectionately known as Brutus, from its robust survival in Rome traffic, but not really made for the family.

We returned determined to adopt a brother or sister for Julia, but surprised ourselves by finding soon after arrival in London that Ann was pregnant. The miracle had happened and seven months later she presented me with a son and Julia with a brother. We named him Robert and, like Julia, he has grown up not only talented but 'honest and true' as my father always enjoined the young to do. So has our third child, Katie, whom we adopted by the same process as Julia two years later to fulfil our wish for three. We have been very fortunate in our children.

Ann and Julia came home by British Overseas Airways latest plane, the Comet, the world's first jet airliner and a source of British national pride. I had travelled on it myself already two or three times. It was a noisy brute, and not all that comfortable, but it had priority of landing at Rome Fumicino and London Heathrow because of its high fuel consumption, which was an advantage to its passengers, and it was a graceful looking bird. Tragically its life as a civil airliner was foreshortened by inadequate knowledge of metal fatigue and two or three consequential total losses with all on board. I believe the RAF still use some of the strengthened version. But it came back into use too late to compete with the American

313

Bidding farewell to 'Brutus', my Healey-Abbott, faithful for ten years, but
no longer family-friendly. 1965.

giants Boeing, McDonnell Douglas and Lockheed. Like so many other
great British inventions since the war, it lacked management and financial
support.

We had a place to go in my old haunt Ashley Court in Victoria, within
walking distance of the FO, but the slightly larger flat I had negotiated
there soon proved inadequate. Instead, we fell upon an old-fashioned
maisonette at the top of 74 Carlisle Mansions, around the corner, and set
about covering its extensive wood floors with one material or another,
repainting the walls and ceilings, installing heaters and furnishing it in
time to have friends and colleagues along for a large flat warming before
the arrival of Robert. I look back on that flat with affection. It did us
well, at reasonable rent, for that spell in London and, sub-let while we
were next abroad, as a base to store things for some years. The only
drawback was the old-fashioned lift which, being rope operated, officially
required the porter of the block to break off his other duties to escort
people to all floors each time they came and went. He was a grumpy old
fellow, but who could blame him? At least, unlike our Rome apartment,
we had a lift of sorts. Also, for all the glory of that 4 Ara Coeli nest, it
had not stopped Ann and Julia being tear-gassed on one occasion when,
watching riots in the Piazza Venezia below, police gas drifted up and sent
them coughing and spluttering indoors. Carlisle Mansions had nothing so
dramatic. But like our flat in Rome, it did have space for family and friends
to visit, a singular pleasure in London after five years abroad.

Equally pleasurable was re-finding the British countryside. Every spell abroad always sharpened our appreciation of the homeland. This time, however, it was not a particularly happy country to come back to. At the helm, Macmillan and the 'never had it so good' period had gone, to be replaced by Sir Alec Douglas-Home, the last unelected politician to be Prime Minister (though he had to give up his peerage and secure election to the Commons to meet that objection). He immediately lost the 1964 election. Labour's Harold Wilson then held power for six years but was hamstrung by recurrent economic difficulties, by City opposition, by overweening trade union power and excesses and by the issue of EEC membership frustrated by de Gaulle. Anglo-American relations had been partly restored by American willingness to provide Polaris to save the so-called independence of the British nuclear deterrent, but as United States combat troops became increasingly involved in the Vietnam war in support of the South against the communist North, and Wilson found himself under Labour pressure to object, relations between him and President Lyndon Johnson, never very good, became strained and remained so. This was also the era of social revolt against convention, the rise of 'flower-power' and anti-Vietnam demonstrations.

In the FO we had a succession of rather ineffectual Foreign Secretaries, beginning with Rab Butler under Douglas-Home's premiership. Butler had become a shadow of his former self, and foreign affairs were not his meat anyway. Then came Patrick Gordon-Walker, under Wilson's premiership. He had lost his seat in the general election and then proceeded to lose a by-election as well, so he had to go. Third came Michael Stewart, a quiet little man with no presence but a keen understanding of foreign affairs and great courage against Labour critics over Viet Nam. A former Ambassador to Washington Sir Nicholas Henderson has described him as 'an unsung Foreign Secretary ... one of the most underestimated I have known', and Harold Wilson himself, in his book on the governments of 1964–70, wrote: 'Recalling now the vilification and violence of the demonstrations [on Vietnam] that marked so much of Michael Stewart's two periods at the FO I have every reason for saying that his critics were as wrong in their misrepresentation of what he was seeking to achieve as in their persistent undervaluation of his untiring efforts, his influence and his achievements.' But Wilson left him at the FO less than two years and then switched him with the Deputy Prime Minister George Brown at the Ministry of Economic Affairs in order to retain the unpredictable Brown in government. Stewart returned for a second two-year spell in the FO in 1968 after Brown's resignation. But Brown's two years at the FO were perhaps the most peppery of his extraordinary political career. Except for Stewart's personal steadfastness, the later 1960s thus left the FO for most of seven important years without the political leadership it had come to expect since the war under Bevin, Eden, Lloyd, and Douglas-Home with

Heath at his side. And this was at a time of turbulence in Anglo-American affairs over Vietnam, in European affairs over membership of the EEC and in Commonwealth affairs over the Rhodesian unilateral declaration of independence (UDI) and the Biafran war in Nigeria. I myself was only back in the FO for the first two of those years, but that was enough to feel the frustration. That low period in the country's foreign affairs continued until Heath as Prime Minister after Wilson made the break-through on membership of the European Community in 1971 and President Nixon brought the Vietnam war to an end in 1973.

My job in the FO was back in my old department Western Organisations. We had acquired the additional function of 'Co-ordination' – entitling us to interfere in every other department's business if we so chose! – in exchange for giving up 'Planning', which had been assigned to the Permanent Under-Secretary's department. I was to be Assistant Head of the WOC department – 'a key job in a key department,' declared Personnel, – covering up for the fact that it was to be the fourth First Secretary job I had had with still no prospect of a Counsellor post. The Counsellor head of the department, John Barnes, was an old friend and colleague, of post-war vintage but older age group. He had a brilliant mind and grasp of foreign affairs, and was enjoying the job enormously, shooting off minutes ('memos') in all directions each morning when he arrived in the office from his place in Sussex, having read the previous day's telegrams before leaving the office the night before, thought about them and scribbled his notes in the commuter train coming up that morning. He was a dynamo. There were double doors separating our adjacent offices, and the space between had come to be known as the 'decompression chamber', so my predecessor sardonically informed me as he took his escape. I had been warned. In fact, Barnes had asked for me and written me a succession of warmly welcoming letters before I came. He had too much on his plate even for him and hoped I would relieve him of some of the load. 'I live in permanent hopes that the future will be less hectic than the present,' he wrote 'but they will probably be disappointed and I shall certainly face the future with complete confidence in your company.'

I was willing, and had written home: 'I'm delighted with the FO job – assistant head of my old department. I shall be dealing with NATO and Western European Union and policy towards Europe, the things that interest me most in present world affairs. As usual it will be a busy job, but I shall be glad to get my teeth into something again after three years of fiddle-faddling in Rome.' I am not sure what that last phrase was meant to convey. It did a little less than justice perhaps to the work at Rome. But I was hoping, I know, for more responsibility. In that I was to be disappointed. As I knew from my two previous stints the FO was a great place to be, congenial, sparkling and at the centre of things, and we were privileged in Western Organisations to be involved in so many things.

We worked direct to the Deputy Under-Secretary (Political) – now the same Lord Hood who had been Assistant Under-Secretary previously – without this time an Assistant Under-Secretary between. But it was still a tall hierarchy to the top, involving sometimes endless minutes and submissions and drafts before something emerged. It worked, and worked brilliantly, no one could deny that, and not only in dealing with problems as they arose around the globe, but in foreseeing them. But for me, I still preferred being my own boss somewhere. We all knew however there was no future in the Service without periods of policy-making at home, and it was nice to be back in my old haunt, overlooking No 10 Downing Street again – and this time with an office of my own.

The members of the department had all changed since I was last there. We had a new bunch of bright young first, second and third Secretaries, a new generation departmental lady named Sabena and a trio of secretaries to match. Several went on later to higher things. Western Organisations department was always a hot-bed of talent. David Goodall rose to be High Commissioner to India; Alan Munro to be Ambassador to Saudi Arabia; David Thomas to the difficult job of Ambassador to Cuba; and John Patterson whom I have mentioned in a previous chapter. Then there was an unusual New Zealander called Bryan Gould who came to us initially, I think, on secondment from industry, but remained a couple of years and then did a spell in the Embassy at Brussels before turning to academic life at Oxford and in due course Labour politics. He was a genial and likeable young man who concealed well his political ambitions. In fact, he rose to be a member of the Labour shadow cabinet, campaign co-ordinator for the Labour general election in 1987 and challenger for the Labour leadership soon after. Unsuccessful in that, he returned to other eminence in New Zealand. There must be something about the air down under that propels so many Australians and New Zealanders into British public life. I do not find I always agree with them, but their dynamism is often compelling.

As we in Britain were going through the doldrums internationally at that time, our work in the FO was rather more defensive than creative. The United States was absorbed in Vietnam. The Soviet Union under Brezhnev (replacing Khrushchev in 1964) was concentrating on outstripping the Americans in military might and in space. France under de Gaulle was busy trying to undermine both NATO and progress in the European Community. Germany was absorbed in its own economic progress. We in Britain were distracted by Rhodesia and our own economic problems. The Western organisations of NATO, Western European Union, OECD, Council of Europe and even the European Community were rather reduced to studying their own roles – always a mark of frustration. Interesting work began to emerge in academic and official circles about disarmament and the nascent concept of détente, to reduce the tensions of the cold war. Still more effort, most necessarily, was going into defence studies and strategies. I attended a Foreign Office Summer School at Cambridge on 'Foreign Policy and Defence' soon after returning from Rome, and it was impressive both in its line-up of eminent British and American officials and academics as speakers and in its content and attendance. Defence in the cold war was the issue of the day. It was about that time that Alastair Buchan, with far-sighted private and official British and American support, set up the Institute for Strategic Studies, which I think remains a world-wide leader in its field today. Barnes and I joined as founder members. There were also university seminars we took it in turns to attend even as far afield as the University of Aberystwyth's country retreat in the mountains of mid-Wales. It was all to prove of value when the era of détente and disarmament finally arrived, although frustratingly remote from attainment in the mid 1960s.

Looking back at my notes of those seminars, it is striking to recall the defence problems of those times. Here are some extracts:

- The Soviet 'deterrent' (nuclear-capable) forces in 1964 included 175 ICBMs trained on US and West European targets and substantial numbers of submarines, bombers and IRBMs directed mostly at Western Europe, and were reckoned to be capable of destroying all targets in Europe and a proportion of those in the USA.

- At the rate the Soviets were expanding, it was likely they would have between two and three times more ICBMs within four years.

- Additionally the Soviets had large and powerful 'defence' forces in submarines, surface ships, missile defence, and air and ground forces, plus Warsaw Pact forces, the only overall weaknesses being in logistics and tactical nuclear weapons.

- Soviet military strategy was in a state of flux. They had no doctrine of limited war or flexible response. It was all or nothing, geared mainly to nuclear war in Europe.

- Soviet policy was nonetheless based on deterrence. This was so since the Cuba crisis (which had contained a large element of bluff, which President Kennedy had successfully called). Soviet policy did not envisage a pre-emptive first strike if threatened. In all Soviet scenarios the West was postulated as the aggressor. Their doctrine was offensive, their strategy defensive.

- In 1964 the United States had as many as 42 Defence Agreements with different countries over the globe. Most had been concluded by Secretary of State Foster Dulles under the Eisenhower Presidency (1953–60). The American military establishment, who had to service the agreements, criticised Dulles for 'Pactomania'. But the agreements did help generally to bolster security.

- The Eisenhower policy of 'massive retaliation' was a declaratory doctrine.

Eisenhower felt strongly the US did not have the resources to meet all threats under all their commitments and therefore devised this policy of main (but not sole) reliance on nuclear weapons. He nonetheless allowed a missile gap to emerge as the Soviet Union drew ahead.

- President Kennedy rectified that rapidly in the early 1960s. He put the American strategic force on more immediate alert as well as strengthening the ICBM, submarine and other forces and improving command and control. In addition the Americans started working on tactical nuclear weapons and began studies of the (British) concept of graduated response.

- The early 1960s, especially post-Cuba, saw an acceleration in the arms race of mounting concern to all involved and beyond.

- The warning time for nuclear attack on the US was 10 minutes, and on the UK 4 minutes.

- The UK, like other allies not in the super-power league, could not hope to keep up. We were already spending 7% of GNP on defence, and costs had risen 30% over the previous few years. However we still had global commitments. We had been involved in 15 conflicts since the War! The big question was whether and how long we could sustain all our defence commitments, bearing in mind rising costs and current economic difficulties (not to mention political difficulties on defence in the governing Labour Party).

It was into this world of politico-military threat and controversy that I found myself pitched this time in the FO. It was all very interesting – not least, for me, the visit we at the Summer School paid to RAF Honington to see our Victor and Vulcan nuclear-capable bombers scrambled and take-off for us. I could not imagine them ever being used in nuclear combat, especially in the shadow of American might and against that of the Soviet Union. But they gave us a seat at the nuclear table. In time I came to doubt the worth of that, especially when mounted in Polaris and Trident submarines, for all the intelligence spin-off it is supposed to give us. But I have never held with unilateral nuclear disarmament. It must be multilateral – and with so much proliferation now, that seems a long way off.

The major military project we had on our departmental plate was an American proposal for a Multilateral nuclear Force (MLF). Barnes was keen on it, and it was being worked out in NATO, which was why we were dealing with it rather than the FO's more specialist defence department. It had been conceived by President Kennedy's advisers to meet the concern of non-nuclear members of the Alliance, and particularly Germany, that they would be the battlefield in any nuclear confrontation with the Soviet Union but had no say in the use of the Allied nuclear deterrent.

The MLF was to be a new sea-borne force with a multi-national crew drawn from participating members of the Alliance – seven in fact, including Britain, Germany, Italy, the Netherlands and Turkey. (It was assumed France would not join.) The argument for it was that, by requiring multi-lateral decision to fire its weapons (by a mechanism to be decided) it would not only give the participants their say in its use but, since the Allied nuclear forces were likely in practice to be interdependent, the participants would thereby have influence on the ultimate American decision to press the button. The arguments against it were that it would be costly (carrier forces were notoriously expensive); probably impractical (there were likely to be serious command and communication problems between the different nationalities, not least in the decision to fire); it would represent the addition of a whole new nuclear weapons system at a time of excessive proliferation anyhow; and, because of its multilateral character, it would be an ambiguous one at that. It might also lead to some dissemination of nuclear weapons – although with the Americans doubtless controlling one end and the Russians certainly expected to control theirs if they set up a Warsaw Pact equivalent, that was perhaps a false argument.

I found it difficult to work up any enthusiasm for the project. We all, in our heart of hearts, felt uncomfortble with the status quo, which in the ultimate left the decision on whether Western Europe would be largely annihilated or not in the hands of the Soviet leaders and, on our side, an American President in Washington with no possible time to consult. Was the MLF or anything like it really going to change that? Even possessing our own British nuclear force, we all knew we had in the crunch to place our trust in the Americans. As Leonard Beaton, the distinguished Canadian Director of Studies at the ISS at the time, put it succinctly: 'Final control must remain in national sovereign hands.'

Barnes was passionately loyal to it and the good American intentions, to the end. He had secured the Foreign Secretary's agreement when Rab Butler was in that post and, in his persistent way, he made sure that no subsequent Foreign Secretary disowned it until it died from other causes. I myself felt loyalty to him, and the Foreign Secretary's decision, and suffered a hard time of it, both with the Chiefs of Staff Committee, although Lord Mountbatten, then Chairman, and Sir Solly Zuckerman, the influential Chief Scientific Adviser to the Government, were courteously kind, and with our own Permanent Under-Secretary at the time, Sir Harold Caccia, who was anything but that – but he was not known for tolerance of opposing opinion. This was while Barnes was on holiday in my second year, and I had to tell him on return he had timed his absence well! The NATO discussions went on for a year and more but revealed so many political and technical problems the project finally ran into the sand and was abandoned. That was after my time. I would have been happier if it had done so earlier. It was well-meant but a monster.

Fortunately, there were other, more enjoyable, things to do in the department, not least negotiation of the first Anglo-French joint strike aircraft venture – the military forerunner of the great Airbus Consortium today. There were also the regular NATO and Western European Union meetings to prepare for and occasionally attend, and European Community relations to help keep alive. Outside Government I found it encouraging to see the European Movement still active and did what I could to support their hard working director-general of that time, Denis Walwin Jones. There was also an active Foreign Affairs dining club created at that time in London, largely on the initiative of Hugh Corbet, an Australian journalist, which attracted eminent speakers from all over the world. I joined it as a founder member. Such voluntary bodies still flourished in London then. That was before the City found it could no longer afford the time to frequent West End clubs, and the IRA bombs in London drove out much of evening life, such as it was beyond theatreland. I found London less of a social desert on return this time, but that was because with a family there were now other things to think about.

The birth of our son, Robert, was first. Having one small child in Rome was one thing, with two adoring Italian servants to help. They called Julia 'occhi vispi' (vivacious eyes) and wanted us to have more. Coping with two little ones in the middle of London, with no help until Ann found a Swiss au pair, was quite another. But millions of other less fortunate parents were doing this. So we adjusted, and diplomatic life outside the office went largely by the board. Fortunately both children were healthy and lively, Robert arriving several weeks early in his haste to remind us that he too was part of the Rome connection. Appropriately enough, Ann always felt, we were due at the theatre that night, with Julia's visiting American godmother, Betty Becker, to see 'A funny thing happened on the way to the Forum'! Happily, the old Westminster hospital still existed then, just a few streets away, and the nurses were first rate. What a pity it was later abandoned in the craze for economies of scale. Robert's godmother was also, by coincidence, an American, Margaret McClure Smith, widow of the former Australian Ambassador to Rome who sadly died in post while we were there. We had happy christenings of Julia in the great St Laurence church at Ludlow and Robert in St Margaret's Westminster.

No sooner were we reasonably settled however, than the FO decided otherwise. This time the intention was good but the execution abysmal. The FO was going through a bad time administratively and we – and no doubt others – paid for it. Our Personnel colleagues always assured us that their career planning for all of us and post selections were done with great care, and so I think most of us felt they were, until the mid-1960s.

They even had a primitive computer to help them. It was affectionately called the knitting-needle machine. We teased them of course. Tell them you were happy to go anywhere in the world except the United States, as one eccentric colleague I remember did, and he was promptly sent to the United Nations in New York! Catch them unprepared as I did on one occasion and out could pop an improbable suggestion like Ecuador. 'Why there?' I asked, mystified, 'I am not a Latin American specialist nor even Spanish-speaking.' It transpired it was simply an association of names. I would have replaced a fellow called Hope-Jones. Fortunately it was not pursued. It prompted some of us to do a little research for fun. We all knew the case of the British Ambassador to Lisbon Sir N. Ronald being replaced by his namesake, Sir N. Ronald, to the confusion of the poor Portuguese. But our researches revealed that we only had one Debenham in the Service and one Freebody, and they were in the same department; we only had one Comfort and one Joy and they too were together. So were Marshall and Snelgrove (then a well-known department store, like Debenham and Freebody, in case any young reader of these lines may not have heard of them). But the crowning case we found was in the heart of Personnel Department itself: They had a Donald and a Duck and had contrived to put them together. Knitting-needle or no, that association of names clearly occasionally triumphed. I spent the rest of my career keeping well away from Hope-Jones, and I am sure he did the same with me.

Christmas 1964, however, brought welcome proof that the FO Administration still had a measure of career planning, at least for some of us. A chosen few in our age group were to be given promotion to Counsellor rank at last – but not yet. It was called notional promotion, and had been invented by the Commonwealth Relations Service. No dividend came with it, just a promise of more responsibility and pay if we behaved ourselves, when they could find suitable posts. But it was welcome news. There were about ten of us selected and I remember feeling pleased that my name appeared second, not for alphabetic reasons but apparently in order of preferment. It was also nice to receive messages of congratulations from old colleagues of past posts, like Derek Riches, now on his third Ambassadorial appointment since he had been my Chargé d'Affaires at Jedda a decade and a half before. The Service was still like a family that way. On the other hand this news meant that we would have to be on the move again as soon as there was a suitable vacancy, almost certainly abroad and after only a year at home.

Things then developed fast. Within a matter of weeks I was offered the improbable but interesting appointment of High Commissioner to Brunei, in South-East Asia. It was improbable because it was a part of the world I had had nothing to do with since my first post in the Economic Relations Department of the FO nearly twenty years before and, of more consequence, it was not an FO but a Commonwealth Relations post. It was to be a guinea-pig cross-posting between the two Services now beginning to merge in accordance with the recommendation of an official Commission under the chairmanship of the eminent public servant Lord Plowden. At that stage the Foreign Office and Commonwealth Relations Office (CRO) remained separate but had created a joint Diplomatic Service Administration Office to engineer the merger. So I would be reporting to a CRO hierarchy of officials and Ministers I had yet to meet, but be responsible administratively to this strange but rapidly growing organisation called the DSAO. In addition, as Brunei was still not wholly independent but a British Protectorate, with Britain responsible for its defence and external affairs, the High Commissioner wore two hats, one as representative of Her Majesty's Government in Brunei and the other as member of the Sultan's Council responsible for defence and foreign affairs. Furthermore, under one of those Treasury imposed financial arrangements only to be found, I feel sure, in the British empire, the High Commission's costs were traditionally borne by the Brunei government, and the Sultan, being rich, liked this because it meant he called the tune. The High Commissioner could not employ staff or entertain or repair his house or launch, without the Sultan's authority. The DSAO determined this must be changed. The appointment clearly had the makings of a little Warren Hastings with not two but four masters (CRO, DSAO, FO and Sultan of Brunei). Add to this that the climate and conditions seemed hardly ideal for untropicalised small children, and we had to take a few days and make enquiries before we felt we could assent. I did so nonetheless.

The appointment was interesting because of its very improbability. The vacancy arose because the existing High Commissioner had somehow earned the displeasure of the Sultan. It was a challenge. Brunei was only a quarter the size of Wales, and a tenth of its population. But, unlike its much larger North Borneo neighbours, Sabah and Sarawak, it was rich in oil and had refused to join the Federation of Malaysia, preferring to keep its wealth to itself and, ultimately, to seek its own independence. Its per capita income was among the highest in the world. It was also at that time militarily important. Indonesia possessed the large southern part of Borneo and coveted the north. Indonesian forces had invaded, drawing Britain into war to defend Malaysia. The Borneo war, as it was called, was at its height. British troops were fighting in the jungle not far from Brunei, and some were stationed there. On the other hand, the CRO believed it time that the Sultan should democratise more. It was one thing for him to provide his part-Malay part-Chinese people with a free health service, secondary education and old age pensions, a golden-domed mosque, plentiful work, and no income tax. It was quite another, the CRO believed, to ignore the political aspirations of the people to participate in government. The then Sultan, Sir Omar Ali Saiffudin, preferred to appoint his own

Council and rule by decree. He was a benign but autocratic ruler, and believed in divine right.

The Secretary of State for Commonwealth Relations approved my nomination, so did the Queen. The Sultan welcomed it and gave his agrément. The CRO and DSAO could not agree a date; one said April the other June/July. But while they argued we set about preparing, as one does. There was information to gather about the place and its facilities, about the office and domestic staff, about adjustments to the accommo-dation necessary for a family, about inoculations, health and, in time, schooling for the children, and so much else. The paucity of briefing material made it almost like going blind to Guinea. We had family and housing affairs to settle at home, having assumed we would be in London longer. We tracked down people who had been there, and I went on an FO seminar on the region. We started learning Malay, and decided, on advice, to find and engage a children's nanny to come with us. By mid-February, I asked for a decision on timing and also permission to start the usual round of interested departments for official briefing. There was no response. Although there were by now CRO officials at every alternate level in the DSAO, they, like some of our FO officials there, seemed to have become detached from their parent departments. It emerged one day from my reading of the daily telegrams that the CRO had decided to invite the Sultan to London to put him on the spot about democratisation and also over who should pay the piper. They eventually persuaded him to come at the end of May. But they failed to shift him on either score. A week later, having picked this up on the grapevine I felt justified in calling both organisations to task in these terms:

## BRUNEI

1. I have not yet been told the outcome of the Sultan's visit to London last week and how it affects my position. Is my appointment as High Commissioner to be confirmed or dropped?

  2. If it is to be confirmed, I hope that we can now fix dates. Four months is a long time to sit in the wings, and my personal affairs have been too long in suspense.

  3. If there has not been agreement on financial responsibility and my appointment has consequently to be dropped, then I should be glad to know right away so that I can put my arrangements into reverse. They have already cost me a tidy sum in various ways.

  4. The absence of an announcement is also embarrassing. As you know, my appointment is now widely known including, to my knowledge, to the *Manchester Guardian* (Clare Hollingworth was recently in Brunei), to several Members of Parliament, to the Diplomatic Corps in London and NATO and to many others. The original telegrams

were given wide circulation in the Office and then the Sultan blew the gaff in Brunei. Curiosity has grown with the waiting, especially since my name did not appear among those listed in *The Times* as attending the official dinner for the Sultan last week. I have hitherto fended off enquiries by saying that it depended on the Sultan's visit. This no longer holds water. If I am not to go, I trust that an acceptable explanation may be agreed right away. The simple thing to say would be that there was deadlock over who should pay me – if this were the case. If I am to go, I hope that an announcement may be made soon.

Mr Muirhead, DSAO                    (W. N. Hugh-Jones) 31 May 1965
Copy to: Sir N. Pritchard, CRO

This time I received a response. The Head of Personnel confirmed that the Commonwealth Office had failed to persuade the Sultan on money or democracy and that, my posting having been linked to successful negotiation with him, it could not now go through. I was offered some weak apologies and told that, as a stop-gap, they were sending in a fellow who had been there before, on the existing 'unacceptable' terms. So there ended my Brunei saga – and, with it, the only occasion in my life when two governments fought for the privilege of paying me and I gained neither! The DSAO offered me the appointment of Deputy High Commissioner in neighbouring Sarawak as consolation but with the right to decline. I did so unhesitatingly. The Borneo war was by then coming to an end, the Indonesians having been successfully repulsed. Brunei would revert to the 'Devil of a State' so bitterly – and no doubt unfairly – portrayed by the novelist Anthony Burgess. The Sultan would go on funding the High Commission, and ruling his state by decree until he abdicated in favour of his son two years later. Brunei became fully independent in 1984. Sarawak remained part of Malaysia and the Deputy High Commissioner there subordinate to the High Commissioner in Kuala Lumpur. They were not for me.

I found this experience disillusioning. So did Ann. We began to wonder whether we really wanted to stay in a Service that was becoming so incompetent and thoughtless. There seemed to be two things wrong. The first was not so much the merger of Services, which was overdue, but the way it was done. The Plowden Commission, appointed by the Prime Minister, at FO suggestion – the FO was always good at foreseeing the need for change – produced a long list of sensible recommendations, from the merger itself to improved terms of service for families abroad and people in unhealthy posts; relaxation of the 'marriage bar' on women diplomats; first charge priority for economic and commercial work; more training; and permission for officers retiring early to draw their pensions at 60. (It is extraordinary to think now that they could not do so until then.) But the Commission fought shy of recommending the simultaneous merger of the FO and CRO at home and so, for five years, while the services were being steadily merged, we had to put up with a three-headed gorgon at home of FO, CRO and joint DSAO. Many former members of the Service like Lord Gladwyn and present members like me warned it was logically and institutionally mistaken. One of the joint Secretaries, Donald Tebbit, an old friend, explained to me that the Commission simply could not get CRO and political agreement to full merger, and to prolong the argument further would have prejudiced the introduction of the other much-needed reforms. They were confident there would be one Ministry as soon as the CRO personnel had got used to being in a single service. They were right in that and, all in all, the Commission was acknowledged to have done a lot of good. But we had five years and more of over-administration and much insensitive muddle in the Service in the meanwhile.

The second thing that seemed to go wrong in the process was a dumbing down of standards. This resulted primarily from trying to be too fair to the Commonwealth Service. Their experience was limited to former British territories (and the English language). Their Trade Commission Service was staffed by the Board of Trade not the CRO. Many of their members were still Home Civil Servants, with no basic obligation to serve wherever they might be needed abroad, as applied in the Diplomatic Service. There were some fine officers I met among them, particularly abroad. But there were some who were given high positions in the merged service at home who were out of their depth. Some of the FO appointments, too, were not perhaps the best the Service could have provided. There was some suspicion of what today might be called cronyism. The then Permanent Under-Secretary was a powerful official, former cricket blue and Ambassador to Washington who did not like dissent. But I feel sure that was unfair and that it was just coincidence. He was replaced on retirement in 1965 by Sir Paul Gore-Booth, who had to live with the DSAO but contrived to restore a little humanity to the system. (How could I say otherwise? He wrote on a telegram I had drafted to Paris on Anglo-French aeronautical collaboration: 'As one recently returned from service abroad I should like to commend this draft very warmly – an ideally comprehensive but concise instruction.' I doubt if it was that good. But he was a very thoughtful PUS.) After his three year stint I think it was the turn, under the merger agreement, for a CRO man to succeed him. I was abroad then and do not know how well he succeeded. But by and large those years of the long drawn out merger were not the happiest for the Service. I was to find on posting to a Commonwealth Relations post in Ottawa in 1968 that there were still strains and stresses all too evident.

My meeting with the Head of Personnel, in June 1965, over the Brunei fiasco, was not the most pleasantly memorable. I expected some contrition but received what seemed to me little but pompous diversion. It was a hot

Summer's day, and I was uncharacteristically driven to speak my mind. (I was much more of a diplomat in those days! – not always given to suffering fools gladly perhaps, but endowed with patience and hating to offend anyone.) Not satisfied with his response, I asked to see his boss, the Chief Clerk, whom I knew, and he found this horrifying. I did in fact go and see the Deputy Chief Clerk, who was a CRO appointee, that being considered more appropriate, and although he conceded nothing, it made me feel a little better about it all. Chewing it over afterwards, however, I determined to take a look at the outside world and see whether we might not be happier in the future if I changed career. Life was not proving easy for Ann in central London with two toddlers after all the Brunei upset, and we opted to try a period in a cottage her brother had spare in the village of Crondall in Hampshire. It was not much fun learning to commute by steam train to Waterloo from the concrete slab of a station at Fleet, where the bowler-hatted and umbrella-carrying City workers lined up and travelled together in total English silence each morning. But it gave me a new perspective on life, and the family loved being in the countryside, with their cousins and their geese, toads, goldfish, bees, gooseberries, village flower shows, Morris dancers, and just space in which to play and walk. It was back to roots.

My initial enquires about alternative occupations and careers soon convinced me that there was plenty out there of interest but none just waiting for me to enter. It would take hard search and time. I decided to tell the FO, whatever the consequences, and ask for six months grace from foreign posting. There was no such thing as sabbatical leave in those days. The search would have to be on top of my daily work. So off I went in late July to see the Head of Personnel, to break the news to him and explain the reasons. He took it disbelievingly, replying that they had an interesting post for me. Curiosity getting the better of me I enquired what it was. 'Hanoi,' he said triumphantly. 'The Prime Minister [Wilson] has been persuaded that Britain could play a useful role in bringing the Vietnam war to an end if we had a representative in Hanoi in direct contact with the Vietminh. We would like you to go and do this, as Consul-General!'

I was taken aback. The challenge was difficult to resist. The Vietnam war was the leading issue of the time. Wilson was under pressure from President Lyndon Johnson to make a military contribution, but also from his own Labour supporters to do the opposite and condemn the American war effort. The British and Soviet Foreign Ministers were still nominally joint chairmen of the Geneva Conference set up in 1954 to encourage peace there and President Johnson was believed not to be averse to the idea of a negotiated settlement. It seemed to me nonetheless, even on the spur of the moment, that the appointment was likely to be mission impossible. It might appease Labour backbench opinion but it was hardly likely to influence a disciplined Vietminh concerned only with driving the Americans out as they had driven out the French before them. But the question I posed was: 'As it clearly could not be a family post what would I be expected to do with my wife and children?' He seemed barely to have thought of that, and suggested it might be possible to house them in Saigon and I could visit them by air. When I pointed out there were hardly likely to be any flights between the two warring capitals, he hastily added, 'via Bangkok, of course.' Wisdom comes easily after the event. I should of course have dismissed the idea on family grounds without more ado. Saigon was an American garrison town, and the flights clearly unknown. I could then have reverted to my purpose of seeking six months more at home to explore other livelihoods. Instead I agreed to consider the proposal with my wife, and give him my response in a day or two. I did so, after the weekend, having by then come to my senses. I confirmed we wished to remain in London another six months.

I was to learn in due course that, in the eyes of the people who ran our Administration at that time, I had committed two grave sins. The first was to dare to think of leaving the Service. They were very possessive. The second was that, in confirming my family objections to Hanoi I had technically rejected a posting. I found that insincere, to say the least. My case was not alone. Other colleagues were complaining of the same. The DSAO did not find anyone to go to Hanoi, but apparently left it to another government department whose representative, I happened to learn later through mutual friends, had a miserable time, poor fellow. The Vietminh proved totally uncooperative, even refusing him possession of a car.

My outside explorations meanwhile progressed slowly. I tried some merchant banks in the City, a few leading companies in industry, the CBI, the British Institute of Management, the Parliamentary Ombudsman, several management selection agencies, some University administration openings, one or two departments of the home civil service, and the Liberal Party. It was there that with the encouragement of Emlyn Hooson, MP for Montgomery and Lord Gladwyn, by then a leading Liberal peer, I nearly found a new home and determined to make it so one day. Lord Ogmore invited me to stand for Folkestone at the coming General Election but, with no private income of my own and little likelihood of winning the seat first time, I had to put that out of mind. Lord Beaumont, head of the Liberal Party Organisation, then invited me to apply for the post of Head of Research and Information at Party headquarters but even after they had stretched the salary for me, it was still below the minimum I could afford with a family. Beaumont did however ask if I would be interested in his own job when he gave it up, and I assured him that I would be. Ten years later I was able to fulful that promise.

The revenge of the DSAO, if that is what it was, came in the New Year of 1966. I was at home in Crondall and received a call from the new Head of Personnel, Muirhead's successor, whose name was Duncan. He was a former Sudan colonial servant and anyone listening would have thought he was fighting the fuzzy-wuzzies. 'Have you made up your mind?' he barked at me. 'Your six months is up and we must know.' As I was still doing my job in Western Organisations department I thought his demand a little abrupt and replied that six months had not proved long enough to explore the outside but I was negotiationg on one invitation and should know in two to three days time (That was the Liberal Party research job and level of salary they could manage.) I would let him know and meanwhile, in case the decision was that I would continue in the Service, I would like to exercise my right to send him my post preferences. He blustered at that but, for what use it proved, I did so. My order of preference was North America where I had never been; Eastern Europe for the same reason; Western Europe; Far East, or South-East Asia or Latin America, where I had not been; and, lowest preference, Africa or Middle East, where I had been. 'But,' I added, 'my overriding preferences are to have my family with me in conditions suitable for small children and to have a lively job of work to do.' A couple of days later I told Duncan I was available for posting – and warned Ann it might be a 'stinker'.

So indeed it proved to be: the Congo! Duncan did not know when he telephoned me, whether I was to be Counsellor in the Embassy in Leopoldville or Consul in the rank of Counsellor at Elizabethville, capital of the Katanga. He had to find out and ring me back, which did not exactly impress me. It turned out to be Elizabethville, and the job would be principally assuring air and rail supplies to neighbouring Zambia which was being starved by Ian Smith's Rhodesia under his unilateral declaration of independence.

So, in the space of one eventful if frustrating year, I found myself successively designated High Commissioner, Deputy High Commissioner, Consul-General and finally Consul, starting with a promised plum job among the high fliers and ending with a prune job among the lower. It took a little swallowing, but I know I could not have lived with myself if I had just let that incompetence and insincerity pass without challenge. Fortunately others, too, took up the cudgels against the DSAO and it was eventually re-absorbed into a merged FO and CRO, cut down to size and re-staffed. I do not think any tears were shed over its demise, and the vast volumes of bureaucratic regulations it bequeathed to us remained I suppose unread. It was a freak in the history of the British Diplomatic Service.

For my part I realised for the first time in my life that I was not accustomed to reverse. But I had at least got a post of my own and promotion and could take the family with me – and there was 'no better 'ole to go to' anyway. So we decided to make the best of it, and give lots of farewell parties to be remembered. Hopefully it was only going to be for a year or two. I wrote to a senior colleague: 'I leave London at this time with some regrets, with an election on too, but a period in the wilderness is probably timely if only to recharge batteries, and with Rhodesia and Tshombe to concern us Elizabethville could be fun ... meanwhile I hope we shall not give de Gaulle an inch on NATO or Europe, but keep our powder dry until he is gone, and direct our policies on Europe to that day.'

# CHAPTER 17

# Congo–Katanga

# 1966–1968

'THIS POST,' wrote my predecessor as HM Consul Elisabethville, 'is not particularly arduous office-wise but pretty hefty after dark on the usual rat race. The powers-that-be have decided that we are a kind of crisis post at present but they didn't hear it from me. Certainly we have odd hectic days but so what?' That did not sound very exciting. Nor was it at that time. Perhaps we were going to have an easy-going tour after all in this former Belgian Shangri-la?

The post report and my predecessor Ken Ritchie between them assured us: 'There can be few more pleasant climates or healthier places anywhere in the world' (being near the Equator but, like Rhodesia, on the high central African plateau) ... 'There is a small number of good European doctors available, though they are overworked, the hospital facilities are rather old-fashioned and there is a shortage of nurses' ... 'Social life is informal and, in a city of 200,000 – the second largest in the Congo – including 10,000 Europeans (70% Belgian), life can be what you make it' ... 'As for culture, there isn't much!' ... But 'sport and recreation facilities include tennis, swimming, an excellent golf course' (designed and laid by a former British Consul in 1930) ... 'Travelling the Consular district of Katanga and Kivu (together the size of Sweden) is fascinating ... though there are no macadamised roads beyond the mining towns of Elisabethville, Jadotville, and Kolwezi, and to the Zambian border. One does not motor for pleasure but only to get somewhere' ... 'There is dancing in the nightclubs and sometimes informally in private ... the "twist" and the "hully-gully" are still popular' ... 'There are three schools to choose from, taking pupils from kindergarten to University entrance ... all in French of course' ... 'The Consul's residence is a four-bedroomed bungalow with a swimming pool in the garden.' It was two miles out of the town, conveniently on the way to the Golf Club. It was rented, with bare Ministry

331

of Works furniture. The occupants would have to bring most things with them. There was some Ministry of Works china (much of it chipped), glassware (some cracked), silverware (odd sets), kitchenware (limited), 'no linen except for 4 badly stained bedspreads and 6 pillows in poor condition, four pictures and no ornaments' ... But there was 'an excellent cook (40 years service) and houseboy' ... 'The only extent to which the Englishman [sic] is expected to modify his way of life is to remember to shake hands on every possible occasion.' They might have added 'but in greeting Belgian ladies it should be a kiss on the cheek, and not once but three and even four times – unless you prefer the gallant kiss on the hand ... But if so, remember to instruct your children or you might (as we did) hear your four year old piping up: "Why is that man smelling your hand, Mummy?".' The perils of living abroad!

We arrived on 21 March and first impressions were good. The flight, via Kano in northern Nigeria and Leopoldville in the lower Congo had been long by propellar-driven Constellation but, as I was now a Counsellor, we were allowed for the first time to travel first class and, except for the cigars the Sabena chief steward seemed to think I must want at four o'clock in the morning, we were well looked after. It was Robert's first flight and Julia's third. Helped by a splendid nanny, Maureen, we had found to come with us, they took it well. At Elisabethville, there was brilliant sunshine, glorious white cumulus clouds I had not seen outside Snowdonia, a very competent Vice-Consul and staff and a friendly chief of protocol of the Katangan Governor there to greet us. It all seemed a little improbable. We were able to go straight into the residence, with its Union Jack flying, Ritchie and his wife having generously offered to move into a guest house for the short period of our overlap. Both of us would have preferred no handover. They were an unnecessary pain, in my experience, and I have found no reason to change that view since. On this occasion we did it to oblige the Ambassador in Leopoldville, John Cotton, who turned out to be a bristly old stager with his own ideas on most things, not always the same as mine. But the Embassy was a thousand miles away, and the Elisabethville Consulate had the unusual but important right of direct reporting to London. That turned out to be very necessary as events in the Katanga and beyond hotted up.

After a couple of weeks Ann wrote her first impressions:

Our residence is a modern bungalow, open to the airport road but standing back, with a crescent-shaped lawn in front framed by a whole semi-circle of beautiful English rose bushes ... The back is dominated by the swimming pool (which Hugh has arranged to have covered when not in use, for the sake of the children), and a wonderful mixture of English flowers (planted by a succession of nostalgic British Consuls) and tropical plants ... The town is large and the central and European parts modern, built criss-cross so that every street is at right angles to the next, and lined with flowering blue jacaranda and red flame trees and attractive houses. But the shops are empty and what is available is very expensive, so we do most of our shopping across the border in Zambia – two hours away by car on weekly expeditions by one of the staff. I only buy milk and bread here, and fresh fruit and vegetables from the colourful African market where the women crouch with babies on backs, over their piles of nuts, tomatoes, avocados and pineapples ... The children have settled down happily, though we were all troubled the first week with insect bites and heat bumps. They are devoted to Maureen and I can hardly believe our good luck in finding her ... We have really been delighted to find the climate as perfect as claimed (outside the rainy season), blue skies, fresh air (4000 feet up here), glorious sunshine all day and cool enough for cardigans in the evening and several blankets at night. In fact everything so far has been a pleasant surprise.

She might have added that the Golf Club was very congenial, even to allowing a free drop if your ball landed in a coiled snake or column of red ants! Her letter home continued:

There are crowds of Europeans, literally thousands, including an English-speaking community, everything from mining to trading and banking – many have been here for years and, whatever the troubles, love the climate, spaciousness and easy way of living too much to want to go back to Europe or anywhere else ... So far we have been invited out practically every evening and it has all been most interesting ... On Sunday night we went to a beautiful little theatre to see a play (Fail Safe) put on by the Union Minière (the big mining company). The theatre still bore the bullet holes of the last 'troubles' two years ago, and signs of creeping shabbiness, but it would take a lot of beating anywhere ... There is none of the tension of Guinea here. We went to lunch with the Governor (Godefroid Munongo) at his palace last week and had a pleasant chat with him. He seems a very reasonable and likeable man and Hugh got on well with him straight away.

To all this I added 'The office seems well organised ... but overstaffed for a change. It remains to be seen what job there is for me to do.'

It took a little while for that to emerge. And when it did it was nothing to do with supplies to beleaguered Zambia, which my Vice-Consul Bernard Attwood and pro-consul Jack Eden had well in hand; or with Rhodesia, which was hundreds of miles away south of the Zambezi and isolated from all but South Africa, in its own false independence. Nor was it to do with administration, in the good hands of young Bill Stump, or our communications in the equally good hands of Bert Parfitt, or with the local staff,

My brother Eryl and his two children Ruth and Christopher with Robert
and Julia home on leave from the Congo, 1967.

all trained and competent, from dear Mme L'hoest our dedicated translator
to Cookie and Lamek at the residence and Alphonse, my equally loyal
driver. My predecessor had written to me: 'You will have a fairly good
staff and I shall be leaving this post a damn sight better organised than I
found it.' I did not know how that was but could imagine because his
predecessors had had the successive periods of Katangan upheaval to cope
with whereas his period had been the lull. But he had used it to good
purpose and bequeathed me a well-run ship. So for the first few months
I found myself in the unusual position of having little to do but get to
know the Katangan authorities and personalities; pay courtesy calls on the
leading Chiefs up country; tour the main towns and local authorities of
Katanga by air (which I did with my congenial and able American colleague
Art Tienken); get to know my heterogeneous British community, the
Consular corps, and the leaders of the Union Minière; visit the Ambassador
at Leopoldville and High Commissioner at Lusaka for liaison; play golf,
socialise, and enjoy family life in a warm and pleasant climate.

It was a happy break, not least for my golf handicap which came tumbling
down – until my golf clubs were burgled with my car, and ended up with
the heads sawn off, as officers' swagger canes, in one venal section of the
local Congolese Army. I never did recover any, neither the Police nor I
having the temerity to approach the Army with 'Look here, *mon Capitaine*,
that looks awfully like the Consul's 5 iron under your arm'! There was

indeed a lot of crime, and with unemployment high following the 'troubles', and stark contrast between the poverty of the native townships and the wealth of the European residential areas (although the expatriate housing was all sensibly modest), that was only to be expected. But the hard-hitting Katangan police kept it under some measure of control.

It was not long however, before the inbred turmoil of the Congo began to raise its ugly head again. This time it was the new Leopoldville Government of President Mobutu and his army, student and bas-Congo tribal support who started it, bent – understandably – on asserting their authority over the country but – less understandably – on using vicious means. Their main target was obviously the old enemy the Katanga and its industrial treasure-chest, the Union Minière. I think I was a lone observer in seeing this coming and warning of the consequences to begin with, other of course than Governor Munongo who had every personal reason to fear it. The Americans were sold on Mobutu up to the hilt. So, to a lesser extent, were our own people in Leopoldville and London. The Belgians were more wary but comforted themselves that no government of the Congo could succeed without the established Belgian industries. As the Spring and Summer of 1966 advanced the signs grew that the Katanga and Kivu were in for troubled times again. I was reminded in a letter of well wishes from Ritchie's predecessor, Bill Wilson, by now HM Ambassador to Togo, that I was the sixth HM Consul Elisabethville in six years. It was a salutary warning.

My first concern, alongside our trade and investment interests, had to be for the British community. They numbered about 1000 in Katanga, mainly in business, mining and evangelical missions, counting not only British citizens but British Protected persons and Commonwealth citizens for whom we were responsible. Then there was a further 1000 in the Kivu, mostly East African Asians of the Aga Khan's sect. I found that we had as good lines of communication with the Kivu community, hundreds of miles to the north, as could be expected through a local and respected honorary Vice-Consul Wilson had had the foresight to appoint, H. K. Sheriff. But in Katanga we had nothing beyond the haphazard. So, with the ready cooperation of leading members, I set up a representative committee and simple network of communication throughout the community in case of need. It later proved to be a life-saver.

The Congo covers a huge area of central Africa including the great Congo river, jungle, mountains and savanna. Nine other countries border it. Together they make up most of what we popularly call 'darkest Africa'. It is the third largest country of the continent, only slightly smaller than the Sudan and Algeria but more populated, more diversified, geographically and ethnically, and much richer in natural resources. It equates in size nearly to Western Europe and in population (50 million) nearly to our own in the UK. On the map it is like a great misshapen balloon around the Congo basin with the capital Kinshasa (formerly Leopoldville) incongruously stuck in the neck. It extends from the Atlantic ocean in the west to Lake Tanganyika in the east, and from Sudan in the north to Angola and Zambia (formerly Northern Rhodesia) in the south. It had no entity until King Leopold of Belgium secured it all in the 'Scramble for Africa' in the late nineteenth century. The Belgians ruled it as a colony until it became independent in 1960. They never found it easy to govern and pulled out administratively in rather shameful haste when riots for independence broke out in the late 1950s, leaving few trained officers, civil or serving, or politicians and managers to take over. The result is now histroy: widespread disorder; civil war between the national government at Leopoldville and the secessionist leader Moise Tshombe and his mercenary-led forces in Katanga; secessionist movements also in the Kivu to the North and the Kasai to the West; United Nations military intervention – finally prevailing in 1963. Tshombe then went into exile but, in an attempt at reconciliation, he was invited back the following year by the then President Kasavubu and the Parliamentary Assembly to be Prime Minister of the Congo as a whole. That brought relative peace for a while except for a pro-Marxist rebellion in the North-East. But Tshombe and Kasavubu did not get on and were both ousted in a coup d'état in late 1965 by the Commander-in-Chief of the Congolese forces, Colonel Sese Seko Mobutu.

That event was but five months old when I came to Elisabethville. The secession war was only two years past and, despite the lull while Kasavubu and Tshombe ruled the Congo, it was still fresh in Katangan minds. It had wreaked much damage on the province and brought in its wake much looting and brutality, including regrettably by some of the UN troops. It had been the first, and not an exemplary UN military operation. Nor were the Congolese troops – the ANC – or, for that matter, Tshombe's mercenaries and Katangese Gendarmerie, exactly above reproach. It was a period no-one in Katanga we met wanted to re-live – especially as the secession had failed.

In his book *To Katanga and Back*, about two of those years, 1960–61, Conor Cruise O'Brien, the then Representative of the UN in Katanga, concluded: 'In my opinion the right course and ultimately the most tenable both inside the Congo and diplomatically, is a firm hand both in ending the secession of Katanga and in preventing the entry to it of undisciplined Congolese units.' He went on to suggest that 'these absurd and dangerous forces – both the [Katanga] gendarmerie and the [National] ANC – should be paid off ... and a small well-disciplined force loyal to the Central Government should be trained and built out of the better elements now under arms.' His advice was not heeded. It was not in other respects either – he was sacked by the UN. But in this regard I lived to witness he was right. With few exceptions the Congolese Army (then the largest in black Africa) and particularly the 'elite' Paras, proved to be as ill-trained, ill-disciplined (and over-armed) as any, I would hazard, to be found anywhere. Being far from their homes, amidst alien tribes and languages in the Katanga and Kivu, and doped much of the time, they were easily aroused by their political masters to fear of enemies, real and imaginary. They were nonetheless permitted by their equally ill-trained officers to carry their sub-machine guns in the streets, loaded at the ready, and to molest, beat, loot, rape and murder at will given the chance. They formed a lethal cocktail. In the year we had them rampaging in Katanga, 1966/67, the white community was reckoned to have lost, at their hands, more people murdered than Kenya did at the hands of the Mau Mau in the eight years of that insurrection. The local Katangese suffered even more. So did the people of the Kivu. The Congolese army was virtually lawless.

President Mobutu undoubtedly knew this. He himself had been picked out, in the Leopoldville maelstrom of independence in 1960, by Western representatives, including the British MI6 and very probably the American CIA, as a likely saviour of the Congo. As Conor Cruise O'Brien observed in his book: 'Mobutu [and his colleague] Bomboko and perhaps Ileo have always worked closely with Western Embassies, notably the American Embassy.' He had rapidly achieved command of the post-independence Congolese army. But he had failed to defeat Tshombe's secession, requiring the UN to do the job for him, and had a score to settle with Katanga on that account. He wanted also, as history now confirms, to subjugate the whole Congo to his dictatorship and – although I admit even my prescient observation did not pick this up at the time – to milk the country to his own financial benefit. He was, in many Western and Congolese eyes, in 1960 and even more in 1965 when he seized political power, the 'great black hope' of the Congo. But he never was that in the eyes of the Katanga or Kivu. And although for many years he strutted the stage of Africa as a major leader, he was never remotely a Balewa of Nigeria or Nyerere of Tanganyika or Nkrumah of Ghana or Kaunda of Zambia or Machel of Mozambique or Senghor of Senegal or Houphouet-Boigny of Ivory Coast or even Sekou Touré of Guinea, let alone a Nelson Mandela. He was a smart bas-Congolese who hoodwinked Western governments into supporting him because he displayed drive, army support, political nous in choosing his colleagues and advisers and posed as anti-communist and a patriot. When he was finally ousted in 1997 a typical newspaper headline (the UK *Independent*) read: 'Zaire (Congo) leader leaves behind a bitter nation ruthlessly stripped of all its wealth over 32 years.'

His campaign to break the Katanga and seize its revenues began soon after I arrived, in an attempt to oust Governor Munongo, Tshombe's right-hand man in secession, and replace him with his own nominee. It back-fired. Munongo won the election. Mobutu then turned his propagandists onto attacking the Union Minière for allegedly supporting Tshombe and Munongo. Simultaneously he forced the Leopoldville Parliament to relieve Tshombe of his seat; and, contrary to agreements reached with Belgium by Tshombe when he was Prime Minister, Mobuto began expropriating Belgian enterprises. Aroused by these provocations, a large force of Katangese gendarmerie employed at the time fighting the Mulelist rebels in the North-East, mutinied and took control of the main city of that region, Kisangani (formerly Stanleyville) and the country around. Mobuto blamed this mutiny on Tshombe and the Belgians and stepped up his squeeze on the Katanga.

This was our first crisis in my time there. We had six more in the eighteen months that followed, 'each', as I wrote after the sixth 'uglier than the last'. This first was relatively minor. Although far from the mutineers, the security authorities immediately clamped down on movement in Katanga by closing the airport and borders. In addition, to quote our Leopoldville Embassy's report later: 'the Government put it about that the mutiny was part of a larger plot sponsored by Belgian big business to reinstate Tshombe ... At the height of the Kisangani mutiny few people believed that Mobuto could weather the storm. However, in the event, the mutineers, by their indecision, lost the initiative and, in October, surrendered unconditionally to loyal mercenaries after little or no struggle.' The travel restrictions in Katanga were then lifted. They had only lasted a short time. But being held hostage in effect was not pleasant, particularly for the Union Minière people at whom they were primarily directed. We found also we had acquired another problem to deal with, in the person of one Captain Mika, appointed by Mobutu as his Head of the Sûreté (Security) in Katanga. Mika unashamedly enjoyed imposing the travel restrictions, over the head of the Governor, and obliging the Police to arrest anyone he thought suspicious. That included a well known British subject in Elisabethville who was something of a minor Walter Mitty, but had acted as a back-stop for some of the mercenaries. Mika would have none of the man's protestations that he had nothing to do with Tshombe. Nor would Leopoldville. But I was able to get him out of prison and, with his wife, eventually home to safety in Britain. It was the first of many encounters I had with 'the mad Mika' as he came to be known.

Mobutu's next step was to announce a policy of 'decolonisation' of the country and particularly of Katanga. It soon became clear that the aim was to break Belgian domination of Congo business and industry. This policy aim sat oddly alongside Mobutu's parallel measures to impose central government control of Parliament and all the regions, bringing the country back from the measures of democracy introduced after independence to something very like the old colonial system of administration. He summoned Governor Munongo to Leopoldville and promptly put him under house arrest. Munongo was a man of substance, brother of the paramount chief of the Bayeke tribe, Minister of the Interior in the secessionist Katangan government and a man of whom Tshombe admitted he took orders as often as he gave them. He carried great respect in Katanga and beyond. I was with him the night before he left for Leopoldville. He clearly knew it was a trap but was not a man to run away. With his removal, and short of a complete collapse of the Mobutu regime, Katangan seces-sionism was effectively buried. There was no other leader to take his place. But Mobutu had only just started. To rub in his intentions he dropped the Belgian names of the main cities of the country and reintroduced old Congolese names, so Leopoldville became Kinshasa, Elisabethville became Lubumbashi, and Stanleyville became Kisangani (so breaking the name connection with H. M. Stanley, the explorer and finder of Dr Livingstone). A few years later he changed the name of the country to Zaire and of Katanga to Shaba. Some of us wished he could have chosen a more elegant and pronounceable name for the Katangan capital. I wrote home: 'Just fancy me as HM Consul Lubumbashi!' I do not recall that we bothered the Queen and Secretary of State for Foreign Affairs at home to change my appointment but the Congolese Minister of Foreign Affairs insisted on behalf of President Mobutu on a new exequatur in the name of Lubumbashi, which I still possess.

December 1966 brought a second crisis and this time, fortified by his good fortune and success so far, Mobutu set out to take Katanga and the great Union Miniére by storm. He abolished elected Governorships and provincial Ministers throughout the Congo and substituted his own ap-pointees. In the Katanga we were given military government for a while under the local Army Commander General Massiala. He was a professional soldier from the Belgian days who had achieved rapid promotion to become second in command of the national army but retained an earthy sense of responsibility. We came to know each other quite well, which proved useful both ways in times of crisis when he wanted me to help calm the foreign community and I wanted him to get a grip on the Paras. He was taken off to Kinshasa for a while to fill the post of Chief of the national Army after Mobutu peremptorily sacked the then Chief for sympathising with the mutineer's grievances. He was also transferred later to take command in the Kivu when a further gendarmerie rebellion, this time mercenary led, threatened the whole eastern Congo in July 1967. But, although a man of the Kasai, he preferred the Katanga and always returned there. He was this time given the task of his life, not only military governor of the Katanga at a time when his President was gunning for the province, but in charge of the notorious Paras whom Mobutu had just sent into South Katanga to garrison at Shinkolobwe not far from the main towns. They were to augment units of the regular Army and Katangese gendarmerie already stationed at Lubumbashi.

Mobutu's principal target was now the Union Minière du Haut Katanga (UMHK) and its huge assets, largely owned under a 1906 concession with still 23 years to run, by Belgian corporate and individual interests. The minority shareholders included 20% Congo state, some individual French, and 14% British (through Tanganyika Concessions Ltd – who also owned 90% of the Benguela railway built through Angola to ship UMHK produce to the Atlantic). To quote *Congo 1960*: 'UMHK was the third largest producer of copper in the world … the chief world producer of cobalt … and a producer of zinc, germanium, cadmium and precious metals and uranium-radium ore.' It also, to quote an Embassy report of ours of the time: 'controlled in the Katanga the entire production of hydro-electric power and owned a large share in the metallurgical and chemical industries, maize milling, cattle farming, railways, insurance, explosives, cement, hospitals, schools, real estate and roads.' It was part of my job to keep in touch with the directors because UMHK's activities affected everyone and, more specifically, because the Tanganyika Concessions Board wanted me to do so. (They held 20% voting rights.) The UMHK directors I came to know were all men of substance, rightly proud of UMHK's achievements and modern plant but deeply concerned about the future. Despite three years of secession war ( in which UMHK undoubtedly sided with Tshombe), the Katanga still contributed over 50% to the foreign earnings of the Congo and UMHK still directly employed over 1000 expatriate technicians and many thousands of Katangans, and indirectly many thousands more. They were shrewd operators and loved to recount to me how when the British and Belgians drew the boundaries between their respective Rhodesian and Congolese colonies at the turn of the nineteenth century, the British had employed Army officers using simple rulers while the Belgians had cunningly employed geologists using little hammers. As a result the boundaries alternated between straight lines, where the Belgians did not care, and wiggly ones where they reckoned there might be minerals to exploit. The Belgians did not get the lot, the Zambian copper belt also proved rich. But they did very well out of it – and the Congo/Zambian border lines still bear witness to their story.

Just before Congolese independence the Belgian government legislated to allow companies operating in the Congo to transfer their registered headquarters to Belgium. UMHK smartly did so. Mobutu's first object was to get this reversed so as to make UMHK subject to Congolese control. His second was to exercise that control and start bleeding UMHK for revenue and foreign exchange, over and above the dues already paid. There was urgency about this as the Congolese state coffers were empty and the Congolese currency failing. Throughout 1966 Mobutu built up pressure on UMHK to these ends, eventually forcing UMHK to the negotiating table but only partially succeeding. However, on the eve of Christmas he broke off negotiations and dramatically declared both the abolition of UMHK and the creation of a new Congolese company, to take over UMHK's installations and operations in the Congo. It was a breath-taking move, reminiscent to me of the first ever expropriation of a major oil company by the Saudi Arabian government when I was in Arabia in 1951, except that that had eventually been by agreement whereas this most definitely was not. Moreover Mobutu then followed this by crudely demanding of UMHK's expatriate technicians, on the last day of the year, to choose whether they wanted to continue in service with GECOMIN or have their contracts terminated by UMHK with appropriate compensation. Turmoil ensued. With this gun at their heads most of the technicians opted to leave with compensation. The Congolese Authorities panicked. They knew they could not cope without them. They immediately closed the frontiers and airport again, forcibly preventing all departures, even of families going on leave.

So Christmas 1966, far from being a season of goodwill and cheer, was hostage and crisis time again in Katanga, like the previous August, but this time more direct and vicious. There was no Father Christmas for the children. Instead, we were threatened with the Paras up the road if anyone moved. The head of Security had a field day rounding up anyone suspected of trouble-making or trying to escape. The young Portuguese Consul was expelled, his Embassy in Kinshasa having been attacked by Mobutu's rent-a-mob and relations with Portugal broken off on the pretext (not wholly unfounded) that the Portuguese in Angola preferred Tshombe. Mobutu also expropriated the insurance industry, in Kinshasa, without compensation and threatened to take over assets of the Belgian banking octopus the Société Générale, the parent of UMHK and many other enterprises in the Congo. There was also an extraordinary announcement from Kinshasa that all Consulates in Katanga were to be 'suspended'. It was at this time that the Governor General Massiala appealed to us Consuls to help calm our communities who by now were understandably in a state of some tension. I enjoyed telling him he had better get us 'de-suspended' first, whatever that meant, but added that it was a nonsense we proposed to ignore. He agreed. Apparently some of Mobutu's young turks had dreamt it up in the hope of frightening us into some sort of submission. In time that crisis ended as suddenly as it had started. The Société Générale, acting for UMHK, recognised the take-over and Mobutu recognised he could not do without them. So it was agreed that UMHK would continue to manage and operate the mines, refineries and ancillaries and to market the products for GECOMIN. That agreement not only relieved the increasingly un-pleasant situation in Katanga, it undoubtedly, as our Kinshasa Embassey reported later, saved the Congo from bankruptcy.

I took the family on leave in March while relative peace prevailed, and bought a house on mortgage for us in Guildford and a new set of golf clubs for me on the burglary insurance. The house later proved a blessing to the family and the best thing I ever bought. The clubs were a folly, original Scots Macgregors, far too good for me but much fun.

The FO decided they wanted me to return to Katanga for part of a tour 'for administrative reasons'. The DSAO was in its usual muddle and, like English estate agents, felt it had to construct a chain of moves before it could find me a new place. They sought flatteringly to console me that they and Ambassador Cotton in Kinshasa wanted me to continue in charge while the present uncertainty continued. I reminded them I had been drawn into playing a bigger part in the Katangan troubles than our declining interests justified. It was nice that this seemed to be appreciated by the European as well as British communities and by the Katangan authorities alike. But reduced to its bare bones, the post clearly did not merit its present grading or staffing and, if the Service was looking for economies as we were constantly being reminded, here was one. They responded later by cutting our already meagre allowances but keeping the grading and staffing of the post as it was. I thought that pretty cheap, so did my staff, but par for the course for that wretched DSAO. Their timing was also rather thoughtless. They contrived to inform us of the cuts, including that they were not prepared to compensate us fully for Congolese devaluation, in the midst of our worst crisis, and without a word of regret. They seemed to have lost two of the best traditions of the Service, competence and thoughtfulness. We would have gladly fed them to Mobutu's lions at the time.

We came back from leave in late May to find a new Governor installed in the Lubumbashi residence and things hotting up. Manzikala had been Governor of the North-East province of the Congo, with a reputation for madness, murder and violent treatment of two successive wives. Mobutu had evidently hand-picked him for Katanga. General Massiala was back as local Army Commander. Mika was still head of Security. The Paras were still at Shinkolobwe. Munongo, the elected Governor, and the only really capable one among them had now been imprisoned by Mobutu awaiting trial in Kinshasa, as had a few lesser political figures of the previous regime. Mobutu had promulgated a new Constitution designed to give him virtually dictatorial powers over the country, and had called a national referendum in June to legitimise it. In the event, as our Kinshasa Embassy reported, 'it was so conducted and rigged that the populace had no option but to vote in the affirmative. The methods used to secure an overwhelming majority in its favour ranged from fraud, open intimidation and violence in the Katanga and other lukewarm regions to the murder of the Mayor of Matadi. In Katanga, where Manzikala, the new Governor, had been ruthless in securing the necessary verdict, there remained a lasting legacy of bitterness.'

This time it was the native Katangans who took the brunt. A month later I reported:

Since Mobutu decreed the permutations of Governors and civil servants throughout the country, the upper echelons of the civil administration of this region, provincial, district and municipal are now, like the Army and the Sûreté, wholly staffed from other parts of the Congo and principally from the Bas-Congo. Tribal and historic enmities thus mount on feelings against the regime and the Army. So gloomy is the picture in fact that it was noticeable during the recent crisis how the Balubas of North Katanga and the Kasai huddled with the more Southerly Katangans in common fear and self-interest. This is a rare sight, and it shows that the old Baluba problem of Katanga can now be subsumed in times of stress, in a common front. In the light of past animosity between the other tribes of Katanga and the Balubas, this is quite an achievement for Mobutu's policy of ending tribalism. But it is a unity in adversity against him, not in support of his policies and regime ... I do not think it will explode (into rebellion) in present circumstances. It is more likely to lead to steady emigration into the bush and across the frontiers ... This is why the 1000 trekked from Pweto into Zambia last month. More will follow if there is no manifest change of heart and policy towards Katanga in Kinshasa.

That was crisis number three and we saw for the first time the brutal teeth of both the new Governor Manzikala and the Paras, whom he brought into the towns to assert his authority. They were not pleasant to encounter,

Remonstrating with 'mad Mika', Chief of Security in the Katanga, Lubumbashi, 1967.

preferring to wave their loaded guns at us or hit out with them, than to give way on the pavement, and to stop, search, rob and beat anyone they chose. Apart from constantly having to make representations to the Governor, Army Chief and Head of Security I found I was frequently being called out to help people in distress, sometimes alone if I could not get the Army or Police commanders to accompany me. Each time it meant finding the people who had got a message through to me, and talking to the soldiers who were threatening them, using the little consular pennant on my car as a mark of authority. It was not nice to have their loaded guns in the face, nor to see the often fearful ignorance in their eyes, usually dilated with dope. Their lingo was their own. I had to make up a mixture of pidgin French and English with gestures to persuade them I was the British Consul and we were not enemies. These events became all too disagreeably frequent as things got worse. I was fortunate to possess an innate faith in my own survivability. To show fear before them would have been fatal.

Crisis number four came in July, and this time the Paras were let loose on us in force. Mobutu had contrived the kidnapping of Tshombe in Europe and his incarceration in Algiers, having already had him condemned to death *in abstentia*. Within a week the French-speaking mercenary commando of the Congolese Army mutinied in Kisangani in the north and Bukavu in the east. The mercenaries had originally been recruited by Tshombe through the South African Colonel Mike Hoare and Frenchman Colonel Bob Denard. Mobutu had found it useful to re-engage them against the Mulele rebellion in the north but, under pressure from other African governments, had paid off the English-speaking commando. He had not got around to disbanding the French-speaking commando. They had been invaluable in putting down the gendarmerie revolt in Kisangani the previous year. This time however they responded to Tshombe, rallied the gendarmerie and an additional force of disgruntled North Katangese troops, and routed the Congolese Army (the ANC) in Kisangani and Bukavu. Their leader Denard was wounded in the process and had to be flown out. That set them back. But a Belgian planter Major Schramme, took command and, in early August, issued an ultimatum to President Mobutu to resign or he would march with his 150 mercenaries and 1000 soldiers on Katanga.

The outbreak of that mutiny, this time led by mercenaries, caused panic in Katanga. I will let the report I wrote on 17 July 1967 to the Ambassador Kinshasa, the FO and our Missions in Brussels, Washington and Lusaka, tell the story of the first phase. (Like the other official reports I quote in this chapter, this letter was recently released by the Public Records Office under the 30 year rule - their reference in this case being FCO 25/64):

## CONFIDENTIAL

BRITISH CONSULATE,

LUBUMBASHI
19 July 1967.

KATANGAN SITUATION Before going to the Kivu I ought perhaps to give you a round up of the recent crisis here from the outbreak of the mercenary rebellion in the North to the restoration of relative calm last week. In the rush of events and day and night problems of dealing with them, my telegraphic reports were, I fear, rather bitty.

2. News of the rebellion broke on the 5 July. On instructions from Kinshasa, the Katangan authorities immediately deployed the troops to the towns and other strategic points, whipped up the road barriers, closed all airports, prohibited movement across the frontiers, closed all clubs and imposed a curfew on whites from 9 p.m. My Ismaili community gallantly, or prudently, decided to stand with the rest of the British community and regard themselves as white.

3. I had the leaders of the British community and missionary organisations in straight away and told them to pass the word of prudence throughout the community and as far as possible up country, and to stay in touch. Throughout the subsequent events this organisation, set up last year, proved most effective and the community held together wonderfully. The only bad cases we had were some members and visitors temporarily lost on the morning of 7 July after the (Army) house searching patrols had swept through all the European residential areas, but they were fairly quickly found and released; a bang on the head and kick in the stomach suffered by one of the leading members of my Lubumbashi community who gallantly went to the rescue of some missionaries in trouble with a group of paratroops; and the case of armed robbery and attempted rape reported in my telegram No. 160. For the rest, the community here and in the up-country towns suffered the terror and minor looting of everyone else but contrived to come to no physical harm or serious loss of property. In many cases the Consulate and members of the community were able to give help to other communities and have been thanked for this. The acting Head of GECOMIN has also thanked me for such help as I was able to give.

4. Thursday night 6/7 July was the worst night of terror. Panic and racial animosity had begun to show in the provincial administration, the Sûreté and the Military and throughout the towns during the day, stimulated by intensified security measures, armed patrols in the towns, the import of paratroops from their up-country Shinkolobwe camp, the Government's discriminatory measures against whites and the excreta of Kinshasa and Lubumbashi radios. All foreign farmers in the Lubumbashi area, including non-Congolese Africans, two Tanzanians among them – about fifty in all – were rounded-up without reason, but presumably because their farms could house rebels, and dumped in the Kasapa prison. (They spent several uncomfortable days there before being released, intermittently being dragged out to do labourer's work under armed guard in the fields –

including one old Belgian woman of 74.) This was one of many episodes that day.

5. I called on Governor Manzikala late that afternoon and, as I reported at the time, found him whistling up his courage. He told me that the curfew was being brought forward to 6 o'clock. An announcement was just going out. This was at nearly 5 o'clock. I protested that it had been announced only that morning that it was being brought forward to 7 p.m.; it would be impossible at an hour's notice to warn everyone in time. He said that Mobutu had been on the telephone to him all day, at half hourly intervals and in a raging mood, and among other things, had insisted on the curfew beginning here at 6 o'clock, like everywhere else in the Congo. So it had to be, but he implied there would be some licence to offenders that evening. We hurriedly put the word out to as many as possible of the British community to be in by 6 o'clock.

6. The only licence given was, in fact, to the Military and Sûreté. The paratroop patrols pounced at 6 p.m., arrested any white face they could find, beat a good few, forced others to give up their valuables and money and generally began the rampage. Other troops joined in. The police were powerless. One group of paratroops rounded up nine whites in the centre of town, and made off with them in a lorry out of town; the group, all apparently Belgian and Greek, included a girl of 21 and a boy of 14, son of a Belgian technician in GECOMIN who was also in the group. For some reason the girl was pitched out on the way out of town, relatively unharmed. Her fiancé was with the other eight. They were taken into the bush 15 kms. out of town, not far from where the power pylons were blown up last month, and there mercilessly butchered with bayonet and bullet. One escaped wounded, a remarkable old Belgian of 78, and found his way to safety and to report to my Belgian colleague the following morning. He is still in hospital. A Belgian major attached to the ANC and a Member of the Belgian Consulate-General went out to the site straight away, risking attack for breaching the ban on movement out of town. They found three bodies, bayoneted and bullet ridden but otherwise barely identifiable as the bush had been set alight to finish them off. Not far away they found the body of the boy. The others have still to be found.

7. That same night beginning at 4 in the morning, joint military/police and civilian patrols began house to house searches throughout the European residential areas. Dozens were taken off to prison or the police and military cells for possessing pistols or shot-guns they were supposed, at 24 hours notice, to have handed in the previous day, or for possessing anything remotely military, from boots to khaki coloured shirts. Many others were taken in that night and the following days, on other obscure grounds of suspicion. In all, including the farmers, they eventually numbered in the hundreds.

8. The same thing happened in varying degrees throughout the other main towns of the Katangan copperbelt. Kolwezi was the worst after Lubum-

bashi. There, as I reported at the time, the GECOMIN European Managers were ridiculed in public, beaten and tortured. By night fall all GECOMIN European employees had decided to strike in protest. They were eventually talked out of this by Gonze, the General Manager, but resigned instead. That is another story we are still living with.

9. On the Friday afternoon, 7 July, my American and Belgian colleagues and I decided that we must have it out with the Governor before things got worse. We gathered the other career Consuls and descended on the Governor en bloc to lodge a strong protest about these excesses, and particularly the murders, and to demand proper measures for the safety and security of foreigners and fair treatment for those caught infringing the emergency regulations. Manzikala was taken aback. This was a new experience to him. He kept us waiting an hour and finally appeared flanked by his Vice-Governor, the Provincial Inspector of Police and leading representatives of the local press. He was evasive about the murders, shielding himself behind the Army's yarn that they had been committed by villagers angered by last month's dynamiting of the pylons. In the end, for what it was worth, he took our points and undertook to provide facilities for a group to go out and search for the remaining missing. But despite constant pressure by my Belgian, Greek and American colleagues and from GECOMIN, it still took another two days before these facilities were accorded, by which time the bodies had vanished as well as the missing. The military had covered up, and the full enquiry Manzikala later agreed to institute has still not produced anything. Nor, I feel sure, is it ever likely to.

10. That day and night groups of paratroops started open robberies in the streets and night marauding in the European residential areas. Racial tension was high, inflamed by President Mobutu's declarations and the Kinshasa and Lubumbashi radios. Whites who ventured into the centre of town in day time did so at their risk. The same applied in Kolwezi.

11. By Saturday morning 8 July Lubumbashi was in uproar. Panic spread further with radio announcements (since traced to the mad Mika, our provincial head of Sûreté, but fairly clearly authorised by Manzikala) confining Europeans to their houses from 2 p.m., with lights out from 6 p.m. (which is Sunset at present). On the Swahili radio programme it was announced that the masses were to foregather in town the following morning with their primitive weapons to defend the Republic. Panic rose to hysteria. For many Europeans, these were signs that a massacre of whites was imminent. More dangerous, the riff-raff of the town had clearly picked up the scent. This was evident in the Communes and in the streets. The Consulates were inundated with *cris de coeur*. It was clear that something drastic would have to be done, and quickly, or the situation would be totally out of hand.

12. It fell to my American colleague and me to take the initiative. Our Belgian colleague was overwhelmed and in any case ostracised by Manzikala; our new French colleague is rather an old fuddy-duddy and our

other colleagues generally eschew the lead. Harrop and I agreed that I
would tackle General Massiala and he Governor Manzikala.

13.  By good fortune I was able to catch Massiala on the telephone right away.
He had been incommunicado since the outbreak of the crisis, preferring
to let Manzikala (whom he cannot abide) and Col. Ikuku of the paratroops
stew in it, while he concerned himself with his own affairs. I told him
that in our judgement and that of the other leaders of the foreign
communities, a grave situation threatened; it was imperative that the
troops should be brought under proper control immediately, the morning's
announcements rescinded, and vigorous efforts made by all the authorities
concerned to restore some semblance of calm before things exploded.
Recalling the times when he had appealed to Consuls to help restore
calm in previous – though lesser – crises last year, I said it was now our
turn to call on him. I begged him in the name of the Consular Corps
and foreign community to take control immediately and firmly. He responded without hesitation, doubtless glad that someone had asked him
to take over. What he did precisely we may never know. I have barely
seen him since. But we do know that he tackled Manzikala immediately
(and probably enjoyed doing so) and that as a result firm orders went out
from the Residence soon afterwards to the radio and loudspeaker vans to
deny outright, in the Governor's name, the first two of the morning's
announcements, and to the paratroops that they were confined to barracks
at night.

14.  Harrop saw Manzikala in the afternoon and rubbed it home in appropriate
terms. He warned the Governor that the situation was serious and that
American public opinion would already be revolted by news of the
Thursday night murders without adding to the list. Manzikala claimed
disingenuously that the morning's radio announcements were not his
doing but Mika's (and he had now had them formally denied). He also
claimed that he had already prepared an appeal for calm to be delivered
on the radio later in the afternoon. It seemed to Harrop that he had in
fact just done this, probably after seeing Massiala, but, we imagine, also
after getting the green light from Mobutu to put the stops on. This is
then what he proceeded to do, belatedly but effectively. His radio appeal,
repeatedly broadcast in the late afternoon and evening, was forceful, and
favourable to the Europeans. It must have hurt him to deliver it. But in
the knowledge, I presume, that Mobutu had enough trouble on his hands
with the rebellion in the North not to want his inflammatory measures
and declarations to lead to a blood-bath in Katanga, Manzikala evidently
realised in the nick of time that his own head was at stake. He did the
right things when forced and, aided by the simultaneous collapse of the
rebellion in the North, did them effectively. He also had it announced
firmly that there was to be no meeting of the masses the following day.
But no one I have spoken to since, European or American or Katangan,
will readily forget how he let things go to the limit. Nor, for that matter,
do they forgive Massiala – or, of course, Mika.

15. Relative calm has now returned, and we are picking up the bits. It was a nasty episode, certainly much nastier for the foreign community than any last year (and that is saying something) and, in the view of the old timers, nastier than anything they have previously encountered since the 1960 mutiny. Before, they have always had some sympathy and security from the provincial if not the Central Government – in the Mutiny, the secession war and the Mulelist rebellion. Under the Mobutu regime and especially since Munongo left and was ultimately replaced by Manzikala, they have had the reverse. This, as I have explained in my tel. No. 200, is the real reason for the mass decision in GECOMIN and elsewhere in the foreign community of Katanga after this episode to up stumps and quit. How many will actually go remains to be seen. Time, the blue sky, and the restoration of calm may bring second thoughts to many. But there is one case that I regard as symbolic. The best known doctor in the region, Dr Questiaux, born in the Congo and renowned for his devotion to medicine and charity in the Congolese service, has announced after much heart-searching that he must start afresh elsewhere for the sake of his family and cause. This may have quite an effect on others. For its excesses, the Congo is losing one of its best doctors. Everywhere one goes it is the same story; the wives and families are booking passages out, as they become available; the men are weighing up the prospects. One or two prominent members of the British community are pulling out. I do not feel I can discourage them. The choice is theirs. But I cannot in all honesty pretend to them that this is a place, in present circumstances, for British investment. On the past year's experience the risk element is altogether too high.

(W. N. HUGH-JONES)

This report evoked a letter from the Permanent Under-Secretary of the Foreign Office, Sir Paul Gore-Booth, saying they had not previously appreciated just how dreadful things were in the Congo and expressing his deep appreciation of all we were doing in such difficult circumstances. That letter was addressed, according to protocol, to the Ambassador in Kinshasa. For some reason he sat on it, although he did later convey to me the gist. I found it by chance thirty years later in the Public Records Office. It was nice to know!

My aside remark in the penultimate paragraph of that report, that the rebellion in the North had collapsed, proved premature. There was a deceptive lull following Denard's departure. But in early August, it started all over again with Schramme's ultimatum to Monutu to abdicate, and we in Katanga were sucked into crisis number five. The strange thing about these episodes was how things went quiet between them. The high plateau was like that. The sunshine, moderate altitude and spaciousness had that calming effect. So of course did experience.

This latest lull lasted a fortnight. Schramme's ultimatum was immediately countered by Mobutu's recently created MPR political party. They publicly threatened reprisals against European residents if the mercenaries moved south. To prove that was no idle threat they then sacked the Belgian Embassy in Kinshasa. Mobutu appealed to the Americans for air transport to move his spare military units up to face Schramme and the Americans responded. 'But for this timely assistance,' our Kinshasa Embassy commented, 'Mobutu and his government might well have fallen.' I was not so sure. At the sharp end in Katanga, it did not look to me quite like that. I found it improbable that Schramme and his force would want to leave their stronghold in the north-east in a vain attempt to conquer the Katanga, however much they might be urged by their paymasters (believed to be Tshombe's brother Tomas and some Belgian backers). Their aim was to bargain for Tshombe's release. However that is not how the excitable Katangan (and Kinshasa) authorities saw it, and it was with them we had to contend.

I had visited the Kivu in the lull in late July, accompanied by our Military Attaché, Colonel Brook-Fox from the Kinshasa Embassy. To get there we had to hitch a lift from Kinshasa to Bukavu in an American Hercules transport plane filled with stinking dried fish to feed the Army and town. Brook-Fox returned after two days, his job of making a military assessment completed. I stayed on to succour the 1000 strong British-protected East African Asian community in Bukavu and Goma, and to negotiate with the provincial Governor Engulu and military chief General Kakudji on their behalf. Also to bring their passports up to date or, in the great majority of cases, to issue them with emergency certificates to see them through the next few months. It proved to be a timely visit.

The Kivu and the bordering countries of Rwanda and Burundi, all formerly Belgian colonial territories, have become over the years since the Belgians pulled out, one of the world's most turbulent regions, with recurrent inter-tribal conflict, massacres, even genocide, principally between the Hutu and Tutsi. It was there, also, that today's Congo civil war started with the Kabila rebellion supported by Rwanda, which brought about the downfall of Mobutu in 1997, but which still continues. It now involves not only rival Congolese factions and so-called 'armed groups', but the forces of six neighbouring states – Rwanda, Burundi, Uganda, Zimbabwe, Angola and Namibia. Most recently the Kivu, and specifically its capital Goma, has also suffered the horror of volcanic eruption. It is a beautiful part of the world, the size of Ghana, encompassing the temperate and volcanic region of Lake Kivu in the east, the tropical forests of Maniema in the west (leading to Kisangani and the upper Congo river); and the pastoral, and in colonial days white settler country bordering on Burundi, Rwanda and Uganda. Coffee, tea and other plantations abounded in those days and the scenery, lakeside resorts and game reserve of Parc Albert drew tourists from far afield. In my visit there in 1967 it was the scene of the mercenary and gendarmerie rebellion, withdrawn momentarily to Punia further north, and of defending Congolese troops scared out of their wits by the mercenary threat and at night firing at anything that moved. Every shot echoed around the hills and valleys, too, so adding to the tension. It was far from the once peaceful place it had been and there was much destruction to be seen from the fighting and looting.

I found Governor Engulu an intelligent and responsible young man but lacking knowledge of what to do. He knew, as I did, that the ANC had run amok in Bukavu once the mercenaries and gendarmerie had withdrawn, committing a catalogue of murders, robbery, looting and rape. He listened to my homily that his civil and military people should put law and order and the safety of people and property first and get a grip on the soldiers. It did not do much good, for Schramme and his mutineers descended on the place again and put them all to flight within three weeks of my visit. The Governor did however respond to my plea to obtain Kinshasa authority to re-open the frontiers. I was able to give him assurances from my honorary Vice-Consul and his community and from all the other local Consuls and hon. Consuls I took it upon myself to convene, on behalf of their communities, that no one would rush to take advantage of the frontiers being re-opened, still less provoke the exodus Engulu feared, unless they genuinely had to flee for their lives. The frontiers were duly re-opened before I left. Sheriff later told me that that measure, and the emergency travel certificates I had given to our people, saved that community. When Schramme descended, they had no choice but to flee or be crushed between the rebels and the ANC. Sheriff led them into Rwanda and Uganda, without a soul being lost (although they all lost property left behind, of course). This was the second time he had had to do this, the previous occasion being during the Mulele rebellion two years earlier. For his leadership and courage I recommended him for an MBE which I am glad to say was eventually conferred. It would be difficult to name one better merited.

My return to Lubumbashi was as round-about as the visit had been adventurous. It involved rough road, in Sheriff's car, to an airstrip in Rwanda (we were in fact the first to cross the re-opened frontier); then an air flight in the co-pilot's seat of a little bush plane to Bujumbura, capital of Burundi; thence, by Fokker to Kampala the capital of Uganda; then Dakota to Lusaka and another to N'dola in Zambia; and by road back to Lubumbashi. I would have preferred the dried fish route via Kinshasa given the option but, in retrospect, would not have wished to miss an extraordinary experience at Bujumburu airport. I was met there by an excited British Chargé d'Affaires who told me the President of Burundi, Captain Michombero, had declared me persona non grata (PNG) so I had better get out fast. I never did discover why. No reason was given, and I did not think it prudent to wait to find out. But, like all diplomats who have experienced it, I quite prize mine.

Back at Lubumbashi the scene had all the signs again of the early July troubles and worse. In the face of Schramme's ultimation to Mobutu, the Governor and Chief of Security were at panic stations, the Kinshasa propaganda machine was deliberately whipping up racial tension and specifically threatening the Katangan whites, and the Paras were out on the streets, beating and robbing at will with, this time, not even a General Massiala in remote control. He had been sent to Bukavu to take command there, and all I could say later for his successor was: 'The new General, Nzoigba, proved to be plain block without tackle and the Paratroop Colonel, Ikuku, a playboy.' We soon had a rapidly escalating series of incidents, mostly involving the Paras in Elisabethville, Jadotville and Kolwezi but also the regular forces and now, additionally, civilian activists of Mobutu's new political party. Up-country as well as in the towns stories were pouring in of murders, some gruesome, physical assaults, some grisly, and rampant robbery and looting. I found myself called out to one case of attempted rape and countless cases of people being molested and robbed at the myriad road blocks the army set up. I also had a Para invasion of my own residence. Ignoring the flag they barged in, rounded up my wife, children, nanny and the two servants, and proceeded to search the place, allegedly looking for arms but brazenly pocketing bits of jewellery in the process. Fortunately I had lodged my pistol in the Consulate safe, being convinced it would be more dangerous to be found with one in the house than to be without it. Ann played it calmly and persuaded the leader to let her telephone me. I spoke to him on the phone, then came straight out and talked him into going. I then rang Governor Manzikala and General Nzoigba, and lodged strong protests. They had no effect. Nor did other protests that I and my Belgian, French, Italian, Greek, Netherlands and United Nations colleagues made about other incidents. The Governor and his civilian and military associates seemed consumed with Mobutu's propaganda that we were all in league with Schramme and the mercenaries. They were by now in any case helpless before the Paras, simply replying to protests that the Army had to root out all arms and mercenaries hidden in the community. Only the Chief of Police kept his head but he admitted total impotence. Law and order had collapsed.

It was clearly crunch time for the foreign communities. Each Consul had to decide for his own. I gave it a day or two more to see if things improved but they grew worse. So I convened the British Committee and advised them that in the circumstances I thought we should evacuate the women and children. I would not order general evacuation as that would put the much larger Belgian community on the spot and almost certainly provoke further Army violence and the closure of frontiers (which had momentarily been forgotten by the authorities). For those same reasons, I counselled against concerted departures but advised what I called 'a thinning out', preferably by road to Zambia – where I had lined up the good Vicar of Bancroft and his community to help people on their way through. The Committee fully agreed and went away to brief people in their own designated areas. It was traumatic for all but most observed it and all bore it with fortitude. Except for those who trickled back, as many did in due course, they were out for two and a half months. That was far longer than I considered necessary, but the Kinshasa Embassy and FO stepped in when I was about to lift the order in September and advised against doing so until the mercenary invasion was completely at an end. In fact, within a week of them authorising me to lift the order eventually, at the end of October, I had to organise a repeat evacuation of the women and children because of a new mercenary invasion from Angola, but that was fortunately over in a week.

We had a bit of an Anglo-American spat over the first evacuation. I had naturally warned my Belgian and other colleagues with communities that we were doing it, partially and discreetly. My Belgian colleague sadly wished he could do the same with his huge community and was understanding. Some other colleagues followed our example. The Americans objected and protested to London from Washington. They were out on a limb at this time, supporting Mobutu and Manzikala and even presuming to be our spokesman with the Governor. I had to tell my American colleague that was presumptuous and mistaken. We spoke for ourselves and our own communities, and were all of the opinion that Manzikala was incapable, dangerous and must go. My American colleague came round to that view himself in due course, and so fortunately did Mobutu. The FO supported me and rejected the American protest. They had briefed the Secretary of State, George Brown, on what I was doing and why, and he approved. The Americans had no leg to stand on anyhow, being in the privileged position of exemption by Mobutu from travel restrictions and, in Katanga, having no community to defend except the Consulate staff and two or three missionaries. Anglo-American accord was happily restored by the time of the next crisis; and the Americans were the first to evacuate when the mercenaries then invaded from Angola. We met up with the Harrops again, and indeed stayed with them at their place at Syracuse in upper New York state when we were in Canada. They were a delightful family and Bill rose eventually to become chief inspector of the American foreign service. In Lubumbashi, when he found himself out on a limb from the rest of us, he was the victim of his own government's folly. As President George W. Bush admitted in the early days of the Afghanistan war in 2001, the Americans, for all their great virtues, are not always very good 'at making other governments', or words to that effect.

Ann, the children and our nanny Gillian (whom we had been fortunate to find on home leave, to succeed Maureen) slipped quietly off to Zambia in mid-August, by car, along with the other Consulate and Community wives and children, all proceeding separately to avoid attention. She drove our rather tinpot early model Cortina but it was all right for the Zambian roads. They went down to the capital, Lusaka, and found a temporary home with kindly colleagues in the High Commission, the Le Bretons, who had visited us at Lubumbashi on liaison duty only the previous month and been stuck with us for nearly a fortnight, poor things, by the Congolese closing the frontiers. He proudly retained as a memento a consular warrant I had issued to make him a Vice-Consul Lubumbashi so he could pass the time of his encagement helping in the office. They had two toddlers of their own in Lusaka so our children had playmates. Our nanny helped both. The Le Bretons were marvellous, Ann was even able to get on with her latest novel and we could, with difficulty, talk occasionally on the telephone. So the first weeks of separation passed without hardship. They did too, in varying degree, for the families of my staff who had opted in one case to return to the UK and the others to stay in temporarily vacant mining houses kindly made available to them by people in the Zambian copperbelt. The community wives and families scattered widely and I heard of no insuperable difficulties.

As the mercenary rebellion in the Kivu and its repercusions in Katanga continued into September and then the Embassy Kinshasa and FO stuck in their oar, all these separations became more painful. My family joined the others at the Zambian towns of Bancroft and Ndola near the border and, at times when the frontier was open, we were occasionally able to drive down for a few hours to see them. But the imposed extension made the separations, discomfort and uncertainties progressively more burdensome and it was not helped in the case of the Consulate, by our enemy number two, the Diplomatic Service Adminstration Office in London (our first enemy had to be the Congolese authorities!). They made us bear most of the expenses of evacuation ourselves, which seemed singularly mean, and argued the detail of the remainder down to the last penny. The correspondence continued long after my departure for home and Ottawa in 1968. Attwood, then acting Consul, put it to them straight: 'During the period of evacuation all the married officers at this post suffered considerable personal and financial hardships, not of their own making. These difficulties were accepted cheerfully, as part of Service life. I sincerely hope that they will be appreciated in DSAO and that subsistence claims submitted will receive the sympathetic consideration which they merit.' They were met in token at the end. I hope any British tax-payer reading these lines will appreciate the lengths to which the Diplomatic Service went to conserve their hard-earned contributions in those days!

The sixth crisis and, for my consular staff the worst, but in fact the turning point, came in the last week of August. The evacuation had been just in time. My report to Kinshasa and London recorded it thus:

CONFIDENTIAL

British Consulate
Lubumbashi
8 September 1967

The Paras have taken again to roughing up the Katangese on every occasion; and, for the Europeans, this time have chosen the principal European residential area, Les Roches as their main marauding area ... When marauding, their custom is to go out in groups of four or five. They hammer on a house or swagger into a restaurant capped, dressed and booted in camouflaged battle-wear, often doped and with loaded sub-machine guns at the ready. They usually claim they are searching for arms but, once in, proceed to loot. If this does not satisfy them, and all too frequently it does not, they drag the householder and, if necessary, his wife outside to threaten them with the bush (i.e. murder). Eventually they may be bought off with money or jewellery. If not, the unfortunates are tortured or beaten (or the worst happens as at Kambove). They then move on to another house or locality, leaving the terrified household to collect its wits and telephone their Consul.

On the evening of 20 August, a Sunday, a group of paratroops in Lubumbashi walked into the popular St Tropez restaurant on the lake below my house, felled the proprietor in a pool of blood and, ignoring telephonic instructions from the Chef d'Etat Major to return to camp, proceeded to herd all the diners into a lorry to drive them off to what all 27 feared was the bush. A paratroop Captain joined them at this point. For some reason, seemingly a lack of decision among the paratroops, the victims were taken round the town in a nightmare drive for a time and then roughly disembarked on one of the main boulevards of another residential area, the Captain then disappearing. Here they were huddled on the pavement while the paratroops debated their fate, breaking off intermittently to threaten the few passers-by also with their lives. Two of my staff were called on this occasion; they were in a near-by house. The rest of the story you know from my telegrams. Attwood and Stump came straight round to me afterwards and the following morning we had a Consular Corps meeting with Manzikala.

(W.N. HUGH-JONES)

Attwood and Stump had had the courage to tackle the Paras. This was in fact their first direct occasion. Attwood, with Stump in support, handled it like a trooper, taking responsiblility for all those under threat irrespective of nationality and standing up to the armed Paras. For their pains they were dragged off and threatened with their lives, but eventually managed to talk the Paras out of it and secured the release of their captives. The news was around Lubumbashi in no time and I was able to secure the ready support of all my consular colleagues, to face Governor Manzikala with a strong and combined protest the following morning. We also agreed to demand that the soldiers concerned be punished and that the Paras be taken off the streets and confined to barracks at least at night and stopped from parading about with their loaded weapons except when genuinely on duty. I led, and demanded a restoration of law and order, intimating that our communities could not be expected to work and stay otherwise. This was the one weapon we had. Mobutu was known to fear that the technicians would leave and his treasure store GECOMIN would collapse. Manzikala wriggled between rage and fear, at one moment signalling to one of his guards standing immediately behind me to do the usual with anyone opposing him and bring the butt down on me but then changed his mind and grabbed his telephone instead. He sought to excuse the soldiers and shift the blame onto Attwood, but got short shrift on that. In the end he was forced to agree to do all he could to meet our demands, although we left with little faith in his capacity to do so. On receiving my telegraphic report the FO immediately instructed the Ambassador in Kinshasa 'to do your utmost, after consulting your American and Belgian colleagues, to see Mobutu or failing him, the highest available authority, to reinforce Mr Hugh-Jones's protest and ask for firm instructions to be sent to Lubumbashi to keep the ANC under control and to prevent them from molesting Europeans.'

Manzikala had in fact lost control and so had the General commanding the ANC and the Colonel commanding the Paras. In the week that followed our meeting, they went to ground, nightly marauding grew, looting spread, some gruesome murders of Europeans occurred in the bush again and the Army started internecine skirmishing between the Paras and the Gendarmerie in Elisabethville. Manzikala fled to Kinshasa. To quote my happy report: 'he went to seek Mobutu's stamp and grace. He secured the stamp but not the grace.' Mobutu had finally sacked him. He was one of the most evil men I think I have ever encountered (second to Mobutu himself of course). Katanga breathed a sigh of relief, and an even bigger one when the acting Governor Kihuyu told us that Mobutu had ordered the Paras back to barracks. But our relief was short-lived. The Paras objected. The Gendarmerie saw their chance. On the night of 26 August, to quote my report: 'Lubumbashi was rocked by machine gun and rifle fire and even mortar. Europeans everywhere ran for cover (and phoned their Consuls non-stop for news and advice). The African communes went wild with fright, many taking flight into the bush; the United Nations war had come again and this time no Tshombe to defend them ... It stopped as suddenly as it started ... We still do not know the casualties ... The ANC has effectively covered up.' It later emerged that the Paras had shot up a unit of the Gendarmerie giving the latter the excuse they had been waiting for to hit back. This incident did however mark the end of the crisis. Mobutu, now intent on putting up a good show for the conference of the Organisation of African Unity he had persuaded his fellow African leaders to hold in Kinshasa, wielded the stick he could have used at any time if he had wanted. To quote my own reports again: 'The Paras moved, with wives, concubines, baggage and the lot to Shinkolobwe ... in an ugly mood, committing another atrocity in Jadotville *en route*.' But they and their officers and Manzikala were gone and, though the mercenary threat remained, Katanga and Elisabethville breathed again. Attwood and Stump were each awarded the MBE for their bravery and devotion to duty, and rightly so.

A new young Governor, Paluku, took over in early September fresh from the South Kivu and Kongo Central, where he had a reasonably good reputation. One of his first acts was to assemble the Consuls and tell us – to quote my report – 'Mobutu had instructed him that peace and security must be restored to Katanga; this was to be his first and main work. He wanted our cooperation in pacifying the foreign community and would be at our disposal at any time. Law, order and justice would be maintained in the proper way, not by unauthorised forces, military or civil, taking things into their own hands. He, as the sole decision maker, under the central Government, was determined to see to that. He had already instructed General Nzoigba in this sense, and had laid it down that henceforth neither troops nor police should carry arms, anywhere in Katanga, when on patrol or walking out. Arms should be confined to barracks and police should henceforth only carry batons.' I commented: 'This is quite a revolution here, and much to the good if soldiers and police will obey. At our Consular request, Paluku has today published the substance of his declaration to us and these measures for all to read.' We remained wary, but it was welcome news. Paluku remained as good as his word. Crisis six was over.

Throughout this period, from the time Schramme issued his ultimatum to Mobutu from Bukavu in early August to in fact early November, the mercenary and gendarmerie rebels in the Kivu made no move, other than to conduct stand-off battles with ANC there. Mobutu meanwhile emerged from the OAU conference strengthened by African support. Under the aegis of the International Red Cross, unofficial negotiations were engaged with Schramme and by the end of October, we knew from those contacts that the force was planning to pull out into Rwanda in early November. Suddenly, however, peace was shattered again, and in Katanga we were into crisis number seven. On 1 November, a new mercenary invasion force, headed by a restored Colonel Denard, appeared out of Angola into south-west Katanga heading for the key mining town of Kolwezi and, supposedly, Elisabethville. Panic returned to the region and particularly the main towns. There was a substantial exodus of the foreign community and Katangans to countries around and beyond. I had to 'thin out' the women and children of the British community again, even though some, like the Consulate wives and children, had only returned the previous week. I advised them this time to stay close in Zambia as I could not see how this mercenary threat could last long. Within days it was clear there were no more than 100 involved, and that it was a last throw by the mercenaries, paid by Tshombe's patrons to support Schramme and his force in the Kivu. It was known Schramme had been calling on Denard for some time to return and at least create a diversion from Angola. But, when it came it was too little and too late and, under pressure from the ANC, Denard's lot vanished back into Angola within the week.

This time, under the new Governor, the authorities kept their heads in Elisabethville and most of Katanga. There were no incidents, no curfews, and no closure of frontiers – a most welcome development of responsibility by the Congolese Authorities. In the area of conflict in the south-west, however, it was the all-too-familiar story of razed villages, murders, rapes and looting, led by the Paras, and thousands of local people were forced to flee temporarily into the bush or across into Angola and Zambia. A few European residents were killed or wounded in the process. Fortunately, once again, no member of the British community fell victim, although the large Garanganzi Mission at Kasaji and smaller one at Mutshatsha only escaped (on my and mercenary advice) in the nick of time and found everything looted when they were able to return. We had a whip-round the community to help them, but they would need much more from their supporters at home.

In reporting on this invasion I concluded: 'The expedition may have given Denard some personal satisfaction at least in so far as it may have saved him from having his throat cut by the embittered mercenaries of Bukavu when they meet again in the bars of Europe. The expedition failed to prompt Mobutu into withdrawing ANC troops from Bukavu but at least it tried. It may also have given satisfaction to the Portuguese Angolan services, who have for so long borne the brunt of rebel Angolan attacks from the Congo. But it is difficult to see what satisfaction it can have given Denard's paymasters, if they be Tomas Tshombe and his friends. It has brought nothing but added misery to their fellow tribesmen of west Katanga.' Schramme and his force in the Kivu decided there and then to quit. They crossed into Rwanda, where they were disarmed and interned. The mercenary led rebellion was over. The cost to the sponsors was reckoned to be in the millions of dollars (a lot of money in those days) and, coupled with Mobutu's gross mismanagement, the cost to the Congolese economy was undoubtedly immense.

In a report before this final crisis I wrote:

In the past eighteen months this region has been through six major crises ... Three have involved closure of the frontiers making the Europeans hostages. The latest in July and August, have involved bloodshed. All have been accompanied by waves of arrests, interrogations, frequent beatings and, in one degree or another, looting. The latest missed massacre by a hairsbreadth. Racial hatred has been created and whipped up to fever pitch. The mob has been held at bay only with difficulty. The economy has degenerated visibly. Twelve Governors and Acting Governors have come and gone. Paluka is the thirteenth. In Union Minère/Gecomin four Directors-General have come and gone. Cayron is the fifth. The European population has fallen from an estimated 30/40,000 to an estimated 15/20,000, that is by half or more. But that is still a large number remaining ... It is a remarkable exercise in tenacity. Katanga was settler country before Congo independence. There are European families going two (and more) generations back, and the spaciousness, climate, good living and good money of pre-independence days are still fresh in many minds. It is quick money, when it can be made, that holds some. It is property, pensions, memories and inertia that hold the majority. Some are already returning after the recent crises. But it is fewer every time and no observer can recall so many really leaving for good this time ... Many could be replaced by the Congolese with an effort (of training) but that effort is required from the Congolese as much as, if not more than from the European employers ... Compared with what it was and what it could become again under good Government, Katanga is a sorry picture ... I have never myself seen anywhere a region like Katanga so fabulously blessed with riches but so reduced to poverty by mismanagement.

I left Elisabethville the following February, by which time it was back to the deceptively calm and pleasant land we had found on arrival two years before. Ann went ahead with the children and Gillian to start the process of adoption of our second daughter we had already named Kate. My next posting was to be Ottawa in Canada. We found Britain not much of a country to go back to at that time, with strikes, devaluation, foot-and-mouth disease and snow, snow and snow. But, as Ann wrote home from Zambia in early November: 'We all went back to Lubumbashi [from evacuation] at the end of October, got settled in, and then the invasion from Angola exploded, and we had to bundle into the car at short notice and come all the way down here again ... Really an awful bore, as the house we had occupied earlier was no longer free – so we had to be taken in by kind souls, all in one little room with mattresses on the floor ... and then move to a rather nasty little place ... All this moving about has been very unsettling and exhausting ... and I hope we have no more before the time comes for us to fly home.' Fortunately they had a house of our own to go to, in Guildford, for the first time. But they had had a rough time.

My final few weeks in Katanga were a little fraught for other reasons. I finally found a better and more secure residence in town and had to knock that into shape and make the move before I left. Then the FO Inspector chose that of all times to make his periodic visit, requiring volumes of paper work in preparation for him and of course hospitality for him and his secretary. Then the FO Under-Secretary, John Henniker, was coming and as he was a colleague I much respected as well as being the FO big cheese on Africa I went to some trouble to prepare. But that was wasted effort, for he could not come in the end. Then finally, Ambassador Cotton insisted on coming in my final week which, with great respect to him (a splendid diplomatic phrase that!), was untimely. I had warned him I was without wife, in a half-equipped new dwelling, in the midst of an inspection, and of farewells and packing. But he came and I am afraid we nearly came to blows. Indeed Attwood claimed afterwards he thought I was going to sock the Ambassador – with good reason, he loyally added. That would really have been one for the Diplomatic Service record book! But I suppose I had about reached the limit of endurance, I did not feel we had had much support from him and to have him come commanding obeisance at that stage and in those circumstances seemed to me inconsiderate. In any case I believe a Consul, like an Ambassador, should be left to his own farewells. However he received a knighthood before retirement and I was glad of that.

I had many nice bouquets before leaving. But the two I most appreciated were, first of all the farewell party the Golf Club gave me which was attended by the new Katanga Governor and all, and they thanked me for all I had done for the whole community during the troubles. They gave me a travelling clock because, although I am normally quite punctual, I never seemed there to be able to get to the tee quite on time.

The second and even more unexpected compliment came in a letter the General Secretary of the Miners' International Federation sent to the Foreign Secretary George Brown extending the 'thanks and deepest gratitude' of that august body 'on behalf of the Miners in 36 countries affiliated to this International', to me for gaining the release from arrest and rough handling by the Security authorities of Jim Roberts, their Africa liaison officer, and to Ann and me for giving him sanctuary in our home for two weeks while I negotiated with the Congolese authorities for his release. Roberts was a remarkable man who piloted himself in a tiny plane around Africa but had drifted off course in Angola and landed at Lubumbashi airport at the very moment the authorities were expecting mercenaries to drop out of the sky from all directions. The Foreign Office subsequently wrote to me: 'Your handling of this case was admirable and is a classic example of what a Consul can do for the protection of his nationals given his firmness of purpose and good relations with local officials. We intend making your report required reading in the Department for future Consular courses.' I do not suppose many budding Consuls ever read it. But that letter to me was the FO at its most thoughtful, and it was nice to receive.

CHAPTER 18

# Canada

# 1968–1970

CANADA was the very antithesis of the Congo. If its climate of long winter, short summer, colourful fall but no spring compared unfavourably, most everything else offered home from home with the added thrill of reaching North America at last. As I landed at Montreal it was the fulfilment of an ambition to see the New World, and in the two years I was to spend there Canada did not disappoint. Overshadowed though it was by its United States neighbour politically and economically, it was still larger geographically and had its own distinct virtues of quiet determination and common sense. It could also occasionally laugh at itself. It was a Canadian journalist who said recently on a BBC television programme: 'Canadians are very forgiving people. We even say thank you to our bank machines.' But it was Churchill who commented away back in 1939: 'That long frontier from the Atlantic to Pacific Ocean, guarded only by neighbourly respect and honourable obligations, is an example to every country and a pattern for the future of the world.' That was a sincere compliment to the United States, too, of course.

No one perhaps would call Canada's capital city Ottawa, where I was to reside and work, the 'flesh-pots', like Paris or Rome, but the country was to be that to me after the jungle of the Congo. Broad and long though it was, its leading cities, Montreal and Toronto, were only hours away by road as were the Great Lakes, Niagara Falls and indeed the United States. And, with jet airliners then coming into use, the prairies, the rocky mountains and the Pacific on the one side and the great St Lawrence Seaway and the Atlantic on the other were now only hours away by flight. (The Yukon and North-west Territories were still another matter.) My job at the British High Commission (the title given to Embassies in Commonwealth countries) was to be Head of Chancery, as at Rome. But I had learnt my lesson, and determined this time to find a way of travelling at least occasionally, instead of being just the High Commission's sitting bull.

My first concern had to be the family. After two separations in the Congo on account of the evacuations, we now had to be apart again for most of five months while Ann prepared at home for our new baby Kate and fulfilled the adoption rules. I caught up with her and the children for a month together in Guildford between posts but then had to go ahead to Ottawa to meet the wishes of the FO and High Commissioner. We were fortunate that the colleague in Personnel handling our transfer, Frank Mills, was familiar with the adoption process and the FO had a Welfare Section who helped liaise with the Adoption Society for us. Without them both, I do not think we would have achieved it. The ponderous DSAO, Mills and Welfare Section apart, seemed too weighed down with their chains of moves to adjust to such considerations. I am sure the old Personnel set-up would have done so without fuss. It was more flexible. I hope today's equivalent is too. However, with the noble help of the Adoption Society, we achieved our wish for a third child by mid-January, the formalities were completed by early May and my wife and the children, now aged five, three, and five months, were able to join me in Ottawa at the end of May. As they sailed up the St Lawrence and docked at Montreal, it was, we hoped, the end of our trials, at least for the time being.

While at home I was surprised to find that my appointment to a leading Commonwealth post brought crumbs of recognition not then accorded to the equivalent FO posts. First came an invitation to attend a BBC TV course to learn how to deal with interviewers (English-speaking that is). One of them threw an outrageous googly at me, as is their wont, but rather smothered me with flattery when I threw it back. Canada was very much in the news at that time, with the emergence as possible Liberal leader and Prime Minister of an enigmatic French-Canadian, Pierre Trudeau. Echoing some of the idiocies about him then appearing in the British popular press, my interviewer asked what would happen if he turned out to be a communist. I knew nothing about him and indeed very little about modern Canada, having had no time yet to brief myself after the Congo. So I resorted to asking him if he could conceive of Canada, of all our allies in the cold war, changing sides? To his credit, he applauded that and I learnt my first lesson in TV interviews: watch for the googly and slog it back for six if you can. The great ones like Robin Day, Ludovic Kennedy and even David Frost did not need to play games like that to extract a story. They did it by diplomacy. Some of their belligerent successors today would in my view do well to go back to those first principles. But I digress. My experience of being interviewed on TV and Radio did not advance much beyond that BBC short course until I changed career. Diplomats were not often in those days dragged before the public gaze as

With Ann, Julia, Robert and Katie in Ottawa in the autumn of 1968.

they are today, and Canadian interviewers were generally very kindly anyhow.

The other tokens of recognition we unexpectedly received after the announcement of my appointment, were an approach by *Who's Who* to appear in their hallowed pages and an invitation from Her Majesty The Queen to a reception at Buckingham Palace. We had only met her once before, at Rome, although I had also met Prince Philip many years before at Jedda. This was how Ann described the reception:

It was so easy, so elegantly informal that it was difficult to believe we were doing anything out of the ordinary. We hired a car and driver and at 6pm drove into Buckingham Palace yard, then a second great courtyard and into an inner rectangle, with an entrance between pillars and steps ... Huge red-carpeted hall with smiling equerries standing under chandeliers with lists in their hands to welcome us. We were amazed to find there were to be only 40 guests – not an enormous reception after all. Up a great branched staircase with a large gentleman in a Scots kilt to direct us to take the right hand sweep of the stairs – and then, at the top, finding ourselves in a long and splendid place, which turned out to be the Picture Gallery and which made me feel at first that somehow we had strayed into an Art Gallery – long polished floor and dazzling chandeliers and huge oils on the walls ... Here the guests gathered and the Gentlemen of the Household rather neatly and unobtrusively split the 40 guests into 5 groups of 8, making introductions so that no one was standing alone. About 10 minutes of quiet talking in groups, then doors opened and we were asked to go through, in pairs, husbands on the left side – I saw why when, forming up in the short line, I saw the Queen and Prince Philip standing to receive us at the entrance to a white and gold drawing room. As the names were called out the husband went forward first to be greeted, then the wife followed. Two of the couples got mixed up and there was some gentle laughter on all sides – Prince Philip greatly enjoying the joke to relax the atmosphere. (Fortunately it wasn't Mr & Mrs Hugh-Jones who got split up!) The Queen looked surprisingly informal and almost girlish in a yellow silk dress (skirt just nicely on the knee!!) and black shoes and bag, and her hair in the same style she wore during the war when she was still a girl – rather large sausagey curls (I felt she needed a good Parisian coiffeur!) A lovely smile for everyone. I remembered my curtsey, but when she said 'How do you do' I automatically replied 'How do you do', quite forgetting to murmur 'Your Majesty', and we all passed on into the White Drawing Room, where waiters (white-gloved and very be-medalled) started handing round drinks and trays of delicious canapés. The whole room dominated by an enormous painting of Princess Alexandra in a white dress on the far wall. Then it was just like any other cocktail party except that the Queen and Prince Philip were circulating among the chattering guests. Hugh had quite a chat with Prince Philip – But not about the Congo. He was down on the guest list as Head of Chancery Ottawa – so our hosts had not been briefed that far! Well it was all an experience – and after that we dined with Margaret McClure Smith and the Canadian High Commissioner – Ritchie – a charming and amusing man who told us a lot about Ottawa.

At the High Commission in Ottawa I was to find things different there too, far plumper and more easy going than any top grade mission I had encountered in our Service. My predecessor Bonar Sykes warned me that he had been the first Head of Chancery they had had there, replacing a second Minister (the first being Deputy High Commissioner). He had been responsible for administration and co-ordination, but not head of the political section. A Commonwealth Service Counsellor, Eleanor Emery, did that. But she would be leaving and the idea was that I should double both jobs. The DSAO Head of Personnel in London told me this too but rather weakly asked me to 'take the reins only when the present rider is willing and then only gently'. What I found was an incumbent who had spent much of her Commonwealth Service career dealing with Canada, loved the country and the people, and did not want to leave. There used to be a saying in the Foreign Service that three years was about the maximum anyone should spend in any one country; by that time you had probably grown either to love it or to hate it, and in either case could no longer be objective about it. There was a lot of truth in that. My new colleague in Ottawa was an able Commonwealth officer and went on to be High Commissioner to Botswana. But, as always when a Head Office shies away from making clean personnel changes, it is the people down the line who suffer. It was not kind on her and it took time and pain to take over. I was nonetheless able to make a grand tour of much of Canada's main provincial capitals before doing so. My only regret was that I never reached the Maritime Provinces – not anyway until a golfing visit to Prince Edward Island twenty years later – and I never reached the Yukon or North West Territories. But most Canadians in Ottawa never had the chance to do so either. I was very fortunate to tour their great country as I did. Come to think of it, I wonder how many Civil Servants and Politicians in London ever have the opportunity to get to know their own country, Britain, extensively?

My predecessor in Ottawa also advised me: 'The other main difference in the office here that is likely to strike you is that the process of integration is still not complete. There are at least four traditions or habits at work – the old Commonwealth Office, the Board of Trade, the old Commonwealth Office Information Service, and the Foreign Service. There is also a large crop of Service (Defence) people, a small British Council office and a substantial Pensions office. So there is a good deal of co-ordinating to be done. There is also an important co-ordinating/liaison function which the Head of Chancery has to perform between the office here and the eight other British Government Offices (not Consulates!) across Canada.' He was right. The High Commission office turned out to be a large brick and glass building, built post-war on a prime site in the centre of Ottawa. It was divided into compartments of people, many from home but many more locally engaged, seemingly representing not so much one Government Service as a conglomerate of home departments. They included, besides the CRO and FO, the Board of Trade, the Commonwealth Information Service, the Ministry of Defence (Navy, Army and Air Force), Defence Equipment (a euphemism for arms sales promotion), Science and Technology, Social Security and the Passport Office, over 300 people in all counting our Trade Commissioners in the provincial capitals. I had not been sent there as hatchet man but to carry on pruning and pulling it together. That was a full time job, as my predesessor had found. But by dint of reform and reorganisation I was able to get it down steadily to half time, leaving me the other half for the political work.

The High Commissioner was a Board of Trade man, Sir Henry Lintott. He had played a part in the first British negotiations to try to get into the European Community and had a strong supporting wife. But he was leaving on retirement that summer and craved only a quiet retreat to his home and garden in Sussex. He was replaced in the autumn by Sir Colin Crowe, a Foreign Office man (third generation in fact, I believe), a former FO Chief of Administration, described by a senior Whitehall colleague as 'simple but shrewd' and, with his very supportive wife, as nice a boss as one could hope to have in the Service. I had known him when first entering the FO twenty years before – and he had not changed his congenial and unassuming manner. He was in fact standing proof that diplomatic dignity does not demand suave aloofness, as many people seem to think. It can sit just as easily, and indeed more pleasingly, on a smiling face – provided of course there is substance behind it! Nelson Mandela must be the supreme example. Crowe was not in his league, but he was a good man and a popular High Commissioner.

His deputy, Tom Rogers, was also an FO man, with a remit to concentrate on trade promotion. I had known him too in the early post-war years when, the roles reversed, he was specialising on political affairs and I on trade and payments. He had been in the Indian Civil Service when India and Pakistan achieved independence, and then transferred to the Foreign Service. His reserved manner concealed a clear head and a life of roving adventure in the Persian Gulf on official public duty during World War II. His book *Great Game, Grand Game* makes interesting reading. He went on to be Ambassador to Colombia, and we stayed in touch for many years. His replacement, just before I left, was a Commonwealth Service man, George Whitehead, and he went on to be Deputy head of Administration in the merged FCO. His Commercial Counsellor, Robin Gray, from the Board of Trade, was also an able man and a little dynamo to boot. So were his two successive assistants, Derek Thomas who went on eventually to be Minister in Washington and John Guinness who rose to be Chairman of British Nuclear Fuels Ltd. They were a bright bunch on that side of the house. So was the head of the large Passport section, Ken Kelley, and the later Administration Officer, Lowe. The Chancery and Information Sections were not so well endowed, except for one young FO man Donald MacLeod, scion of the MacLeods, but I think he retired early to help look after the clan. The Commonwealth Service was not, in my limited experience of it, strong on the political side. Where the High Commission did have strength was among the locally-engaged. Having a common language with the Canadians and a large emigré British community, we were fortunate alongside the other posts I had known, in being able to draw on so much local talent.

It was also our good fortune, of course, that our job was to conduct friendly relations with one of our staunchest allies. An idealist friend of the family, Raymond Field, husband of one of my father's star pupils, Betty, wrote to my by now 80 year old mother: 'I am surprised that Wynn likes Canada. Now that is a very stupid thing to write in one sense, Canada being so big and I not so very familiar with his personal preferences. It is however in such contrast to Africa, where the field of intergovernmental relations, the emergent problems of new nation states as well as the tremendous economic potential would seem to me to make that part of the world unique in opportunity for our diplomatic resources. I know that Wynn saw great opportunities there and that he must have had some scaring experiences in the Congo – a country from which we now seem to be more remote than the moon. His duties in Canada must be very different, and I am sure that you are greatly relieved at his living in a more stable society. His family must be a great joy to you all and a constant source of interest.'

They were. The children adored their grandparents on both sides and wrote messages with every one of our letters, while they, on their side were as proud of them as only grandparents can be. We hoped they would be able to visit us in Canada but sadly that was not to be. None in the end could make the journey. What Raymond Field saw as my preferences were of course right. Canada was a country not only of geographical greatness but enormous potential and challenge for those bent on enterprise or the outback. For a diplomat, engaged as I was essentially in intergovernmental relations, it turned out to be both gratifying and frustrating.

The frustrating part, to get that off the chest first, was not so much to do with Canada as with our own Service and domestic problems. I have always enjoyed administration. It has a satisfaction of its own in achieving practical results. Faced with the reforms needed in the Ottawa High Commission but not being in charge and anyhow bound by a home policy towards merger of the Services of softly-softly-catchy-monkey, it was distinctly thwarting, especially when we knew government economic policy at home was in tatters (that was before Roy Jenkins became Chancellor of the Exchequer) and the cry was to save every penny on foreign expenditure. As in previous posts I was prepared to fight against false economies tooth and nail. But in a hard currency area I did find it extravagant that we were so flush with home departmental representation, and also bound by such out-dated procedures as to be obliged to provide large Passport and Pensions services in Ottawa for British emigrés. It was interesting to find that there were broadly two categories of them to deal with. The first, who rarely bothered us, were those who had come to Canada because they wanted to come to Canada. Most took out citizenship, became Canadians and made their lives there. The second, who did bother us, were those who came to Canada simply to get away from Britain. Many seemed to live in the past, forever complaining about their home country (which is why they left), but complaining also about their country of adoption Canada, because they had come for the wrong reasons, their own fault. As they remained British we had to maintain large Passport and Pensions offices in Ottawa primarily for them. Today I trust these services are provided from home augmented by field consular offices, as in non-Commonwealth countries. The old Commonwealth Service, before merger, was in many ways very backward.

A second frustration lay in the conditions of living we found awaiting us. Someone once described Ottawa as a delightful capital village, and so in many ways it was. Created for the federal government, symbolically sited on the Ontario-Quebec border between English-speaking and French-speaking Canada, gracefully overlooking the Ottawa river and the Rideau canal, it contained little else but government and parliament. But it was rapidly expanding with ancillary occupations and housing had not kept pace. Nor had domestic help especially for children. There was a large preponderance of single women employed as civil service secretaries, Ottawa men all seemed to get married young, and there was no social life after 10pm. Our few single ladies in the High Commission generally found life dull. Our families, on the other hand, saw it as a lovely post if only they could find housing and help. The position I found, exacerbated by inadequate allowances, was that most High Commission wives were tied to domesticity, often unable to help diplomatically, and something like a fifth of the home-based staff were at any one time searching for somewhere to live. It was not an acceptable situation but would take a major effort and time to resolve.

My own was a case in point. My predecessor had spent a year finding a house suitable for family and entertaining but the owner then wanted it back. All I could find in time for the arrival of my family was a wooden cabin up the Gatineau river at Larrimac where no one could sneeze without the foundations and walls shaking and after dark it was a struggle to keep out the blackfly and mosquitoes. We just camped. But in truth, the children loved it, and so did we, it was a beautiful spot, on the river, and we had a nanny temporarily at that time. We were also able to entertain there with barbacues and the like. Canadians enjoyed the outdoors and loved log-cabins. We found why, it was fun – for the short Summer. Come the 'Fall' and Winter however, we had to move into town and all we were able to find there was a small house which, to accommodate our family and our entertainment commitments, I could only describe home as 'a sardine tin'. It served us, uncomfortably, for a year. I wrote: 'The housing situation is the worst I have known in any post ... Everyone just fends for themselves with a resultant appalling amount of frustration and waste of man-hours. I've now geared the whole office and London to deal with it as it should be, and am also seeking to persuade London to go in for a policy of buying a proportion instead of always renting at increasing rents.' It did improve as a result although it was mainly our successors who benefitted.

My third source of quiet disgruntlement, common to all colleagues of my post-war generation in the Service at that time, was to find old friends in the Canadian External Affairs Service (as they called their Foreign Service) and in the Diplomatic Corps in Ottawa filling more senior positions than mine because their Services had moved with the times while ours was still administratively stuck in the mud. Modernisation of our Service was to come with a new fundamental review in 1968/69 but not soon enough for many of us. The Canadians fortunately understood this and I was able to see and entertain Government Ministers, senior Officials, Ambassadors, Editors, University Principals, Provincial Premiers and leading businessmen without problem as the job demanded. Canadians took people as they found them and – unlike the attitude that once plagued English society, 'if you do not find them, don't bother' – the Canadians liked people and bothered. They were also open and hospitable (like the Americans). I believe they still are. Characteristics like that do not change. At any rate that is how we found them and, domestic problems aside, it made for a happy time there.

This was the gratifying side. There could not be many capital cities in the world where, in my first week, attending a reception by the High Commissioner for Canadian defence chiefs at his historic Earnscliffe residence, I found myself afterwards taken off by some of the guests for a scrambled egg supper cooked by an Air Force General and served by an Admiral. Like me they were temporarily wifeless. But it was the spontaneous Canadian hospitality that warmed the cockles. Gerry Edwards, the General, went into history not only for his Air Force exploits but in retirement, as Captain of his British Columbian golf club, when on Captain's drive-in he decided to cede place to his wife Ethel who protested she had never swung a club (as he knew) but proceeded – it was an opening par three – to strike a hole-in-one! It cost him a Canadian dollar or two! Bob Timbrell, the Admiral, also had a distinguished war including skippering one of the little boats that so heroically brought back the troops from Dunkirk in 1940. We still keep in touch through mutual American friends and have even been known to golf Turnberry, Prestwick, Blairgowrie and St Andrews together.

That was years later in a select group of Anglo-American-Canadian golfing maniacs my long standing American friend Mac Johnson and I formed a decade and a half ago and we still meet annually one side of the Atlantic or the other. That friendship was also a product of Ottawa. Mac Johnson was Counsellor (and later Minister) at the American Embassy. We together created a Diplomatic Corps golf society that flourished each summer with matches and socials against the joint services at Canadian

Forces Headquarters (the navy, army and air force being then in the process of merger); the diplomats of External Affairs; and the Ministers, MPs, and Senators of Parliament. They were jolly affairs, regularly augmented by good friends like Jaffrey Wilkins of the Civil Service Commission, ready to be soldier, sailor, politician or diplomat as needed. But they were also keenly competitive. My co-founder still likes to recall a needle foursomes match with the Parliamentarians when he and I, playing last for the Diplomatic Corps, were one stroke up on the 18th hole against the renowned Trade Union leader and Minister of Industry (and discoverer of Mr Trudeau) Jean Marchand and his MP partner. Faced with the crucial putt, he recounts that he turned to me and said, 'Shall we go for it or play diplomatic chicken?' I abruptly replied, so he claims: 'Rule Britannia!' and so impressed was he that he sank the putt without ado, giving the Diplomatic Corps victory and the Canadian Parliament cause to swear they would get their own back next time. I think the story has become a little apocryphal over the years, but it is a happy reminder of the spirit in which those encounters took place. It was in fact the spirit of Ottawa of those days. I feel sure it still is.

Another great pleasure was to run into so many old friends, the product I suppose by then of twenty-one years in the Diplomatic Service. The Deputy Under-Secretary in External Affairs turned out to be my old cricketing colleague in Paris, Basil Robinson – later to become head of the Canadian Native Affairs department, a test of any man's diplomatic skill. The senior official charged with drafting Mr Trudeau's foreign policy review, turned out to be my companion in arms at our first United Nations Conference in 1948, John Halstead. A handsome Ottawa hostess I encountered socially turned out to be Diana Kirkwood, wife of David, by then a senior official in the Privy Council, the central department of the Canadian government, but when I knew them, newcomers to Paris like me. The first secretary in the Nigerian Embassy, Emanuel Oba, had been one of the Commonwealth trainee diplomats I had been commissioned to induct at the Rome Embassy. His Ambassador, Eddy Enahoro, had opened the Nigerian Embassy there, and we remain in touch with him and his wife Katie to this day. The newly arrived French Ambassador, Pierre Siraud, turned out to be none other than my colleague at Conakry. If the world is a small place, the diplomatic world is even smaller, and that was of course one of its attractions – and I hope still is today.

The basic job of a High Commission, like that of any Embassy, apart from trade promotion, was to follow the politics and economics of the country and foster good relations with the government and people of influence at all levels. There was scope for all that in Canada. The 'Trudeau phenomenon', as it was generally called, had just hit the country. Born of a Québécois father and half Scottish mother, Pierre Elliott Trudeau was something new to the Canadian scene, a French Canadian of the modern

generation with a federal outlook and the talent to become Federal Prime
Minister. He had money from his father's industry, education from the
Quebec Jesuits and the universities of Montreal, Harvard, the Sorbonne
and the London School of Economics, a 1960s image of motorbike and
sandals, a bachelor charisma, and an erudite diction in English and French.
But he also had a mysterious reserve. He was an enigma. The Prime
Minister was still Mike Pearson, a statesman of world renown but wise
enough to make way for younger blood when the Provinces started complaining of the Ottawa 'Old Guard'. He had announced his intention to
retire and indicated his preference for Trudeau to succeed him. A convention of the governing Liberal Party had been called for early April, to
be held in Ottawa. I arrived in time to attend it, and rather wished I
hadn't. It turned out to be pantomine North American style with the
candidates in turn marching into a converted sports hall, accompanied by
a drum beat and troupe of majorettes. Each addressed the throng of Party
delegates from all over the country, said to be 1000 strong but many clearly
found the corridors and caucus meetings more interesting, for the hall
never seemed full. However, after four ballots and seven hours of voting
Trudeau won on a platform of 'one nation' (meaning Quebec should remain
in Canada but Canada should be bilingual and bicultural); reform of
government (meaning, among other things, that Members of Parliament
should be given work in committees instead of wrangling on the floor);
and a 'Just Society' (which some took to mean socialism but others saw
as progressive liberalism). He had in fact already shown some of his colours
as Pearson's Minister of Justice, in promoting civil liberties and pragmatic
fairness.

Trudeau's rise to power, after only three years in Parliament, had been
meteoric. He immediately called a General Election for June, and secured
an absolute Liberal majority, for the first time in ten years. Flamboyant
premiers were not unknown in Canada, especially at Provincial level in
the West and Newfoundland, and there had been a Conservative Prime
Minister ten years previously, John Diefenbaker, who had blazed a romantic
trail. But in the words of one of the Provincial leaders I met on my tour
in May: 'Trudeau was in a class on his own. He was Diefenbaker with
bells on.' He turned out of course to be far more than that, and went on
to win three successive general elections, losing momentarily to the Conservatives in 1979 but leading the Liberals back to power again the following
year. His greatest achievement was to hold Quebec within the confeder-
ation, which some might say gives Canada its root distinction from the
United States. He thereby saved Canadian unity, against the separatist
tendencies of that Province which had emerged from General de Gaulle's
mischievous encouragement and, more profoundly, from its own quiet
revolution of the 1960s. It was then that the Liberals had gained power
in Quebec and replaced the dead hand of the old Quebec regime and

catholic church. But that revolution had also released a new assertive generation of 'free Quebec' protagonists and they were to become Canada's and Trudeau's problem for years to come.

Between Trudeau's assumption of the Prime Ministership and the General Election I was able to secure agreement and fit in a grand tour of the leading six provinces – Quebec, Ontario, Manitoba, Sasketchewan, Alberta and British Columbia. It was May and, from the Atlantic to the Rockies, the land was awakening from the long winter. Through the good offices of our so-called Trade Commissioners in each of the provincial capitals, I was able to meet everyone and anyone of importance from the Premiers and Lt. Governers downwards, and enjoyed frank and informative talks with each and all – except one, I shall come to, in British Columbia. We talked about their provincial problems and politics, federal problems, and relations with Britain. Their openness was refreshing after my experiences of the Middle East, Africa and even Europe. So was their interest in Britain and their sympathy with us in the economic crisis we were then suffering. The main topics were inevitably the economic recession at the time, which was widespread, Trudeaumania and Quebec. I found the general attitude to the new Prime Minister ranged widely, from wariness in Quebec to enthusiasm in Ontario to feigned indifference in British Columbia, although no one professed to have made him out. That was before Trudeau's grand electoral tour, but I do not think it changed much throughout his first two years. He remained a puzzling Prime Minister. I found the same marked difference of interest across the Provinces in the subject of Quebec. It was obviously intense in Quebec itself, but otherwise ranged from deep concern in Ontario to almost blind indifference in the west. 'Canada has had enough of Quebec,' declared the Premier of Saskatchewan when I asked his opinion. 'If the Quebecois want to go their own way they can do so. English-speaking Canada can get along without them.' His name was Thatcher, and a right die-hard he was too! The Alberta Lt. Governor, a Scot by the name of His Honour Dr Grant MacEwan, expressed more interest in Scottish and Welsh nationalism than in Quebec. Premier (or Prime Minister as he preferred to be called) Wacky Bennett of British Columbia simply professed indifference. 'Quebec is on the other side of the Rockies and of no concern to British Columbia,' he declared.

Mr Bennett was a Canadian apart. He had been Social Credit boss of beautiful British Columbia seemingly for ever and I think his father was before him. I had to be vetted by his Permanent Secretary before he would receive me. I found him – to quote my report – 'very much the centrepiece of British Columbia politics, full of blah and vigour, manipulating the strings with remarkable application. His office and those around him bore the air of high, if conspiratorial efficiency – in marked contrast to the easy-going informality of the offices of his Prairie counterparts.' Unlike everyone I had met in the other Provinces, he refused to recognise there was a recession. But so did a prominent Vancouver newspaper editor I met. 'British Columbia is fortunate to be endowed with everything; you name it, we have it,' he claimed – with some justice perhaps.

One of my most interesting discoveries of that tour was how confederal Canada worked – a matter of relevance and interest to Britain one day when we would finally come around to accept the wisdom of Gladstone's devolved regionalism. The Canadian constitution had been described as 'the loosest in the World'. Yet it worked and held together, despite the vastness of the country, the thinness of the population stretched mainly along the border with the United States (and fewer in numbers than the state of California), the wide range of outlooks, the multiracialism (Inuits and Indians, Chinese and others as well as Quebecois) and the seemingly perpetual arguments over Quebec and the Federal/State division of powers. The answer, I think, as I put in our 1969 Annual Report, was: 'Canada is a greatly favoured country. She is remote from the flashpoints of the world and sheltered by the United States. She has enormous area and vast resources. She is one of the wealthest countries in the world and growing richer by leaps and bounds, yet as she goes into the '70s there is deep introspection as to whether she can survive. Can she meet the challenge from Quebec and hold off the separatists? Can she prevent herself being submerged by the United States? Has she a role to play in the world? The answer to these questions must be yes. There is a cohesiveness and tenacity about Canadians that is often under-estimated, most of all perhaps by themselves. They need leadership and strong Government to give the affirmative answers. 1970 should show whether the Trudeau Government have it in them to provide it.'

The successive Trudeau Governments assuredly did have it in them and so, happily, in varying degrees, have their successor governments. The lesson I learnt on that tour was that however much the Provinces kicked against Ottawa and the Federal government, they wanted strong federal government. It was Premier Thatcher of Saskatchewan who was constrained to admit that, adding: 'At least with Trudeau I get a yes or a no, mostly no, whereas when I came away from Pearson I had to stop and think what had been agreed.' That remark hardly did justice to Pearson, to whom Canada, the Atlantic Alliance and the Commonwealth owed so much. But confederalism and strong central government were to be proven afresh by Trudeau's Canada to be compatible and healthily so.

The related discovery of that tour was to find that having one political party in power at federal level and different political parties in power in the different provinces also worked. Canada showed it was not necessary to have political uniformity as those opponents of devolution in Britain protested. At that time the Canadian Federal Government was Liberal and so was Quebec (although its own very independent variety), Ontario was Conservative, and so was Manitoba. Saskatchewan was right-wing Liberal,

British Columbia and Alberta were Social Credit, and the four Maritime Provinces were each something else. It was quite common for people to vote for one party in the federal elections and another in the provincial elections – just as, in fact, people often do in Britain today between national, local and European elections. For my personal preference I would of course like to see them all vote Liberal! But, short of that, we should heed the Canadian example, which is – or was, in my observation – not what our psephologists like to call 'tactical voting' but genuine voting for people and policies they considered best for their different levels of government. Since the Scotland and Wales Acts of 1998 we are at last beginning to see this in Britain, although it has been evident in local government for years. Anyhow, that tour of Canada taught me much, and I like to think my reports opened a window or two in the High Commission too.

Prime Minister Trudeau was not always a comfortable partner in the North Atlantic Alliance or the Commonwealth, as Pearson had so long been. He insisted on looking at everything afresh, commissioning reviews and task forces on a scale not even the 1997 Blair government of Britain matched. We all know Gaius Petronius Arbiter's alleged observation some time in the first century BC: 'We tend to meet any new situation by reorganising, and a wonderful method it can be for creating the illusion of progress while producing confusion, inefficiency and demoralisation.' Less well known is my own – quite irrelevant – anagram of 'Houses of Parliament': 'Loonies far up Thames!' But the first Trudeau Government were no innocents to management. The backlog of legislation they had inherited from their predecessors was cleared in no time, Parliamentary procedures were reformed, bilingualism was introduced (meaning that French became an official language alongside English), the machinery of government was tightened and the offices of the Prime Minister made almost presidential. When it came to defence and foreign affairs however, our conclusion, in our Annual Review for 1969 was less complimentary: 'It has been an unhappy year. The much touted review of foreign policy has yet to be completed but the review of defence led to the decision to reduce Canadian forces in Europe by half and ... the defence programme has been cut by some 5–10%.' This fulfilled Trudeau's intention from the start to reduce Canada's commitment to NATO. 'There was a feeling that Europe could contribute more, while Canada for her part must look more widely about her, to the Pacific, to the Arctic and to Latin America and not be quite so Europe-orientated as it had been in the past.' Trudeau's Canada also broke ranks with the USA by recognising Communist China (although President Nixon followed not long afterwards). The External Affairs budget was cut drastically, although the country maintained its important contribution to UN and other peace-keeping forces.

Today, in retrospect, those changes were probably fair and timely for Canada. It was a period of world change. There was a world recession, and then the dubious American and European decisions to abandon fixed exchange rates and float currencies. Politically and militarily the United States, leader of the Alliance and Canada's neighbour, was in turmoil with the assassination of Martin Luther King and consequent black riots, the assassination also of the democratic Presidential candidate Robert Kennedy, continuing riots and demonstrations against the war in Vietnam, the advent of President Nixon and the beginning of the process of withdrawal from Vietnam. Trudeau's focus had to be on the American continent, on the repercussions on Canada of events in the USA, on standing up to the big American corporations which were so pervasive, on assuaging but controlling the emergent Quebecois while also maintaining Western Canada on board, above all on maintaining Canadian unity in a rapidly changing world. Before leaving Canada I drafted a report on Quebec, which concluded: 'As an Atlantic ally, close Commonwealth friend and major trading partner, it has always been taken as read that [the maintenance of] Canadian unity is in the British interest. I am sure that this must remain so. And it must remain so in the interest of the Western world as a whole. Canada is an integral part of that world ... However, we must not on any account intervene [in Quebec]. For us as Anglais to do so would be disastrous.' The FCO welcomed and endorsed those conclusions. The term 'Anglais' was how the Quebecois always referred to the British ever since our conquest of French Quebec and Canada in 1759. They had long memories, as we were to find later that year when their extremists kidnapped our official representative in Montreal. Trudeau won through in the end, and also won respect world-wide, including a place for Canada in the elite Group of 7. I am sure that was also warmly welcomed in London. Canada and Britain have always been close friends.

We had many visitors from home in our time at Ottawa, a few personal like Eric and Ann Bruton who never failed to come and see us wherever we were – except in the Congo but that was not for their want of trying. Most of them were however official, and they seemed to come in an endless stream. There were Ministers and officials of any number of home departments come to exchange views with their Canadian counterparts, and there were defence officials, scientists, technologists, industrialists, financiers, reverse brain-drain organisers, cultural event organisers, and the inevitable FO inspectors – my 8th inspection in six posts abroad I calculated. We also had the Foreign Secretary, Michael Stewart, and enjoyed his visit. He was not easy in company but came out with his wife and staff to our cabin on the Gatineau and everyone found him sincere and quietly impressive. I cannot say quite the same of Prime Minister Harold Wilson, when he came. Congenial, cocksure, impressive certainly but perhaps to be judged as much by his entourage as himself. Asked once by someone why he surrounded himself with second-rate advisers he is alleged to have replied, 'I do not need brains around me. I have them myself. I need loyalty.' We had to admire his intellectual and political skill but I for one did not take to him then, or later.

One thing he did do however – apart from winning four elections! – was to appoint in 1968 yet another review of the Diplomatic Service which, unintentionally, was to be of great benefit to the Service in time. Its purpose, ominously, was 'to achieve British overseas representation at lesser cost'. We were rather more heartened when we heard that the Foreign Secretary had secured the appointment to the Commission of Sir Val Duncan, a much travelled and wise chairman of RTZ, Sir Frank Roberts, a former Ambassador to Moscow and live-wire member of countless businesses and good causes in retirement, and Andrew Shonfield, a much-respected Director of the Royal Institute of International Affairs. After preparatory work and interviews at home they set out to visit a variety of posts abroad, beginning with us in Ottawa. They had not wanted to come our way but did so, en route to Washington, in deference to our new High Commissioner, Colin Crowe, as a former Chief of FO administration. Their visit was a near-disaster. I went to Montreal airport to meet them, taking the High Commissioner's gold painted Austin Princess he had inherited from his predecessor, and an old Wolseley saloon and small Hillman pick-up which made up the whole of our so-called car pool. Half way to Ottawa on a gentle hill the Princess slowly choked to a stop. I remember noticing the signs on the side of the road incongruously pointed to villages called Como and Lucerne, and cars passing us turned and laughed at our broken down convoy led by a golden hearse. There was no option but to bundle the drivers and visiting staff off to Como with the pick-up and Austin to fend for themselves, and take the three Commissioners and secretary on in the Wolseley, driving myself.

They had only agreed to stay one night so time was precious. They gamely crowded into the back seat, leaving the lady secretary in the front and, as it was too uncomfortable for any of them to nod off after their Atlantic flight, I thought it might keep them occupied if I seized the opportunity to put to them a few of my own ideas on Service reform. They responded splendidly, doubtless glad of something to talk about instead of the absurdity of our position. I had no need to tell them the High Commission's cars were a disgrace and needed replacing. More important, I put to them first the case, as I saw it, for completing the merger of the Foreign and Commonwealth Offices without further delay, and the early abolition of the DSAO as a high priority. Second, I suggested the abolition of the cumbrous old UK passport and substitution of the simpler computer-printed style used by the Americans and others. Third, I begged them to remove responsibility for officially owned property overseas from the dead hand of the Ministry of Works to an FO or associated Agency. And fourth, I pleaded for more delegation of financial authority from the Treasury to the FO and from the FO to posts. To my agreeable surprise I found them not only interested but enthusiastic on all counts, and we passed the remaining hour of the journey in ardent discussion of each. At their request I even gave them a memorandum on the property question, before they left. I cannot claim responsibility for the outcome but like to think my six-pennyworth on that memorable journey helped. All four proposals appeared in the Commission's final recommendations and were then put into effect (except, temporarily, the passport change as the next Foreign Secretary, Sir Alec Douglas-Home, found it too much for his sentimental taste). In their swipe at the DSAO they declared, in a masterful piece of under-statement: 'We found evidence of over-administration ... and now feel this is a greater danger than under-administration in the past.' Perhaps today's Foreign and Commonwealth Office administration which, from some accounts, has again become bloated, this time by consultants, might want to heed the Duncan Commission advice afresh in this regard.

The Commission report was full of good sense. Above all it at last pointed up the absurd log-jam on promotion, built up since the post-war reforms without redress and now blatantly out of line with the Home Civil Service and everyone else. In particular it told how to deal with it by releasing willing horses, with fair compensation, as the Armed Services had long done. Altogether the report was a breath of fresh air, although inevitably it took a few years for the recommendations to be put into effect. Those three Commissioners and their Secretary, Robert Wade-Gery, and those in the FO who carried through their conclusions, no doubt against Treasury, Civil Service Department, Ministry of Works and political opposition, deserved the thanks of all to come. The nation's diplomatic service is too important to be subject either to bureaucratic possession or to political and managerial whims and fancies.

For me personally all this came just too late. But I leave that story and my farewell to friendly Canada to the next chapter.

PART THREE

# Europe and Change of Career, 1970–1973

CHAPTER 19

# The Turning Point

## 1970–1971

L IFE IN THE DIPLOMATIC SERVICE is great as long as your health holds and your family can stand it.' That is what we maintained, and I dare say it is what our successors still find today. The key to the life we led was to keep fit.

The Service I knew recognised this and, the DSAO period aside, it was consciously caring. If it was also inclined to be paternalistic and possessive that had advantages and disadvantages. The downside was that our lives were rarely our own. Contrary to the public image, the social round was on top of the day's work, not in substitution of it, and was of course duty not just pleasure. Abroad we were always on call, at home too when necessary and even sometimes on leave. It was a way of life with, underlying it, the fundamental commitment to go anywhere in the world we were asked unless we had very good reason not to. Few of the more junior members of the Service had a home of their own and, when abroad, home was in any case just a base rented out to strangers (and sometimes difficult to repossess on return after the Wilson government's Tenant Protection Act of the late 1960s). Abroad we lived in locally rented flats or houses we usually had to find for ourselves or, in the more senior positions in the longer established posts, in official residences, sometimes grand which meant they became an hotel for visiting dignitaries, sometimes less so. Every two to three years we moved to another country, dealing with different peoples, different languages, different customs and different conditions of living.

Few posts outside the English-speaking world had local schools suitable for our children, either because their standards were different or because the instruction was only in the local language, or both. So most children had to be sent home to boarding school whatever the parents' wishes, and they saw each other only once a year in the post-war years, later improved

381

to twice a year, unless the parents could afford to pay for the journeys themselves. A few opted to keep their children with them wherever they went, but they would be the first to admit privately that it tended to retard the children's education – and indeed that was sometimes obvious. Most importantly, the wives were expected to play their full part in the diplomatic life, supporting their husbands and the Embassy, prohibited from taking paid employment of their own when abroad, and assessed along with the husband on his record. So it could be tough on family life and particularly on the wife, with limitations on three of the things that normally matter most: freedom, family life and a home of one's own. Pay and allowances were limited too. We could count on going into debt in the first year of each post, as we bore the expense of uprooting from one and settling into the next, and of leave in between if we could get it. Looking back, it may seem a wonder that we all, and particularly the wives, put up with it. Some did not, and fell by the wayside, but as much for health as any other reasons.

The upside was the interest of the work. It could be very fulfilling, and most families joined in. That not only kept us devoted but helped to create a reputation that has made the Diplomatic Service the number one career choice of young people leaving university since the war – a remarkable record of which the FO and FCO can be justly proud. There was the perceived glamour of travelling the world, of representing one's country abroad and of mixing with the great. But there was also endlessly changing work and great camaraderie. For my part, as the preceeding chapters have recorded, most of it, despite the restrictions and hardships, was fun. A good deal of the credit for that lay in the self-organisation of the Service. If it was authoritarian, it was also traditionally benign. Our administrators were but colleagues taking their turn. It was not two and more services, one home and the others abroad, as it once had been, but one collective Service. And although the wives had no say in the administration, not at any rate until they formed their own Diplomatic Wives Association in the 1960s, they were key to that collective. None of the Missions I served could have functioned without their loyal participation. They deserve a diplomatic history of their own.

It may be a little different today. Forty years ago our Chargé d'Affaires in Saigon, Cosmo Stewart, wrote a despatch I am sure all members of the Service of that generation would remember. In humorous detail he re-counted the deliberations of the diplomatic Heads of Mission and Vietnamese Protocol on how they should treat the husband of the first ever lady Ambassador when she arrived (from the Philippines). With true gallic logic the French Ambassador finally brought the issue to a conclusion that probably still guides protocol in such cases today: 'It is evident,' he declared. 'The man should be treated as the husband of his wife!' It would be interesting to know what they would have made of the modern day partners, lovers, mistresses, call them what you will, who apparently now accompany some Ambassadors.

The Service had its own wry humour, another attractive feature, shared to some extent with other diplomatic services whatever the common language. That tongue in my day was increasingly English, though in my early years it was still formally French. The Service also, and perhaps outstandingly, maintained a high professionalism, and was renowned for it. That made for good understanding, whatever the problem, and justified pride.

Today the FCO doubtless offers rather better terms, conditions and facilities, not least for spouses and families, although the security restrictions against terrorism some have to endure abroad must be onerous and, under recent Governments, the meddling of Ministers and Treasury-imposed Consultants in administrative matters they know little about must be a trial. The opening of plum posts to people of limited diplomatic experience and even, if I am not mistaken, to outsiders seems to me singularly ill-judged, paving the way to cronyism and to the abuse of political appointments which so plagues the American Foreign Service. I am glad to see it is still nonetheless possible for a Permanent Under-Secretary and Head of the Diplomatic Service to write of the Service in the FCO house magazine: 'We are privileged to work in this organisation: look at the recruitment numbers, people want to work here ... There are a hundred applicants for every job ... We handle things that matter to people: entry clearance, consular and commercial work, and foreign policy. Our tasks matter and it is our responsibility to give them our best shot.'

The health facilities must particularly have improved with the great advance in modern medicine, including tropical medicine, and in transport facilities for evacuating the sick when necessary. That was much needed. We had no hospital or penicillin in Jedda, nor a competent Embassy doctor in Paris (but that was our fault), nor anything but basic medicine in Conakry, nor physicians and surgeons who did not take us for fair game and gain in Rome, nor good medical facilities in the Katanga by the end of my time there, nor first-class health and surgical care in Ottawa that did not, under the North American system, charge an arm and a leg for everything. So we had to stay fit, and so did our families, or when necessary fly home for National Health treatment if the Treasury Medical Adviser could get a hospital bed for us. The Diplomatic Wives Association helped there once they were formed. The Service nonetheless accumulated its crocks. That was inevitable, and most of the time it tried to look after them if they could still do a job of work. I have described in my Rome chapter the high proportion of staff I found at the Embassy there recovering from unhealthy post service. In Oslo, regarded as an even better convalescent post, I recall the FCO Head of Personnel telling me in 1970 he had just received an appeal from the Embassy there for an archivist or secretary capable of lifting a typewriter, as they had none currently fit enough to do so!

I myself was lucky, and so was my family, until Ottawa. My wife and I survived Guinea, Rome and the Congo without medical mishap, and all three of our children suffered no more ailments in babyhood than seemed normal, Julia in Rome and onwards, Robert in London and onwards and Katie in Ottawa. But there our luck broke. We lived an active outdoor life, weather permitting, as we had wherever we were, and the children remained well. But there were signs that the excitement of frequent change was giving way to confusion, and there were now three of them aged 6, 4 and 1. The crunch came when Ann herself suffered first a hysterectomy and then prolonged breathing complications, not helped by the domestic problems of finding suitable dwellings and mother's helps. It became evident the Congo had taken its toll on the family, with the turmoil and evacuations, as had the vagrant life we had led since. In all we had lived in as many as thirteen different dwellings between us in three years. Ann had to return to England from Ottawa for nearly two months for her operation and treatment, taking our two elder children with her. Our youngest stayed with me, helped by two worthy shift minders aged 16 and 73. Ann had to return home briefly again later that year, 1969, when her father developed a brain tumour and died. That was also distressing.

By March 1970 we were due for home leave and instinct told me to claim as much as I could. With accumulated entitlement, duty consultations with departments at home, and useful courses and conferences to attend, I was able to amass four months, to mid-July and this was agreed. As things turned out we needed every minute of it. That leave was the turning point in our lives.

By the time it arrived we had come to realise that we could not carry on as we were. Fond as we had become of Canada and the Canadians, it would be folly for me to bring the family back without assurance of home and help. I had at last found an appropriate house, large enough for the family and for entertaining, well situated in Rockcliffe and at reasonable rent, but while the owner wanted to sell it to us and everyone including the FCO and Treasury agreed it would be a good buy for the future, the Ministry of Works in one of its last gasps before being relieved of responsibility for official overseas property, decided as usual that it would prefer to architect and build its own – which of course it never did. So HMG and the High Commission lost a good investment and I lost the prospect of bringing my family back.

Forseeing this, and with confirmatory local medical advice that Ann and the children needed for the sake of their health and happiness, to settle down, I wrote to the Head of Personnel in London: 'My wife and I find this a very happy post and in normal circumstances would be glad to return for another tour. But we have had a run of personal problems –

housing, health and so forth ... the Katanga ... 13 different dwellings between us in three years ... disturbing for our young children ... I am planning to come back to Ottawa after home leave of course ... The High Commissioner will then be on leave ... But I do not expect to be able to bring the family back, and I would hope that we would not have to be separated for too long.' I went on to ask that I be transferred to home or Europe next for family reasons, including being near to my increasingly invalid mother in Shropshire, and I took the opportunity to remind him: 'As the Department knows, I have been in the vanguard for fifteen years of those who consider that our national future lies in Europe. Now that the door is at last opening, those with whom I have been associated in this cause over the years would rather expect me to be making what contribution I can and I would certainly like to be doing so ... either in the negotiating team for our entry into the Common Market, or behind or forward of it, economic or political.'

I had no thought at that time of leaving the Service. That only emerged as the leave progressed. I knew from the soundings I had made after the Brunei/Hanoi episode in 1965 that changing jobs in an established career

With Robert on Llangollen bridge, 1970.

was one thing, changing career in middle age was quite another. In any case there were more immediate things to think about, like re-occupying our house in Guildford, where we had never lived but only briefly camped, finding local schools for the two elder children and a mother's help, settling in, visiting my mother in Ludlow and my brother in Liverpool who was also ill and whose marriage had sadly broken up. There was business to do in the FCO on behalf of the High Commission, a defence seminar they wanted me to attend as FCO representative at Cambridge, and others planned on Africa, Europe and Export Promotion. Remembering that I had only paid one visit home in three years and that had been brief, between the Congo and Canada, there was family business to review, friends and acquaintances to see and visits to be paid. There would be no time for golf or any other sport, but the garden demanded attention.

To add to the mix, the Office suddenly announced they were appointing Sir Colin Crowe as UK Permanent Representative to the United Nations in New York and replacing him, as High Commissioner in Ottawa, by Sir Peter Hayman, a Deputy Under Secretary in the FCO. I had known him many years previously in Paris when he was a Ministry of Defence counsellor in our delegation to NATO. He had since joined the Diplomatic Service as a late entrant. He asked me to meet in London and brief him on Ottawa and Canada. I came away dismayed by his outlook. Knowing from the FCO my circumstances he nonetheless urged that I should come back to Ottawa for a full tour to help him, leaving my family abandoned in Guildford. I declined of course. He was a strange man, as subsequent events in his life revealed. The over-age entry into the Service, begun in a limited way in the late 1950s, was not in his case a great success.

By the end of April, six weeks after our return home, it was plain that the family had found its haven in Guildford. No 1 Poyle Road was a solid house, friendly and just the right size, built by a far-sighted previous owner in the early 1930s when labour and materials were cheap, but instead of economising he had invested in the robust. Modifying it proved correspondingly hard work but it adapted well. Perched high above the town with a splendid view and the privacy of a cul-de-sac, it was nonetheless only short walking distance to schools for the children, the town and the station to London. Ann's health had some way to go to recover but began to improve immediately. Mother's helps were available. The children took to the place and found friends and delights everywhere, and stability. It became evident that I could not without disruption uproot the family again, after all they had been through, not simply to return to Canada but in the years immediately ahead to the wilderness again or at least beyond Western Europe. Medical opinion confirmed this. That meant that I myself could not either.

The choice was stark. I had long maintained the view in the Service that if one could not fulfil the obligation to go anywhere in the world one should get out. Now I was faced with just that. The FCO had been as sympathetic as they could be on my return. They were open that I was slated to become a senior Ambassador. The congestion at the top remained solid but the prospects were easing following some recent blood-letting, and mine would not be prejudiced by a spell at home. They had no suitable vacancies in sight in Europe, so it would mean marking time for a while wherever I was. Over the weeks that followed I found myself steadily facing up to the need to break the umbilical cord. I had after all had an interesting and successful diplomatic career over four continents, some exciting times, and been head of Mission twice including an Embassy. I could still perhaps play a continuing part on Europe from some different base. The family concern dictated a break. Better it be clean than long drawn out. A whole new life beckoned – like the abyss.

One day I happened by chance upon an advertisement in *The Times* for the post of Director of the Nuffield Trust, an esteemed grant-giving trust disbursing between £1m and £3m each year to research and innovation in the sciences, social sciences and education, based in Regent's Park, paying even less in salary than the FCO but enough; age under 55; requiring, in the rather exaggerated terms of job descriptions of that time 'high administrative and intellectual capacity, breadth of interest, enthusiasm and keen critical judgement', also, importantly, the capacity to get on well with Universities, Government, the Royal Society and major Foundations. It seemed somehow made for me, if only to test the water. The Chairman was a merchant banker, Sir Geoffrey Gibbs, and the other members of the Board all Vice-Chancellors, Rectors or Professors of leading Universities. Through the intermediary of an Oxford friend I made contact with one of them, Sir Kenneth Wheare, Rector of Exeter College, Oxford and he was encouraging. He had already admitted to a mutual friend, however, that 'We don't really know what kind of man we are looking for.' I also saw the outgoing director Brian Young, who was moving on to become Director-General of the Independent Television Authority, and he too was encouraging. So I decided to take the plunge and apply.

It took a week or two to compile a c.v., and to secure referees – which, looking back, made quite an impressive list, including as it did the Vice-Chancellor of Cambridge University, Professor Owen Chadwick; the Provost of Oriel and former Vice-Chancellor of Oxford University, Kenneth Turpin; the Pro-Vice-Chancellor of Liverpool University, Professor Desmond Farmer; a Vice-President of McKinsey, the Management Consultants, and former Chief Scientific Officer of the Ministry of Technology, Dr Alcon Copisarow; the Director-General of the British Council, Sir John Henniker-Major; a Director of the Bank of England and Chairman of the Book Development Council, Sir Eric Roll; and the Permanent Under-Secretary of the FCO and Head of the Diplomatic Service, Sir Denis Greenhill. My application read quite well, and was delivered in good time – although I remember having to steady my hand to sign it. I had told the Foreign Office I was doing so and the reasons. That was necessary to get the Permanent Under-Secretary to act as a referee. But, as a believer in openness, I determined to do so anyway. I had by then made my decision to change career and although the FCO repeatedly assured me they wanted me to stay and that the door remained open, I knew in my heart now there was no going back, not on anything but a temporary basis anyhow.

The Nuffield in fact proved a busted flush. I record that harshly not because they did not choose me. With 230 applicants, most proposed by Universities, I would have understood if they had had good reason to prefer another. But they displayed an administrative amateurishness that would surely have dismayed their benefactor Lord Nuffield. Apart from the private admission that they knew not what they wanted, applications were acknowledged only with a third person note: 'The Chairman is grateful for your letter ... He will in early June be getting in touch with those the Trustees would like to interview ... if you do not hear from him please take it they are pursuing other possibilities.' I heard not a dicky-bird, which seemed to me, accustomed to the politeness and efficiency of the diplomatic service, a discourtesy to my distinguished referees apart from me, and I conveyed this to the Chairman through friends. He then wrote ponderously, 'Although I said I would not be writing if the answer was a disappointing one, I felt that it was only right to send this line to you and some others whose distinguished record would naturally lead them to expect an interview.' It was a lesson I was to learn repeatedly in my search for a new career that, at that time at any rate, the world at home was rather full of goldfish bowls, each shoal swimming around in its own circle, unaware of the others except through distorting glass – and still conducting senior recruitment very much on the old boy net. Today they have head-hunters to do it for them, but the principle remains. I had occasion, fifteen years later, to consult the Director of Pro-Ned, an organisation set up to encourage and help leading companies to recruit non-executive directors to their boards. He found generally the same introspection. It had not changed. Perhaps it now has. I hope so.

This first immersion in the problems ahead was dismaying but also a challenge. With the wise advice of friends like Peter Pattrick, personnel director of Bowaters and a golfing buddy of old, I took a deep breath and proceeded to write to everyone I knew who might have openings or contacts to suggest; to all the banks and related companies in the City; to the Chairmen or Managing Directors of The Times top 100 companies; to every job advertisement I could find remotely interesting; and to every institution and voluntary organisation that might conceivably be looking for a director. It became a major operation. But it could not be done by halves, unless I was prepared to risk missing something I might later regret.

It was a new career I was looking for, something that might lead on to other things, not just a dead-end job. For I was still only 46, and with young children to bring up I needed to work to at least 60. Also there were still things to do in life and I craved interesting work. It proved quite hard going getting this exploration under way, amidst family and official preoccupations and with no secretarial assistance. But I managed it before returning to Canada in July, and was able to continue it from Ottawa, and from Management School and successive one-off FCO jobs I undertook on return.

My records of that career search and the countless interviews involved still fill a filing cabinet. It was a testing time but worth the effort both in the outcome and the fascinating insight it gave me into the worlds of so many industrial, commercial and financial companies, public corporations, institutions, representative bodies, public services and agencies, consultances and – my initial and ultimate preferred area – voluntary organisations. I shall recount a few of the more interesting experiences later.

The FCO were sympathetic when I first announced my decision to retire. They repeatedly urged me to stay and assured they could put me into home-based appointments until the family position improved. But they finally accepted my decision. I was perhaps fortunate that a new team had taken over the administration on the demise of the ill-gotten Diplomatic Service Administration Office, and they were bright and far-seeing. They included people of vision and understanding like the Permanent Under Secretary, Sir Denis Greenhill; the Chief Clerk, Donald Tebbit, later to become High Commissioner to Australia and, in retirement, Chairman of the English Speaking Union; David Cole from the former Commonwealth Service, as his deputy; and Derek Day and John Leahy as Heads respectively of the Personnel Operations and Establishment & Organisation Departments, who I believe went on to become High Commissioners to Canada and Australia respectively.

They and others had the task of negotiating the Duncan Commission recommendations which included, for the first time, redundancies on compensatory terms. We, outside the Administration, knew nothing of this beyond Duncan's report. It was too sensitive to divulge to us. My financial calculations for the future were based on the simple assumption that the salary of my new career or job would be my all, until at any rate I qualified for pension at 60. I did detailed cash flows for five, ten and fifteen years ahead on this basis to gauge the minimum salary I could afford to take if we were not to sink into debt. This meant I had to turn down an otherwise attractive job as Director of International Affairs with the British Red Cross. The Chairman then was a former Ambassador Sir Evelyn Shuckburgh with whom I had twice enjoyed working in the Service. But beggars must be choosers if they have obligations.

I had written to Colin Crowe in Ottawa in May to tell him of developments and that I would be returning to Ottawa as promised but alone and I hoped not for long. My letter continued: 'The Office are prepared to give me a spell in London and this could greatly help. But the trouble and risk lie in the post after that, abroad again, probably on promotion, and therefore too much to count on somewhere acceptable to Ann's health and the happiness of the children, two of whom will then be prep school age. Moreover I should then be rising 50, the worst age at which to seek jobs outside if we found that we could not fulfil the obligation to go where we were told.' He wrote back: 'I can see why you feel you want to get out – you and your family have certainly taken a fearful beating these last few years, but for myself I can only say how frightfully sorry I am to hear it. I myself shall miss you terribly, but more important so will the Service ... I am sure the Office can find something to carry you through until you are properly satisfied ... I am so glad they are being sympathetic ... but so they ought to be! Your troubles after all arise from service to HMG.' As a former Chief of Administration of the Service his reassurance was good to have.

I returned to Ottawa in mid July, concerned about the rigidity that seemed suddenly to have entered into the FCO attitude once they had studied the regulations and realised their limited discretion in the case of someone opting to leave. The system was built for possession not release. But at least I was secure in the knowledge that the family was settled at Guildford, that I would be returning in September, that I had FCO agreement then to use accumulated leave to take myself off to Management School for a refresher course and that, all being well, the FCO might then find me a 3 to 4 month job while I concluded my search for a new career. It was not a happy position to be in, three thousand miles from home, but I could in spare time continue to explore openings at home by mail, and so I did.

My two months back in Ottawa went quickly. The 30 Lakeview house had no view of any lake but was otherwise a good place to be. The High Commissioner and Lady Crowe had lodged there happily in my absence, while their official residence was being redecorated. But it was empty without the family, and not my idea of fun cooking and fending for myself on top of everything else. Fortunately Canadian and other friends rallied round and I was soon, in any case, into a round of farewell dinners and parties that warmed the cockles as well as fed the brute. The news from home was not always good. Robert developed tonsillitis and a foolish doctor declared his illness to be 'the nearest [to a] mastoid I ever was up against'. I am all for medical frankness, but not such dramatisation. Robert had an unhappy experience and a week in hospital. But it was acute tonsillitis not, fortunately, anything life-threatening. It was nonetheless difficult not to be concerned occasionally. All three children had been pushed around in their short lives and though, as my doctor brother used to say, most small children are like rubber balls and usually bounce back, we never knew until they fully settled whether they had picked up any problems in the process. Fortunately Robert's bout turned out to be the only one, except that he and Julia did find, on entering British schools, that they had to catch up a year. (The Canadians tended to take more time than us over primary education, perhaps wisely.) Ann wrote: 'I know we are making the right decision. Apart from health it would be just bleak and impossible for us to be sweating it out in not too desirable foreign posts from now on, while the children grew up separately in England.' She had great faith in my capacity to find a rewarding new career!

We had many messages of sympathy and support. One old friend of my mothers's wrote to her: 'I was so very distressed to hear of your sad news about Wynn and family. What a very difficult decision for him to have to make. He has got on so well in the Foreign Service with such a bright future ahead. And yet he must consider Ann and the children. Canada, I am sure, would be quite out of the question for them as things are at present, and Wynn would not feel happy leaving them alone in England.' She wrote that in November and the 'as things are at present in Canada' referred to an event there, after I had left, that was to change the lives of diplomats world wide.

Jasper Cross was our Trade Commissioner and effectively Consul-General in Montreal, and had been so for three years or more. He and his wife Barbara were our representatives in Quebec, and were well liked. A terrorist wing of the Quebec liberation movement conceived the evil notion of kidnapping him, to draw international attention to their cause, and to hold him to ransom against Canadian government concessions to Quebec. No one foresaw this. No one had had experience of how to deal with it. It was to be the forerunner of many kidnappings of diplomats by terrorist groups world-wide in the years to come. This was the first. By unhappy coincidence, the second to suffer kidnapping some months later, Geoffrey Jackson, HM Ambassador to Uruguay, was at this time also a colleague, as Trade Commissioner in Toronto. I spent the evening with Jasper and Barbara Cross at their modest house in Montreal before catching the plane home from the airport there, in late September, not long before the event. They had no security guards of course. None but the High Commission residence and office did in those days. That was the same worldwide. It became very different once the terrorist habit spread. A few years later when I re-visited the Paris Embassy, it was sad to see the residence had become like a prison and the Ambassador and his wife unable to go places without guards. All that started at Montreal, and poor Jasper and Barbara Cross were the victims. The Canadian government and police handled the affair with their accustomed professionalism. It was new to them too, and took months. But they found and released Jasper in the end, and he then returned to London to achieve in due course a senior position in his home department the Board of Trade. It was a grim ordeal for him and Barbara that many others like John McCarthy and Terry Waite have since endured. No one but they can begin to describe it. Jasper and Barbara Cross to my knowledge never did publicly. They deserve to be remembered as a very courageous couple. I prayed for them many times that winter – and counted my own blessings.

Packing up and saying farewell to everyone at Ottawa was initially more of an anti-climax than climax, after the hectic four months at home. Also it was the Canadian Summer holiday period when all who could do so repaired to their log cabins on the lakes and rivers up-country. We had given up our summer cabin on the Gatineau although Canadian friends, like Jaffrey and dear Jo Wilkins, made me at home in theirs. I wrote to my aged mother at the end of August:

> It isn't as if I've been unduly busy – once at any rate that awful process of packing for the last time in this Service was over. It nearly broke my heart disposing of some of the children's things when we were so well prepared for another year here – Robert's skis for instance, when he was getting so keen by the end of last Winter. And despatching our best china and glass which we shan't use again for years now. And breaking up this house which, despite the unhappiness of last Winter, is just the house I had dreamt of having here. Also I've been deep in my spare time preparing a more professional curriculum vitae and statement of aim and what I think I can offer, to send this week with about 60 more letters I am preparing to personalities I hope will help. Yes, I have been busy. But it is the interminable unsettlement which has curbed my doing the things I wanted to do – like writing to you. And the house is like a morgue, I hate being in it alone. Now the Crowes are back to say farewell before going to New York. And farewell parties for me have already started. Anyhow only another 4 weeks now, and I'll be on my way home – by weekend 26/27 September ... I shall only have a few days at home, and then slap into the intellectual bath I've set myself at the Oxford Centre for Management Studies until Christmas. So I shall probably not be able to come and see you until after that is over, but at least we can talk on the telephone ... It's all going to be so much better.

Ann wrote consolingly: 'Don't forget that in spite of everything we did have a good 2 years in Canada and lots of happiness. Those things of the children, skis and skates etc, mark two years when they had a grounding at a lovely school and made friends and got their confidence and did a lot of growing up ... Now we have a lovely house here [in Guildford] with, once we get you back, everything we need for health and happiness ... So just enjoy your last weeks in Canada.'

I think I did. My farewell parties were heart-warming. So was the invitation I had from the Chairman of the Canadian Civil Service Commission to consider settling in Canada and joining their service, which I had to decline. So also was the letter I had from Sir Colin Crowe when he took up his new post at the United Nations in New York but nonetheless found time to write. 'My dear Hugh ... New York has enmeshed us with a bang (if that is what a net can do). But I can't really say final farewell to Ottawa without thanking you for all your unfailing help and advice all our time there. You really have been an absolute pillar to the whole High Commission and to me particularly – we should have been lost without you. I only wish things had been easier for you at home, but you and Ann were incredibly brave and uncomplaining. I do hope things will settle down now and that you will find something that will meet all your wishes.' I replied that his letter 'reminded me all too forcibly how deeply we shall miss all the best in the Service'. I knew it was unlikely I would find quite the same civility and camaraderie in the world that now beckoned.

Yet another nice farewell message I retain was from a French-Canadian newspaper editor in Montreal: 'Knowing you and a few other blokes prevents me from being too much of a French-Canadian nationalist. God bless you, and may you survive Mr Wilson's administration. *Mes meilleurs voeux*. Willie Chevalier.' But I suppose my most abiding memory was a party with some of my closest Ottawa friends at a favourite bistro of mine in the village of Wakefield up the Gatineau. It had no licence so we had to bring the drink ourselves. The young 'patron' was a born chef. After his meal we went out on the old wooden balcony overlooking the river for brandy and coffee. Night had just fallen. As if by magic the sky suddenly lit up in great bands of multicolours which continued to ebb and flow for at least an hour. We were entertained to the most glorious display of the Northern Lights any of us had ever seen. It was just like friendly Canada to see me out of my diplomatic career abroad in such a blaze!

From that sublime moment and then the pleasure of being with the family again once home, I had rapidly to adjust on return, to the Oxford Centre for Management Studies, a newly established but already well reputed business school, which today is a fully-fledged College of the University called, after its benefactor, Templeton. I had explored Harvard but the timing and cost were prohibitive, also Manchester, Cranfield and Insead at Fontainebleau but all three had few vacancies at that notice and, like so much of business and industry at that time, they were going through a short-sighted phase of questioning the worth of anyone over 45. In this they were blindly copying the Americans, unaware, as anyone coming from that continent knew, that the tide had already turned. America had rediscovered that the dynamism of youth was all very well in times of boom, but come the recession business and industry were searching again for experienced greyheads. Britain followed suit eventually, but far from being young middle-aged I soon found in my career search at that particular time that 46 was very nearly over the top! It added one more hurdle.

Norman Leyland, the director and founder of the Oxford Centre, was too wise for that. He believed in casting his net wide and not only contrived to find me a place on his six-monthly Senior Management Development Programme starting in early October but kindly agreed that if I was unable to do the second part in the new year he would understand. That was important as the FCO, although prepared to sponsor me to meet the School's requirement of employer support, felt they 'could not agree to meet my expenses on the course from official funds given the knowledge that you would not be coming back to the Service for any appreciable length of time after the management course'. The concept that good employers should give retraining help to redundant employees had not yet penetrated this country, or certainly not the Civil and Diplomatic Service. So I paid my own way at Oxford for the first instructional part, and had to miss the second, the project part, in the new year.

Under the School's rules the project, sensibly, would have related to my work but the FCO foresaw security problems there anyhow. In those days whatever we did in the Office, even if it was not classified secret or confidential, was not for public knowledge. Except for Ministers, and the News Department who dealt with journalists and the press, our lips were sealed outside the Office – even on trivialities like tea-breaks in case newspaper gossip columnists might mock them! So on the management course I was on my own, with only limited spare time to pursue the career search, and suddenly a hardening of the FCO attitude under their rules. They now said that come Christmas I would either have to leave the Service, or commit myself to staying on in the FCO for another year or two subject to the availability of suitable jobs for me. Rules or no rules it was not a nice position to be in, I felt, especially after doing my duty by returning to Ottawa. It was not a happy 'Senior Manager' who set off for Oxford. Optimistic as ever, however, I determined to make the most of it and meanwhile to keep urging the FCO to find me a temporary job thereafter, leading to retirement in the Spring.

Reinforced by talking to people who had themselves changed career, I was concerned not to find myself cast adrift if I could help it. Apart from not wanting to be unemployed even for a short time I was warned of the unwritten law of management employment in Britain that you must belong to something to be worth considering. If it still holds, it seems to me a foolish principle especially now with so many redundant managers of quality around, and to be singularly British, not American. But I found it very prevalent at that time, and suspect it still is. A good friend of mine, Freddie Braybrook, Managing Director of Shell Chemicals, offered himself for the 'Great and Good List' at a time when George Brown's Ministry of Economic Affairs was looking for experienced industrialists willing to give voluntary time to the national Economic Plan for Britain. His offer was warmly welcomed, so he took early retirement from Shell and presented himself for national duty. The response was a closed door. In due course he learnt it was because he 'no longer belonged'. So he promptly found himself a non-executive directorship with a small chemical company. And lo and behold the doors of the great Economic Plan fraternity opened to him, and he was welcomed within. Many Management Selection Agencies I came to know, which were proliferating fast at that time, confirmed the same advice. So I hung on in with the FCO, and by Christmas was rewarded with the offer of a temporary job until the Spring, which should see me out. It proved a very interesting job too, working with all the national and regional broadcasting companies, television and radio, and some on the Continent too. But that is for my next chapter.

Today, management is a subject of study and research in all Universities and Business Schools. Thirty years ago it was a relatively new import from the United States, and still so weak that come a recession the secondment of people to such courses was generally an employer's lowest priority. Oxford University did not even recognise the subject until the late 1960s when Norman Leyland, then an outstandingly successful bursar of Brasenose College, launched the idea and found benefactors to establish the Oxford Centre. This was in singularly ugly but functional modern buildings at Kennington, not far from Cowley. He recruited a good teaching and administrative staff, and an excellent chef for he believed in high culinary standards. The core activity was the six-monthly Senior Managers Programme, limited to ten or so people to maintain the Oxford tradition of personal tuition. The participants were drawn from leading companies and institutions country-wide. My course was a mixed and congenial group of managers from ICI, Cunard, the RAF, Glendevon Farms in Scotland and a range of construction and other companies. The staff knew their subjects, and we studied everything then in vogue: financial analysis, cost accounting, investment appraisal, budget control, management accounting, quantitative methods of control, company organisation, marketing, industrial relations; and an introduction to the new thing called computers. Also the latest popular idea called 'management by objectives' – actually a much more common-sense principle, invented by that remarkable American thinker Peter Drucker, than some of its successors, so beloved of politicians looking for easy answers, like the 'comparability of wages' craze and today's 'flexible labour markets' and 'performance-related pay'. When will politicians understand that management demands experience and hard work not facile ideas and that 'a week may be a long time in politics' (Harold Wilson's words) but 'a year is a short time in management' (my words)?

The thing I gained most from the Oxford Centre was, like my previous university courses, not so much the detailed knowledge as the discipline, language and way of thinking. It was a useful addition to my curriculum vitae that I had been to management school – and now to Oxford as well as Cambridge! More important, it was refreshing to discover not only new thinking about management but that one's own ideas were not isolated but part of a corpus of experience that was being widely researched and taught. It boosted self-confidence whether one's destination was to new worlds or back to one's own. My colleagues all felt the same, I think. I enjoyed meeting them again a quarter of a century later at the celebration, attended by the then Deputy Prime Minister, Michael Heseltine, and many others, of the granting of the Royal Charter to the School's successor Templeton College, in 1995. It was only a pity that Norman Leyland did not live to see this coming of age of his worthy child.

Thus reinforced, and with by December the offer by the FCO of a temporary job until the Spring, I was able to step up the search for a new career with renewed vigour. The main problem, I had discovered, was that there was just no established mechanism for doing this, as I think there is today. In those days loyalty and duty to your company or organisation still counted for something – and more is the pity, in my view, that the Thatcherite 'enterprise culture' years did so much to displace such motives by mammon-worship. An American friend of mine in Shell who had worked in many countries, recounted to me when I asked his advice, that he had that day run into a colleague in trauma after deciding to move. 'What company are you joining then?' enquired my friend encouragingly. 'I am not changing company,' replied the colleague, horrified at the very thought, 'just another department of Shell.' It seemed that many companies and institutions in those days tended at management level to be like clams when outsiders appeared, just as labour liked to practise the 'closed shop' at floor level. The arrival of head-hunting consultancies did not help much, as they earned their money from companies and organisations looking to fill specific vacancies, and their expertise lay in identifying and winkling out people in comparable jobs. They were not geared to helping people search for new careers. So, friends advised me and I soon learnt, it had to be the hard way.

My records reveal that over the nine months July 1970 to April 1971, despite the interruptions, I must have approached directly or through intermediaries, some 45 banks, 100 industrial and commercial companies (including a handful of foreign companies operating in Britain), 10 public corporations, 10 public agencies, 15 institutions, 10 consultancies and, although I was not keen on transferring to the home Civil Service for fear of being stuck in a great hierachy, some 10 home Departments. That was about 200 organisations in all. Some 50 invited me to interview mostly at Board or MD level. For each that meant briefing myself not just on where they were – it would not do to be lost and late – but of course on their affairs. To break through the barriers I had to persuade them I wanted to join, that my diplomatic service had taught me to be a maid of all trades and to adapt, and that I could bring something useful to them. In a few cases I failed altogether, in others we agreed amicably or implicitly that we were not made for each other. In the majority they had no suitable vacancies but would keep me in mind. In half a dozen there were interesting prospects and in another half dozen good fall-back prospects. The crunch choice came in the Spring of 1971, with my deadline then imminent. But it was not to be. The FCO suddenly invited me back to work on entry into Europe and, as I had given my word and warned prospective new employers of this, my next chapter became not one of industry, overseas development or consultancy but of Europe.

Before I come to that there are just a few interesting tales to tell of the interviews. Those in that remarkable square mile called the City of London came first. I knew some of the banks, and not least the Bank of England, and some of the insurance companies from official dealings in Whitehall and abroad, and knew too, from Whitehall, the powerful influence the City collectively exerted on government. But the closed nature of their society was a surprise. It has all changed since. In those days, before 'The Big Bang', it was another world. The then chairman of Barings, Lord Cromer invited me to lunch with some of his senior staff but looked me up and down disdainfully in my slightly crumpled suit (I had just flown in from Canada) and the conversation never recovered. He had recently been Governor of the Bank of England and had just secured the job of Ambassador in Washington, an unusual political appointment by Edward Heath for services rendered. I met him again in the FCO the following week but he did not know me. I do not think he was a great success in Washington. Some of the other merchant banks were more welcoming. All were British owned, unlike today. They included Warburg (where I knew several of the directors), Lazard, Schroder Wagg, Hill Samuel, Kleinwort Benson, Ansbacher, Charterhouse, Brandt, Singer & Friedlander, Orion and, in Wales, the Hodge Group. But none had suitable vacancies, except two and neither of them appealed.

The first of these was the Channel Tunnel Group of banks, led by Morgan Grenfell & Flemings who were looking for someone to liaise with the Ministry of Transport on this great project. We met several times but the construction arm (RTZ I think) put paid to it by insisting on appointing their own man. I withdrew with relief, unconvinced that the Channel Tunnel would be built in that decade. The second opening was with a smaller merchant bank seeking help to expand abroad. We parted when the chairman asked me frankly whether with my public service background I could throw myself into developing financial business that 'would not always be in the national interest'. It was a foretaste of the great floating currency speculation to come. It was not for me. Nor, for different reasons, were the clearing banks. Several interviewed me but I think more out of courtesy to intermediaries who had kindly recommended me than from

genuine interest. The National Westminster chairman and board by coincidence received three recommendations about me in the space of a few
days and evidently felt they had to show some interest. Unlike most others
however they did not so much invite as summon me to interview. It was
early on a Monday morning, and it was not with any directors but with
three senior managers. I found them seated, three little men together,
behind a huge desk in the corner of a large room, just like 'See no evil,
speak no evil and hear no evil'. 'Why would I want to join them?' they
kept asking in surprise. Eventually I asked whether they had ever recruited
anyone to management level from outside? After much thought one said
to the others: 'There was that Army Major we took in once, do you
remember? But that was at lower level!' So I thanked them and took my
leave. It was the goldfish bowl at its most opaque. I suppose it must be
clearer today, especially under that bank's new Scottish owners.

My interviews with industrial and commercial companies were more
down to earth. The British Aircraft Corporation, precursor of British
Aerospace, immediately responded to my approach by inviting me to
interview with the Deputy Managing Director, Arthur Greenwood, to
consider becoming co-ordinator of the pan-European Tornado fighter-
bomber project based in Munich. The different nationalities involved were
not co-operating well. It needed a diplomat to bring them together, BAC
thought. I was interested, despite the unattractive commuting involved
and we agreed in principle to carry it forward. Later that very week British
Airways chose to cancel their outstanding order for more BAC 111
short-haul planes, leaving the British Aircraft Corporation with no option
but to cut staff heavily at Bristol. Greenwood telephoned me to regret
that he thought the co-ordination job would probably now be impossible
to fulfil by someone brought into the company from outside when many
of BAC's own managers were going begging and the workforce bitter. I
felt I had to agree.

BAC's approach to things was refreshingly professional after that of the
City. So by and large was that of companies like Wates, Glaxo, Plessey,
EMI, Metal Box, Blackwood Hodge, RTZ, British Rail, de la Rue and ICL.
At each interview we explored possibilities rather than just the bland
'what do you think you can bring to us?' Where it emerged there were
none, we agreed so or they let me know. Where there was a suitable
opening we pursued it. ICL came closest. Indeed after several meetings
they invited me to join Peter Hall, the director responsible for their
government and international relations, to help develop those sides of
their affairs. My recall by the FCO to work on Europe then intervened,
or I might well have found my future with that good company. We remained
in touch for a long time.

Broadcasting, on the face of it, was another obvious field to explore,
especially after my work in that world for the FCO. But it turned out not

to be. I was not a producer or a journalist, and broadcasting management was then a closed shop. The World Service had earlier put me on their books as a possible commentator on international affairs, but that was short-lived when one day they pulled me out of class at the Oxford Management Centre – to everyone's intense curiosity – to ask if I would come to London and do a piece on the Gabon for President Bongo's imminent visit to Britain. All I knew about the Gabon then was unprintable African gossip. So I had to decline. Other institutions who interviewed me included the British Institute of Management and the Henley Administrative Staff College, both of whom wanted to expand internationally, the City University, the Royal Chemical Society and the Poultry Federation, each of whom were looking for a new executive director, and the International Development Studies Institute at Brighton who were looking for research staff. Then there was a range of public agencies who showed interest: the Crown Agents, the Commonwealth Development Corporation, the Science Research Council, the National Research Development Corporation, the RAC and even the Duchy of Cornwall.

One that I was short-listed for when recalled to the FCO was director of TETOC, the Ministry of Overseas Development's agency for British assistance in technical education and training to third-world countries. That could have been interesting but the interview fell in my first week on the Europe job and my mind was rather on other things; they had their favoured internal candidate anyway, although I apparently ran him to within one vote on the very large interview board. That, too, might have been my destiny. So might one of the Management Consultancies, McLintock Mann and Whinney Murray, with whom I had established a close understanding. It was all coming to a head on cue by Easter 1971, with the fall-back of joining the home Civil Service or possibly in due course the European Commission in Brussels once we had joined. I was ready for the plunge. Then the call on Europe unexpectedly came. It meant giving up the openings so laboriously gained, informing all those who had so kindly helped me that it was all off, and then some time ahead re-starting the search all over again when released to do so. I wrote letters of explanation and thanks to all but added that I would be back on the market after the entry into Europe. My turning point had come, and there was no going back, but it would take a while yet to complete the change.

# CHAPTER 20

# The World of Television

# 1971

THE INTERIM JOB the FCO gave me to do in 1971 was to conduct an informal study of BBC Television and Independent Television to see how relations with them could be improved. At that time there was formal contact at Director-General and Diplomatic Unit levels but virtually none at the working level, as the FCO customarily had with the Press and BBC Radio. This seemed silly as both BBC TV and the ITV companies were impacting more and more on Britain's relations with other countries, both by their increasing film reporting on countries in the news and by their growing export of drama, feature, documentary and other films to foreign broadcasting companies. They seemed to feel that using the expertise and facilities of the FCO and its Missions abroad would prejudice their statutory independence.

There was some silliness on the FCO side, too. I was not told this at the time, and only learnt it thirty years later when the papers were released by the Public Records Office. The then Deputy Under-Secretary in charge of the FCO information and cultural services, Sir James Johnston, evidently considered that BBC journalists represented 'a larger collection of prima donnas than has ever graced Covent Garden'; that television attracted 'ambitious and often self-opinionated individuals out to make personal reputations for themselves'; and that complaining all the time to top BBC executives to issue instructions to their staff was counterproductive because those staff 'were not amenable to regular direction'. Johnston's internal memo concluded more moderately that FCO officials should have 'close and friendly contacts at the editorial, i.e. producer level', and that would be the most effective means of 'influencing the content, emphasis and balance of (relevant) BBC programmes'. Norman Reddaway, the wise-headed Assistant Under-Secretary (Information), later my mentor in other helpful directions and still later himself to become Ambassador to Poland, then apparently took charge of the matter. He badgered the FCO Administration to find somebody to work up better relations with the BBC and Independent television, and in due course they found me available and willing to take it on.

The world of broadcasting and particularly television was not entirely new to me. I had had dealings with correspondents and stations abroad and visited BBC TV before going to Ottawa. But my knowledge of what went on inside was zero and I was intrigued to find out. My contacts with the BBC in my own career search had been limited to the Director of Public Affairs, Kenneth Lamb, in Broadcasting House and, through him, with the World Service. They had not reached television, or home radio. BBC TV and ITV were to me – as to the FCO generally it seemed – large goldfish bowls of their own. I determined to start at the top and meet as many of the senior executives and producers as I could, both in the BBC and in the leading IT companies, and then, if possible, go and see what the impact of television on foreign relations looked like through the eyes of leading German, French, Belgian and Dutch television corporations. Living in Guildford, reunited with my family, I would have to commute to London and beyond daily, which never did appeal to me, but it would be useful to re-learn that habit for the future. Operating from the FCO, I would have a useful base and part-time secretary, which were boons after working without them at Guildford and Oxford.

Britain was in political turmoil at the time, the Heath government having inherited from the Wilson government it defeated in 1970, a Trade Union movement out of control, but with no more idea of how to deal with it than Mr Wilson. Go-slow strikes throughout the electricity industry had reduced many cities to blackouts, new pay computers to impotence and hospitals to despair. The *Guardian* reported: 'Nationwide power cuts averaged 31% yesterday, with 40% in some areas, and hospitals faced their most critical 24 hours of the strike so far with staff struggling to keep going by candle and battery power.' My problems paled into insignificance alongside this daily diet of national misery. Fortunately the transport services kept running.

My first port of call in BBC TV was the Managing Director Huw Wheldon. It was a happy coincidence that we knew each other of old through our respective families in Wales, and that he was a man of great vision and understanding who grasped the point of my mission straight away. We had a jolly lunch – everything about Huw Wheldon was big and jolly – he would have made a great Director-General of the BBC and many I know to this day regret that the Governors played safe instead. After lunch he whistled up the senior assistant in his TV Liaison Section, John Goss, to be my guide, and gave instructions that all doors were to be opened to me. It was apparently unprecedented. He knew I would not abuse it but, in addition, as he divulged to me later, he thought my observations of the TV world, as an outsider looking in, could possibly be illuminating. Looking through his office window across the great bull-ring interior of the White City headquarters I remember him saying with his trademark bellow of laughter: 'Look how they are all watching each other across this place. It's like that.'

From him I went on a few days later to have talks with David Attenborough, then Director of TV Programmes – we forget perhaps when we see him still making superb wild life programmes thirty years on that he was already second in command of BBC TV then but chose to go back to producing – and the Controllers of BBC 1 Paul Fox, BBC 2 Robin Scott, and of Administration, S. G. Williams. Together with Huw Wheldon they formed the managing board of BBC TV then. I also had meetings with Joanna Spicer, their long-term planner, and the Heads of TV News, Derrick Amoore; Current Affairs Group, John Grist; Features Group, A. E. Singer; Documentaries Department, E. R. Cawston; Outside Broadcasts Peter Dimmock; Light Entertainment Group, Bill Cotton; TV Enterprises, D. G. Scuse; Co-productions, J. J. Stringer; and several of the leading Current Affairs and News producers and staff like R. T. Frances (Assistant Head), Brian Wenham (*Panorama*), A. D. Smith (*24 Hours*), John Heuston (Foreign News Editor), and Alan Protheroe (Assistant News Editor). In addition there was Robin Day I found on his own at a social function and, in the studios, a range of producers, all markedly individualistic. Together with the administrative and engineering staff they formed a large but impressively talented body – although probably about as difficult to manage as an assembly of soloist musicians! But Wheldon was a powerful manager who contrived to work them as a team and seemingly get the best out of them at all levels. That was of course the great period of BBC TV, before in due course the Thatcher Broadcasting Act encouraged the ratings war with ITV and the 'dumbing down' that seems to have occurred ever since.

The world of Independent TV also proved impressive, for different reasons. There were then 16 companies, each with a region of its own, except that Thames and London Weekend shared the London region, and ITN produced the national and international news for all the others and was jointly owned by them. They were all lightly controlled by the Independent Television Authority with Lord Aylestone, a former Labour Minister, as Chairman; and there were joint bodies called the ITC and ITA which agreed networking and other relations between them. While the BBC was, and remains today, a public corporation funded largely by public subscription through the TV licence, the IT companies were, and of course remain today, commercial corporations funded largely by advertising revenue. I found them each much smaller and in the main tighter ships than the BBC, the big five Thames, LWT, ATV (Midland), Granada (North-west) and Yorkshire being no larger than destroyers alongside the great BBC aircraft-carrier, while the others ranged from corvette size Scottish, Harlech, Anglia, Tyne-Tees, Southern and Ulster to the mine-sweeper size Grampian, Westward, Border and Channel. Some like Granada specialised in Current Affairs or like ATV in Features, over and above their regional programmes, others in light entertainment or drama, the great thing being to get programmes onto the lucrative IT network where they were shown country-wide. ITN was always on network, and highly regarded. I was able to meet both its Editor and deputy Editor, Nigel Ryan and David Nicholas, and several of its presenters; and among the regional companies, Denis Forman the Managing Director of Granada and Jeremy Wallington director of their *World in Action* programme; Howard Thomas and Jeremy Isaacs of Thames; and Messrs Hughes of London Weekend, Ryder and Flanagan of ATV (the famous Lew Grade was away, as often, in the USA), Cox and Baverstock of Yorkshire, Buxton and Connell of Anglia, Bredin of Border, Brown of Scottish, Goddard of HTV, Smith and Johnson of Southern, Jelly and Clifford of Tyne-Tees and Cadbury of Westward; also Weltman of the IBA and Copplestone of ITA. Many of them had been in on the creation of ITV, and shared responsibility for its vigorous growth.

With each and all I was able to discuss the make-up of their programmes and their impact on our foreign relations. In the case of ATV this was nothing new to them, Lew Grade being the pioneer of exporting TV films to the USA. In most others, it was a novel perspective, their focus, like that of BBC TV, being always on the domestic audience. They were intrigued that the FCO should send someone to see them. A few responded positively to the idea of more regular contact, and followed it up afterwards (notably Granada, Anglia and of course ITN). Others just took note and I felt would do nothing until some event made it worth their while. Unbeknown to them or me at that time, that event was about to come in the shape of the Great Debate on entry into Europe. My contacts with them and the BBC were then to prove doubly useful.

My visits to some of the leading television stations on the continent proved valuable from a different viewpoint. It was interesting to have their comments on British television, which most regarded as of the highest standard; on how much of it they were able to see, which was, partly for language reasons, distinctly more than we in Britain saw of theirs; and how conscious they were of the growing impact of TV on foreign relations. In that they were well ahead of us. They not only exchanged programmes across frontiers more than we did but, using high masted receivers when necessary it was not uncommon to find entrepreneurs picking up British programmes across the Channel and piping them around coastal Belgian and Dutch towns (as, I discovered, Dublin was also doing, on the other side). The days of satellite and cable TV were still some way off. But while we in Britain saw foreign films only when bought in, sometimes for news from different sources and more often for entertainment from the United States, people in parts of Belgium were regularly picking up German, Dutch and French broadcasts terrestrially on their simple domestic sets. We in Britain, as ever, were apart. But the message was clear: transfrontier television was coming, so the impact of TV on our foreign relations would grow.

The conclusions of my study were that television had now become 'the most powerful medium for conveying news and views on foreign as on domestic events, and for portraying the affairs and culture of foreign countries, as of Britain itself, to the British public' ... 'What it screens and says on any particular country will often be reported back to the government of that country and occasionally to its press' ... 'BBC TV and ITV activities abroad are now fairly extensive' (2500 and more visits abroad each year, in addition to their resident correspondents, Visnews, camera-men, and stringers in some countries) ... 'Britain is now the world's leading exporter of television news items' ... 'Sales and purchases of programmes across frontiers could develop further when the market in video-cassettes, videodiscs or holograms breaks in perhaps three or four years' time' ... 'With the notable exception of ITN however, relations between BBC TV, ITV and the FCO are largely confined to formal channels' ... Operating abroad 'in the more sensitive countries and this means nowadays the majority of nations, what BBC TV and ITV select to film and whom they choose to interview may at minimum attract official attention and in some cases require official sanction' ... 'British Missions abroad exist to help British interests in any way they can. But, except for ITN, contact and cooperation with them by travelling BBC TV and ITV crews and journalists appear to be growing less rather than greater, especially among the less experienced' ...

My conclusions invited attention to the fact that, at home 'the FCO has a wealth of expertise and factual knowledge on foreign countries which BBC TV and ITV are welcome to draw on, in the same way as do the Press, BBC External Broadcasting Service and ITN. At present BBC TV and ITV make little use of this service' ... 'Few foreigners understand the BBC's unique constitutional status and independence of government. Still fewer understand the deep delegation of authority over programme content and creative competitiveness which form its mainspring.' (That was the BBC ethos then, but much less so since Birt I believe.) 'Likewise, few understand the statutory independence of the IT companies from each other or the constitutional position of their supervisory body the Inde-pendent Television Authority' ... 'British television presents a singularly bewildering pattern of independencies and dependencies' ... 'It remains important to uphold and explain these principles abroad. But independence is one thing; inter-dependence is another. Whether it be between different parts of the BBC, or between different IT companies, or between the BBC,

IT and the Government, there is no credibility abroad in denying their interdependence (nor is there any necessity)' ... 'For three such important British institutions (BBC TV, ITV and FCO) with common interests abroad to remain quite so far apart would seem to be to the benefit of none, nor in the general interest.'

I went on to recommend a number of practical measures to establish working relations between BBC TV and the FCO and between the IT companies and the FCO, which I think were put into effect. At least the shouting matches ceased! No doubt today it is all harmony and light. I hope so.

Huw Wheldon entertained me to tea to receive my report and recommendations. By chance he chose as venue the English-Speaking Union off Berkeley Square, which I was to come to know intimately as Director-General of that organisation two years later. It was my first visit, and it was rather dowdy. Like so may others who used it, he was a member through an aunt or other elder of the family. He probed me as much on how I had found the people and ways and workings of his empire as on cooperation with the FCO. I told him that from all those I had talked to outside as well as inside the BBC, and on the Continent, BBC TV drama, features, documentaries, outside broadcasts and light entertainment had no equal, and current affairs were not far behind. In the field of TV news broadcasting however, ITN impressed most. They were a model of professionalism with high grade journalists not only preparing but presenting the news (whereas BBC TV in those days used actors). Not long afterwards I was glad to see BBC TV changed to journalist presenters, and the standard (and ratings) I think leapt. ITN have since sadly gone commercial and downhill. News to me is news, not entertainment and I think Wheldon agreed. On the matter of relations with the FCO, he summed up my recommendations in his own inimitable way: 'The name of the game is pressure, dear boy. Thanks.'

# CHAPTER 21

# The Great Debate on Europe

# 1971

IN LATE MAY 1971 the third British attempt to negotiate entry into the European Economic Community suddenly promised breakthrough. Prime Minster Heath found President Pompidou of France more amenable than his predecessor General de Gaulle and returned from a meeting in Paris convinced that the negotiations already under way in Brussels would this time succeed. He instructed that the time had come to present the case for membership of the Community to the British public and Parliament, and that an information campaign should be mounted throughout the country to achieve this. Some groundwork had already been laid both within the Government and outside in the European Movement, and a limited information effort was already under way. The campaign now had to be greatly enlarged and all possible elements and contributions pulled together, in time for the whole to be launched just as soon as the terms of British membership were settled with the EEC, and a White Paper prepared for Parliament. It was hoped that would be by early July. There was not much time.

Public opinion on Europe was then as divided as at any time since 1960. So was Parliamentary opinion. The information campaign would need to last until Parliament voted on the issue. Mr Heath initially wanted that to be by the end of July, but was soon persuaded that the debate was too big to be rushed and must run through to October. The anti-European forces were already grouping to mount strong opposition, with much of the Labour Party and Trade Union Movement on their side. The Government had only a 25 majority in the House of Commons and numerous dissenters in their ranks. The media had become bored with the subject over the years of frustrated negotiations but would soon rise to the issue once they scented major political conflict. It was they in fact who came to dub it 'The Great Debate', and in those days that was a term of respect, unsullied by the over-use it has today. It was to determine, at last, Britain's post-war place in the world and future in Europe.

I was in Ludlow visiting my mother that Whitsun weekend, having just completed as far as I could the job of improving FCO relations with the TV media and, simultaneously, my own search for a new career. The job options now lay before me and I was preparing for the plunge. At the eleventh hour the FCO called. They had tracked me down and, in the voice of Assistant Under-Secretary Norman Reddaway, wanted to know if I would take on the Europe campaign as Official Co-ordinator, working with Anthony Royle MP, Parliamentary Under-Secretary in the FCO who would be Minsterial Co-ordinator, and William Whitelaw MP, Lord President of the Council in the Heath Government, Leader of the Commons and Minister responsible for Information. I hesitated only long enough to flash through the loss of outside careers now open to me, and agreed to take it on willy-nilly. I had given my word to put the cause of Britain in Europe first and this was it. My personal future would have to be put on ice again. I agreed to return to London and start right away.

It is perhaps worth rehearsing briefly the sequence of events that led to this Great Debate and its historic significance. The idea of securing the future peace of Europe by binding its member states together in some form of union was given wings, paradoxically in the light of subsequent history, by a British statesman, Winston Churchill, in Zurich in 1946 and it was he who presided over the establishment of the European Movement at the Hague Conference the following year. He even talked of a United States of Europe. But it was never clear whether he envisaged Britain as a part of it or just as one of its 'sponsors and guardians together with the USA, the Commonwealth and perhaps even the USSR'. His initiative was nonetheless taken in Europe to mean that, although the Attlee Labour government would have no truck with it, Britain under a Conservative government would participate. There was all the more dismay on the Continent when Churchill's subsequent government and then the Eden government declined to join the successive initiatives of France, Germany, Italy and the three Benelux countries in forming first a European Coal and Steel Community in 1951, then the still-born European Defence Community in 1952 and, most important of all, the European Economic Community, or Common Market as it came to be known, in 1957. Indeed the Eden government went so far as to advise the governments of the Six that we thought they were making a big mistake in launching the EEC which would not succeed.

We were wrong. The EEC proved to be a great success and Britain was left trying to save what we could by forming a European Free Trade area with some of the outer states of Europe, and then, in 1961, after much soul-searching by the Macmillan government, applying ourselves to join after all. As Lord Gladwyn commented in a 1966 essay on the European

With my mother, Ann, Robert, Julia and Katie in Ludlow, 1971.

Idea: 'Few people across the Channel, few perhaps in Britain itself, realised the magnitude of the change in British policy which had been accomplished. Virtually it meant that in the face of a potential menace exerted by a super-power which had already occupied a great part of Eastern Europe, the British Government were abandoning the policy of European balance which they had successfully pursued for something like four hundred years.' It also meant facing up to the supranationality of the Community, although the effects of this were generally exaggerated by the anti-Europeans; and a pooling of sovereignty, although in essence perhaps no more than we had long done on defence in NATO and, as Eden himself had aptly put it to Parliament in 1945: 'Every succeeding scientific discovery makes greater nonsense of old-time conceptions of sovereignty.' (To my knowledge there is no legal definition of that emotive term in Britain anyhow.)

This historic development was not however to be achieved for another ten years. Negotiations with the Six were engaged in 1961, led on the British side by Edward Heath then Lord Privy Seal in the Macmillan government. But in January 1963 President de Gaulle pronounced a French veto. He repeated that act again in November 1967, after the Wilson Labour government had unexpectedly picked up the baton and deposited a new British application to join. Three years later, with de Gaulle now back in retirement at Colombey-les-deux-Églises, the Heath government followed this up with the third application, and negotiations with the Six began again, this time led on the British side first by Anthony Barber and then, more substantively, by Geoffrey Rippon, Chancellor of the Duchy of Lancaster. They were well advanced when Mr Heath finally secured the green light from Monsieur Pompidou at the end of May 1971.

Legend tends today to jump those years of historic decision, 1971/2, and ascribe the real determination of British membership of the European Community to the subsequent popular Referendum of 1975. That is not of course correct. The decision of principle to join was taken in October 1971 and to enact the European Communities Bill in 1972, both by Parliament in our traditional way, although after a public debate of unparalleled fullness and allocation of Parliamentary time greater than any since the pre-war India Act. The 1975 Referendum was not on the principle of membership or on the European Communities Act but on the financial, agricultural, regional and Commonwealth terms of British accession which the Wilson government had marginally renegotiated with our European partners to get themselves off the hook of continued internal Labour dispute over membership. It is true that by bringing the pro-Europeans together again from all political Parties and all sections of the Community and securing a resounding two-to-one public majority, the Referendum settled the continuing dispute for that time, and it is remembered by all who took part, pro and anti, as an exciting cross-party campaign. It was consultative, the final decision resting with Parliament (as it must always do under the British constitution unless Parliament decides otherwise). No government of course, having called a referendum, could politically afford to ignore an adverse result. I believe it inconceivable however that if the 1975 Referendum had unexpectedly gone against him Harold Wilson would have promptly sought the agreement of Parliament to renege on the Treaty and pull Britain out of the Community. What he or his successor James Callaghan would almost certainly have done would have been to seek from Brussels still further 'improvements' in the terms and then go back to Parliament or the electorate for approval. Mr Wilson indicated clearly on the last day of the 1971 Great Debate his intentions. He would not want to withdraw from Europe but would emulate de Gaulle to get better terms. By 1975 too much water had flowed under the Channel for there to be any turning back. That in effect is what the British public said in the 1975 Referendum. They had made their decisions through Parliament in 1971/2.

One reason why the 1975 Referendum lives fresher in people's minds than the previous debates on Europe is no doubt because it was novel, the first in the line of six referenda we have had in the UK in recent years, not counting local polls, and still the only national one (the others being regional). Another reason is that while the pro-Europeans certainly drew heavily in the Referendum on the experience of the 1971 Great Debate (I know this personally from the late Sir Con O'Neill, their co-ordinator), and probably the anti-Europeans did too, there was this time less wariness among politicians of different parties about the novelty of campaigning together in public, and most found the experience memorable. Yet another reason must be that whereas the Referendum has been fully written up and analysed publicly, the 1971 Great Debate has to my knowledge never been so (except two instant and rather uninformed accounts in otherwise worthy books by David Spanier and Uwe Kitzinger on the membership negotiations). There was an official report, now doubtless covered in dust in the official archives. It was written by me as Official Co-ordinator. I recall that it was flatteringly judged by Geoffrey Rippon as 'most interesting' and by Anthony Royle as 'quite excellent', and that Royle expressed the hope that it would one day be published. In default of that I have compiled from research and recollection the account in this chapter.

The Great Debate was, and still remains I believe, the largest information campaign ever conducted in this country in peace-time. Notwithstanding the 1975 Referendum and the advance in campaigning techniques since, it may still perhaps carry a lesson or two for the impending Referendum on the Euro or other national single issue campaigns of the future. In the following pages I seek to recall the make-up of the pro-campaign, the opposition, the principal personalities involved, the political egos and bureaucratic cross-currents we occasionally had to bear but, overall, the remarkable spirit of common cause that inspired the whole effort, and the final great result in Parliament.

None of us, inside or outside the Government, had conducted a campaign like this before. Some of course could draw on election experience, but this was to be government-led not party-led and in the national not party cause. Some of us had never conducted a campaign at all. We soon learnt. In its scale, complexity and cross-Party ramifications, there were no peace-time precedents. Nor was there even a war-time precedent, for public television had not then existed and, as the Conservatives and Labour had just discovered in the 1970 general election, TV had now become much the most powerful medium. The 1961/63 and 1967 EEC information campaigns provided a few pointers to what was required; and we had some foundation to build on in the preparations laid by a few far-sighted people before June 1971. But in the autumn of 1970 Ministers had confirmed an earlier strategic decision not to deploy the full weight of support and argument for entry until the case was assured and known. Full planning and co-ordination had to wait for that – which is where I came in at the beginning of June 1971. We then had to build fast. The case for public presentation could not be completed while the negotiations continued in Luxembourg, for fear of getting it wrong or undermining Mr Rippon's negotiating position there. It was 23 June before the main terms were finally agreed. Anticipating this, Prime Minister Heath announced the programme in outline to the House of Commons a few days earlier: there would be a White Paper by 7 July; then public and parliamentary consideration of the issue and terms over four months, including a 4-day exploratory ('take-note') Parliamentary debate in late July; and the final debate and decision in Parliament after the Recess in late October. It would be all go through the summer and autumn.

The task the Prime Minister and his colleagues set was in fact mountainous. It was 'to convince Members of Parliament that the tide of public opinion was moving in favour of joining the EEC ... and to achieve the maximum vote in favour in the House of Commons.' That was easy to say at the time. But, in the country, public opinion polls showed a massive three-to-one majority against the venture. And in the House of Commons all the Parties were split on the issue, and there was far from being an assured majority in favour. Throughout the first half of the year, public opinion surveys by the four leading polling organisations, taken together, had consistently shown between 60% and 65% against and only 18% to 25% in favour. (A poll-of-polls and ORC chart of the time is reproduced later in this chapter.) There was some improvement after the Prime Minister's meeting with President Pompidou in late May and a further improvement when it was announced that the negotiations had been successfully concluded. But at the start of our campaign in early July the polls were still showing over 50% against and only 30% in favour. The one encouraging feature was that survey research confirmed that, except for those dead-set against membership, the more people were informed on the issue the more favourable they tended to become. We were to work on that basis throughout. We eschewed polemics and what today is called 'spin' in our briefings and literature and stuck to substantive argument and fact. That did not stop us devising an effective quick-reaction system to counter promptly, through speeches and the press, contentious arguments and points made by the opposition. But the level of debate never descended on our side (nor, to my recollection, on the side of the opposition) to the acrimonious or personal, as it seems to do so often in election campaigns.

A particular problem of our own making was that some time previously Mr Heath had injudiciously declared that he would want the 'full-hearted consent of the British people' to take Britain into the EEC. That remark was to be held against him when, despite the remarkable turn-round in public opinion our campaign did achieve, we never quite fulfilled that dream. With hindsight it would have been better if he had added 'as expressed in our traditional way through Parliament', which is what he had in mind. That we certainly achieved.

No one knew the precise state of opinion in Parliament when we started. There were no polls or even Whips' counts, and anyhow it was early days. But there were back-benchers on both sides busily sounding opinion and, on the most favourable count there were only about 45% in favour (mainly Conservative but also some 50 Labour and a few Liberals), with about 35% against (including nearly 40 Conservatives and at least 170 Labour). The remaining 20% were judged to be 'in varying degrees of doubt'. The hard core anti-marketeers (as they came to be known) on the Government benches were more numerous than the Government majority in the House, so it was clear from the outset that the Government would have to depend in the crunch on a band of Labour pro-marketeers prepared if necessary to defy their own party leadership. Harold Wilson and many of his colleagues, despite their earlier conversion to EEC membership, were now moving steadily against, under Trade Union and left wing pressure. It was a sad sight. The pro-market Labour Committee for Europe did well to find in late June as many as 100 Members of the Parliamentary Labour Party willing to sign an advertisement in the *Guardian* supporting EEC membership. But many of those subsequently fell by the wayside, as their official Party position hardened. The pro-Committee was led by Roy Jenkins, then deputy Leader of the Party, and included George Thomson, Harold Lever, Michael Stewart, Shirley Williams, George Brown, Roy Mason, Bill Rodgers, David Owen, Roy Hattersley, John Mackintosh, Gwyn Morgan, Tom McNally and their Secretary and co-ordinator, Alan Lee Williams. I came to work with many of them again in the Liberal/SDP Alliance in later years. It cannot have been easy for them, hardened politicians though they were, holding to their convictions against the views and pressure of their majority Party colleagues – any more, in fairness, than it must have been for the Conservative anti-marketeers in their Party. I learnt a lot about internal Conservative and Labour party goings-on and arm-twisting in those months. It was not always savoury.

Our preparations in June got off to a good start, so much so that we were emboldened after two weeks to set phases and targets. Phase 1 would be from early July to the Recess and holiday season, 6 August. By then we hoped public opinion in the polls would have reached at least 40% in favour and, Ministers agreed, 'if we reach parity we shall have done very well'. We did in fact do so. It was an extraordinary turn-round in public support.

The second phase would cover the holiday season until mid-September. The aim would be to consolidate and develop support in the country so that the Party Conferences in late September/early October might be held against a background of clear public opinion in favour. We did not quite achieve that target. There was inevitable loss of momentum and public interest in the holiday period; the economic situation became a distraction; and Labour opposition hardened. But we did maintain majority public support, and pro and wavering MPs back in their constituencies were bucked by the state of opinion they found.

The third phase, mid-September to end-October, would concentrate on the Party Conferences and the final Parliamentary debate. No target was set for the desired Parliamentary majority. Apart from constitutional objections that would have been folly given the still fluid state of opinion in some sections of the Commons. But it was agreed that the aim must be a decisive majority. Without that, it would be difficult and divisive to proceed to signature of the Treaty of Accession, to the passage of a European Communities Bill to give domestic legal force to the obligations and rights of membership, and to full preparedness for entry on 1 January 1973. The outcome would need to be clear to everyone, at home and abroad.

The preparations in June were hectic but enjoyable – as indeed was the whole campaign. Thrown in at the deep end, it did not take me long to find out what was already in hand, and to decide the priorities. There was everyone to meet, the who-was-doing-what to be absorbed, the logistics to be established including an operations room which would be my base, and a small staff of three to be found to join me: John Crosby, a young diplomat who made a useful deputy, Susan James, also a young diplomat who made a charming and efficient assistant, and Patricia Stanton who put up with us as typist. We were seconded to the Lord President's office although, for practical reasons, accommodated in a spare conference room in the FCO. There were Anthony Royle's and my terms of reference to be written up for the benefit of interested Departments, which caused a little scratchiness at first from those who thought we were treading on their territory, but that was soon resolved. It was decided to keep the information effort separate from the negotiations, so as to leave each side a freer hand in their respective fields. But close working relations would be essential, and they were in fact maintained throughout, from Ministerial down to desk level, without more than minor skirmishes. I personally had also to bring myself rapidly up to date on the issues and learn some principles of campaigning. Two timely seminars I discovered that first week helped, one by the Federal Trust on management aspects of the EEC and the other by the Bridge Foundation, run by my future Liberal friends Bill Pearson and David Griffiths, at, by another coincidence, the English-Speaking Union. It was on the relative response rates achieved by voluntary organisation campaigns using the different available media: advertising, literature, meetings, personal contact, radio and television. The TV came out streets ahead.

That confirmed my determination to make TV my first priority, and to get on with it immediately. With the ready agreement of Ministers and my colleagues I was able rapidly to meet or talk on the telephone to most of the people I had come to know from my last job, and others, in BBC TV and Radio, ITN and twelve of the fifteen ITV regional companies (I never did reach Grampian, Ulster and Channel until later) at management and Head of News and Current Affairs levels. This was to forewarn them of what was coming and to engage their interest. The Prime Minister's Chief Press Secretary, Donald Maitland, did the same with the national newspapers and many regional newspapers, at management and reporter levels. That early media initiative paid handsome dividends. *The Times, Guardian, Economist, Daily Mail, Mirror, Sun, Sunday Times* and *News of the World* declared themselves editorially favourable, and I think all remained so. The *Daily Telegraph* and *Financial Times* felt it necessary to strike an editorial balance, but on the favourable side. The main regional newspapers also responded favourably. The *Daily Express, Spectator, New Statesman* and *Morning Star* remained anti. Television and Radio, bound by their rules of editorial impartiality, were not expected to take sides. All nonetheless showed interest and some keen interest – the campaign was after all likely to generate big news and feature material through to October. BBC TV and BBC Radio decided to give it top priority, and ITN and Southern TV top priority plus. The remainder indicated they would work on it. All pleaded for events to report and build on. This convinced me we would need a rolling Diary of Events circulated regularly every fortnight to the media as well as to everyone involved in our campaign, including all Ministerial offices and the non-governmental organisations and groups taking part. It became the one executive job I took into my office, and it proved invaluable to the campaign. The art of co-ordination, I knew from past experience, was to get the executive jobs done by other people and not to get bogged down trying to do them ourselves. There were countless willing departments, groups and people prepared to help, and what better than to get them all involved. That became my next priority.

Meanwhile, in the media, ITN immediately displayed that high TV news leadership and professionalism that so marked them in those days. They produced in quick time a series of twenty 5-minute programmes on different aspects of the EEC and British entry, for inclusion night after night in the middle of News at Ten through late June and early July. For each the audience was up to 11 million. It was an astonishing achievement and, although strictly balanced in its presentation, it undoubtedly had a profoundly favourable public impact by simply showing people in illustrated form what the European Community was about, the arguments for and against British entry, the terms negotiated and how each major sector of the British economy might be affected. The producers were Peter Snow, the now well known and eternally young BBC producer and presenter, and Julian Haviland who went on to become *The Times* political editor. They came to see me a few days after I had briefed David Nicholas, their deputy Editor, to say that ITN had decided straight away that the campaign merited the big treatment. They asked if I could arrange factual briefing for them on the understanding of course that they would use it as they chose and we might not always like the product. I put them in touch with the FCO and Cabinet Office officials co-ordinating the negotiations and those officials did all that was asked of them on this basis. Peter Snow and his graphics have since become famous. His and his colleague's outstanding journalistic and producer talents should not be overlooked. To this day I have never myself seen the equal of that News at Ten series for sheer professional brilliance.

BBC TV also mounted a special programme presenting the White Paper on 7 July, with an estimated audience of 9 million, and a marathon Great Debate of its own adversarial making in early October which was not so successful – the studio audience was supposed to vote before and after but Gallup's counting broke down at the end and the presenter, Robin Day, made history by describing it in anger on the air as 'The Great Cock-up'. It was like Uncle Mac's famous comment I remember he broadcast inadvertently after one of his much-loved Children's Hour programmes before the war: 'That should keep the little b ... s quiet for another night!'. In fairness, however, BBC TV, like ITN and the 15 ITV regional companies, found countless other occasions throughout the Great Debate to report events and speeches or to mount their own news, current affairs and features programmes. So did BBC Radio. And so, of course, did the Press, national, regional and technical. The Debate was rarely out of the news from June to October.

The second priority was organisation. We had to bring together in a simple structure those who would have the greatest practical contribution to make, and establish flexible procedures for involving others and campaigning together. The basis had been laid in the preliminary Group and its line to the Lord President involving, unusually but sensibly, Ministers, officials and non-governmental organisations mixed together. We built on this. It became the Campaign Group, meeting regularly at the beginning of each week and sometimes again before the weekend. It consisted of the chairman, Anthony Royle, myself as official co-ordinator, three or four of the principal officials involved, leading representatives of the Conservative Central office, the Conservative Group for Europe, the Labour Committee for Europe, the British Council of the European Movement (BCEM) and one or two non-governmental people for their individual expertise. It was a working campaign group, not a talking shop, and the meetings were short. The officials included the Prime Minister's Chief Press Secretary, Donald Maitland, who went on to a distinguished career in both the Diplomatic and Civil Services; Norman Reddaway, Assistant Under-Secretary and brain behind the preparations; a head or two of the negotiating departments to maintain liaison; and an able drafter called James Adams, later to become Ambassador to Egypt, who edited the Factsheets for popular distribution and periodic messages for Ministerial speakers. The FCO was shy of publicly participating because the campaign was on the home front. I respected their wish, but today wonder what can be wrong in a government department responsible for our international relations being involved in presenting the case at home for some proposed international development. Perhaps there are fewer such Whitehall hang-ups today. Certainly the Great Debate campaign would not have been so successful without FCO initiative, and the Minister charged with opening the Parliamentary debate in October was of course the Secretary of State for Foreign Affairs, Sir Alec Douglas-Home. Also I do not think Anthony Royle found any difficulty in being simultaneously Ministerial co-ordinator of the Campaign and FCO Parliamentary Under-Secretary. He was a Byronesque figure, with a disabling limp but an infectious enthusiasm and perhaps absence of high political ambition which together made him popular in the Tory ranks. His politics and mine privately were well apart but except when he once dismissed my pleading on behalf of some worthy group with the die-hard dictum 'But life is unfair, isn't it!', we got on extremely well. He made an excellent chairman.

The Cabinet Minister in charge, William ('Willie') Whitelaw also proved a pleasure to work with. An avuncular but shrewd landowner from Penrith, son of a former Scottish MP and railway (LNER) chairman, he concealed behind his large frame and jovial manner a golfer of no mean worth, past Captain of the Royal and Ancient, and a successful Chief Tory Whip for several years. He went on of course to become a distinguished Deputy Prime Minister to Margaret Thatcher, and perhaps the only man besides her husband and President Reagan who found how to deal with her. Anthony Royle and I met with him first thing each week and at other times when necessary. In the chair he was like a great owl, coming out occasionally with a wise hoot but never missing a thing. I also met regularly with the director and staff of the British Council of the European Movement and occasionally its chairman Lord Harlech and, whenever necessary, with other groups and individuals involved or willing to be involved, including the chief information officers of the Treasury, Department of Trade and Industry, Ministry of Agriculture, Departments of Employment, Health and Social Security and the Scottish and Welsh Offices. Then there was an informal breakfast group, run by an advertising man and former director of public relations at Conservative Central Office, Geoffrey Tucker, which took no executive part but was useful in bringing in a few people of position and influence in the media, politics and industry. It was through that group that I was initially able to bring in David Steel, then Chief Whip of the Liberal Party, and his assistant (now MP) Archie Kirkwood.

The non-governmental members of the Campaign Group included the Director of the European Movement, Ernest Wistrich, a stalwart worker in the European cause for many years. His organisation had steadfastly carried the public banner through thick and thin in the 1960s, sometimes confined by lack of resources and public interest to just maintaining the faithful, at other times as each new government revived the cause of EEC membership, widening its public support and activities at national and local level. With the government now taking the lead, the BCEM had to adapt to a supporting role, reducing its speech programmes and the like that government and others could do better but expanding those of its activities that government could not or preferred not to undertake, including advertising in the national and local press (particularly lists of prominent supporters), sponsored articles, posters, conferences, seminars, mobile vans, letters to the press and MPs, and other popular and grass-roots activities. They had also over the years invaluably brought into being a Conservative Group for Europe and a Labour Committee for Europe each operating fairly independently of the BCEM but still member bodies of that Movement.

The Conservative Group for Europe was strong and active in both Houses of Parliament, with at least 130 MPs among its membership. They were represented on our Campaign Group by their chairman Col. Sir Tufton Beamish, MP for a Sussex constituencey and a man of his word and military efficiency, and occasionally by the brilliant Norman St John Stevas, whom we affectionately called the Archbishop because he did tend to prolong our meetings with sermons. He went on of course to much greater things briefly in the Thatcher government and then in the arts world. Also in the Campaign Group were the Conservative Central Office and Research Centre, represented by that pillar of the Conservative Party, its deputy Chairman, Sir Michael Fraser, and their director of public relations, Don Harker, and deputy head of research Michael Niblock. Their participation in the campaign was of great importance providing as they did, through their constituency organisations, the platforms for most of our Ministerial speaker meetings and, through their research department, extra briefing for Ministerial and MP speakers. They also ran a day-to-day question and answer service for their MPs throughout the campaign, and, in the later stages, a channel for feeding points to speakers at short notice when opposition arguments and press deadlines made this desirable. They were unstinting and, with few exceptions, dependable in their support.

The Labour Committee for Europe provided the meeting ground for those Labour MPs and Peers who believed Britain's future lay in Europe and were prepared to fight for it. Their Secretary and representative on our campaign group was Alan Lee Williams, MP for Hornchurch, Essex, a Thames 'Waterman' and a man of vision, courage and good humour. I came to enjoy his cooperation and friendship again in later years, in international voluntary organisations, and he succeeded me but one, as Director General of the English-Speaking Union. To these Labour pro-marketeers, having common cause with a Conservative-led campaign was one thing. Co-operating with it was quite another. In most other countries of the Western world I doubt if that would have posed any great problem. In our country, under our absurdly adversarial system, it was like supping with the devil. Liaison and co-operation grew hesitantly at first. The broad church character of our Campaign Group helped, so in particular did the encouragement given them by the BCEM and, I think, those of us in a central but politically neutral position to do so. But it was Alan Lee Williams and, behind him, a handful of his colleagues who blazed the trail and, paradoxically, it was when their Party moved towards formal opposition, that they themselves found their home fully in our joint campaign. In the final phase there was mutual trust and confidence across this political divide, and it was to play a vital part in the outcome.

The Campaign Group also included occasional people in their personal capacities, like Geoffrey Tucker already mentioned (who came to be known as the Cardinal because he too liked to pontificate) and Michael King, Information Officer of the CBI. The membership was kept flexible, like the structure, and our ways of working were informal, somewhat in contrast to those of the bureaucratic world in which we were based. From the start we agreed that as much as possible of the organisation and co-ordination should be conducted orally and as little as possible on paper. That probably meant more time in meetings and discussion, but it made easier both the task of marrying working methods between the non-governmental and governmental organisations involved, and of creating an intimacy of liaison and co-ordination. Campaign developments and reactions were anyhow often too rapid to be handled otherwise. Everyone adapted extraordinarily well. Time was never in fact taken to define the organisational, as distinct from the campaigning, tasks. They just emerged. In essence they were: to establish a common purpose and drive among all concerned; to plan and build the primary Governmental contribution to the campaign; to adjust and develop the roles and activities of the non-Governmental organisations; to engage the support of business, professional, social and other community groups as widely as possible; and to fill gaps. By and large I think all these organisational aims were achieved with remarkably few hitches or argument. The only dispute I recall was whether we should break for August or carry on. The advertising element thought we should stop. I took the management view that with so many thousands of people now involved we could not possibly rebuild the momentum for the final phase if we closed down completely for a month. Ministers agreed. So, fortunately as it turned out, we kept on campaigning through the holiday season.

But that is jumping ahead. The launch of the Great Debate was early July. By then we were ready. The central text and starting point was the White Paper 'The United Kingdom and the European Communities', prepared in the Cabinet Office and agreed by Ministers. It concluded:

'Every historic choice involves challenge as well as opportunity. Her Majesty's Government are convinced that the right decision for us is to accept the challenge, seize the opportunity and join the European Communities.' It was presented to Parliament on 7 July. Our campaign then opened up with full media briefings, more literature distribution countrywide, a major programme of speaker-meetings, participation in TV and Radio debates as they arose, statements in Parliament when called for and the BCEM national and local activities. All government Ministers had been asked by the Lord President to take part, and to co-ordinate their plans for speeches and TV and Radio appearances with my office. Central to our briefing arrangements for them and all participants was a Message our scribes prepared and agreed with Ministers for each of the main phases of the campaign, setting out themes and the main points to get across. In addition, weekly speaking notes were circulated, and occasional one-point notes also. Our rolling Diary of Events kept everyone and the Media informed. It was a huge programme in July, lesser in the holiday season of August, and full again in September leading up to the Party Conferences. In all some 70 Ministers, 25 Labour and Liberal pro-Europe leaders, 200 or more back-bench MPs and a substantial number of peers and non-Party BCEM speakers took part; many several times over. In addition many MPs held meetings of their own in their constituencies. The anti-marketeers also of course held many meetings up and down the country.

Our literature campaign was also massive. Every household in the land received over the months eleven small Factsheets, distributed through the Post Office, explaining 'What is the Common Market', 'How the Common Market works', 'The Background to Britain's application', and such aspects as 'Industry', 'Trade', 'Social Security', 'Agriculture and Fisheries', 'Community Finance', 'The Industrial Arguments', 'Some Questions Asked', and 'Free Movement of Labour'. They were strictly factual, and the distribution of some had begun in March. It continued right through except for August. In addition, a popular and illustrated short version of the White Paper was distributed widely in July. All were advertised by the Central Office of Information in the national press and by poster in the main towns through the summer and in late September. We did not suppose that everyone read them all, but the feedback was widely appreciative. The possibility was explored of advertising them on television but, despite the uncontroversial nature of the Factsheets, that was ruled out by the IT Authority on statutory grounds. I learnt soon after appointment that Ministers had also earlier considered engaging a public relations firm for the campaign, on the precedent of the Decimal Currency operation. That too was rejected – happily and sensibly, in my view – on the grounds that it would not have been proper before Parliament had approved the Government's policy in principle – which was not until October.

The Messages we sought to get across throughout the campaign were intended to be coherent and simple. They were conveyed at two levels, the high political and the low detail. The main Message was that as a member of the EEC 'Britain would have a more prosperous and secure future and Britain's views would once again be listened to in the world', whereas 'Outside the Communities, Britain would decline'. On the detailed issues our brief was always to explain, and to seek to allay anxieties not to dismiss them. The main ones I recall were feared loss of identity, loss of sovereignty, adverse impact on Commonwealth trade and an expected increase in prices.

The problems we faced of course were more than just argument. There was first the hugely adverse state of public opinion and divided state of Parliamentary opinion I have already mentioned and, with it, the traditional British resistance to anything smacking of Government propaganda, at least in peace-time. There was widespread scepticism after the previous two French rebuffs. There was a populist undercurrent fanned by Mr Wedgwood Benn and others, for the issue to be put to a national referendum. Both the Government and Labour Opposition firmly rejected that and it never actually achieved more than about 10% public support in the polls. It nonetheless demanded attention right through the campaign and in Parliament.

Then, there was the very complexity of the issue. As John Davies, the Secretary of State for Trade and Industry, said in the final Parliamentary debate: 'Time and again the spotlight of public interest (during the Great Debate) has shifted from one central issue to some other no less fundamental: sovereignty, continental defence, the cultural and scientific survival of Europe, the under-developed world, the economic consequences for Britain, short and long-term, the repercussions on the Commonwealth. The inescapable conclusion was that one way or the other, every facet of our future is deeply affected by this decision.' He could have added to his list of major aspects raised: peace and security in Europe, prices, employment, regional policy, social security and pensions, fisheries and many more. The 'take note' debate in the Commons at the end of July lasted four days with 90 speeches. The final debate at the end of October lasted six days – the longest on any single issue since the war – with 177 speeches. The Lords debates in July and October involved 107 and 82 speeches. The BBC TVs own Great Debate in October programmed for a full evening ran on until two o'clock in the morning. The national Great Debate continued in all its complexity to the end.

A third problem was the standing of the Government in the country at the time. In Robert Worcester's *How to win the Euro Referendum. Lessons from 1975*, he remarks: 'Europe is not an "issue-issue" with the British people. It is an "image-issue" – which will be decided as much on the credibility of those putting each side of the argument as on the merits of the case that they argue.' That was undoubtedly true of the Great Debate.

The Heath Government was not overly strong in the public image in July 1971, nor was the economic situation although the Chancellor's measures in mid July improved the atmosphere temporarily. Moreover the threat of higher prices and alleged threat to jobs remained obstinately the main causes of popular opposition to the end. On the other hand there was never any public doubt of the Government's firmness of intention. A striking feature of the polls throughout was that, however people felt about the issue, never less than 80% expected the Government to take the country into the Communities in the end. This proved crucial.

A fourth problem lay in the strength of the anti-Europe organisations. They were led by the Common Market Safeguards Campaign which in August, under its Secretary Mr Frere Smith, absorbed the others – the Commonwealth Industries Association, Keep Britain Out, Women against the Common Market and the Anti-Common Market League. They had been founded at various times since the Macmillan Government's original application in 1961, and were well entrenched, including in television and radio where they had secured parity of representation with the Government and our campaign in any broadcast debate. They were also quite effectively organised in parts of the country at grass roots. Their leaders were the Shadow Labour Ministers Peter Shore and Douglas Jay and the Conservative back-bencher Neil Marten. Their supporters included many strange bed-fellows like Enoch Powell and the Trade Union leader Clive Jenkins, but also a solid body of long-standing opponents. They rather faded under the impact of our campaign in July but reorganised in August and came back in association with Labour and the Trades Union Congress leadership in September. Their campaign included leaflets, pamphlets, speeches, conferences, appearances on TV and radio, letters to the press and MPs, constituency referenda and direct canvassing of MPs.

Fifth, and much the main problem from late July onwards, was the decision by Harold Wilson, forewarned at a special Labour Party conference in mid-July and confirmed by the Party National Executive on 28 July, to oppose the Government on the terms of entry. This greatly strengthened the anti-marketeers but also polarised the issue in the country and Parliament on party lines. It was a volte-face by Messrs Wilson, Callaghan, Healey and other Labour leaders from the position they had held in government in 1967 and in the 1970 General Election. The main reason given was that the terms were unsatisfactory, although three previous Labour Foreign Secretaries (Lord George Brown, Michael Stewart and Patrick Gordon Walker) and both former Labour negotiators (Lord Chalfont and George Thomson) publicly acknowledged that these terms were within the negotiating intentions of Labour when in power. Other reasons given, that the Common Agricultural and Regional policies of the Community and the home economy had developed unfavourably, were also contested by the minority pro-market Labour leaders. The all powerful

TUC had come out against joining at all. That was the major reason. Harold Wilson at least avoided going that far, which enabled him to do a reverse volte-face when he came back to power three years later. But it sharpened the 1971 Great Debate as nothing else could.

Opposition leaders like the old socialists Peter Shore and Michael Foot and the Trade Union barons Jack Jones and Hugh Scanlon made no bones about their basic reason. They wanted to retain power in Westminster, or more precisely in Whitehall, to bring about a socialist society in Britain. I am sure they were equally opposed to devolution of power to the regions and local authorities of Britain. Right wing Conservatives today, like Lady Thatcher and Ian Duncan Smith, seem to me motivated by a similar purpose. They want power to be retained in London to carry out their goals, in their case old fashioned freedom of the Market, the reverse of socialism. They may pay lip service to the principle of subsidiarity (doing things at the appropriate level) but basically seem to want a 'little England' centralised on London. That is how the main Opposition case came across in the Great Debate. It seems to be still the same today, although now more right wing than left.

The July phase of our campaign nonetheless exceeded all expectations. By the end of that month the poll of polls was showing near parity of public opinion and some polls were even showing, for the first time, a majority in favour. That to us confirmed the willingness of the people to be convinced by clear leadership and the facts, despite the barrage of opposition. It also demonstrated, as never before in peace-time, the enormous power of government to persuade public opinion of a cause if they marshalled their information resources effectively. It was gratifying for me to be at the wheel and on such an historic voyage.

The second phase through August and early September was less thrilling. The Recess and Holiday season made it hard to sustain momentum and the Labour National Executive decision of 28 July, presented by the Chairman Mr Mikardo and others as Labour Party policy against the Government's proposals, gave a large fillip to the opposition cause. The polls turned against us, not by more than 10% but enough to give concern. We stepped up our efforts again, including the BCEM at grass roots, and even brought in speakers from the Continent to explain life in the Community. By the end of August the polls were once again showing us in the lead, and even the anti-market Beaverbrook Press acknowledged 'rapidly growing support on the Common Market … over the Summer holidays'. We had attained Ministers' target of majority public opinion support by the start of the Party Conference season.

The third phase, mid-September to late October, was conducted at three levels: the national, the local and the political Parties. By and large the results in the former two, that is in the country, were this time disappointing, but our main focus had now to be on the Parties and specifically those in

Parliament who were going to make the final decision. In that overriding aim we succeeded. But that was still a month ahead. By mid-September we were again campaigning in the country at full strength with resumed literature distribution to households; hundreds of speaker meetings (especially in Scotland where we were able to catch up important lost ground); press briefings; participation in TV and Radio debates; BCEM newsheets, leaflets, advertising, rallies and letters; some 50 additional pamphlets by private organisations, banks and research centres; and recruitment of support, notably the National Farmers' Union, the CBI, the Associated Chambers of Commerce, the International Department of the British Council of Churches, the British Youth Council and many more influential bodies. But public interest at large had waned – a fact also reflected in local audiences. Unemployment, prices and Northern Ireland had come to preoccupy people more. The regional press by and large kept up their coverage but the national media flagged, keeping their powder dry for the final phase in Parliament. The debate was now politically loaded by Labour and Trade Union opposition. Our support in the polls declined.

The fourth and final phase was directed, on both sides, at the Parties and Parliament, and particularly at the 625 MPs whose votes pundits now busied themselves trying to forecast, with wide margins of the unknown. Most expected a majority for the Government's proposals, but all, from the Prime Minister downwards, recognised that it must be a good majority to be convincing. Estimates ranged from an inadequate 25 to a more than adequate 110.

The Conservative Central Council started the conference round with a one-day special meeting on the subject in Glasgow. The Co-operative Congress followed, also with a one-day special conference, and came out in qualified support (the London Co-operative Society dissenting). The Trades Union Congress held a perfunctory half-day debate at its annual conference and voted massively against EEC membership, although not without some dissent. The Liberal Party gave a day of its annual conference to the subject and voted almost unanimously in favour. The Labour Party despatched the subject on the first day of its annual conference as quietly as the militant left on the one hand and Lord George Brown and a few other pro-Europe stalwarts would let it. The vote was 5 to 1 against entry into Europe on the Government's negotiated terms. That was on 4 October and brought the Labour Party formally into opposition. It also split the Party wide open. As The Times commented: 'Mr Roy Jenkins and the Labour Europeans are caught in a dilemma. The issue between them and their party majority is so extensive and deep that in an earlier and less ideological age we should have seen a realignment of the main parties, as backbenchers crossed the floor in both directions (the Conservative hard-line opponents included). No such resolution is conceivable today.' The seeds were nonetheless sown at this time for the ultimate schism in the

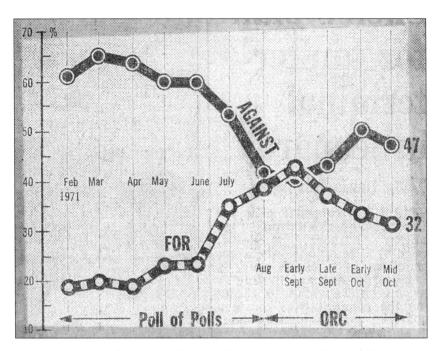

Labour Party and departure of Roy Jenkins, Shirley Williams, Bill Rodgers, David Owen, and some forty other Labour MPs to found the Social Democratic Party ten years later. At this juncture, however, this pro-European minority was constrained both by agreement between Mr Wilson and Mr Jenkins to refrain from campaigning further on the issue in order not to widen the Party split, and by public and private pressure brought to bear on the minority by the majority. The Conservative Party Conference on the other hand devoted its whole first day to the subject and, exceptionally, took a vote. The result was a solid 8 to 1 majority in favour. This meant that the 110 or more opposed or doubtful Conservative MPs estimated in June had been whittled down to about 40. It was accordingly now clear that, even on the most cautious estimate of Labour supporters and abstainers and Liberal supporters, the Government was assured a good Parliamentary majority. The Prime Minister immediately seized the initiative by declaring that the vote on the Government side would not be whipped but free. The effect was dramatic, and was welcomed not only by the dissident minorities on both sides but generally in the country. The Labour opposition was caught on the wrong foot and had to settle on its side for a ragged 3-line whip. It was a masterful stroke by Mr Heath.

The final House of Commons debate starting on 21 October was a six-day marathon, of high standard throughout. On the fourth day, Roy Jenkins declared he would vote with the Government and so did Douglas Houghton, Chairman of the Parliamentary Labour Party. Labour support gathered pace thereafter. Conservative waiverers had already begun to come over. At the end, Mr Heath wound up the debate with these words: 'I do not think any Prime Minister has stood at the dispatch box in time of peace and asked the House to take a positive decision of such importance as I am asking tonight and I am well aware of the responsibility ... I have always made it plain to the British people that consent to this would be given by Parliament. Parliament is part of the people. Tonight, when Parliament endorses this motion, many millions of people across the world will rejoice that Britain will be taking up her rightful place in the true European unity which we are going to seek.' The motion was then put, on 28 October, that British entry into the European Communities be agreed in principle on the arrangements negotiated by the Government. Amidst great excitement, it was carried by a majority of 112, more than anyone had expected. (My own best estimate before the debate had been between 75 and 110. Whitelaw's had been lower still, and he lost a bet on it!) It was also more than four times the Government's normal majority. Of the 622 MPs able to vote, 356 did so in favour including 69 Labour and 5 Liberal; 244 voted against including 39 Conservative, 6 Independents and 1 Liberal; and 22 abstained, including 20 Labour and 2 Conservative. The House of Lords also voted in favour by the massive majority of 451 to 58. The decision of Parliament was overwhelming 'Aye'.

Our campaign had succeeded in all its aims, except in maintaining majority public support in the last phase particularly among Labour voters but that returned once Parliament had voted. The polls then showed a clear popular majority both that EEC entry was in Britain's national interest (50% for, 30% against) and that the opponents should now accept the verdict of Parliament (50% for, 35% against). The Government thus had popular support as well as its Parliamentary mandate to proceed with preparations for entry. The cardinal achievements of the campaign had been to turn around public opinion in July and August from 25% in favour and 60% against to a vastly different 45% in favour and 40% against; and then to win Parliamentary approval, against the odds, by such a decisive majority.

This success was attributable to several factors but most of all, in my view, to three: firm leadership by the Prime Minister and Government, against a formidable but ultimately divided opposition; the maintainance throughout of a simple and clear message that Britain needed to be in Europe; and the massive effort we put into it.

The main elements of that effort were the media and particularly the television coverage achieved; the literature, and particularly the vast household distribution; and the speech programme, involving as it did hundreds of meetings (and press briefings) up and down the country. The European Movement's many activities at all levels provided another essential element, as did the support of so many other non-governmental bodies.

The financial cost was modest. The opposition complained of heavy governmental and BCEM expenditure, ignoring the fact that they themselves had TUC funding. In fact the cost of the Government part of the campaign was less than £½ million and that of the BCEM less than £¼ million. For the greatest peace-time information campaign this country has ever seen, that was I think a particular source of public service satisfaction (I believe the Decimal Currency information campaign of 1970, which was smaller but used commercial agencies, cost more than twice as much, £2 million).

The one disappointing feature of the Great Debate was the decision of Harold Wilson and many of his Labour and Trade Union colleagues, to continue the battle after Parliament had settled the issue. TUC opposition did not stop the General Secretary, Vic Feather, declaring on their behalf: 'I have no doubt the British unions will be able to work within the structure of the [Common] Market and influence its development. We shall help them to reach their aims.' Similarly, on the extreme right, the proprietor of the *Daily Express*, Sir Max Aitken, who had long campaigned through his newspapers against Britain joining the Common Market, wrote: 'The Daily Express accepts the verdict of the freely elected British Parliament.' Even Mr Wilson, to quote the *Daily Telegraph* at the time: 'after some backing and filling was compelled to admit that Labour favoured entry if the terms were satisfactory, and would abide by the Treaty and continue British Membership.' But he also maintained that no Parliament could bind its successor and a future Labour government 'would immediately give notice we could not accept the terms negotiated by the Conservatives, and in particular the unacceptable burdens arising out of the financial arrangements, the Common Agricultural Policy, the blows to the Commonwealth and any threats to our essential regional policies ... If the Community then refused to negotiate or if negotiations were to fail, we would sit down amicably and discuss the situation with them. We should make it clear from that moment that our posture, like that of the French (President de Gaulle) after 1958, would be rigidly directed towards the pursuit of British interests ... The Community could accept, or decide that we should agree to part. That would depend on them ... Today is not an end. It is a beginning' – by which he was referring to his Labour Opposition's intention to attack the Government's consequential legislation, the European Communities Bill, when it came before the House in the New Year. To me, his use of the word 'posture' said it all. It had more to do with partisan politics and the short-term interest of Labour Party and Trades Union unity than with the long-term future of Britain in Europe – just as thirty years later, the Conservative leader William Hague talked big for a time about re-negotiating Britain's Treaty commitments to Europe, in the hope of currying right wing Conservative and populist opinion domestically. Looking back I am sure that Mr Wilson's manoeuvring and re-negotiation weakened the British hand in Europe. However the Great Debate decision of 1971 survived, and despite periodic sniping from the extremes of British politics, I have no doubt it will continue to do so. Britain is, to its enormous benefit, now an established member of the European Union.

We had quite modest celebrations after the 28 October vote, a party with the Prime Minister and rather larger one at the European Movement, and lots of gratifying letters of mutual congratulations and thanks. But the general tone was 'on with the next job', the European Communities Bill. For me it was writing the official report and then, so I thought, back once more to finding a new career. The Great Debate had been an exciting and fulfulling task.

CHAPTER 22

# Entry into Europe

## 1972–1973

THE CALL TO CONTINUE WORKING on Europe came unexpectedly just as I was winding up the Great Debate job and reviewing afresh my prospective change of career. 'Would I be willing to join the Whitehall team responsible for the European Communities Bill, and be their chief press spokesman?', I was asked. The job would be for about six months, in the Cabinet Office, working with the Chancellor of the Duchy of Lancaster, Geoffrey Rippon, the Solicitor General, Sir Geoffrey Howe, the deputy Under-Secretary (Europe) in the Cabinet Office, Peter Thornton, an Assistant Under-Secretary seconded from the Home Office, Brian Cubbon, a lawyer seconded from the Treasury Solicitors' department, Derek Rippengal and a small supporting staff. The terms would be to get this essential legislation through Parliament without defeat. Failure would wreck the whole process of entry into Europe.

The Prime Minister had announced the weekend after the great 28 October vote that the Government's legislative programme for the new session would be largely devoted to 'the demands which are now about to be made upon a modern Britain moving into the European Community.' This foreshadowed the early tabling of a European Communities Bill which would 'enable the UK to comply with the obligations entailed by membership of the European Coal & Steel Community, the European Economic Community and the European Atomic Energy Community, and to exercise the rights of membership.' There would be four months of Parliamentary scrutiny and debate on the Bill, longer than on any other since the war. It would start in mid-January. There was no time to lose if British accession to Community membership and the beginning of our complex transitional arrangements were to be achieved by the planned date of 1 January 1973. But there was to be no rushing Parliamentary time on the Bill. It was too important for that, and the pundits were forecasting war from the Labour

Opposition and Tory anti-marketeers at every turn. In the event the passage of the Bill did produce moments of high drama both in some early cliff-hanging votes and later in the collapse of Labour unity. But no one could foretell that when I was appointed in late November. The word then was that we should prepare for everything. The drafting of the Bill and the preparation of briefs for Ministers were already under way.

I did not this time wholly relish the prospect of being involved. The job appealed to me as another challenge on Europe, and in Parliament. But I had not seen much of home and family for months (my club, the Anglo-Belgian in Belgrave Square, had been my haven when I was too pressed to commute to Guildford). I was overdue for an operation on a sinus, damaged by a fight with a cricket ball some time previously. I wanted to get my future settled. And, while I enjoyed dealing with the media and it would be interesting to become more intimately acquainted with that remarkable institution the 'Parliamentary Press Lobby', my career search had taught me that my first choice of job would always be managerial. I had no burning desire to be spokesman, chief or otherwise. However, there it was, and I felt obliged to stay with the cause. An incentive was that the FCO and Civil Service Department had now begun planning the recruitment of candidates to fill the vacancies that would be open to Britain in the European Commission and the Council of Ministers' Secretariat in Brussels when we entered, and the FCO suggested they propose me for a senior post there subject to suitable vacancies. I weighed this up, decided it made sense, and informed the firms and organisations who had shown interest in having me that I was no longer available. At the same time I wrote to the thirty and more eminent friends who had helped: 'I am now joining the Rippon group in the Cabinet Office for the legislative phase and am then slated for Brussels subject to suitable vacancies. I have accepted this risk and called off the opportunities in industry and man-agement consultancy which emerged in the Spring and Autumn, as I think it should resolve my family and career problem in the most logical way. It will be pioneering in a cause I have long put first, but static and near home so all right for the family. Anyhow it is fingers crossed for it … Thank you again for all your kindness and help.' All replied encouragingly.

The two Ministers I was to work with, Geoffrey Rippon and Geoffrey Howe, were both outstanding in their own ways, but as alike as chalk and cheese. Geoffrey Rippon's constituency was in Northumberland and his political base, I think, in local government national associations. He was a shrewd choice by Prime Minister Heath both to lead the Brussels negotiations and to take the legislation through the House. Convivial and laid back, he gave the impression of easy-going and at times even indolence, driving his official negotiating team in Brussels sometimes to distraction by appearing not to have bothered to read his briefs. But he had in fact a remarkable capacity to absorb the issues, judge his negotiating and debating opponents and sense the political occasion. I saw more of him in later years when he was chairman of the prestigious European-Atlantic dining Group and I was one of its vice-chairmen. After the European Communities Bill he invited me to join him at the Department of the Environment when he became Secretary of State there, but I was unable to do so. He did not find favour with Mrs Thatcher when she became Prime Minister because, to his credit and I think her discredit, he remained loyal to Edward Heath and Europe. He later, I believe, sadly fell foul of Robert Maxwell, like so many others. I enjoyed working with him.

I cannot quite say the same of Geoffrey Howe. He was courteous enough, and brilliant both on the legal drafting and presentation of the Bill and in absorbing and arguing the detailed issues in the House. But I found him a little cerebral and remote. Conservative Parliamentary gossip had him marked at the time as one of two up-and-coming future Tory Prime Ministers, the other being Christopher Chataway, one of Roger Bannister's pace-makers in the first one-minute mile and a popular Postmaster-General in Mr Heath's government. The would-be king- and queen-makers of the Conservative party also talked at the time of an up-and-coming woman MP called Margaret Thatcher, but as a possible future Chancellor of the Exchequer rather than Prime Minister. I never really got to know Geoffrey Howe, either then or later but, like so many others, came to admire his ultimate stand against an overweening Prime Minister Thatcher on Europe and in Parliament.

Officialdom in the Cabinet Office was a new world to me. Everyone wanted to work there as it was the centre of things. Few could do so because it was policy to keep its functions to the Cabinet Secretariat and, in lodger units, some only temporary, to such co-ordination functions as could not be performed effectively in any of the other great Departments of State but had to be done centrally. No. 10 Downing Street staff were also in those days strictly limited – to the Prime Minister's personal staff, press office and, a new innovation, a 'central policy review unit' of bright young things under an imported member of the Rothschild family. Today that chick seems to have given place to a whole brood of No. 10 units. I wonder whether so much centralisation is a good thing – and where they are accommodated, No. 10 being but a big town house. The Cabinet Office had to be selective because that building too, situated on the corner of Downing Street and Whitehall, was small, so much so in fact that the then Cabinet Secretary Sir Burke Trend (who was also Head of the Civil Service) felt obliged to determine the allocation of offices personally.

In the year I was there on the European Communities Bill and then on preparations for membership, he moved me and my small staff four times. My first two offices were little rabbit warrens. The third was more wholesome, but only lasted a few weeks before the Prime Minister appointed a Minister of Information and he took precedence over me. My last office, indeed my last-ever office in Whitehall, made up for all the others. It was a large, rather fusty but otherwise sumptuous office overlooking both Downing Street and Whitehall, at first floor level, and intended for a Minister. Some rebellious farmers and other disgruntled groups had taken at that time to protesting vehemently at the entrance to Downing Street, which had no gates as it does now, and it was considered preferable that an official like me should be in the firing line of any bricks they might throw, rather than a Minister. None in fact came my way, so my final weeks in the Cabinet Office were spent in relative comfort.

I cannot quite say the same of the nights, when I had to be in the House late and could not commute to Guildford. Instead of running up bills at my club, I discovered a corner of the Cabinet Office the Cabinet Secretary did not seem to know about, the boiler room, and secured permission to bunk down there on a camp bed whenever necessary. The boilermen let me use their bathroom facilities. They were a congenial bunch of troglodytes but, like everyone else in the place, kept their own company. There was little corporate spirit to be found in the Cabinet Office, as there was in the FCO and most other Departments. There were too many temporary lodgers for that. But we in the Rippon group in time created our own, even if rather painfully at first.

Peter Thornton was used to all this. He had been head of the EEC Unit in the Cabinet Office, co-ordinating the negotiations with Brussels, before over-seeing this task. He was keenly conscious of his responsibility and a bit fretful in his management. At our first encounter he understandably wanted me to start immediately but, less understandably, asked me to cancel my sinus operation to do so. I declined and it took him a little time to understand my commitments both personal and to Europe. But we got on well in the end. He went on to become Permanent Secretary of the Department of Trade & Industry. His number two, Brian Cubbon, was also very able and ambitious. He had come from the Department most officials in Whitehall regarded as the backwater, the Home Office, and optimistically wanted to be considered for the post of Ambassador or Minister in our delegation to the EEC. Instead he went on to become Permanent Secretary of the Northern Ireland Office, and was injured by an IRA car-bomb in Dublin. This was the attack in which our Ambassador, Christopher Ewart-Biggs, was killed. Happily Cubbon recovered and subsequently I think became Permanent Secretary of the Home Office. The third senior member of the group, Derek Rippengal, was equally able in his own legal field and beyond, but not involved in the Whitehall rat race. He went on to be Counsel to the Chairman of Committees of the House of Lords, and was a pleasure to work with from the start. But we all, and the two responsible Ministers and their private offices, jelled together once the trauma of preparing the Bill and voluminous brief was over, and the Bill successfully launched. The press presentation went very well. I shall come back to that.

Another feature of Cabinet Office life I found surprising was the rigidity of the internal administration. This doubtless derived from the small and exclusive nature of that Office as it was then – and is probably quite different today. My job was both executive in organising the press launch and briefing the press, and co-ordinating in securing a common approach by the information and press officers of all the many Departments of government involved. I needed only a staff of two, an assistant and a secretary, but it was like moving a mountain to get them and I had to rely on the temporary loan of staff from a much more overstretched FCO in the meanwhile. Eventually the Department of Trade & Industry came to my rescue. The point of light relief however, came when I asked for a tape-call-maker to save me time dialling my many daily contacts, and a Xerox copier to save queueing at the EEC unit's communal photocopier two floors up. The Administration Officer's reply on the latter was to offer service at 'the main reproduction centre to which work may be sent, or in cases of extreme urgency where work may be taken by your PA for an instant service'. On the former his reply was even more painstakingly negative:

> In the Cabinet Office the Call Maker is not the sort of equipment that we consider justified for the following reasons:
>
> (1) Senior Officers are provided with Personal Secretaries in order to save their time. The PS is expected to make the out-going call right through to the stage when the person called is on the line. The Call Maker machine may save some time in the actual dialling out process but this is by no means the only unproductive part of making the telephone call.
>
> (2) The Cabinet Office has private lines to several Government Departments which avoids exchange dialling.
>
> (3) We find that by making the calls the Personal Secretaries become more involved in the work of their masters [sic], and monitoring at least the first moments of a call is mutually advantageous.
>
> I hope that you can agree with our view which incidentally is shared by the Civil Service Department Management Services whose advice has been sought by our Organisation & Methods Officer.

That was in mid-January 1972. With time then running out before the launch of the Bill I resorted to invoking the intercession of No. 10. All three requests – staff, photocopier and call-maker – were suddenly met like magic. Such were the ways of our bureaucracy, both at its best, in the comprehensive briefing mounted in quick time for Ministers Rippon and Howe on the Bill, and at its worst, in the hierarchical and penny-pinching resistance to innovative organisation. The Cabinet Office administration was I think glad to see the back of me and my small unit when we eventually left. But in fairness, I suppose it was not much fun for them coping with an endless stream of temporary lodger units all demanding different things. And I confess to a measure of pride in having actually served a year in that holy of holies. It was certainly an experience – of the great and the small!

The European Communities Bill was 'to give legal effect to the arrangements made for British membership under the accession Treaty', which was signed by Mr Heath and the leaders of the Six in Brussels on 22 January. The Bill could probably have been limited to three clauses together with annexes. The idea had grown publicly however that it might be a 'thousand clause Bill'. The Government, forewarned by Mr Wilson at the end of the Great Debate that the Labour Opposition 'would challenge it clause by clause and line by line', decided on a short single Bill of twelve clauses and four annexed schedules. Most of the clauses dealt with definitions, the European Court, and amendments to UK law to conform to existing Community law in particular areas like customs, import duties, sugar, food and drugs, road transport, application of the Common Agricultural Policy, film quotas, company law and restrictive trade practices. The key clause was 2 which in the space of only eighty-six short lines, gave in sub-section 1 the force of law in the UK to such present and future Community law as, under the Community Treaties, applied direct; and, in sub-section 2, authorised the Government to apply other Community obligations and rights by Orders in Council and regulations. It also provided for financial contributions to the Community and acceptance of any receipts.

There was an immediate outcry from the Labour opposition and anti-marketeers that it was a lawyer's conjuring trick designed to limit debate on this fundamental feature of Community membership. This was a warning of things to come in Parliament. Outside, the press happily took it differently. There was sneaking admiration for the brilliance of the Bill, no criticism, and it fell like a lead balloon. My colleagues and Geoffrey Howe were a bit taken aback and I think disappointed there was no limelight, but soon came round to recognise it was just what we wanted. My press arrangements could not, paradoxically, have gone better. We could now concentrate on the impending battle in Parliament and, press-wise, on the Parliamentary lobby.

I had worked quite hard for this result. The legislation was unusual in involving so many Departments and issues, and in being handled from the Cabinet Office, which had no Press Office of its own. The briefs my colleagues produced for Ministers ran to hundreds of pages filling two fat volumes of spring-back binders. They covered every aspect of our future relationship with the complex of Community affairs that might be raised in the Parliamentary debates. A set of summary briefs had to be prepared for the Press launch and, as with the Ministerial briefs, they each had to be cleared with the Departments concerned. There were leading editors and writers to contact, people like David Wood and David Spanier of *The*

*Times*, David Watt of the *Financial Times*, Ian Aitken of the *Guardian*, Harry Boyne of the *Daily Telegraph*, Andrew Knight of the *Economist*, Nora Beloff of the *Observer*, Ronald Butt of the *Sunday Times*, Walter Terry of the *Daily Mail*, Willy Woolf of the *Daily Mirror* and Anthony Shrimsley of the *Sun*, all of them distinguished in the newspaper world but new to me because the press briefing of the Great Debate had been done by No. 10 and the principal Departments and Organisations concerned. Then there were the 100 and more Parliamentary Lobby correspondents to list and the leading ones to get to know. They were a world of their own, accustomed to mixing with the Parliamentary great and to being spoon-fed. There were also the leading foreign correspondents in London to involve. Last but not least there were my television and radio contacts to renew. The Cabinet Office having no press facilities and contact lists of its own, I had to draw on the help of other Departments concerned and particularly No. 10 where Donald Maitland and his assistant (and future successor as Chief Press officer) Tom McCaffrey were as ever unfailing. We were creating a press office in the Cabinet Office from scratch. The press launch had to be organised in a borrowed hall. It was very well attended and gave the Bill and its Ministerial movers, Mr Rippon and Sir Geoffrey Howe, a favourable send-off. I was relieved.

My job thereafter was merely to maintain these contacts, be available to them either in the Cabinet Office or in the Press Gallery of the House of Commons, maintain inter-departmental press co-ordination, and advise our two Ministers and my colleagues on press relations. Once the launch was achieved this work became largely routine. The media showed little interest in the substance of the debates. They were more concerned, as ever under our adversarial political system, with the strategy and tactics of both sides and the chance of dramatic votes and possible rebuffs to the Government. The many hours I spent with them in the House, listening to their gossip and analyses, aroused my interest in weighing the political moves and prospects for our side. Politics and Parliament had interested me from childhood and in earlier years I had dreamt of being there. Many times over the years I had visited the House either in the gallery or, when serving in the FO and FCO as adviser to one or other of our Ministers, in the advisers' box. The great occasions still held me. But those days, nights and weeks I spent on the European Communities Bill, listening to the spinning of adversarial debate (I prefer the probing of committee discussion myself) and observing the contortions of Parliamentary procedure, only served to confirm my desire to help manage politicians (and specifically of course the Liberals) rather than be one of them. More immediately however I found I could make myself useful to the Rippon team advising on strategy and tactics and drafting occasional speeches for them. It became an interesting part of my job.

The progress of the Bill through the procedure of 2nd Reading on the floor of the House, detailed consideration in Committee, back to the Chamber to debate amendments, then to the Lords and back for 3rd Reading, offered endless opportunity to a determined opposition to make trouble. The Government still had only a 25 majority, and some of them seemed determined to maintain their anti-market opposition. To make matters worse the Government was in trouble in the country, with much industrial unrest and economic discontent. The miners' strike cast widespread gloom and rising unemployment generated still more despondency. Mr Heath had made it plain that if the vote on the 2nd Reading of the Bill went against the Government, he would call a general election. The Labour Party saw this as a possible opportunity to drive the Government out and come back to power themselves. The vote was taken on 17 February. The House was packed. Mr Wilson beat the drum that the Bill imposed an alien system of government. Geoffrey Howe tellingly rejoined that the system was no different from that the Wilson Government had declared they wished to join in 1967. Mr Heath reaffirmed that he and his colleagues were at one that there would have to be a General Election if this vote was lost. The division was called amid tense excitement (and after frantic activity by the Whips on both sides). The Government scraped home by 8 votes. All but four of the pro-Europe Labour minority (plus Ray Gunter who resigned on it) voted against in deference to their Party unity. Some fifteen die-hard Conservatives went with them, leaving the Liberals to save the day by voting 5 to 1 in favour. Their Leader, Jeremy Thorpe, suffered physical as well as verbal abuse from angry Labour members for having the courage of his convictions. It was not a pleasant sight.

There were also scares and alarms in the Committee stage which lasted until April. In all some 24 divisions were called in the period to Easter, the Government majority falling at times to 11, 13 and 14 – figures which would have been lower still but for Liberal support. An acute new problem lay with the 8 Ulster Unionist MPs who had turned against the Government, carrying a few right-wing Conservatives with them, over the Government's decision to suspend the Stormont Assembly and impose direct rule from Westminster. Two had voted against and one abstained on 2nd Reading. Now all 8 were in doubt. The Government decided to win back their support by promising an increase in Northern Ireland's representation in the House of Commons (it is now 17). Back on the floor of the House the tightest vote of all was, predictably, on the catch-all Clause 2. My recollection is that it was a majority of four. It was certainly touch-and-go. But, as Churchill used to say, under our political system all that is needed is a simple majority of one. So, happily, the Bill continued on its way, amendment after amendment being proposed by the Opposition and rejected by the Government, brief after brief being updated by my colleagues for our Ministers, only to find at the last moment that the Speaker, under our tortuous Parliamentary procedure, had selected some but omitted others, so officials' work was partly wasted – the theory being, I was told by the House of Commons clerks, that it kept Ministers on their toes – which of course it did not for they were on their toes already, dealing with the amendments that had been selected.

The course of the Bill has been fully documented in Hansard and beyond. Parliamentary approval was finally secured in July and the Act came into force in September in good time for entry into membership of the Community on the planned date of 1 January 1973. To me the most interesting feature of the whole process, aside from the opportunity to observe the workings of Parliament from within and to be party to getting the European Communities Bill through, was the conduct of the Labour opposition throughout. It was a study in itself.

It early became obvious that Labour strategy and tactics on the Bill could only be gauged in the light of their own internal divisions and struggle. The Parliamentary Labour Party fell broadly into three groups. The smallest but, because of strong Trade Union support, the increasingly powerful, was the left-wing, mainly Tribune, group of committed anti-marketeers, some 50 in number, led by Michael Foot and Peter Shore. Acting no doubt on the principle that the best way to deal with trouble-makers was to load them with responsibility, Wilson gave Foot and Shore the job of conducting the parliamentary opposition to the Bill. It did not quite work out as he intended. They failed to bring defeat on the Government or the Bill but, as the *New Statesmen* reflected half way through, 'the function of the Opposition is not only to oppose but to clarify, and it is being highly successful at this.' In the process they clearly enhanced their standing in the Party. Everyone knew Peter Shore's ability and diligence. Michael Foot was a dedicated socialist and brilliant speaker, but no one had seen him lead before. People in the House began saying that perhaps his capacity for responsible leadership on the front bench had been underestimated after all. He went on, seven years later, of course, to become the Party's leader, though a far from successful one. His rise up the ladder began on the European Communities Bill.

The middle and largest group in the Parliamentary Labour Party at that time numbered about 145. With Mr Wilson they put the unity of the Party first, and supported the Party's official position on Europe. That was acceptance of entry but opposition to the terms. The Foot-Shore group were opposed to entry on any terms.

The third group, numbering about 90 and led by the Party deputy leader Roy Jenkins, were the pro-marketeers. Many had found traumatic the experience of rebelling against their whips in the Great Debate vote of the previous October, and were glad when Douglas Houghton, chairman of the Parliamentary Party (and himself a pro-marketeer) proposed a closing of ranks against the Government on the consequential legislation except where the principle of entry was involved. That formula was never accepted by the anti-marketeers or adopted by the PLP but it served as a guide to the pro-marketeers. They dropped any intention of playing an active part on the Bill, and the Government lost any hope of their support (though a handful continued to abstain). They numbered among them more Shadow Ministers than the anti-market group, though not enough for a majority in the Shadow Cabinet. In February, after publication of the Bill, they did succeed in blocking an attempt by the anti-market group to establish the Opposition line as one of root and branch opposition to the Bill. Up to Easter, however, they clearly lost credibility and ground to the Foot-Shore group.

The struggle between the Opposition and the Government on the Bill thus concealed an equally bitter battle within the Labour Party between the anti-marketeers who were looking to persuade the next Party Conference to vote for outright withdrawal from the European Communities and the pro-marketeers who believed in Europe. Even more, it was the rising battle of the left to gain control of the Party. The Bill gave their leadership not just a platform to shine in Parliament and the Party but the opportunity to take the debate outside when they saw advantage and to embarrass and discredit the Jenkins group when they could.

Mr Wilson's position in all this was clear: the sooner, in party terms, this deeply divisive issue of Europe was out of the way the better. He supported Mr Foot and Mr Shore in harassing the Government, inside and outside Parliament, whenever the occasion looked fruitful or, alternatively, whenever there was complaint that he was not giving the support he should. His main interests were Party unity and Northern Ireland. The European issue was an embarrassment to him. On the other hand he remained firm on the Party line that the terms were wrong, not the concept of membership, and when challenged in the 2nd Reading debate to endorse a call by Mr Shore 'to renegotiate and relegislate' he declined to do so. He remained firmly against the left-wing aim to carry the Party Conference totally against Europe. He doubtless saw that a Party decision of that nature would land him with a problem every bit as great as Hugh Gaitskell's had been on unilateral nuclear disarmament.

The crunch came in the Spring when President Pompidou suddenly gave new credibility to the idea of a referendum. Officially Monsieur Pompidou wanted a display of public support in France for his policy on Europe. In fact, like his predecessor, General de Gaulle, the referendum was designed just to boost his domestic political position. Seizing this development however, Wedgwood Benn immediately revived his proposal to have a referendum on Europe in this country and persuaded the Labour Party National Executive, of which he was now chairman, to drop its previous opposition to the idea. Mr Wilson unexpectedly followed suit and the Shadow Cabinet adopted the proposal by eight votes to six. To Roy Jenkins this was one step too far. It was, he said, not the way an

Opposition should be run. On 10 April he resigned as deputy leader of the Party and member of the Shadow Cabinet and retired to the back benches. Harold Lever and George Thomson accompanied him. It was the parting of the ways. The Labour Party's internal conflict on Europe had now split it apart. Their spokesmen on the Bill continued to fight their corner against the Government, but the sword was blunted. As for the Party, that split was to haunt them for years to come.

We celebrated the successful passage of the Bill more modestly even than the Great Debate. In diplomatic tradition I had the leading press men and members of our team to a party at my house in Guildford and we were blessed with a balmy evening warm enough to sit out late in the garden overlooking the lights of Guildford. It was a happy occasion. As it turned out, it was also the last diplomatic dinner my wife and I gave before leaving government service. My records tell me that the team had some official 'jollifications' in late September when the Bill was finally passed, but by then I was on to my next job. I had some very nice letters and messages of thanks from Rippon, Thornton, Cubbon and others, Cubbon remarking, 'Throughout the exercise Ministers and I have been greatly indebted to you for your wise and perceptive advice on the tactics to be employed ... the final success of the Bill owes as much to the employment of the right tactics as to anything else. Moreover I do not think I can recall any significant press criticisim of what we were doing on the Bill, and this too is your work.' That was very nice of him. The substantive work was of course done by Cubbon himself, Thornton and their colleagues and the two Ministers.

In July I was asked by Anthony Royle and others to take on a third job on Europe. The Prime Minister wanted a special information and educative effort conducted in the country after the enactment of the Bill and in the interval between the European Summit meeting planned to be held in Paris on 19–20 October, and British entry into the Community on 1 January. The purpose would be to encourage business, industry, the professions and all other sectors of the country likely to be affected, to step up their preparations for Community membership. The Summit was relevant because, apart from being the first a British Prime Minister had attended, it was expected to mark another major development of the Community. The Heads of Government did in fact decide that the whole complex of relations between the countries of the Community should be transformed into a European Union by the end of the decade; that the objective of economic and monetary union in Europe should be attained by 1980; and that a programme of action should be worked out for the removal of fiscal, legal and technical barriers to internal trade and industrial co-operation within the Community. The enlarged Community could not stand still while the new members, the UK, Ireland, Denmark and Norway (though in the event Norway failed to ratify), were settling in. Apart from internal considerations this was the year when the world abandoned Bretton Woods in favour of floating currencies which was to affect the Community profoundly.

At home there was all too much evidence that many medium and small businesses and industries had still not prepared themselves either to face the consequences of a common market or to take advantage of it. The Government could not do it for them. What we could do, and this was the Prime Minister's wish, was to mount a short information and educative campaign between October and January directed at the sectors most concerned to stimulate and help them. Anthony Royle was to be Ministerial co-ordinator and chairman of a mixed ministerial and official committee representing all the 15 principal Departments concerned (mostly at Senior Information Officer level), and I was to be official co-ordinator and deputy to him.

We agreed in early August that the first and main task should be to beef-up departmental campaigning by each of the Departments concerned to their own sectors – DTI to industry and commerce; MAFF to agriculture, fisheries & food; the Treasury to financial services; DOE to transport and, on the environmental consequences, to industry and agriculture; DES to universities, colleges and local education authorities; the Lord Chancellor's Department to the courts and legal profession; and so forth. The second element would be a campaign of ministerial speeches up and down the country, centrally co-ordinated. The third would be a centrally organised publicity effort to draw attention to the whole. And the fourth would be to enlist the fullest support of trade and industrial associations, interested voluntary organisations and the media. Ministers approved this framework and the Lord President, now Robert Carr, wrote to all his senior Ministerial colleagues in mid-August for their support and participation.

The Departmental programmes were each considered and approved by our Committee, gaps filled and all brought into force by the end of October. They encompassed leaflets, pamphlets, booklets and other explanatory literature; liaison with trade, industrial and professional associations; press briefings and radio participation; visits, conferences and seminars; enquiry points; and Ministerial articles and statements. Ministerial speech programmes were organised for October, November and December, involving altogether 50 Ministers and 270 speeches. General speaking notes were compiled centrally including on the outcome of the Summit meeting, but platforms were arranged by Departments. Conservative Central office also helped with meetings and briefing notes.

When we considered what was most needed for the centrally organised element of the campaign, we soon concluded it was a handy Checklist and Guide to key sources of information and advice available to firms, institutions and people to find what they needed to know about Community practices and law, about the transitional arrangements, and about the opportunities presented. This may now sound simple enough. But, with so many aspects of national affairs affected – the Community, after all, was not in its infancy when we joined but fifteen years into the development of common market laws and practices – and also so many departments of government involved, it proved quite a task to plan, agree and condense all this into a slim booklet. We achieved it by the dead-line of 26 October. The Prime Minister approved. Money was found for central costs by the three Departments most concerned – the DTI, MAFF and DOE – and for a TV and Press advertising campaign to accompany the Checklist, to a total of £350,000. Parliament was informed. So was the Parliamentary press lobby and the sectoral press by central and departmental press briefings. In addition we organised a reception by Ministers for editors, leader writers and radio and TV correspondents. All this was done, as planned, in the week following the European Summit. To begin with the Checklist was sent free, with Ministerial exhortations to prepare, to some 350,000 selected company executives, financial service managers, education officers, local authorities and libraries, and trade, industrial and professional associations. The advertising went on intermittently until early December.

We had no means of monitoring the results. It was administratively and financially impractical to mount any special arrangements to assess the impact. But the indicators were all favourable. Demand for the Checklist reached ¾ million and required a reprint. Enquiries on specific issues poured in to the main Departments. There was no press, radio or television criticism but, on the contrary, a favourable response to our appeal to them to help by stepping-up their own contributions to the 'Are we ready for Europe' campaign. The European Movement and a number of banks, firms and trade associations helpfully joined in. I think we had one letter of complaint from the public – that the Checklist was too much like hard work or something like that. We could not expect to please all the people all the time! Otherwise, the feedback was all favourable and appreciative. How much our efforts actually helped to ensure preparedness we shall never know. Ministers, from the Prime Minister down, counted it well designed and effective. So even did the deputy head of the Cabinet Office, John Hunt, who was initially sceptical but in due course commented, 'Excellent. You must be pleased.' I suppose I was. That concluded my succession of jobs on entry into Europe.

Reflecting now on the historic debates and decisions of that time but the sad rumbling and grumbling that still domestically seems to accompany our membership of the European Community, I am left wondering why we must for ever be wasting time raking over the tired arguments about sovereignty, independence, Germany, 'damn foreigners' and the like, instead of getting on in there and taking the lead, as successive governments have at different times declared we would do. In the 1970s the so-called 'sceptics' were on the left of our political spectrum supported by the Trade Unions. Now they are on the right, supported paradoxically by a largely foreign-owned press. Of course the Community structure and mode of operation have faults. So do our own in this country. They both need reform – but hardly abandonment. No one can surely deny that this country has benefitted enormously from 30 years of Community membership, and can expect to go on doing so if we play our full part. As I write, our present Foreign Secretary Jack Straw, formerly sceptical, now acknowledges 'the benefits of the European Union for ordinary people are many: peace and security, a single market guaranteeing freedom to work and travel, 3 million British jobs, cleaner air and water, the collaborative effort to fight crime, and greater rights to equality for women at work.' Instead of familiarity breeding contempt, it seems it can breed understanding! A case in point is the so-called 'Brussels Commission', the power-house of the Union. Far from being a monster, as so many of our politicians love to call it, it is in fact no larger I believe than the city Council of Bristol, and that includes its sizeable translation staff. But the argument of the sceptics seems peppered with such myths. Some opponents for years argued that Parliament was not told, when entry was being debated in 1971/72, that the Community planned to evolve from a Customs Union into an Economic and Monetary Union. That was incorrect. The House was told clearly by the Prime Minister in 1971 that 'we would play our full part in the progress towards economic and monetary union.'

What is true is that few if any foresaw then a common currency, the Euro. We in Britain were at that time preoccupied with what were called 'the external characteristics of sterling,' and particularly an orderly run-down of the sterling balances still held by some countries in London as their reserves. But those days are now long gone, as are the Bretton Woods arrangements that gave the world some measure of currency stability for twenty years after the war. We did not fuss about the sovereign independence of sterling then. We were only too glad of international support. If we want currency stability today, not just for internal benefit to trade and tourism but for common strength against the enormous growth of today's world speculators (or 'movers of investment capital, as some pundits now euphemistically call them), a common European currency is, to my thinking, a necessity and it is sad that at this time of writing, we are once again hanging back instead of leading. It is to be hoped we can re-kindle on this issue the spirit of the Great Debate and courage of the 1971/72 Parliament (and of the 1975 Referendum.)

If, this time, there has to be a national referendum before Parliament decides, so be it. Personally I believe referenda are useful for regional issues where there is no regional Parliament, as in Scotland and Wales before devolution and Northern Ireland on the Peace Agreement. But where there is a Parliament, where we do exercise Parliamentary Democracy, then we should surely use it. If it is felt our political system has become unrepresentative, untrusted and ineffectual, the answer is straightforward.

In the traditional British way we should reform it, not bypass it. The reforms needed are all well known: electoral reform to establish fair and proportional representation, democratic reform to re-assert Parliamentary control of 'elective dictatorship' governments (as Lord Hailsham called them), devolution of regional matters down to regional assemblies (and European matters up to the European Parliament), elective reform of the House of Lords, and procedural reform in the House of Commons to foster more thoughtful discussion and less posturing debate. We could then again have a Parliament the public respects.

But that will take time. If meanwhile, to decide to join the Euro, there has to be a national referendum, it is as well to remember that, led by the Government as it must be, it will be first and foremost a popular vote of confidence in the Government, over the head of Parliament. General de Gaulle knew that about national referenda very well. The Irish Government has re-learnt it recently over the Nice Treaty. To use a cricketing analogy, the choice of wicket is obviously important and, in the case of the Euro, it may be sticky if only because of all the rubbish that Euro opponents have been left free to heap on it for so long. But it is the general batting record of the Government that will be the over-riding issue. It was so in 1975, and I am sure it will be the same whenever the Euro referendum is held. However capable we the public may believe we are today of judging complex national issues for ourselves, the fact is that we elect people to listen to us but do the deciding for us. That is our national way. As Churchill is alleged to have said: 'Parliamentary democracy has many faults, but no one has yet found a better way of governing ourselves'. That I think was one constitutional lesson of 1971. The other was that the European Community may have its faults but no one has found a better place for Britain to be in the modern world. So my message to posterity is: let's get on with it, and remember the old Welsh saying: 'Where there is no vision the people perish.'

# CHAPTER 23

# Change of Career

# 1973

B Y LATE 1972, as we wound down the official 'Prepare for Europe' campaign, it was clear that I too needed to get on with things, and settle my own future. The FCO confirmed they had proposed me for the first wave of British appointments to the European Commission. It now lay with the Civil Service Department and a Board set up for the purpose of handling the appointments, under the chairmanship of the 2nd Permanent Secretary in the Cabinet Office, John Hunt, soon to become Cabinet Secretary and Head of the Civil Service. The FCO was represented on this board by its second highest official, Sir Tom Brimelow, later to become Permanent Under Secretary. The FCO had recommended me as a 'very strong candidate' and everyone expected me to go if I was willing which I had declared I was. It was my hope to take the family with me, failing which I would commute home at weekends as was the custom in the Community.

The Board's first task, with the support of the Civil Service Department, was to determine the posts in each of the Community institutions we wanted for British candidates within the outline quotas already agreed in Brussels, and to direct the negotiations for them with the Commission. Those negotiations were under the aegis of the UK Permanent Delegation to the Communities, whose newly appointed Head, Michael Palliser, was a colleague of long-standing. He personally welcomed the news that I would be coming, generously adding that the Commission 'truly needs people of your calibre'. By coincidence, the Commission on its side appointed as adviser none other than the same personnel consultant Harry Hoff who, with C. P. Snow, had guided me into the RAF in 1943 and whom I had come to know when he appeared in Ottawa in 1968 working to reverse the brain-drain to Canada. Unfortunately I did not see him this time. We were enjoined to put our faith in the Whitehall machine.

The Board's second job was to receive and sift applications invited within government through Departments and outside government through advertisement. It was expected there might be twenty senior appointments (and many more middle and junior). The final selection would be by interview with Sir Christopher Soames, the former Conservative government Minister and more recently Ambassador to Paris, and George Thomson, the former Labour government Minister, whom Prime Minister Heath had appointed to be the first British Commissioners on the European Commission. Both were staunch pro-marketeers and were appointed on that basis.

In early November some twenty senior officials from as many as fourteen different departments of the government were selected, on application, to pay a 'familiarisation' visit to Brussels. I was one of them, as was one other diplomatic colleague. We never learnt how many of that group were eventually appointed. Probably few, for as things turned out it had little relevance to the outcome. I took advantage of the visit to meet old friends and several senior staff members of the Commission including the Secretary General Emile Noel. One or two of the Directors-General were wary, obviously fearful of their jobs, but not M. Noel who welcomed my observation that with enlargement there might be a need to strengthen the co-ordinating role of his office by the appointment of an additional Deputy to him. There was in fact much criticism around at the time that the eighteen or so Directors-General, heads of the different services in the Commission, needed tighter co-ordination. Noel knew this but did not have the resources to achieve it. He probably also saw subsidiary advantage in my suggestion, that it would not mean displacing anyone, as all other senior appointments from Britain, Denmark and Ireland threatened to do. Whatever the reason, he expressed the hope that he would have me as a colleague, and I warmly reciprocated.

I returned home happy in the prospect and promptly registered with the FCO and Whitehall machine the suggestion that this new post should be proposed and, although a co-ordinating role is rarely popular in any organisation, I would be willing to take it on. I added several second preferences like External Relations, Overseas Aid and, in the Council of Ministers Secretariat, External Relations & Trade, just in case – but not Commission Press Spokesman the FCO had at one time suggested as I wanted to get back to management. While in Brussels I was also able to explore housing, community life there and schools for the children, and was well satisfied on all counts. The British School had an excellent reputation and I promptly registered the children.

Unbeknown to us at that time, but we were told by the FCO on return: 'there is a lot of negotiating and in-fighting to be done, and we are unlikely to know the outcome before January at the earliest.' It sounded slightly ominous but nothing to what we soon learnt was actually happening. Within government many departments were now wheeling and dealing to get their own officials on secondment into key Commission policy posts of interest to them and, in negotiation with the Commission, the Whitehall machine had decided to demand the full 18% notional quota of Commission jobs at all levels from the outset and the senior ones of their preference. In addition, and contrary to their original policy that 'volunteers prepared to make a career of it would have the edge', they had decided to prefer people prepared to go on secondment, retaining their careers at home to come back to. Altogether this went even further than the French were notorious in the Community for always seeking, and caused uproar when it became known in Brussels. On 1 December most of the Commission's 5000 staff came out on strike and the Council of Ministers staff followed them, in protest at the British approach to the issue. Their trade union leaders claimed Britain was challenging the tradition of the Community to appoint people on 'a permanent career basis with no problem of divided loyalties'. Britain was accused of 'endangering the [Community] service by parachuting Whitehall civil servants into Brussels for relatively short spells – three or four years – then withdraw them to continue their careers in Whitehall.'

In fact, the Commission had acknowledged that for a new member state the process of finding staff willing to make it a career would take time and most of the first senior British appointments would probably have to be seconded officials. Also, there were additional reasons for the strike, notably over pay and allowances (which were even lower than our own), and fear of redundancies because of a Community decision not to increase overall numbers to accommodate the British, Danish and Irish entrants. But the seeming arrogance and insularity of the British demands created much bitterness. The warm welcome that I knew from friends in the Commission awaited British entry, even if it meant loss of some jobs, suddenly froze. Our demands not only conflicted with the spirit of the Community, held dear by so many Community officials, but were unrealistic. Whatever the French might do, the training of British civil servants was always to serve their political masters of the day loyally whoever they were and whatever their policies. The job of the Director-General of Agriculture or Regional Policy or External Relations in the Commission was to serve his Commissioner and the Commission, not his home department and government, and I feel sure that is how most of the British appointees soon learnt to conduct themselves. If not they would not have lasted long there. Of course it was expected they would keep in touch with home. But that was very different from being at their own government's beck-and-call. This was an established principle in every international organisation, but most of all in the European Communities.

It was foolish of the Whitehall machine and the Commissioners-designate (with, it has to be admitted the support of some on the economic side of the FCO), to ignore this Community principle and try to out-French the French. It back-fired, and the Commissioners then, so we learnt later from the FCO Administration, tried to redress the situation by 'arbitrarily scratching around at the last moment for people they could think of in any walk of life outside officialdom'. There were also Administration complaints of 'capriciousness and secretiveness' against the responsible department (the Civil Service Department was new to the game having only been created under the previous Government. It was abolished ten years later). Altogether the handling of the operation left much dissatisfaction at home and in Brussels. No doubt the lesson was learnt for the future, but it was not the happiest start to British membership.

Nor was it the happiest start for me. As New Year 1973 and accession to the Community approached I waited for the invitation to interview with our Commissioners-designate, but none came. There was an embarrassed wall of silence. I made noises and an invitation finally arrived just before Christmas. It was to see Soames, who was not accompanied by Thomson, but by a Civil Service Department adviser. It turned out to be a sham. They made a bow to my experience and we ran through the posts I could fill beginning with the Deputy Secretary-Generalship. But they left me with the disquieting feeling that all had been stitched up already and they had not the courage to tell me so. I had not met Soames before, and was not impressed. He seemed to suffer rather an exaggerated opinion of his own importance. But that was probably mutual! My disquiet was in due course confirmed by the FCO (and eventually by Soames himself – two months later!). Preference had been given to those who 'had the advantage of being in the work', meaning those who would remain British officials on secondment. The Whitehall machine had taken up my suggestion of creating an additional post of Deputy Secretary-General and agreed it with Brussels, but had chosen to fill it with an official plucked out of one of our Embassies in Europe who would remain in the FCO career. Debrett's now tells me that the official concerned did not in fact come back from Brussels but stayed in the Commission until retirement. Doubtless some others did too, contrary to the Whitehall policy. It could have been predicted.

But that was not the whole story. There was something still missing. The FCO could after all have kept candidates intending to make a career in the Community temporarily on their books, thus fulfilling the requirement nominally, and we knew they were willing to do this if necessary. There was a suspicion that when the Whitehall machine decided to prefer seconded officials they also determined to exclude anyone actively pro-European, but were keeping this secret for fear of public objection. Incredibly, this turned out to be true. We learnt it authoritatively months later. It was a very silly decision because, apart from being offensive both to the Community tradition of commitment and to those in Britain who had worked for membership, it ruled out some excellent British candidates with practical experience of working in the European Community and other European institutions as well as those, like me, who were ready to do so. How those responsible seriously thought this would help Whitehall get its own way in Brussels, and how they reconciled it with Soames's and Thomson's own pro-Europe credentials as Commissioners, indeed how Soames himself did so, I do not know. Unfortunately or fortunately, depending on one's viewpoint, it was water under the bridge by the time this truth came out. Otherwise it might well have produced a sequel outcry to that in December, but this time at home as well as in Brussels. By any standards, it was a deplorable piece of bureaucratic chicanery to no official advantage.

For myself, I had to register my dismay with the FCO Administration – which prompted the revelation of their own criticism of the process I have already quoted. There was no point in grieving. I consoled myself I would not really have wanted to go to Brussels with a Whitehall halter round my neck. But it was annoying to say the least. I would take a holiday with my wife in the Canaries and then wind myself up to resume, for the third time, the search for a new career. It was not a prospect that exactly fired me. But at least that New Year, as I attended the official celebration Gala of Accession at Covent Garden, I could look around and feel I had done my little bit for Britain's future in Europe. Others could now carry that forward.

Those first few months of 1973 were the nadir. The FCO in the persons of the Chief of Administration, Donald Tebbit, and the new Head of Personnel, Richard Parsons, were helpful as ever. They again offered me a continued diplomatic career, with early promotion prospects, but I knew that remained impracticable given my family circumstances and they accepted my decision. Instead they undertook to recommend me to the home Civil Service, while I reopened my own exploration of business, industry and the institutional and voluntary world. It is curious that we call the former the 'Public' Sector, and the latter the 'Private' Sector, whereas in the educational world private schools are called Public and public schools are called State. But then we do in this country enjoy making difficulties for ourselves, and still more for foreigners, by some of our traditional appellations. How for instance is anyone supposed to know what a Lord Privy Seal does in the Cabinet, when he is rarely a Lord, and manifestly never a privy nor a seal? The French or the Americans would simply call him (or her) 'Minister of ...' or 'Secretary of State for ...'. But I would not want ours changed. They add eccentricity to life. But I digress, to lighten the story.

My family situation also took a turn for the worse at this time. My wife decided she wanted separation and I had to accept that this had become inevitable. She had found comfort in her own circle of friends while I had to spend so much of my time in London and would have to do so again in the new job once found. We agreed to separate amicably. The important thing was to cause the children minimum upset. They had settled happily in Guildford and for me the one good feature of those 1973 months was that I was able to spend time with them. In fact they took it well. I suppose they were so used to upheaval. This all developed during 1973. It was not the outcome we could have foreseen, or wanted. In principle it released me to go abroad again if I wished but that would have meant leaving the children for long periods and I could not contemplate that. Their interest and welfare had to come first. So my decision to retire from the FCO remained firm and I went through with it in my 26th year of service, eleven years short of the normal age limit. In recommending me to the home Civil Service the FCO summed me up in officialese as 'having had a good career, done effective jobs wherever he had been ... was only leaving the Service for family reasons ... would by now have been promoted to Under Secretary or equivalent Ambassadorship if he had not contracted out three years ago ... and as promotion in the Foreign and Commonwealth Service is 4 to 5 years behind that of the Civil Service, they would do well to grab him!'. That was nice of them.

The job interviews I had this time could fill another chapter. But I shall recount only the high and the low. Most came this time through intermediaries or advertisments. I had written to all those 'good and great' friends who had previously been so helpful. It was rather humiliating to have to tell them that Brussels had fallen through. But it brought in response many heartening letters of support, with some caustic comments on the change of Whitehall policy that had excluded me and others. This time two or three 'head hunters' also showed interest. More and more companies were waking up to the fact that they were now in the European Community and needed people to advise them. There seemed also to be more organisations prepared to recruit people over 45 (except the Treasury, I discovered, who for some reason still lagged behind). The mood was changing. I had pleasing interest from the International Chamber of Commerce, the Metals Society, Rank Xerox, Oxfam, my old friends the Management Consultants, McLintock Mann & Whinney Murray, the Henley Administrative College, the Plastics Federation, British Rail, the Electricity Council, the Central Electricity Generating Board (CEGB) and others. Also, within the government, the Department of the Environment (DOE), the Welsh Office, the DHSS and the Northern Ireland Office. In the institutional field, I regretfully had to decline two interesting posts because they could not offer the minimum salary I needed. For the Oxfam directorship, I was just too late, discovering it only on my return from the Canaries; their Board were nice enough to regret that too. I would have enjoyed it. In the business field, they seemed to move slower, and two or three, particularly the interesting Rank Xerox invitation, came too late because by then I was committed. This, I had learnt, was one of the problems of job hunting. You could go for weeks, sitting at home by the phone or, to save money on London calls, standing in the telephone booth of your club in London feeding sixpences (as they were in those days) into the meter, telephoning people – or hesitating to 'phone them – and hearing nothing but 'we have you in mind'. At more favourable times, you suddenly found two, three or more possibilities maturing together and were left worrying which you most wanted and how to keep the others warm in case you did not get your preference. Fortunately I did not nail-bite or I fancy I would have had none left.

There was little difficulty of decision in some cases, like British Rail and the Metals Society. We just agreed amicably that we were not meant for each other. I was never a rail buff or a metallurgist. There was more to the Department of the Environment, Welsh Office and Northern Ireland Office jobs. All three were interesting. In the DOE, Geoffrey Rippon, now Secretary of State, wanted a trouble-shooter to find administrative and legislative ways of accelerating the process of appeals against housing developments in what were then called 'white lands'. It was described to me as a 'hot seat', both because it involved co-ordination of various directorates and authorities in that huge department and locally and, more particularly, because it was bound to arouse strong environmental and political opposition. As a challenge it appealed to me. As a conservationist it appalled me. Consulting an old friend in the Civil Service Department I learnt that there was an interesting Whitehall rule that an official could refuse an appointment on grounds of conscience once in his or her career without prejudice. I never did discover whether that was a written or unwritten rule, and do not know if it still applies today. With some trepidation I invoked it and was relieved to find Rippon and the DOE hierarchy fully understanding. It was an interesting experience.

The Northern Ireland Office wanted me in Belfast, and that too appealed, especially as direct rule had just been imposed in the troubled circumstances of the time. But it soon became obvious that I could neither take the family with me nor commute regularly. So that ruled that out. The Welsh Office, for their part, wanted me in Cardiff, to help deal with Welsh local government and, on the horizon, devolution. They were somewhat fearful of that, particularly the mayhem they envisaged if there was one party in control of national government in Westminster and another in control of provincial government in Cardiff. We discussed how it worked in Canada, Australia, the USA and Germany, and they decided I could perhaps help. Sadly, for a return to Wales held out many attractions, I was unable to see devolution coming in my time there or any career in the tiny Welsh Office in the meanwhile. So that prospect too fell.

While all this was going on an interesting opportunity emerged in the electricity industry, then nationalised of course, to help develop their growing international relations both in consultancy and in Brussels and other international organisations concerned with energy. The Electricity Council was first in the field but flatteringly found me 'too big for the job', a term I had encountered before and learnt to mean they had decided after all to keep the job in their own goldfish bowl. One of the interviewers however, Mr W. D. Fenton, Vice-chairman of the Central Electricity Generating Board, had other ideas. He rang me to ask if I would be interested in becoming Director Overseas Relations of the CEGB, with similar functions to the Electricity Council post but, the CEGB being the monopoly provider of electricity in England and Wales and second only to the Soviet Board as the biggest generating body in the world, it would be on a grander scale. I would be the CEGB's 'ambassador' in its European and international relations. They would have to go through the motions of trawling the industry for any in-house candidates first, but he thought I had just the experience needed and he would hope to see me appointed. He would be in touch in a month when the trawl was completed.

He had struck me at interview as a man of international experience and understanding – which he was frank in telling me his colleagues, first-class engineers though they all were, tended to lack in their dealings with consultancy clients abroad and Brussels. I had put a lot of work into preparing for the Electricty Council job and was now near the end of my FCO leave. So I agreed to stand. This meant continuing to brief myself, from experts I found in and out of government, on UK and EEC energy policies and people, international electrical energy associations and agreements, nuclear energy prospects (then in vogue) and the CEGB's links abroad, also of course on the CEGB structure and personalities. I was warned the chairman, Arthur Hawkins, was a difficult man. It was early July before he finally invited me to a Board lunch and interview, and it turned out to be an extraordinary affair. Flanked by his embarrassed colleagues he proceeded to tell me the Soviets really knew how to build and manage industry, and nearly exploded when I challenged that view as tactfully as I could by instancing the growing evidence of Soviet economic collapse. He then contrived, over the main course, to denounce civil servants as 'brain-pickers and paper-pushers', diplomats as 'arrogant', bankers as 'mealy-mouthed', the EEC as 'skulduggery' and foreigners generally as beneath contempt.

This tirade over (and after rudely staring to see how I ate my asparagus!), the Chairman demanded to know how I would conduct the job of Director Overseas Relations. He was not prepared to take questions but expected me to know it all and, once in the job, to operate alone on my own budget. That did not make much sense to me (or to Mr Fenton). But by now he seemed bent on demolition, which I had been warned was his wont, and with an aggression and intensity that bordered on the bizarre. I was assured later it was not just me, and that others too wondered how such a man had come to be head of such a powerful nationalised industry.

I suppose that is what any in-bred organisation risks. He had the courtesy to meet with me for a few minutes after lunch but only to tell me the obvious, they would find someone from within after all. Mr Fenton and the Board's Personnel Director were dismayed and apologetic. For my part I could only register it as one more novel experience. But it was a trying waste of time and effort, and my only consolation was the comment afterwards of friends who knew Hawkins's reputation, that the outcome was probably a blessing in disguise – to which I could only respond, as our lights flickered again in the acute fuel shortage of those days, that so long as he kept them burning that was one small mercy. He did not I think last much longer as Chairman, and the CEGB was of course broken up and privatised ten years later.

By this time FCO grace was understandably running out. They were still geared to the possession of people not to the shedding of them and once I had declared for premature retirement I was out of their possession rules and on my way. They remained helpful but the lengthy CEGB affair had set me back and I would probably have to seize one or other of the offers still open to me. Then an attractive new one emerged. The prestigious English-Speaking Union wanted a Director-General to run their new England and Wales organisation, which was in fact the heart of the parent ESU of the Commonwealth, and they were reorganising and thinking also of expanding into Europe. They already had sister ESUs in the United States, Canada, Australia, New Zealand and Pakistan. They were a voluntary organisation, devoted to fostering international understanding between peoples, particularly through student and other educational exchanges. The prospect took me back to the Nuffield Foundation opening that had started me on my quest for a new career three years previously. It had come full circle. Additionally, however, the ESU was truly international and open to development. It had a distinguished former Ambassador to Washington, Sir Patrick Dean, as Chairman. Encouraged by my old friend Norman Reddaway in the FCO, who knew it well, I applied, and was duly interviewed. The salary was poor but they raised it to meet me. I liked the atmosphere. It was both challenging and welcoming. The Board promptly offered me the appointment. I decided it was what I had been looking for, and accepted. It turned out to be more demanding than they or I envisaged, but it happily settled at last my change of career.

Later it occurred to me to jot down the lessons I had learnt of searching for a new career in middle age and, encouraged by friends in management consultancy, we even talked of a booklet on the subject. But there was never time to write it, and today the employment market is altogether different. For what interest it may still hold, however, here in brief are the main precepts I found:

- Think through what you want to do, but exclude nothing. You may be surprised what comes up.

- Choose a time of economic upsurge if you can. If times are bad, be prepared to take temporary jobs, but be careful to keep in the swim of opportunities.

- Conduct your search professionally. Your CV, your engagement of intermediaries and references, your research and approaches to the companies, institutions or other organisations you think might be interested, need all to be done well and methodically.

- Cast your net wide. Do not be afraid of rebuff or no reply. Remember, you are not looking just for a ready-made slot. You can sometimes inspire companies and other organisations to create one for you if they are sufficiently impressed by your experience and talents.

- Don't be shy. Get people involved in the areas of your choice to talk about you, so your availability becomes more widely known.

- Prepare thoroughly for interviews. Present yourself as they would wish, and do your homework on them beforehand. Remember however hard they may appear, they are still human and will be looking for evidence not just that you know what their company or organisation is about, but that you really want to join them.

- Prepare to be asked what you believe you can contribute to their company or organisation, and how you would approach any job with them.

- Keep your pecker up! Do not, whatever the circumstances, allow depression to show through. Repeat to yourself it is the system that is wrong, not you. If you are middle-aged and the young are pushing up relentlessly, counter with the wisdom and guile of your age.

- Be prepared if necessary to do what the French call 'reculer pour mieux sauter' (take a backward step in order the better to jump forward).

- When you find a company or organisation that seems to want you, remember that is half the battle. Apart from the welcome that brings, they then have an extra stake in your success.

- On the other hand, if you are the employer or manager doing the interviewing, remember it might be you on the other side one day!

No doubt today's 'human resources managers' and 'head-hunters' will find these simple principles out of date, and I am sure they are. But shed of modern jargon I wonder how their substitute principles would read? In essence most employment encounters must be between a proposer and a disposer, between an asker and a giver (except perhaps at 'fat-cat' level), and those rules are eternal. Or so it seems to me. But I am quite open to be told, as I am by my children, that things have changed since my day!

I left the Diplomatic Service in September 1973 with many happy memories but no time for regrets. Most diplomats find, or used to find, that the career ran to the age of 60, that being the Civil Service limit, and then came the void as they looked around for non-executive directorships or other things to do. In his delightful memoirs *Diplomat in a Changing World*, Sir Bernard Burrows puts it succinctly thus: 'One day you are in correspondence with the higher reaches of government and taking part in decision-making. The next day nobody wants to hear from you again. Admittedly you get a nice pension, but the sudden separation from the corridors of power is painful. Some countries ease the transition by giving retiring officers temporary posts as consultants or such like. We do not.' I myself perforce was spared that. Given the option, however, I have little doubt I would have enjoyed going the full course with the prospect, if all went well, of heading a major embassy or delegation before the retirement let-down. That would also have left me much better off financially, although in the event I was fortunate to find myself an unexpected beneficiary of the new blood-letting retirement rules introduced in 1972/3, thanks to the Duncan Commission and the example of the Armed Services. The new rules allowed appropriate people to go early with a modest handshake and pension, fixed to aged 55 but indexed thereafter. That made a great difference to the jobs I could afford to take in the voluntary sector thereafter.

Pitched into this new world at 49 left me no time to indulge in reminiscence or regret. The FCO in those days had no formal association for former members and their contact with us was scant. On reaching old age pension I had to seek official records of my Diplomatic and Air Force service. The RAF responded by return. The FCO had to labour months to oblige. All that has now changed with the creation of a flourishing FCO Association, run voluntarily but as professionally as everything else the FCO does. Thirty years ago, however, aside from old friendships and occasional business contacts, the break was clean. It had to be in my case. The new world of voluntary organisation and, ultimately, politics, was too all-absorbing to allow otherwise. But that is another story to come.

When I left the Diplomatic Service the then Head and Permanent Under-Secretary, Sir Denis Greenhill, sent me a farewell letter which I reproduce not so much for its content, reasonable summary of my service though it may have been, but for the courtesy and camaraderie it enshrined as a feature of that great Service as it was – and I hope still is.

The author of that letter I had known since his Paris days in the UK delegation to NATO and mine in the Embassy there. He was, as his obituarist said when he died in 2000, 'an unusual man ... never been an Ambassador abroad (but had nonetheless a very distinguished and interesting career) ... chosen for the job by George Brown partly it seems because Brown, then foreign secretary, mistakenly thought his father had been an engine driver ... But regarded by many of us as one of the best,

Foreign and Commonwealth Office

London S.W.1

8 October 1973

W N Hugh-Jones Esq MVO
1 Poyle Road
Guildford
Surrey
GU1 3SL

*Dear Hugh,*

Now that you are leaving us on retirement, I should like
to thank you for the loyal and valuable work you have done
during your career under the Crown.   You have had a successful
career, with a number of highlights.   Sir John Ward was full
of praise for what you did as Head of Chancery in Rome and
Sir Colin Crowe for your good work in Ottawa.   But I suppose
the job on which you may look back with greatest satisfaction
was the special assignment you took on in the last couple of
years in the Cabinet Office, when you played a most useful
part in the public relations aspects of our entry into Europe.

    We are indeed sorry that your family circumstances make
it impossible for you to continue to fulfil the obligations
of overseas service, and that you are therefore retiring early at
your own wish.   I am delighted that you have taken up so
important a post as that of Director-General of the English
Speaking Union.   The Service will look forward to keeping in
touch with you in this function.   I wish you and your wife
every happiness for the future.

*yours ever*

*Denis*

Denis Greenhill

if not the best, PUSs since the War.' He was the ninth in my time in the
service. Even PUSs had to retire at 60. I enjoyed meeting him again from
time to time at one voluntary function or another in later years. He never
failed to recognise old colleagues even when in old age he was nearly
blind.

There was one other valedictory message that I shall quote. It was from
the Head of the Civil Service, Sir Burke Trend, thanking the FCO for

lending me to the Cabinet Office. On my European Communities Bill press job he judged it to have been 'a notable success.' On my preparations for the Community job he commended the way I had performed it 'with characteristic enthusiasm and energy.' That oft-quoted French politician and diplomat, Talleyrand, would not have approved of a diplomat so described. 'Never show zeal,' he is alleged to have counselled. But campaigning, which is what my Europe jobs were about, demanded a rather more exuberant approach than diplomacy, and I found that fun. I suppose we all harbour in us the unorthodox, and some more than others. Apart from fulfilment of a cause, it also proved a happy transition into the voluntary world and politics which were to follow.

I enjoyed my diplomatic career, the rough and the smooth, as these pages have recalled. My good wishes go out to all who represent their country in the Foreign and Commonwealth Service today. I hope that, any present trials and tribulations apart, they will find it as fulfilling as I did, foreshortened though mine was.

My good wishes for health and happiness go out also to everyone who has read this book. The next, if they are still interested, will be on life in the voluntary movement and particularly the English-Speaking Union in the 1970s, the Liberal Party and the remarkable Liberal/SDP Alliance in the decade 1977–87, the Avebury in Danger campaign in the late 1980s, lecturing in the United States and other causes I have enjoyed serving this last quarter century.

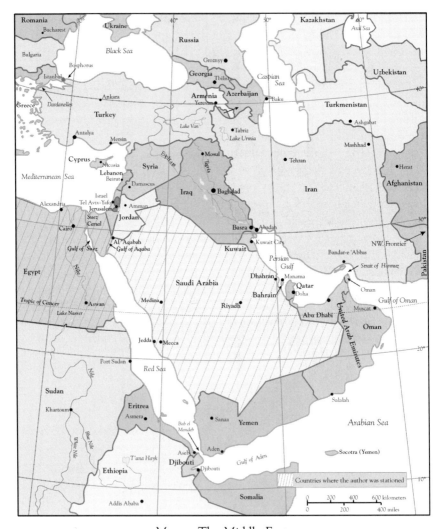

Map 1. The Middle East.

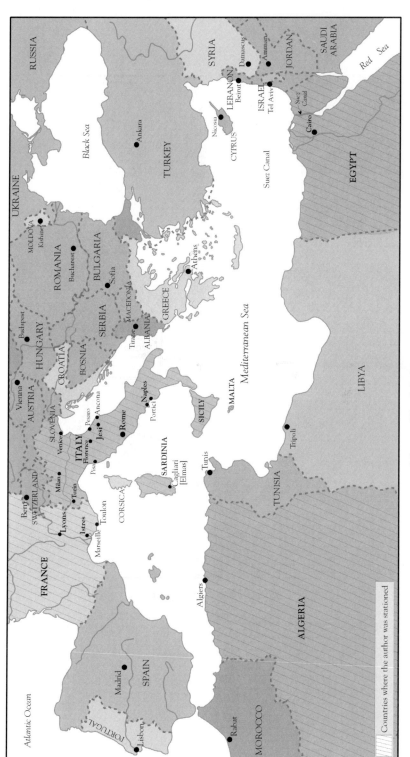

Map 2. The Mediterranean.

Map 3. Africa.

# Index